The original Farm Holiday Guide to Coast & Country Holidays 2004

England, Scotland, Wales & Ireland

with
Farms • Hotels • Guest Houses • Self-catering • Caravan & Camping • Activity Holidays • Country Inns •

For Contents see Pages 2 & 3
For Index of towns/counties see back of book

FHG Publications
Paisley

Part of IPC Country and Leisure Media

CONTENTS

The Farm Holiday Guide to
COAST & COUNTRY HOLIDAYS 2004

Colour Section 1-60
Guide to Tourist Board Ratings 64
Readers' Offer Vouchers 67-94
Family-friendly Pubs and Inns 335-344
Website Directory 345-373
Index of Towns/Counties 375-378

ENGLAND

BOARD
Bedfordshire 95
Cambridgeshire.................................96
Cheshire 98
Cornwall 100
Cumbria..108
Derbyshire......................................115
Devon 119
Dorset 129
Durham 135
Essex..136
Gloucestershire...............................137
Hampshire......................................141
Herefordshire 144
Hertfordshire..................................146
Isle of Wight 146
Kent..147
Lancashire......................................150
Leicestershire.................................151
Lincolnshire....................................151
Norfolk 153
Northamptonshire..........................155
Northumberland 156
Nottinghamshire 157
Oxfordshire 158
Shropshire 160
Somerset..164
Staffordshire..................................170
Suffolk 171
Surrey 172
East Sussex....................................172
West Sussex...................................173
Warwickshire 174
West Midlands 175
Wiltshire 175
Worcestershire...............................177
North Yorkshire 179

SELF-CATERING
Cornwall 186
Cumbria..195
Derbyshire......................................202
Devon 205
Dorset 214
Durham 218
Gloucestershire...............................219
Hampshire......................................220
Herefordshire 221
Isle of Wight 222
Kent..223
Lancashire......................................224
Lincolnshire....................................226
Norfolk 228
Northumberland 230
Oxfordshire 233
Shropshire 234
Somerset..236
Staffordshire..................................239
Suffolk 240
East Sussex....................................242
Warwickshire 243
Wiltshire 243
East Yorkshire 245
North Yorkshire 245
West Yorkshire 252

CARAVANS & CAMPING................253

ACTIVITY HOLIDAYS......................264

CONTENTS

The Farm Holiday Guide to
COAST & COUNTRY HOLIDAYS 2004

SCOTLAND

BOARD
Aberdeen, Banff & Moray 267
Argyll & Bute 268
Ayrshire & Arran 270
Borders 271
Dumfries & Galloway.........................272
Dundee & Angus 273
Edinburgh & Lothians 274
Fife 275
Highlands (North) 276
Highlands (South) 277
Perth & Kinross 278
Stirling & The Trossachs 279
Scottish Islands.................................280

SELF-CATERING
Aberdeen, Banff & Moray 282
Argyll & Bute 284
Ayrshire & Arran 288
Borders 290
Dumfries & Galloway.........................291
Dundee & Angus 291
Highlands (North) 293
Highlands (Mid).................................294
Highlands (South) 295
Lanarkshire 296
Perth & Kinross 297
Scottish Islands.................................297

CARAVANS & CAMPING 298

WALES

BOARD
Anglesey & Gwynedd 303
North Wales 304
Carmarthenshire 305
Ceredigion...306
Pembrokeshire 307
Powys 309
South Wales 313

SELF-CATERING
Anglesey & Gwynedd 316
North Wales 319
Carmarthenshire 320
Ceredigion...321
Pembrokeshire 322
Powys 325

CARAVANS & CAMPING 327

REPUBLIC OF IRELAND

BOARD 328   **SELF-CATERING** 328   **CARAVANS & CAMPING** ..328

COUNTRY INNS

England / Scotland / Wales.........329

ENGLAND and WALES Counties

NORTH WALES
1. Denbighshire
2. Flintshire
3. Wrexham

SOUTH WALES
4. Swansea
5. Neath and Port Talbot
6. Bridgend
7. Rhondda Cynon Taff
8. Merthyr Tydfil
9. Vale of Glamorgan
10. Cardiff
11. Caerphilly
12. Blaenau Gwent
13. Torfaen
14. Newport
15. Monmouthshire

© MAPS IN MINUTES™ 2003

Please mention Farm Holiday Guide when enquiring

YORKSHIRE DALES to SCOTTISH HIGHLANDS

SELF-CATERING

Over 600 superb, personally inspected, self catering holiday properties in beautiful rural and coastal locations. From Yorkshire's Dales and Moors, the Lakes and Cumbria, through Northumbria and the Borders to Scotland's Highlands and Islands. Cosy cottages to country houses, many welcome pets and short breaks are available.

0870 909 9500

Skipton, North Yorkshire, BD23 2AA.

www.dalesholcot.com

SELF-CATERING

Every kind of property for every kind of holiday

BRITAIN'S FAVOURITE COTTAGE HOLIDAYS

With over 3,000 quality graded cottages throughout the UK, catering from two to twenty-two, you're sure to find the right property for you. Many of our properties also accept pets so none of your family need miss out.

Look & Book at: www.country-holidays.co.uk or call 0870 442 5240 for your **2004** brochure.

London

Chase Lodge Hotel
An Award Winning Hotel
with style & elegance, set in tranquil surroundings at affordable prices

10 Park Road Hampton Wick Kingston-Upon-Thames KT1 4AS
Tel: 020 8943 1862 . Fax: 020 8943 9363
E-mail: info@chaselodgehotel.com Website: www.chaselodgehotel.com

*Quality en suite bedrooms
Full English Breakfast
A la carte menu
Licensed bar
Wedding Receptions
Honeymoon suite
available with jacuzzi & steam area
20 minutes from Heathrow Airport
Close to Kingston town centre & all major transport links.*

AA * * * Les Routiers RAC * * *

All major credit cards accepted

The Farm Holiday Guide to Coast & Country Holidays 2004

Bedfordshire/Berkshire/Cornwall

COUNTRY INNS

THE Globe INN

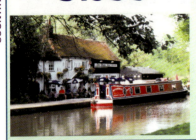

Globe Lane, Stoke Road, Old Linslade,
Leighton Buzzard, Bedfordshire LU7 7TA

★ Canal-side location with access over own bridge.
★ Beer garden with outdoor eating facilities
★ Bar/Lounge open all day, every day
★ Children welcome ★ Children's play area
★ Dining area with non-smoking section
★ Excellent choice of food served
12 noon to 9pm daily
★ Booking Highly Recommended

Tel: 01525 373338 • Fax: 01525 850551

BOARD

Discover Rose-in-Vale – The Hotel in the Valley

Hiding away in its own 11-acre valley, deep in the heart of the country, yet with the magnificent North Cornish coast right on the doorstep. There is a choice of 18 bedrooms and suites, all en suite, with central heating, TV, radio, hairdryer and beverage tray; three ground floor rooms are suitable for less able guests. The Rose Suite offers a queen-size four-poster bed, separate sitting room, spa bath, walk-in-shower and some special touches, and Master Rooms feature four-poster or half-tester beds. Dining in the Valley Restaurant is a particular pleasure, with the emphasis on locally produced foods wherever possible, complemented by an interesting selection of fine wines. Special diets catered for.

Cocktail Bar • Library • Drawing Room
• Outdoor heated pool
• Croquet and badminton in the grounds
• Sauna.

Rose-in-Vale Country House Hotel
Mithian, St Agnes TR5 0QD
Tel: 01872 552202 • Fax: 01872 552700
www.rose-in-vale-hotel.co.uk
reception@rose-in-vale-hotel.co.uk

ETC/AA/RAC ★★★   RAC 2 Dining Awards

BOARD

Boscean Country Hotel
St Just, Penzance, Cornwall TR19 7QP • Tel/Fax 01736 788748

The Boscean Country Hotel, located amidst some of the most dramatic scenery in West Cornwall, is somewhere very special just waiting to be discovered. This country house offers a wonderful combination of oak panelled walls, a magnificent oak staircase and open log fires. The natural gardens, extending to nearly three acres, are a haven for wildlife including foxes and badgers. Situated on the Heritage Coast in an Area of Outstanding Natural Beauty close to Cape Cornwall and the Coastal Footpath, this is an ideal base from which to explore the Land's End Peninsula. The moors of Penwith are rich in Iron and Bronze Age relics dating back to 4000BC. Penzance, St Michael's Mount, St Ives, Land's End and the Minack Theatre are all a short distance away. 12 en suite rooms, centrally heated throughout, licensed bar. Excellent home cooking using fresh local produce. ***Unlimited Desserts!!*** Open all year. ETC ◆◆◆◆

Bed & Breakfast £23.00 • Dinner, Bed & Breakfast £36.00
E-mail: Boscean@aol.com • Website: www.bosceancountryhotel.co.uk

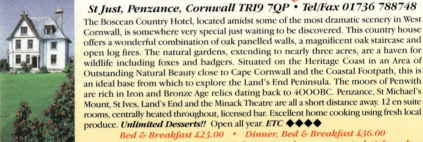

Publisher's Note

While every effort is made to ensure accuracy, we regret that FHG Publications cannot accept responsibility for errors, omissions or misrepresentations in our entries or any consequences thereof. Prices in particular should be checked because we go to press early. We will follow up complaints but cannot act as arbiters or agents for either party.

Cornwall

Penrose Burden Holiday Cottages

St Breward, Bodmin, Cornwall PL30 4LZ
Tel: 01208 850277 / 850617; Fax: 01208 850915
www.penroseburden.co.uk

Situated within easy reach of both coasts and Bodmin Moor on a large farm overlooking a wooded valley with own salmon and trout fishing. These stone cottages with exposed beams and quarry tiled floors have been featured on TV and are award-winners. Home-made meals can be delivered daily. All are suitable for wheelchair users and dogs are welcomed. Our cottages sleep from two to seven and are open all year.

Please write or telephone for a colour brochure.   Nancy Hall

Close to The Eden Project

Self-catering & Camping with country views and within easy reach of the sea. Tennis court, heated swimming pool & fishing lakes etc

ONE OF CORNWALL'S FAVOURITE FAMILY HOLIDAY PARKS

Trencreek Farm Holiday Park
Hewaswater, St Austell, Cornwall PL26 7JG
Tel: 01726 882540 Website: www.trencreek.co.uk

Viscar Farm
HOLIDAY COTTAGES
NEAR FALMOUTH

Set in 22 acres, the three cottages are full of character - open beamed ceilings, stone walls, inglenook fireplace, slate floors, double glazed, attractive wall lighting, pine furniture, well equipped.
There is a wealth of wildlife to be seen, an ideal location for beaches and touring. Sleep 2-4 + cot.
Available all year, short winter breaks.
Linen and towels provided; welcome tray.

For brochure tel: 01326 340897

e-mail: BiscarHols@amserve.net
www.viscarfarm-cottages.co.uk

Cornwall

BOARD

Little Larnick Farm
Pelynt, Looe, Cornwall PL13 2NB

Telephone: 01503 262837

Little Larnick is situated in a sheltered part of the West Looe river valley. Walk to Looe from our working dairy farm and along the coastal path to picturesque Polperro. The character farmhouse and barn offers twin, double and family en suite rooms. The bedrooms are superbly equipped and decorated to a high standard. The family room is in a downstairs annexe overlooking the garden. Our newly renovated barn offers three self-contained bedrooms with their own lounge areas. Cycling shed, drying room and ample parking. No pets. No smoking. Bed and Breakfast from £22.50 to £27.50 Open all year. Contact: **Mrs Angela Eastley.**

SELF-CATERING

Falmouth

Detached bungalow and gardens, shower room, bathroom and separate wc. Close to Falmouth Town Centre in residential area. Sleeps 2 to 6. Garage and parking. From £350 to £600 per week incl. Unlimited electricity and hot water.

Booking Office:
Creation Accommodation, 96 Market Street, Penryn TR10 8BH
Tel: 0800 298 6465 • Fax: 01326 375088
e-mail: hq@encompasstravel.com

SELF-CATERING

Tredragon Lodge

Five Serviced Self-Catering Lodges
between Newquay & Padstow at Mawgan Porth, Cornwall
200 yards from the beach

Fully Equipped • Dishwashers • Daily Maid Service • Linen Provided

Contact: J. MCLUSKIE - 01637 881610
www.tredragonlodge.co.uk • Email: tredragonlodge@hotmail.com

SELF-CATERING

Trenannick Cottages

Five delightful cottages converted from 18th century farm buildings, standing at the end of a private, tree-lined drive, in a quiet rural setting. All cottages have small private gardens, and access to barbecue area, children's playing field, and small copse. Ideal touring base for North Cornish coast, two miles from A39, with Crackington Haven, Bude, and Boscastle all nearby. Accommodation varies from two to six persons per cottage, with wheelchair access in the Roundhouse. Open throughout the year, with log fires for those colder evenings. Short Breaks available. Pets welcome in certain cottages. Rates from £130 to £475 per week.

Details from **Mrs L. Harrison, Trenannick Farmhouse, Warbstow, Launceston PL15 8RP** • Tel: 01566 781443
e-mail: lorraine.trenannick@il2.com • website: www.trenannickcottages.co.uk

Cornwall

Hollyvagg Farmhouse

Part of cosy 17th century Listed Farmhouse in 80 acres of fields and woods. Working farm with rare breed sheep, horses, geese, dogs and cats. Central to North and South coasts, Bodmin Moor, and the fabulous Eden Project. Golf and riding nearby. All modern conveniences. Sleeps 5. Prices from £180.00. Also available luxury mobile home, sleeps 4, in idyllic private location.

Hollyvagg Farmhouse
Lewannick, Launceston, Cornwall PL15 7QH
Mrs Anne Moore • 01566 782309

SELF-CATERING

"One of the most beautifully situated hotels in England"

Willapark Manor is a lovely character house in a beautiful setting amidst 14 acre grounds, overlooking Bossiney Bay. Surrounded by woodland, it is secluded and has direct access to the coastal path and beach. It is a family-run hotel with a friendly and informal atmosphere, excellent cuisine and a well stocked cocktail bar. Beautifully appointed bedrooms, all en suite and with colour TV and tea/coffee making facilities. Some four-posters. A warm welcome and a memorable holiday assured.

Willapark Manor Hotel
Bossiney, Tintagel, Cornwall PL34 0BA
Tel: 01840 770782
www.willapark.co.uk

BOARD

TREMAINE GREEN
for MEMORABLE HOLIDAYS

"A beautiful private hamlet" of 11 award-winning traditional cosy **Cornish** craftsmen's cottages between **Looe** and **Polperro**. Clean, comfortable and well equipped, with a warm friendly atmosphere, for pets with 2 to 8 people. Set in lovely grounds, only 14 miles from the **Eden Project** with country and coastal walks nearby. Pets £16 pw; owners from only **£112:**

• Towels, Linen, Electricity & Central Heating included • Dishwashers in larger cottages • Power shower Baths • Launderette
• Games Room • Tennis Court • TV/Videos • Cots & Highchairs available • Pubs & Restaurants in easy walking distance

Mr & Mrs J Spreckley, Tremaine Green Country Cottages, Pelynt, Near Looe, Cornwall PL13 2LT
Tel: 01503 220333 • e-mail: stay@tremainegreen.co.uk • web: www.tremainegreen.co.uk

SELF-CATERING

Polgrain Holiday Cottages

Nestling on the outskirts of the tiny village of St Wenn, our beautiful barn conversions offer a high degree of comfort in well-appointed character cottages. They are superbly positioned for touring and walking: Newquay, the dramatic coastline, many tourist attractions including the Eden Project all within 10 miles. Ideal for family seaside holidays or romantic country breaks - the perfect destination at any time of year. Each has:

• fully fitted kitchen with microwave and washing machine
• living room with TV, video, CD; three cottages have open fires
• bathroom with bath and shower • patio with BBQ

Polgrain Holiday Cottages, Higher Polgrain, St Wenn, Cornwall PL30 5PR
01637 880637 • Fax: 01637 881644 • www.selfcateringcornwall.uk.com
e-mail: Polgrainholidaycottages@ukgateway.net

• Laundry room • Children's play area • **INDOOR HEATED POOL**

SELF-CATERING

The Farm Holiday Guide to Coast & Country Holidays 2004

Cumbria

COUNTRY INN

THE Sun Inn
Pooley Bridge, Penrith CA10 2NN
017684 86205 • Fax: 017684 86913

Dating from the mid 1700s, the inn has nine bedrooms, all en suite, comprising five doubles, one twin, two singles and a family room. There is a no smoking policy in the bedrooms and also in the 30 seater dining room, the lobby and the lounge bar. The Public bars attract the colourful local people, walkers, fishermen and sportsmen who enjoy rugby and football on our big screen. The inn enjoys a certain atmosphere, especially in busy times during the season. Visitors are encouraged to enjoy the inn and the area in winter when we offer special rates. Children and dogs are most welcome.

e-mail: michaeljane66@btopenworld.com

SELF-CATERING

Our range includes three very comfortable, large Coach Houses, two stone built Cottages with open fires, three three-bedroomed pine Lodges, six two-bedroomed cedar Chalets, a unique detached converted Dairy and two converted Bothies which make ideal, low cost accommodation for two people.

All set in a private 300-acre estate between Lake Ullswater and Helvellyn and containing a working hill farm, a Victorian waterfall wood, private lake foreshore for guests to use for boating and fishing, and 100 acres of designated ancient woodland for you to explore. Children welcome. Dogs by appointment in some of the accommodation. Colour TV, central heating, launderette, payphone; daytime electricity metered. Linen hire available.

Weekly prices from £145 to £465.
Please phone for full brochure.
e-mail: welcome@patterdalehallestate.com
website: www.patterdalehallestate.com   ETC ★★/★★★

Patterdale Hall Estate

The Estate Office, Patterdale Hall Estate, Glenridding, Penrith, Cumbria CA11 0PJ
Tel: 017684 82308 • Fax: 017684 82867

B&B BOARD

SANDOWN
Lake Road, Windermere, Cumbria LA23 2JF • Tel: 015394 45275

Superb Bed and Breakfast accommodation. All rooms en suite with colour TV and tea/coffee making facilities. Situated two minutes from Lake Windermere, shops and cafes. Many lovely walks. Open all year. Special out of season rates, also two-day Saturday/Sunday breaks. From £22 to £32 per person, excluding Bank Holidays. Well behaved dogs welcome. Each room has own safe private car parking. SAE or telephone for further details.

Proprietors: Irene and George Eastwood

BOARD

Lightwood Country Guest House
Cartmel Fell, Grange-over-Sands LA11 6NP

Built in 1656, Lightwood maintains original features and charm whilst offering modern home comforts. A family business for over 50 years the Cervettis offer warm hospitality and excellent home cooking with Italian inspiration, using homegrown and local produce. All diets catered for. Set in two acres of beautiful natural and landscaped gardens. Excellent fell walking area. Only 2.5 miles from Lake Windermere. Six individually decorated en suite bedrooms with countryside views. On-site complementary therapies. A recipe for wellbeing and relaxation. Children welcome. Which? Hotel Guide recommended.

B&B from £23pppn • D,B&B from £40.90pppn for weekly stay
Short Break rates • Closed December

Tel & Fax: 015395 31454
enquiries@lightwoodguesthouse.com
www.lightwoodguesthouse.com

Cumbria

SELF-CATERING

HODYOAD COTTAGES

Hodyoad stands in its own private grounds, with extensive views of the surrounding fells in peaceful rural countryside. Mid-way between the beautiful Lakes of Loweswater and Ennerdale, six miles from Cockermouth and 17 from Keswick. Fell walking, boating, pony trekking and trout fishing can all be enjoyed within a three-and-a-half mile radius.

Each cottage is fully centrally heated and has two bedrooms to sleep five plus cot. All linen provided. Lounge with colour TV. Kitchen with fitted units, cooker and fridge. Bathroom with shower, washbasin, toilet, shaver point. Laundry room with washing machine and tumble dryer. Car essential, ample parking. Sea eight miles. Open all year. From £200 to £360 per week. For further details please contact:

Mrs J. A. Cook, Hodyoad House, Lamplugh, Cumbria CA14 4TT • Tel: 01946 861338

COUNTRY INNS

The Blacksmiths Arms

Talkin Village, Brampton, Cumbria CA8 1LE
Tel: 016977 3452 • Fax: 016977 3396
e-mail: info@blacksmithstalkin.co.uk
www.blacksmithstalkin.co.uk

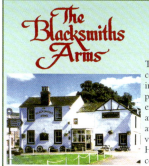

The Blacksmith's Arms offers all the hospitality and comforts of a traditional country inn. Enjoy tasty meals served in the bar lounges, or linger over dinner in the well-appointed restaurant. The inn is personally managed by the proprietors, Anne and Donald Jackson, who guarantee the hospitality one would expect from a family concern. Guests are assured of a pleasant and comfortable stay. There are five lovely bedrooms, all en suite and offering every comfort. Peacefully situated in the beautiful village of Talkin, the inn is convenient for the Borders, Hadrian's Wall and the Lake District. There is a good golf course, walking and other country pursuits nearby.

BOARD

Greenah Crag

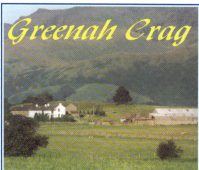

Enjoy a relaxing break at Greenah Crag, a 17th century former farmhouse peacefully located in the Lake District National Park, just 10 miles from Keswick and only eight miles from the M6 motorway. Ideal for exploring Northern Lakes, Eden Valley, Carlisle, Hadrian's Wall and the Western Pennines. Accommodation is in two double bedrooms with bathroom en suite, and one twin-bedded room with washbasin, all with tea/coffee making facilities. The guests' sittingroom with TV and woodburning stove is a cosy place on the coldest days! A full breakfast is served in the oak-beamed diningroom. Pub/restaurant three-quarters-of-a-mile. Regret no pets or smoking in the house. Bed and Breakfast from £19 pp. Please telephone for brochure.

Mrs Maureen Dix, Greenah Crag, Troutbeck, Penrith CA11 0SQ (017684 83233)

SELF-CATERING

Brook House Cottage Holidays

Location! Location! Location!

c/o Bassenthwaite Hall Farm, Bassenthwaite Village, Near Keswick, Cumbria CA12 4QP

By a stream with ducks! Delightful cottages charmingly restored and cared for in this attractive hamlet near Keswick. Various cottages sleep 2-10, ideal for reunions or family get-togethers. Short Breaks available. Excellent food at village pub. Ideally situated 2 miles from Skiddaw and Bassenthwaite lake. Keswick 6 miles.

Mid-week and weekend breaks from £80 to £250 available. Open all year.

Tel & Fax: 017687 76393
website: www.holidaycottageslakedistrict.co.uk
e-mail: a.m.trafford@amserve.net

Cumbria

NEW HOUSE FARM
BUTTERMERE/LORTON VALLEY, COCKERMOUTH, CUMBRIA CA13 9UU
web: www.newhouse-farm.co.uk • e-mail: hazel@newhouse-farm.co.uk
Tel: 01900 85404
Fax: 01900 85478
(See Map 5 Ref C3)

SITUATED IN THE QUIETEST AND MOST BEAUTIFUL PART OF THE LAKES, NEW HOUSE FARM HAS 15 ACRES OF OPEN FIELDS, PONDS, STREAMS AND WOODS WHICH GUESTS AND DOGS MAY WANDER AROUND AT LEISURE AND THERE IS EASY ACCESS TO NEARBY LAKES AND FELLS. ALL BEDROOMS ARE EN SUITE. THERE IS A COSY DINING ROOM AND THREE COMFORTABLE SITTING ROOMS WITH OPEN LOG FIRES. THE FOOD SERVED IS FINE TRADITIONAL FARE.
BED & BREAKFAST FROM £46, DINNER, BED & BREAKFAST FROM £68.

Good Hotel Guide   Which? Hotel Guide   AA ♦♦♦♦♦

"THE LORTON VALE — A PLACE FOR ALL SEASONS"

Lane Ends Cottages

The cottages are situated next to "Fellside" on the edge of Elterwater Common. Two cottages accommodate a maximum of four persons: double bedroom, twin bedded room; fully equipped kitchen/diningroom; bathroom. Third cottage sleeps five: as above plus single bedroom and separate diningroom. Electricity by meters. The cottages provide an ideal base for walking/touring holidays with Ambleside, Grasmere, Hawkshead and Coniston within a few miles. Parking for one car per cottage, additional parking opposite. Open all year; out of season long weekends available. Rates from £200 per week. Brochure on request (SAE please).

Mrs M. E. Rice, "Fellside", Elterwater, Ambleside LA22 9HN • 015394 37678

CONISTON COUNTRY COTTAGES
LITTLE ARROW, CONISTON, CUMBRIA LA21 8AU
Tel & Fax: 015394 41114
e-mail: enquiries@conistoncottages.co.uk
www.conistoncottages.co.uk

A selection of tastefully furnished cottages set amidst the beautiful lake and mountain scenery of Coniston. Central location provides easy access for exploring the Lake District. Ideal base for fell walking, mountain-biking, climbing and sailing, or simply to relax and enjoy the scenery. Complimentary leisure club membership.

Quality cottages in superb surroundings

Cumbria/Derbyshire

CARAVANS

Greenhowe Caravan Park
Great Langdale, English Lakeland.

Greenhowe Caravan Park
Great Langdale, Ambleside,
Cumbria LA22 9JU

Greenhowe is a permanent Caravan Park with Self Contained Holiday Accommodation. Subject to availability Holiday Homes may be rented for short or long periods from 1st March until mid-November. The Park is situated in the Lake District half-a-mile from Dungeon Ghyll at the foot of the Langdale Pikes. It is an ideal centre for Climbing, Fell Walking, Riding, Swimming, Water-Skiing. **Please ask about Short Breaks.**

For free colour brochure
Telephone: (015394) 37231 • Fax: (015394) 37464 •
Freephone: 0800 0717231

SELF-CATERING

Howscales sits in open, tranquil countryside in the heart of the Eden Valley, yet is only 15 miles from the M6. Originally a 17th century farm, the buildings have been converted into five self-contained cottages, catering for 2-4, each with their own character. The cottages are set around a cobbled courtyard and are surrounded by lawns, gardens and magnificent views. Each cottage is centrally heated, comfortably furnished, with well-equipped kitchens that provide all the comforts of home. Howscales is an ideal base to explore the Eden Valley, Lakes, Pennines and Hadrian's Wall.

• Non-smoking • Open all year • Short Breaks
• Brochure available • Pets by arrangement • Resident owner

Liz Webster, Howscales, Kirkoswald, Penrith CA10 1JG • Tel: 01768 898666 • Fax: 01768 898710
e-mail: liz@howscales.fsbusiness.co.uk • website: www.eden-in-cumbria.co.uk/howscales

---

BOARD

BIGGIN HALL
Biggin-by-Hartington, Buxton SK17 0DH

Tel: 01298 84451 • Fax: 01298 84681
website: www.bigginhall.co.uk

Tranquilly set 1,000 ft up in the White Peak District National Park, 17th century Grade II* Listed Biggin Hall – now one of the 'World's Best Loved Hotels' where guests experience the full benefits of the legendary Biggin Air – has been sympathetically restored, keeping its character while giving house room to contemporary comforts. Rooms are centrally heated with bathrooms en suite, colour TV, tea-making facilities, silent fridge and telephone. Those in the main house have stone arched mullioned windows, others are in converted 18th century outbuildings. Centrally situated for stately homes and for exploring the natural beauty of the area. Return at the end of the day to enjoy your freshly cooked dinner alongside log fires and personally selected wines. Well-behaved pets are welcome by prior arrangement.

ETC ★★

BOARD/SELF-CATERING

Near Dovedale and Manifold Valley • B&B and Self-catering

On a working farm in quiet countryside, within easy reach of Alton Towers, stately homes and places of historic interest. Ideal touring centre.

• **B&B** – 4 double/twin rooms (2 en suite), dining/sitting room with TV. Tea/coffee making; full central heating; open fire. Terms from £27 pppn; reduced rates for children; cot and high chair available.

• **Self-catering** – Cottage (sleeps 7), two farmhouses (sleep 12). Sitting rooms and dining rooms (kitchen/diner in cottage). Electric cookers, fridges, washing machine and dryer. Car essential; nearest shops 3 miles. Pay phone. Pets permitted. ETC ★★★/★★★★

Details from Mrs M.A. Richardson, Throwley Hall Farm, Ilam, Near Ashbourne, Derbyshire DE6 2BB
Tel: 01538 308202/308243 • Website: www.throwleyhallfarm.co.uk
e-mail: throwleyhall@talk21.com or throwley@btinternet.com

Derbyshire/Devon

BOARD

Stone Cottage

A charming cottage in the quiet village of Clifton, one mile from the Georgian market town of Ashbourne.
Each bedroom is furnished to a high standard with all rooms en suite, all with four-poster bed. TV and coffee making facilities.
A warm welcome is assured and a hearty breakfast in this delightful cottage.
There is a large garden to relax in.
Ideal for visiting Chatsworth House, Haddon Hall, Dovedale, Carsington Waters and the theme park of Alton Towers.
B&B from £21 per person. Good country pubs nearby serving evening meals.
Enquiries to: Mrs A. M. Whittle, Stone Cottage, Green Lane, Clifton, Ashbourne, Derbyshire DE6 2BL • Telephone: 01335 343377
Fax: 01335 347117 • E-mail: info@stone-cottage.fsnet.co.uk

SELF-CATERING

WOLFSCOTE GRANGE FARM COTTAGES
Hartington, Near Buxton, Derbyshire SK17 0AX
Tel & Fax: 01298 84342

Charming cottages nestling beside the beautiful Dove Valley in stunning scenery. Cruck Cottage is peaceful 'with no neighbours, only sheep' and a cosy 'country living' feel. Swallows Cottage offers comfort for the traveller and time to relax in beautiful surroundings. It sparkles with olde worlde features, yet has all modern amenities including en suite facilities and spa bathroom. The farm trail provides walks from your doorstep to the Dales. Open all year.
Weekly terms from £180 to £450 (sleeps 4) & £180 to £550 (sleeps 6).

ETC ★★★★
e-mail: wolfscote@btinternet.com
website: www.wolfscotegrangecottages.co.uk

BOARD

SAND PEBBLES HOTEL & RESTAURANT

Hope Cove, near Salcombe. Friendly family-run Hotel 300 yards from delightful sandy beaches and coastal walks. Refurbished 2003. Relaxing restaurant renowned for excellent food and service. Come and stay with us and...

"Let Us Spoil You"
Telephone: 01548 561673
website: www.sandpebbleshotel.co.uk
SEE OUR ENTRY UNDER DEVON – SALCOMBE

SELF-CATERING

Mount Folly Farm
Bigbury-on-Sea • 01548 810267

Please write or telephone for a brochure.
Mrs J. Tucker, Mount Folly Farm, Bigbury-on-Sea, Near Kingsbridge Devon TQ7 4AR
SEE ALSO MAIN ENTRY UNDER DEVON/KINGSBRIDGE

A delightful family farm, situated right on the coast, overlooking the sea and sandy beaches of Bigbury Bay and the River Avon. Lovely coastal walks. Ideal base for the South Hams.

The spacious wing comprises half of the farmhouse and is completely self-contained.

Toad Hall Cottages

200 fabulous and unusual properties situated in truly beautiful waterside, rural and village locations in Devon, Cornwall & Exmoor.

For our full colour brochure please call

08700 777345

www.toadhallcottages.com
email: thc@toadhallcottages.com

BONEHAYNE FARM
COLYTON, DEVON EX24 6SG

COTTAGE: CARAVAN: BOARD

- Family 250 acre working farm • Competitive prices
- Spectacular views • South facing luxury caravan
- Cottage with four-poster and central heating
- Four miles to the beach • Five minutes from Colyton
- Spacious lawns/gardens • Laundry room, BBQ, picnic tables
- Good trout fishing, woods to roam, walks

Mrs Gould
Tel: 01404 871396/871416

website: www.bonehayne.co.uk • e-mail: gould@bonehayne.co.uk

WULFRUNA
HOLIDAY APARTMENTS
9 Esplanade Road, Paignton TQ4 6EB

Tel: 01803 212660

Apartments for couples and families
Prices from £95 per week
A warm welcome, comfort and cleanliness assured
Brochure from
Lynne and Ian Macrae

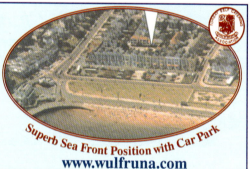

Superb Sea Front Position with Car Park

www.wulfruna.com

Lifton Hall Hotel
Lifton, Devon PL16 0DR

ETC/AA ★★

Tel: 01566 784863 • Fax: 01566 784770 • relax@liftonhall.co.uk • www.liftonhall.co.uk

A 300-year old manor house where old-fashioned values of service, style and comfort can still be enjoyed. On the Devon/Cornwall border, ½ mile off the A30, it offers the perfect opportunity to explore the West Country. The 9 tastefully furnished bedrooms (including 3 superior rooms) have en suite bath or shower and a full range of amenities; there is also a light and airy residents' lounge, a stylish dining room and a cosy bar. Meals are an essential part of the Lifton Hall experience, with something to suit every taste and appetite, using only the best quality local produce. A carefully chosen and reasonably priced wine list provides the perfect accompaniment.

Owners Andrew and Glenys Brown extend an invitation to you to experience the charm and beauty of the area whilst enjoying their unique hospitality and personal service at Lifton Hall.

Devon

COLLACOTT FARM Quality Country Cottages

Eight delightful country cottages sleeping 2-12 set around a large cobbled courtyard, amidst twenty acres of tranquil Devon countryside. All are well equipped with wood-burning stove, dishwasher, heating, bed linen, and their own individual patio and garden. A tennis court, heated swimming pool, games room, children's play area, trampoline room and BHS approved riding centre make Collacott an ideal holiday for the whole family.

Jane & Chris Cromey-Hawke, Collacott Farm,
King's Nympton, Umberleigh, North Devon EX37 9TP
Tel: 01769 572491 • e-mail: jane@collacott.co.uk
website: www.collacott.co.uk

Instow Beach Haven Cottage

View from balcony of beach and sea

Seafront cottage overlooking the sandy beach. Instow is a quiet yachting village with soft yellow sands and a pretty promenade of shops, old houses, pubs and cafés serving drinks and meals. Beach Haven has extensive beach and sea views from the house and garden, sleeps 5, own parking, gas fired central heating, colour TV, washing machine. Lawned garden overlooking sea with terrace and garden furniture. Coastal walks and cycle trails, boat to Lundy Island. Dog welcome. Other sea front cottages available.

Ring 01237 473801 for prices and vacancies only or send SAE for brochure to Mrs F.I. BARNES, 140 Bay View Road, Northam, Bideford, Devon EX39 1BJ

Churchwood Valley

Seven times David Bellamy Gold Award Winner

Relax in one of our comfortable log cabins, set in a peaceful wooded valley near the beach. Enjoy wonderful walks in woods and along the coast. Abundance of birds and wildlife. Up to two pets per cabin. Open April to January including special Christmas and New Year Breaks.

Wembury Bay, South Devon PL9 0DZ

e-mail: Churchwoodvalley@btinternet.com • Tel: 01752 862382

Cider Room Cottage Hasland Farm, Membury, Axminster.

This delightfully converted thatched cider barn, with exposed beams, adjoins main farmhouse overlooking the outstanding beauty of the orchards, pools and pastureland, and is ideally situated for touring Devon, Dorset and Somerset. Bathing, golf and tennis at Lyme Regis and many places of interest locally, including Wildlife Park, donkey sanctuary and Forde Abbey. Membury Village, with its post office and stores, trout farm, church and swimming pool is one mile away. The accommodation is of the highest standard with the emphasis on comfort. Two double rooms, cot if required; shower room and toilet; sitting/diningroom with colour TV; kitchen with electric cooker, microwave, washing machine, fridge. Linen supplied if required. Pets by arrangement. Car essential.
Open all year • No smoking • Terms from £135 to £270 • SAE, please, to

Tel: 01404 881558   Mrs Pat Steele, Hasland Farm, Membury, Axminster EX13 7JF

Devon

SELF-CATERING

"**West Ridge**" bungalow stands on elevated ground above the small coastal town of Seaton. It has one-and-a-half-acres of lawns and gardens and enjoys wide panoramic views of the beautiful Axe Estuary and the sea. Close by are Axmouth, Beer and Branscombe. The Lyme Bay area is an excellent centre for touring, walking, sailing, fishing, golf, etc. This comfortably furnished accommodation is ideally suited for two to four persons. Cot can be provided. Available March to October. £195 to £425 weekly (fuel charges included). Full gas central heating. Colour TV. SAE for brochure.

Mrs E.P. Fox, "West Ridge", Harepath Hill, Seaton EX12 2TA (Tel & Fax: 01297 22398)
e-mail: foxfamily@westridge.fsbusiness.co.uk
website: www.cottageguide.co.uk/westridge

SELF-CATERING

Watermill Cottages

Down a narrow lane lies a secret valley just over a mile inland from Slapton Sands. There you will find the six delightful **Watermill Cottages** on the banks of a small river by an old mill house. A peaceful haven with wonderful walks and freedom for children to explore. Home cooking available. Winter breaks from **£95**.

Hansel, Dartmouth, South Devon TQ6 0LN
website: www.watermillcottages.co.uk

For our colour brochure call 01803 770 219 or e-mail: graham@hanselpg.freeserve.co.uk

---

COUNTRY INN

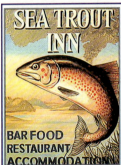

SEA TROUT INN
Staverton, Near Totnes, Devon TQ9 6PA
Tel: 01803 762274 • Fax: 01803 762506
website: www.seatroutinn.com

The Inn has two well-appointed bars with oak beams and real log fires, both pleasant places to relax and unwind after a day's walking or touring. 10 bedrooms, delightfully decorated in a comfortable cottage style, have private bathrooms, central heating, direct-dial telephone, tea/coffee making facilities and colour TV.

Guests dining in the Hotel may choose from the award winning restaurant or the relaxing and leisurely atmosphere of the bars or, on warmer summer days, the attractive patio garden. An extensive menu ranges from light snacks to full meals, with vegetarian dishes always available.

SELF-CATERING

CHICHESTER HOUSE HOLIDAY APARTMENTS

Quiet, relaxing, fully furnished apartments. Opposite Barricane Shell Beach – central seafront position with outstanding sea and coastal views.

Watch the sun go down into the sea from your own balcony.

• Open all year • Free parking • Pets by arrangement.
SAE to resident proprietor, Joyce Bagnall.
Off-peak reductions. Short Break details on request.

**The Esplanade, Woolacombe EX34 7DJ
Tel: 01271 870761**

Devon

Higher Coarsewell Farm
Ugborough, Near Ivybridge, Devon PL21 0HP

Part of a traditional family-run dairy farm situated in the heart of the peaceful South Hams countryside, near Dartmoor and local unspoilt sandy beaches.

Bed and Breakfast from £18 daily; optional Evening Meal extra. Open all year.

Very spacious bungalow with beautiful garden and meadow views. Double room with bathroom en suite and en suite family room. Guest lounge/dining room. Good home cooked food, full English breakfast served. Children welcome.

Mrs Susan Winzer
e-mail: susan_winzer@hotmail.com

Tel: 01548 821560

We have a lovely farm set at the head of the Fuchsia Valley of Lee, with views across the Atlantic. Our four fully furnished cottages and two holiday homes are so popular we have erected a log cabin to accommodate all the visitors who want to keep coming to stay in this peaceful corner of Devon, surrounded by our special animals and the beautiful wildlife - deer, badgers, geese and buzzards to name but a few.
The beaches of Lee Woolacombe are close by.
Meals and cream teas are available, by arrangement, in our conservatory.

Lower Campscott Farm
Lee, Ilfracombe, Devon EX34 8LS
Tel: 01271 863479
e-mail: holidays@lowercampscott.co.uk
website: www.lowercampscott.co.uk

Working farm in South Huish Valley, one mile from the fishing village of Hope Cove, three miles from famous sailing haunt of Salcombe. Walking, beaches, sailing, windsurfing, bathing, diving, fishing, horse-riding – facilities for all in this area. We have a dairy herd and two flocks of pedigree sheep. Guests are welcome to take part in farm activities when appropriate. Traditional farmhouse cooking and home produce. Country restaurant on site serving freshly cooked meals using local produce. Lunches, cream teas, dinner, children's meals. Access to rooms at all times. Tea/coffee making facilities and TV in rooms, all of which are en suite. Games room. Non-smoking. Open all year, except Christmas. Warm welcome assured. Self-catering cottages also available. Dogs by arrangement. Details and terms on request. Bed and Breakfast from £30 to £35 pp.

e-mail: anne@burtonfarm.co.uk • website: www.burtonfarm.co.uk
Anne Rossiter, Burton Farm, Galmpton, Kingsbridge TQ7 3EY • 01548 561210

The nearest camping and caravan park to the sea, in perfectly secluded beautiful coastal country. Our family-run park, adjoining National Trust land, is only 500 yards from Rockham Beach, yet only five minutes' walk from the village of Mortehoe with a Post Office, petrol station/garage, shops, cafes and pubs – one of which has a children's room. Four to six berth holiday caravans for hire and pitches for tents, dormobiles and touring caravans, electric hook-ups available. We have hot showers and flush toilets, laundry room, shop and off-licence; Calor gas and Camping Gaz available; children's play area. Dogs accepted but must be kept on lead. Open Easter to end September. Brochure available.

**North Morte Farm Caravan & Camping,
Dept. FHG, Mortehoe,
Woolacombe EX34 7EG (01271 870381)**

Devon

SELF-CATERING

DEVONCOAST HOLIDAYS

We are an experienced Holiday Letting Agency, with properties ranging from one bedroom flats to three bedroomed houses, all in **Sunny South Devon**. Some have sea views. All are fully equipped with CTV and car parking. Children and pets are welcome. Mini Breaks.
We are open all year. Free brochure & map.

**P. O. BOX 14, BRIXHAM, DEVON TQ5 9AB
Tel: 07050 33 8889   www.devoncoast.com**

BOARD

Harton Farm
Oakford, Tiverton EX16 9HH (01398 351209)

Come and enjoy a unique rural experience on our traditional non-intensive working farm near Exmoor; peace and quiet for adults, and for the children, a chance to meet the animals. 17th Century stone farmhouse, secluded but accessible, ideal touring centre. Comfortable accommodation in three double bedrooms with washbasin and tea making facilities; luxury bathroom with a view; dining room serving real country cooking with farm-produced additive-free meat and organic vegetables; home baking a speciality; guests' lounge with colour TV. Home spun wool. Garden. Children over four welcome. Pets accepted. Car essential - parking. Open for Evening Meal, Bed and Breakfast from £26; Bed and Breakfast from £18. Reductions for children. Farm walks. Fishing, shooting, riding can be arranged. Vegetarian meals available on request.

e-mail: lindy@HARTONFARM.co.uk   web: www.hartonfarm.co.uk

SELF-CATERING

A most attractive, well equipped, south-facing cottage with large garden, on edge of the village of Bishop's Nympton, three miles from South Molton.

Ideal holiday centre, easy reach of Exmoor, the coast, sporting activities and places of interest.

• Three bedrooms: one double, one twin-bedded with washbasin and one single.
• Two bathrooms with toilets.

Court Green, Bishop's Nympton, Near South Molton • Sleeps 5

• Sitting and dining rooms, large kitchen. Central heating, electric wood/coal effect fires, TV.

One mile sea trout/trout fishing on River Mole. Well behaved pets welcome. Terms April to October £200 to £240.

Mrs J. Greenwell, Tregeiriog, Near Llangollen LL20 7HU
Tel: 01691 600672

SELF-CATERING

**HOPE BARTON BARNS
Tel: 01548 561393
www.hopebarton.co.uk
★★★★ Open All Year**

Nestling in its own valley close to the sandy cove, Hope Barton Barns is an exclusive group of 17 stone barns in two courtyards and three luxury apartments in the converted farmhouse. Superbly furnished and fully equipped, accommodation ranges from a studio to four bedrooms, sleeping two to 10. Heated indoor pool, sauna, gym, lounge bar, tennis court, trout lake and a children's play barn. We have 35 acres of pastures and streams. Farmhouse meals. Ample parking. Golf, sailing and coastal walking nearby. A perfect setting for family summer holidays, walking in Spring/Autumn or just a "get away from it all" break. Free range children and well behaved dogs welcome. For full colour brochure please contact: **Mike or Judy Tromans.**

Hope Cove – Near Salcombe - South Devon – TQ7 3HT

Devon

SELF-CATERING

Lookweep Farm
Dartmoor National Park

Lookweep Farm is set within Dartmoor National Park and is perfectly placed for exploration of Dartmoor, the stunning coastline, charming villages and towns of South Devon. *Shippen* and *Dairy* cottages are two attractive, well-equipped stone cottages surrounded by open farmland and woods in this tranquil setting near Bovey Tracey and just a two mile drive from Haytor. Own gardens, ample parking, heated pool and outstanding walks right on your doorstep. Children welcome (high chairs and cots available). Pets by arrangement. Short breaks available. Mastercard and Visa accepted. Sleeps 5. Please phone or write for brochure.

**John and Helen Griffiths, Lookweep Farm, Liverton,
Newton Abbot TQ12 6HT • 01626 833271 • Fax: 01626 834412
e-mail: holidays@lookweep.co.uk • website: www.lookweep.co.uk**

BOARD/SELF-CATERING

2002 Golden Achievement Award of Excellence for Quality and Service

Winner of the 2002 Golden Achievement Award of Excellence for Quality and Service, this tastefully refurbished 16th century farmhouse is situated close to the road between Barnstaple and Bideford on the lovely Taw/Torridge estuary, immediately adjacent to the Tarka Trail. Open all year, the rooms are fully modernised, with colour TV and en suite facilities. With courtyard parking, this is an ideal base for touring Devon and Cornwall. It is within a mile of the sandy beach at Instow, and excellent pubs and restaurants. A self-catering cottage (ETC ★★★) is also available, and there are many leisure activities close at hand. For details contact:

**Peter Day, Lower Yelland Farm, Fremington, Barnstaple EX31 3EN
Tel: 01271 860101 / 07803 933542
e-mail: peterday@loweryellandfarm.co.uk
www.loweryellandfarm.co.uk**

COUNTRY INNS

The Castle Inn Hotel
Lydford, Okehampton, Devon EX20 4BH
Tel: 01822 820241 • Fax: 01822 820454

One of the finest traditional wayside inns in the West Country, this romantic Elizabethan hostelry is featured in Conan Doyle's 'The Hound of the Baskervilles'. First-class food in a bar and restaurant with slate floors, bowed ceilings, low, lamp-lit beams and fascinating antiques; dining by candlelight from imaginative table d'hôte and à la carte menus. Guest rooms, decorated in individual style, are beautifully furnished and equipped. A wonderful place to shake off the cobwebs of urban existence and appreciate the really worthwhile things of life.

e-mail: castleinnlyd@aol.com

BOARD

Great Sloncombe Farm
Moretonhampstead Devon TQ13 8QF
Tel: 01647 440595

Share the magic of Dartmoor all year round while staying in our lovely 13th century farmhouse full of interesting historical features. A working mixed farm set amongst peaceful meadows and woodland abundant in wild flowers and animals, including badgers, foxes, deer and buzzards. A welcoming and informal place to relax and explore the moors and Devon countryside. Comfortable double and twin rooms with en suite facilities, TV, central heating and coffee/tea making facilities. Delicious Devonshire suppers and breakfasts with new baked bread.

**Open all year~No smoking~Farm Stay UK
e-mail: hmerchant@sloncombe.freeserve.co.uk • website: www.greatsloncombefarm.co.uk**

The Farm Holiday Guide to Coast & Country Holidays 2004

Devon

SELF-CATERING

WIDMOUTH FARM
Watermouth, Near Ilfracombe
Devon EX34 9RX
Tel: 01271 863743 Fax: 01271 866479

Widmouth Farm has 35 acres of gardens, woodland, pastures and a private beach on National Heritage Coastline. There are 10 one, two and three bedroom cottages, some early Victorian, some conversions from farm buildings. All are comfortable and well equipped. We have sheep, goats, chickens, ducks, rabbits, guinea pigs and much wildlife (seals sometimes play off our coast). The surroundings are tranquil, the views superb and access easy (on the A399 between Ilfracombe and Combe Martin). Ideal for walking (the coastal footpath runs around the property), bird watching, painting and sea fishing. Ilfracombe Golf Club in walking distance. Pets welcome.

e-mail: holiday@widmouthfarmcottages.co.uk   website: www.widmouthfarmcottages.co.uk

---

SELF-CATERING

Stressed out?   Let Narramore work its magic on you!

Six comfortable cottages situated on 107-acre horse stud/alpaca farm. A really warm pool, bubbling hot spa, games/laundry room, play area, fishing pool, boat, barbecue, small animals, plus the opportunity to badgerwatch amidst glorious countryside – all these make us special. Colour brochure. Open all year. Terms from £100 to £660. Short breaks available.

Narramore Farm Cottages, Narramore Farm,
Moretonhampstead, Devon TQ13 8QT
01647 440455 • Fax: 01647 440031
e-mail: sue@narramorefarm.com
website: www.narramorefarm.co.uk

Mrs Sue Horn

Holiday and Accommodation guides 2004

Each year FHG Publications produce a large range of attractive holiday accommodation guides for all kinds of holiday opportunities throughout Britain. They are great value for money and are available in most bookshops and larger newsagents at the following prices.

Please mention Farm Holiday Guide when enquiring

Dorset

REDLANDS FARM CARAVAN PARK
...for Personal Service
and Easiest Access to
Weymouth Beach...

Very conveniently situated in a semi-rural location backing onto open fields, yet not too far from the town centre and 1½ miles from the seafront. Buses stop just outside the park entrance and serve not only the town centre but much of Dorset. Ideal for day trips exploring the lovely countryside.

- Thirty 4 - 8 berth modern luxury caravans for hire with all services plus colour TV and fridge • Friendly family-run park • Launderette facilities • Supermarkets close by • Personal supervision • Caravan sales • Children and Pets welcome • Plenty of official footpaths and country walks to explore • Car parking alongside caravans • Open March to November
- Terms per week £130 – £420

SAE for enquiries.

REDLANDS FARM CARAVAN PARK
DORCHESTER ROAD, WEYMOUTH, DORSET DT3 5AP
Tel: 01305 812291 • Fax: 01305 814251

Redlands Sports Club is opposite the park where club, bar and sports facilities are available. Membership open to all visitors.

Dorset

SELF-CATERING

Little Hewish Barn

A 150 year old brick and flint barn, converted to provide comfortable accommodation of a very high standard, including oil-fired central heating. There are two double bedrooms (one converts to twin), both with en suite bath/shower facilities. Spacious open-plan living/dining area features a wood-burning stove, fully-equipped kitchen, dishwasher, washer/dryer, TV/video, stereo etc. Children and well-behaved pets are very welcome. Fully-enclosed patio garden and ample on-site parking. Prices are all inclusive – no hidden extras. 'Per person per night' pricing outside of peak periods.

Little Hewish Barn, Milton Abbas, Blandford Forum, Dorset DT11 0DP
Tel: 01258 881235 • Fax: 01258 881393 • E-mail: terry@littlehewish.co.uk

---

BOARD

Pennhills Farm

Pennhills Farmhouse set in 100 acres of unspoiled countryside, is situated one mile from the village of Shillingstone in the heart of the Blackmore Vale, an ideal peaceful retreat, short break or holiday. It offers spacious comfortable accommodation for all ages; children welcome, pets by arrangement. One downstairs bedroom. All bedrooms en suite with TV and tea/coffee making facilities, complemented by traditional English breakfast with home produced bacon and sausages. Vegetarians catered for. Good meals available locally. Brochure sent on request. A warm and friendly welcome is assured from your host Rosie Watts. From £22 per person.

Mrs Rosie Watts, Pennhills Farm, Sandy Lane,
Off Lanchards Lane, Shillingstone, Blandford DT11 0TF
Tel: 01258 860491

BOARD/SELF-CATERING

B&B £22–£27 per person

Cardsmill Farm Holidays

Whitchurch Canonicorum, Charmouth
Bridport, Dorset DT6 6RP
Tel & Fax: 01297 489375 • e-mail: cardsmill@aol.com
website: www.farmhousedorset.com

Stay on a real working family farm in the Marshland Vale, an Area of Outstanding Natural Beauty. Enjoy country walks to the village, coast and around farm and woods. Watch the daily milking, see baby calves and lambs, and seasonal activities here on this 590 acre farm. En suite family and double rooms available with CTV, tea/coffee trays.

Also available, three large, rural quiet farmhouses. Each has half-acre garden, double glazed conservatory and parking space. Taphouse farmhouse has six bedrooms, three bathrooms, lounge, 22x15 ft kitchen/diner, games room, oil-fired Rayburn, log fire and central heating. Courthouse has four bedrooms, two bathrooms, lounge, kitchen/diner and full central heating. All available all year for long or short stays. Phone for a brochure.

CARAVANS

WOOLSBRIDGE MANOR

FARM CARAVAN PARK AA▶▶▶ ETC ★★★

Situated approximately three-and-a-half-miles from the New Forest market town of Ringwood – easy access to the south coast. Seven acres level, semi-sheltered, well-drained spacious pitches. Quiet country location on a working farm, ideal and safe for families. Showers, mother/baby area, laundry room, washing up area, chemical disposal, payphone, electric hook-ups, battery charging. Children's play area on site. Site shop. Dogs welcome on leads. Fishing adjacent. Moors Valley Country Park golf course one mile. Pub and restaurant 10 minutes' walk.

Three Legged Cross, Wimborne, Dorset BH21 6RA   Telephone: 01202 826369

Dorset

where the forest meets the sea...

here is a peaceful place for the WHOLE family

To the North as you look...
The New Forest is waiting to be explored!

To the East as you look...
Maritime history in the making - Southampton.

To the West as you look...
The unspoilt beauty of the Isle of Purbeck.

And to the south there is the wide open sea, **so why are you still reading this?**

01202 428 717 / 417 757 www.**bournecoast**.co.uk

Bournecoast

Est. 1960
K.W. Simmons MBE

Superior Self-Catering Holiday Cottages

Set in the heart of the beautiful and unspoilt Dorset countryside with stunning views and a peaceful, traffic free environment. Luccombe offers quality accommodation for 2 to 8 people in a variety of converted and historic farm buildings, with original timbers and panelling. Well equipped kitchens. Large shower or bath. Cosy lounge/dining with colour TV. Bed linen, duvets, towels provided. Laundry room. Children and well behaved pets welcome. Ample parking. Disabled access. Riding, tennis, games room. Clay pigeon shooting and fishing nearby. Post office and village stores in local village. Open throughout the year. Group/family enquiries welcome. Short breaks available. Magnificent heated, indoor swimming pool, sauna and gymnasium on site.

Luccombe Country Holidays

Luccombe, Milton Abbas, Blandford Forum, Dorset DT11 OBE • Tel: 01258 880558
Fax: 01258 881184   E-mail: info@luccombeholidays.co.uk   Web: www.luccombeholidays.co.uk

ETC ★★★★ SELF-CATERING

"Dormer Cottage", Woodlands, Hyde, Near Wareham

This secluded cottage, cosy and modern, is a converted old barn of Woodlands House. Standing in its own grounds, it is fronted by a small wood with a walled paddock at the back. Pleasant walks in wooded forests nearby. In the midst of "Hardy Country" and ideal for a family holiday and for those who value seclusion. All linen included, beds ready made on guests' arrival and basic shopping arranged on request. Amusements at Bournemouth, Poole and Dorchester within easy reach. Five people and a baby can be accommodated in two double and one single bedrooms; cot and high chair available. Bathroom, two toilets; lounge and diningroom, colour TV. Kitchen with cooker, fridge, washing machine, small deep freeze, etc. Pets welcome. Open all year. Golf course half-mile; pony trekking, riding nearby. SAE, please, for terms.

Mrs M.J.M. Constantinides, "Woodlands", Hyde, Near Wareham BH20 7NT (01929 471239)

Dorset

Isle of Purbeck
Downshay Farm

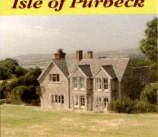

Working dairy farm in the heart of beautiful Isle of Purbeck, midway between Corfe Castle and Swanage. This Victorian Purbeck stone farmhouse has a family room en suite and one double with private shower room close by. Both rooms have colour TV and tea/coffee making facilities.

Steam railway within walking distance, coastal path and sandy beaches three miles away. Excellent pubs and restaurants to be found locally. Open Easter to October for Bed and Breakfast from £20 per person.

e-mail: downshayfarm@tiscali.co.uk
**Mrs Justine Pike, Downshay Farm,
Haycrafts Lane, Harmans Cross, Swanage BH19 3EB
Tel: 01929 480316**

Built in 1892, **HOLLY HEDGE FARM** is situated next to Bulbury Woods Golf Course, set in 11 acres of wood and grassland adjacent to lake. We are just 15 minutes away from the Purbecks, the beach and the forest. The area is ideal for walking or cycling and Poole Quay and Harbour are also nearby.
Accommodation comprises two double/family rooms, one twin and one single, all with en suite showers, colour TV, tea/coffee making facilities, radio alarms and central heating.

- Prices for a single room £30, double £52 per night.
- Open all year round for summer or winter breaks.
- Full English or Continental breakfast served.

**Mrs Stephenson
Holly Hedge Farm
Bulbury Lane, Lytchett Matravers,
Poole, Dorset BH16 6EP
Tel: 01929 459688**

Stocks Farm
Tel & Fax: 01202 888697

Stocks Farm is a family-run farm and nursery situated in peaceful countryside just one-and-half miles from the lovely country town of Wimborne Minster, off the B3078. Surrounded by lovely Dorset countryside and pretty villages; coastline, beaches and New Forest within easy reach.

Bed and Breakfast accommodation consists of one double en suite bedroom and one twin bedroom with private bathroom, both on ground level. Disabled guests are very welcome. Tea and coffee making facilities in both rooms. All accommodation is non-smoking. Situated in secluded garden with patio for guests to enjoy breakfast outside. Local pubs and restaurants offer varied menus. Bed and Breakfast from £20 per person per night.
Mrs King, Stocks Farm, Furzehill, Wimborne BH21 4HT

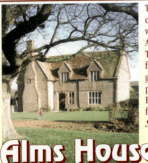

Alms House Farm

This charming old farmhouse was a monastery during the 16th century, restored in 1849 and is now a Listed building. A family-run working dairy farm, 140 acres overlooking the Blackmoor Vale. Accommodation is in three comfortable en suite rooms with colour TV and tea/coffee making facilities. Diningroom with inglenook fireplace, lounge with colour TV, for guests' use at all times. Also garden and lawn. Plenty of reading material and local information provided for this ideal touring area. Bed and Breakfast from £24. Excellent evening meals in all local inns nearby. Situated six miles from Sherborne with its beautiful Abbey and Castle.

SAE for further details. Mrs Jenny Mayo
**Hermitage, Holnest,
Sherborne DT9 6HA**
(Tel and Fax: 01963 210296)

Dorset

Brambles

Set in beautiful, tranquil countryside, Brambles is a pretty, thatched cottage offering every comfort, superb views and a friendly welcome. There is a choice of en suite twin, double or single rooms, all very comfortable and with colour TV and tea/coffee making facilities. Pretty garden available for relaxing in. Full English or Continental breakfast served. Evening meals available by prior arrangement. There are many interesting places to visit and wonderful walks for enthusiasts. B&B £27 per person.

Woolcombe, Melbury Bubb, Dorchester DT2 0NJ • Tel: 01935 83672

New House Farm
Mangerton Lane, Bradpole, Bridport DT6 3SF

Stay in a modern, comfortable farmhouse on a small working farm set in the rural Dorset hills and become one of the family. A large wild garden where you are welcome to sit or stroll round. Two large rooms available, both en suite, both with lovely views over the surrounding countryside, both with television and tea/coffee making facilities. We are near to Bridport and the seaside, golf courses, fossil hunting, beautiful gardens, wonderful walking, coarse fishing lake – lots to do. Simple traditional farmhouse evening meals can be provided, subject to booking. B&B from £35.

e-mail: jane@mangertonlake.freeserve.co.uk
website: www.mangertonlake.co.uk • Tel & Fax: 01308 422884

Hemsworth Manor Farm
Witchampton, Wimborne BH21 5BN

Our lovely old Manor Farmhouse which is mentioned in the Domesday Book, is situated in an exceptionally peaceful location, yet is only half-an-hour's drive from Salisbury, Dorchester, Poole, Bournemouth and the New Forest. Hemsworth is a working family farm of nearly 800 acres, providing some lovely walks. The farm is mainly arable, but is also home to sheep, horses, ponies and various domestic pets. We have three fully equipped en suite bedrooms, all with colour TV. Separate lounge for guests' use. There are excellent pubs locally. Brochure available.

Tel: 01258 840216 •• Fax: 01258 841278

Publisher's Note

While every effort is made to ensure accuracy, we regret that FHG Publications cannot accept responsibility for errors, omissions or misrepresentations in our entries or any consequences thereof. Prices in particular should be checked because we go to press early. We will follow up complaints but cannot act as arbiters or agents for either party.

The Farm Holiday Guide to Coast & Country Holidays 2004

Durham/Essex/Gloucestershire

BOARD

Bee Cottage Farmhouse

Charming farmhouse situated in peaceful, picturesque surroundings on the edge of the beautiful Durham Dales. We offer good food and are happy to cater for vegetarians; residential and restaurant licence. Bed and Breakfast; dinner available. Northumbria boasts over 80 golf courses, and the Beamish Open Air Museum, Hadrian's Wall and the Metro Centre are all under 20 miles. Walking, cycling and fishing available nearby. Great for pets.

**BEE COTTAGE FARMHOUSE,
CASTLESIDE, CONSETT, DURHAM DH8 9HW
Telephone: 01207 508224**
e-mail: welcome@beecottagefarmhouse.freeserve.co.uk
web: www.SmoothHound.co.uk/hotels/beecottage.html

SELF-CATERING

East Briscoe Farm Cottages
Baldersdale
Barnard Castle
Co. Durham
DL12 9UL

Emma Wilson
01833 650087

In a beautiful situation central to the North of England. The six stone-built cottages offer superb accommodation on a stunning riverside estate which offers walks and fishing. A place to relax and explore the North.
Sleep 2-6. Open all year.
Pets welcome in two of the cottages.
Terms from £120
Winner of the Northumbria TB 'Self-Catering of the Year' 1999

fax: 01833 650027 • e-mail: info@eastbriscoe.co.uk • www.eastbriscoe.co.uk

---

SELF-CATERING

Sudgrove Cottages

Self-catering in the Heart of the Cotswolds
ETC ★★★   Open all year

3 stone cottages, each with its own garden, set in a peaceful hamlet on a hill between two unspoilt valleys. Relax in the garden, explore the Cotswolds, Severn Vale and beyond by car, or walk the many footpaths that radiate from Sudgrove. A warm welcome awaits all year.

Prices: 2 bedroom cottages (sleep 4) £200-£300 per week
3 bedroom cottage (sleeps 6) £225-£410 per week

Contact: Carol Ractliffe, Sudgrove, Miserden, Glos. GL6 7JD • Tel/Fax: 01285 821322
e-mail: enquiries@sudgrovecottages.co.uk • website: www.sudgrovecottages.co.uk

---

Looking for Holiday Accommodation?

for details of hundreds of properties throughout the UK including comprehensive coverage of all areas of Scotland try:

www.holidayguides.com

Please mention Farm Holiday Guide when enquiring

Gloucestershire

A warm and friendly welcome awaits you at our completely refurbished 15th century Grade II Listed farmhouse, in the heart of this beautiful village. Spacious beamed rooms, inglenook fireplace in dining room where a full English breakfast is served. Large private car park at rear. All bedrooms are en suite and have coffee/tea making facilities, TV, radio and hairdryer.

Accommodation comprises one double, two twin and one family suite consisting of a single and a double room en suite. Sorry no pets allowed in the house. Non-smoking
Terms per night: £55 per double bedded suite, 2 persons sharing. More than two nights £50. Twin-bedded rooms are £50 or single occupancy £40. Family room for 3 persons sharing £80.

Veronica Stanley, Home Farm House, Ebrington, Chipping Campden GL55 6NL
Tel & Fax: 01386 593309
e-mail: willstanley@farmersweekly.net • website: www.homefarminthecotswolds.co.uk

POOL FARM
Bath Road, Wick, Bristol BS30 5RL
Tel: 0117 937 2284

Welcome to our 350 year old Grade II Listed farmhouse on a working farm. On A420 between Bath and Bristol and a few miles from Exit 18 of M4, we are on the edge of the village, overlooking fields, but within easy reach of pub, shops and golf club. We offer traditional Bed and Breakfast in one family and one twin room with tea/coffee facilities and TV; guest lounge. Central heating. Ample parking. Open all year except Christmas. Terms from £20.

A large, quiet farmhouse set in 350 acres, built on the site of monastery between the Malverns and Cotswolds, half a mile M5-M50 junction. Six en suite bedrooms with colour TV and tea making facilities. Centrally heated. Open all year except Christmas. Large lounge with open fire and colour TV. Spacious diningroom. Licensed bar. Good home cooked food in large quantities, home produced where possible. Children's own TV room, games room and playroom. Tennis lawn. Play area and lawn. Cot and high chair available. Laundry facilities. Ideally situated for touring with numerous places to visit. Swimming, tennis, sauna, golf within three miles. Coarse fishing available on the farm.

Bed and Breakfast from £19 to £21. Reduced rates for children and Senior Citizens.

Mrs Bernadette Williams, Abbots Court, Church End, Twyning, Tewkesbury GL20 6DA
Tel & Fax: 01684 292515 • e-mail: bernie@abbotscourt.fsbusiness.co.uk

The Bowl Inn & Lilies Restaurant

16 Church Road, Lower Almondsbury, Bristol BS32 4DT
Tel: 01454 612757
Fax: 01454 619910
e-mail: reception@thebowlinn.co.uk
website: www.thebowlinn.co.uk

- 13 double/twin rooms, all en suite
- Lunch & Evening Meal available
- Special rates for Weekend Breaks
- Open all year

Whether travelling on business or just taking a leisurely break, you will find all the comforts of modern life housed in this historic 12th century village inn.

- Real ales • Fine wines
- Extensive bar fayre
- A la carte restaurant
- 5 Minutes J16 M5.

Gloucestershire/Hampshire

COUNTRY INNS

❖ THE OLD NEW INN ❖
Bourton-on-the-Water, Gloucestershire GL54 2AF
Tel: 01451 820467 • Fax: 01451 810236 • www.theoldnewinn.co.uk

The Old New Inn is a traditional country Inn. It has log fires and three bars where guests can enjoy a drink and a chat. In the heart of the Cotswolds, close to the River Windrush, Bourton-on-the-Water is an ideal centre for a country holiday. All bedrooms (one with four-poster) are en suite and all have TV and tea/coffee making facilities. The Hotel has a spacious lounge for residents. There is a car park and a large attractive beer garden. A comprehensive table d'hôte dinner menu is available in the evening – bar meals are served at lunch times and evening.

e-mail: reception@theoldnewinn.co.uk

BOARD

Tel & Fax: 01452 840224

Quality all ground floor accommodation. "Kilmorie" is Grade II Listed (c1848) within conservation area in a lovely part of Gloucestershire. Double, twin, family or single bedrooms, all having tea tray, colour TV, radio, mostly en suite. Very comfortable guests' lounge, traditional home cooking is served in the separate dining room overlooking large garden. Perhaps walk waymarked farmland footpaths which start here. Children may "help" with our child's pony, and hens. Rural yet perfectly situated to visit Cotswolds, Royal Forest of Dean, Wye Valley and Malvern Hills. Children over five years. No smoking, please. Ample parking.

Bed, full English Breakfast and Evening Dinner from £29;
Bed and Breakfast from £20.

S.J. Barnfield, "Kilmorie Smallholding", Gloucester Road, Corse, Staunton, Gloucester GL19 3RQ
e-mail: sheila-barnfield@supanet.com

BOARD/SELF-CATERING

Fritham Farm

Lovely farmhouse on working farm in the heart of the New Forest. Peace and tranquillity in this wonderful area of natural beauty. Three twin/double rooms, all en suite with king-size beds and tea/coffee making facilities. Large lounge with TV. There is also a very comfortable cottage (sleeps 2) on the farm with views across green fields to the Forest beyond. No smoking. Children 10 and over welcome. Come and enjoy a relaxing stay in this lovely corner of England – perfect for walking/cycling/riding/touring.

B&B £22 to £24 per person.
Cottage £250 to £350 per week.

John & Penny Hankinson, Fritham Farm, Fritham, Lyndhurst, Hampshire. S043 7HH
Tel & Fax: 023 8081 2333 • E-mail: frithamfarm@supanet.com

BOARD

Mays Farm
Longwood Dean, Near Winchester SO21 1JS
Tel: 01962 777486 & Fax: 01962 777747

Twelve minutes' drive from Winchester, (the eleventh century capital city of England), Mays Farm is set in rolling countryside on a lane which leads from nowhere to nowhere. The house is timber framed, originally built in the sixteenth century and has been thoroughly renovated and extended by its present owners, James and Rosalie Ashby. There are three guest bedrooms, (one double, one twin and one either), each with a private bathroom or shower room. A sitting room with log fire is usually available for guests' use. Ducks, geese, chickens and goats make up the two acre "farm". Prices from £23 per person per night for Bed and Breakfast.

Booking is essential • Please telephone or fax for details

Herefordshire

An historic, comfortable and spacious home, tastefully renovated. We offer two large double bedrooms with en suite facilities and TV, and a smaller twin-bedded room with private bathroom. All have central heating and tea/coffee making facilities. The dining room has an open inglenook fireplace and the large sittingroom has an inviting woodburner. Wide range of country pubs, inns and hostelries nearby. Children welcome; dogs can be accommodated in an adjacent building. There are plenty of nearby places of interest, as well as golf, fishing, bowls, tennis, horse racing and cricket, wonderful walks and wildlife. Ample car parking; transport service available.

Sheila and Roger Steeds, Linton Brook Farm, Bringsty, Bromyard WR6 5TR • Tel & Fax: 01885 488875

BOARD

Mainoaks Farm Cottages
Goodrich, Ross-on-Wye

Six units sleeping two, four, six and seven. Mainoaks is a 15th century listed farm which has been converted to form six cottages of different size and individual character. It is set in 80 acres of pasture and woodland beside the River Wye in an Area of Outstanding Natural Beauty and an SSSI where there is an abundance of wildlife. All cottages have exposed beams, pine furniture, heating throughout, fully equipped kitchen with microwave, washer/dryer etc, colour TV. Private gardens, barbecue area and ample parking. Linen and towels provided. An ideal base for touring the local area with beautiful walks, fishing, canoeing, pony trekking, golf, bird-watching or just relaxing in this beautiful tranquil spot. Open throughout the year. Short breaks available. Pets by arrangement. Brochure on request.

Mrs P. Unwin, Hill House, Chase End, Bromsberrow, Ledbury, Herefordshire HR8 1SE
Telephone 01531 650448   ETC ★★★ to ★★★★ Highly Commended

SELF-CATERING

THE LODGE

The Lodge, being the former Verger's cottage, can be found in a tranquil setting just eight miles north of the historic cathedral town of Hereford. Peacefully located next to the Parish Church. Guests can enjoy the pleasure of the gardens of Felton House, the stone-built former Rectory. The Lodge has been completely renovated and restored to its Victorian character but with the convenience of central heating, a modern kitchen, two shower rooms, a diningroom and a sittingroom with TV and video. There are three bedrooms with accommodation for five people (one double room, one twin, one single), and in addition a cot is available. Linen may he hired. Children, and pets with responsible owners, are most welcome. Private parking, patio and garden. The Lodge is a cosy, restful cottage, spotlessly clean. Short Breaks catered for and weekly terms range from £150 to £275 per week, exclusive of electricity. Brochure available.

Marjorie and Brian Roby, Felton House, Felton HR1 3PH   Tel/Fax: (01432) 820366
e-mail: bandb@ereal.net   website: www.SmoothHound.co.uk/hotels/felton.html

SELF-CATERING

Sink Green Farm

Rotherwas, Hereford HR2 6LE • Tel: 01432 870223
e-mail: enquiries@sinkgreenfarm.co.uk
website : www.sinkgreenfarm.co.uk

A friendly welcome awaits you at our 16th century farmhouse overlooking the picturesque Wye Valley, yet only three miles from Hereford. Our individually decorated, en suite rooms, one four-poster, all have tea/coffee making facilities, colour TV and central heating. Relax in our extensive garden, complete with summer house and hot tub, or enjoy a stroll by the river.
Prices from £23 per person. Children welcome. Pets by arrangement.

♦♦♦♦

BOARD

Herefordshire/Hertfordshire/Isle of Wight

Thatch Close
Llangrove, Ross-on-Wye, Herefordshire

Secluded, peaceful, comfortable Georgian farmhouse, yet convenient for A40 and M4, M50. Our three lovely bedrooms, each with its own bathroom (two en suite), have magnificent views over the unspoilt countryside. Relax in the visitors' lounge or sit in the shade of mature trees in our garden. You may be greeted by our dog or free-flying parrot.
Telephone or e-mail for brochure.
Mrs M. E. Drzymalski, Thatch Close, Llangrove, Ross-on-Wye, Herefordshire HR9 6EL
Telephone: 01989 770300
e-mail: thatch.close@virgin.net
website: www.thatchclose.com

COUNTRY INNS

SALISBURY ARMS HOTEL
Fore Street, Hertford, Hertfordshire SG14 1BZ
Tel: 01992 583091 • Fax: 01992 552510
www.salisbury-arms-hotel.co.uk
e-mail: reception@salisbury-arms-hotel.co.uk

Hertford's oldest hostelry offers guests excellent food, traditional local ales and an extensive list of wines available by the glass and bottle in surroundings that have character and charm. This is complemented by great service. The two bars and the lounge are excellent for winding down and putting the world to rights. The wood panelled, air-conditioned restaurant has an excellent value table d'hôte and à la carte menu that offers a combination of traditional and contemporary dishes and is well known for its superb food. The rooms are all en suite with satellite TV. Two rooms have been specially designed for those who require disabled facilities. The meeting room can accommodate up to 40 people for conferences/company dinners or celebration parties. The surrounding area has much to offer in terms of places of interest. Green fee discounts are available to guests with booked tee times at many of the surrounding golf clubs. Central London is 35 minutes away by train.   ETC/AA ★★★

SELF-CATERING

Isle of Wight   ETC ★★★/★★★★★   Island Cottage Holidays

Charming individual cottages in lovely rural surroundings and close to the sea.

Over 50 cottages situated throughout the Isle of Wight. Beautiful views, attractive gardens, delightful country walks. All equipped to a high standard and graded for quality by the Tourist Board. £132 to £1195 per week. Short breaks available in low season from £89 to £395 (three nights). For a brochure please contact:

Mrs Honor Vass, The Old Vicarage, Kingston, Wareham, Dorset BH20 5LH
Tel: 01929 480080 • Fax: 01929 481070
e-mail: enq@islandcottageholidays.com
website: www.islandcottageholidays.com

BOARD

Alvington Manor Farm
Manor Farm Lane, Carisbrooke, Newport PO30 5SP
Tel: 01983 523463

Alvington Manor is a 17th century manor farmhouse, situated in the centre of the Isle of Wight, near Carisbrooke Castle and the start of the Tennyson Trail. We have five en suite bedrooms, four with bathrooms, one with a shower room. All rooms have televisions and tea/coffee making facilities. There is a guest sitting room, gardens and car parking. Good food pubs nearby. We are open all year round.
Prices from £20 per person per night, inclusive of full English breakfast. Children welcome, price on application.

For ferry booking from Portsmouth and Lymington • phone 01990 827744
from Southampton • phone 01703 334010

Please mention Farm Holiday Guide when enquiring

Kent/Lancashire

Bower Farmhouse — Stelling Minnis, Near Canterbury CT4 6BB

Anne and Nick Hunt welcome you to Bower Farm House, a traditional 17th century Kentish farmhouse situated in the midst of Stelling Minnis, a medieval common of 125 acres of unspoilt trees, shrubs and open grassland; seven miles south of the cathedral city of Canterbury and nine miles from the coast.

The house is heavily beamed and maintains its original charm. A full traditional English breakfast is served. Children welcome; pets by prior arrangement. Open all year (except Christmas). Car essential. Excellent pub food five minutes away. Bed and Breakfast from £24 per person.

Telephone: 01227 709430
e-mail: book@bowerbb.freeserve.co.uk
website: www.bowerfarmhouse.co.uk

Residential Park Homes, Leisure Homes and Tourist Park.

Beautiful setting for a peaceful and relaxing holiday, set in the heart of the Kent countryside. An ideal base for visiting the many attractions nearby, from historic castles to quaint villages. Electric hook-ups available. A friendly welcome awaits you. Terms on request.

Tel: 01580 291216
e-mail: info@campingsite.co.uk
web: www.campingsite.co.uk

Woodlands Park
Tenterden Road, Biddenden
Kent TN27 8BT

Blakey Hall Farm » 01282 863121

B&B and Luxury Self-Catering

Delightful old farmhouse offers B&B in picturesque surroundings. Private TV lounge and dining room for guests. TV, tea and coffee in all rooms. No smoking. ETC ♦♦♦

Duke of Lancaster Luxury Apartment
2 en suite bedrooms ♦ All linen and towels provided
♦ Full central heating ♦ Well equipped kitchen ♦ No pets

Duke of York Luxury Apartment
First floor apartment with balcony and stunning views
♦ 2 en suite bedrooms ♦ Fully fitted kitchen with dishwasher etc

A warm welcome awaits ♦♦ Contact Mrs Rachel Boothman for details
Blakey Hall Farm, Red Lane, Colne, Lancashire BB8 9TD

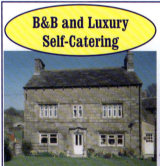

Woodside & Parkside   ETC ★★★★ SELF CATERING
High Bentham, Lancaster LA2 7BN • Contact: Thomas & Jane Marshall
Tel/Fax: 015242 62163 • www.riversidecottages.co.uk

Large stone barn converted into two properties with interconnecting doors so they can be let separately for 6 and 8, or let together to accommodate 14. Mainly en suite bathrooms.

Parkside has a ground floor bedroom and bathroom. Set in beautiful countryside yet within walking distance of the market town. Colour brochure. Open all year. Short Breaks or weekly lets.

The Farm Holiday Guide to Coast & Country Holidays 2004

Leicestershire/Lincolnshire/Norfolk

BOARD

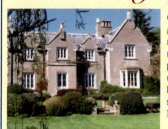

The Old Rectory
Belton-in-Rutland, Oakham LE15 9LE
Tel: 01572 717279 • Fax: 01572 717343

RAC Guest Accommodation

Guest accommodation. Victorian country house and guest annexe in charming village overlooking Eyebrook valley and rolling Rutland countryside. Comfortable and varied selection of rooms, mostly en suite, with direct outside access. Prices from £20 per person per night including breakfast. Small farm environment (horses and sheep) with excellent farmhouse breakfast. Public House 100 yards. Lots to see and do: Rutland Water, castles, stately homes, country parks, forestry and Barnsdale Gardens. Non-smoking. Self catering also available.

e-mail: bb@iepuk.com

SELF-CATERING

WOODTHORPE HALL
COUNTRY COTTAGES

Very well appointed luxury one and three bedroomed cottages, overlooking the golf course, all with central heating, colour TV, microwave, washer, dryer, dishwasher and fridge freezer. Woodthorpe is situated approximately six miles from the coastal resort of Mablethorpe and offers easy access to the picturesque Lincolnshire Wolds. Adjacent facilities include golf, fishing, garden centre, aquatic centre, snooker, pool and restaurant with bar and family room. ETC ★★★★. For further details contact:
Woodthorpe Hall, Woodthorpe, Near Alford, Lincs LN13 0DD • Tel: 01507 450294
Fax: 01507 450885 • e-mail: enquiries@woodthorpehall.com • www.woodthorpehall.com

---

BOARD

**Mrs S. Evans, Willow Farm,
Thorpe Fendykes, Wainfleet,
Skegness PE24 4QH
Tel: 01754 830316
Email: willowfarmhols@aol.com
Website: www.willowfarmholidays.co.uk**

In the heart of the Lincolnshire Fens, Willow Farm is a working smallholding with free range hens, goats, horses and ponies. Situated in a peaceful hamlet with abundant wildlife, ideal for a quiet retreat – yet only 15 minutes from the Skegness coast, shops, amusements and beaches.

Bed and Breakfast is provided in comfortable en suite rooms from £17 per person per night, reductions for children (suppers and sandwiches can be provided in the evening on request). Rooms have tea and coffee making facilities and a colour TV and are accessible to disabled guests. Friendly hosts! Ring for brochure.

BOARD/SELF CATERING

HOLMDENE FARM
BEESTON, KING'S LYNN PE32 2NJ

17th century farmhouse situated in central Norfolk within easy reach of the coast and Broads. Sporting activities available locally, village pub nearby. One double room, one twin and two singles. Pets welcome. Bed and Breakfast from £20 per person; Evening Meal for £15. Weekly terms available and child reductions. Two self-catering cottages. Sleeping 4/8. Terms on request. ETC ★★★

MRS G. DAVIDSON • Tel: 01328 701284
e-mail: holmdenefarm@farmersweekly.net
website: www.northnorfolk.co.uk/holmdenefarm

Norfolk/Northumberland

4B&B STRENNETH Country Bed and Breakfast
Airfield Road, Fersfield, Diss, Norfolk IP22 2BP

STRENNETH is a well-established, family-run business, situated in unspoiled countryside just a short drive from Bressingham Gardens and the picturesque market town of Diss. Offering first-class accommodation, the original 17th Century building has been carefully renovated to a high standard with a wealth of exposed oak beams and a newer single storey courtyard wing. There is ample off-road parking and plenty of nice walks nearby. All seven bedrooms, including a Four-Poster and an Executive, are tastefully arranged with period furniture and distinctive beds. Each having remote colour television, hospitality trays, central heating and full en suite facilities. The establishment is smoke-free and the guest lounge has a log fire on cold winter evenings. There is an extensive breakfast menu using local produce. Ideal touring base. Pets most welcome. Outside kennels with runs if required. Bed and Breakfast from £25.00.

Telephone: 01379 688182 • Fax: 01379 688260
E-mail: pdavey@strenneth.co.uk • Website: www.strenneth.co.uk

Holiday Cottages - near Hadrian's Wall, Northumberland
Ald White Craig

- Wren's Nest sleeps 1/2 • Smithy Cottage sleeps 2/3
- Cobblestones Cottage sleeps 4 • Coach House sleeps 5
- Shepherd's Heft sleeps 6. ETC up to ★★★★

On the edge of Northumberland National Park, a superb base for exploring Hadrian's Wall and Roman museums. Lake District, Scottish Borders and Northumberland coast all approx. one hour's drive. B&B also available.

For further information contact: **C. Zard, Ald White Craig Farm, Shield Hill, Near Hadrian's Wall, Haltwhistle NE49 9NW**
Tel: 01434 320565 • Fax: 01434 321836

e-mail: whitecraigfarm@yahoo.co.uk • www.hadrianswallholidays.com

Comfortable farmhouse accommodation on working mixed farm situated on the Heritage Coast between the villages of Craster and Howick. Ideal base for walking, golfing, bird-watching or exploring the coast, moors and historic castles. The Farne Islands, famous for their colonies of seals and seabirds, and Lindisfarne (Holy Island) are within easy driving distance. Accommodation is in two double rooms with washbasins. Guests have their own TV lounge/dining room with full central heating. Bed and Breakfast from £20.00. Open Easter to November. Non-smoking.

Howick Scar Farm House
Craster, Alnwick NE66 3SV
Tel & Fax: 01665 576665
e-mail: stay@howickscar.co.uk
website: www.howickscar.co.uk

On the banks of the River Tweed with stunning scenery and beautiful walks.

Three miles from Berwick-upon-Tweed. Seven well-equipped cottages. Sleeping 2-6. Warm, comfortable and attractive. Fishing, tennis court, good beaches nearby. Pets welcome in some cottages. Well placed for visiting the Scottish Border towns, the Cheviots and Lindisfarne.

For further details contact: Mrs Carol Lang
Tel: 01289 386631 • Fax: 01289 386800
E-mail: stay@westord.co.uk
Website: www.westord.co.uk

West Ord Holiday Cottages
West Ord Farm
Berwick upon Tweed
Northumberland TD15 2XQ

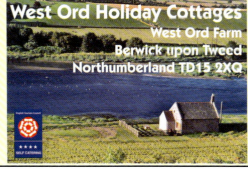

Northumberland/Nottinghamshire/Oxfordshire

Waren House Hotel

Waren Mill, Belford, Near Bamburgh,
Northumberland NE70 7EE
Tel: 01668 214581 • Fax: 01668 214484
e-mail: enquiries@warenhousehotel.co.uk
website: www.warenhousehotel.co.uk

Set in six acres of mature wooded grounds, Waren House has been reborn under the talented and loving hands of owners, Anita and Peter Laverack. Beautifully presented food is served in the elegant dining room, and the wine list is a most fascinating read. Probably the icing on the cake is that the beauty of this uncrowded Heritage Coast makes it much like the Lake District was 40 years ago, before it was well and truly discovered.

*Please do "discover" Waren House –
it will be a choice you will never regret.*

Enjoy a break on the Northumberland Coast

Choose from twelve family-owned and managed cottages along the Northumberland coast.
Three-day short breaks from £70 per cottage during low season.
Beautiful rugged coastline, fishing villages little changed in 100 years, golden beaches, historic castles, wildlife, walks, cycling, fishing, golf, Alnwick Castle & Gardens, National Park, Kielder Water and Forest.

**For details and bookings contact: Heritage Coast Holidays,
6G Greensfield Court, Alnwick, Northumberland NE66 2DE
01670 787864 24-hour enquiry line • Tel: 01665 606022 (office hours)
Fax: 01670 787336 • e-mail: paulthompson@alncom.net**

Visit our website• www.northumberland-holidays.com

Laurel Farm is an old farmhouse in approximately three acres of land. All rooms are spacious, with en suite or private facilities. Teatrays, TV, hair dryer and bath robes for non en suite room. Laurel Farm is on a quiet lane with easy access from M1, A46 and A606. Convenient for tourist attractions. Breakfast is served in a spacious dining room and only local produce and our own free-range eggs used. Laurel Farm rooms are for non-smokers only and are therefore 'asthma friendly'. Double/ twin from £25.00 per person per night, single occupancy from £38.00 per person per night.

Mrs V. Moffat, Laurel Farm, Browns Lane, Stanton-on-the-Wolds, Nottingham NG12 5BL

Laurel Farm
0115 9373488

The Close Guest House

Witney Road
Long Hanborough
Oxfordshire
OX8 8HF

We offer comfortable accommodation in house set in own grounds of one-and-a-half acres. Three family rooms, four double rooms; all standard en suite; one double and one single. All have colour TV and tea/coffee making facilities. Lounge. Full central heating. Use of garden and car parking for eight cars. Close to Woodstock, Oxford and the Cotswolds. Babysitting. Open all year except Christmas. Bed and Breakfast from £20.
Mrs I.J. Warwick (01993 882485).

Shropshire

Red House Farm

Red House Farm is a late Victorian farmhouse in Longdon-on-Tern, a small village noted for the aqueduct built by Thomas Telford in 1796 to carry the Shropshire Union Canal over the River Tern.

Visit the world famous Ironbridge Gorge with its industrial museums

- Friendly welcome • Spacious rooms
- Home comforts • Families welcome
- Local pubs serving good food
- Bed & Breakfast from £20 per person

Tel: 01952 770245

Contact Mrs Mary Jones, Red House Farm, Longdon-on-Tern, Wellington, Telford, Shropshire TF6 6LE
website: www.virtual-shropshire.co.uk/red-house-farm • e-mail: rhf@virtual-shropshire.co.uk

---

Shuttocks Wood is a Scandinavian house in woodland setting situated within easy travelling distance of the Long Mynd and Stiperstones Hills. Accommodation consists of two double and two twin-bedded rooms, all en suite and with tea/coffee facilities and colour TV. Good walks and horse riding nearby and a badger set just 20 yards from the door! Ample parking. Non-smoking establishment. Children over 12 years welcome. Sorry, no pets. Open all year. Bed and Breakfast from £25 per person per night. Credit cards accepted.

Shuttocks Wood
Norbury, Bishop's Castle SY9 5EA
Tel: 01588 650433 • Fax: 01588 650492

Malt House Farm
Lower Wood, Church Stretton, Shropshire SY6 6LF
Prop. Mrs Lyn Bloor
Tel: (01694) 751379
AA ♦♦♦

Olde worlde beamed farmhouse situated amidst spectacular scenery at the lower slopes of the Long Mynd Hills. We are a working farm producing beef cattle and sheep. One double bedroom and one twin, both with en suite bathroom, colour TV, hairdryer and tea tray. Good farmhouse cooking is served in the dining room. Private guests' sitting room. Non-smoking. Regret no children or pets. Now fully licensed.
Bed and Breakfast from £20pppn • Evening Meal from £15.00pp.

Looking for Holiday Accommodation?

for details of hundreds of properties throughout the UK including comprehensive coverage of all areas of Scotland try:

www.holidayguides.com

The Farm Holiday Guide to Coast & Country Holidays 2004

Somerset

Worldwide Footprints
Presents
Motion Postcards

The new and exciting way to share your holiday with family and friends. Sealed inside each postcard is a CD-Rom movie which takes you on a relaxing tour, accompanied by gentle background music.

Order now online to preview your destination before you go or to keep as a souvenir of memories past. Alternatively look out for them in the shops when you visit.

www.worldwidefootprints.com
Tel/Fax: 01884 839723
5 Dukes Mead, Meadow Lane, Cullompton, Devon EX15 1QT

BOARD/SELF-CATERING

Real Farm – Real Food – Relax

Escape to where the buzzards soar and red deer roam. B&B and Self-catering. Charming cottage and 18th century farmhouse on our 500-acre organic stock farm adjoining heather moors, South West coast path, and thatched village of Selworthy for 'scrummy' cream teas. All within National Trust Estate – wonderful walks and riding, bring dogs and horses. Waymarked farm trail with picnic wood. Organic lamb, Aberdeen Angus beef, free-range pork, bacon, ham, sausages, and more, all available in our farm shop. Free organic produce basket for self-catering accommodation guests; organic breakfasts also available. Minehead three miles, Dunster Castle six miles. Award winners from Exmoor National Park for conservation.

ETC ★★★ / ★★★★

Penny & Roger Webber, Hindon Organic Farm, Near Selworthy TA24 8SH • Tel & Fax: 01643 705244
e-mail: info@hindonfarm.co.uk • website: www.hindonfarm.co.uk

---

BOARD

On Devon/Somerset borders, 230 acre family-run farm with cattle, sheep, poultry and horses. Ideal for walking, touring Exmoor, Quantocks, both coasts and many National Trust properties. Pleasant farmhouse, tastefully modernised but with olde worlde charm, inglenook fireplaces and antique furniture, set in large gardens with lawns and flower beds in peaceful, scenic countryside. Two family bedrooms with private facilities and tea/coffee making. Large lounge, separate dining room offering guests every comfort. Noted for relaxed, friendly atmosphere and good home-cooking.

Bed and Breakfast from £22; Dinner £10 per person.
Reductions for children.

tel: 01398 361296
e-mail: lowerwestcott@aol.com
Brochure on request

Mrs Ann Heard, Lower Westcott Farm,
Ashbrittle, Wellington
Somerset TA21 0HZ

BOARD

Hungerford Farm is a comfortable 13th century farmhouse on a 350-acre mixed farm, three-quarters of a mile from the West Somerset Steam Railway. Situated in beautiful countryside on the edge of the Brendon Hills and Exmoor National Park. Within easy reach of the North Devon coast, two-and-a-half miles from the Bristol Channel and Quantock Hills. Marvellous country for walking, riding, and fishing on the reservoirs. Family room and twin-bedded room, both with colour TV; own bathroom, shower, toilet. Own lounge with TV and open fire. Children welcome at reduced rates, cot and high chair. Sorry, no pets. Open February to November. B&B from £20; reduced rates for longer stays.

Hungerford Farm, Washford, Watchet TA23 0JZ
Tel: 01984 640285 • e-mail: sarah.richmond@virgin.net

Somerset

Withy Grove Farm

SELF-CATERING

Come and enjoy a relaxing and friendly holiday "Down on the Farm" set in beautiful Somerset countryside. Peaceful rural setting adjoining River Huntspill, famed for its coarse fishing. The farm is ideally situated for visiting the many local attractions including Cheddar Gorge, Glastonbury, Weston-super-Mare and the lovely sandy beach of Burnham-on-Sea. Self-catering cottages are tastefully converted, sleeping 4-5. Fully equipped with colour TV

★ Heated Swimming Pool ★ Games Room
★ Licensed Bar and Entertainment (in high season)
★ Skittle Alley ★ Laundry

For more information please contact: Mrs Wendy Baker, Withy Grove Farm, East Huntspill, Near Burnham-on-Sea, Somerset TA9 3NP • Telephone: 01278 784471

SELF-CATERING

Gothic House is a Victorian former farmhouse with two self-contained units available. Well-equipped kitchens with washing machine, microwave, cooker, fridge. Free central heating. Comfortably furnished sitting rooms with colour TV. Bed linen and bathroom towels provided. It is situated on the edge of the Somerset Levels in the unspoilt village of Muchelney. Within the village are the ruins of a medieval Abbey and also the medieval priest house belonging to the National Trust.

Gothic House can be found two-and-a-half miles south of Langport and is next door to well-known potter John Leach. Ideal for touring, cycling, fishing, walking and birdwatching.

Terms from £160 to £295 per week.

Mrs J. Thorne,
Gothic House,
Muchelney,
Langport, Somerset
TA10 0DW

01458 250626 • e-mail: joy-thorne@totalserve.co.uk

Leigh Farm Pensford, Near Bristol BS39 4BA
Telephone or Fax: 01761 490281

BOARD

200-year old comfy, natural stone built farmhouse. Guest lounge with open fire in cold weather; TV, video. Bedrooms with TV and beverage trays. Keys for access at all times. Double en suite, family room with cot and private bathroom. Extra bedrooms can be facilitated (subject to availability) at short notice on empty self-catering properties with private facilities. Menu available and breakfasts freshly cooked to order.

Working livestock farm • Cows with calves and growing stock • A few free-range pigs and chickens.
Credit cards accepted • Regret no pets • B&B from £27.00pp.

The Castle Hotel
Porlock, Somerset TA24 8PY
Tel & Fax: 01643 862504

BOARD

The Castle Hotel is a small, fully licensed family-run hotel in the centre of the lovely Exmoor village of Porlock. It is an ideal holiday location for those who wish to enjoy the grandeur of Exmoor on foot or by car. The beautiful villages of Selworthy and Dunster with its castle are only a short distance away. There are 13 en suite bedrooms, all fully heated, with colour TV and tea/coffee making facilities. The Castle Hotel has a well-stocked bar with Real Ale. Draught Guinness and Cider. A full range of Bar Meals is available at lunchtimes and evenings or dine in our Restaurant. Children and pets are most welcome. Family room available. Darts, pool and skittles.

❖❖ *Special Breaks available* ❖ *Extremely low rates* ❖❖

Somerset/Staffordshire/Suffolk

KNOWLE FARM

  ETC ★★★

Four cottages superbly converted from old barns and furnished to a high standard. Pretty gardens to relax in and separate play area for children. Two cottages have kitchen/diner, separate lounge, colour TV, the other two have kitchen, lounge/diner, colour TV. Cot, highchair by prior arrangement. Bed linen supplied, towels by request. Situated in quiet secluded countryside yet close to Wells, Glastonbury, Bath, etc. Area also has a wide selection of family attractions. Sorry, no pets. Terms from £150 to £450. Car essential, ample parking. Payphone for guests. Open all year. Cottages sleep two/five/six.

www.knowle-farm-cottages.co.uk

West Compton, Shepton Mallet BA4 4PD • Tel: 01749 890482 • Fax: 01749 890405

Exmoor •• The Pack Horse
Allerford, Near Porlock, Somerset TA24 8HW
Tel/Fax: 01643 862475
www.thepackhorse.net • e-mail: holidays@thepackhorse.net

Our self-catering apartments and cottage are situated in this unique location within a picturesque National Trust village which has local amenities. The Pack Horse sits alongside the shallow River Aller, overlooking the famous bridge. Enjoy immediate access from our doorstep to the beautiful surrounding countryside, pretty villages, spectacular coast, and Exmoor.

Terms from £220 to £450 per week
OPEN ALL YEAR • PRIVATE PARKING • SHORT BREAKS
Very warm welcome assured

Offley Grove Farm, Adbaston, Eccleshall, Staffs ST20 0QB

Tel/Fax: 01785 280205

You'll consider this a good find! Quality accommodation and excellent breakfasts. Small traditional mixed farm surrounded by beautiful countryside. The house is tastefully furnished and provides all home comforts. Whether you are planning to book here for a break in your journey, stay for a weekend or take your holidays here, you will find something to suit all tastes among the many local attractions. Situated on the Staffordshire/Shropshire borders we are convenient for Alton Towers, Stoke-on-Trent, Ironbridge, etc. Reductions for children. Play area for children. Open all year. Bed and Breakfast all en suite from £24pp. Many guests return. Self-catering cottages available.

Brochure on request.
e-mail: accomm@offleygrovefarm.freeserve.co.uk
website: www.offleygrovefarm.co.uk

THE GROVE COTTAGES

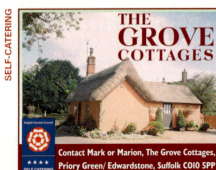

Enjoy the romantic atmosphere of your own 300-year-old farm cottage, with ancient oak beams, open log fires, period furniture, ducks, roses and a touch of luxury. Set in lovely Suffolk countryside, just 90 minutes from London or 60 minutes from Cambridge, our seven cottages are close to the beautiful medieval villages of Lavenham, Long Melford and Kersey. Bikes and canoes are available to explore 'Constable Country'. Pets are welcome. The cottages sleep from 2-6. Please visit our New Superfast Website at www.grove-cottages.co.uk where you will find lots of photos, information and prices, plus an Availability Calendar. Short Breaks are always welcome.

website: www.grove-cottages.co.uk
e-mail: mark@grove-cottages.co.uk
Tel: 01787 211115 or
International: 0044 1787 211115

Contact Mark or Marion, The Grove Cottages, Priory Green/Edwardstone, Suffolk CO10 5PP

Suffolk/East Sussex

SOUTHWOLD/WALBERSWICK

Furnished Holiday Cottages, Houses and Flats available in this charming unspoilt seaside town. Convenient for sandy beaches, with safe bathing, sailing, fishing, golf and tennis. Near to 300 acres of open Common. Attractive country walks and historic churches are to be found in this area, also the fine City of Norwich, the Festival Town of Aldeburgh and the Bird Sanctuary at Minsmere, all within easy driving distance.

**H.A. Adnams, Estate Agents,
98 High Street,
Southwold IP18 6DP
Tel: 01502 723292
Fax: 01502 724794
www.haadnams.com**

SAE, please, for brochure with full particulars.

SELF-CATERING

Signposted on B1119, Fiddlers Hall is a 14th century, moated, oak-beamed farmhouse set in a beautiful and secluded position. It is two miles from Framlingham Castle, 20 minutes' drive from Aldeburgh, Snape Maltings, Woodbridge and Southwold. A Grade II Listed building, it has lots of history and character. The bedrooms are spacious; one has en suite shower room, the other has a private bathroom. Use of lounge and colour TV. Plenty of parking space. Lots of farm animals kept. Traditional farmhouse cooking. Bed and Breakfast terms from £25 per person.

Mrs Jennie Mann, Fiddlers Hall, Cransford, Near Framlingham, Woodbridge IP13 9PQ • 01728 663729

BOARD

...family fun in a fantastic seaside setting
- four indoor fun pools
- adjacent golden beach
- bar & entertainment venues
- sauna, spa bath & solarium
- Dylan's kids club & play areas
- convenience store
- local water sports

Nr Rye, East Sussex

Great Value Breaks

GREAT BRITISH *Holiday Parks*

Tel: 0870 442 9284 ★ www.gbholidayparks.co.uk

CARAVANS

**Mr and Mrs G. Burgess
Polhills
Arlington, Polegate
East Sussex BN26 6SD
01323 870004**

Idyllically situated on shore of reservoir and edge of Sussex Downs within easy reach of the sea. Fully furnished period cottage (approached by own drive along the water's edge) available for self-catering holidays from April to October (inclusive). Fly fishing for trout can be arranged during season. Accommodation consists of two main bedrooms; tiled bathroom. Lounge with colour TV; large well-fitted kitchen with fridge freezer, electric cooker, microwave, put-u-up settee; sun lounge. washing machine; dining room with central heating. Linen supplied. Most rooms contain a wealth of oak beams. Children and pets welcome. Car essential. Ample parking. Shops two miles. Golf, hill climbing locally. Sea eight miles.

Weekly terms from £220 to £295 (electricity included).

SELF-CATERING

The Farm Holiday Guide to Coast & Country Holidays 2004

East Sussex/West Sussex/Tyne & Wear

BOARD/CARAVANS

Westwood Farm

Farm with pigs, sheep, chickens, etc. Quiet rural location off country lane half a mile from B2093 approximately two miles from seafront and town centre. Golf course nearby. Central position for visiting places of interest to suit all ages. Elevated situation with outstanding views over Brede Valley. Double, twin, family rooms with en suite and private facilities. Colour TV, tea/coffee in all rooms, two bedrooms on ground floor. Full English breakfast. Off-road parking.
Bed and Breakfast from £20 to £27pp for two persons sharing. Reduced rates for weekly booking. Also available six-berth self-catering caravan – details on request.

Mr & Mrs S. York,
Westwood Farm,
Stonestile Lane,
Hastings.
TN35 4PG

- Tel & Fax: 01424 751038
- e-mail: york@westwood-farm.fsnet.co.uk
- website: www.SmoothHound.co.uk/hotels/westwoodf.html

BOARD

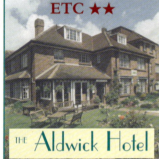

ETC ★★

Aldwick Road, Aldwick, Bognor Regis, West Sussex PO21 2QU

Bognor Regis, sunniest town in mainland Britain, provides a splendid point from which to explore the coast and countryside of West Sussex and Hampshire. The Aldwick Hotel has been caring for the needs of holidaymakers since 1947, and is well practised in providing home-from-home comforts, quality food and service. So whether visiting the seaside for sunshine; Chichester for its history, Cathedral and Festival Theatre; or Goodwood for historic car racing on circuit and hill climb, and horse racing over arguably Britain's most scenic racecourse, choosing the Aldwick Hotel will ensure your comfort for short breaks and holidays.

Tel: 01243 821945 • Fax: 01243 821316
e-mail: info@aldwickhotel.com • website: www.aldwickhotel.com

CARAVANS

...Premier park in a prime location

Great Value Breaks

★ indoor swimming pool
★ family & adult bar
★ evening entertainment
★ Dylan's children's club
★ fantastic local attractions
★ Café & take away
★ multi-sports court

Whitley Bay, Tyne and Wear

Tel: 0870 442 9282 ★ www.gbholidayparks.co.uk

FHG

Visit the FHG website
www.holidayguides.com
for details of the wide choice of accommodation featured in the full range of FHG titles

West Sussex

COUNTRY INNS

Horse & Groom

17th Century Inn with Restaurant & Accommodation

Located in the quiet West Sussex village of East Ashling, the Horse & Groom is a traditional 17th Century inn with separate en suite accommodation in a converted barn and new wing. Only a few miles from the historic city of Chichester, it makes the perfect place to stay for an unforgettable break, to simply relax and unwind.

The bar has all the charm of a traditional English country pub, with original flagstones and a baker's oven set into the wall. It offers an excellent selection of real ales, chilled lagers, fine wines and spirits for your enjoyment.

The light and airy restaurant makes a wonderful place to enjoy lunch or have dinner, and for lighter meals, bar snacks are also available.

For a memorable break or short overnight stay we offer 11 en suite twin/double rooms, each with colour television and tea/coffee making facilities. Five rooms have been converted from the adjoining old flint barn.

Open January – December. Bed & Breakfast from £40 per room (single), £60 (double).

❖ **Horse & Groom** ❖

East Ashling, near Chichester, West Sussex PO18 9AX

Tel: 01243 575339 • Fax: 01243 575560

E-mail: horseandgroomea@aol.com

www.horseandgroom.sageweb.co.uk • www.thehorseandgroomchichester.com

The Farm Holiday Guide to Coast & Country Holidays 2004

Warwickshire/Worcestershire

Holly Tree Cottage
Birmingham Road, Pathlow, Stratford-upon-Avon CV37 0ES
Tel & Fax: 01789 204461

Period cottage dating from the 17th Century, with antiques, paintings, collection of porcelain, fresh flowers, tasteful furnishings and friendly atmosphere. Picturesque gardens, orchard, paddock and pasture with wildlife and extensive views over open countryside. Situated 3 miles north of Stratford-upon-Avon towards Henley-in-Arden on A3400. Rooms have television, radio/alarm, hospitality trays and hairdryers. Breakfasts are a speciality. Pubs and restaurants nearby. Ideally located for Theatre, Shakespeare Country, Heart of England, Cotswolds, Warwick Castle, Blenheim Palace and National Trust Properties. Well situated for National Exhibition Centre, Birmingham and National Agricultural Centre, Stoneleigh. Children welcome, pets by arrangement. Non-smoking. Bed and Breakfast from £27 per person.

e-mail: john@hollytree-cottage.co.uk • website: www.hollytree-cottage.co.uk

---

Two miles south of Stratford-upon-Avon on the A3400 is Monk's Barn, a 75 acre mixed farm welcoming visitors all year. The farm dates back to the 16th century, although the pretty house is more recent. The double, single and twin rooms, most with en suite facilities, are provided in the main house and the cleverly converted milking parlour. The two ground floor rooms are suitable for some disabled guests. Visitors' lounge. Beautiful riverside walk to the village. Tea/coffee making facilities and colour TV in rooms. Sorry, no pets. Non-smokers preferred. Details on request. Bed and Breakfast from £18 to £20.

Mrs R.M. Meadows, Monk's Barn Farm
Shipston Road, Stratford-upon-Avon CV37 8NA
Tel: 01789 293714 • Fax: 01789 205886

AA ♦♦♦♦ Guest Accommodation

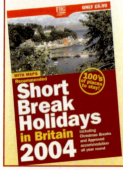

BRICKBARNS, a 200-acre mixed farm, is situated two miles from Great Malvern at the foot of the Malvern Hills, 300 yards from the bus service and one-and-a half miles from the train. The house, which is 300 years old, commands excellent views of the Malvern Hills and guests are accommodated in one double, one single and one family bedrooms with washbasins; two bathrooms, shower room, two toilets; sittingroom and diningroom. Children welcome and cot and babysitting offered. Central heating. Car essential, parking. Open Easter to October for Bed and Breakfast from £16 nightly per person. Reductions for children and Senior Citizens. Birmingham 40 miles, Hereford 20, Gloucester 17, Stratford 35 and the Wye Valley is just 30 miles.

Mrs J.L. Morris, Brickbarns Farm, Hanley Road, Malvern Wells WR14 4HY
Tel: 016845 61775 • Fax: 01886 830037

Recommended
Short Break Holidays in Britain 2004

Specifically designed to cater for the most rapidly growing sector of the holiday market in the UK. Illustrated details of hotels offering special "Bargain Breaks" throughout the year.

Available from bookshops and larger newsagents for £6.99

FHG PUBLICATIONS LTD
Abbey Mill Business Centre, Seedhill, Paisley, Scotland PA1 1TJ
www.holidayguides.com

East Yorkshire/North Yorkshire

SELF-CATERING

With delightful views overlooking the Yorkshire Wolds, ideally situated for touring the East Coast, Bridlington, Scarborough, Moors and York, this secluded and private four-bedroomed farmhouse is set in its own acre of woodland lawns and orchard, with garden furniture, summerhouse and children's play area. Games room in converted Granary in the main farm area 200 yards away. Clean and comfortable and very well-equipped including dishwasher, microwave, automatic washing machine and dryer; two bathrooms, payphone, TV and video. Fully centrally heated. Beds are made up for your arrival; cots and high chair available. Three miles to the nearest village of Kilham with Post Office, general stores, garage and public houses. Available all year. Terms per week from £230 to £380 (low season), from £380 to £540 (high season). Brochure on request.

Mrs P.M. Savile, Raven Hill Farm, Kilham, Driffield YO25 4EG
Tel: 01377 267217

CARAVANS

just 5 miles ...*from the centre of York!*

NEW 2003

This all-new park, which is open all year, has superb facilities including a full length Golf Driving Range and a 9 hole Putting Course.

Tel: **01904 499275**
www.yorkcaravansite.co.uk

BOARD

Furnace Farm
Fryup, Lealholm, Whitby,
North Yorkshire YO21 2AP
Tel/Fax: **01947 897271**
E-mail: furnacefarm@hotmail.com

A warm Yorkshire welcome to our working family farm in the peaceful Esk Valley. Close to Moors and Coast, with beautiful views. Ideal base for walking and touring. Woodland river walk on farm, day fishing available. Whitby 10 miles, 'Heartbeat Country' and Steam Railway 5 miles, Danby Moors Centre 2 miles. Accommodation consists of two tastefully colour-coordinated rooms – a family room with cot available, and a double/twin. One en suite and one with private bathroom. Both rooms have hospitality trays with fresh milk, colour TV and central heating. Delicious full English Breakfast served in cosy dining room/lounge with log fires. Use of large garden. Secure cycle storage. Dogs by arrangement. Non-smoking.

B&B £22.50 - £25.00 • Open all year • Contact: Peter & Jane Dowson

BOARD

Carr House Farm
Ampleforth, Near Helmsley YO6 4ED
Tel: **01347 868526** or **07977 113197**
e-mail: enquiries@carrhousefarm.co.uk
website: www.carrhousefarm.co.uk

Sunday Observer recommends:
"Fresh air fiends' dream – good food, good walking, warm welcome"
In idyllic 16th century farmhouse, sheltered in Herriot/Heartbeat countryside, half an hour to York, ideal to enjoy Moors, Dales, National Parks, coasts, famous abbeys, castles and stately homes. Romantics will love four-poster bedrooms en suite and medieval-styled bedroom in comfortable relaxing home, with large garden.
Enjoy full Yorkshire Breakfasts — own produce used whenever possible and served in oak-panelled, beamed dining room with flagstoned floor, inglenook and original brick bread oven. Aromatherapy beauty treatments and massage available. No children under seven, no smoking and no pets. Bed and Breakfast from £22.50. Evening meal £12.50.
Open all year **Which?** • **BBC Good Food Magazine 2002** • Contact: **Annabel Lupton**

North Yorkshire

SELF-CATERING

Cissy's Cottage

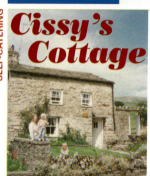

Hardraw, Hawes, North Yorkshire. Sleeps 4

A delightful 18th century cottage of outstanding character. Situated in the village of Hardraw with its spectacular waterfall and Pennine Way. Market town of Hawes one mile. This traditional stone built cottage retains many original features including beamed ceilings and an open fire. Sleeping four in comfort, it has been furnished and equipped to a high standard using antique pine and Laura Ashley prints. Equipped with dishwasher, microwave and tumble dryer. Outside, a south-facing garden, sun patio with garden furniture, and a large enclosed paddock make it ideal for children. Cot and high chair if required. Open all year. Terms £120-£295 includes coal, electricity, linen and trout fishing. For brochure, contact:
Mrs Belinda Metcalfe, Southolme Farm, Little Smeaton, Northallerton DL6 2HJ Telephone 01609 881302/881052

SELF-CATERING

Panoramic views, waterfalls, wild birds and tranquillity

Stone farmhouse with panoramic views, high in the Yorkshire Dales National Park (Herriot family's house in 'All Creatures Great and Small' on TV). Three bedrooms (sleeps 6-8), sitting and dining rooms with wood-burning stoves, kitchen, bathroom, WC. House has electric storage heating, cooker, microwave, fridge, washing machine, colour TV, telephone. Garden, large barn, stables. Access from lane, private parking, no through traffic. Excellent walking from front door, near Wensleydale. Pets welcome. Self-catering from £400 per week.

Westclose House (Allaker),
West Scrafton, Coverdale, Leyburn, North Yorks DL8 4RM
For bookings telephone 020 8567 4862
e-mail: ac@adriancave.com • www.adriancave.com/yorks

SELF-CATERING

Fern Croft

2 Mill Lane, Askrigg
Sleeps 4

A modern cottage enjoying quiet location on edge of village with open fields rising immediately behind. Attractive and compact, this Wensleydale village is an ideal centre for the Dales, with facilities for everyday needs, including two shops, Post Office, restaurant and a couple of pubs. Furnished to a high standard for four, ground floor accommodation comprises large comfortable lounge/diner with colour TV and well-equipped kitchen. Upstairs there are two double bedrooms with a double and twin beds respectively, and modern bathroom. Storage heating included, other electricity by meter. Regret no pets. Terms from £140 to £270 weekly. Brochure:
Mr and Mrs K. Dobson • 01689 838450

BOARD

Unique Bed & Breakfast accommodation.

En suite for 2 people only. Own private lounge. Located on the clifftop with access to the golden sands of Filey Bay. Quiet location. Good Yorkshire food, 3-course English breakfast. Bookings for evening meals as required.

Sea Cabin

The perfect venue for a relaxing break.
• Private parking • Pets welcome
By car: 5 mins Filey, 10 mins Flamborough,
15 mins Bridlington, 20 mins Scarborough.
For brochure and terms:
Leonard & Diane Hunter, "Sea Cabin" 16 Gap Road, Hunmanby Gap, Near Filey YO14 9QP (01723 891368)

North Yorkshire/West Yorkshire

New Close Farm

A supa dupa cottage on New Close Farm in the heart of Craven Dales with panoramic views over the Aire Valley. Excellent area for walking, cycling, fishing, golf and touring.
- Two double and one single bedrooms; bathroom.
- Colour TV and video.
- Full central heating and double glazing.
- Bed linen, towels and all amenities included in the price.
- Sorry, no young children, no pets.
- Non-smokers preferred.
- From £250-£300. Winter Short Breaks available.

The weather can't be guaranteed but your comfort can

Kirkby Malham, Skipton BD23 4DP
Tel: 01729 830240 • Fax: 01729 830179
e-mail: brendajones@newclosefarmyorkshire.co.uk
website: www.newclosefarmyorkshire.co.uk

FHG DIPLOMA AWARD WINNER

SELF-CATERING

Garth End Cottage
Staithes

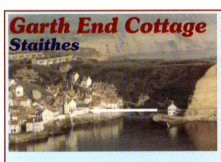

Georgian cottage situated on sea wall in this old fishing village in the North York Moors National Park. Excellent walking centre. Small sandy beach with numerous rock pools. Cottage has feature fireplace, beamed ceilings, pine panelled room, well-equipped kitchen including microwave. Warm, comfortable, well-equipped with central heating, electricity and bed linen included in rent. Two lounges, front one with picture window giving uninterrupted panoramic views of sea, harbour and cliffs. Dining kitchen; bathroom with toilet; three bedrooms - one double, one twin, one single (two with sea views); colour TV/video. Front terrace overlooking the sea. Sorry, no pets.

Terms from £220 • Sleeps 5/6 • Apply Mrs Hobbs (01132 665501)

SELF-CATERING

Summerwine Cottages

Shepley, Near Holmfirth, Huddersfield, West Yorkshire
Set in 6 acres of Pennine farmland, deep in the heart of 'Summer Wine' country. The 3 self-contained cottages, *Granary* (1 double room), *Harvest* (1 double, 1 twin) and *Winnow* (1 double, 1 twin), can accommodate up to 4 adults. Each has central heating and double glazing, as well as ample off-road parking and telephone. Furnishings and decor are of a high standard, with TV, video, washer/dryer and microwave. Cot, high chair etc available on request. Pubs, restaurants and shops are only a short walk; surrounding villages well served by public transport. Open all year; minimum let two nights. Terms from £150 to £325 per week.

www.summerwinecottages.co.uk

Details from **Mrs S. Meakin, West Royd Farm, Marsh Lane, Shepley, Huddersfield HD8 8AY**
Tel: 01484 602147 • Fax: 01484 609467 • e-mail: summerwinecottages@lineone.net

SELF-CATERING

Looking for Holiday Accommodation?

for details of hundreds of properties throughout the UK including comprehensive coverage of all areas of Scotland try:

www.holidayguides.com

Anglesey & Gwynedd/North Wales/Pembrokeshire

SELF-CATERING

BRYN BRAS CASTLE
Listed Building Grade II★

LLANRUG, Near CAERNARFON, NORTH WALES LL55 4RE
Tel & Fax: Llanberis (01286) 870210

This romantic neo-Romanesque Castle is set in the gentle Snowdonian foothills near North Wales' mountains, beaches, resorts and heritage. Built in 1830, on an earlier structure, the Regency castle reflects peace not war - it stands in 32 acres of tranquil gardens, with views. Bryn Bras offers distinctive and individual Apartments, for 2-4 persons, within the castle, each having spacious rooms radiating comfort, warmth and tranquillity and providing freedom and independence.

Open all year including for Short Breaks.
website: www.brynbrascastle.co.uk
BROCHURE SENT WITH PLEASURE.

Many inns and restaurants nearby. This welcoming castle, still a family home, particularly appeals to romantic couples.

SELF-CATERING

Listen to the Views...

SPRING   SUMMER   AUTUMN   WINTER

all through the year...

...Spring breaks, Summer holidays, Autumn leaves or Winter weekends... Whatever time of year you choose, our wide selection of self-catering properties throughout North Wales is sure to include just the right place for you.

Tel: **08707 559888**
Web: www.northwalesholidaycottages.co.uk

NORTH WALES Holiday Cottages & Farmhouses

BOARD

There is a genuine welcome to our mixed working family farm. Quietly set in beautiful countryside surrounded by animals and wild life. Comfortable, well-appointed accommodation. Bedrooms with tea/coffee tray, radio, TV and en suite. Excellent quality food using home and local produce. Families welcome. Deductions for children and Senior Citizens. Open January to December. Pretty flowers, lawns in relaxed surroundings. Personal attention. Unrestricted access. Ideally situated in central Pembrokeshire for coastline walks. Sandy beaches. Bird islands, castles, city of St David's, Tenby. Bed and Breakfast; Bed, Breakfast and Evening Dinner. Terms on application.

Mrs M. E. Davies, **Cuckoo Mill Farm**
Pelcomb Bridge, St David's Road,
Haverfordwest SA62 6EA • Tel: 01437 762139

GOLD WELCOME HOST AWARD • TASTE OF WALES
★★★

SELF-CATERING

Furzewood, Granary & Stables Cottage, Amroth

In a spectacular setting of nine acres overlooking the bay with views to Caldey Island and the Gower, all our cottages offer 5 star comfort all year round. Just minutes from the safe sandy beach, Amroth village and the Pembrokeshire Coast Path and adjacent to Colby Estate, with its lovely sheltered wooded walks. We welcome children, pets and their owners! We have a large safe garden play area and fields to walk the dogs. Short Breaks available out of season. *For brochure contact:*
Mrs Green, Furzewood Farm, Amroth, Pembrokeshire SA67 8NQ
Tel: 01834 814451 • e-mail: info@amrothcottages.co.uk • www.amrothcottages.co.uk

★★★★★

48   Please mention Farm Holiday Guide when enquiring

Pembrokeshire/Powys

Croft Farm & Celtic Cottages
• Pembrokeshire •

SELF-CATERING

Croft makes the ideal place for a main holiday or short break. Delightful barn conversions provide superbly comfortable accommodation. Enjoy the luxury indoor heated pool, sauna, spa pool and gym facilities. Close to sandy beaches, bays and coastal National Park. Good walking country. Indoor and outdoor play areas. Colourful gardens. Friendly farm animals. Pets welcome.

For a brochure please contact Andrew and Sylvie Gow,
Croft Farm & Celtic Cottages, Croft, Near Cardigan, Pembrokeshire SA43 3NT
Tel/Fax: 01239 615179 • www.croft-holiday-cottages.co.uk
• e-mail: croftfarm@compuserve.com

CRUNWERE & HAYLOFT COTTAGES
WTB ★★★★★

BOARD/SELF-CATERING

Two charming cottages privately situated and ideally located for exploring Pembrokeshire. The resorts of Saundersfoot and Tenby are close at hand with the seaside resort of Amroth and the coastal path just minutes away. Each cottage sleeps four to five adults, cots and high chairs also provided. All facilities including fully fitted kitchens, central heating, colour televisions are included. There is ample private parking plus a lawned garden area and patio with garden furniture provided. Farmhouse B&B also available.

Contact: John & Carol Lloyd, East Llanteg Farm, Llanteg, Amroth SA67 8QA
Tel: 01834 831336

e-mail: john@pembrokeshireholiday.co.uk • website: www.pembrokeshireholiday.co.uk

---

Gwarmacwydd

SELF-CATERING

Gwarmacwydd is a country estate of over 450 acres, including two miles of riverbank. See a real farm in action, the hustle and bustle of harvest, newborn calves and lambs. Children are welcomed. On the estate are six character stone cottages. Each cottage has been lovingly converted from traditional farm buildings, parts of which are over 200 years old. Each cottage is fully furnished and equipped. All electricity and linen included. All cottages are heated for year-round use. Colour brochure available.

Tel: 01437 563260 Fax: 01437 563839
e-mail: info@a-farm-holiday.org
website: www.a-farm-holiday.org
Cottages 1-5 WTB ★★★★ SELF CATERING

Mrs Angela Colledge,
Llanfallteg, Whitland,
Pembrokeshire SA34 0XH

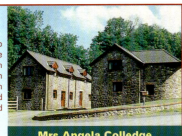

Caebetran Farm

BOARD

A warm welcome, a cup of tea and home-made cakes await you when you arrive at Caebetran. Well off the beaten track, where there are breathtaking views of the Brecon Beacons and the Black Mountains, and just across a field is a 400 acre common, ideal for walking, bird-watching or just relaxing. The rooms are all en suite and have colour TV and tea making facilities. The dining room has separate tables, there is also a comfortable lounge with colour TV and video. Caebetran is an ideal base for exploring this beautiful, unspoilt part of the country with pony trekking, walking, birdwatching, wildlife, hang-gliding and so much more. For a brochure and terms please write, telephone or fax.

"Arrive as visitors and leave as our friends".
Winners of the 'FHG Diploma' for Wales 1998/99. Welcome Host.

Gwyn and Hazel Davies
Caebetran Farm, Felinfach, Brecon, Powys LD3 0UL
(Tel & Fax: 01874 754560) • e-mail: hazelcaebetran@aol.com

BOARD

Powys

Tastefully restored Tudor farmhouse on working farm in peaceful location. En suite bedrooms with breathtaking views over fields and woods, colour TV, beverage trays. Two lounges with log fires. Renowned for excellent food. Wonderful area for wildlife, walking, cycling, near Red Kite feeding station. Safe parking. Brochure on request.

Bed, Breakfast and Evening Meal weekly from £220 to £245. Bed and Breakfast from £22 to £26 per day.

Mrs Ruth Jones, Holly Farm, Howey, Llandrindod Wells LD1 5PP
Tel & Fax: 01597 822402 • Taste of Wales Tourism Award • Farm Stay UK Member

BOARD/SELF-CATERING

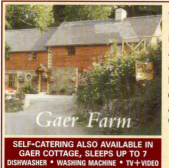

A warm welcome awaits you from Patricia and Phillip Harley and family. Nestling in a quiet valley, a haven for wildlife, Gaer Farm is a working farm with a variety of animals for all the family. Accommodation is in two family rooms and one single room, all en suite with tea-making facilities and TV. Non-smoking. Evening meals and packed lunches by prior arrangement. Within easy reach are salmon fishing, golf, pony trekking, walking and a range of indoor and outdoor sports facilities.

GAER FARM, HUNDRED HOUSE, LLANDRINDOD WELLS, POWYS LD1 5RU
TEL/FAX: 01982 570208
e-mail: relax@gaerfarm.co.uk
www.gaerfarm.co.uk

SELF-CATERING ALSO AVAILABLE IN GAER COTTAGE, SLEEPS UP TO 7
DISHWASHER • WASHING MACHINE • TV+VIDEO

CARAVANS

Co.Kerry

West's Caravan Park

Killarney Road, Killorglin,
Ring of Kerry, SW Ireland
Tel: 00 353 66 9761240

Mobile Homes for hire on family-run park situated on banks of River Laune overlooking Ireland's highest mountain. Pool table, tennis, table-tennis, laundry. Town one mile.
Ideal touring centre for Ring of Kerry, Dingle Peninsula, Cork, Blarney Stone, Killarney National Park and Tralee.
Ferry and mobile home price available.

Mobile Homes from £150 - £350 Sterling p.w.

FHG

Publisher's Note

While every effort is made to ensure accuracy, we regret that FHG Publications cannot accept responsibility for errors, omissions or misrepresentations in our entries or any consequences thereof. Prices in particular should be checked because we go to press early. We will follow up complaints but cannot act as arbiters or agents for either party.

Aberdeen, Banff & Moray/Argyll & Bute

Forglen Country Cottages

SELF-CATERING

The Estate lies along the beautiful Deveron River and our traditional stone cottages nestle in individual seclusion. Visitors can explore one of the ancient baronies of Scotland. The sea is only nine miles away, and the market town of Turriff only two miles, with its golf course, swimming pool, etc. Places of interest including the Cairngorms, Aviemore, picturesque fishing villages and castles, all within easy reach on uncrowded roads. See our Highland cattle. 6 miles of own walks. Wildlife haven.

Terms: from £159 weekly. Special Winter lets. 10 cottages sleeping 6-9. Children and reasonable dogs welcome. STB Inspected.

For a brochure contact: **Mrs P. Bates, Holiday Cottages, Forglen Estate, Turriff, Aberdeenshire AB53 4JP**
Tel: 01888 562918/562518 • Fax: 01888 562252 • Web: www.forglen.co.uk

---

Inistrynich
Dalmally, Argyll PA33 1BQ

SELF-CATERING

Two cottages overlooking Loch Awe surrounded by beautiful scenery, the perfect retreat for a peaceful holiday.

Garden Cottage (sleeps 8) • Millside Cottage (sleeps 4)

Dalmally 5 miles, Inveraray 11 miles, Oban 28 miles. Both have garden area, convector heaters in all rooms, open fire in living rooms, electric cooker, fridge, immersion heater, electric kettle, iron, vacuum cleaner, washing machine, colour TV. Cot and high chair by request. Dogs allowed by arrangement. Car essential, ample parking. Ideal for touring mainland and Inner Hebrides. Good restaurants, hill walking, forest walks, fishing, boat hire, pony trekking. National Trust gardens and golf within easy reach. Open Easter to November.

Colour brochure available, contact: Mrs E. Fellowes

Tel: 01838 200256 • Fax: 01838 200253
E-mail: dlfellowes@supanet.com
Web: www.loch-awe.com/inistrynich

BOARD

A warm welcome awaits you in this delightful bungalow set in 20 acres of farmland where we breed our own Highland cattle which graze at the front. It is a peaceful location as we are set back from the road, and an ideal spot for touring, with the main ferry terminal at Oban just 10 minutes away.

Our luxurious rooms have their own special sitting room attached where you can enjoy your coffee or a glass of wine in peace.

MRS J. CURRIE, HAWTHORN, 5 KEIL CROFTS, BENDERLOCH, OBAN, ARGYLL PA37 1QS

Hawthorn
Tel: 01631 720452

SELF-CATERING

Situated on beautiful Seil Island with wonderful views of surrounding countryside. These lovingly restored cottages (one detached and one attached to the main croft house) retain their traditional character while incorporating all modern facilities. The cottages are near to each other and ideal for two families on holiday together. Seil is one of the most peaceful and tranquil spots in the West Highlands, with easy access to neighbouring Isles of Luing and Easdale. Oban, the hub for trips to Mull and Iona, is half an hour's drive away over the famous 18th century "Bridge Over The Atlantic". Wonderful area for hillwalking, cycling, fishing and bird watching.

Short breaks from £35.00 per day.

Kilbride Croft
Balvicar, Isle of Seil, Argyll PA34 4RD
contact: Mary & Brian Phillips
tel: 01852 300475
e-mail: kilbridecroft@aol.com
website: www.kilbridecroft.fsnet.co.uk

Kilbride Cottage

Croft Cottage

The Farm Holiday Guide to Coast & Country Holidays 2004

Argyll & Bute

SELF-CATERING

The Highland Estate of

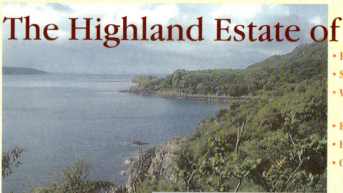

- PEACE
- SECLUSION
- VARIETY OF INTERESTS
- FREEDOM
- HISTORY
- OUTSTANDING SCENERY

Ellary

and Castle Sween

This 15,000 acre Highland Estate lies in one of the most beautiful and unspoilt areas of Scotland and has a wealth of ancient historical associations within its bounds.

There is St Columba's Cave, one of the first places of Christian Worship in Britain, also Castle Sween, the oldest ruined castle in Scotland, and Kilmory Chapel where there is a fascinating collection of Celtic slabs. There is a wide range of accommodation, from small groups of cottages, many of the traditional stone-built estate type, to modern holiday chalets and super luxury caravans at Castle Sween.

Most of the cottages accommodate up to six, but one will take eight.

All units fully equipped except linen. Television reception is included.

Ellary is beautiful at all times of the year and is suitable for windsurfing, fishing, swimming, sailing and the observation of a wide variety of wildlife; there are paths and tracks throughout the estate for the visitor who prefers to explore on foot, and guests will find farmers and estate workers most helpful in their approach.

For further details, brochure and booking forms, please apply to:

ELLARY ESTATE OFFICE, by LOCHGILPHEAD, ARGYLL PA31 8PA

Tel: 01880 770232/770209 or 01546 850223

info@ellary.com • www.ellary.com

Argyll & Bute/Ayrshire & Arran

Rockhill Waterside Country House
Ardbrecknish, By Dalmally, Argyll PA33 1BH Tel: 01866 833218

17th century guest house in spectacular waterside setting on Loch Awe with breathtaking views to Ben Cruachan, where comfort, peace and tranquillity reign supreme. Small private Highland estate breeding Hanoverian competition horses. 1200 metres free trout fishing. Five delightful rooms with all modern facilities. First-class highly acclaimed home cooking with much home-grown produce. Wonderful area for touring the Western Highlands, Glencoe, the Trossachs and Kintyre. Ideal for climbing, walking, bird and animal watching. Boat trips locally and from Oban (30 miles) to Mull, Iona, Fingal's Cave and other islands. Dogs' Paradise! Also Self-Catering Cottages.

website: www.rockhillhanoverianstud.co.uk

ARDTUR COTTAGES

Two adjacent cottages in secluded surroundings on promontory between Port Appin and Castle Stalker. Ideal for hill walking, climbing, pony trekking, boating and fly-fishing. (Glencoe and Ben Nevis half-hour drive). Tennis court by arrangement. Direct access across the field to sea (Loch Linnhe). First cottage is suitable for up to 8 people in one double and three twin-bedded rooms, large dining/sittingroom/kitchenette and two bathrooms. Second cottage is suitable for 6 people in one double and two twin-bedded rooms, dining/sittingroom/kitchenette and bathroom. Everything provided except linen. Shops one mile; sea 200 yards. Pets allowed. Car essential, parking. Open March/October. Terms from £165 to £375 weekly.

SAE, please for details to Mrs J. Pery, Ardtur, Appin PA38 4DD (01631 730223 or 01626 834172)
e-mail: pery@eurobell.co.uk

Welcome to Dunduff Farm where a warm, friendly atmosphere awaits you. Situated just south of Ayr at the coastal village of Dunure, this family-run beef and sheep unit of 600 acres is only 15 minutes from the shore providing good walks and sea fishing and enjoying close proximity to Dunure Castle and Park. Accommodation is of a high standard yet homely and comfortable. Bedrooms have washbasins, radio alarm, tea/coffee making facilities, central heating, TV, hair dryer and en suite facilities (the twin room has private bathroom). There is also a small farm cottage available sleeping two/four people. Bed and Breakfast from £25 per person; weekly rate £170. Cottage from £250 per week. Colour brochure available.
Mrs Agnes Gemmell

Dunduff Farm, Dunure, Ayr KA7 4LH
01292 500225 • www.gemmelldunduff.co.uk

NOTE

All the information in this guide is given in good faith in the belief that it is correct. However, the publishers cannot guarantee the facts given in these pages, neither are they responsible for changes in ownership or facilities that may take place after the date of going to press. Readers should always satisfy themselves that the facilities they require are available and that the terms, if quoted, still apply.

The Farm Holiday Guide to Coast & Country Holidays 2004

Edinburgh & Lothians/Fife/Highlands

01875 833665

We are situated on the A68, three miles south of Pathhead at the picturesque village of Fala. The house is an 18th century coaching inn (Listed building). All bedrooms have washbasins and tea/coffee making facilities; one is en suite. All the rooms are comfortably furnished. We are within easy reach of Edinburgh and the Scottish Borders. A warm welcome is extended to all our guests – our aim is to make your stay a pleasant one. Cost is from £18.50 per person; children two years to 12 years £11.50, under two years FREE.

Mrs Anne Gordon, "Fairshiels", Blackshiels, Pathhead EH37 5SX

Only two miles from St Andrews on the picturesque A917 road to Crail, Spinkstown is a uniquely designed farmhouse with views of the sea and surrounding countryside. Bright and spacious, it is furnished to a high standard. Accommodation consists of double and twin rooms, all en suite, with tea/coffee making facilities and colour TV; diningroom and lounge. Substantial farmhouse breakfast to set you up for the day. The famous Old Course, historic St Andrews and several National Trust properties are all within easy reach, as well as swimming, tennis, putting, bowls, horse riding, country parks, nature reserves, beaches and coastal walks. Plenty of parking available. Bed and Breakfast from £24.

e-mail: anne@spinkstown.com
website: www.spinkstown.com
Mrs Anne Duncan, Spinkstown Farmhouse, St Andrews KY6 8PN
Tel & Fax: 01334 473478

Achnahaird Farm Cottages are situated right beside a large, sandy beach and sand dunes, with stunning panoramic views of the bay and the mountains beyond.
CUL MOR, CUL BEAG and SUILVEN COTTAGES, a recent conversion of a 200 years' old traditional Highland Lodge, offer quality STB 4-star accommodation, sleeping 2-4 guests. All have full oil-fired central heating and open fire, making these cottages a comfortable retreat at any time of the year
THE FARM COTTAGE, sleeping 5, is a spacious well-equipped STB 3-star family cottage with cosy multi-fuel stove in the lounge. All bed linen and towels are supplied in all cottages.
Children and well-behaved pets are welcome.
Price range £250 -£420 per week.
For further details contact: Mrs Marilyn Mackenzie, Achnahaird, Achiltibuie, Ross-shire, IV26 2YT
Tel/Fax: 01854 622458 • e-mail: Mackenzie@achnahaird.freeserve.co.uk • web: www.achnahairdfarm.com

Dunain Park Hotel

A small, luxury, family-owned and run country house hotel, secluded in beautiful gardens. Two miles from Inverness, five miles from Loch Ness. High standards of comfort and service; cuisine is Scottish/French. Open fires, over 200 malt whiskies. Indoor heated swimming pool, sauna. Accommodation includes 6 suites, four-poster bedroom, two self-catering cottages.

DUNAIN PARK HOTEL, INVERNESS IV3 8JN
www.dunainparkhotel.co.uk
e-mail: dunainparkhotel@btinternet.com

Tel: 01463 230512
Fax: 01463 224532

Highlands

Conchra Farm Cottages
Open all year
STB ★★ Self-catering

Comfortable, fully modernised traditional farm cottages adjacent to working farm. Tranquil lochside setting, convenient for exploring Skye and the Highlands. Fully equipped; central heating, electricity and bed linen incl. Excellent value for money and ideal for families, walking and activity holidays.

Gardener's Cottage • 2 single, one double, one twin
Shepherd's Cottage • one family, one twin
Farmer's Cottage • one double, one single, one family. For details contact:

£175-£415 per week

Conchra Farm Cottages, Tigh-na-Coille, Argyll IV40 8DZ
Tel & Fax: 01599 555474 • www.conchracottages.co.uk
e-mail: enquiries@conchracottages.co.uk

Crubenbeg Holiday Cottages

Rural self-catering cottages in the central Highlands where one can relax and stroll from the doorstep or take part in the choice of many sporting activities in the area. We have a children's play area, a Games Room, Pond stocked with trout for fishing and a barbecue. Pets welcome.

Newtonmore, Inverness-shire PH20 1BE
Tel: 01540 673566 • Fax: 01540 673509
E-mail: enquiry@crubenbeg.com • Website: www.crubenbeg.com

BROOMVIEW & SUNSET

Enjoy peace and tranquillity in the North West Highlands in the comfort of our accommodation. These properties overlook picturesque Loch Broom where panoramic views and spectacular sunsets can be seen. Broomview is on the ground floor. One double en suite bedroom, one double and one single bedroom both with wash hand basins. Bathroom, utility, spacious, well-equipped kitchen/dining room, lounge with colour TV and video. Sunset is on the upper floor with a double and single bedroom, shower room, utility, kitchen and lounge with colour TV and video. Ideal base for touring. Children welcome. Sorry, no pets. Colour brochure available. Broomview from £250 to £365, Sunset £195 to £290. For further information contact: **Mrs Linda Renwick, Spindrift, Keppoch Farm, Dundonnell, By-Garve, Ross-shire IV23 2QR (Tel & Fax: 01854 633269).**

FHG
Visit the FHG website
www.holidayguides.com
for details of the wide choice of accommodation featured in the full range of FHG titles

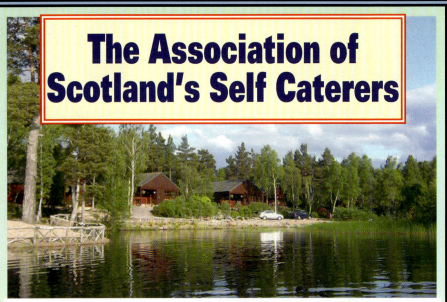

The Association of Scotland's Self Caterers

Selected Self-Catering Holidays in Scotland

Members of the ASSC are committed to high and consistant standards in self catering. Contact your choice direct and be assured of an excellent holiday.

Brochures: 0990 168 571 • Web site: www.assc.co.uk

Owner-Operators ready to match our standards and interested in joining are requested to contact our Secretary for information – 0990 168 571

ASSC/Aberdeen, Banff & Moray/Argyll & Bute

Tulloch Lodges • *Peace, Relaxation and Comfort in Beautiful Natural Surroundings*
One of the loveliest self-catering sites in Scotland. Modern, spacious, attractive and beautifully equipped Scandinavian lodges for up to 6 in glorious woodland/water setting. Perfect for the Highlands and Historic Grampian, especially the Golden Moray Coast and the Golf, Castle and Malt Whisky Trails. £240-£675 per week. Brochure:
Tulloch Lodges, Rafford, Forres, Moray IV36 2RU
Tel: 01309 673311 • Fax: 01309 671515   STB ★★★/★★★★ *Self-Catering*
E-mail: enquiries@tullochlodges.com • web: www.tullochlodges.com

THE GREENKNOWE

A comfortable, detached, renovated cottage in a quiet location at the southern edge of the village of Kintore. Ideally situated for touring castles and pre-historic sites or for walking, fishing and golfing. The cottage is on one level with large sittingroom facing south and the garden. Sleeps four plus cot.
• Walkers Welcome Scheme •
Terms £275–£475 per week including electricity and linen.
Mr & Mrs P. A. Lumsden, Kingsfield House, Kingsfield Road, Kintore, Aberdeenshire AB51 0UD
Tel: 01467 632366 • Fax: 01467 632399 • e-mail: kfield@clara.net

The Robert Gordon University in the heart of Aberdeen offers a variety of accommodation in the city centre to visitors from June through to August. Aberdeen is ideal for visiting Royal Deeside, castles and historic buildings, playing golf or touring the Malt Whisky Trail. The city itself is a place to discover, and Aberdonians are friendly and welcoming people. We offer Two Star self-catering accommodation for individuals or groups at superb rates, in either en suite or shared facility flats. Each party has exclusive use of their own flat during their stay. The flats are self-contained, centrally heated, fully furnished and suitable for children and disabled guests. All flats have colour TV, microwave, bed linen, towels, all cooking utensils, and a complimentary 'welcome pack' of basic groceries. There are laundry and telephone facilities on site as well as ample car parking spaces.

Contact: The Robert Gordon University, Business & Vacation Accommodation, Schoolhill, Aberdeen AB10 1FR • Tel: 01224 262134 • Fax: 01224 262144
e-mail: p.macinnes@rgu.ac.uk • website: www.scotland2000.com/rgu

Mr & Mrs E. Crawford
Blarghour Farm
Loch Awe-side, by Dalmally, Argyll PA33 1BW
Tel: 01866 833246 • Fax: 01866 833338
E-mail: blarghour@btconnect.com
www.self-catering-argyll.co.uk

At Blarghour Farm one may choose from four centrally heated and double glazed holiday homes sleeping from two to six people, all enjoying splendid views of lovely Loch Awe. Kitchens are well appointed, lounges tastefully decorated and furnished with payphone, TV and gas fire, beds are made up and towels supplied while the two larger houses have shower rooms in addition to bathrooms, all with shaver point. The two larger houses are suitable for children and have cots and high chairs. No pets are allowed. Open all year. Centrally situated for touring. Illustrated brochure on request.

When making postal enquiries, remember that a stamped, addressed envelope is always appreciated

ASSC/Argyll & Bute/Ayrshire & Arran/Borders/Highlands

Cologin Country Chalets Oban
All Scottish Glens have their secrets: let us share ours with you – and your pets!

Call now for our colour brochure and find out more
Open all year round. Rates from £180 to £510 per week.
Autumn Gold breaks and mid-week deals also available
MRS LINDA BATTISON, COLOGIN FARMHOUSE, LERAGS GLEN,
BY OBAN, ARGYLL PA34 4SE Tel: (01631) 564501 • Fax: (01631) 566925
e-mail: cologin@west-highland-holidays.com
web: www.west-highland-holidays.co.uk

STB ★★★ to ★★★★ Self Catering

Five cottages in architect designed conversion of home farm. Spacious accommodation for 2-8 persons. Stone fireplaces for log fires. Bird-watching, fishing and walking. Easy access to island ferries. Pets welcome. Open all year. Colour brochure. From £175-£490. STB ★★
Contact: Amanda Minshall, Dunmore Court, Kilberry Road,
Near Tarbert, Argyll PA29 6XZ
e-mail: dunmorecourtsc@aol.com • www.dunmorecourt.com
WEST LOCH TARBERT, ARGYLL • DUNMORE COURT Tel: 01880 820654

ArranHideAways
www.arran-hideaways.co.uk
Arran's *Local* Accommodation Booking Service

Properties throughout the Island
All villages – all dates
STB Quality Assured*
Short Breaks available
Major credit cards accepted

our staff are here 7 days a week
01770 302303/302310
www.arran-hideaways.co.uk • on-line booking & availability
Invercloy House, Brodick, Isle of Arran KA27 8AJ
* All our properties have applied for grading under the STB Quality Assurance Scheme

Mill House, Letterbox & Stockman's Cottages
– Three recently renovated, quality Cottages, each sleeping four, on a working farm three miles from Jedburgh. All ideal centres for exploring, sporting holidays or getting away from it all. Each cottage has two public rooms (ground floor available). Minimum let two days. Terms £190–£350. Open all year. Bus three miles, airport 54 miles.
Mrs A. Fraser, Overwells, Jedburgh, Roxburghshire TD8 6LT
Telephone: 01835 863020 • Fax: 01835 864334
e-mail: abfraser@btinternet.com • www.overwells.co.uk

Innes Maree Bungalows, Poolewe IV22 2JU
Only a few minutes' walk from the world-famous Inverewe Gardens in magnificent Wester Ross. A purpose-built complex of six superb modern bungalows, all equipped to the highest standards of luxury and comfort. Each bungalow sleeps six with main bedroom en suite. Children and pets welcome. Terms from £190 to £425 inclusive of bed linen and electricity. Brochure available. Tel & Fax 01445 781454
E-mail: fhg@poolewebungalows.com • Website: www.poolewebungalows.com
STB ★★★★

SUMMER WATERSPORTS AND WINTER SKIING
Just six miles south of Aviemore these superb log chalets are set in 14 acres of woodland in the magnificent Spey Valley, surrounded on three sides by forest and rolling fields with the fourth side being half a mile of beach frontage. Free watersports hire for guests, 8.30-10am/4-5.30pm daily. Sailing, windsurfing, canoeing, salmon fishing, archery, dry ski slope skiing. Hire/instruction available by the hour, day or week mid April to end October. Boathouse Restaurant on the shore of Loch Insh offering coffee, home-made soup, fresh salads, bar meals, children's meals and evening à la carte. Large gift shop and bar. Three Children's Adventure Areas, 3km Lochside/Woodland Walk/Interpretation Trail, Ski Slope, Mountain Bike Hire and Stocked Trout Lochan are open all year round. Ski, snowboard hire, and instruction available December-April.

Loch Insh Log Chalets, Kincraig,
Inverness-shire PH21 1NU
Tel: 01540 651272
e-mail: office@lochinsh.com
website: www.lochinsh.com

ASSC/Highlands/Lanarkshire/Perth & Kinross

BLACKPARK FARM Westhill, Inverness IV2 5BP
This newly built holiday home is located one mile from Culloden Battlefield with panoramic views over Inverness and beyond. Fully equipped with many extras to make your holiday special, including oil fired central heating to ensure warmth on the coldest of winter days. Ideally based for touring the Highlands including Loch Ness, Skye etc. Extensive information is available on our website.
A Highland welcome awaits you.
Tel: 01463 790620 • Fax: 01463 794342 • e-mail: i.alexander@blackpark.co.uk • website: www.blackpark.co.uk

Cuilcheanna Cottages
Onich, Fort William
Inverness-shire PH33 6SD
A small peaceful site for self catering with three cottages and eight caravans (6 x 2003 models). Situated in the village of Onich, 400 yards off the main road. An excellent centre for touring and hill walking in the West Highlands.
For further details please phone
01855 821526 or 01855 821310
e-mail: onichholidays@mail.com

Arisaig House Cottages – *luxurious secluded accommodation in mature woodland*

- **ACHNAHANAT** in the grounds of Arisaig House, sleeps up to 8
- **THE BOTHY** set at the end of the walled gardens, sleeps up to 8
- **THE COURTYARD** self-contained apartment on first floor, sleeps 2
- **FAGUS LODGE** set in mature gardens, sleeps up to 6
- **GARDENER'S COTTAGE** set in gardens off small courtyard, sleeps up to 3
- **ROSHVEN** overlooks walled gardens of Arisaig House, sleeps up to 4

Set in an area of breathtaking coastal and hill scenery, and wonderful sandy beaches. Mountain bike hire, and fishing on Loch Morar can be arranged. Golf 7 miles, swimming pool 13 miles. Hard tennis court. Day trips to the Small Isles and to Skye. ON-LINE BOOKING.

Details from: **Andrew Smither, Arisaig House, Beasdale, Arisaig, Inverness-shire PH39 4NR**
Tel/Fax: 01687 462 686
e-mail: enquiries@arisaighouse-cottages.co.uk • www.arisaighouse-cottages.co.uk

CARMICHAEL COUNTRY COTTAGES
Westmains, Carmichael, Biggar ML12 6PG • Tel: 01899 308336 • Fax: 01899 308481
200 year old stone cottages in this 700 year old family estate. We guarantee comfort, warmth and a friendly welcome in an accessible, unique, rural and historic time capsule. We farm deer, cattle and sheep and sell meats and tartan - Carmichael of course. Open all year. Terms from £190 to £535.
15 cottages with a total of 32 bedrooms. Private tennis court and fishing loch, cafe, farm shop and visitor centre
e-mail: chiefcarm@aol.com • website: www.carmichael.co.uk/cottages

LAIGHWOOD HOLIDAYS
NEAR DUNKELD
For your comfort and enjoyment

We can provide properties from a large de luxe house for eight to well-equipped cottages and apartments for two to six, some open all year. All are accessible by tarmac farm roads. Laighwood is centrally located for sightseeing and for all country pursuits, including golf, fishing and squash. Sorry, no pets. Brochure on request from:

Laighwood Holidays, Laighwood, Dunkeld PH8 0HB.
Telephone: 01350 724241 • Fax: 01350 724212
e-mail: holidays@laighwood.co.uk • website: www.laighwood.co.uk

The Farm Holiday Guide to Coast & Country Holidays 2004

FHG PUBLICATIONS 2004

Your guides to Good Holidays

Recommended COUNTRY HOTELS
a quality selection of Britain's best Country Houses and Hotels

Recommended COUNTRY INNS & PUBS
accommodation, food and traditional good cheer

CARAVAN & CAMPING HOLIDAYS
covers every type of caravan and camping facility

BED & BREAKFAST STOPS
ever more popular independent guide with over 1000 entries

THE GOLF GUIDE Where to Play / Where to Stay
a detailed list covering virtually every club and course in the UK with hotels and other accommodation nearby,
– recommended by golfers, to golfers.

CHILDREN WELCOME!
Family Holiday and Days Out guide

PETS WELCOME!
the pet world's version of the ultimate hotel guide,
over 1000 properties where pets
and their owners are made welcome

Recommended SHORT BREAK HOLIDAYS
approved accommodation all year round for short breaks

BRITAIN'S BEST HOLIDAYS
user-friendly guide to all kinds of holiday opportunities

COAST & COUNTRY HOLIDAYS
holidays for all the family, from traditional farm houses
to inns, guesthouses and small hotels

SELF CATERING HOLIDAYS
one of the best and perhaps the widest selection
of self-catering accommodation

*Available from bookshops
or larger newsagents*

FHG PUBLICATIONS LTD
Abbey Mill Business Centre,
Seedhill, Paisley PA1 1TJ
www.holidayguides.com

**The best-selling series
of UK Holiday Guides**

Other FHG Publications

Recommended Country Hotels of Britain
Recommended Country Inns & Pubs of Britain
Recommended Short Break Holidays in Britain
Pets Welcome!
The Golf Guide: Where to Play/Where to Stay
Self-Catering Holidays in Britain
Britain's Best Holidays
Guide to Caravan and Camping Holidays
Bed and Breakfast Stops
Children Welcome! Family Holiday and Days Out Guide

ISBN 185055 353 X
© IPC Media Ltd 2004

Cover photographs:
Milford Haven: supplied by Graham Bell
Cover design: Focus Network
No part of this publication may be reproduced by any means or transmitted without the permission of the Publishers.

Maps: ©MAPS IN MINUTES™ 2003. ©Crown Copyright, Ordnance Survey Northern Ireland 2003 Permit No.NI 1675

Typeset by FHG Publications Ltd, Paisley.

Printed and bound in Great Britain by William Clowes, Beccles, Suffolk

Distribution. Book Trade: NBN Plymbridge, Plymbridge House, Estover Road, Plymouth PL6 7PY
Tel: 01752 202300; Fax: 01752 202333
News Trade: Market Force (UK) Ltd, 5th Floor Low Rise, King's Reach Tower, Stamford Street, London SE1 9LS
Tel: 0207 633 3450; Fax: 0207 633 3672

Published by FHG Publications Ltd., Abbey Mill Business Centre, Seedhill, Paisley PA1 ITJ (Tel: 0141-887 0428; Fax: 0141-889 7204).
e-mail: fhg@ipcmedia.com

US ISBN 1-58843-361-7
Distributed in the United States by
Hunter Publishing Inc., 130 Campus Drive, Edison, N.J. 08818, USA

The Original Farm Holiday Guide to Coast & Country Holidays is an FHG publication, published by IPC Country & Leisure Media Ltd, part of IPC Media Group of Companies.

The Original Farm Holiday Guide to
Coast & Country Holidays 2004

As its name suggests *The Farm Holiday Guide to COAST & COUNTRY HOLIDAYS* offers an excellent selection of holiday accommodation, mostly situated in the countryside or near the sea. There's something to suit everyone, from hotels and B&Bs, to self-catering and caravan holidays, and a selection of country inns and pubs. The entries are well described and generally give an indication of rates. Our proprietors extend the warmest of welcomes to their guests, and provide clean, comfortable accommodation and good wholesome food.

No holiday is complete without exploring the surrounding area, and you will usually find some general information within the entries to help you plan ahead. Our Readers' Offer Vouchers may save you some money on family outings and, should you wish to stop for a meal or snack, our Family Friendly Pubs, Inns and Hotels supplement lists a range of establishments which make an extra effort to cater for parents and children.

ENQUIRIES AND BOOKINGS. Give full details of dates (with an alternative), numbers and any special requirements. Ask about any points in the holiday description which are not clear and make sure that prices and conditions are clearly explained. You should receive confirmation in writing and a receipt for any deposit or advance payment. If you book your holiday well in advance, especially self-catering, confirm your arrival details nearer the time. Some proprietors, especially for self-catering, request full payment in advance but a reasonable deposit is more normal.

CANCELLATIONS. A holiday booking is a form of contract with obligations on both sides. If you have to cancel, give as much notice as possible. The longer the notice the better the chance that your host can replace your booking and therefore refund any payments. If the proprietor cancels in such away that causes serious, inconvenience, he may have obligations to you which have not been properly honoured. Take advice if necessary from such organisations as the Citizen's Advice Bureau, Consumer's Association, Trading standards Office, Local Tourist Office, etc., or your own solicitor. It is possible to insure against holiday cancellation. Brokers and insurance companies can advise you about this.

COMPLAINTS. It's best if any problems can be sorted out at the start of your holiday. If the problem is not. solved, you can contact the organisations mentioned above. You can also write to us. We will follow up the complaint with the advertiser – but we cannot act as intermediaries or accept responsibility for holiday arrangements.

FHG Publications Ltd. do not inspect accommodation and an entry in our guides does not imply a recommendation. However our advertisers have signed their agreement to work for the holidaymaker's best interests and as their customer, you have the right to expect appropriate attention and service.

THE FHG DIPLOMA. Every year we award a small number of Diplomas to holiday proprietors who have been specially recommended to us by readers. The names of our 2003 Diploma winners are listed in this book and we will be happy to receive your recommendations for 2004.

Please mention *The Farm Holiday Guide to COAST AND COUNTRY HOLIDAYS* when you are making enquiries or bookings and don't forget to use our Readers' Offer Voucher/Coupons if you're near any of the attractions which are kindly participating.

Anne Cuthbertson,
Editor

Ratings You Can Trust

ENGLAND

The **English Tourism Council** (formerly the English Tourist Board) has joined with the **AA** and **RAC** to create a new, easily understood quality rating for serviced accommodation, giving a clear guide of what to expect.

HOTELS are given a rating from One to Five **Stars** – the more Stars, the higher the quality and the greater the range of facilities and level of services provided.

GUEST ACCOMMODATION, which includes guest houses, bed and breakfasts, inns and farmhouses, is rated from One to Five **Diamonds**. Progressively higher levels of quality and customer care must be provided for each one of the One to Five Diamond ratings.

HOLIDAY PARKS, TOURING PARKS and CAMPING PARKS are now also assessed using **Stars**. Standards of quality range from a One Star (acceptable) to a Five Star (exceptional) park.

Look out also for the new **SELF-CATERING** Star ratings. The more **Stars** (from One to Five) awarded to an establishment, the higher the levels of quality you can expect. Establishments at higher rating levels also have to meet some additional requirements for facilities.

SCOTLAND

Star Quality Grades will reflect the most important aspects of a visit, such as the warmth of welcome, efficiency and friendliness of service, the quality of the food and the cleanliness and condition of the furnishings, fittings and decor.

**THE MORE STARS,
THE HIGHER THE STANDARDS.**

The description, such as Hotel, Guest House, Bed and Breakfast, Lodge, Holiday Park, Self-catering etc tells you the type of property and style of operation.

WALES

Places which score highly will have an especially welcoming atmosphere and pleasing ambience, high levels of comfort and guest care, and attractive surroundings enhanced by thoughtful design and attention to detail

STAR QUALITY GUIDE FOR

HOTELS, GUEST HOUSES AND FARMHOUSES
SELF-CATERING ACCOMMODATION
(Cottages, Apartments, Houses)
CARAVAN HOLIDAY HOME PARKS
(Holiday Parks, Touring Parks, Camping Parks)

★★★★★ Exceptional quality
★★★★ Excellent quality
★★★ Very good quality
★★ Good quality
★ Fair to good quality

In England, Scotland and Wales, all graded properties are inspected annually by Tourist Authority trained Assessors.

FHG Diploma Winners 2003

Each year we award a small number of diplomas to holiday proprietors whose services have been specially commended by our readers. The following were our FHG Diploma Winners for 2003.

England

DERBYSHIRE

Mr Tatlow
Ashfield Farm, Calwich
Near Ashbourne
Derbyshire DE6 2EB

DEVON

Mrs Tucker
Lower Luxton Farm, Upottery
Near Honiton
Devon EX14 9PB

◆

Royal Oak
Dunsford Near Exeter
Devon EX6 7DA

GLOUCESTERSHIRE

Mrs Keyte
The Limes, Evesham Road
Stow-on-the-Wold
Gloucestershire GL54 1EN

HAMPSHIRE

Mrs Ellis, Efford Cottage,
Everton, Lymington,
Hampshire SO41 0JD

◆

R. Law
Whitley Ridge Hotel
Beauly Road, Brockenhurst
Hampshire SO42 7QL

HEREFORDSHIRE

Mrs Brown
Ye Hostelrie, Goodrich
Near Ross on Wye
Herefordshire HR9 6HX

NORTH YORKSHIRE

Charles & Gill Richardson
The Coppice, 9 Studley Road
Harrogate
North Yorkshire HG1 5JU

◆

Mr & Mrs Hewitt
Harmony Country Lodge
Limestone Road, Burniston,
Scarborough
North Yorkshire YO13 0DG

Wales

POWYS

Linda Williams
The Old Vicarage
Erwood, Builth Wells
Powys LD2 3SZ

Scotland

ABERDEEN, BANFF & MORAY

Mr Ian Ednie
Spey Bay Hotel
Spey Bay
Fochabers
Moray IV32 7PJ

PERTH & KINROSS

Dunalastair Hotel
Kinloch Rannoch
By Pitlochry
Perthshire PH16 5PW

HELP IMPROVE BRITISH TOURISM STANDARDS

As recommendations are submitted from readers of the FULL RANGE of FHG titles the winners shown above may not necessarily appear in this guide.

THE FHG DIPLOMA

HELP IMPROVE BRITISH TOURIST STANDARDS

You are choosing holiday accommodation from our very popular FHG Publications.
Whether it be a hotel, guest house, farmhouse or self-catering accommodation, we think you will find it hospitable, comfortable and clean, and your host and hostess friendly and helpful.
Why not write and tell us about it?

As a recognition of the generally well-run and excellent holiday accommodation reviewed in our publications, we at FHG Publications Ltd. present a diploma to proprietors who receive the highest recommendation from their guests who are also readers of our Guides. If you care to write to us praising the holiday you have booked through FHG Publications Ltd. – whether this be board, self-catering accommodation, a sporting or a caravan holiday, what you say will be evaluated and the proprietors who reach our final list will be contacted.

The winning proprietor will receive an attractive framed diploma to display on his premises as recognition of a high standard of comfort, amenity and hospitality. FHG Publications Ltd. offer this diploma as a contribution towards the improvement of standards in tourist accommodation in Britain. Help your excellent host or hostess to win it!

FHG DIPLOMA

We nominate

Because

Name ....

Address..

....

Telephone No...

FHG READERS' OFFER 2004

Leighton Buzzard Railway
Page's Park Station, Billington Road,
Leighton Buzzard, Bedfordshire LU7 4TN
Tel: 01525 373888
e-mail: info@buzzrail.co.uk • website: www.buzzrail.co.uk
One free adult/child with full-fare adult ticket

valid from 16/3/04 – 29/10/04

NOT TO BE USED IN CONJUNCTION WITH ANY OTHER OFFER

FHG READERS' OFFER 2004

Bekonscot Model Village
Warwick Road, Beaconsfield, Buckinghamshire HP9 2PL
Tel: 01494 672919 • e-mail: info@bekonscot.co.uk
website: www.bekonscot.com
One child FREE when accompanied by full-paying adult

valid February to October 2004

NOT TO BE USED IN CONJUNCTION WITH ANY OTHER OFFER

FHG READERS' OFFER 2004

Buckinghamshire Railway Centre
Quainton Road Station, Quainton, Aylesbury HP22 4BY
Tel & Fax: 01296 655720
e-mail: bucksrailcentre@btopenworld.com
website: www.bucksrailcentre.org.uk
One child FREE with each full-paying adult

not valid for special events

NOT TO BE USED IN CONJUNCTION WITH ANY OTHER OFFER

FHG READERS' OFFER 2004

Sacrewell Farm & Country Centre
Sacrewell, Thornhaugh, Peterborough PE8 6HJ
Tel & Fax: 01780 782254
e-mail: wsatrust@supanet.com • website: www.sacrewell.org.uk
One child FREE with one full paying adult

valid from March 1st to October 1st 2004

NOT TO BE USED IN CONJUNCTION WITH ANY OTHER OFFER

FHG READERS' OFFER 2004

Tamar Valley Donkey Park
St Ann's Chapel, Gunnislake, Cornwall PL18 9HW
Tel: 01822 834072
e-mail: info@donkeypark.com • website: www.donkeypark.com
50p OFF per person, up to six persons

valid from Easter until the end of October 2004

NOT TO BE USED IN CONJUNCTION WITH ANY OTHER OFFER

A 65-minute journey into the lost world of the English narrow gauge light railway. Features historic steam locomotives from many countries.

PETS MUST BE KEPT UNDER CONTROL AND NOT ALLOWED ON TRACKS

Open: Sundays and Bank Holiday weekends 16 March to 29 October. Additional days in summer.

Directions: On A4146 towards Hemel Hempstead, close to roundabout junction with A505.

FHG PUBLICATIONS, ABBEY MILL BUSINESS CENTRE, PAISLEY PA1 1TJ

Be a giant in a magical miniature world of make-believe depicting rural England in the 1930s.
"A little piece of history that is forever England."

Open: 10am to 5pm daily mid February to end October.

Directions: Junction 16 M25, Junction 2 M40.

FHG PUBLICATIONS, ABBEY MILL BUSINESS CENTRE, PAISLEY PA1 1TJ

A working steam railway centre. Steam train rides, miniature railway rides, large collection of historic preserved steam locomotives, carriages and wagons.

Open: Sundays and Bank Holidays April to October, plus Wednesdays in June, July and August 10.30am to 5.30pm.

Directions: off A41 Aylesbury to Bicester Road, 6 miles north west of Aylesbury.

FHG PUBLICATIONS, ABBEY MILL BUSINESS CENTRE, PAISLEY PA1 1TJ

Farm animals, 18th century watermill and farmhouse, farm artifacts, caravan and camping, children's play area. Restaurant and gift shop.

Open: all year 9.30am to 5pm.

Directions: signposted off both A47 and A1.

FHG PUBLICATIONS, ABBEY MILL BUSINESS CENTRE, PAISLEY PA1 1TJ

Cornwall's only Donkey Sanctuary set in 14 acres overlooking the beautiful Tamar Valley. Donkey rides, rabbit warren, goat hill, children's playgrounds, cafe and picnic area.

Open: Easter to end of October and February half-term - daily from 10am to 5.30pm. November to March open weekends. Closed January.

Directions: Just off A390 between Callington and Gunnislake at St Ann's Chapel.

FHG PUBLICATIONS, ABBEY MILL BUSINESS CENTRE, PAISLEY PA1 1TJ

FHG READERS' OFFER 2004

Cars of the Stars Motor Museum
Standish Street, Keswick, Cumbria CA12 5HH
Tel: 017687 73757
e-mail: cotsmm@aol.com • website: www.carsofthestars.com

One child free with two paying adults

Valid 2004

NOT TO BE USED IN CONJUNCTION WITH ANY OTHER OFFER

FHG READERS' OFFER 2004

Windermere Steamboats & Museum
Rayrigg Road, Windermere, Cumbria LA23 1BN
Tel: 015394 45565 • e-mail:steamboat@ecosse.net
website: www.steamboat.co.uk

Two for the price of one (adults) OR 25% off family ticket

valid March to October 2004

NOT TO BE USED IN CONJUNCTION WITH ANY OTHER OFFER

FHG READERS' OFFER 2004

Blue-John Cavern
Castleton, Hope Valley, Derbyshire S33 8WP
Tel: 01433 620642 • e-mail: lesley@bluejohn.gemsoft.co.uk
website: www.bluejohn-cavern.co.uk

One child free with every paying adult

Valid until end 2004

NOT TO BE USED IN CONJUNCTION WITH ANY OTHER OFFER

FHG READERS' OFFER 2004

Crich Tramway Village
Crich, Matlock, Derbyshire DE4 5DP
Tel: 0870 7587267 • Fax: 01773 852326
e-mail: info@tramway.co.uk • website: www.tramway.co.uk

One child FREE with every full paying adult

valid during 2004

NOT TO BE USED IN CONJUNCTION WITH ANY OTHER OFFER

FHG READERS' OFFER 2004

Treak Cliff Cavern
HOME OF BLUE JOHN STONE
Castleton, Hope Valley, Derbyshire S33 8WP
Tel: 01433 620571
e-mail: treakcliff@bluejohnstone.com • website: www.bluejohnstone.com

10% discount (not valid on Special Events days)

valid during 2004

NOT TO BE USED IN CONJUNCTION WITH ANY OTHER OFFER

A collection of cars from film and TV, including Chitty Chitty Bang Bang, James Bond's Aston Martin, Del Boy's van, Fab1 and many more.

PETS MUST BE KEPT ON LEAD

Open: Daily 10am-5pm. Closed February half term. Weekends only in December.

Directions: In centre of Keswick close to car park.

FHG PUBLICATIONS, ABBEY MILL BUSINESS CENTRE, PAISLEY PA1 1TJ

World's finest steamboat collection and premier all-weather attraction. Swallows and Amazons exhibition, model boat pond, tea shop, souvenir shop. Free guided tours. Model boat exhibition.

Open: 10am to 5pm 3rd weekend in March to last weekend October.

Directions: on A592 half-a-mile north of Bowness-on-Windermere.

FHG PUBLICATIONS, ABBEY MILL BUSINESS CENTRE, PAISLEY PA1 1TJ

Large range of natural water-worn caverns featuring mining equipment, stalactites and stalagmites, and fine deposits of Blue-John stone, Britain's rarest semi-precious stone.

DOGS MUST BE KEPT ON LEAD

Open: 9.30am to 5.30pm.

Directions: Situated 2 miles west of Castleton; follow brown tourist signs.

FHG PUBLICATIONS, ABBEY MILL BUSINESS CENTRE, PAISLEY PA1 1TJ

A superb family day out in the atmosphere of a bygone era. Explore the recreated period street and fascinating exhibitions. Unlimited tram rides are free with entry. Play areas, shops, tea rooms, pub, restaurant and lots more.

Open: daily April to October 10 am to 5.30pm, weekends in winter.

Directions: Eight miles from M1 Junction 28, follow brown and white signs for "Tramway Museum".

FHG PUBLICATIONS, ABBEY MILL BUSINESS CENTRE, PAISLEY PA1 1TJ

An underground wonderland of stalactites, stalagmites, rocks, minerals and fossils. Home of the unique Blue John stone – see the largest single piece ever found. Suitable for all ages.

Open: Opens 10am. Enquire for last tour of day and closed days.

Directions: Half-a-mile west of Castleton on A6187 (old A625)

FHG PUBLICATIONS, ABBEY MILL BUSINESS CENTRE, PAISLEY PA1 1TJ

FHG	**Coldharbour Mill Museum**	
READERS' OFFER 2004	Coldharbour Mill, Uffculme, Cullompton, Devon EX15 3EE Tel: 01884 840960 • e-mail: info@coldharbourmill.org.uk website: www.coldharbourmill.org.uk TWO adult tickets for the price of ONE	valid during 2004

NOT TO BE USED IN CONJUNCTION WITH ANY OTHER OFFER

FHG	**The Big Sheep**	
READERS' OFFER 2004	Bideford, Devon EX39 5AP Tel: 01237 472366 Admit one child FREE with each paying adult	valid during 2004

NOT TO BE USED IN CONJUNCTION WITH ANY OTHER OFFER

FHG	**The Gnome Reserve & Wild Flower Garden**	
READERS' OFFER 2004	West Putford, Near Bradworthy, Devon EX22 7XE Tel: 01409 241435 • e-mail: info@gnomereserve.co.uk website: www.gnomereserve.co.uk One FREE child with full paying adult	Valid during 2004

NOT TO BE USED IN CONJUNCTION WITH ANY OTHER OFFER

FHG	**Killhope Lead Mining Museum**	
READERS' OFFER 2004	Cowshill, Upper Weardale, Co. Durham DL13 1AR Tel: 01388 537505 e-mail: killhope@durham.gov.uk • website: www.durham.gov.uk/killhope One child FREE with full-paying adult (not valid for Park Level Mine)	valid April to October 2004

NOT TO BE USED IN CONJUNCTION WITH ANY OTHER OFFER

FHG	**BARLEYLANDS FARM**	
READERS' OFFER 2004	Barleylands Road, Billericay, Essex CM11 2UD Tel: 01268 290229 • e-mail: info@barleylands.co.uk website: www.barleylands.co.uk FREE adult ticket when accompanied by one child	Valid 1st March to 31st October. Not special event days

NOT TO BE USED IN CONJUNCTION WITH ANY OTHER OFFER

A picturesque 200-year old woollen mill with machinery that spins yarn and weaves cloth.
Mill machinery, restaurant, exhibition gallery, shop and gardens in a waterside setting.

Open: February to December daily 10.30am to 5pm.

Directions: Two miles from Junction 27 M5; follow signs to Willand (B3181) then brown tourist signs to Working Woollen Mill.

FHG PUBLICATIONS, ABBEY MILL BUSINESS CENTRE, PAISLEY PA1 1TJ

"England for Excellence" award-winning rural attraction combining traditional rural crafts with hilarious novelties such as sheep racing and duck trialling, Indoor adventure zone for adults and children.

Open: daily, 10am to 6pm April - Oct Phone for Winter opening times and details.

Directions: on A39 North Devon link road, two miles west of Bideford Bridge.

FHG PUBLICATIONS, ABBEY MILL BUSINESS CENTRE, PAISLEY PA1 1TJ

Visit 1000+ gnomes and pixies in two acre beech wood. Gnome hats are loaned free of charge - so the gnomes think you are one of them - don't forget your camera! Also 2-acre wild flower garden with 250 labelled species.

Open: Daily 10am to 6pm 21st March to 31st October.

Directions: Between Bideford and Bude; follow brown tourist signs from A39/A388/A386.

FHG PUBLICATIONS, ABBEY MILL BUSINESS CENTRE, PAISLEY PA1 1TJ

Britain's best preserved lead mining site – and a great day out for all the family, with lots to see and do. Underground Experience – Park Level Mine now open.

Open: April 1st to September 30th 10.30am to 5pm daily. Weekends and half term in October

Directions: Alongside A689, midway between Stanhope and Alston in the heart of the North Pennines.

FHG PUBLICATIONS, ABBEY MILL BUSINESS CENTRE, PAISLEY PA1 1TJ

Craft Village with animals, museum, blacksmith, glassblowing, miniature railway (Sundays and August), craft shops, tea room and licensed restaurant.

DOGS MUST BE KEPT ON LEAD

Open: Craft Village open all year. Farm open 1st March to 31st October.

Directions: M25, A127 towards Southend. Take A176 junction off A127, 3rd exit Wash Road, 2nd left Barleylands Road.

FHG PUBLICATIONS, ABBEY MILL BUSINESS CENTRE, PAISLEY PA1 1TJ

FHG NATIONAL WATERWAYS MUSEUM
READERS' OFFER 2004
Llanthony Warehouse, Gloucester Docks, Gloucester GL1 2EH
Tel: 01452 318200 • website: www.nwm.org.uk
e-mail: bookingsnwm@thewaterwaystrust.org

20% off museum admission (excludes combination tickets)

valid during 2004

NOT TO BE USED IN CONJUNCTION WITH ANY OTHER OFFER

FHG Cider Museum & King Offa Distillery
READERS' OFFER 2004
21 Ryelands Street, Hereford HR4 0LW
Tel: 01432 354207 • Fax: 01432 371641
e-mail: info@cidermuseum.co.uk • website: www.cidermuseum.co.uk

50p reduction on entry fee

valid during 2004

NOT TO BE USED IN CONJUNCTION WITH ANY OTHER OFFER

FHG Verulamium Museum
READERS' OFFER 2004
St Michael's, St Albans, Herts AL3 4SW
Tel: 01727 751810 • e-mail: museum@stalbans.gov.uk
web: www.stalbansmuseums.org.uk

"Two for One"

valid from 1/8/04 until 31/12/04

NOT TO BE USED IN CONJUNCTION WITH ANY OTHER OFFER

FHG Museum of Kent Life
READERS' OFFER 2004
Lock Lane, Sandling, Maidstone ME14 3AU
Tel: 01622 763936 • Fax: 01622 662024
e-mail: enquiries@museum-kentlife.co.uk • website: www.museum-kentlife.co.uk

Two tickets for the price of one (cheapest ticket FREE)

valid from March to November 2004

NOT TO BE USED IN CONJUNCTION WITH ANY OTHER OFFER

FHG Docker Park Farm

READERS' OFFER 2004
Arkholme, Carnforth, Lancashire LA6 1AR
Tel & Fax: 015242 21331
e-mail: info@dockerparkfarm.co.uk • website: www.dockerparkfarm.co.uk

One FREE child per one paying adult (one voucher per child)

valid from January to December 2004

NOT TO BE USED IN CONJUNCTION WITH ANY OTHER OFFER

On three floors of a Listed Victorian warehouse telling 200 years of inland waterway history. • *Historic boats* • *Boat trips available (Easter to October)* • *Painted boat gallery* • *Blacksmith* • *Archive film* • *Hands-on displays "A great day out"*

Open: every day 10am to 5pm (excluding Christmas Day).

Directions: Junction 11A or 12 off M5 – follow brown signs for Historic Docks. Railway and bus station - 15 minute walk. Free coach parking.

FHG PUBLICATIONS, ABBEY MILL BUSINESS CENTRE, PAISLEY PA1 1TJ

Discover the fascinating history of cider making. There is a programme of temporary exhibitions and events plus free samples of Hereford cider brandy.

Open: April to Oct 10am to 5.30pm (daily)
Nov to Dec 11am to 3pm (daily)
Jan to Mar 11am to 3pm (Tues to Sun)

Directions: situated west of Hereford off the A438 Hereford to Brecon road.

FHG PUBLICATIONS, ABBEY MILL BUSINESS CENTRE, PAISLEY PA1 1TJ

The museum of everyday life in Roman Britain. An award-winning museum with re-created Roman rooms, hands-on discovery areas, and some of the best mosaics outside the Mediterranean.

Open: Monday to Saturday 10am-5.30pm
Sunday 2pm-5.30pm.

Directions: St Albans.

FHG PUBLICATIONS, ABBEY MILL BUSINESS CENTRE, PAISLEY PA1 1TJ

Kent's award-winning open air museum is home to a collection of historic buildings which house interactive exhibitions on life over the last 150 years.

Open: Seven days a week from March to November. 10am to 5.30pm.

Directions: Junction 6 off M20, follow signs to Aylesford.

FHG PUBLICATIONS, ABBEY MILL BUSINESS CENTRE, PAISLEY PA1 1TJ

We are a working farm, with lots of animals to see and touch. Enjoy a walk round the Nature Trail or refreshments in the tearoom. Lots of activities during school holidays.

Open: Summer: daily 10.30am to 5pm
Winter: weekends only 10.30am to 4pm.

Directions: Junction 35 off M6, take B6254 towards Kirkby Lonsdale, then follow the brown signs.

FHG PUBLICATIONS, ABBEY MILL BUSINESS CENTRE, PAISLEY PA1 1TJ

FHG DONINGTON GRAND PRIX COLLECTION

DONINGTON PARK
Castle Donington, Near Derby, Leics DE74 2RP
Tel: 01332 811027 • e-mail: enquiries@doningtoncollection.co.uk
website: www.doningtoncollection.com

READERS' OFFER 2004

One child FREE with each full-paying adult

valid until 01/01/05

NOT TO BE USED IN CONJUNCTION WITH ANY OTHER OFFER

FHG Snibston Discovery Park

Ashby Road, Coalville, Leicestershire LE67 3LN
Tel: 01530 278444 • Fax: 01530 813301
e-mail: snibston@leics.gov.uk • website: www.leics.gov.uk/museums

READERS' OFFER 2004

One FREE child with every full paying adult

valid until June 2004

NOT TO BE USED IN CONJUNCTION WITH ANY OTHER OFFER

FHG Skegness Natureland Seal Sanctuary

North Parade, Skegness, Lincolnshire PE25 1DB
Tel: 01754 764345
e-mail: natureland@fsbdial.co.uk • website: www.skegnessnatureland.co.uk

READERS' OFFER 2004

Free entry for one child when accompanied by full-paying adult.

Valid during 2004

NOT TO BE USED IN CONJUNCTION WITH ANY OTHER OFFER

FHG Museum in Docklands

No. 1 Warehouse, West India Quay, Hertsmere Road, London E14 4AL
Tel: 0870 4443855 • Fax: 0870 4443858
e-mail: info@museumindocklands.org.uk

READERS' OFFER 2004

TWO adult tickets for price of ONE. Children go FREE

valid from 01/08/04 to 31/12/04

NOT TO BE USED IN CONJUNCTION WITH ANY OTHER OFFER

FHG PLEASURELAND

Marine Drive, Southport, Merseyside PR8 1RX
Tel: 08702 200204 • Fax: 01704 537936
e-mail: mail@pleasurelandltd.freeserve.co.uk • website: www.pleasureland.uk.com

READERS' OFFER 2004

3 for 2, if two all day wristbands purchased, third provided FREE
• offer not valid on Bank Holiday Weekends

valid from March to November 2004

NOT TO BE USED IN CONJUNCTION WITH ANY OTHER OFFER

The world's largest collection of Grand Prix racing cars – over 130 exhibits within five halls, including McLaren Formula One cars.	**Open:** Daily 10am to 5pm (last admission 4pm). Closed Christmas/New Year. **Directions:** 2 miles from M1 (J23a/24) and M42/A42; to north-west via A50.

FHG PUBLICATIONS, ABBEY MILL BUSINESS CENTRE, PAISLEY PA1 1TJ

Located in 100 acres of landscaped grounds, Snibston is a unique mixture, with historic mine buildings, outdoor science play areas, wildlife habitats and an exhibition hall housing five hands-on galleries. Cafe and gift shop. Plus new for 2003 - Toy Box (gallery for under 5s & 8s).	**Open:** Seven days a week 10am to 5pm. **Directions:** Junction 22 from M1, Junction 13 from M42. Follow Brown Heritage signs.

FHG PUBLICATIONS, ABBEY MILL BUSINESS CENTRE, PAISLEY PA1 1TJ

Well known for rescuing and rehabilitating orphaned and injured seal pups found washed ashore on Lincolnshire beaches. Also: penguins, aquarium, pets' corner, reptiles, Floral Palace (tropical birds and butterflies etc).	**Open:** Daily from 10am. Closed Christmas/Boxing/New Year's Days. **Directions:** At the north end of Skegness seafront.

FHG PUBLICATIONS, ABBEY MILL BUSINESS CENTRE, PAISLEY PA1 1TJ

The Museum In Docklands unlocks the history of London's river, port and people in a nineteenth century warehouse, originally used to house imports of exotic spices, rum and cotton. It now holds a wealth of objects from whale bones to WWII gas masks.	**Open:** open 7 days 10am to 6pm. **Directions:** furthest warehouse along quayside from West India Quay DLR over footbridge from Canary Wharf shopping centre.

FHG PUBLICATIONS, ABBEY MILL BUSINESS CENTRE, PAISLEY PA1 1TJ

Over 100 rides and attractions, including the Traumatizer - the UK's tallest, fastest suspended looping coaster and the Lucozade Space Shot. New for 2003 - Abdullah's Dilemma	**Open:** March to November, times vary.

FHG PUBLICATIONS, ABBEY MILL BUSINESS CENTRE, PAISLEY PA1 1TJ

FHG READERS' OFFER 2004

Southport Zoo and Conservation Trust
Princes Park, Southport, Merseyside PR8 1RX
Tel: 01704 548894 • Tel & Fax: 01704 538102
e-mail: info@southportzoo.com • website: www.southportzoo.com

FREE Zoo Pack per family

valid during 2004 except Bank Holidays

NOT TO BE USED IN CONJUNCTION WITH ANY OTHER OFFER

FHG READERS' OFFER 2004

DINOSAUR ADVENTURE PARK
Weston Park, Lenwade, Norwich NR9 5JW
Tel: 01603 876310 • Fax: 01603 876315
e-mail: info@dinosaurpark.co.uk • website: www.dinosaurpark.co.uk

50p off standard admission prices for up to six people

Easter 2004 till end of October 2004

NOT TO BE USED IN CONJUNCTION WITH ANY OTHER OFFER

FHG READERS' OFFER 2004

The Collectors World of Eric St John-Foti
Hermitage Hall, Downham Market PE38 0AU
Tel: 01366 383185 • Fax: 01366 386519
website: www.collectors-world.org

50p off adult admission - 25p off child admission

valid during 2004

NOT TO BE USED IN CONJUNCTION WITH ANY OTHER OFFER

FHG READERS' OFFER 2004

Chesters Walled Garden
Chollerford, Hexham NE46 4BQ
Tel: 01434 681483 • e-mail: mail@chesterswalledgarden.co.uk
website: www.chesterswalledgarden.co.uk

One FREE adult with one paying adult

valid Easter to end of August 2004

NOT TO BE USED IN CONJUNCTION WITH ANY OTHER OFFER

FHG READERS' OFFER 2004

Newark Air Museum
The Airfield, Winthorpe, Newark, Nottinghamshire NG24 2NY
Tel: 01636 707170
e-mail: newarkair@lineone.net • website: www.newarkairmuseum.co.uk

Party rate discount for every voucher
(50p per person off normal admission).

Valid during 2004

NOT TO BE USED IN CONJUNCTION WITH ANY OTHER OFFER

Lions, snow leopards, chimpanzees, otters, reptiles, aquarium and lots more, set amidst landscaped gardens. Gift shop, cafe and picnic areas.	**Open:** all year round from 10am **Directions:** on the coast 16 miles north of Liverpool; follow the brown and white tourist signs

FHG PUBLICATIONS, ABBEY MILL BUSINESS CENTRE, PAISLEY PA1 1TJ

It's time you came-n-saurus for a monster day out set in over 100 acres of parkland. Enjoy the adventure play areas, dinosaur trail, secret animal garden and lots more.	**Open:** Please call for specific opening times or see our website. **Directions:** Nine miles from Norwich, follow the brown signs to Weston Park from the A47 or A1067

FHG PUBLICATIONS, ABBEY MILL BUSINESS CENTRE, PAISLEY PA1 1TJ

The collections of local eccentric Eric St John-Foti (Mr Norfolk Punch himself!) on view (over 80) and the Magical Dickens Experience. Two amazing attractions for the price of one. Somewhere totally different, unique and interesting.	**Open:** 11am to 5pm (last entry 4pm) Open all year. **Directions:** one mile from town centre on the A1122 Downham/Wisbech Road.

FHG PUBLICATIONS, ABBEY MILL BUSINESS CENTRE, PAISLEY PA1 1TJ

Beautiful walled garden with famous collections of herbs and herbaceous plants, including Roman Garden, National Thyme and Marjoram Collections. Nursery and Gift shop.	**Open:** From Easter to the end of October 10am to 5pm daily. **Directions:** Six miles north of Hexham off B6318 next to Chesters Roman Fort.

FHG PUBLICATIONS, ABBEY MILL BUSINESS CENTRE, PAISLEY PA1 1TJ

A collection of 65 aircraft and cockpit sections from across the history of aviation. Extensive aero engine and artefact displays.	**Open:** Daily from 10am (closed Christmas period). **Directions:** Follow brown and white signs from A1, A46, A17 and A1133.

FHG PUBLICATIONS, ABBEY MILL BUSINESS CENTRE, PAISLEY PA1 1TJ

FHG READERS' OFFER 2004

Galleries of Justice
Shire Hall, High Pavement, Lace Market, Nottingham NG1 1HN
Tel: 0115 9520555 • e-mail: info@galleriesofjustice.org.uk
Fax: 0115 9939828 • website: www.galleries of justice.org.uk

TWO for ONE with full paying adult one free visit per voucher

Valid from Jan to Dec 2004, not Bank Holidays

NOT TO BE USED IN CONJUNCTION WITH ANY OTHER OFFER

FHG READERS' OFFER 2004

The Tales of Robin Hood
30 - 38 Maid Marian Way, Nottingham NG1 6GF
Tel: 0115 9483284 • Fax: 0115 9501536
e-mail: robinhoodcentre@mail.com • website: www.robinhood.uk.com

One FREE child with full paying adult per voucher

valid from January to December 2004

NOT TO BE USED IN CONJUNCTION WITH ANY OTHER OFFER

FHG READERS' OFFER 2004

The White Post Modern Farm Centre
Farnsfield, Nottingham NG22 8HL
Tel: 01623 882977 • e-mail: tim@whitepostfarmcentre.co.uk
Fax: 01623 883499 • website: www.whitepostfarmcentre.co.uk

10% off entry to the farm with voucher

valid during 2004

NOT TO BE USED IN CONJUNCTION WITH ANY OTHER OFFER

FHG READERS' OFFER 2004

Cogges Manor Farm Museum
Church Lane, Witney, Oxfordshire OX28 3LA
Tel: 01993 772602 • website: www.cogges.org

Two for the price of one

Valid April to end of November 2004

NOT TO BE USED IN CONJUNCTION WITH ANY OTHER OFFER

FHG READERS' OFFER 2004

Avon Valley Railway
Bitton Station, Bath Road, Bitton, Bristol, BS30 6HD
Tel: 0117 932 5538
e-mail: enquiries@avonvalleyrailway.co.uk • website: www.avonvalleyrailway.co.uk

One FREE child ticket with every fare-paying adult
(Not valid for "Day out with Thomas Events")

valid from May to October 2004

NOT TO BE USED IN CONJUNCTION WITH ANY OTHER OFFER

Journey with us through 300 years of Crime and Punishment on this unique atmospheric site. Witness a real trial in the authentic Victorian courtroom. Prisoners and gaolers act as guides as you become part of history.

Open: Tuesday to Sunday 10am to 5pm peak season 10am to 4pm off-peak.

Directions: from Nottingham city centre follow the brown tourist signs.

FHG PUBLICATIONS, ABBEY MILL BUSINESS CENTRE, PAISLEY PA1 1TJ

Travel back in time to the dark and dangerous world of intrigue and adventure of Medieval England's most endearing outlaw - Robin Hood. Story boards, exhibitions and a film show all add interest to the story.

Open: 10am -6pm, last admission 4.30pm.

Directions: Follow the brown and white tourist information signs whilst heading towards the city centre.

FHG PUBLICATIONS, ABBEY MILL BUSINESS CENTRE, PAISLEY PA1 1TJ

A modern working farm with displays indoors and outdoors designed to help visitors listen, feel and learn whilst having fun. Daily baby animal holding sessions plus a large indoor play barn.

Open: Daily 10am to 5pm.

Directions: 12 miles from Nottingham on A614 or follow Robin Hood signs from J27 of M1.

FHG PUBLICATIONS, ABBEY MILL BUSINESS CENTRE, PAISLEY PA1 1TJ

Historic manor house and farm with traditional animals. Work in the Victorian kitchen every afternoon.

Open: April to 2nd December: Tuesday to Friday 10.30am to 5.30pm. Saturday and Sunday 12-5.30pm.

Directions: Just off A40 Oxford to Cheltenham road at Witney.

FHG PUBLICATIONS, ABBEY MILL BUSINESS CENTRE, PAISLEY PA1 1TJ

The Avon Valley Railway offers a whole new experience for some, and a nostalgic memory for others. Steam trains operate every Sunday Easter to October, plus Bank Holidays and Christmas.
PETS MUST BE KEPT ON LEADS AND OFF TRAIN SEATS

Open: Steam trains operate every Sunday Easter to October plus Bank Holidays and Christmas

Directions: On the A431 midway between Bristol and Bath at Bitton

FHG PUBLICATIONS, ABBEY MILL BUSINESS CENTRE, PAISLEY PA1 1TJ

FHG READERS' OFFER 2004

The Helicopter Museum

The Heliport, Locking Moor Road, Weston-Super-Mare BS24 8PP
Tel: 01934 635227 • Fax: 01934 645230
e-mail: office@helimuseum.fsnet.co.uk • website: www.helicoptermuseum.co.uk

One child FREE with two full-paying adults

valid from April to October 2004

NOT TO BE USED IN CONJUNCTION WITH ANY OTHER OFFER

FHG READERS' OFFER 2004

Easton Farm Park

Easton, Near Wickham Market, Ipswich, Suffolk IP13 0EQ
Tel: 01728 746475 • e-mail: easton@eastonfarmpark.co.uk
website: www.eastonfarmpark.co.uk

£1 per person off for up to 4 full paying admissions

Valid until end 2004

NOT TO BE USED IN CONJUNCTION WITH ANY OTHER OFFER

FHG READERS' OFFER 2004

New Pleasurewood Hills

Leisure Way, Corton, Lowestoft, Suffolk NR32 5DZ
Tel: 01502 508200 • Fax: 01502 567393
e-mail: info@pleasurewoodhills.com • website: www.pleasurewoodhills.com

'3 for 2' One FREE adult/child with two full paying adults

valid during 2004, except special events and at Christmas

NOT TO BE USED IN CONJUNCTION WITH ANY OTHER OFFER

FHG READERS' OFFER 2004

PARADISE PARK & GARDENS

Avis Road, Newhaven, East Sussex BN9 0DH
Tel: 01273 512123 • Fax: 01273 616000
e-mail: enquiries@paradisepark.co.uk • website: www.paradisepark.co.uk

Admit one FREE adult or child with one adult paying full entrance price

valid during 2004

NOT TO BE USED IN CONJUNCTION WITH ANY OTHER OFFER

FHG READERS' OFFER 2004

Buckley's Yesterday's World

High Street, Battle, East Sussex TN33 0AQ
Tel: 01424 775378   e-mail: info@yesterdaysworld.co.uk
website: www.yesterdaysworld.co.uk

50p off each admission

Valid until end 2004

NOT TO BE USED IN CONJUNCTION WITH ANY OTHER OFFER

The world's largest helicopter collection - over 70 exhibits, includes two royal helicopters, Russian Gunship and Vietnam veterans plus many award-winning exhibits. Cafe, shop. Flights.

PETS MUST BE KEPT UNDER CONTROL

Open: Wednesday to Sunday 10am to 5.30pm. Daily during school Easter and Summer (open till 6.30pm) holidays and Bank Holiday Mondays. (10am to 4.30pm November to March)

Directions: Junction 21 off M5 then follow the propellor signs.

FHG PUBLICATIONS, ABBEY MILL BUSINESS CENTRE, PAISLEY PA1 1TJ

Lots of baby animals. FREE pony rides, face painting, green trail, 'pat-a-pet', indoor children's soft play area; gift shop, tearoom, pets' paddocks

DOGS MUST BE KEPT ON LEADS

Open: March to October 10.30am to 6pm

Directions: Follow brown tourist signs off A12 and other roads

FHG PUBLICATIONS, ABBEY MILL BUSINESS CENTRE, PAISLEY PA1 1TJ

With over forty rides, shows and attractions set in fifty acres of parkland - you'll have everything you need for a brilliant day out. The mixture of old favourites and exciting new introductions are an unbeatable combination.

Open: From 10am. Closing time varies depending on season.

Directions: Off A12 between Great Yarmouth and Lowestoft.

FHG PUBLICATIONS, ABBEY MILL BUSINESS CENTRE, PAISLEY PA1 1TJ

A plant lover's paradise with outstanding themed gardens and extensive Museum of Natural History. Conservatory gardens contain a large and varied collection of the world's flora. Sussex History Trail. Dinosaur Museum and park. Rides and amusements.

Open: Open daily, except Christmas Day and Boxing Day.

Directions: Signposted off A26 and A259.

FHG PUBLICATIONS, ABBEY MILL BUSINESS CENTRE, PAISLEY PA1 1TJ

The past is brought to life at the top attraction in the South East 2002 (England for Excellence Awards). Step back in time and wonder through over 30 shop and room settings.

PETS NOT ALLOWED IN CHILDREN'S PLAY AREA

Open: 9.30am to 6pm (last admission 4.45pm, one hour earlier in winter).

Directions: Just off A21 in Battle High Street opposite the Abbey.

FHG PUBLICATIONS, ABBEY MILL BUSINESS CENTRE, PAISLEY PA1 1TJ

FHG READERS' OFFER 2004

Wilderness Wood
Hadlow Down, Near Uckfield, East Sussex TN22 4HJ
Tel: 01825 830509 • Fax: 01825 830977
e-mail: enquiries@wildernesswood.co.uk • website: www.wildernesswood.co.uk

TWO for the price of ONE

valid during 2004

NOT TO BE USED IN CONJUNCTION WITH ANY OTHER OFFER

FHG READERS' OFFER 2004

The New Metroland
39 Garden Walk, Metrocentre, Gateshead NE11 9XY
Tel: 0191 4932048 • e-mail: enquiries@metroland.uk.com
Fax: 0191 4932904 • website: www.metroland.uk.com

TWO Gold All Day Passes for the price of ONE

valid until 31/12/04 except Bank Holiday Weekends

NOT TO BE USED IN CONJUNCTION WITH ANY OTHER OFFER

FHG READERS' OFFER 2004

Wildfowl & Wetlands Trust
District 15, Washington, Tyne & Wear NE38 8LE
Tel: 0191 416 5454
e-mail: val.pickering@wwt.org.uk • website: www.wwt.org.uk

One FREE admission with full-paying adult

valid from 1st Jan 2004 to 30th Sept 2004

NOT TO BE USED IN CONJUNCTION WITH ANY OTHER OFFER

FHG READERS' OFFER 2004

Stratford Butterfly Farm
Swans Nest Lane, Stratford-upon-Avon, Warwickshire CV37 7LS
Tel: 01789 299288 • e-mail: sales@butterflyfarm.co.uk
website: www.butterflyfarm.co.uk

One child free with each paying adult

Valid during 2004

NOT TO BE USED IN CONJUNCTION WITH ANY OTHER OFFER

FHG READERS' OFFER 2004

Cholderton Rare Breeds Farm Park
Amesbury Road, Cholderton, Wiltshire SP4 0EW
Tel: 01980 629438
e-mail: sales@rabbitworld.co.uk • website: www.choldertonfarm.co.uk

One person FREE with two paying adults
(not valid on Public Holidays or weekends during July and August)

valid June to November 3rd 2004

NOT TO BE USED IN CONJUNCTION WITH ANY OTHER OFFER

Wilderness Wood is a unique family-run working woodland in the Sussex High Weald. Explore trails and footpaths, enjoy local cakes and ices, try the adventure playground. Many special events and activities. Parties catered for.	**Open:** daily 10am to 5.30pm or dusk if earlier. **Directions:** On the south side of the A272 in the village of Hadlow Down. Signposted with a brown tourist sign.

FHG PUBLICATIONS, ABBEY MILL BUSINESS CENTRE, PAISLEY PA1 1TJ

Europe's largest indoor family funfair, with exciting rides like the New Rollercoaster, Disco Dodgems and Swashbuckling Pirate Ship. There's something for everyone whatever the weather!	**Open:** Daily except Christmas Day. Mon - Wed & Fri - Sat 10am to 8pm. Thurs 10am - 9pm, Sun 11am to 6pm. (Open from 12 noon Monday to Friday during term time). **Directions:** Signposted from the A1.

FHG PUBLICATIONS, ABBEY MILL BUSINESS CENTRE, PAISLEY PA1 1TJ

100 acres of parkland, home to hundreds of duck, geese, swans and flamingos. Discovery centre, cafe, gift shop; play area.	**Open:** Every day except Christmas Day **Directions:** Signposted from A19, A195, A1231 and A182.

FHG PUBLICATIONS, ABBEY MILL BUSINESS CENTRE, PAISLEY PA1 1TJ

Wander through a lush landscape of exotic foliage where a myriad of multi-coloured butterflies sip nectar from tropical blossoms. Stroll past bubbling streams and splashing waterfalls; view insects and spiders all safely behind glass.	**Open:** 10am to 6pm summer, 10am to dusk winter.

FHG PUBLICATIONS, ABBEY MILL BUSINESS CENTRE, PAISLEY PA1 1TJ

Lovely rural farm with 50 breeds of rabbit, and several breeds of poultry, pig, sheep, goat, horses and ponies. Iron Age Roundhouse. Cafe, craft shop, events throughout holidays, famous pig races, nature trail, indoor and outdoor play.	**Open:** 10.30am to 6pm in season, weekends 10am to 4pm in winter. **Directions:** Near Stonehenge, just off the A303 at the intersection with A338 Salisbury/Swindon Road.

FHG PUBLICATIONS, ABBEY MILL BUSINESS CENTRE, PAISLEY PA1 1TJ

FHG READERS' OFFER 2004

The Deep
Hull, HU1 4DP
Tel: 01482 381000 • Fax: 01482 381018
e-mail: info@thedeep.co.uk • website: www.thedeep.co.uk

One FREE child for each two full paying adults

valid until Dec 2004 (after 2pm only)

NOT TO BE USED IN CONJUNCTION WITH ANY OTHER OFFER

FHG READERS' OFFER 2004

Embsay & Bolton Abbey Steam Railway
Bolton Abbey Station, Skipton, N. Yorkshire BD23 6AF
Tel: 01756 710614 • website: www.embsayboltonabbeyrailway.org.uk

One adult travels FREE when accompanied by a full fare paying adult

valid during 2004, does not include Special Event Days

NOT TO BE USED IN CONJUNCTION WITH ANY OTHER OFFER

FHG READERS' OFFER 2004

Museum of Rail Travel
Ingrow Railway Centre, Near Keighley, West Yorkshire BD22 8NJ
Tel: 01535 680425 • e-mail: admin@vintagecarriagestrust.org
website: www.vintagecarriagestrust.org

"ONE for ONE" free admission

Valid during 2004 except during special events (ring to check)

NOT TO BE USED IN CONJUNCTION WITH ANY OTHER OFFER

FHG READERS' OFFER 2004

The Colour Museum
Perkin House, PO Box 244, Providence Street, Bradford BD1 2PW
Tel: 01274 390955 • Fax: 01274 392888
e-mail: museum@sdc.org.uk • website: www.sdc.org.uk

TWO for ONE

valid during 2004

NOT TO BE USED IN CONJUNCTION WITH ANY OTHER OFFER

FHG READERS' OFFER 2004

Thackray Museum
Beckett Street, Leeds LS9 7LN
Tel: 0113 244 4343 • Fax: 0113 247 0219
e-mail: info@thackraymuseum.org • website: www.thackraymuseum.org

TWO for ONE on the purchase of a full price adult ticket

valid until July 2004 excluding Bank Holidays

NOT TO BE USED IN CONJUNCTION WITH ANY OTHER OFFER

The Deep is the world's only submarium. Here you can discover the story of the world's oceans on a dramatic journey from the beginning of time and into the future.
You can also explore the wonders of the oceans, from the tropical lagoon to the icy waters of Antarctica.

Open: daily 10am to 6pm (last entry at 5pm).
Closed Christmas Eve and Christmas Day
Directions: from the North take A1/M, M62/A63. From the South take A1/M, A15/A63 follow signs to Hull city centre, then local signs to The Deep.

FHG PUBLICATIONS, ABBEY MILL BUSINESS CENTRE, PAISLEY PA1 1TJ

Steam trains operate over a 4½ mile line from Bolton Abbey Station to Embsay Station. Many family events including Thomas the Tank Engine take place during major Bank Holidays.

Open: steam trains run every Sunday throughout the year and up to 7 days a week in summer. 10.30am to 4.30pm
Directions: Embsay Station signposted from the A59 Skipton by-pass; Bolton Abbey Station signposted from the A59 at Bolton Abbey.

FHG PUBLICATIONS, ABBEY MILL BUSINESS CENTRE, PAISLEY PA1 1TJ

A fascinating display of railway carriages and a wide range of railway items telling the story of rail travel over the years.

ALL PETS MUST BE KEPT ON LEADS

Open: Daily 11am to 4.30pm
Directions: Approximately one mile from Keighley on A629 Halifax road. Follow brown tourist signs

FHG PUBLICATIONS, ABBEY MILL BUSINESS CENTRE, PAISLEY PA1 1TJ

The Colour Museum is unique. Dedicated to the history, development and technology of colour, it is the ONLY museum of its kind in Europe. A truly colourful experience for both kids and adults, it's fun, it's informative and it's well worth a visit.

Open: Tuesday to Saturday 10am to 4pm (last admission 3.30pm).
Directions: just off Westgate on B6144 from the city centre to Haworth.

FHG PUBLICATIONS, ABBEY MILL BUSINESS CENTRE, PAISLEY PA1 1TJ

A fantastic day out for all at the lively and interactive, award-winning Thackray Museum. Experience life as it was in the Victorian slums, discover how medicine has changed our lives and the incredible lotions and potions once offered as cures. Try an empathy belly and explore the interactive bodyworks gallery.

Open: daily 10am till 5pm, closed 24th - 26th and 31st December and 1st January.
Directions: from M621 follow signs for York (A64) then follow brown tourist signs. From the north, take A58 towards city and then follow brown tourist signs.

FHG PUBLICATIONS, ABBEY MILL BUSINESS CENTRE, PAISLEY PA1 1TJ

FHG READERS' OFFER 2004

The Grassic Gibbon Centre
Arbuthnott, Laurencekirk, Aberdeenshire AB30 1PB
Tel: 01561 361668 • e-mail: lgginfo@grassicgibbon.com
website: www.grassicgibbon.com

TWO for the price of ONE entry to exhibition (based on full adult rate only)

Valid during 2004 (not groups)

NOT TO BE USED IN CONJUNCTION WITH ANY OTHER OFFER

FHG READERS' OFFER 2004

Oban Rare Breeds Farm Park
Glencruitten, Oban, Argyll PA34 4QB
Tel: 01631 770608
e-mail: info@obanrarebreeds.com • website: www.obanrarebreeds.com

20% DISCOUNT on all admissions

valid during 2004

NOT TO BE USED IN CONJUNCTION WITH ANY OTHER OFFER

FHG READERS' OFFER 2004

Dunaskin Heritage Centre
Waterside, Patna, Ayrshire KA6 7JF
Tel: 01292 531144
e-mail: dunaskin@btconnect.com • website: www.dunaskin.org.uk

TWO for the price of ONE

valid from 1st May to 31st October 2004

NOT TO BE USED IN CONJUNCTION WITH ANY OTHER OFFER

FHG READERS' OFFER 2004

Kelburn Castle & Country Centre
Fairlie, Near Largs, Ayrshire KA29 0BE
Tel: 01475 568685 • e-mail: info@kelburncountrycentre.com
website: www.kelburncountrycentre.com

One child FREE for each full paying adult

Valid until October 2004

NOT TO BE USED IN CONJUNCTION WITH ANY OTHER OFFER

FHG READERS' OFFER 2004

Scottish Maritime Museum
Harbourside, Irvine KA12 8QE
Tel: 01294 278283 • e-mail: smm@tildesley.fsbusiness.co.uk
website: www.scottishmaritimemuseum.org • Fax: 01294 313211

TWO for the price of ONE

Valid from January to December 2004

NOT TO BE USED IN CONJUNCTION WITH ANY OTHER OFFER

Visitor centre dedicated to the much-loved Scottish writer Lewis Grassic Gibbon. Exhibition, cafe, gift shop. Outdoor children's play area. Disabled access throughout.

Open: Daily April to October 10am to 4.30pm. Groups by appointment including evenings.

Directions: On the B967, accessible and signposted from both A90 and A92.

FHG PUBLICATIONS, ABBEY MILL BUSINESS CENTRE, PAISLEY PA1 1TJ

Rare breeds of farm animals, pets' corner, conservation groups, tea room, woodland walk in beautiful location

Open: 10am to 6pm mid-March to end October

Directions: two-and-a-half miles from Oban along Glencruitten road

FHG PUBLICATIONS, ABBEY MILL BUSINESS CENTRE, PAISLEY PA1 1TJ

Set in the rolling hills of Ayrshire, Europe's best preserved ironworks. Guided tours, audio-visuals, walks with electronic wands. Restaurant/coffee shop.

Open: April to October daily 10am to 5pm.

Directions: A713 Ayr to Castle Douglas road, 12 miles from Ayr, 3 miles from Dalmellington.

FHG PUBLICATIONS, ABBEY MILL BUSINESS CENTRE, PAISLEY PA1 1TJ

The historic home of the Earls of Glasgow. Waterfalls, gardens, famous Glen, unusual trees. Riding school, stockade, play areas, exhibitions, shop, cafe and The Secret Forest.

PETS MUST BE KEPT ON LEAD

Open: daily 10am to 6pm Easter to October.

Directions: On A78 between Largs and Fairlie, 45 mins drive from Glasgow.

FHG PUBLICATIONS, ABBEY MILL BUSINESS CENTRE, PAISLEY PA1 1TJ

Scotland's seafaring heritage is among the world's richest and you can relive the heyday of Scottish shipping at the Maritime Museum.

Open: all year except Christmas and New Year Holidays. 10am - 5pm

Directions: Situated on Irvine harbourside and only a 10 minute walk from Irvine train station.

FHG PUBLICATIONS, ABBEY MILL BUSINESS CENTRE, PAISLEY PA1 1TJ

FHG READERS' OFFER 2004

Almond Valley Heritage Centre
Millfield, Livingston, West Lothian EH54 7AR
Tel: 01506 414957
e-mail: info@almondvalley.co.uk • website: www.almondvalley.co.uk

Free child with adult paying full admission

Valid during 2004

NOT TO BE USED IN CONJUNCTION WITH ANY OTHER OFFER

FHG READERS' OFFER 2004

MYRETON MOTOR MUSEUM
Aberlady, East Lothian EH32 0PZ
Tel: 01875 870288

One child FREE with each paying adult

valid during 2004

NOT TO BE USED IN CONJUNCTION WITH ANY OTHER OFFER

FHG READERS' OFFER 2004

Loch Ness 2000 Exhibition Centre
Drumnadrochit, Inverness-shire, IV63 6TU
Tel: 01456 450573 • Fax: 01456 450770
e-mail: info@loch-ness-scotland.com • website: www.loch-ness-scotland.com

Two for one OR one child free per full paying adult

valid until 31/12/04

NOT TO BE USED IN CONJUNCTION WITH ANY OTHER OFFER

FHG READERS' OFFER 2004

Speyside Heather Garden & Visitor Centre
Speyside Heather Centre, Dulnain Bridge, Inverness-shire PH26 3PA
Tel: 01479 851359 • Fax: 01479 851396
e-mail: enquiries@heathercentre.com • website: www.heathercentre.com

FREE entry to 'Heather Story' exhibition

valid during 2004

NOT TO BE USED IN CONJUNCTION WITH ANY OTHER OFFER

FHG READERS' OFFER 2004

Highland and Rare Breeds Farm
Elphin, Near Ullapool, Sutherland IV27 4HH
Tel: 01854 666204

One FREE adult or child with adult paying full entrance price

valid May to September 2004

NOT TO BE USED IN CONJUNCTION WITH ANY OTHER OFFER

An innovative museum exploring the history and environment of West Lothian on a 20-acre site packed full of things to see and do, indoors and out.

Open: Daily (except Christmas and New Year) 10am to 5pm.

Directions: 15 miles from Edinburgh, follow "Heritage Centre" signs from A899.

FHG PUBLICATIONS, ABBEY MILL BUSINESS CENTRE, PAISLEY PA1 1TJ

On show is a large collection, from 1899, of cars, bicycles, motor cycles and commercials. There is also a large collection of period advertising, posters and enamel signs.

Open: Daily April to October 11am to 4pm; November to March: Sundays 1pm to 3pm or by special appointment.

Directions: Off A198 near Aberlady. Two miles from A1.

FHG PUBLICATIONS, ABBEY MILL BUSINESS CENTRE, PAISLEY PA1 1TJ

World famous attraction at Loch Ness. Centre includes shopping complex, coffee shop, restaurants, hotel and boat cruises throughout the summer. Don't miss the Highlands most popular tourist attraction.

Open: all year - times vary.

Directions: 14 miles south of Inverness on the A82 main road.

FHG PUBLICATIONS, ABBEY MILL BUSINESS CENTRE, PAISLEY PA1 1TJ

Award-winning attraction with unique 'Heather Story' exhibition, gallery, giftshop, large garden centre selling 300 different heathers, antique shop, children's play area and famous Clootie Dumpling restaurant.

Open: All year except Christmas Day.

Directions: Just off A95 between Aviemore and Grantown-on-Spey.

FHG PUBLICATIONS, ABBEY MILL BUSINESS CENTRE, PAISLEY PA1 1TJ

Highland croft open to visitors for "hands-on" experience with over 30 different breeds of farm animals "stroke the goats and scratch the pigs". Farm information centre and old farm implements. For all ages, cloud or shine!

Open: July and August 10am to 5pm.

Directions: On A835 15 miles north of Ullapool

FHG PUBLICATIONS, ABBEY MILL BUSINESS CENTRE, PAISLEY PA1 1TJ

FHG READERS' OFFER 2004

Landmark Forest Theme Park
Carrbridge, Inverness-shire PH23 3AJ
Tel: 01479 841613 • Freephone 0800 731 3446
e-mail: landmarkcentre@btconnect.com • website: www.landmark-centre.co.uk

10% DISCOUNT for pet owners. Free admission for pets! Maximum of four persons per voucher

Valid during 2004

NOT TO BE USED IN CONJUNCTION WITH ANY OTHER OFFER

FHG READERS' OFFER 2004

New Lanark World Heritage Site
New Lanark Mills, New Lanark, Lanarkshire ML11 9DB
Tel: 01555 661345 • Fax: 01555 665738
e-mail: visit@newlanark.org • website: www.newlanark.org

One FREE child with every full price adult

valid until 31st October 2004

NOT TO BE USED IN CONJUNCTION WITH ANY OTHER OFFER

FHG READERS' OFFER 2004

Finlaystone Country Estate
Langbank, Renfrewshire PA14 6TJ
Tel & Fax: 01475 540505
e-mail: info@finlaystone.co.uk • website: www.finlaystone.co.uk

Two for the price of one

valid until April 2004

NOT TO BE USED IN CONJUNCTION WITH ANY OTHER OFFER

FHG READERS' OFFER 2004

Llanberis Lake Railway
Gilfach Ddu, Llanberis, Gwynedd LL55 4TY
Tel: 01286 870549 • e-mail: info@lake-railway.co.uk
website: www.lake-railway.co.uk

One pet travels free with each full fare paying adult

Valid Easter to October 2004

NOT TO BE USED IN CONJUNCTION WITH ANY OTHER OFFER

FHG READERS' OFFER 2004

MUSEUM OF CHILDHOOD MEMORIES
1 Castle Street, Beaumaris, Anglesey LL58 8AP
Tel: 01248 712498
website: www.aboutbritain.com/museumofchildhoodmemories.htm

One child FREE with two adults

valid during 2004

NOT TO BE USED IN CONJUNCTION WITH ANY OTHER OFFER

Great day out for all the family. Wild Water Coaster*, Microworld exhibition, Forest Trails, Viewing Tower, Climbing Wall*, Tree Top Trail, Steam powered Sawmill*, Clydesdale Horse*. Shop, restaurant and snackbar.
(* Easter to October)
DOGS MUST BE KEPT ON LEADS

Open: Daily (except Christmas Day and attractions marked*).

Directions: 23 miles south of Inverness at Carrbridge, just off the A9.

FHG PUBLICATIONS, ABBEY MILL BUSINESS CENTRE, PAISLEY PA1 1TJ

A beautifully restored cotton mill village close to the Falls of Clyde. Explore the fascinating history of the village, try the 'New Millennium Experience', a magical ride which takes you back in time to discover what life used to be like.

Open: 11am to 5pm daily. Closed Christmas Day and New Year's Day.

FHG PUBLICATIONS, ABBEY MILL BUSINESS CENTRE, PAISLEY PA1 1TJ

Colourful gardens, imaginative woodland play areas and tumbling waterfalls. The Estate combines history with adventure in a fun day out for all the family, where your dog can run freely. Step back in time and uncover its secrets.

Open: Daily 10.30am to 5pm

Directions: Off A8 west of Langbank, 20 minutes west of Glasgow Airport.

FHG PUBLICATIONS, ABBEY MILL BUSINESS CENTRE, PAISLEY PA1 1TJ

A 60-minute ride along the shores of beautiful Padarn Lake behind a quaint historic steam engine. Magnificent views of the mountains from lakeside picnic spots.
DOGS MUST BE KEPT ON LEAD AT ALL TIMES ON TRAIN

Open: Most days Easter to October. Free timetable leaflet on request.

Directions: Just off A4086 Caernarfon to Capel Curig road at Llanberis; follow 'Country Park' signs.

FHG PUBLICATIONS, ABBEY MILL BUSINESS CENTRE, PAISLEY PA1 1TJ

Nine rooms in a Georgian house filled with items illustrating the happier times of family life over the past 150 years. Joyful nostalgia unlimited.

Open:
March to end October

Directions:
opposite Beaumaris Castle

FHG PUBLICATIONS, ABBEY MILL BUSINESS CENTRE, PAISLEY PA1 1TJ

| **FHG**
READERS'
OFFER
2004 | *Alice in Wonderland Centre*
3/4 Trinity Square, Llandudno, Conwy, North Wales LL30 2PY
Tel: 01492 860082 • e-mail: alice@wonderland.co.uk
website: www.wonderland.co.uk
One child FREE with two paying adults. Guide Dogs welcome
NOT TO BE USED IN CONJUNCTION WITH ANY OTHER OFFER | valid during 2004 |

| **FHG**
READERS'
OFFER
2004 | **Celtica**
Y Plas, Machynlleth, Powys SY20 8ER
Tel: 01654 702702   e-mail: celtica@celtica.wales.com
website: www.celtica.wales.com
Child FREE when accompanied by full-paying adult
NOT TO BE USED IN CONJUNCTION WITH ANY OTHER OFFER | valid during 2004 |

| **FHG**
READERS'
OFFER
2004 | **National Cycle Collection**
Automobile Palace, Temple Street, Llandrindod Wells, Powys LD1 5DL
Tel: 01597 825531
e-mail: cycle.museum@care4free.net • website: www.cyclemuseum.org.uk
TWO for the price of ONE
NOT TO BE USED IN CONJUNCTION WITH ANY OTHER OFFER | Valid during 2004 except Special Event days |

| **FHG**
READERS'
OFFER
2004 | **Rhondda Heritage Park**
Lewis Merthyr Colliery, Coed Cae Road, Trehafod, Near Pontypridd CF37 7NP
Tel: 01443 682036 • e-mail: info@rhonddaheritagepark.com
website: www.rhonddaheritagepark.com
Two adults or children for the price of one when accompanied by a full paying adult
NOT TO BE USED IN CONJUNCTION WITH ANY OTHER OFFER | Valid until end 2004 for full tours only. Not valid on special event days. |

FHG PUBLICATIONS
publish a large range of well-known accommodation guides. We will be happy to send you details or you can use the order form at the back of this book.

Walk through the Rabbit Hole to the colourful scenes of Lewis Carroll's classic story set in beautiful life-size displays. Recorded commentaries and transcripts available in several languages.

Open: All year 10am to 5pm but closed Sundays in winter and Christmas/Boxing Day/New Year's Day.

Directions: situated just off the main street, 250 yards from coach and rail stations.

FHG PUBLICATIONS, ABBEY MILL BUSINESS CENTRE, PAISLEY PA1 1TJ

A unique theme attraction presenting the history and culture of the Celts. Audio-visual exhibition, displays of Welsh and Celtic history, soft play area, tea room and gift shop. Events throughout the year.

Open: 10am to 6pm daily (last admission to exhibitions 4.40pm)

Directions: in restored mansion just south of clock tower in town centre; car park just off Aberystwyth road

FHG PUBLICATIONS, ABBEY MILL BUSINESS CENTRE, PAISLEY PA1 1TJ

Journey through the lanes of cycle history and see bicycles from Boneshakers and Penny Farthings up to modern Raleigh cycles. Over 250 machines on display

PETS MUST BE KEPT ON LEADS

Open: 1st March to 1st November daily 10am onwards.

Directions: Brown signs to car park. Town centre attraction.

FHG PUBLICATIONS, ABBEY MILL BUSINESS CENTRE, PAISLEY PA1 1TJ

Make a pit stop whatever the weather! Join an ex-miner on a tour of discovery, ride the cage to pit bottom and take a thrilling ride back to the surface. Multi-media presentations, period village street, children's adventure play area, restaurant and gift shop. Disabled access with assistance.

Open: Open daily 10am to 6pm (last tour 4.30pm). Closed Mondays October to Easter, also Dec 25th to 1st Jan inclusive.

Directions: Exit Junction 32 M4, signposted from A470 Pontypridd. Trehafod is located between Pontypridd and Porth.

FHG PUBLICATIONS, ABBEY MILL BUSINESS CENTRE, PAISLEY PA1 1TJ

Visit the FHG website
www.holidayguides.com
for details of the wide choice of accommodation featured in the full range of FHG titles

ENGLAND
Board Accommodation

BEDFORDSHIRE

SANDY
Mrs M. Codd, Highfield Farm, Tempsford Road, Sandy SG19 2AQ (01767 682332; Fax: 01767 692503). Tranquil welcoming atmosphere on attractive arable farm. Set well back off A1 giving quiet, peaceful seclusion yet within easy reach of the RSPB, the Shuttleworth Collection, the Greensand Ridge Walk, Grafham Water and Woburn Abbey. Cambridge 22 miles, London 50 miles. All rooms have tea/coffee making facilities, all have bathroom en suite and some are on the ground floor. There is a separate guests' sitting room with TV. Family room. Dogs welcome by arrangement. No smoking. Most guests return! Prices from £27.50 per person per night. ETC ♦♦♦♦ SILVER AWARD, GUESTACCOM "GOOD ROOM" AWARD. BEST ETC B&B REGIONAL WINNER FOR EASTERN COUNTIES.
e-mail: margaret@highfield-farm.co.uk

Whipsnade Wild Animal Park • *Dunstable, Bedfordshire* • *01582 872171*
website: www.whipsnade.co.uk
See rare and endangered species from around the world. Visitors can take a trip through the Woodland Bird Walk and visit the children"s farm in 600 acres of parkland.

One free adult/child with full-fare adult at
Leighton Buzzard Railway
see our READERS' OFFER VOUCHERS for full details

FHG PUBLICATIONS publish a large range of well-known accommodation guides. We will be happy to send you details or you can use the order form at the back of this book.

CAMBRIDGESHIRE

CAMBRIDGE
Mrs Jean Wright, White Horse Cottage, 28 West Street, Comberton, Cambridge CB3 7DS (01223 262914). A 17th century cottage with all modern conveniences situated in a charming village four miles south-west of Cambridge. Junction 12 off M11 – A603 from Cambridge, or A428 turn-off at Hardwick turning. Accommodation includes one double room, twin and family rooms. Own sitting room with colour TV; tea/coffee making facilities. Full central heating; parking. Golfing facilities nearby. Excellent touring centre for many interesting places including Cambridge colleges, Wimpole Hall, Anglesey Abbey, Ely Cathedral, Imperial War Museum at Duxford, and many more. Bed and Breakfast from £22.50 per person sharing a double. Children welcome.

CAMBRIDGE (near)
Vicki Hatley, Manor Farm, Landbeach, Cambridge CB4 4ED (01223 860165). Five miles from Cambridge and 10 miles from Ely. Vicki welcomes you to her carefully modernised Grade II Listed farmhouse, which is located next to the church in this attractive village. All rooms are either en suite or have private bathroom and are individually decorated. TV, clock radios and tea/coffee making facilities are provided in double, twin or family rooms. There is ample parking and guests are welcome to enjoy the walled gardens. Bed and Breakfast from £25 per person double, and £35 single.

ELY
Mrs Linda Peck, Sharps Farm, Twenty Pence Road, Wilburton, Ely CB6 3PX (01353 740360). Between Ely (six miles) and Cambridge (12 miles) our modern farmhouse offers guests a warm welcome and a relaxed atmosphere. All rooms have en suite or private bathroom, central heating, colour TV, radio alarm, tea/coffee making facilities, hair dryer and views over surrounding countryside. Breakfast is served in the Conservatory, with home-made preserves and free range eggs. Special diets catered for. Disabled facilities. Ample parking. No smoking. Bed and Breakfast from £24.00 per person. Short Breaks available.
e-mail: sharpsfarm@yahoo.com

ELY
Mrs C. H. Bennett, Stockyard Farm, Wisbech Road, Welney, Wisbech PE14 9RQ (01354 610433). A warm welcome awaits you at this comfortable former farmhouse in the heart of the Fens, equidistant from Ely and Wisbech. The house makes an ideal base from which to explore the numerous historic sites, watch wildlife at the nearby nature reserves or fish the famous fenland waters. Whatever your interests, Cindy and Tim can offer advice and information. One double and one twin bedroom, both with handbasin, radio, hairdryer and hot drink facilities. Breakfast is served in the conservatory adjoining the guests' TV lounge. Vegetarian breakfast a speciality. Free-range produce. Central heating. Private parking. No smoking. Pets welcome. B&B from £18 per person.

Readers are requested to mention this guidebook when seeking accommodation (and please enclose a stamped addressed envelope).

ENGLAND / Board   Cambridgeshire

WICKEN
Mrs Valerie Fuller, Spinney Abbey, Wicken, Ely CB7 5XQ (01353 720971). Working farm. Spinney Abbey is an attractive Grade II Listed Georgian stone farmhouse with views across pasture fields. It stands in a large garden with tennis court next to our dairy farm which borders the National Trust Nature Reserve Wicken Fen. One double and one family room, both en suite, and twin-bedded room with private bathroom, all with TV, hospitality tray, etc. Full central heating, guests sittingroom. Regret no pets and no smoking upstairs. Situated just off A1123, half-a-mile west of Wicken. Open all year. Bed and Breakfast from £25 per person. **ETC ♦♦♦♦**
e-mail: spinney.abbey@tesco.net
website: www.spinneyabbey.co.uk

WISBECH
Jayne Best, Four Winds, Mill Lane, Newton, Wisbech PE13 5HZ (01945 870479; Fax: 01945 870274). Charming country house situated in the midst of the Fens countryside, although only four miles from Wisbech and close to King's Lynn, Norfolk coast (28 miles). Ideally situated for touring, fishing and cycling. Accommodation comprises one double en suite with shower, one twin en suite with bath, two singles with washbasins and one main bathroom with Airspa. Private parking. Terms from £23.

One child FREE with one full paying adult at
Sacrewell Farm & Country Centre
see our READERS' OFFER VOUCHERS for full details

Fitzwilliam Museum • *Cambridge, Cambridgeshire* • *01223 332904*
website: www.fitzmuseum.cam.ac.uk
One of the UK's finest collections of armour, antiquities, sculpture, furniture, pottery, paintings, prints, coins and much more.

 Other specialised **FHG PUBLICATIONS** published annually: available in all good bookshops or direct from the publisher.

PETS WELCOME! £7.99
Recommended COUNTRY HOTELS OF BRITAIN £6.99
Recommended COUNTRY INNS & PUBS OF BRITAIN £6.99
Recommended SHORT BREAK HOLIDAYS IN BRITAIN £6.99

FHG Publications Ltd, Abbey Mill Business Centre,
Seedhill, Paisley, Renfrewshire PAI ITJ
Tel: 0141-887 0428 • Fax: 0141-889 7204
e-mail: fhg@ipcmedia.com • website: www.holidayguides.com

CHESHIRE

CHESTER
Mrs Anne Arden, Newton Hall, Tattenhall, Chester CH3 9NE (01829 770153; Fax: 01829 770655). Part 16th century oak-beamed farmhouse set in large well kept grounds, with fine views of historic Beeston and Peckforton Castles and close to the Sandstone Trail. Six miles south of Chester off A41 and ideal for Welsh hills. Rooms are en suite or have adjacent bathroom. Colour TV in all bedrooms. Guests' own lounge. Fully centrally heated. Bed and Breakfast from £25. Children and pets welcome. Open all year. **ETC** ♦♦♦♦
e-mail: newton.hall@farming.co.uk

CONGLETON
Mrs Sheila Kidd, Yew Tree Farm, North Rode, Congleton CW12 2PF (01260 223569; Fax: 01260 223328). Discover freedom, relaxation, wooded walks and beautiful views. Meet a whole variety of pets and farm animals on this friendly working farm. One double and one triple room, both en suite. Your comfort is our priority and good food is a speciality. Generous scrummy breakfasts and traditional evening meals. A true taste of the countryside — just for you! Bed and Breakfast £25 to £30; optional Evening Meal £12. Brochure on request. **ETC** ♦♦♦♦
e-mail: yewtreebb@hotmail.com
website: www.yewtreebb.co.uk

HESWALL
Church Farm, Church Lane, Thurstaston, Wirral CH61 0HW (0151-648 7838; mobile: 0780 1037483; Fax: 0151-648 9644). Sleeps 2. Exceptional fitted en suite room with beautiful views, situated on an organic farm overlooking the River Dee and North Wales. Organic breakfast. Own produce available to buy in new farm shop. Organic coffee and refreshments in coffee shop. Farm animals to watch and pet. Also camping and caravanning available. Bed and Breakfast from £30 to £40. Non-smoking. Children welcome. Open all year except Christmas and New Year. Contact **Steve and Brenda Ledsham.**
e-mail: sales@churchfarm.org.uk
website: www.churchfarm.org.uk

HYDE (near Manchester)
Mrs Charlotte R. Walsh, Needhams Farm, Uplands Road, Werneth Low, Gee Cross, Near Hyde SK14 3AQ (0161 368 4610; Fax: 0161-367 9106). Working farm. A cosy 16th century farmhouse set in peaceful, picturesque surroundings by Werneth Low Country Park and the Etherow Valley, which lie between Glossop and Manchester. The farm is ideally situated for holidaymakers and businessmen, especially those who enjoy peace and quiet, walking and rambling, golfing and riding, as these activities are all close by. At Needhams Farm everyone, including children and pets, receives a warm welcome. Good wholesome meals available in the evenings from Monday to Friday. Weekends by arrangement. Residential licence and Fire Certificate held. Open all year. Bed and Breakfast from £24 single minimum to £36 double maximum; Evening Meal £7. **ETC/AA** ♦♦♦
e-mail: charlotte@needhamsfarm.co.uk
website: www.needhamsfarm.co.uk

Terms quoted in this publication may be subject to increase if rises in costs necessitate

ENGLAND / Board   Cheshire   99

KNUTSFORD

Steve & Jane, Pickmere House, Park Lane, Pickmere, Knutsford WA16 0JX (01565 733433; Fax: 01565 734202). A Listed Georgian farmhouse in rural village close to Arley Hall and Tatton Park, two miles west of M6 Junction 19 on B5391 giving swift access to airport and all major north west towns and tourist attractions. Spacious en suite rooms with TV, tea/coffee trays and hairdryers, overlooking farmlands. Parking at rear. Residents' Bar. Bed and Breakfast £25 to £35 single, £50 double/twin. **AA** Approved.
website: www.pickmerehouse.co.uk

NANTWICH

Mrs Jean E. Callwood, Lea Farm, Wrinehill Road, Wybunbury, Nantwich CW5 7NS (01270 841429; Fax: 01270 841030). Charming farmhouse set in landscaped gardens, where peacocks roam, on 150 acre family farm. Working farm, join in. Spacious bedrooms, colour TVs, electric blankets, radio alarm and tea/coffee making facilities. Centrally heated throughout. Family, double and twin bedrooms, en suite facilities. Luxury lounge, dining room overlooking gardens. Pool/snooker; fishing in well stocked pool in beautiful surroundings. Bird watching. Children welcome, also dogs if kept under control. Help feed the birds and animals and see the cows being milked. Near to Stapeley Water Gardens, Bridgemere Garden World. Also Nantwich, Crewe, Chester, the Potteries and Alton Towers. Bed and Breakfast from £21 per person. Children half price. Weekly terms available. **AA ♦♦♦**
e-mail: contactus@leafarm.co.uk

NORTHWICH

Mrs T.H. Campbell, Manor Farm, Cliff Road, Acton Bridge, Northwich CW8 3QP (Tel & Fax: 01606 853181). Peaceful, rural, elegantly furnished traditional country house with open views from all rooms. Situated away from roads down a long private drive, above the wooded banks of the River Weaver. Absorb the tranquillity of our garden providing access to a private path through our woodland into the picturesque valley. In the heart of Cheshire, we are an ideal location for business or pleasure. Within easy reach of Chester, Merseyside, Manchester/ Liverpool Airports and the motorway network (M56 Junction 10). All rooms have en suite/private bathroom and beverage tray and TV. Ample safe parking. Bed and Breakfast from £24. **ETC ♦♦♦**, *WELCOME HOST*.
e-mail: terri.mac.manorfarm@care4free.net

The **FHG**
GOLF
GUIDE
Where to Play
Where to Stay

Available from most bookshops, THE GOLF GUIDE (published annually) covers details of every UK golf course – well over 2800 entries – for holiday or business golf. Hundreds of hotel entries offer convenient accommodation, accompanying details of the courses – the 'pro', par score, length etc.

In association with 'Golf Monthly' and including Holiday Golf in Ireland, France, Portugal, Spain, The USA, South Africa and Thailand

£9.99 from bookshops or from the publishers (postage charged outside UK) • FHG Publications, Abbey Mill Business Centre, Paisley PA1 1TJ

CORNWALL

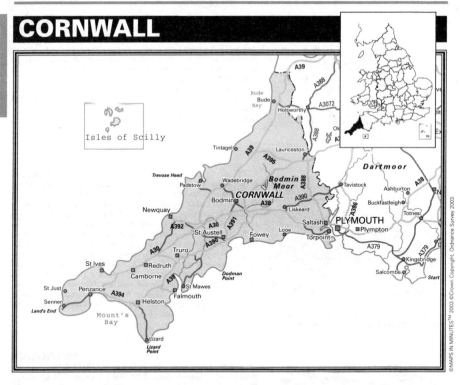

BODMIN

Mrs Margaret Oliver, Tremeere Manor, Lanivet, Near Bodmin PL30 5BG (01208 831513). Tremeere is a 17th Century Manor House set in a 240-acre dairy farm in mid-Cornwall on the halfway mark for the Saints Way, 15 minutes' drive from the Eden Project. There are spacious comfortable rooms comprising two double en suite bedrooms and one twin-bedded room, all with TV, and with lovely views of the surrounding countryside. Central heating, tea/coffee making facilities and a comfortable guests' lounge with TV. Prices are from £22 per person for a double or twin room and £25 per person for a single. No smoking. Nearby is Bodmin town with its ancient Gaol and Steam Railway. Lanhydrock House (NT), The Lost Gardens of Heligan or walking on Bodmin Moor and visiting the famous Jamaica Inn. Coastal walks and beaches are within easy reach as well as walking the Camel Trail. **ETC**

BUDE

Margaret and Richard Heard, Trencreek Farmhouse, St Gennys, Bude EX23 0AY (01840 230219). Comfortable farmhouse which offers a homely and relaxed family atmosphere. Situated in quiet and peaceful surroundings yet within easy reach of Crackington Haven. Well placed for easy access to coastal and countryside walks. Family, double and twin-bedded rooms, most en suite, all with tea and coffee making facilities. Two comfortable lounges. Games room. Separate diningroom. Generous portions of home-cooked farmhouse food are always freshly prepared. Children welcome, special rates for under twelves. Spring and Autumn breaks available. Non-smoking. Sunday lunches and midday lunches optional.

ENGLAND / Board   Cornwall 101

BUDE
Mrs Pearl Hopper, West Nethercott Farm, Whitstone, Holsworthy (Devon) EX22 6LD (01288 341394). Working farm, join in. Personal attention and a warm welcome await you on this dairy and sheep farm. Watch the cows being milked, help with the animals. Free pony rides, scenic farm walks. Short distance from sandy beaches, surfing and the rugged North Cornwall coast. Ideal base for visiting any part of Devon or Cornwall. We are located in Cornwall though our postal address is Devon. The traditional farmhouse has washbasins and TV in bedrooms; dining room and separate lounge with colour TV. Plenty of excellent home cooking. Access to the house at anytime. Bed and Full English Breakfast from £16, Evening Meal and packed lunches available. Children under 12 years reduced rates. Weekly terms available.
e-mail: pearl@westnethercott.fsnet.co.uk

BUDE
Mrs Sylvia Lucas, Elm Park, Bridgerule, Holsworthy EX22 7EL (01288 381231). Elm Park is a 205 acre dairy, beef and sheep farm. Six miles from surfing beaches at Bude and ideal for touring Devon/Cornwall. Children are especially welcomed, with pony rides. Games room available with snooker, table skittles, darts, etc, and golf putting. There are spacious family rooms (two en suite) and a twin-bedded room, all with colour TV and tea/coffee making facilities. Ample four-course dinners with freshly produced fare and delicious sweets. Bed and Breakfast from £18. Reductions for children and everyone is made welcome and comfortable. Brochure available.

BUDE (near)
Mrs & Mrs R. Holmes, Bears & Boxes Country Guest House, Dizzard, St Gennys, Near Bude EX23 0NX (Tel & Fax: 01840 230318). Friendly, comfortable accommodation is available in our cottage situated in a peaceful, rural Area of Outstanding Natural Beauty on Cornwall's Heritage Coast, a few minutes' walk from the spectacular Coastal Path. All rooms are equipped with hostess tray, TV and other luxuries; most are en suite. Cot and high chair available. Lounge, reading room and dining room for guests' use. Safe bathing, very good surfing, sea and fly fishing, horse riding, golf and trekking within easy reach; Widemouth Bay, Bude and Boscastle a short drive away. Evening meals by arrangement. No smoking. Pets welcome by arrangement. Open all year. B&B from £25pppn. **ETC** ◆◆◆
website: www.bearsandboxes.com

FOWEY
Mrs S.C. Dunn, Menabilly Barton, Par PL24 2TN (01726 812844). Working farm. Menabilly Barton is a secluded farmhouse set in a wooded valley leading to a quiet sandy beach. Spacious dining room, lounge with TV, peaceful garden open during the day. Good traditional farmhouse food. Three large bedrooms, en suite available. Bathroom with shower, two toilets. Facilities for making drinks and microwave if required. Coastal walks, National Trust properties, Heligan Gardens and The Eden Project all nearby. Local village pub serves good food. Historic port of Fowey three miles, North Coast only 40 minutes' drive. Bed and full English Breakfast. Reductions for children. Colour brochure on request.
e-mail: R.Dunn@Agriplus.net

When making enquiries or bookings, a stamped addressed envelope is always appreciated

HELSTON

Mrs P. Roberts, Hendra Farm, Wendron, Helston TR13 0NR (01326 340470). Hendra Farm, just off the main Helston/Falmouth road, is an ideal centre for touring Cornwall; three miles to Helston, eight to both Redruth and Falmouth. Safe sandy beaches within easy reach – five miles to the sea. Two double, one single, and one family bedrooms with washbasins and tea-making facilities; bathroom and toilets; sittingroom and two diningrooms. Cot, babysitting and reduced rates offered for children. No objection to pets. Car necessary, parking space. Enjoy good cooking with roast beef, pork, lamb, chicken, genuine Cornish pasties, fish and delicious sweets and cream. Open all year except Christmas. Evening Dinner, Bed and Breakfast from £150 per week which includes cooked breakfast, three course evening dinner, tea and home-made cake before bed. Bed and Breakfast only from £15 per night also available.

LAUNCESTON

Hurdon Farm, Launceston PL15 9LS (01566 772955). Elegant Listed 18th century farmhouse, idyllically tucked away amidst our 500 acre mixed working farm. Centrally positioned on Devon/Cornwall border, it is ideally located for exploring the many attractions in both counties. Near the Eden Project. Six luxurious and spacious en suite bedrooms, all with colour TV, radio, tea/coffee facilities and central heating. Comfortable guests' lounge. Superb English breakfasts and delicious four-course dinners, freshly prepared and cooked, are served at separate tables in the dining room. Open May till November. Bed and Breakfast from £23. **AA ♦♦♦♦**

LAUNCESTON

Mary Rich, "Nathania", Altarnun, Launceston PL15 7SL (01566 86426). A warm welcome awaits you, for accommodation on a small farm on Bodmin Moor within easy reach of coast, moors, towns, lakes and fishing. Visit King Arthur country – Tintagel, Dozmary Pool, the famous Jamaica Inn, Wesley Cottage and cathedral of the moors. One mile from A30, very quiet, ideal for overnight stop for West Cornwall and for Eden Project. Double room en suite, twin rooms with bathroom adjoining. Tea making facilities and TV. Payphone. Conservatory and lounge for quiet relaxation. We look forward to meeting you for one night, or why not book your holiday with us and tour Cornwall. You will enjoy the quiet, happy, relaxing atmosphere. Prices from £12.50 per person per night. Also camping and caravan site. Please telephone, or write, for details – SAE, thank you.

LOOE

See also Colour Display Advertisement

Mrs Angela Eastley, Little Larnick Farm, Pelynt, Looe PL13 2NB (01503 262837). Little Larnick is situated in a sheltered part of the West Looe river valley. Walk to Looe from our working dairy farm and along the coastal path to picturesque Polperro. The character farmhouse and barn offers twin, double and family en suite rooms. The bedrooms are superbly equipped and decorated to a high standard. The family room is in a downstairs annexe overlooking the garden. Our newly renovated barn offers three self-contained bedrooms with their own lounge areas. Cycling shed, drying room and ample parking. No pets. No smoking. Bed and Breakfast from £22.50 to £27.50. Open all year. **ETC ♦♦♦♦** *SILVER AWARD.*

Readers are requested to mention this guidebook when enquiring about accommodation

LOOE

Mrs D. Eastley, Bake Farm, Pelynt, Looe PL13 2QQ (01503 220244). Working farm. This is an old farmhouse, bearing the Trelawney Coat of Arms (1610), situated midway between Looe and Fowey. The two double en suite bedrooms and the family room with private bathroom are all decorated to a high standard and have tea/coffee making facilities and TV. Sorry, no pets, no smoking. Open from March to October. A car is essential for touring the area, ample parking. There is much to see and do here – horse riding, coastal walks, golf, National Trust properties, the Eden Project and Heligan Gardens are within easy reach. The sea is only five miles away and there is shark fishing at Looe. Bed and Breakfast from £21 - £25. Brochure available on request. **ETC ♦♦♦♦**

MEVAGISSEY

Mrs Dawn Rundle, Lancallan Farm, Mevagissey, St Austell PL26 6EW (Tel & Fax: 01726 842284). Lancallan is a large 17th century farmhouse on a working 700 acre dairy and beef farm in a beautiful rural setting, one mile from Mevagissey. We are close to Heligan Gardens, lovely coastal walks and sandy beaches, and are well situated for day trips throughout Cornwall. Also six to eight miles from the Eden Project (20 minutes' drive). Enjoy a traditional farmhouse breakfast in a warm and friendly atmosphere. Accommodation comprises one twin room and two double en suite rooms (all with colour TV and tea/coffee facilities); bathroom, lounge and diningroom. Terms and brochure available on request. SAE please.
e-mail: dawn@lancallan.fsnet.co.uk

MULLION

Mrs Joan Hyde, Campden House, The Commons, Mullion TR12 7HZ (01326 240365). Campden House offers comfortable accommodation in a peaceful setting with large gardens and a beautiful sea view. It is within easy reach of Mullion, Polurrian and Poldhu Coves, and is ideally situated for exploring the beautiful coast and countryside of the Lizard. Mullion golf course is less than one mile away. All eight bedrooms have handbasin with hot and cold water and comfortable beds; some rooms have en suite shower. There is a large sun lounge, TV lounge with colour TV and a large dining room and bar. Guests have access to the lounges, bedrooms and gardens at all times. Children and pets welcome. Bed and Breakfast from £17.50 to £22 (en suite).

NEWQUAY

Mike and Alison Limer, Alicia, 136 Henver Road, Newquay TR7 3EQ (Tel & Fax: 01637 874328). A warm welcome from your hosts Mike and Alison, who offer you a relaxed and friendly atmosphere in the comfort of their home. Traditional full English breakfast. Four en suite bedrooms, all tastefully furnished, with TV, clock/radio, hairdryer and refreshment tray; one standard with private facilities, iron provided. Relax in the conservatory or spacious lounge. Choose between the golden beaches along Newquay's coastline or a breathtaking coastal walk to Watergate Bay. The Eden Project, quaint fishing villages and the spectacular Cornish coastline, are all within 30 minutes' car ride. Open all year and fully centrally heated. Bed and Breakfast from £20 per person daily. Please telephone or write for brochure. **ETC ♦♦♦♦**
e-mail: aliciaguesthouse@mlimer.fsnet.co.uk   website: www.cornishlight.freeserve.co.uk/alicia.htm

---

50p OFF per person, up to six persons at
Tamar Valley Donkey Park
see our READERS' OFFER VOUCHERS for full details

NEWQUAY

Mrs B. L. Harvey, Shepherds Farm, Fiddlers Green, St Newlyn East, Newquay TR8 5NW (01872 540502). Working farm. A warm welcome awaits you on our family-run 600 acre mixed working farm. Come and share our warm and friendly atmosphere with first class service in affordable quality accommodation. Cleanliness guaranteed. All rooms en suite and have colour TV and tea making facilities. Large garden. Central location, ideal for touring. The farm is set in rural, small hamlet of Fiddlers Green three miles from beautiful Cornish coastline, five miles from Newquay; 20 minutes from south coast. Glorious sandy beaches, ideal for surfing, little rivers for the very young. Beautiful breathtaking views and walks along scenic clifftops. One-and-a-half miles from National Trust property of Trerice. Good pub food close by. Come and join us! Discounted golf. Bed and Breakfast from £20 to £22. ETC ♦♦♦♦

NEWQUAY

Ms Jill Brake, Bre-Pen Farm, Mawgan Porth, Newquay TR8 4AL (01637 860420). A warm Cornish welcome awaits you from Rod and Jill in a friendly farmhouse on a working farm. The National Trust Coastal Path skirts the farm, making it an ideal walking area. The beaches of Mawgan Porth and Watergate Bay are within easy walking distance, both ideal for surfing. A short drive east takes you to the historic fishing port of Padstow, Bedruthan Steps and many glorious sandy beaches. Ideally situated for visiting the many attractions of Cornwall. Horse riding and riding holidays now available. Riding on farm, beach etc for novice or experienced riders. Pub lunch or picnic rides. Dog kennels available. Double en suite rooms, twin and family suite, all with tea/coffee facilities and colour TV. Traditional farmhouse breakfast; vegetarians catered for. ETC ♦♦♦♦

PADSTOW

Mrs Sandra May, Trewithen Farm, St Merryn, Near Padstow PL28 8JZ (01841 520420). Trewithen farmhouse is a renovated Cornish Roundhouse, set in a large garden and situated on a working farm enjoying country and coastal views. The picturesque town of Padstow with its pretty harbour and narrow streets with famous fish restaurants is only three miles away. St Merryn Parish boasts seven beautiful sandy beaches and bays. Also coastal walks, golf, fishing and horse riding on neighbouring farm. Hire a bike or walk along the Camel Trail cycle and footpath - winding for 18 miles along the River Camel. The accommodation has been tastefully decorated to complement the exposed beams and original features. All bedrooms are en suite or have private facilities, TV and hot drinks tray. Parking. Full English breakfast. TV lounge. Bed and Breakfast from £25 - £30 per person per night. Weekly rates and Winter weekend breaks available. ETC ♦♦♦♦

See also Colour Display Advertisement

PENZANCE

Mr Wilson, Boscean Country Hotel, St Just, Penzance TR19 7QP (Tel & Fax: 01736 788748). The Boscean Country Hotel, located amidst some of the most dramatic scenery in West Cornwall, is somewhere very special just waiting to be discovered. This country house offers a wonderful combination of oak panelled walls, a magnificent oak staircase and open log fires. The natural gardens, extending to nearly three acres, are a haven for wildlife including foxes and badgers. Situated on the Heritage Coast in an Area of Outstanding Natural Beauty close to Cape Cornwall and the coastal footpath, this is an ideal base from which to explore the Land's End Peninsula. The moors of Penwith are rich in Iron and Bronze Age relics dating back to 4000 BC. Penzance, St Michael's Mount, St Ives, Land's End and the Minack Theatre are all a short distance away. Twelve en suite rooms, centrally heated throughout, licensed bar. Excellent home cooking using fresh local produce. Open all year. Bed and Breakfast £23. Dinner, Bed and Breakfast £36. ETC ♦♦♦♦
e-mail: Boscean@aol.com   website: www.bosceancountryhotel.co.uk

ENGLAND / Board Cornwall 105

PENZANCE
Mrs M. D. Olds, Mulfra Farm, Newmill, Penzance TR20 8XP (01736 363940). Near Mulfra Quiot, this hill farm, with cows and calves, high on the edge of the Penwith moors, offers superb accommodation which attracts many of our guests to return year after year. The 17th century, stone built, beamed farmhouse, with far-reaching views, offers two double en suite bedrooms with tea and coffee facilities, TV; comfortable guests' lounge with inglenook fireplace and Cornish stone oven, dining room and sun lounge. Car essential, ample parking, friendly atmosphere, good food, beautiful walking country. Ideal centre for exploring west Cornwall. St Ives eight miles. Eden Project one hour. Bed and Breakfast from £22 - £25. *CORNWALL TOURIST BOARD HIGHLY COMMENDED.*

PENZANCE
Mrs Penny Lally, Rose Farm, Chyanhal, Buryas Bridge, Penzance TR19 6AN (01736 731808). Rose Farm is a small working farm in a little hamlet close to the picturesque fishing villages of Mousehole and Newlyn and seven miles from Land's End. The 200-year-old granite farmhouse is cosy with pretty, en suite rooms. One double, one family suite and a romantic 15th century four-poster room in barn annexe. We have all manner of animals, from pedigree cattle to pot-bellied pigs! Open all year (closed Christmas). **ETC/AA** ◆◆◆
website: www.rosefarmcornwall.co.uk

ROSELAND PENINSULA
Mrs Shirley E. Pascoe, Court Farm, Philleigh, Truro TR2 5NB (01872 580313). Working farm. Situated in the heart of the Roseland Peninsula, undoubtedly one of the loveliest parts of Cornwall with safe, unspoilt beaches on the seaward side, and the beautiful River Fal on the other. The traditionally run farm extends to about 250 acres, 50 of which border the upper reaches of the estuary, providing superb walking and bird watching, while down river is excellent for sailing, fishing, water skiing etc. The spacious old farmhouse, with over an acre of garden and plenty of parking space, lies in the quiet little village of Philleigh with its lovely old Norman Church and 17th century 'Roseland Inn'. There are plenty of good pubs and restaurants within a few miles. For horse owners who fancy a riding holiday we specialise in providing first class facilities for you and your horse(s). There is also a 6-bed cottage available for holiday letting. Please write or phone for brochure and terms.
e-mail: courtfarm@philleigh.freeserve.co.uk

ST AUSTELL
Mrs Liz Berryman, Polgreen Farm, London Apprentice, St Austell PL26 7AP (01726 75151). Polgreen is a family-run dairy farm nestling in the Pentewan Valley in an Area of Outstanding Natural Beauty. One mile from the coast and four miles from the picturesque fishing village of Mevagissey. A perfect location for a relaxing holiday in the glorious Cornish countryside. Centrally situated, Polgreen is ideally placed for touring all of Cornwall's many attractions. Cornish Way Leisure Trail adjoining farm. Within a few minutes' drive of the spectacular Eden Project and Heligan Gardens. All rooms with private facilities, colour TV, tea/coffee making facilities, guest lounge, children welcome. Terms from £23 per person per night. **ETC** ◆◆◆◆
e-mail: polgreen.farm@btclick.com
website: www.polgreenfarm.co.uk

Cornwall — Board / ENGLAND

Discover Rose-in-Vale – The Hotel in the Valley

Hiding away in its own 11-acre valley, deep in the heart of the country, yet with the magnificent North Cornish coast right on the doorstep. There is a choice of 18 bedrooms and suites, all en suite, with central heating, TV, radio, hairdryer and beverage tray; three ground floor rooms are suitable for less able guests. The Rose Suite offers a queen-size four-poster bed, separate sitting room, spa bath, walk-in-shower and some special touches, and Master Rooms feature four-poster or half-tester beds. Dining in the Valley Restaurant is a particular pleasure, with the emphasis on locally produced foods wherever possible, complemented by an interesting selection of fine wines. Special diets catered for.

Rose-in-Vale Country House Hotel
Mithian, St Agnes TR5 0QD
Tel: 01872 552202 • Fax: 01872 552700
www.rose-in-vale-hotel.co.uk
reception@rose-in-vale-hotel.co.uk

Cocktail Bar • Library • Drawing Room
• Outdoor heated pool
• Croquet and badminton in the grounds
• Sauna
ETC/AA/RAC ★★★   RAC 2 Dining Awards

See also Colour Advertisement

ST IVES

Roslyn & Keith Pester, Coombe Farmhouse B&B, Lelant Downs, St Ives TR27 6NW (01736 740843). Built of sturdy granite, Coombe is an early 19th century farm house tucked away at the foot of Trencrom Hill, an ancient hill fort owned by the National Trust. The remaining aspects look out across local farmland which provides a constantly changing vista. Rooms have fresh flowers, cosy beds with crisp cotton sheets and patchwork quilts. A substantial breakfast with home-baked bread and eggs from our own free-range hens is served in the old dairy. St Ives with its sandy beaches and cobbled streets is a short drive over the hill. Well placed for a variety of pursuits; walking, riding, bird watching and sketching. Alternatively relax in the garden with a good book. Coombe is the ideal spot from which to explore the splendid rugged scenery of West Cornwall. Bed and Breakfast from £25. Non-Smokers only please. No children under 12. *CORNWALL TOURIST BOARD APPROVED ACCOMMODATION.*

ST IVES

Linda & Bob Gale, Fairfield House, Porthrepta Road, Carbis Bay, St Ives TR26 2NZ (01736 793771). Linda and Bob welcome you to their homely Edwardian Guest House with fabulous sea views. Ideally situated close to Carbis Bay beach in St Ives Bay, voted one of the most beautiful bays in the world. Two minutes' walk to the Coastal Path, beach and rail line (branch line to St Ives takes three minutes) or walk the beautiful Coastal Path to St Ives. Visit the galleries including the famous Tate, the cobbled streets and harbour, with its many restaurants/pubs. Fairfield House has been recently refurbished with new en suite rooms added in 2003. Lovely rooms, most with sea views across the bay to St Ives. Non-smoking guest house with emphasis on comfort, cleanliness and personal service. Cream teas served in our lovely garden. Bed and Breakfast with varied menus from £22.00 per person per night.
e-mail: info@fairfieldhouse.net
website: www.fairfieldhouse.net

ST MAWES/TRURO

Mrs A. Palmer, Trenestrall Farm, Ruan High Lanes, Truro TR2 5LX (01872 501259). Working farm, join in. A tastefully restored 200 year old barn, now a farmhouse offering comfortable accommodation on a 300 acre mixed working farm. Situated on beautiful Roseland Peninsula, within easy reach of St Mawes and Truro and amenities such as Heligan Gardens and the Eden Project, at the same time not being too far from attractions further west. Close to safe beaches and beautiful Fal estuary for sailing, bird watching etc. Accommodation consists of double, family or twin rooms all en suite, with tea/coffee facilities; sittingroom with TV and an open fire for chilly days. Children welcome, babysitting service. Pets accepted. Phone or write for details of Bed and Breakfast from £22.50 per person per night.

ENGLAND / Board   Cornwall 107

See also Colour Display Advertisement

TINTAGEL
Willapark Manor Hotel, Bossiney, Tintagel PL34 0BA (01840 770782). Willapark Manor is a lovely character house in a beautiful setting amidst 14 acre grounds, overlooking Bossiney Bay. Surrounded by woodland, it is secluded and has direct access to the coastal path and beach. It is a family-run hotel with a friendly and informal atmosphere, excellent cuisine and a well stocked cocktail bar. Beautifully appointed bedrooms, all en suite and with colour TV and tea/coffee making facilities. Some four-posters. A warm welcome and a memorable holiday assured. One of the most beautifully situated hotels in England.
ETC ★★
website: www.willapark.co.uk

TRURO
Mrs Pamela Carbis, Trenona Farm, Ruan High Lanes, Truro TR2 5JS (01872 501339). Enjoy a relaxing stay at Trenona Farm, a mixed farm situated on the unspoilt Roseland Peninsula midway between the Cathedral city of Truro and the town of St Austell, home of the acclaimed Eden Project. The farmhouse is Victorian and has four guest bedrooms, all of which are double/family rooms with colour TV and tea/coffee making facilities. Three rooms have en suite facilities and the fourth has a private bathroom. There is a separate TV lounge and dining room, together with gardens and a patio. Children and pets are welcome. Brochure available. Open March to November.
e-mail: info@trenonafarmholidays.co.uk
website: www.trenonafarmholidays.co.uk

WADEBRIDGE
Mrs E. Hodge, Pengelly Farm, Burlawn, Wadebridge PL27 7LA (01208 814217). A Listed Georgian farmhouse on a working dairy farm, in a quiet location overlooking wooded valleys. Tastefully decorated and centrally heated throughout, offering one double and one twin room, both en suite with TV, radio, hairdryer and beverage trays. Full English breakfast, using mainly local produce, is served in the traditional style diningroom. Special diets by prior arrangement. Comfortable lounge with TV/video. Large garden with outstanding views for relaxing. An ideal walking, touring and cycling base, only six miles from the coast, with sailing, surfing, golf, riding and coastal walks; Camel Trail, the Saints' Way and Pencarrow House nearby. The Eden Project 35 minutes' drive, Padstow 20 minutes, Wadebridge one and a half miles, with shopping, pubs, restaurants, leisure facilities and The Camel Trail. New 2004 static caravan also available. ETC ◆◆◆◆
e-mail: hodgepete@hotmail.com
website: www.pengellyfarm.co.uk

WHITSAND BAY - DOWNDERRY
Mrs S.M. Hoskin, The Copse, St Winnolls, Polbathic, Torpoint PL11 3DX (01503 230205). The Copse is situated in peaceful, unspoilt countryside midway between Plymouth and Looe. The beaches and the golf course at Whitsand Bay are two miles away. We offer en suite rooms with colour television and drinks-making facilities. The Copse is an ideal base for touring Cornwall and South Devon, and visiting the Eden Project. Non-smoking. Regret, no pets. Tariff: £10 to £22 per person per night.

National Maritime Museum • *Falmouth, Cornwall* • *01326 313388*
website: www.nmmc.co.uk
A gateway to the maritime world with interactive displays of boats and their place in the nation's life.

CUMBRIA

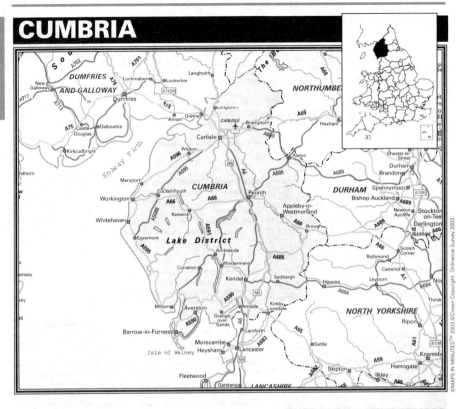

BOWNESS-ON-WINDERMERE

Holly Cottages Guest House, 2 Holly Cottages, Rayrigg Road, Bowness-on-Windermere LA23 3BZ (015394 44250). Guest House in the centre of Bowness-on-Windermere, offering four double en suite rooms with colour TV and tea making facilities. Centrally situated to all shops and restaurants. Lake Windermere and boat trips five minutes away. Excellent position for exploring the Lake District. If you enjoy walking, cycling, shopping, steam power, visiting houses and gardens, viewing wonderful scenery or simply pottering about, there is something here for any age or ability. We look forward to welcoming you soon. Sorry, no smoking in house. Private parking and access at all times. Dogs by arrangement. Contact: **Jan or Jim Bebbington (015394 44250).**
website: www.hollycottageguesthouse.co.uk

BRAMPTON

Mrs Elizabeth Woodmass, Howard House Farm, Gilsland, Brampton CA8 7AJ (016977 47285). Working farm. A 250 acre mixed farm with a 19th century stone-built farmhouse situated in a rural area overlooking the Irthing Valley on the Cumbria/Northumbria border. Half-a-mile from Gilsland village and Roman Wall; Haltwhistle five miles and the M6 at Carlisle, 18 miles. Good base for touring – Roman Wall, Lakes and Scottish Borders. Trout fishing on farm. Guests' lounge with colour TV where you can relax anytime in comfort. Diningroom. One double room en suite, one twin and one family room with washbasins, bath or shower. All bedrooms have tea/coffee making facilities. Bathroom with shower, toilet. Children welcome at reduced rates. Sorry, no pets. Car parking. Open January to December for Bed and Breakfast from £23 to £26. Weekly terms available. SAE or telephone for brochure. **ETC ♦♦♦♦ SILVER AWARD.**

ENGLAND / Board   Cumbria   109

The Buttermere/Lorton Vale

- A Place for All Seasons

AA New House Farm, Lorton, Buttermere,
Near Cockermouth, Cumbria CA13 9UU
✦✦✦✦
Guest Accommodation
Tel: 01900 85404 • Fax: 01900 85478

Situated in the quietest and most beautiful part of the Lakes, New House Farm has 15 acres of open fields, ponds, streams and woods, which guests may wander around at leisure and there is easy access to nearby lakes and fells. All bedrooms are en suite. There is a cosy dining room and three comfortable sitting rooms with open log fires. The food served is fine traditional fare.
Which? Hotel Guide Hotel of the Year Award Winner(Cumbria)
e-mail: hazel@newhouse-farm.co.uk
website: www.newhouse-farm.co.uk

See also Colour Advertisement

CARLISLE

Mrs Dorothy Nicholson, Gill Farm, Blackford, Carlisle CA6 4EL (01228 675326; mobile: 07808 571586). In a delightful setting on a beef and sheep farm, this Georgian style farmhouse dated 1740 offers a friendly welcome to all guests breaking journeys to or from Scotland or having a holiday in our beautiful countryside. Near Hadrian's Wall, Gretna Green and Lake District. Golf, fishing, swimming and large agricultural auction markets all nearby; also cycle path passes our entrance. Accommodation is in one double room en suite, one family and one twin/single bedrooms. All rooms have washbasins, shaver points and tea/coffee making facilities. Two bathrooms, shower; lounge with colour TV; separate diningroom. Open all year. Reductions for children; cot provided. Central heating. Car essential, good parking. Pets permitted. Bed and Breakfast from £19 to £24. Telephone for further details or directions.

CARLISLE

Mrs Georgina Elwen, New Pallyards, Hethersgill, Carlisle CA6 6HZ (01228 577308). Working farm. Farmhouse filmed for BBC TV. Relax and see beautiful North Cumbria and the Borders. A warm welcome awaits you in our country farmhouse tucked away in the Cumbrian countryside, yet easily accessible from M6 Junction 44. In addition to the surrounding attractions there is plenty to enjoy, including hill walking, peaceful forests and sea trout/salmon fishing or just nestle down and relax with nature. Bed and Breakfast: Two double en suite, two family en suite rooms and one twin/single bedroom, all with tea/coffee making equipment. Bed and Breakfast from £25 per person, Dinner £14; Dinner, Bed and Breakfast weekly rates from £170 to £180. Menu choice. Self-catering offered. Disabled facilities. We are proud to have won a National Salon Culinaire Award for the "Best Breakfast in Britain". **ETC ✦✦✦✦** *GOLD AWARD WINNER.*
e-mail: info@newpallyards.freeserve.co.uk   website: www.newpallyards.freeserve.co.uk

CALDBECK

Mr and Mrs A. Savage, Swaledale Watch, Whelpo, Caldbeck CA7 8HQ (Tel & Fax: 016974 78409). Ours is a mixed farm of 300 acres situated in beautiful countryside within the Lake District National Park. Central for Scottish Borders, Roman Wall, Eden Valley and Lakes. Primarily a sheep farm (everyone loves lambing time). Visitors are welcome to see farm animals and activities. Many interesting walks nearby or roam the peaceful northern fells. Enjoyed by many Cumbrian Way walkers. Very comfortable accommodation with excellent home cooking. All rooms have private facilities. Central heating. Tea making facilities. We are a friendly Cumbrian farming family and make you very welcome. Bed and Breakfast from £19 to £25; Evening Meal from £12 to £15, Tuesday, Wednesday, Thursday and Saturday only. **ETC/AA ✦✦✦✦**
e-mail: nan.savage@talk21.com   website: www.swaledale-watch.co.uk

CARTMEL FELL

Lightwood Country Guest House, Cartmel Fell, Grange-over-Sands LA11 6NP (Tel & Fax: 015395 31454). Built in 1656, Lightwood maintains original features and charm whilst offering modern home comforts. A family business for over 50 years the Cervettis offer warm hospitality and excellent home cooking with Italian inspiration, using homegrown and local produce. All diets catered for. Set in two acres of beautiful natural and landscaped gardens. Excellent fell walking area, only 2.5 miles from Lake Windermere. Six individually decorated en suite bedrooms with countryside views. On-site complementary therapies – a recipe for wellbeing and relaxation. Children welcome. B&B from £23pppn; D,B&B from £40.90pppn for weekly stay. Short Break rates. Closed December. **ETC ♦♦♦♦. WHICH?**

See also Colour Display Advertisement

HOTEL GUIDE RECOMMENDED.
e-mail: enquiries@lightwoodguesthouse.com
website: www.lightwoodguesthouse.com

COCKERMOUTH (near)

Mrs Nicholson, Swinside End Farm, Scales, High Lorton, Near Cockermouth CA13 9VA (01900 85134; Fax: 01900 85410)). Working farm situated in a peaceful part of Lorton Valley, the perfect base for your Lakeland holiday. Ideal for hill walking and touring around the Lake District. All rooms have TV, central heating, washbasins, tea/coffee making facilities and hairdryer. TV lounge with open fire. Magnificent views. Packed lunches available. A warm welcome awaits you. Open all year. Pets by arrangement. Bed and Breakfast from £20 - £22 per person per night.
e-mail: swinside@supanet.com

COCKERMOUTH (near)

Mrs Bridget Woodward, Whitekeld Farm, Ullock, Near Cockermouth CA14 4RJ (01946 861171). Beautiful double room with large en suite wet room/bathroom in converted sandstone farm outbuildings. Complete privacy and self-contained with magnificent views. Open May 2004, along with two converted barns, each for two people, with en suites and top facilities. Terms from £30 to £40 per person per night. Please telephone or e-mail for more details.
e-mail: LBWoodward@aol.com
website: www.whitekeldfarm.co.uk

One child FREE with two paying adults at
Cars of the Stars Motor Museum
see our READERS' OFFER VOUCHERS for full details

Holker Hall & Gardens • *Near Newby Bridge, Cumbria* • *015395 58328*
website: wwwholker-hall.com
A historic hall set in 25 acres of beautiful gardens, plus the Lakeland Motor Museum featuring the Campbell Bluebird Exhibition.

Cumberland Pencil Museum • *Keswick, Cumbria* • *017687 73626*
website: www.pencils.co.uk
The fascinating history of the humble pencil, from the discovery of Borrowdale graphite to present day manufacture. See the world's largest colouring pencil, Shop.

ENGLAND / Board   Cumbria   111

KENDAL

Hollin Root Farm, Garth Row, Skelsmergh, Kendal LA8 9AW (01539 823638). Dating from 1844 Hollin Root Farm is a typical Lakeland farmhouse set in beautiful open countryside with land down to the river. Tranquil settings and large gardens make this an ideal place for longer stays and a good base from which to explore the Lake District. There are many footpaths near the farm including the 84 mile Dales Way. Accommodation consists of three en suite rooms all with colour TV and tea/coffee making facilities. Excellent breakfasts. Packed lunches available. Private car park, safe cycle storage. Children and vegetarians welcome. Open all year. Non-smoking establishment. B&B from £22 to £28 pppn. ETC ♦♦♦♦
e-mail: b-and-b@hollin-root-farm.freeserve.co.uk
website: www.hollinrootfarm.co.uk

KESWICK

Mrs M. M. Beaty, Birkrigg Farm, Newlands, Keswick CA12 5TS (017687 78278). Birkrigg is very pleasantly and peacefully situated, with an excellent outlook in the lovely Newlands Valley. Five miles from Keswick between Braithwaite and Buttermere. Being in a beautiful mountainous area makes this an ideal place to stay especially for those wishing to walk or climb. Centrally located for touring the many beauty spots in the Lake District. Clean, comfortable accommodation awaits you. A good Breakfast is offered at 8.30am, Evening Tea at 9.30pm. Packed Lunches available. Sorry, no Evening Meals. Local inns all provide good food, two to four miles away. Open March to November. **ETC** ♦♦♦

KESWICK

Rickerby Grange, Portinscale, Keswick CA12 5RH (017687 72344). Set within its own garden with private car parking, in the picturesque village of Portinscale near the shores of Lake Derwentwater within walking distance of the market town of Keswick. Ideally situated for exploring all parts of the Lakes. Offering comfort, friendly service, these being the essential qualities provided by the resident proprietor. A well-stocked bar offering draught beers; comfortable lounge and elegant dining room where a four course dinner can be enjoyed with a varied selection of wines. A la carte also available. Three ground floor bedrooms, all rooms en suite with tea and coffee making facilities, colour TV, direct dial telephone. DB&B from £49, Winter rates available (Special Breaks). Open all year, including Christmas and New Year.

Brochure on request. Contact **Val. AA/ETC** ♦♦♦♦, **RAC** ♦♦♦♦ *SPARKLING DIAMOND AWARD.*
e-mail: val@ricor.co.uk
website: www.ricor.co.uk

KESWICK

Colin and Lesley Smith, Mosedale House, Mosedale, Mungrisdale CA11 0XQ (017687 79371). Traditional 1862 built, lakeland farmhouse. A smallholding with donkeys, ducks and hens. It enjoys a magnificent position, nestling at the foot of Carrock Fell, overlooking the river Caldew, three-and-a-half miles from the A66 Keswick to Penrith road. Four-course dinners, licensed, vegetarians welcome. Home-baked bread, our own free-range eggs. Packed Lunches. No smoking. En suite rooms. Attractive lounge. Bed and Breakfast from £25. Dinner £16. Delightful two bedroomed self catering cottage. Peaceful location, fell-walking from the door. Abundant wildlife. Visit us on our website below. Grade One facilities for disabled guests. **ETC** ♦♦♦♦

e-mail: mosedale@northlakes.co.uk
website: www.mosedalehouse.co.uk

The FHG Directory of Website Addresses

on pages 345 - 373 is a useful quick reference guide for holiday accommodation with e-mail and/or website details

Cumbria

KESWICK

Mrs Deborah Mawson, Highside Farm, Bassenthwaite, Keswick CA12 4QG (017687 76952/76328). Fantastic 17th century period working farmhouse, tastefully renovated to the highest standards, featuring oak beams and Inglenook fireplace. Ideally situated for walking, sightseeing, cycling, touring, etc. The farm nestles at the foot of Skiddaw and Ullock Pike, and has tremendous views towards Bassenthwaite Lake. Highside offers a family room sleeping up to four, a double bedroom and a ground-floor bedroom. All rooms are en suite. Highside is the ideal base for your holiday in the Lake District – a hidden jewel waiting to be discovered. Strictly non-smoking. Terms from £27 per person per night. Three night specials £78.
e-mail: deborah@highside.co.uk
website: www.highside.co.uk

NEWBIGGIN ON LUNE

Mrs Brenda Boustead, Tranna Hill, Newbiggin on Lune, Kirkby Stephen CA17 4NY (015396 23227 or 07989 892368). Tranna Hill offers a relaxing and friendly atmosphere in a non-smoking environment. Five miles from M6 Junction 38, ideal base for all activities with Howgill Fells Nature Reserve, fish farm and golf course only minutes away. Well placed for breaking your journey or touring the Lakes and Dales. Private parking and large gardens. En suite rooms furnished to a high standard with TV, refreshment trays, central heating and beautiful views. Delicious breakfasts. All for £20pppn. ETC ◆◆◆◆
e-mail: trannahill@hotmail.com
website: www.trannahill.co.uk

PENRITH

Mrs Sheila Robinson, Skygarth Farm, Temple Sowerby, Penrith CA10 1SS (01768 361300). A working farm on the outskirts of Temple Sowerby in the beautiful Eden Valley, ideal for a stopover en route to or from Scotland. A warm and friendly welcome awaits all guests arriving at our spacious 17th century farmhouse. Relax and watch TV in our comfortable guest sitting room, which has tea/coffee making facilities, or sit in the garden and savour the quiet tranquillity of the Eden Valley. We have two spacious family rooms which look out over the garden, with central heating, TV, and tea/coffee facilities. A hearty farmhouse breakfast starts your day. AA ◆◆◆
e-mail: enquire@skygarth.co.uk
website: www.skygarth.co.uk

PENRITH

Mrs Brenda Preston, Pallet Hill Farm, Penrith CA11 0BY (017684 83247). Pallet Hill Farm is pleasantly situated two miles from Penrith on the Penrith-Greystoke-Keswick road (B5288). It is four miles from Ullswater and has easy access to the Lake District, Scottish Borders and Yorkshire Dales. There are several sports facilities in the area - golf club, swimming pool, pony trekking. Good farmhouse food and hospitality with personal attention. An ideal place to spend a relaxing break. Double, single and family rooms; TV lounge and dining room. Children welcome, cot, high chair. Sorry, no pets. Car essential, parking. Open Easter to November. Bed and Breakfast £14 (reduced weekly rates), reduced rates for children.

FHG

FHG PUBLICATIONS publish a large range of well-known accommodation guides. We will be happy to send you details or you can use the order form at the back of this book.

ENGLAND / Board   Cumbria **113**

PENRITH
Mrs Mary Teasdale, Lisco Farm, Troutbeck, Penrith CA11 0SY (017687 79645). Lisco has beautiful views of Saddleback and the Fells. Three miles from Keswick Golf Club, six miles from Derwentwater and five from Ullswater. A good base for touring lovely Lakeland. Comfortable accommodation offered in one double and two en suite family rooms, all with tea/coffee making facilities and washbasins. Bathroom with shower. Lounge and separate diningroom. Bed and Breakfast, optional Evening Meal. Good home cooking. Colour TV. Children welcome. Outside accommodation available for dogs if required. Large dogs also welcome. SAE or phone for further information.

PENRITH
Beckfoot Country House, Helton, Penrith CA10 2QB. (01931 713241; Fax: 01931 713391). A beautiful Victorian country house set in three acres of gardens, with wonderful views of the Lowther valley, a tranquil and unspoilt corner of the Lake District National Park. All rooms are en suite, spacious and well appointed with TV, hospitality tray and complimentary toiletries; luxurious executive suite with four-poster. Ironing facilities available. Cumbrian breakfast and home-cooked evening meals served in the oak-panelled diningroom. Activities nearby include walking, cycling, horse riding, fishing, golf, swimming and paragliding, or visit Hadrian's Wall and the Scottish Borders, Eden Valley, historic Carlisle city, historic castles and gardens. Special three night breaks available. AA ◆◆◆◆
e-mail: info@beckfoot.co.uk
website: http//www.beckfoot.co.uk

See also Colour Display Advertisement

RAVENGLASS
George and Cath Jones, Holly House Hotel, Main Street, Ravenglass CA18 1SQ. (01229 717230). A small privately-run hotel in a quiet village overlooking the broad estuary on the Irish Sea coast, where visitors will receive a warm welcome and excellent service. Accommodation comprises seven comfortable bedrooms, four en suite, the other three have wash basins. All have colour TV and tea/coffee making facilities. Family rooms available. Ideally situated for walking, fishing and boating activities as well as many places of interest to visit. The cosy public bar offers a wide selection of wines, spirits, beers and real ale. Wholesome home-made food available throughout the day catering for all tastes including a special children's menu. B&B from £21 pppn.
website: www.thehollyhousehotel.com

TROUTBECK
Mrs Maureen Dix, Greenah Crag, Troutbeck, Penrith CA11 0SQ (017684 83233). Enjoy a relaxing break at Greenah Crag, a 17th century former farmhouse peacefully located in the Lake District National Park, just 10 miles from Keswick and only eight miles from the M6 motorway. Ideal for exploring Northern Lakes, Eden Valley, Carlisle, Hadrian's Wall and the Western Pennines. Accommodation is in two double bedrooms with bathroom en suite, and one twin-bedded room with washbasin, all with tea/coffee making facilities. The guests' sittingroom with TV and woodburning stove is a cosy place on the coldest days! A full breakfast is served in the oak-beamed diningroom. Pub/ restaurant three-quarters-of-a-mile. Regret no pets or smoking in the house. Bed and Breakfast from £19 pp. Please telephone for brochure.

Terms quoted in this publication may be subject to increase if rises in costs necessitate

SANDOWN

Lake Road, Windermere, Cumbria LA23 2JF • Tel: 015394 45275

Superb Bed and Breakfast accommodation. All rooms en suite with colour TV and tea/coffee making facilities. Situated two minutes from Lake Windermere, shops and cafes. Many lovely walks. Open all year. Special out of season rates, also two-day Saturday/Sunday breaks. From £22 to £32 per person, excluding Bank Holidays. Well-behaved dogs welcome. Each room has own safe private car parking. SAE or telephone for further details.

Proprietors: Irene and George Eastwood

See also Colour Advertisement

WINDERMERE

Mrs Dorothy Heighton, Beckmead House, 5 Park Avenue, Windermere LA23 2AR (Tel & Fax: 015394 42757). A small family-run guest house with quality accommodation, delicious breakfasts and a relaxed friendly atmosphere. Single, double or family rooms, with en suite or private showers, all decorated to a high standard with central heating, electric blankets, tea/coffee making facilities, colour TV, hairdryers and clean towels daily. Comfortable residents' lounge. Walking, climbing, sailing, water skiing, pony trekking, golf nearby, or visit historic houses, gardens and museums. **ETC ♦♦♦♦**
e-mail: beckmead_house@yahoo.com
website: www.beckmead.co.uk

WINDERMERE

Mr and Mrs D. Lennon, Meadow Cottage, Ratherheath Lane, Crook LA8 8JX (015398 21269). Sandra and David Lennon extend a warm welcome to guests who stay at Meadow Cottage. Set in one and a half acres, this old Lakeland cottage has spectacular views and is the ideal location when visiting this beautiful region. All bedrooms are en suite, have tea and coffee facilities and colour TV. We provide Aga-cooked vegetarian or English breakfasts. Some five miles from Lake Windermere, the popular heart of the Lake District, we are conveniently placed for touring, walking or cycling exploration. A flexible service is provided in this non-smoking guest house. Please enquire for brochure. Prices from £25 per person.

Two for the price of one (adults) OR 25% of family ticket at

Windermere Steamboats & Museum

see our READERS' OFFER VOUCHERS for full details

FHG

FHG PUBLICATIONS publish a large range of well-known accommodation guides. We will be happy to send you details or you can use the order form at the back of this book.

ENGLAND / Board   Derbyshire 115

DERBYSHIRE

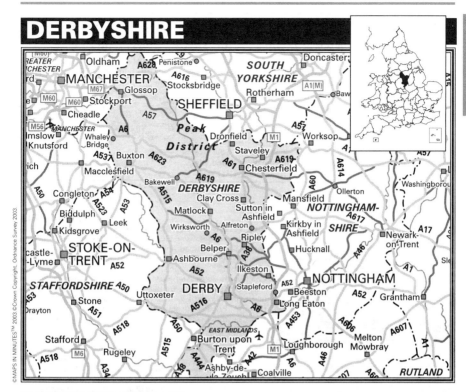

ASHBOURNE
Mrs A.M. Whittle, Stone Cottage, Green Lane, Clifton, Ashbourne DE6 2BL (01335 343377; Fax: 01335 347117).
A charming cottage in the quiet village of Clifton, one mile from Georgian market town of Ashbourne. Ideal for visiting Chatsworth House, Haddon Hall, Dovedale, Carsington Waters and the theme park of Alton Towers. Each bedroom is furnished to a high standard; all rooms en suite with four-poster beds, TV and coffee making facilities. Large garden to relax in. A warm welcome is assured and a hearty breakfast in our delightful cottage. Nearby good country pubs serving evening meals. Bed and Breakfast from £21 per person. Please write or telephone for further details.
ETC/AA ♦♦♦
e-mail: info@stone-cottage.fsnet.co.uk

ASHBOURNE
Mrs M. Richardson, Throwley Hall Farm, Ilam, Ashbourne DE6 2BB (01538 308202 or 308243). Our Bed and Breakfast accommodation is set in the heart of rural England in the Peak District National Park. Situated on our family farm where the sheep and cattle are nurtured in easy harmony with abundant wildlife and wild flowers. Within a few miles of the nationally renowned beauty of the Manifold Valley and Dovedale. In the spring and summer months you can enjoy watching the new lambs and calves. The bedrooms are comfortable, well-equipped, spacious. All have wash basins, tea and coffee facilities, and are en suite or have private bathrooms. Despite their peaceful rural location we're within easy reach of Alton Towers theme park as well as Chatsworth and the historic pottery works of Stoke-on-Trent. Nearby the charming local market towns of Ashbourne, Leek and Buxton move at a gentler pace. Tariffs from £27 pppn with reduced rates for children.
e-mail: throwleyhall@talk21.com or throwley@btinternet.com
website: www.throwleyhallfarm.co.uk

116 Derbyshire   Board / ENGLAND

BIGGIN HALL
Tel: 01298 84451 • Fax: 01298 84681
Biggin-by-Hartington, Buxton SK17 0DH   **website: www.bigginhall.co.uk**

Tranquilly set 1,000 ft up in the White Peak District National Park, 17th century Grade II* Listed Biggin Hall – now one of the 'World's Best Loved Hotels' where guests experience the full benefits of the legendary Biggin Air – has been sympathetically restored, keeping its character while giving house room to contemporary comforts. Rooms are centrally heated with bathrooms en suite, colour TV, tea-making facilities, silent fridge and telephone. Those in the main house have stone arched mullioned windows, others are in converted 18th century outbuildings. Centrally situated for stately homes and for exploring the natural beauty of the area. Return at the end of the day to enjoy your freshly cooked dinner alongside log fires and personally selected wines. Well-behaved pets are welcome by prior arrangement. ETC ★★

See also Colour Advertisement

BAKEWELL
Mrs Alison Yates, Smerrill Grange, Middleton, By Youlgreave, Bakewell DE45 1LQ (01629 636232). Working farm. Traditional bed and breakfast on beef cattle and sheep farm. Beautiful setting in heart of Peak District. Very old farmhouse. Many tourist attractions within short driving distance, eg Chatsworth House and Haddon Hall. Bakewell and Matlock six miles. Glorious walks in Derbyshire Dales. Double en suite, double and twin bedrooms with private bathroom. Tea/coffee making facilities. Private guests' sitting and dining rooms. Bed and Breakfast from £17. Reductions for children. Dogs by arrangement.

BASLOW
Mrs S. Mills, Bubnell Cliff Farm, Wheatlands Lane, Baslow, Bakewell DE45 1RF (01246 582454). Working farm. A 300 acre working farm situated half-a-mile from the village of Baslow in the beautiful Derbyshire Peak District. Guests can enjoy, from their bedroom window, breathtaking views of Chatsworth Park and surrounding area. Chatsworth House, the majestic home of the Duke of Devonshire, medieval Haddon Hall and the traditional market town of Bakewell (famous for its puddings), are all close by. Accommodation comprises two double rooms, guests' lounge/dining room with TV and log fires in the winter. NON-SMOKERS ONLY. Bed and Breakfast from £17.50 per person with shared bathroom. Reductions for children. Varied breakfast menu.

BUXTON
Mrs Jane Pilkington, Bank Top Farm, Pilsbury Road, Hartington, Buxton SK17 0AD (01298 84205; mobile: 07751 766872). Lying between the hills, almost off the beaten track, we entrance the imagination of those who wish to relax in a peaceful garden with English afternoon tea. Dovedale is ideal for walking, cycling, and touring the area's unspoilt villages, market towns and historic houses. In our farmhouse we offer warm hospitality and hope to fulfil your (reasonable) desires. Open all year. Bed and Breakfast from £24pp; Evening Meal available. Non-smoking. ETC ◆◆◆
e-mail: owenjane@farming.co.uk
website: www.banktophartington.freeserve.co.uk

CHINLEY (near Buxton)
Mrs Barbara Goddard, Moseley House Farm, Maynestone Road, Chinley, High Peak SK23 6AH (01663 750240). Enjoy a stay on our farm set in a special landscaped area in the lovely Peak District. We offer comfort and hospitality in spacious family/twin and double rooms, some en suite. Colour TV, central heating. Delicious breakfasts. Children welcome. Village half a mile away. Open all year except Christmas. Also newly-built self-catering cottage suite designed for two plus sofa bed. Fabulous views. Weekly lets or short breaks. Bed and Breakfast from £20 to £23. ETC ◆◆◆
e-mail: moseleyhouse@supanet.com

DOVEDALE (near Ashbourne)

Derek & Susan Cockayne, St. Leonard's Cottage, Thorpe, DE6 2AW (01335 350224). One of the oldest cottages in the village, St Leonard's stands in its own grounds of one third of an acre and overlooks the village green. Thorpe Cloud rises in the background. Footpaths start on the village green with one mile to the famous stepping stones in Dovedale. Available to walkers and cyclists of all ages are the Tissington, High Peak and Manifold old railway trails. Carsington Water is close by, suitable for walking, cycling, fishing and sailing. Ideally situated for touring the Peak District, with many historic houses to visit, i.e. Chatsworth, Haddon and Kedleston. St Leonard's Cottage is fully modernised but retains the original oak beams. Three en suite bedrooms with full sized bathrooms, tea/coffee making facilities. Centrally heated throughout. Dining and sitting room with colour TV and library. Open to guests all day. Private parking. For a friendly holiday, midweek or weekend break, please ring Derek or Susan. Refreshments available on arrival. Bed and Breakfast from £25 per person per night. Sorry, no pets. A non-smoking cottage.

GLOSSOP

Graham and Julie Caesar, Windy Harbour Farm Hotel, Woodhead Road, Glossop SK13 7QE (01457 853107). Situated in the heart of the Peak District on the B6105, approximately one mile from Glossop town centre and adjacent to the Pennine Way. Our 10-bedroom hotel with outstanding views of Woodhead and Snake Passes and the Longdendale Valley is an ideal location for all outdoor activities. A warm welcome awaits you in our licensed bar and restaurant serving a wide range of excellent home-made food. Bed and Breakfast from £25 per night.

KIRK LANGLEY

Mrs Diane Buxton, New Park Farm, Lodge Lane, Kirk Langley DE6 4NX (01332 824262 or 07779 845611). Working farm. An early 19th century farmhouse situated seven miles from Ashbourne and four miles from Derby, within easy reach of Alton Towers and The American Adventure Park, Dovedale, Carsington Water, two miles from Kedleston Hall. Good food is served in hotels and pubs only a few miles away. Accommodation consists of two double and two single rooms with a shared bathroom and toilet. All rooms have a TV and tea/coffee making facilities. Parking is off-road, close by the house. Situated in peaceful surroundings overlooking Kirk Langley village and countryside. Bed and Breakfast from £15 per person. Reductions for children. Open all year. Write or telephone for details.

MATLOCK

Mrs D. Wootton, Old School Farm, Uppertown Lane, Uppertown, Ashover, Near Chesterfield S45 0JF (01246 590813). Working farm, join in. This working farm in a small hamlet on the edge of the Peak District enjoys unspoilt views. Ashover is three miles away and mentioned in the Domesday Book; Chatsworth House, Haddon Hall, Hardwick Hall, Matlock Bath and Bakewell all within seven miles. Accommodation comprises two family rooms with en suite facilities, one double, one single rooms. Washbasin in two of the rooms; shared bathroom for guests' use only. Plenty of hot water; fitted carpets; large livingroom/diningroom with colour TV. Car essential. No smoking in bedrooms. NO PETS. Disabled guests welcome. Children welcome. Open from April to October. Bed and Breakfast from £22 per person per night; Bed, Breakfast and Evening Meal £34 per person per night. Evening meal minimum two persons. Reductions for children. Take the B5057 Darley Dale Road off the A632 Chesterfield to Matlock main road. Take second left. Keep on this road for approximately one mile. Old School Farm is on left opposite the stone water trough. **ETC/RAC ♦♦♦♦,** *SPARKLING DIAMOND AWARD.*

FREE or REDUCED RATE entry to Holiday Visits and Attractions — see our READERS' OFFER VOUCHERS on pages 67-94

118 Derbyshire   Board / ENGLAND

MATLOCK
Mrs Linda Lomas, Middlehills Farm Bed and Breakfast, Grange Mill, Matlock DE4 4HY (01629 650368). We know the secret of contentment - we live in the most picturesque part of England. Share our good fortune, breathe the fresh air, absorb the peace, feast your eyes on the beautiful scenery that surrounds our small working farm, with our pot bellied pig who just loves to have her ears scratched, and Bess and Ruby who are ideal playmates for children of all ages. Retire with the scent of honeysuckle and waken to the aroma of freshly baked bread and sizzling bacon then sample the delights of the Peak District and Derbyshire Dales such as Dovedale, Chatsworth and Haddon Hall.

MELBOURNE (near)
Mrs Mary Kidd, Ivy House Farm, Stanton-by-Bridge, Near Melbourne DE73 1HT (Tel & Fax: 01332 863152). Working farm, join in. Ivy House Farm is a 400 acre arable farm with horses at livery. The farmhouse, converted in 2000, has three en suite double rooms and we have also converted some cowsheds into chalets, all of which are en suite with tea/coffee making facilities and TV. Each chalet has a theme – Cowshed, Sheep Pen, Stable and Pigsty. The area has lots to do and see, such as Calke Abbey, ski slopes, Alton Towers, motor racing at Donington Park. There are also lots of places to eat. Children are welcome, but we are strictly non-smoking. Ample off-road parking. Bed and Breakfast from £25. ETC *SILVER AWARD*.
e-mail: mary@guesthouse.fsbusiness.co.uk
website: www.ivy-house-farm.com

FHG

Other specialised
FHG PUBLICATIONS

Published annually: available in all good bookshops or direct from the publisher.

PETS WELCOME! £7.99
Recommended **COUNTRY HOTELS** OF BRITAIN £6.99
Recommended **COUNTRY INNS & PUBS** OF BRITAIN £6.99
Recommended **SHORT BREAK HOLIDAYS** IN BRITAIN £6.99

FHG PUBLICATIONS LTD,
Abbey Mill Business Centre,
Seedhill, Paisley, Renfrewshire PA1 1TJ
Tel: 0141-887 0428 • Fax: 0141-889 7204
e-mail: fhg@ipcmedia.com
website: www.holidayguides.com

DEVON

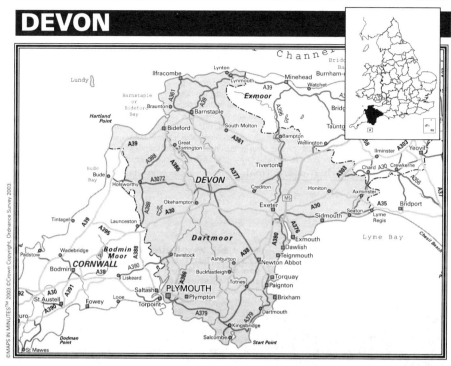

ASHBURTON

Mr and Mrs Richards, Gages Mill, Buckfastleigh Road, Ashburton TQ13 7JW (Tel & Fax: 01364 652391). Relax in the warm and friendly atmosphere of our lovely 14th century former wool mill, set in over an acre of gardens on the edge of the Dartmoor National Park. Eight delightful en suite rooms, one on the ground floor; all with tea and coffee making facilities, central heating, hairdryers, radio and alarm clocks. We have a large comfortable lounge with corner bar and granite archways leading to the dining room and a cosy sittingroom with colour TV. Home cooking of a very high standard. Licensed. Ample car parking. Being one mile from the centre of Ashburton, this is an ideal base for touring South Devon or visiting Exeter, Plymouth, Dartmouth, the many National Trust properties and other places of interest. Children over 12 years welcome. Sorry no pets. Bed, Breakfast and Evening Meal or Bed and Breakfast only. **ETC/AA ◆◆◆◆, ETC** *SILVER AWARD FOR EXCELLENCE.*

Admit one child FREE with each paying adult at

The Big Sheep

see our READERS' OFFER VOUCHERS for full details

One FREE child with full paying adult at

The Gnome Reserve & Wild Flower Garden

see our READERS' OFFER VOUCHERS for full details

Harton Farm
Oakford, Tiverton EX16 9HH (01398 351209)

Come and enjoy a unique rural experience on our traditional non-intensive working farm near Exmoor; peace and quiet for adults, and for the children, a chance to meet the animals. 17th Century stone farmhouse, secluded but accessible, ideal touring centre. Comfortable accommodation in three double bedrooms with washbasin and tea making facilities; luxury bathroom with a view; dining room serving real country cooking with farm-produced additive-free meat and organic vegetables; home baking a speciality; guests' lounge with colour TV. Home spun wool. Garden. Children over four welcome. Pets accepted. Car essential - parking. Open for Evening Meal, Bed and Breakfast from £26; Bed and Breakfast from £18. Reductions for children. Farm walks. Fishing, shooting, riding can be arranged. Vegetarian meals available on request.

e-mail: lindy@HARTONFARM.co.uk   web: www.hartonfarm.co.uk

See also Colour Advertisement

BARNSTAPLE (near)
Mrs J. Ley, West Barton, Alverdiscott, Near Barnstaple EX31 3PT (Tel & Fax: 01271 858230). Our family-run working farm of 240 acres, with a pedigree herd of suckler cows and sheep, is situated in a small rural village between Barnstaple and Torrington on the B3232. It is an ideal base for your holiday, within easy reach of Exmoor and many sandy beaches on our rugged coastline; also near RHS Rosemoor Gardens, Dartington Glass, the Tarka Trail, golf courses and many beauty spots. Comfortable accommodation with family room, twin beds, single and double rooms available. Guest lounge with TV and tea/coffee making facilities. Good farmhouse cooking including a variety of our own produce when available. Ample parking. Sorry, no pets. No smoking. B&B from £18, Evening Meal optional. Reduced rates for children under 12; weekly terms on request.

BIDEFORD (near Clovelly)
Mrs Yvonne Heard, West Titchberry Farm, Hartland Point, Near Bideford EX39 6AU (Tel & Fax: 01237 441287). Situated on the rugged North Devon coast, West Titchberry is a traditionally run stock farm, half a mile from Hartland Point. The South West Coastal Path skirts around the farm making it an ideal base for walkers. The three guest rooms comprise an en suite family room; one double and one twin room both having wash basins. All rooms have colour TV, radio, hairdryer, tea/coffee making facilities; bathroom/toilet and separate shower room on the same floor. Outside, guests may take advantage of a sheltered walled garden and a games room for the children. Hartland village is three miles away, Clovelly six miles, Bideford and Westward Ho! sixteen miles and Bude eighteen miles. Bed and Breakfast from £20 pppn. Evening meal £10. Children welcome at reduced rates for under 12s. Open all year except Christmas. Sorry, no pets.

BRAUNTON
Mrs Roselyn Bradford, "St Merryn", Higher Park Road, Braunton EX33 2LG (01271 813805). Set in a beautiful, sheltered garden of approximately one acre, with many peaceful sun traps to sit and relax. Open all year. Ros extends a warm welcome to all her guests. Accommodation (£20–£25 per person) includes single, double and family rooms, all en suite or with private bathroom. All rooms non-smoking, centrally heated, with colour TV and tea/coffee facilities. Guest lounge with books, games, colour TV/video/DVD. Swimming pool, fish ponds, hens and thatched summerhouse, barbecue facilities. Excellent parking.
e-mail: Ros@st-merryn.co.uk
website: www.st-merryn.co.uk

COLYTON

Mrs Ruth Gould, Bonehayne Farm, Colyton EX24 6SG. (01404 871396). Working farm. Bonehayne Farm, situated in beautiful Coly Valley, set amidst 250 acres dairy farmland on banks of the River Coly, where daffodils are a feature in springtime, and Mallard duck and Kingfishers are a common sight. Trout fishing freely available. Woodlands to explore. Visitors welcome to participate in some farm activities and make friends with the animals. One family, one double bedroom, with washbasins; bathroom, toilet. Spacious, homely lounge with inglenook fireplace, TV. A good English breakfast. Lawn and play area for children with extended large lawn overlooking surrounding countryside. Reduced rates, cot, high chair. Parking. Farway Country Park, riding school, Honiton Golf Course, coastal area, all within four-and-a-half miles. Open April to October. Bed and Breakfast; Evening Meal optional. Terms on request.
e-mail: gouldrl@hotmail.com
website: www.bonehayne.co.uk

COLYTON

Mrs Norma Rich, Sunnyacre, Rockerhayne Farm, Northleigh, Colyton EX24 6DA (01404 871422). Working farm, join in. A warm and friendly welcome awaits you. Come and enjoy a relaxing holiday on our working farm, which is set in an Area of Outstanding Natural Beauty amongst the rolling hills of East Devon. Local villages include the fishing village of Beer and picturesque Branscombe. If you enjoy walking, there are plenty of country walks and we are close to the coastal footpaths. There is a Full English Breakfast. Fresh and mainly homegrown produce is used to make excellent and varied Evening Meals. Sweets are all homemade. Early morning tea. Evening drinks. Three bedrooms with washbasin, separate w.c. TV in lounge, games room, sun room, Wendy house, sandpit. Cot and high chair available. Please enquire for reasonable rates.

CREDITON

Mrs M Reed, Hayne Farm, Cheriton Fitzpaine, Crediton EX17 4HR (01363 866392). Guests are welcome to our 17th century working beef and sheep farm, situated between Cadeleigh and Cheriton Fitzpaine. Exeter nine miles, Tiverton eight miles. South and North coast, Exmoor and Dartmoor within easy reach. Three local pubs nearby. Good farm fayre. Fishing lake; summer house overlooking duck pond. Bed and Breakfast from £20, reduction for children.

EXETER

Mrs Sally Glanvill, Rydon Farm, Woodbury, Exeter EX5 1LB (01395 232341). Working farm. Guests return time and time again to our delightful 16th century Devon longhouse. We offer a warm and friendly family welcome at this peaceful dairy farm. Three miles from M5 Junction 30 on B3179. Ideally situated for exploring the coast, moors and the historic city of Exeter. Only 10 minutes' drive from the coast. Inglenook fireplace and oak beams. All bedrooms have central heating, private or en suite bathrooms, hair dryers and tea/coffee making facilities. One room with romantic four-poster. A traditional farmhouse breakfast is served with free range eggs and there are several excellent pubs and restaurants close by. Pets by arrangement. Open all year. Highly recommended. Bed and Breakfast from £26 to £35. **ETC/AA** ♦♦♦♦, *FARM STAY UK MEMBER.*

World of Country Life • *Exmouth, Devon* • *01395 274533*
website: www.worldofcountrylife.co.uk
All-weather attraction with Victorian street, vintage cars, indoor play area, pets centre, safari deer train, plus lots more. Something for all the family!

EXETER
Karen Williams, Stile Farm, Starcross, Exeter EX6 8PD (Tel & Fax: 01626 890268). Enjoy a peaceful break in beautiful countryside. Close to the Exe Estuary and only two miles to the nearest sandy beach. Take a stroll to the village (only half a mile) to discover many eating places, or a little further to some specially recommended ones. Birdwatching, golf, fishing, racing, etc. all nearby, and centrally situated for exploring all the lovely countryside and coastline in the area. Good shopping in Exeter. Comfortable rooms, guests' lounge, English breakfast. Nice garden. Plenty of parking. NON-SMOKING. Personal service and a 'home from home' atmosphere. Bed and Breakfast from £20 per person per night.
website: www.stile-farm.co.uk

EXETER
Mrs Dudley, Culm Vale Guest House, Stoke Canon, Exeter EX5 4EG (Tel & Fax: 01392 841615; mobile: 07855 481765). A fine old country house of great charm and character, giving the best of both worlds as we are only three miles to the north of the Cathedral city of Exeter, with its antique shops, yet situated in the heart of Devon's beautiful countryside on the edge of the pretty village of Stoke Canon. An ideal touring centre. Our spacious comfortable Bed and Breakfast accommodation includes full English breakfast, colour TV, tea/coffee facilities, washbasin and razor point in all rooms, some with bathrooms en suite. Full central heating. There is ample free parking. Bed and Breakfast £19 to £35pppn according to room and season. Credit cards accepted. **ETC ♦♦♦, AA** *THREE RED DIAMONDS*.

EXMOUTH
Devoncourt Hotel, Douglas Avenue, Exmouth EX8 2EX (01395 272277; Fax: 01395 269315). Standing in four acres of mature subtropical gardens, overlooking two miles of sandy beach, yet within easy reach of Dartmoor and Exeter, Devoncourt provides an ideal base for a family holiday. Single, double and family suites, all en suite, well furnished and well equipped; attractive lounge bar and restaurant. Recreational facilities include indoor and outdoor heated pools, sauna, steam room, spa and solarium; snooker room; putting, tennis and croquet; golf, sea fishing and horse riding nearby. Bed and Breakfast from £70 single, £105 double; Self-catering /room only from £55 single, £80 double. Weekly rates available.

GREAT TORRINGTON
Mrs Beryl Heard, Furze Farm Bed and Breakfast, Great Torrington EX38 7HA (01805 623360). A warm welcome is assured at this homely, long established B&B situated one and a half miles from the historic town of Great Torrington. Lovely old character farmhouse with spacious en suite rooms in the heart of Tarka country. Accommodation consists of two double, one family room all with private facilities, TV and tea tray. A hearty breakfast with home-baked bread is provided. Ideal location for RHS Rosemoor Gardens and the Tarka Trail, popular with cyclists and walkers. Cycle hire nearby. Clovelly, Atlantic Village Designer Outlet, Westward Ho!, Instow and Appledore are a short drive away. Bideford, Barnstaple and Holsworthy are within thirty minutes' drive. Dartmoor and Exmoor within easy reach. Non-smoking establishment. B&B £44 double, £25 single.
e-mail: beryl@furze-farm.co.uk

The FHG Directory of Website Addresses
on pages 345 - 373 is a useful quick reference guide for holiday accommodation with e-mail and/or website details

ENGLAND / Board   Devon **123**

HARTLAND
Mrs A. Heard, Greenlake Farm, Hartland, Bideford EX39 6DN (01237 441251). Greenlake is a mixed farm set in approximately 250 acres of unspoilt countryside, just two miles from Hartland on the North Devon coast. While the farmhouse retains its original character with features such as oak beams in some of the rooms, it also offers every facility for your comfort. Some accommodation offers en suite facilities, while all rooms have fitted carpets, TV and tea/coffee equipment. There is a television lounge and a separate dining room. Guests are welcome to watch the farm work in progress. Ideally situated for touring North Devon and North Cornwall; the popular sandy beaches of Bude and Westward Ho! are only a short drive away, as are the market towns of Bideford and Holsworthy.

HONITON/TAUNTON
Mrs Elizabeth Tucker, Lower Luxton Farm, Upottery, Honiton EX14 9PB (01823 601269). Working farm. If you are looking for a quiet, peaceful and relaxing holiday, come to Lower Luxton Farm, where a warm and friendly welcome awaits you. Situated in an area of outstanding natural beauty in the centre of the Blackdown Hills, overlooking the Otter Valley. Ideal centre for touring. Carp and tench fishing in our farm pond. Olde worlde farmhouse with inglenook and beams, fully modernised and offering family, double or twin rooms with tea/coffee making facilities, TV, en suite/private bathroom. Good home cooking assured and plenty of it! Bed and Breakfast from £18 per night. Weekly Bed and Breakfast with six Evening Dinners from £140 per week. Children and pets welcome. Open all year. SAE, or telephone, for our brochure.

ILFRACOMBE
Alison and Adrian Homa, Mullacott Farm, Mullacott Cross, Ilfracombe EX34 8NA (01271 866877). Stay on a family-run working farm in the recently converted barn adjacent to the farmhouse. We have many friendly animals to see. It is an ideal base for the beach, walking and riding. All the tastefully decorated rooms have beamed ceilings, with en suite facilities, colour TV and hospitality tray. Ground floor rooms are available. Guests are given their own key. A scrumptious home-produced breakfast, including home-made bread and preserves, our own sausages, bacon and free-range eggs, complements the very high standards of cleanliness and comfort to be found at Mullacott Farm. Children are welcome. Non-smoking. Bed and Breakfast from £25 per person. Special offers available.

IVYBRIDGE
Mrs P. Stephens, Venn Farm, Ugborough, Ivybridge PL21 0PE (01364 73240). Working farm. Enjoy a rural retreat at Venn, yet only three miles from dual carriageway. We are 20 minutes from beaches and South Dartmoor is visible from the farm. We have two family bedrooms, and a separate garden cottage which has two twin ground floor bedrooms overlooking a large pond. We also have self-catering for eight, four and two persons, again with ground floor bedrooms. Brochure on request from: **Pat Stephens (01364 73240). ETC ♦♦♦ (★★★★ *SELF-CATERING), DISABLED CATEGORY 2 ACCESSIBILITY.*
website: www.SmoothHound.co.uk/hotels/vennfarm**

*When making enquiries or bookings,
a stamped addressed envelope is always appreciated*

IVYBRIDGE (near)

Mrs Susan Winzer, Higher Coarsewell Farm, Ugborough, Near Ivybridge PL21 0HP (01548 821560). Working farm. Higher Coarsewell Farm is part of a traditional family-run dairy farm situated in the heart of the peaceful South Hams countryside, near Dartmoor and local unspoilt sandy beaches. It is a very spacious bungalow with beautiful garden and meadow views. One double room with bathroom en suite and one en suite family room. Guest lounge/dining room. Good home cooked food, full English breakfast served. Children welcome - cot, high chair and babysitting available. Bed and Breakfast from £18 daily; optional Evening Meal extra. Open all year. A3121 turn-off from the main A38 Exeter to Plymouth road.
e-mail: susan_winzer@hotmail.com

KINGSBRIDGE

Mrs Angela Foale, Higher Kellaton Farm, Kellaton, Kingsbridge TQ7 2ES (Tel & Fax: 01548 511514). Working farm. Smell the fresh sea air and enjoy the delicious Aga-cooked breakfast in the comfort of this lovely old farmhouse. Nestled in a valley, our farm with friendly animals welcomes you. Spacious, well-furnished rooms, en suite, colour TVs, tea/coffee making facilities, own lounge, central heating and log fires. Flexible meal times. Attractive walled garden. Safe car parking. Situated between Kingsbridge and Dartmouth. Visit Salcombe by ferry. One-and-a-half miles to the lost village of Hallsands and Lannacombe Beach. Beautiful, peaceful, unspoilt coastline with many sandy beaches, paths, wild flowers and wildlife. Ramblers' haven. Good pubs and wet-weather family attractions. Open Easter to October. Non-smoking. Bed and Breakfast from £20. ETC ◆◆◆
e-mail: higherkellatonfarm@agriplus.net   website: www.welcome.to/higherkellaton

KINGSBRIDGE

Mrs B. Kelly, Blackwell Park, Loddiswell,Kingsbridge TQ7 4EA (01548 821230). Bed and Breakfast and optional Evening Meal is offered at Blackwell Park, a 17th century farmhouse situated five miles from Kingsbridge. Seven bedrooms, some en suite, and all with washbasins and tea-making facilities. Games room; large garden, also adjoining 54 acres of woodland/nature reserve. Ample food with a choice of menu. CHILDREN AND PETS ESPECIALLY WELCOME; babysitting, dogsitting. Pets welcome FREE of charge. Dartmoor, Plymouth, Torbay, Dartmouth and many beaches lie within easy reach.

KINGSBRIDGE

Mrs M. Darke, Coleridge Farm, Chillington, Kingsbridge TQ7 2JG (01548 580274). Coleridge Farm is a 600 acre working farm situated half-a-mile from Chillington village, midway between Kingsbridge and Dartmouth. Many safe and beautiful beaches are within easy reach, the nearest being Slapton Sands and Slapton Ley just two miles away. Plymouth, Torquay and the Dartmoor National Park are only an hour's drive. Visitors are assured of comfortable accommodation in a choice of one double and one twin-bedded rooms; private shower; toilet; shaver points and tea/coffee making facilities. Spacious lounge with TV. A variety of eating establishments in the locality will ensure a good value evening meal. Children welcome. Small dogs by arrangement. Terms on request.

TWO Adult tickets for the price of one at
Coldharbour Mill Visitor Centre & Museum
see our READERS' OFFER VOUCHERS for full details

ENGLAND / Board   Devon **125**

Lifton Hall Hotel   Lifton, Devon PL16 0DR   ETC/AA ★★
Tel: 01566 784863 • Fax: 01566 784770 • relax@liftonhall.co.uk • www.liftonhall.co.uk

A 300-year old manor house where old-fashioned values of service, style and comfort can still be enjoyed. On the Devon/Cornwall border, ½ mile off the A30, it offers the perfect opportunity to explore the West Country. The 9 tastefully furnished bedrooms (including 3 superior rooms) have en suite bath or shower and a full range of amenities; there is also a light and airy residents' lounge, a stylish dining room and a cosy bar. Meals are an essential part of the Lifton Hall experience, with something to suit every taste and appetite, using only the best quality local produce. A carefully chosen and reasonably priced wine list provides the perfect accompaniment.

Owners Andrew and Glenys Brown extend an invitation to you to experience the charm and beauty of the area whilst enjoying their unique hospitality and personal service at Lifton Hall.

See also Colour Advertisement

See also Colour Display Advertisement

KINGSBRIDGE
Anne Rossiter, Burton Farm, Galmpton, Kingsbridge TQ7 3EY (01548 561210). Working farm in South Huish Valley, one mile from the fishing village of Hope Cove, three miles from famous sailing haunt of Salcombe. Walking, beaches, sailing, windsurfing, bathing, diving, fishing, horse-riding – facilities for all in this area. We have a dairy herd and two flocks of pedigree sheep. Guests are welcome to take part in farm activities when appropriate. Traditional farmhouse cooking and home produce. Country restaurant on site serving freshly cooked meals using local produce. Lunches, cream teas, dinner, children's meals. Access to rooms at all times. Tea/ coffee making facilities and TV in rooms, all of which are en suite. Games room. Non-smoking. Open all year, except Christmas. Warm welcome assured. Self-catering cottages also available. Dogs by arrangement. Details and terms on request. Bed and Breakfast from £30 to £35 per person. **ETC ♦♦♦♦** *SILVER AWARD.*
e-mail: anne@burtonfarm.co.uk   website: www.burtonfarm.co.uk

KINGSBRIDGE (near)
Mrs M. Newsham, Marsh Mills, Aveton Gifford, Kingsbridge TQ7 4JW (Tel & Fax: 01548 550549). Georgian Mill House, overlooking the River Avon, with mill pond, mill leat and duck pond. Small farm with friendly animals. Peaceful and secluded, just off A379, Kingsbridge four miles, Plymouth 17 miles. Bigbury and Bantham with their beautiful sandy beaches nearby, or enjoy a walk along our unspoilt river estuary, or the miles of beautiful South Devon coastal paths. We are only eight miles from Dartmoor. One double and one double/twin room, both en suite; other rooms have washbasin, and there is a guest bathroom with additional separate WC. All bedrooms have tea/coffee making facilities, colour TV and room heaters. Guests have their own lounge/dining room with colour TV. Beautiful gardens, ample car parking. Bed and Breakfast from £20 per night. Phone, fax or SAE for brochure or enquiries.
e-mail: newsham@marshmills.co.uk   website: www.marshmills.co.uk

LYNMOUTH
Tricia and Alan Francis, Glenville House, 2 Tors Road, Lynmouth EX35 6ET (01598 752202). Idyllic riverside setting for our delightful Victorian house built in local stone, full of character and lovingly refurbished, at the entrance to the Watersmeet Valley. Award-winning garden. Picturesque village, enchanting harbour and unique water-powered cliff railway nestled amidst wooded valleys. Beautiful area where Exmoor meets the sea. Breathtaking scenery, spectacular views to the heather-clad moorland. Peaceful, tranquil, romantic - a very special place. Tastefully decorated bedrooms, most with pretty en suites. Elegant lounge overlooking river. Enjoy a four-course breakfast in our attractive dining room. Non-smoking. Licensed. Bed and Breakfast from £25 per person per night. **AA ♦♦♦♦**
e-mail: tricia@glenvillelynmouth.co.uk   website: glenvillelynmouth.co.uk

LYNMOUTH

Rock House, Lynmouth EX35 6EN (01598 753508; Fax: 01598 753472). Share the magic of living at the water's edge in a Grade II Listed building which stands alone at the harbour entrance. Offering peace and tranquillity, it is the perfect place to relax. All rooms have sea views, are centrally heated, en suite, with TV, hairdryer, alarm clock and tea/coffee making facilities. Fresh ingredients used in all meals; vegetarian and special diets catered for. Superb wine list. Fully licensed bar. Putting, tennis and numerous woodland, coastal and riverside walks nearby. Explore the Heritage Coast by boat; ideal for birdwatching. Visit the Valley of Rocks and Doone Valley; the heart of Exmoor is only a short journey away by car or bus.
e-mail: enquiries@rock-house.co.uk
website: www.rock-house.co.uk

LYNTON

Cliff Bench, Valley House, Lynbridge Road, Lynton EX35 6BD (01598 752285). A secluded Victorian country house, five minutes' walk from Lynton. Set into the rock face high above the West Lyn River, with magnificent views of the National Trust Woodland and sea. All rooms are stylishly decorated, en suite with tea/coffee making facilities, hairdryer, colour TV and beautiful views. Interesting breakfast menu; scrumptious evening meals most days; packed lunches available. Relax in the bar/lounge, the new conservatory room or the front terrace. A walkers' paradise, with some of the best horse riding in the country; also golf and surfing. Rates from £20 pppn. RAC ◆◆◆◆
e-mail: info@valley-house.co.uk
website: www.valley-house.co.uk

See also Colour Display Advertisement

MORETONHAMPSTEAD

Mrs T. M. Merchant, Great Sloncombe Farm, Moretonhampstead TQ13 8QF (01647 440595). Working farm. Share the magic of Dartmoor all year round while staying in our lovely 13th century farmhouse full of interesting historical features. A working mixed farm set amongst peaceful meadows and woodland abundant in wild flowers and animals, including badgers, foxes, deer and buzzards. A welcoming and informal place to relax and explore the moors and Devon countryside. Comfortable double and twin rooms with en suite facilities, TV, central heating and coffee/tea making facilities. Delicious Devonshire suppers and breakfasts with new baked bread. Open all year. No smoking. **ETC** ◆◆◆◆ *SILVER AWARD*, **AA** ◆◆◆◆, *FARM STAY UK MEMBER*.
e-mail: hmerchant@sloncombe.freeserve.co.uk
website: www.greatsloncombefarm.co.uk

OTTERTON

Mrs E.J. Earl, Ropers Cottage, Ropers Lane, Otterton, Budleigh Salterton EX9 7JF (01395 568826; Fax: 01395 568206). In the centre of Otterton, a picturesque village close to the coast, Ropers Cottage waits to welcome you. A quiet retreat to explore East Devon's gentle pleasures, riverside walks, the coastal path, beaches, heathland and never far away, Exeter, the county town, and the seaside resorts of Sidmouth, Exmouth and Budleigh Salterton. Guests have a separate entrance. The dining room has separate tables. There is one double and one single en suite room, both with TV, tea/coffee making facilities and shaver point. Secure off-road parking. Full English Breakfast is served. Snacks and evening meals are available at the King's Arms in the village.

Terms quoted in this publication may be subject to increase if rises in costs necessitate

ENGLAND / Board   Devon 127

PLYMOUTH

Mrs Margaret MacBean, Gabber Farm, Down Thomas, Plymouth PL9 0AW (01752 862269). Working farm. Come and join us on this 120 acre working farm in an Area of Outstanding Natural Beauty with lovely walks on the farm and coast. It is ideally situated for touring and near the historic city of Plymouth. Good food and a warm welcome are assured with Bed and Breakfast or Bed, Breakfast and Evening Meal available. One double and one family room en suite, one single, one twin and one family room with washbasins. All have tea/coffee making facilities, TV and clock radio. Iron, ironing board, hairdryer available. TV lounge, dining room. Fire Certificate. Bed and Breakfast from £18 to £20. Special rates for Senior Citizens and children. Brochure available on request.

See also Colour Display Advertisement

SALCOMBE

Sand Pebbles Hotel & Restaurant, Hope Cove TQ7 3HF (01548 561673). Sand Pebbles stands in its own grounds with twelve en suite rooms overlooking the sea or countryside with colour televisions, radios and beverage trays. Our lovely restaurant overlooks open countryside and has an enviable reputation for serving superb food. We are just 300 yards from one of the safe, sandy beaches that Hope Cove is renowned for, and the coastal walks which give some of the most spectacular views in the south west. Hope Cove has a timeless quality all of its own and is one of England's most delightful places to retreat for a short break or a long holiday. There's nowhere else quite like it. Well-behaved children and dogs are welcome. Please call Steve or Lorraine for a brochure.
website: www.sandpebbleshotel.co.uk

SIDMOUTH

Mrs Elizabeth Tancock, Lower Pinn Farm, Peak Hill, Sidmouth EX10 0NN (01395 513733). Working farm. Lower Pinn is in an Area of Outstanding Natural Beauty, two miles west of the unspoilt coastal resort of Sidmouth and one mile to the east of the pretty village of Otterton. Comfortable, spacious en suite rooms with colour TV, hot drink facilities, electric blankets and central heating. Guests have their own keys and may return at all times throughout the day. Ample parking. Substantial breakfast served in dining room. Local inns and restaurants nearby provide excellent evening meals. Children and pets welcome. Open all year. Bed and Breakfast from £23 to £26. Full details on request. **ETC ♦♦♦♦**
e-mail: liz@lowerpinnfarm.co.uk
website: www.lowerpinnfarm.co.uk

SIDMOUTH

Mrs Betty S. Sage, Pinn Barton, Peak Hill, Sidmouth EX10 0NN (Tel & Fax: 01395 514004). A 330-acre farm set peacefully just off the coastal road, two miles from Sidmouth and close to the village of Otterton. Safe beaches and lovely cliff walks. Pinn Barton has been highly recommended, and offers a warm welcome in comfortable surroundings with good farmhouse breakfast. All bedrooms have bathrooms en suite; fridge; colour TV; central heating; free hot drinks facilities, electric blankets. Children very welcome. Reductions for children sharing parents' room. Open all year. Bed and Breakfast including bedtime drink from £22 to £24. Own keys provided for access at all times. **ETC ♦♦♦♦** *SILVER AWARD.*
website: www.pinnbartonfarm.co.uk

FREE or REDUCED RATE entry to Holiday Visits and Attractions – see our READERS' OFFER VOUCHERS on pages 67 - 94

SOUTH MOLTON (near)

Hazel Milton, Partridge Arms Farm, Yeo Mill, West Anstey EX36 3NU (01398 341217; Fax: 01398 341569). Now a working farm of over 200 acres, four miles west of Dulverton, "Partridge Arms Farm" was once a coaching inn and has been in the same family since 1906. Genuine hospitality and traditional farmhouse fare await you. Comfortable accommodation in double, twin and single rooms, some of which have en suite facilities. There is also an original four-poster bedroom. Children welcome. Animals by arrangement. Residential licence. Open all year. Fishing and riding available nearby. Bed and Breakfast from £22 to £27; Evening Meal from £10.50. *FARM HOLIDAY GUIDE DIPLOMA WINNER.*
e-mail: bangermilton@yahoo.co.uk

TAVISTOCK

Hilary Tucker, Beera Farm, Milton Abbot, Tavistock PL19 8PL (Tel & Fax: 01822 870216). Beera is situated on a working farm in the heart of the peaceful Tamar valley, with beautiful panoramic views over the Devon/Cornwall border. It provides an ideal base for touring the West Country, with the Eden Project, Lost Gardens of Heligan, Dartmoor, National Trust properties, Morwellham Quay and the historic towns of Launceston and Tavistock all within easy reach. Excellent evening meals by prior arrangement using local and home-grown produce; packed lunches available. The rooms are well appointed and beautifully decorated, with Laura Ashley and Dorma furnishings. We have two doubles (one king-size four-poster) and one twin; all rooms en suite. Children welcome. Credit/debit cards accepted. Bed and Breakfast from £25 to £30; reductions for longer stays. Evening Meal from £14. **ETC ♦♦♦♦ *GOLD AWARD.***
e-mail: Hilary.Tucker@farming.co.uk
website: www.beera-farm.co.uk

TIVERTON

Mrs L. Arnold, The Mill, Lower Washfield, Tiverton EX16 9PD (01884 255297). A warm welcome awaits you at our newly converted mill, beautifully situated on the banks of the picturesque River Exe. Wonderful views to the National Trust's Knightshayes Court and on the route of the Exe Valley Way. Easy access to both the north and south coasts, Exmoor and Dartmoor. Only two-and-a-half miles from the market town of Tiverton. Relaxing and friendly atmosphere with delicious farmhouse fare. En suite bedrooms with TV and tea/coffee making facilities. Bed and Breakfast from £24.

TORQUAY

Aveland Hotel, Aveland Road, Babbacombe, Torquay TQ1 3PT (Tel/minicom: 01803 326622; Fax: 01803 328940). A warm and friendly welcome awaits you in this family-run licensed hotel. Set in a quiet, level location close to Cary Park, tennis courts and bowling green. Within easy walking distance of Babbacombe Downs with panoramic views across Lyme Bay, with "Blue Flag Beaches" ideal for swimming, watersport or just relaxing in the sun. All rooms are en suite with shower and tea/coffee making facilities. There are two comfortable TV lounges as well as a cosy bar to relax in. Full central heating, car park and gardens. Family rooms available. Well-behaved children welcome. Ideal location to explore the many local attractions, the South West Coastal Walks and Dartmoor National Park. Rates from £20 to £26 B&B pppn. All major credit/debit cards accepted. TCHA recommended. Sign Language OCSL stage one. **AA ♦♦♦♦ *WELCOME HOST AND COMMITMENT TO QUALITY AWARDS.***
e-mail: avelandhotel@aol.com
website: www.avelandhotel.co.uk

Quince Honey Farm • *South Molton, Devon* • *01769 572401*
website: www.quincehoney.co.uk
The world's largest living honey bee exhibition, where the hives can be viewed in complete safety. Ideal for all ages, with fascinating videos and well-stocked shop.

ENGLAND / Board   Dorset 129

DORSET

BLANDFORD FORUM

Mrs C.M.Old, Manor House Farm, Ibberton, Blandford Forum DT11 0EN (01258 817349). Working farm, dairy and sheep. Situated nine miles west of Blandford Forum. Small 16th century manor house, now a farmhouse, surrounded by large colourful garden in a quiet unspoilt village which at one time was given to Katherine Howard by Henry VIII. The oak beams and nail studded doors confirm its centuries-old past. One double bedroom, one double or twin (both en suite), and one twin bedroom (separate bathroom); all with tea making facilities. Bathroom and toilet; lounge with TV, diningroom with separate tables. Children welcome, cot and high chair provided. Bed and Breakfast from £17 to £20. Open all year. No evening meal. Good food at Crown Inn nearby. Self catering accommodation also available.

See also Colour Display Advertisement

BRIDPORT

Jane Greening, New House Farm, Mangerton Lane, Bradpole, Bridport DT6 3SF (Tel & Fax: 01308 422884). Stay in a modern, comfortable farmhouse on a small working farm set in the rural Dorset hills and become one of the family. A large wild garden where you are welcome to sit or stroll round. Two large rooms available, both en suite, both with lovely views over the surrounding countryside, both with television and tea/coffee making facilities. We are near to Bridport and the seaside, golf courses, fossil hunting, beautiful gardens, wonderful walking, coarse fishing lake – lots to do. Simple traditional farmhouse evening meals can be provided, subject to booking. Bed and Breakfast from £25. **ETC/AA ◆◆◆ FARM STAY UK MEMBER, WELCOME HOST.**

e-mail: jane@mangertonlake.freeserve.co.uk   website: www.mangertonlake.co.uk

130 Dorset   Board / ENGLAND

BRIDPORT (near)

Mrs Sue Norman, Frogmore Farm, Chideock, Bridport DT6 6HT (01308 456159). Working farm. Set in the rolling hills of West Dorset, enjoying splendid sea views, our delightful 17th century farmhouse offers comfortable, friendly and relaxing accommodation. An ideal base from which to ramble the many coastal and country footpaths of the area (nearest beach Seatown one-and-a-half miles) or tour by car the interesting places of Dorset and Devon. Bedrooms with en suite shower rooms, TV and tea making facilities. Guests' dining room and cosy lounge with woodburner. Well behaved dogs welcome. Open all year; car essential. Bed and Breakfast from £18. Brochure and terms free on request.

CERNE ABBAS

Mrs T. Barraclough, Magiston Farm, Sydling St Nicholas, Dorchester DT2 9NR (01300 320295). Working farm. Magiston is a 400 acre working farm with a comfortable 17th century cob and brick farmhouse set deep in the heart of Dorset. Large garden with river. Half-an-hour's drive from coast and five miles north of Dorchester. The farmhouse comprises double, twin and single bedrooms including a twin on the ground floor. Delicious evening meals served. Children over 10 years and pets welcome. Central heating. Open January to December. Bed and Breakfast from £20 per person per night. Evening Meal, three courses £12.00. Please write or telephone for further details. **ETC** ♦♦♦

CHARMOUTH

Mrs S. M. Johnson, Cardsmill Farm, Whitchurch Canonicorum, Charmouth, Bridport DT6 6RP (Tel & Fax: 01297 489375). Working farm, join in. A Grade II Listed comfortable quiet farmhouse in the picturesque Marshwood Vale, three miles from Charmouth. Ideal location for touring, safe beaches, fossil hunting, golf and walking the coastal path. See the farm animals, pets and crops. Family and double en suite rooms available, each with CTV, shaver points, tea/coffee trays. Cot available. Full central heating and double glazed windows throughout. Lounge with Inglenook fireplace, woodburning stove, oak beams, colour TV, games and books. Dining area with separate tables. English and varied breakfasts. Access at all times. Children and well behaved pets welcome. Large garden with patio, picnic table and seats. Bed and Breakfast from £22 to £27 per person per night. Open February till end of November. Brochure available. Also three self-catering farmhouses to sleep 12–12/14 and 16 plus cots, for long or short stays all year. **ETC** ♦♦♦
e-mail: cardsmill@aol.com   website: www.farmhousedorset.com

DORCHESTER

Mrs V.A. Bradbeer, Nethercroft, Winterbourne Abbas, Dorchester DT2 9LU (01305 889337). This country house with its friendly and homely atmosphere welcomes you to the heart of Hardy's Wessex. Central for touring the many places of interest that Dorset has to offer, including Corfe Castle, Lyme Regis, Dorchester, Weymouth, Lulworth Cove, etc. Lovely country walks and many local attractions. Two double rooms, one single, en suite or separate bathroom. TV lounge, dining room. Large garden. Open all year. Central heating. Car essential, ample parking. Bed and Breakfast from £18. Take A35 from Dorchester, we are the last house at the western edge of the village.
e-mail: v.bradbeer@ukonline.co.uk

A useful index of towns and counties appears at the back of this book on pages 375 - 378. Refer also to Contents Pages 2 and 3.

ENGLAND / Bo...

See also Colour Display Advertisement

Mrs Anita Millorit, Brambles, Wool.., Dorchester DT2 0NJ (01935 83672). countryside, Brambles is a pretty, thatched comfort, superb views and a friendly welco.. of en suite twin, double or single rooms, all v.. with colour TV and tea/coffee making facilit.. available for relaxing in. Full English or Cont.. served. Evening meals available by prior arrange.. ..e are many interesting places to visit and wonde.. walks for enthusiasts. B&B £27 per person.

DORCHESTER (near)

Michael and Jane Deller, Churchview Guest House, Winterbourne Abbas, Near Dorchester DT2 9LS (Tel & Fax: 01305 889296). Our 17th century Guest House, noted for warm hospitality and delicious breakfasts and evening meals, makes an ideal base for touring beautiful West Dorset. Our character bedrooms are all comfortable and well appointed. Meals, served in our beautiful diningroom, feature local produce, with relaxation provided by two attractive lounges and licensed bar. Your hosts Jane and Michael Deller are pleased to give every assistance with local information to ensure a memorable stay. NON SMOKING. Terms: Dinner, Bed and Breakfast £41 to £52; Bed and Breakfast £27 to £37. Short Breaks available, please call for further details. ETC/AA ♦♦♦♦
e-mail: stay@churchview.co.uk
website: www.churchview.co.uk

See also Colour Display Advertisement

FURZEHILL

Mrs King, Stocks Farm, Furzehill, Wimborne BH21 4HT (Tel & Fax: 01202 888697). Stocks Farm is a family-run farm and nursery situated in peaceful countryside just one-and-half miles from the lovely country town of Wimborne Minster, off the B3078. Surrounded by lovely Dorset countryside and pretty villages; coastline, beaches and New Forest within easy reach. Bed and Breakfast accommodation consists of one double en suite bedroom and one twin bedroom with private bathroom, both on ground level. Disabled guests are very welcome. Tea and coffee making facilities in both rooms. All accommodation is non-smoking. Situated in secluded garden with patio for guests to enjoy breakfast outside. Local pubs and restaurants offer varied menus. Bed and Breakfast from £20 per person per night.

See also Colour Display Advertisement

POOLE

Mrs Stephenson, Holly Hedge Farm, Bulbury Lane, Lytchett Matravers, Poole BH16 6EP (01929 459688). Built in 1892, Holly Hedge Farm is situated next to Bulbury Woods Golf Course, set in 11 acres of wood and grassland adjacent to lake. We are just 15 minutes away from the Purbecks, the beach and the forest. The area is ideal for walking or cycling and Poole Quay and Harbour are also nearby. Accommodation comprises two double/family rooms, one twin and one single, all with en suite showers, colour TV, tea/coffee making facilities, radio alarms and central heating. Prices for a single room £30, double £52 per night. Open all year round for summer or winter breaks. Full English or Continental breakfast served.

Sherborne Castle • *Sherborne, Dorset* • *01935 813182*
website: www.sherbornecastle.com
Built by Sir Walter Raleigh in 1594 and home to the Digby family since the early 17th century. Splendid collection of art, furniture and porcelain.

Board / ENGLAND

Fyrnhams • Sheila and David Taylor

A spacious and non-smoking guesthouse, in quiet and unspoilt surroundings with gardens and grounds of about seven acres, with lovely views. Situated about three miles from Lyme Regis and Charmouth, ideal for touring, beaches, fishing, golf course and fossil hunting. Private parking. Access to house all day. A warm and friendly welcome awaits in a real home from home. Excellent accommodation in a comfortable, and well furnished bungalow with one double room with en suite bathroom, one double room with king size and single bed with private facilities, bathroom including a shower. All rooms have CTV, tea/coffee making facilities, clock/radio, hairdryer, towels, heating. Lounge with widescreen TV/ video, overlooks rear patio and gardens. Dining area – we serve a good English farmhouse breakfast. Nearby pub for evening meals. B&B from £20.

Raymonds Hill, Near Axminster EX13 5SZ
Tel/Fax: 01297 33222 or e-mail: sheilataylor@fyrnhams.fsnet.co.uk

PORTLAND
Alessandria Hotel, 71 Wakeham, Easton, Portland DT5 1HW (01305 822270/820108; Fax: 01305 820561). This former 18th century inn is situated in a quiet location. Comfortable accommodation, most rooms en suite, colour TV, tea/coffee. Ground floor rooms. Free parking. Children welcome. Bed and Breakfast at reasonable prices. Warm and friendly hospitality. ETC/AA/RAC ♦♦♦
website: www.s-h-systems.co.uk/hotels/alessand.html

See also Colour Display Advertisement

SHERBORNE
Mrs J. Mayo, Alms House Farm, Hermitage, Holnest, Sherborne DT9 6HA (Tel & Fax: 01963 210296). This charming old farmhouse was a monastery during the 16th century, restored in 1849 and is now a Listed building. A family-run working dairy farm, it is surrounded by 140 acres overlooking the Blackmoor Vale, just one mile off the A352. Accommodation is in three comfortable en suite rooms with colour TV and tea/coffee making facilities. Diningroom with inglenook fireplace, lounge with colour TV, for guests' use at all times. Also garden and lawn. Plenty of reading material and local information provided for this ideal touring area. Bed and Breakfast from £24. Excellent evening meals in all local inns nearby. Situated six miles from Sherborne with its beautiful Abbey and Castle. SAE for further details. **ETC/AA ♦♦♦♦, ETC GOLD AWARD.**

SHERBORNE
Mrs E. Kingman, Stowell Farm, Stowell, Near Sherborne DT9 4PE (01963 370200). A 15th century former Manor House that has retained some lovely historical features. Now a farmhouse on a family-run dairy and beef farm. It is in a beautiful rural location yet only five miles from the A303, two miles from A30 and two hours by train from London. An ideal place to relax and unwind, enjoy traditional home baking and a warm friendly atmosphere. Close to the abbey town of Sherborne, National Trust Properties and many other places of interest to suit all people. Accommodation – one twin room en suite, one double room with a private bathroom, lounge with colour TV and log fires. Bed and Breakfast from £22 to £25 per person per night, reductions for children under 10 years. AA ♦♦♦♦
e-mail: kingman@stowell-farm.freeserve.co.uk

**When making enquiries or bookings,
a stamped addressed envelope is always appreciated**

ENGLAND / Board   Dorset **133**

See also Colour Display Advertisement

SHILLINGSTONE
Mrs Rosie Watts, Pennhills Farm, Sandy Lane, off Lanchards Lane, Shillingstone, Blandford DT11 0TF (01258 860491). Pennhills Farmhouse set in 100 acres of unspoiled countryside, is situated one mile from the village of Shillingstone in the heart of the Blackmore Vale, an ideal peaceful retreat, short break or holiday. It offers spacious comfortable accommodation for all ages; children welcome, pets by arrangement. One downstairs bedroom. All bedrooms en suite with TV and tea/coffee making facilities, complemented by traditional English breakfast with home produced bacon and sausages. Vegetarians catered for. Good meals available locally. Brochure sent on request. A warm and friendly welcome is assured from your host Rosie Watts. From £22 per person per night.

STUDLAND
Mrs F. Higgins, The Old School House, School Lane, Studland BH19 3AJ (01929 450691). We offer a warm welcome and very comfortable en suite accommodation with country views. The Old School House is five minutes from the National Trust beaches and Downs. Lovely position with pub and hotel food five minutes' walk. Guests' own diningroom, and special diets catered for. TV and video in bedroom. Good for touring the Jurassic Coast or walking the South West Coastal Path. Cooking course available - January to March and September to November. Non-smoking. No pets. Open January to November.
ETC ♦♦♦
e-mail: tony.higgins@tesco.net
website: www.quarrcottage.co.uk

SWANAGE
Mrs Rosemary Dean, Quarr Farm, Valley Road, Swanage BH19 3DY (01929 480865). Quarr is a working family farm steeped in history dating back to the Domesday Book. Animals kept naturally – cows, calves, horses, poultry. Bring your children to feed ducks, chickens, peacocks and watch steam trains passing through our meadows. Accommodation in family room with en suite bathroom, own sitting room with colour TV, real log fire, tea making facilities. Two rooms with shared bathroom. Ideal for families, or friends wishing to holiday together. Cot available. Easy reach high class restaurants, pubs; sea three miles. Studland, sandy beach just five miles away. Ideal for walking, cycling, coastal path, RSPB Reserves, golf courses, riding. Bed and Breakfast. Please telephone for further details and terms

---

FHG
Other specialised **FHG PUBLICATIONS**
Published annually: available in all good bookshops or direct from the publisher.

PETS WELCOME! £7.99
Recommended **COUNTRY HOTELS** OF BRITAIN £6.99
Recommended **COUNTRY INNS & PUBS** OF BRITAIN £6.99
Recommended **SHORT BREAK HOLIDAYS** IN BRITAIN £6.99

**FHG Publications Ltd, Abbey Mill Business Centre, Seedhill, Paisley, Renfrewshire PA1 1TJ
Tel: 0141-887 0428 • Fax: 0141-889 7204**
e-mail: fhg@ipcmedia.com • website: www.holidayguides.com

134 Dorset   Board / ENGLAND

See also Colour Display Advertisement

SWANAGE

Mrs Justine Pike, Downshay Farm, Haycrafts Lane, Harmans Cross, Swanage BH19 3EB (01929 480316). Working dairy farm in the heart of beautiful Isle of Purbeck, midway between Corfe Castle and Swanage. This Victorian Purbeck stone farmhouse has a family room en suite and one double with private shower room close by. Both rooms have colour TV and tea/coffee making facilities. Steam railway within walking distance, coastal path and sandy beaches three miles away. Excellent pubs and restaurants to be found locally. Open Easter to October for Bed and Breakfast from £20 per person.
e-mail: downshayfarm@tiscali.co.uk

See also Colour Display Advertisement

WIMBORNE

Mrs A. C. Tory, Hemsworth Manor Farm, Witchampton, Wimborne BH21 5BN (01258 840216; Fax: 01258 841278). Our lovely old Manor Farmhouse which is mentioned in the Domesday Book, is situated in an exceptionally peaceful location, yet is only half-an-hour's drive from Salisbury, Dorchester, Poole, Bournemouth and the New Forest. Hemsworth is a working family farm of nearly 800 acres, providing some lovely walks. The farm is mainly arable, but is also home to sheep, horses, ponies and various domestic pets. We have three fully equipped en suite bedrooms, all with colour TV. Separate lounge for guests' use. There are excellent pubs locally. Brochure available. **ETC ♦♦♦♦**

• • *Some Useful Guidance for Guests and Hosts* • •

Every year literally thousands of holidays, short breaks and overnight stops are arranged through our guides, the vast majority without any problems at all. In a handful of cases, however, difficulties do arise about bookings, which often could have been prevented from the outset.
It is important to remember that when accommodation has been booked, both parties – guests and hosts – have entered into a form of contract. We hope that the following points will provide helpful guidance.

GUESTS:
* When enquiring about accommodation, be as precise as possible. Give exact dates, numbers in your party and the ages of any children.
* State the number and type of rooms wanted and also what catering you require – bed and breakfast, full board etc. Make sure that the position about evening meals is clear – and about pets, reductions for children or any other special points.
* Read our reviews carefully to ensure that the proprietors you are going to contact can supply what you want. Ask for a letter confirming all arrangements, if possible.
* If you have to cancel, do so as soon as possible. Proprietors do have the right to retain deposits and under certain circumstances to charge for cancelled holidays if adequate notice is not given and they cannot re-let the accommodation.

HOSTS:
* Give details about your facilities and about any special conditions. Explain your deposit system clearly and arrangements for cancellations, charges etc. and whether or not your terms include VAT.
* If for any reason you are unable to fulfil an agreed booking without adequate notice, you may be under an obligation to arrange suitable alternative accommodation or to make some form of compensation.

While every effort is made to ensure accuracy, we regret that FHG Publications cannot accept responsibility for errors, omissions or misrepresentations in our entries or any consequences thereof. Prices in particular should be checked because we go to press early. We will follow up complaints but cannot act as arbiters or agents for either party.

DURHAM

Bee Cottage Farmhouse

See also Colour Advertisement

Charming farmhouse situated in peaceful, picturesque surroundings on the edge of the beautiful Durham Dales. We offer good food and are happy to cater for vegetarians; residential and restaurant licence. Bed and Breakfast; dinner available. Northumbria boasts over 80 golf courses, and the Beamish Open Air Museum, Hadrian's Wall and the Metro Centre are all under 20 miles. Walking, cycling and fishing available nearby. Great for pets.

**BEE COTTAGE FARMHOUSE,
CASTLESIDE, CONSETT, DURHAM DH8 9HW
Telephone: 01207 508224**
e-mail: welcome@beecottagefarmhouse.freeserve.co.uk
web: www.SmoothHound.co.uk/hotels/beecottage.html

STANLEY

Mrs P. Gibson, Bushblades Farm, Harperley, Stanley DH9 9UA (01207 232722). Ideal stop-over when travelling north or south. Only 10 minutes from A1(M) Chester-le-Street. Durham City 20 minutes, Beamish Museum two miles, Metro Centre 15 minutes, Hadrian's Wall and Northumberland coast under an hour. Comfortable Georgian farmhouse set in large garden. Twin ground floor en suite room plus two double first-floor bedrooms. All rooms have tea/coffee making facilities, colour TV and easy chairs. Ample parking. Children welcome over 12 years. Sorry, no pets. Bed and Breakfast from £25 to £30 single, £39 to £45 double. Self-catering accommodation also available. Leave A1(M) at Chester-le-Street for Stanley on the A693, then Consett. Half-a-mile after Stanley follow signs for Harperley. Farm on right half-a-mile up from crossroads. ETC ◆◆◆

WEARDALE

Judith & Martyn Moss, High Liathe, Hill End, Frosterley, Weardale DL13 2SX (01388 526421). High Liathe is peacefully situated, overlooking Frosterley village and has wonderful, panoramic views of fields and wooded slopes in Weardale. An interesting stone-built barn, High Liathe is now a comfortable home, offering high standard accomodation for visitors. The bedrooms consist of a single and a double. Private bathroom, with shower. All accomodation centrally heated. All rooms have views of the garden and valley beyond. Private parking. This a small working farm. High Liathe provides an excellent base for walking, cycling and touring "The land of the Prince Bishops". At the end of the day relax in comfort, sit in the garden and if you wish, have an evening meal. ETC ◆◆◆

e-mail: elizabethmoss@bushinternet.com   website: www.high-liathe.co.uk

---

One child FREE with full-paying adult (not valid for Park Level Mine) at
Kilhope Lead Mining Museum
see our READERS' OFFER VOUCHERS for details

ESSEX

COLCHESTER
Mrs Jill Tod, Seven Arches Farm, Chitts Hill, Lexden, Colchester CO3 9SX (01206 574896). Working farm.
Georgian farmhouse set in large garden close to the ancient town of Colchester. The farm extends to 100 acres and supports both arable crops and cattle. Private fishing rights on the River Colne, which runs past the farmhouse. This is a good location for visits to North Essex, Dedham and the Stour Valley which have been immortalised in the works of John Constable, the landscape painter. Children and pets welcome. Open all year. Bed and Breakfast from £25; Evening Meal from £5. Twin room £40; family room en suite. Static caravan on caravan site also available.

WESTCLIFF-ON-SEA
The Balmoral Hotel, 32-36 Valkyrie Road, Westcliff-on-Sea SS0 8BU (01702 342947; Fax: 01702 337828). The warmest welcome awaits you at the most luxuriously appointed hotel in Southend. Situated just a short walk from Westcliff's main shopping centre and within easy reach of all major attractions in the area. The hotel offers a range of bedrooms from singles to executive suites, all with full en suite facilities, colour TV with cable channels, tea/coffee tray, direct dial telephone, radio, hairdryer and writing desk. The Sovereigns Restaurant offers a variety of superb cuisine complemented by a selection of fine wines from around the world. The hotel bar offers a choice of wines, beers and spirits as well as tempting bar snacks. Weddings and conferences are catered for. On-site car park.

B&B from £48 single, £73 double. **AA/RAC ★★**
e-mail: enquiries@balmoralsouthend.com
website: www.balmoralsouthend.com

PUBLISHER'S NOTE

While every effort is made to ensure accuracy, we regret that FHG Publications cannot accept responsibility for errors, misrepresentations or omissions in our entries or any consequences thereof. Prices in particular should be checked because we go to press early. We will follow up complaints but cannot act as arbiters or agents for either party.

Colchester Zoo • *Colchester, Essex* • *01206 331292*
website: www.colchester-zoo.co.uk
Set in 60 acres of grounds, over 150 species in award-winning enclosures. Over 15 unique daily displays from elephant bathtime to penguin parades.

FREE adult ticket when accompanied by one child at
Barleylands Farm
see our READERS OFFER VOUCHERS for details

GLOUCESTERSHIRE

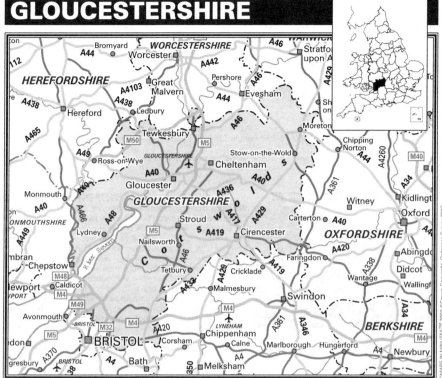

BATH (near)

Mrs Pam Wilmott, Pool Farm, Bath Road, Wick, Bristol BS30 5RL (0117 937 2284). Welcome to our 350 year old Grade II Listed farmhouse on a working farm. On A420 between Bath and Bristol and a few miles from Exit 18 of M4, we are on the edge of the village, overlooking fields, but within easy reach of pub, shops and golf club. We offer traditional Bed and Breakfast in one family and one twin room with tea/coffee facilities and TV. Guest lounge. Central heating. Ample parking. Open all year except Christmas. Terms from £20.

BRISTOL

Mayfair Lodge, 5 Henleaze Road, Westbury on Trym, Bristol BS9 4EX (Tel & Fax: 0117 962 2008). A charming Victorian house located in a smart residential area between Westbury on Trym and Clifton. Family-run with a friendly and relaxed atmosphere. Built in 1886 Mayfair Lodge is tastefully furnished retaining much of the character of the period. All rooms have comfortable beds, remote-control TV, hairdryer and hospitality tray. Some are en suite. Telephone facilities readily available to guests. Antiques are themed throughout the house. Conveniently situated for the city, university, theatres and Bristol Zoo and easily reached from the M4 and M5. Terms from £29 single, twin or double £55. Car parking available at rear of property. AA ♦♦♦

e-mail: avril@akitching.fsnet.co.uk   website: www.s-h-systems.co.uk/hotels/mayfairlodge.html

138 Gloucestershire   Board / ENGLAND

COTSWOLD COUNTRY BED AND BREAKFAST

Bathrooms - three en suite, two shared. B&B: single £24-£38, double £38-£50. Brochure available. Credit cards accepted. **ETC ♦♦♦♦**
e-mail: enquiries@brymbo.com

CHIPPING CAMPDEN
Mrs Gené Jeffrey, Brymbo, Honeybourne Lane, Mickleton, Chipping Campden GL55 6PU (01386 438890; Fax: 01386 438113). A warm and welcoming farm building conversion with large garden in beautiful Cotswold countryside, ideal for walking and touring. Close to Stratford-upon-Avon, Broadway, Chipping Campden and with easy access to Oxford and Cheltenham. All rooms are on the ground floor, with full central heating. The comfortable bedrooms all have colour television and tea/coffee making facilities. Sitting room with open log fire. Breakfast room. Children and dogs welcome. Parking. Maps and guides to borrow. Sample menus from local hostelries for your information. Home-made preserves a speciality. FREE countryside tour of area offered to three-night guests. Rooms: two double, two twin, one family.

website: www.brymbo.com

See also Colour Display Advertisement

three persons sharing, £80. **ETC ♦♦♦♦**
e-mail: willstanley@farmersweekly.net

CHIPPING CAMPDEN
Veronica Stanley, Home Farm House, Ebrington, Chipping Campden GL55 6NL (Tel & Fax: 01386 593309). A warm and friendly welcome awaits you at our completely refurbished 15th century Grade II Listed farmhouse, in the heart of this beautiful village. Spacious beamed rooms, inglenook fireplace in dining room where a full English breakfast is served. Large private car park at rear. All bedrooms are en suite and have coffee/tea making facilities, TV, radio and hairdryer. Accommodation comprises one double, two twin and one family suite consisting of a single and a double room en suite. Sorry, no pets allowed in the house. Non-smoking. Terms per night: £55 per double bedded suite, two persons sharing; more than two nights £50. Twin bedded rooms are £50, or single occupancy £40. Family room for

website: www.homefarminthecotswolds.co.uk

e-mail: milton@farmersweekly.net

FAIRFORD
Suzie Paton, Milton Farm, Fairford GL7 4HZ (01285 712205; Fax: 01285 711349). Located in the picturesque Cotswolds, Milton Farm has an impressive Georgian farmhouse with very spacious and distinctive en suite bedrooms and a comfortable guest lounge with large open fireplace. Warm hospitality and breakfast with locally sourced, quality produce, ensure a memorable stay. Quiet, pleasant outlook on edge of most attractive Cotswold market town with numerous beautiful walks from the farm, across meadowland beside the River Coln. Family, twin and double rooms available with comfortable furniture, remote-controlled TV, tea/coffee making facilities, central heating. All rooms are non-smoking. Fishing can be arranged. Stables available for horse guests. **ETC ♦♦♦♦**
website: www.milton-farm.co.uk

25% off museum admission (excludes combination tickets at
National Waterways Museum
see our READERS' OFFER VOUCHERS for details

The FHG Directory of Website Addresses
on pages 345 - 373 is a useful quick reference guide for holiday accommodation with e-mail and/or website details

ENGLAND / Board   Gloucestershire   139

See also Colour Display Advertisement

perfectly situated to visit Cotswolds, Royal Forest of Dean, Wye Valley and Malvern Hills. Children over five years. No smoking, please. Bed, full English Breakfast and Evening Dinner from £29; Bed and Breakfast from £20. Ample parking.
ETC ♦♦♦
e-mail: sheila-barnfield@supanet.com

GLOUCESTER (near)
S.J. Barnfield, "Kilmorie Smallholding", Gloucester Road, Corse, Staunton, Gloucester GL19 3RQ (Tel & Fax: 01452 840224). Quality all ground floor accommodation. "Kilmorie" is Grade II Listed (c1848) within conservation area in a lovely part of Gloucestershire, deceptively spacious yet cosy, and tastefully furnished. Double, twin, family or single bedrooms, all having tea tray, colour TV, radio, mostly en suite. Very comfortable guests' lounge, traditional home cooking is served in the separate dining room overlooking large garden where there are seats to relax, watch our free range hens (who provide excellent eggs for breakfast!) or the wild birds and butterflies we encourage to visit. Perhaps walk waymarked farmland footpaths which start here. Children may "help" with our child's pony, and hens. Rural yet

walk away. ETC/AA ♦♦♦
e-mail: farmhouse@corshamfield.co.uk

STOW-ON-THE-WOLD
Robert Smith and Julie-Anne, Corsham Field Farmhouse, Bledington Road, Stow-on-the-Wold GL54 1JH (01451 831750; Fax: 01451 832247). A traditional farmhouse with spectacular views of Cotswold countryside. Quiet location one mile from Stow. Ideally situated for exploring all Cotswold villages including Bourton-on-the-Water, Broadway, Burford and Chipping Campden. Within easy reach of Cheltenham, Oxford and Stratford-upon-Avon; also places of interest such as Blenheim Palace, Warwick Castle and many National Trust houses and gardens. Family, twin and double bedrooms; mostly en suite. TV, tea tray and hairdryer in all rooms. Relaxing guest lounge/dining room. Pets and children welcome. Open all year for Bed and Full English Breakfast from £22 (reductions for children). Excellent pub food five minutes'

website: www.corshamfield.co.uk

STOW-ON-THE-WOLD
South Hill Farmhouse, Fosseway, Stow-on-the-Wold, GL54 1JU (01451 831888; Fax: 01451 832255). Siân and Mark Cassie welcome you to South Hill Farmhouse. The house is a Listed Cotswold stone farmhouse (no longer a working farm) situated on the ancient Roman Fosse Way on the outskirts of Stow-on-the-Wold. There is ample parking for guests, and it is only 10 minutes' walk to the pubs, restaurants and shops of Stow-on-the-Wold. 2004 prices: single £38, double/twin £52, family (three) £66 per room per night, including generous breakfast. Non-smoking house. ETC ♦♦♦
e-mail: info@southhill.co.uk
website: www.southhill.co.uk

See the *Family-Friendly Pubs & Inns*
Supplement on pages 335 - 344 for establishments
which really welcome children

**When making enquiries or bookings,
a stamped addressed envelope is always appreciated**

140 Gloucestershire   Board / ENGLAND

STROUD
Mrs Salt, Beechcroft, Brownshill, Stroud GL6 8AG (01453 883422). Our Edwardian house is quietly situated in a beautiful rural area with open views, about four miles from Stroud. The house is set in an attractive garden with mature trees, shrubs and herbaceous borders. We are in the midst of good walking country, for which we can lend maps and guides. We provide a full cooked breakfast or fruit salad and rolls with home-made bread and preserves. We welcome the elderly and small children. We are within easy reach of Cheltenham, Gloucester, Cirencester and Bath, also Berkeley Castle, Slimbridge and the North Cotswolds. We are a non-smoking establishment. Evening meal by prior arrangement. Bed and Breakfast from £22.

See also Colour Display Advertisement

TEWKESBURY
Mrs Bernadette Williams, Abbots Court, Church End, Twyning, Tewkesbury GL20 6DA (Tel & Fax: 01684 292515). Working farm. A large, quiet farmhouse set in 350 acres, on the site of monastery between the Malverns and Cotswolds, half a mile M5-M50 junction. Six en suite bedrooms with colour TV and tea making facilities. Centrally heated. Open all year except Christmas. Large lounge with open fire and colour TV. Spacious diningroom. Licensed bar. Good home cooked food in large quantities, home produced where possible. Children's own TV room, games room and playroom. Tennis lawn. Play area and lawn. Cot and high chair available. Laundry facilities. Ideally situated for touring with numerous places to visit. Swimming, tennis, sauna, golf within three miles. Coarse fishing available on the farm. Bed and Breakfast from £19 to £21. Reduced rates for children and Senior Citizens. **ETC ♦♦♦**
e-mail: bernie@abbotscourt.fsbusiness.co.uk

The **FHG**
GOLF GUIDE
Where to Play
Where to Stay

Available from most bookshops, **THE GOLF GUIDE** (published annually) covers details of every UK golf course – well over 2800 entries – for holiday or business golf. Hundreds of hotel entries offer convenient accommodation, accompanying details of the courses – the 'pro', par score, length etc.

In association with 'Golf Monthly' and including Holiday Golf in Ireland, France, Portugal, Spain, The USA, South Africa and Thailand

**£9.ial from bookshops or from the publishers (postage charged outside UK) • FHG Publications, Abbey Mill Business Centre, Paisley PA1 1TJ

PLEASE NOTE

All the information in this book is given in good faith in the belief that it is correct. However, the publishers cannot guarantee the facts given in these pages, neither are they responsible for changes in policy, ownership or terms that may take place after the date of going to press. Readers should always satisfy themselves that the facilities they require are available and that the terms, if quoted, still apply.

ENGLAND / Board   Hampshire 141

HAMPSHIRE

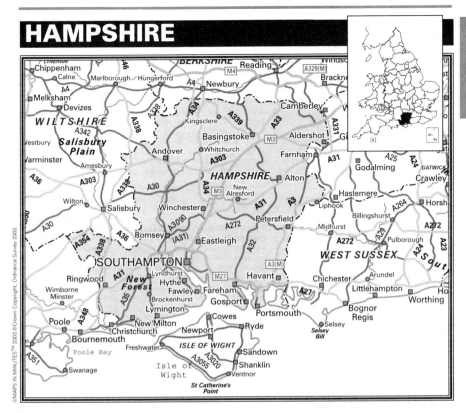

BROCKENHURST (New Forest)

Hilden, Southampton Road, Boldre, Brockenhurst (New Forest) SO41 8PT (01590 623682; Fax: 01590 624444).
Hilden is a friendly Edwardian home in two-and-a-half acres of gardens and paddock, 50 yards from the open New Forest, offering wonderful cycling, riding and walking. Both the pretty Georgian sailing town of Lymington and the New Forest village of Brockenhurst (80 minutes to Waterloo by train) are about two miles away. There are numerous very good pubs and restaurants nearby, including The Hobler Inn, which serves excellent food, under 200 yards away. Children and dogs welcome, stabling can be arranged, as can cycle hire, and riding from various local stables within five minutes' drive.
website: www.newforestbandb-hilden.co.uk

FHG **FHG PUBLICATIONS** publish a large range of well-known accommodation guides. We will be happy to send you details or you can use the order form at the back of this book.

The **FHG** Directory of Website Addresses
on pages 345 - 373 is a useful quick reference guide for holiday accommodation with e-mail and/or website details

LYMINGTON

Mrs Patricia Ellis, Efford Cottage, Everton, Lymington SO41 0JD (01590 642315; Fax: 01590 641030/642315). Our friendly, award-winning guest house is a spacious Georgian cottage, standing in an acre of garden. All rooms are en suite with many extra luxury facilities. We offer a four-course, multi-choice breakfast, with homemade bread and preserves. Patricia is a qualified chef and uses our homegrown produce. An excellent centre for exploring both the New Forest and the South Coast with sports facilities, fishing, bird watching and horse riding in the near vicinity. Private parking. Dogs welcome. Bed and Breakfast from £25 to £34 per person. Sorry no children under 14 years. *RAC SPARKLING DIAMOND AND WARM WELCOME ACCOLADES, WELCOME HOST, ENGLAND FOR EXCELLENCE AWARD, FHG DIPLOMA WINNER 1997, 1999 AND 2000.* ETC ♦♦♦♦ *GOLD AWARD*
e-mail: effordcottage@aol.com
website: www.effordcottage.co.uk

LYNDHURST

Penny Farthing Hotel, Romsey Road, Lyndhurst SO43 7AA (023 8028 4422; Fax: 023 8028 4488). The Penny Farthing is a cheerful small Hotel ideally situated in Lyndhurst village centre, the capital of "The New Forest". The Hotel offers en suite single, double, twin and family rooms with direct-dial telephones, tea/coffee tray, colour TV and clock radios. We also have some neighbouring cottages available as Hotel annexe rooms or on a self-catering basis. These have been totally refitted, much with "Laura Ashley" decor, and offer quieter, more exclusive accommodation. The hotel has a licensed bar, private car park and bicycle store. Lyndhurst has a charming variety of shops, restaurants, pubs and bistros and "The New Forest Information Centre and Museum". All major credit cards accepted. **AA/ RAC/ ETC** ♦♦♦♦
website: www.pennyfarthinghotel.co.uk

NEW FOREST (Fritham)

John and Penny Hankinson, Fritham Farm, Fritham, Lyndhurst SO43 7HH (Tel & Fax: 023 8081 2333). Lovely farmhouse on working farm in the heart of the New Forest. Peace and tranquillity in this wonderful area of natural beauty. Three twin/double rooms, all en suite with king-size beds and tea/coffee making facilities. Large lounge with TV. There is also a very comfortable cottage (sleeps 2) on the farm with views across green fields to the Forest beyond. No smoking. Children 10 and over welcome. Come and enjoy a relaxing stay in this lovely corner of England – perfect for walking/cycling/riding/touring. B&B £22 to £24 per person. Cottage £250 to £350 per week. **ETC/AA** ♦♦♦♦
e-mail: frithamfarm@supanet.com

SOUTHAMPTON

Dormy House Hotel, 21 Barnes Lane, Sarisbury/Warsash, Southampton SO31 7DA (01489 572626; Fax: 01489 573370). The Dormy House Hotel is a tranquil Victorian House, set in a quiet residential area, fully modernised and located within half a mile of the River Hamble and Warsash, perfect for all activities on the river. Accommodation consists of a charming dining room, comfortable lounge, twelve tastefully decorated, en suite bedrooms, each with tea/coffee making facilities, direct-dial telephones and remote-control TV. Ground floor bedrooms have access to the attractive and peaceful garden. Fully licensed. Local restaurants offer a broad range of traditional, light or ethnic menus. Easy access to the many attractions along the South Coast, Isle of Wight and the New Forest and within easy reach of Business Parks at Whitely, Segensworth and Hedge End. **AA** ♦♦♦♦
e-mail: dormyhousehotel@warsash.globalnet.co.uk   website: www.dormyhousehotel.net

ENGLAND / Board   Hampshire 143

See also Colour Display Advertisement

WINCHESTER (near)
Mays Farm, Longwood Dean, Near Winchester SO21 1JS (01962 777486; Fax 01962 777747). Twelve minutes' drive from Winchester, (the eleventh century capital city of England), Mays Farm is set in rolling countryside on a lane which leads from nowhere to nowhere. The house is timber framed, originally built in the sixteenth century and has been thoroughly renovated and extended by its present owners, James and Rosalie Ashby. There are three guest bedrooms, (one double, one twin and one either), each with a private bathroom or shower room. A sitting room with log fire is usually available for guests' use. Ducks, geese, chickens and goats make up the two acre "farm". Prices from £23 per person per night for Bed and Breakfast. Booking is essential. Please telephone or fax for details.

Marwell • *Near Winchester, Hants* • *07626 943163*
website: www.marwell.org.uk
World famous for its dedication to the conservation of endangered species.
Nearly 1000 animals in acres of beautiful parkland.

Other specialised
FHG PUBLICATIONS
Published annually: available in all good bookshops or direct from the publisher.

PETS WELCOME! £7.99
Recommended **COUNTRY HOTELS** OF BRITAIN £6.99
Recommended **COUNTRY INNS & PUBS** OF BRITAIN £6.99
Recommended **SHORT BREAK HOLIDAYS** IN BRITAIN £6.99

FHG PUBLICATIONS LTD,
Abbey Mill Business Centre,
Seedhill, Paisley, Renfrewshire PA1 ITJ
Tel: 0141-887 0428 • Fax: 0141-889 7204
e-mail: fhg@ipcmedia.com
website: www.holidayguides.com

When making enquiries or bookings,
a stamped addressed envelope is always appreciated

HEREFORDSHIRE

See also Colour Display Advertisement

BROMYARD
Sheila and Roger Steeds, Linton Brook Farm, Bringsty, Bromyard WR6 5TR (Tel & Fax: 01885 488875). An historic, comfortable and spacious home, tastefully renovated. We offer two large double bedrooms with en suite facilities and TV, and a smaller twin-bedded room with private bathroom. All have central heating and tea/coffee making facilities. The dining room has an open inglenook fireplace and the large sittingroom has an inviting woodburner. Wide range of country pubs, inns and hostelries nearby. Children welcome; dogs can be accommodated in an adjacent building. There are plenty of nearby places of interest, as well as golf, fishing, bowls, tennis, horse racing and cricket, wonderful walks and wildlife. Ample car parking; transport service available.

See also Colour Display Advertisement

HEREFORD
David Jones, Sink Green Farm, Rotherwas, Hereford HR2 6LE (01432 870223). Working farm. A friendly welcome awaits you at this our 16th century farmhouse overlooking the picturesque Wye Valley, yet only three miles from Hereford. Our individually decorated en suite rooms, one four-poster, all have tea/coffee making facilities, colour TV and central heating. Relax in our extensive garden, complete with summer house and hot tub, or enjoy a stroll by the river. Prices from £23 per person. Children welcome. Pets by arrangement. **AA ♦♦♦♦**
e-mail: enquiries@sinkgreenfarm.co.uk
website: www.sinkgreenfarm.co.uk

ENGLAND / Board   Herefordshire 145

LEOMINSTER

Catherine and Marguerite Fothergill, Highfield, Newtown, Ivington Road, Leominster HR6 8QD (01568 613216). Highfield stands in a large garden with unspoilt views of open farmland and distant hills, just one and a half miles from the old market town of Leominster. Accommodation comprises one twin en suite, and one twin and one double room with private facilities, all with radio alarm and tea/coffee making facilities. Guests are requested not to smoke in bedrooms. There are two sitting rooms, one with TV and French windows opening onto the patio, and both with open fires for chillier seasons. Full central heating. Meals are prepared from fresh ingredients, using local produce where possible. Ample parking. Regret no children and no dogs. Prior booking essential. **ETC** ♦♦♦

e-mail: info@stay-at-highfield.co.uk   website: www.stay-at-highfield.co.uk

LEOMINSTER

Mrs Jenny Davies, Holgate Farm, Kingsland, Leominster HR6 9QS (01568 708275). Working farm. Set amidst the beautiful North Herefordshire countryside on a family-run stock and arable farm, this attractive 17th Century farmhouse offers a warm, friendly welcome. Within easy reach of the Welsh border country, Hereford, Leominster and Ludlow. Spacious and well appointed bedrooms with tea and coffee trays. Guests own bathroom and sitting room. Open all year except Christmas and New Year. This is a no smoking house. B&B £20 per person per night, single room £22. Reductions for children.

LONGTOWN

Mrs I. Pritchard, Olchon Cottage Farm, Longtown, Hereford HR2 0NS (Tel & Fax: 01873 860233). Working farm. Small working farm. An ideal location for a peaceful holiday in lovely walking country close to Offa's Dyke Path and Welsh Border. The farmhouse is noted for its good, wholesome, home produced food and many guests return to enjoy the homely, relaxing atmosphere. Magnificent views and many places of interest to visit. Accommodation comprises two family bedrooms (also used as singles/doubles) both en suite with colour TV, radio, hairdryer and tea/coffee facilities. Guests' sittingroom and diningroom with separate tables. Towels provided. Reductions for children under 10 years; cot, high chair and babysitting offered. Open all year except Christmas. Bed, Breakfast and Evening Meal or Bed and Breakfast from £22. Car essential, parking. Terms on application, with stamp for brochure please. Welcome Host Award. **ETC** ♦♦♦

website: www.golden-valley.co.uk/olchon

See also Colour Display Advertisement

ROSS-ON-WYE

Mrs M.E. Drzymalski, Thatch Close, Langrove, Ross-on-Wye HR9 6EL (01989 770300). Secluded, peaceful, comfortable Georgian farmhouse, yet convenient for A40 and M4, M50. Our three lovely bedrooms, each with its own bathroom (two en suite), have magnificent views over the unspoilt countryside. Relax in the visitors' lounge or sit in the shade of mature trees in our garden. You may be greeted by our dog or free flying parrot. Telephone or e-mail for brochure. **ETC** ♦♦♦♦

e-mail: thatch.close@virgin.net
website: www.thatchclose.com

50p reduction on entry fee at
Cider Museum & King Offa Distillery
see our READERS' OFFER VOUCHERS for details

HERTFORDSHIRE

WATFORD
Grove End Hotel, 73 Bushey Hall Road, Bushey, Watford WD23 2EN (01923 226798; Fax: 01923 210877). Situated in an acre of lovely gardens, this small, welcoming, family-run establishment has been in business for the past 35 years. It has 29 rooms to suit most people's pockets and taste, from basic single rooms to family rooms through to en suite. All rooms have satellite TV, washhand basin, and tea making facilities. En suite rooms also have shower, toilet, hairdryer, direct-dial phone and radio alarm. All rooms include a full English cooked buffet breakfast. There is a small bar, open from Monday to Thursday, which serves bar food from a varied menu. Weekend stays on a Bed and Breakfast basis only.
e-mail: grove.end@ntlworld.com
website: www.groveendhotel.co.uk

ISLE OF WIGHT

See also Colour Display Advertisement

NEWPORT
Alvington Manor Farm, Manor Farm Lane, Carisbrooke, Newport PO30 5SP (01983 523463). Alvington Manor is a 17th century manor farmhouse, situated in the centre of the Isle of Wight, near Carisbrooke Castle and the start of the Tennyson Trail. We have five en suite bedrooms, four with bathrooms, one with a shower room. All rooms have televisions and tea/coffee making facilities. There is a guest sitting room, gardens and car parking. Good food pubs nearby. We are open all year round. Prices from £20 per person per night, inclusive of full English breakfast. Children welcome, price on application. **ETC ♦♦♦**
For ferry booking from Portsmouth and Lymington phone 01990 827744; from Southampton phone 01703 334010.

"Two for One" at
Verulamium Museum
see our READERS' OFFER VOUCHERS for details

Knebworth House • *Near Stevenage, Herts* • *01438 812661*
website: www.knebworthhouse.com
Home of the Lytton family since 1490, with fine collections of manuscripts, portraits and furniture. Set in 250 acre country park with formal gardens and large adventure playground. Gift shop and cafeteria.

Isle of Wight Waxworks • *Brading, Isle of Wight* • *0870 458 4817*
website: www.iwwaxworks.co.uk
See the Rectory Mansion, The Chamber of Horrors, and The World of Nature. Demonstrations the fascinating art of candle carving.

ENGLAND / Board   Kent 147

KENT

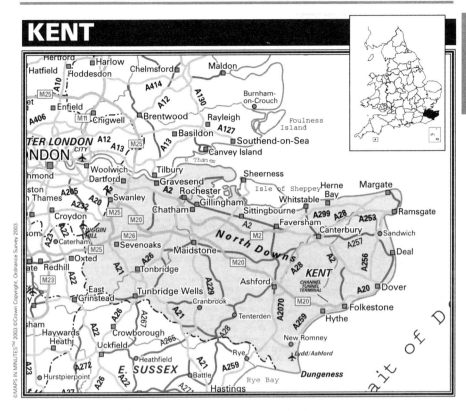

BROADSTAIRS
Keston Court Hotel, 14 Ramsgate Road, Broadstairs CT10 1PS (01843 862401). The Keston Court is a small hotel of charm and character, with friendly service and a homely atmosphere. It is only five minutes' walk to the shops and beach. Parking is free, and our licensed bar will cater for all your needs. All rooms have tea/coffee making appliances, also colour TV. The hotel holds a full fire certificate. Central heating in all rooms. Adults only. Closed during winter months.
e-mail: kestoncourt@tinyonline.co.uk
website: www.SmoothHound.co.uk/hotels.html

CANTERBURY
Mr and Mrs R. Linch, Upper Ansdore, Duckpit Lane, Petham, Canterbury CT4 5QB (01227 700672; Fax: 01227 700840). Beautiful secluded Listed Tudor farmhouse with various livestock, situated in an elevated position with far-reaching views of the wooded countryside of the North Downs. The property overlooks a Kent Trust Nature Reserve, it is five miles south of the cathedral city of Canterbury and only 30 minutes' drive to the ports of Dover and Folkestone. The accommodation comprises three double and one twin bedded room, and a family room. All have shower, WC en suite and tea-making facilities. Dining/sittingroom, heavily beamed with large inglenook. Car essential. Bed and Full English Breakfast from £22.50 per person. Credit Cards accepted. **AA ♦♦♦**

CANTERBURY

See also Colour Display Advertisement

Mrs A. Hunt, Bower Farmhouse, Stelling Minnis, Near Canterbury CT4 6BB (01227 709430). Anne and Nick Hunt welcome you to Bower Farm House, a traditional 17th century Kentish farmhouse situated in the midst of Stelling Minnis, a medieval common of 125 acres of unspoilt trees, shrubs and open grassland; seven miles south of the cathedral city of Canterbury and nine miles from the coast; the countryside abounds in beauty spots and nature reserves. The house is heavily beamed and maintains its original charm. The accommodation comprises a double room and a twin bedded room, both with private facilities. Full traditional English breakfast is served with home-made bread, marmalade and fresh free-range eggs. Children welcome; pets by prior arrangement. Open all year (except Christmas). Car essential. Excellent pub food five minutes away. Bed and Breakfast from £24 per person. **ETC** ♦♦♦ *SILVER AWARD*
e-mail: book@bowerbb.freeserve.co.uk   website: www.bowerfarmhouse.co.uk

CANTERBURY

Mrs Lewana Castle, Great Field Farm, Canterbury CT4 6DE (01227 709223). Situated in beautiful countryside, our spacious farmhouse is about eight miles from Canterbury and Folkestone, 12 miles from Dover and Ashford. We are a working farm with some livestock including friendly ponies and chickens. We provide a friendly and high standard of accommodation with full central heating and double glazing, traditional breakfasts cooked on the Aga, courtesy tray and colour TV in each of our suites/bedrooms. Our annexe suite has a private staircase, lounge, kitchen, double bedroom and bathroom and is also available for self-catering holidays. Our cottage suite has its own entrance, stairs, lounge, bathroom and twin-bedded room. Our large double/family bedroom has en suite bathroom and air-bath. There is ample off-road parking and good pub food nearby. Bed and Breakfast from £25 per person; reductions for children. Non-smoking establishment. **ETC** ♦♦♦♦ *SILVER AWARD*.

Lullingstone Roman Villa • *Near Dartford, Kent* • *01322 863467*
website: www.english-heritage.org.uk
See how middle-class Romans lived at one of England's most important examples of a Roman villa, complete with mosaics.

Two tickets for the price of one (cheapest ticket free) at
Museum of Kent Life
see our READERS' OFFER VOUCHERS for details

FHG
FHG PUBLICATIONS
publish a large range of well-known accommodation guides. We will be happy to send you details or you can use the order form at the back of this book.

BLERIOT'S - DOVER

A Victorian Residence set in a tree-lined avenue, in the lee of Dover Castle. Within easy reach of trains, bus station, town centre, Hoverport and docks. Channel Tunnel approximately 10 minutes' drive. Off-road parking. We specialise in one night 'stop-overs' and Mini Breaks. Single, Double, Twin and Family rooms with full en suite. All rooms have colour TV, tea and coffee making facilities, and are fully centrally heated. Full English Breakfast served from 7am. Reduced rates for room only. Open all year.

Rates: Bed & Breakfast: £23 to £26 per person per night.
Mini-Breaks: January-April and October-December £20 per person per night.
Mastercard and Visa Accepted   ETC ♦♦♦
47 Park Avenue, Dover, Kent CT16 1HE   Telephone (01304) 211394

DOVER

St Mark's Guest House, 23 Castle Street, Dover CT16 1PT (01304 201894). St Mark's Guest House in White Cliffs country is within sight of the famous Dover Castle and in walking distance of the ferry port and town centre with all its shops and cosmopolitan restaurants. Fifteen minutes' drive from the Channel Tunnel. We offer a comprehensive range of facilities. Most rooms are en suite and all have showers and washbasins. All rooms have tea/coffee making facilities, TV and are clean, comfortable and centrally heated. We offer an excellent English breakfast and cater for vegetarians. Bed and Breakfast from £18 to £27 pppn. Family rooms available.

DOVER

Alkham Court, Meggett Lane, South Alkham, Near Dover CT15 7DG (01303 892056). Peaceful location in an Area of Outstanding Natural Beauty overlooking the Alkham Valley, with ponies and sheep on our farm, and a homely atmosphere. Hearty English breakfasts with local produce served in our conservatory dining room which enjoys spectacular views. Excellent accommodation comprising double/family room with en suite facilities, and double room with private bathroom. Ground floor rooms with antique furniture and private entrance. Ideal touring base; Dover Castle and White Cliffs nearby; 10 minutes from Eurotunnel and ferries, 20 minutes Canterbury. ETC ♦♦♦♦
e-mail: wendy.burrows@alkhamcourt.co.uk
website: www.alkhamcourt.co.uk

TUNBRIDGE WELLS

Manor Court Farm B&B and Camping. Georgian farmhouse on a working 350-acre sheep and arable farm priding itself on its warm and friendly atmosphere, spacious rooms and lovely views of Medway Valley. Various animals such as dogs, cats, horses, guinea fowl, chickens etc. Tennis and swimming available by arrangement. Large secluded garden with ponds and orchard area. Secluded space for tents and caravans with new facilities. Excellent base for walking, cycling and touring the south east of England. Chartwell, Leeds Castle, Sissinghurst, Hever etc, are all within easy reach and London 45 minutes by train from Tonbridge. Bed and Breakfast from £24 per person per night (three rooms available), camping from £6 per person per night. Children welcome. Pets by arrangement. You will find us on the A264 road, five miles west of Tunbridge Wells at Stone Cross. ETC ♦♦♦ Contact: **Julia Soyke or Becky Masey** **(01892 740279; Fax: 01892 740919).**
e-mail: jsoyke@jsoyke.freeserve.co.uk   website: www.manorcourtfarm.co.uk

LANCASHIRE

CHORLEY

Mrs K. Motley, Parr Hall Farm, Eccleston, Chorley PR7 5SL (01257 451917; Fax: 01257 453749). Within an hour of the Lake District, Yorkshire Dales, Peak District, Chester and North Wales, Parr Hall Farm is an ideal base for touring the local area. Attractions nearby include Camelot Theme Park, Martin Mere, Southport, Blackpool and antiques at Bygone Times, Heskin Hall, Park Hall and Botany Bay. All rooms are en suite, with central heating. Children are welcome, regret no pets. No smoking. Camping facilities also available. From M6 take A5209 for Parbold, then immediately take B5250 right turn for Eccleston. After five miles, Parr Lane is on the right, the house is first on the left. Bed and Breakfast from £25 per person, reductions for children.

COLNE

Patricia Hodgson, Parson Lee Farm, Wycoller, Colne BB8 8SU (01282 864747). There is a warm welcome at our peacefully located, 260-year old farmhouse on the edge of Wycoller Country Park, which is perfect for walking, being on the Brontë and Pendle Ways. Walking breaks with transport, and fully inclusive tours are available. Accommodation is available in en suite bedrooms with tea/coffee making facilities. There is a guest lounge with TV and books. Open all year. Bed and Breakfast from £19pp. ETC ♦♦♦
e-mail: pathodgson@hotmail.com
website: www.parsonleefarm.co.uk

SOUTHPORT

Mrs Wendy E. Core, Sandy Brook Farm, 52 Wyke Cop Road, Scarisbrick, Southport PR8 5LR (Tel & Fax: 01704 880337). Bill and Wendy Core offer a homely, friendly atmosphere at Sandy Brook, a small working farm situated three-and-a-half miles from the seaside resort of Southport and five miles from the historic town of Ormskirk. Motorways are easily accessible, and the Lake District, Trough of Bowland, Blackpool and North Wales are within easy reach. Six en suite bedrooms with colour TV and tea/coffee making facilities. Central heating throughout. Sittingroom with colour TV; diningroom. High chairs and cots available. Room available for disabled guests. Open all year except Christmas. Bed and Breakfast from £19. Reductions for children. Weekly terms on request. ETC ♦♦♦, *NWTB SILVER AWARD WINNER "PLACE TO STAY" FARMHOUSE CATEGORY.*

TODMORDEN

Mrs L. Parkinson, Cross Farm, Mankinholes, Todmorden OL14 6HP (01706 813481). Stunning views. Lovely interiors. good home-cooking unit. Local produce. Ideal for walking and touring.

LEICESTERSHIRE

See also Colour Display Advertisement

BELTON-IN-RUTLAND (near Uppingham)
The Old Rectory, Belton-in-Rutland, Oakham LE15 9LE (01572 717279; Fax: 01572 717343). Guest accommodation. Victorian country house and guest annexe in charming village overlooking Eyebrook valley and rolling Rutland countryside. Comfortable and varied selection of rooms, mostly en suite, with direct outside access. Prices from £20 per person per night including breakfast. Small farm environment (horses and sheep) with excellent farmhouse breakfast. Public House 100 yards. Lots to see and do: Rutland Water, castles, stately homes, country parks, forestry and Barnsdale Gardens. Non-smoking. Self catering also available. **RAC ◆◆◆**
e-mail: bb@iepuk.com

MELTON MOWBRAY
Hillside House, 27 Melton Road, Burton Lazars, Melton Mowbray LE14 2UR (01664 566312; Fax: 01664 501819). Situated on the edge of the village with views over rolling countryside, Hillside House is a comfortable, converted old farm building, offering one double and one twin room both en suite, and one twin with private bathroom. All have colour TV and tea/coffee making facilities. There is a guests' lounge; Rutland Water, Geoff Hamilton's Garden and Belvoir Castle are close by. Melton Mowbray with its bustling market is one and a half miles away. Bed and Breakfast from £21 to £24pp. Children over ten only. Closed Christmas and New Year. **ETC ◆◆◆◆**
e-mail: hillhs@aol.com
website: www.hillside-house.co.uk

LINCOLNSHIRE

ALFORD (near)
Nev and Jill Brown, Wellbeck Farmhouse, Well, Near Alford LN13 9LT (Tel & Fax: 01507 462453). Nev and Jill welcome you to their farmhouse, set in a large peaceful garden within easy reach of the beautiful Lincolnshire Wolds and the superb beaches. Lincoln 35 miles, Alford one and a half miles. There are two family rooms and one single, with tea and coffee making facilities and colour TV. Full English breakfast is served. Pets by arrangement. Ample parking. Terms from £18 per person; reductions for children.

CONINGSBY
Mrs C. Whittington, High House Farm, Tumby Moorside, Near Coningsby, Boston PE22 7CT (01526 345408). An early 18th century Listed farmhouse with spacious en suite bedrooms and original beamed ceilings. Enjoy a generous farmhouse breakfast using fresh local produce. Centrally located for five 'Bomber Country' museums, championship golf at Woodhall Spa, antiques at Horncastle and local fishing. Historic pubs nearby serving excellent evening meals. Within easy reach of the east coast and the Lincolnshire Wolds. One double and one twin bedroom. Central heating, tea and coffee facilities and colour TV. Open all year except Christmas. No smoking. Children welcome. B&B from £20pp; reductions for three days or more.
e-mail: HighHousefarm@aol.com

152 Lincolnshire   Board / ENGLAND

GAINSBOROUGH
The Black Swan Guest House, 21 High Street, Marton, Gainsborough DN21 5AH (Tel and Fax: 01427 718878). We offer a warm and friendly stay at our delightfully converted 18th century coaching inn, so get away from the 'hurly burly' of modern life, and escape to the peace and quiet, although Lincoln is only 12 miles away and many other attractions are nearby. All our rooms are en suite, with full facilities; we also have a comfortable guest lounge with ample reading matter. Our breakfasts are made with the best quality local produce and should set you up for the day. We are a non-smoking establishment. Single from £30, double from £55. **AA ♦♦♦♦**
e-mail: info@blackswan-marton.co.uk

HORNCASTLE
Mrs Judy Bankes Price, Greenfield Farm, Mill Lane/Cow Lane, Minting, Horncastle LN9 5PJ (Tel & Fax: 01507 578457; mobile: 07768 368829). Enjoy a quiet stay at our lovely spacious home surrounded by extensive grounds and a wonderful wildlife pond. Centrally placed and easy to find, (A158 one mile). Lincoln Cathedral is 15 minutes' drive and the Wolds five minutes. Close to the aviation trails, antique centres and Cadwell Park. The bedrooms comprise two doubles and one twin, all en suite. They have wonderful views, TV, tea trays and modern en suite shower rooms. There is ample easy parking and a tennis court. Non-smoking household. Two pubs within one mile. Bed and Breakfast from £24. **AA ♦♦♦♦**
e-mail: greenfieldfarm@farming.co.uk

See also Colour Display Advertisement

THORPE FENDYKES
Mrs S. Evans, Willow Farm, Thorpe Fendykes, Wainfleet, Skegness PE24 4QH (01754 830316). In the heart of the Lincolnshire Fens, Willow Farm is a working smallholding with free range hens, goats, horses and ponies. Situated in a peaceful hamlet with abundant wildlife, ideal for a quiet retreat - yet only 15 minutes from the Skegness coast, shops, amusements and beaches. Bed and Breakfast is provided in comfortable en suite rooms from £17 per person per night, reductions for children (suppers and sandwiches can be provided in the evening on request). Rooms have tea and coffee making facilities and a colour TV and are accessible to disabled guests. Friendly hosts! Ring for brochure.
e-mail: willowfarmhols@aol.com
website: www.willowfarmholidays.co.uk

Free entry for one child when accompanied by full-paying adult at
Skegness Natureland Seal Sanctuary
see our READERS' OFFER VOUCHERS for details

National Fishing Heritage Centre • *Grimsby, N.E. Lincs* • *01472 323345*
http://welcome.to/NFHCentre
Tells the story of fishermen, their boats, and the waters they fished in.
The dangers and hardships of life at sea are vividly re-created.

A useful index of towns and counties appears at the back of this book on pages 375 - 378. Refer also to Contents Pages 2 and 3.

ENGLAND / Board   Norfolk 153

NORFOLK

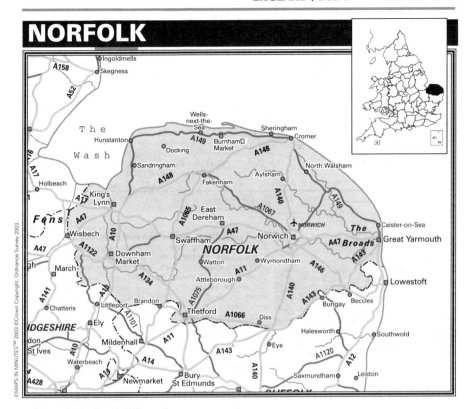

See also Colour Display Advertisement

DISS
4B&B Strenneth Country Bed & Breakfast, Airfield Road, Fersfield, Diss IP22 2BP (01379 688182; Fax: 01379 688260). Well-established, family-run businesss, situated in unspoiled countryside, a short drive from Bressingham Gardens and the picturesque market town of Diss. Offering first-class accommodation, the original 17th century building has been renovated to a high standard with exposed oak beams and a newer single storey courtyard wing. There is ample off-road parking and plenty of nice walks nearby. All seven bedrooms, including a four-poster and an executive, are tastefully furnished, each having colour TV, hospitality trays, central heating and full en suite facilities. The establishment is smoke-free and the guest lounge has a log fire on cold winter evenings. Extensive breakfast menu using local produce. Ideal touring base. Pets most welcome. Outside kennels with runs if required. Bed and Breakfast from £25. **ETC ♦♦♦♦**
e-mail: pdavey@strenneth.co.uk
website: www.strenneth.co.uk

FAKENHAM
Julie Sadler, The Boar Inn, Great Ryburgh, Fakenham NR21 0DX (01328 829212; Fax: 01328 829421). The Boar Inn, with its Listed Frontage nestles in the verdant Wensum Valley, close by the round towered Saxon Church in the heart of Norfolk.The five en suite rooms all have television and tea/coffee making facilities. Meals are served in the beamed bar and in the newly refurbished restaurant. Well situated for tourist attractions in Norfolk; wild life park close by. The resident ghost is more mischievous than troublesome. **ETC ♦♦♦**

154 Norfolk   Board / ENGLAND

Holmdene Farm
Mrs G. Davidson, Holmdene Farm, Beeston, King's Lynn, Norfolk PE32 2NJ

Holmdene Farm is a small livestock farm situated in central Norfolk within easy reach of Coast and Broads. Sporting activities are available locally and the village pub is nearby. The 17th century beamed farmhouse is comfortable and welcoming with log fires for those chilly evenings. One double, one twin and two single rooms, all with beverage trays. Pets welcome. B & B from £20 per person. Evening meal from £15. Weekly terms and child reduction available.
Two self catering cottages, one sleeping five and the other up to eight persons. Terms on request. Please telephone for further details.

ETC ★★★   **Working Farm • Cycles for hire**
                     Telephone: 01328 701284
E-mail: holmdenefarm@farmersweekly.net   Website: www.northnorfolk.co.uk/holmdenefarm
See also Colour Advertisement

HOLT
Mrs Lynda Mack, Hempstead Hall, Holt NR25 6TN (01263 712224). Working farm. Enjoy a relaxing holiday with a friendly atmosphere in our 18th century flint farmhouse, beautifully set on a 300 acre arable farm with ducks, donkeys and large gardens. Close to the north Norfolk coast and its many attractions. Take a ride on the steam train or a boat trip to Blakeney Point Seal Sanctuary. Spot the wild deer or the barn owl on the circular walk through our conservation award-winning farm to Holt Country Park. Large en suite family room (children over 8 years only please), double with private bathroom. Colour TV, tea/coffee facilities. Large lounge with log burning stove. Non-smoking. Sorry, no pets indoors. Bed and Breakfast from £22 per person. Children's reductions. **ETC ♦♦♦♦,** *FARM STAY UK MEMBER.*
website: www.broadland.com/hempsteadhall

KING'S LYNN (near)
Amanda Case, Lower Farm, Harpley, King's Lynn PE31 6TU (01485 520240). Lower Farm is a lovely old farmhouse with large, comfortable rooms. Two double rooms en suite, and one double room with private bathroom. It is close to Sandringham and Houghton Hall; the Peddars Way is nearby for walkers, and there is good golfing, sailing and shooting in the area. It is 20 minutes from the coast, where there are good pubs, also Burnham Market with good shopping. Stabling available; dogs must be kept outside. Terms from £25 to £28 per person, single £30 to £35.

NORFOLK BROADS (Neatishead)
Alan and Sue Wrigley, Regency Guest House, The Street, Neatishead, Near Norwich NR12 8AD (Tel & Fax: 01692 630233). An 18th century guest house in picturesque, unspoilt village in heart of Broadlands. Personal service top priority - same owners for 25 years. Long established name for very generous English Breakfasts. 20 minutes from medieval city of Norwich and six miles from coast. Ideal base for touring East Anglia - a haven for wildlife, birdwatching, cycling and walking holidays. Number one centre for Broads sailing, fishing and boating. Guesthouse, holder of "Good Care" award for high quality services, has three bedrooms (king-size double or twin en suite, double en suite, and standard king-size or twin), individually Laura Ashley-style decorated and tastefully furnished with TV and tea/coffee making facilities. Two main bathrooms. Separate tables in beamed ceiling breakfast room. Guests' sittingroom. Cot, babysitting. Reduced rates on stays of more than one night. Pets welcome. Parking. Open all year. Fire Certificate held. There are two good eating places within walking distance of guest house. Bed and Breakfast from £22. **AA/ETC ♦♦♦♦**
e-mail: regencywrigley@btopenworld.com   website: www.norfolkbroads.com/regency

ENGLAND / Board   Norfolk / Northamptonshire

NORWICH
Foxwood Guest House, Fakenham Road, Taverham, Norwich NR8 6HR (01603 868474). For those preferring the country rather than the city, why not try Foxwood Guest House. We are set in the middle of twenty acres of woodland, on the outskirts of the village of Taverham, approximately six miles from Norwich. All rooms have comfortable beds and tea/coffee making facilities; en suite available. There are many rivers and lakes nearby for the fishermen as well as many golfing areas and a new Sportspark. In Norwich there are lots of restaurants, café/bars, shops, art galleries and the Maddermarket Theatre, Castle Museum and cathedrals; National Trust properties miles of coastline, bird reserves and many other places of interest in the area. Bed & Breakfast from £25 single, £50 double.
e-mail: yvonne@foxwoodguesthouse.fsnet.co.uk

WYMONDHAM
Mrs Joy Morter, Home Farm, Morley, Wymondham NR18 9SU (01953 602581). Comfortable accommodation set in four acres, quiet location, secluded garden. Conveniently situated off A11 between Attleborough and Wymondham, an excellent location for Snetterton and only 20 minutes from Norwich and 45 minutes from Norfolk Broads. Accommodation comprises two double rooms and one twin-bedded room, all with TV, tea/coffee facilities and central heating. Children over five years old welcome, but sorry no animals and no smoking. Bed and Breakfast from £22 to £24 per person per night.

NORTHAMPTONSHIRE

KETTERING
Mrs A. Clarke, Dairy Farm, Cranford St Andrew, Kettering NN14 4AQ (01536 330273). Enjoy a holiday in our comfortable 17th century farmhouse with oak beams and inglenook fireplaces. Four-poster bed now available. Peaceful surroundings, large garden containing ancient circular dovecote. Dairy Farm is a working farm situated in a beautiful Northamptonshire village just off the A14, within easy reach of many places of interest or ideal for a restful holiday. Good farmhouse food and friendly atmosphere. Open all year, except Christmas. Bed and Breakfast from £22 to £35 (children under 10 half price); Evening Meal from £14. **ETC** ♦♦♦ *SILVER AWARD.*

Visit the **FHG** website
www.holidayguides.com
for details of the wide choice of accommodation featured in the full range of FHG titles

NORTHUMBERLAND

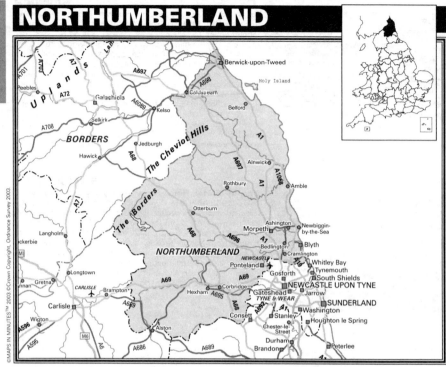

See also Colour Display Advertisement

ALNWICK (near)
Mrs Celia Curry, Howick Scar Farm House, Craster, Alnwick NE66 3SU (Tel & Fax: 01665 576665). Comfortable farmhouse accommodation on working mixed farm situated on the Heritage Coast between the villages of Craster and Howick. Ideal base for walking, golfing, bird-watching or exploring the coast, moors and historic castles. The Farne Islands famous for their colonies of seals and seabirds, and Lindisfarne (Holy Island) are within easy driving distance. Accommodation is in two double rooms with washbasins. Guests have their own TV lounge/dining room with full central heating. Non-smoking. Bed and Breakfast from £20. Open Easter to November. ETC ♦♦♦, *FARM STAY UK*.
e-mail: stay@howickscar.co.uk
website: www.howickscar.co.uk

See also Colour Display Advertisement

BAMBURGH
Waren House Hotel, Waren Mill, Belford, Near Bamburgh NE70 7EE (01668 214581; Fax: 01668 214484). Set in six acres of mature wooded grounds, Waren House has been reborn under the talented and loving hands of owners, Anita and Peter Laverack. Beautifully presented food is served in the elegant dining room, and the wine list is a most fascinating read. Probably the icing on the cake is that the beauty of this uncrowded Heritage Coast makes it much like the Lake District was 40 years ago, before it was well and truly discovered. Please do "discover" Waren House – it will be a choice you will never regret.
ETC/AA/RAC ★★★
e-mail: enquiries@warenhousehotel.co.uk
website: www.warenhousehotel.co.uk

ENGLAND / Board   Northumberland / Nottinghamshire 157

HALTWHISTLE
Saughy Rigg Farm, Twice Brewed, Haltwhistle NE49 9PT (01434 344120/344746). Saughy Rigg Farm is situated about half a mile north of Hadrian's Wall within the National Park, and all the most important Roman sites are within four miles. Accommodation is available in double, family or twin en suite rooms, all with TV and tea/coffee making facilities. There is a cosy guest lounge/dining room. Breakfasts are freshly cooked to order, and packed lunches and evening meals are also available on request. Young children and well-behaved pets are welcome. Baggage transport is available for walkers and cyclists. Bed and Breakfast from £17.50pppn. **ETC ♦♦♦♦**
e-mail: kathandbrad@aol.com
website: www.saughyrigg.co.uk

HEXHAM
Mrs Ruby Keenleyside, Struthers Farm, Catton, Allendale, Hexham NE47 9LP (01434 683580). Struthers Farm offers a warm welcome in the heart of England, with many splendid local walks from the farm itself. Panoramic views. Situated in an area of outstanding beauty. Double/twin rooms, en suite, central heating. Good farmhouse cooking. Ample safe parking. Come and share our home and enjoy beautiful countryside. Children welcome, pets by prior arrangement. Open all year. Bed and Breakfast from £22; Evening Meal from £12.

HEXHAM
Mr & Mrs D Maughan, Greencarts Farm, Humshaugh, Hexham NE46 4BW (01434 681320; mobile: 07752 697355). Greencarts is a working farm situated in Roman Wall country, ideally placed for exploring by car, bike or walking. It has magnificent views of the Tyne Valley. It is warm and homely with central heating and log fires. Home cooked food is provided. En suite accommodation with safe car/bike parking. Convenient for Hexham Racecourse. Fishing available locally. All welcome. Bed and Breakfast from £22 to £25. Open all year
e-mail: Sandra.Maughan2@200m.co.uk.

NOTTINGHAMSHIRE

See also Colour Display Advertisement

STANTON-ON-THE-WOLDS
Mrs V. Moffat, Laurel Farm, Browns Lane, Stanton-on-the-Wolds, Nottingham NG12 5BL (0115 9373488). Laurel Farm is an old farmhouse in approximately three acres of land. All rooms are spacious, with en suite or private facilities. Teatrays, TV, hair dryer and bath robes for non en suite room. Laurel Farm is on a quiet lane with easy access from M1, A46 and A606. Convenient for tourist attractions. Breakfast is served in a spacious dining room and only local produce and our own free-range eggs used. Laurel Farm rooms are for non-smokers only and are therefore 'asthma friendly'. Double/twin from £25.00 per person per night, single occupancy from £38.00 per person per night. **ETC ♦♦♦**

OXFORDSHIRE

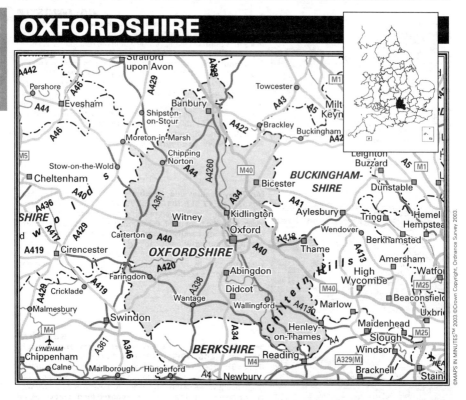

BANBURY (near)
Mrs E. J. Lee, The Mill Barn, Lower Tadmarton, Near Banbury OX15 5SU (01295 780349). Tadmarton is a small village, three miles south-west of Banbury. The Mill, no longer working, was originally water powered and the stream lies adjacent to the house. The Mill Barn has been tastefully converted, retaining many traditional features such as beams and exposed stone walls, yet it still has all the amenities a modern house offers. Two spacious en suite bedrooms, one downstairs, are available to guests in this comfortable family home. Base yourself here and visit Stratford, historic Oxford, Woodstock and the beautiful Cotswolds, knowing you are never farther than an hour's drive away. Open all year for Bed and Breakfast from £25, reductions for children. Weekly terms available.

HENLEY-ON-THAMES
The Old Bakery, Skirmett, Near Henley-on-Thames RG9 6TD (01491 638309; Fax: 01491 638086). This welcoming family house is situated on the site of an old bakery, seven miles from Henley-on-Thames and Marlow; half-an-hour from Heathrow and Oxford; one hour from London. It is in the Hambleden Valley in the beautiful Chilterns, with many excellent pubs selling good food. Excellent village pub in Skirmett within easy walking distance. One double en suite, one twin-bedded room and one double with use of own bathroom. All with TV and tea making facilities. Open all year. Parking for five cars (car essential). Children and pets welcome. Bed and Breakfast from £30 single; £60 double, £75 en suite. ETC ◆◆◆◆
e-mail: liz.roach@euphony.net

ENGLAND / Board   Oxfordshire **159**

See also Colour Display Advertisement

LONG HANBOROUGH
Mrs I.J. Warwick, The Close Guest House, Witney Road, Long Hanborough OX8 8HF (01993 882485). We offer comfortable accommodation in house set in own grounds of one-and-a-half acres. Three family rooms, four double rooms, all are en suite; one double and one single. All have colour TV and tea/coffee making facilities. Full central heating. Use of garden and car parking for eight cars. Close to Woodstock, Oxford and the Cotswolds. Open all year except Christmas. Bed and Breakfast from £20. **ETC** ♦♦♦

OXFORD
D. J. Underwood, Conifer Lodge, 159 Eynsham Road, Botley OX2 9NE (01865 862280; Fax: 01865 865135). Luxury stone house on the outskirts of Oxford city, only two and a half miles bus route to the city centre, yet in the peace and quiet of the countryside. Very accessible to all tourist areas. Central heating in all rooms, double glazed throughout, colour television, large garden and patio, plenty of parking space. Bed and breakfast, business persons welcome, reasonable rates. **ETC** ♦♦♦
website: www.smoothhound.co.uk/oxford

WOODSTOCK
The Leather Bottel, East End, North Leigh, Near Witney OX8 6PY (01993 882174). Joe and Nena Purcell invite you to The Leather Bottel guest house situated in the quiet hamlet of East End near North Leigh, convenient for Blenheim Palace, Woodstock, Roman Villa, Oxford and the Cotswolds. Breathtaking countryside walks. Two double en suite bedrooms, one family room with own bathroom, one single bedroom, all with colour TV and tea/coffee making facilities. Bed and Breakfast £30 per night for single room, from £45 for double. Children welcome. Open all year. Directions: follow signs to Roman Villa off A4095. **ETC** ♦♦♦

Two for the price of one at
Cogges Manor Farm Museum
see our READERS' OFFER VOUCHERS for details

See the *Family-Friendly Pubs & Inns*
Supplement on pages 335 - 344 for establishments
which really welcome children

SHROPSHIRE

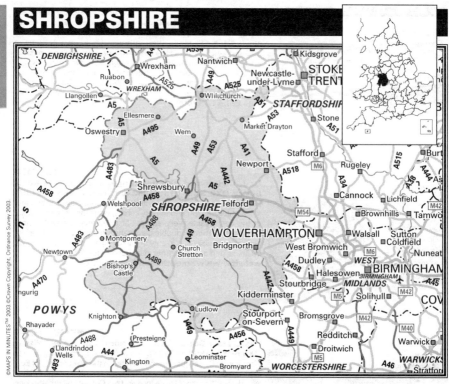

BISHOP'S CASTLE

Mrs Ann Williams, Shuttocks Wood, Norbury, Bishop's Castle SY9 5EA (01588 650433; Fax: 01588 650492). Shuttocks Wood is a Scandinavian house in woodland setting situated within easy travelling distance of the Long Mynd and Stiperstone Hills. Accommodation consists of two double and two twin-bedded rooms, all en suite and with tea/coffee facilities and colour TV. Good walks and horse riding nearby and a badger set just 20 yards from the door! Ample parking. Non-smoking establishment. Children over 12 years welcome. Sorry, no pets. Open all year. Bed and Breakfast from £25 per person per night. Credit cards accepted.

CHURCH STRETTON

Mrs Mary Jones, Acton Scott Farm, Acton Scott, Church Stretton SY6 6QN (01694 781260; Fax: 0870 129 4591). Working farm. Lovely 17th century farmhouse in peaceful village amidst the beautiful hills of South Shropshire, an Area of Outstanding Natural Beauty. The house is full of character; the rooms, which are all heated, are comfortable and spacious. Bedrooms have washbasin and tea/coffee making facilities; en suite or private bathroom. Colour TV lounge. Children welcome, pets accepted by arrangement. We are a working farm, centrally situated for visiting Ironbridge, Shrewsbury and Ludlow, each easily reached within half-an-hour. Visitors' touring and walking information available. Bed and full English Breakfast from £20 per person. Non-smoking. Open all year excluding November, December and January. ETC ◆◆◆, *FARM STAY UK MEMBER.*
e-mail: bandb@actonscottfarm.co.uk   website: www.actonscottfarm.co.uk

ENGLAND / Board   Shropshire   **161**

See also Colour Display Advertisement

CHURCH STRETTON
Mrs Lyn Bloor, Malt House Farm, Lower Wood, Church Stretton SY6 6LF (01694 751379). Olde worlde beamed farmhouse situated amidst spectacular scenery on the lower slopes of the Long Mynd hills. We are a working farm producing beef cattle and sheep. One double and one twin bedrooms, both with en suite bathrooms, colour TV, hairdryer and tea tray. Good farmhouse cooking is served in the dining room. Private guests' sitting room. Non-smoking. Regret no children or pets. Bed and Breakfast from £20 per person per night; Evening Meal from £15.00 per person. Now fully licensed. **AA** ◆◆◆

CLUN
Mrs M. Jones, Llanhedric, Clun, Craven Arms SY7 8NG (01588 640203). Working farm. Put your feet up and relax in the recliners as the beauty of the garden, the trickle of the pond, and the views of Clun and its surrounding hills provide solace from the stress of modern day life. Receive a warm welcome at this traditional oak-beamed farmhouse set back from the working farm. Three bedrooms, double en suite, tea/coffee facilities and good home cooking. Visitors' lounge with inglenook fireplace; separate dining room. Walks, history and attractions all close by. Bed and Breakfast from £22. Reductions for children. Non-smoking household. Regret no dogs in house. Open April to October. **ETC** ◆◆◆

CRAVEN ARMS
Mrs I.J. Evans, Springhill Farm, Clun, Craven Arms SY7 8PE (Tel & Fax: 01588 640337). Springhill Farm is a working farm in an idyllic situation on the Offa's Dyke footpath in glorious South Shropshire countryside with panoramic views over hills and valleys. Walks from the front door. This is a place to relax and unwind away from the pressures of life. Close by are Ludlow, Church Stretton, Ironbridge. All rooms en suite. Evening meals are provided. For reservations contact **Ingrid Evans.**

IRONBRIDGE
Jutta and Alan Ward, Linley Crest, Linley Brook, Near Bridgnorth WV16 4SZ (Tel & Fax: 01746 765527). Very convenient for the medieval towns of Shrewsbury, Bridgnorth, Much Wenlock, Ludlow, Ironbridge and the dramatic landscape of the Long Mynd. We offer three generous double rooms with TV, beverage tray, hairdryer – two of which have a shower en suite, guest-controlled heating and EASY ACCESS; additionally, one has a private conservatory. The third bedroom has a private bathroom. Delicious English breakfast provided and special diets catered for. Winners of the Bridgnorth District Council Healthy Eating Gold Award since 1999. Pub serving food within staggering distance. Open all year, off-road parking; drying facilities, No smoking, no pets, no cards. Children very welcome. From £22.50 per person per night. Weekly rate available. Euro payment accepted. Wir sprechen Deutsch – Herzlich willkommen! Warm welcome assured. **ETC** ◆◆◆ SILVER AWARD.
e-mail: linleycrest@easicom.com   website: www.linleycrest.co.uk

---

The FHG Directory of Website Addresses
on pages 345 - 373 is a useful quick reference guide for holiday accommodation with e-mail and/or website details

LUDLOW (Near)

Mrs Rachel Edwards, Haynall Villa, Little Hereford, Near Ludlow SY8 4BG (Tel & Fax: 01584 711589). Relax in our early 19th century farmhouse, with many original features, oak stairs lead to comfortable rooms (one en suite), all with tea/coffee making facilities, with views over the beautiful, unspoilt countryside. We have a large attractive garden and private fishing (carp). We are ideally situated, approximately two miles from the A49, within easy reach of Ludlow, National Trust Properties, gardens and lovely villages. Walk by the river or experience panoramic views from the Shropshire hills. Sample the local foods. Combine your visit with the Ludlow Festival or one of its many events. Bed and Breakfast from £19 per person per night. Evening meal - check price and availability. Non-smoking. Pets by arrangement. Children over six years welcome. **AA ◆◆◆**
e-mail: rachelmedwards@hotmail.com   website: www.haynallvilla.co.uk

NEWPORT

Sambrook Manor, Sambrook, Newport TF10 8AL (01952 550256; mobile: 07811 915535). Sambrook is centrally situated in the heart of Shropshire, 15 minutes from Telford and Market Drayton, and 30 minutes from Shrewsbury, Potteries, Stafford, and 40 minutes from Birmingham, Alton Towers and the Welsh Borders. The Manor House, which is a Listed building, is the focal point of the farm which has beef and dairy cattle, sheep, horses and of course the farm dogs. On the ground floor is a large sitting room and conservatory for guests' use, while upstairs are three guest bedrooms, all en suite. Full English Breakfast cooked to your individual taste. Visitors' room with colour TV. Tea and coffee facility in bedrooms. Private parking. Stabling available for horses – many accessible bridle paths. Bed and Breakfast £25, reduction for children. **ETC ◆◆◆**
website: www.go2.co.uk/sambrookmanor

OSWESTRY (near)

Pam Morrissey, Top Farm House, Knockin, Near Oswestry SY10 8HN (01691 682582). Full of charm and character, this beautiful 16th century Grade 1 Listed black and white house is set in the delightful village of Knockin. Enjoy the relaxed atmosphere and elegant surroundings of this special house with its abundance of beams, open fires in winter, and fresh flowers all year round. Sit in the comfortable drawing room where you can read, play the piano, listen to music, or just sit and relax. Hearty breakfasts from our extensive menu are served in the lovely dining room which looks out over the flower-filled garden. The large bedrooms are all en suite, attractively decorated and furnished. All have tea/coffee making facilities, colour TV, etc. The main bathroom has a sauna cabinet and spa bath for guests' use. Convenient for the Welsh Border, Shrewsbury, Chester and Oswestry. Bed and Breakfast from £24 to £35 per person **ETC ◆◆◆◆ SILVER AWARD, AA FOUR RED DIAMONDS.**
e-mail: p.a.m@knockin.freeserve.co.uk

PLEASE NOTE

All the information in this book is given in good faith in the belief that it is correct. However, the publishers cannot guarantee the facts given in these pages, neither are they responsible for changes in policy, ownership or terms that may take place after the date of going to press. Readers should always satisfy themselves that the facilities they require are available and that the terms, if quoted, still apply.

ENGLAND / Board   Shropshire 163

SHREWSBURY
Mrs Sheila Griffiths, Sowbath Farm, Shawbury, Shrewsbury SY4 4ES (Tel & Fax: 01939 250064). Set in 120 acres of farmland, centrally located in the heart of the beautiful county of Shropshire, in a peaceful location with easy access to the local towns and attractions. Accommodation consists of one single room, one double room, two twin rooms, one on the ground floor with an en suite bathroom and Mobility 1 Access. Lounge and dining area. Attractions in the area include Hodnet Hall Gardens, Hawkstone Park Follies, Ironbridge Gorge museums, Secret Hills – the Shropshire Hills Discovery Centre, and Shrewsbury town centre shopping. **ETC ♦♦♦**
e-mail: info@sowbathfarm.co.uk
website: www.sowbathfarm.co.uk

See also Colour Display Advertisement

TELFORD
Mrs Mary Jones, Red House Farm, Longdon-on-Tern, Wellington, Telford TF6 6LE (01952 770245). Red House Farm is a late Victorian farmhouse in the small village of Longdon-on-Tern, noted for its aqueduct, built by Thomas Telford in 1796. Two double bedrooms have private facilities, one family room has its own separate bathroom. All rooms are large and comfortable. Excellent Breakfast. Farm easily located, leave M54 Junction 6, follow A442, take B5063. Central for historic Shrewsbury, Ironbridge Gorge museums or modern Telford. Several local eating places. Open all year. Families most welcome, reductions for children. Pets also welcome. Bed and Breakfast from £20.
e-mail: rhf@virtual-shropshire.co.uk
website: www.virtual-shropshire.co.uk/red-house-farm

FHG
Other specialised
FHG PUBLICATIONS
Published annually: available in all good bookshops or direct from the publisher.

PETS WELCOME! £7.99
Recommended **COUNTRY HOTELS** OF BRITAIN £6.99
Recommended **COUNTRY INNS & PUBS** OF BRITAIN £6.99
Recommended **SHORT BREAK HOLIDAYS** IN BRITAIN £6.99

FHG PUBLICATIONS LTD,
Abbey Mill Business Centre,
Seedhill, Paisley, Renfrewshire PA1 1TJ
Tel: 0141-887 0428 • Fax: 0141-889 7204
e-mail: fhg@ipcmedia.com
website: www.holidayguides.com

SOMERSET

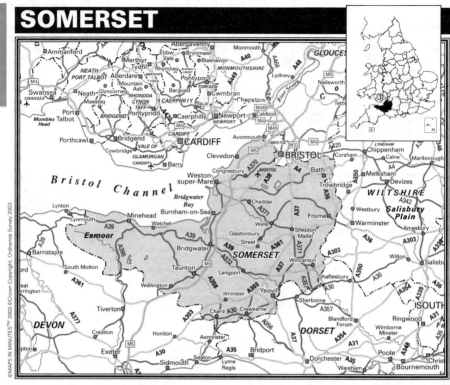

See also Colour Display Advertisement

ASHBRITTLE
Mrs Ann Heard, Lower Westcott Farm, Ashbrittle, Wellington TA21 0HZ (01398 361296). On Devon/Somerset borders, 230 acre family-run farm with cattle, sheep, poultry and horses. Ideal for walking, touring Exmoor, Quantocks, both coasts and many National Trust properties. Pleasant farmhouse, tastefully modernised but with olde worlde charm, inglenook fireplaces and antique furniture, set in large gardens with lawns and flower beds in peaceful, scenic countryside. Two family bedrooms with private facilities and tea/coffee making. Large lounge, separate dining room offering guests every comfort. Noted for relaxed, friendly atmosphere and good home-cooking. Brochure by request. Bed and Breakfast from £22; Dinner £10 per person. Reductions for children. ETC ◆◆◆◆
e-mail: lowerwestcott@aol.com

Haynes Motor Museum • *Near Yeovil, Somerset* • 01963 440804
website: www.haynesmotormuseum.co.uk
Magnificent collection of over 250 vintage, veteran and classic cars, and 50 motorcycles.

West Somerset Railway • *Bishops Lydeard (near Taunton) to Minehead* • 01643 704996
Enjoy 20 miles of glorious Somerset countryside as the steam train gently rolls back the years. Break your journey at any one of ten restored stations along the route. For 24hr talking timetable call 01643 707650.

Worldwide Footprints
Presents
Motion Postcards

The new and exciting way to share your holiday with family and friends. Sealed inside each postcard is a CD-Rom movie which takes you on a relaxing tour, accompanied by gentle background music.

Order now online to preview your destination before you go or to keep as a souvenir of memories past. Alternatively look out for them in the shops when you visit.

www.worldwidefootprints.com
Tel/Fax: 01884 839723
5 Dukes Mead, Meadow Lane, Cullompton, Devon EX15 1QT

BATH (near)
Jackie Bishop, B&B and Self Catering Cottages, Toghill House Farm, Freezing Hill, Wick, Near Bath BS15 5RT (01225 891261; Fax: 01225 892128). Warm and cosy 17th century farmhouse on working farm with outstanding views, yet only three miles north of the historic city of Bath. All rooms en suite with tea making facilities and colour TV, or choose one of our luxury self-catering barn conversions which are equipped to a very high standard and include all linen. Children and pets welcome.

BATH (near)
Mrs Barbara Keevil, Eden Vale Farm, Mill Lane, Beckington, Near Frome BA11 6SN (01373 830371). Eden Vale Farm nestles down in a valley by the River Frome. Enjoying a picturesque location, this old watermill offers a selection of rooms including en suite facilities, complemented by an excellent choice of full English or continental breakfasts. Beckington is an ideal centre for visiting Bath, Longleat, Salisbury, Cheddar, Stourhead and many National Trust Houses including Lacock Village. Only a ten minute walk to the village pub, three-quarters of a mile of river fishing. Local golf courses and lovely walks. Very friendly animals. Dogs welcome. Please phone or write for more information. Open all year. **ETC ◆◆◆**

BRIDGWATER
The Cottage, Fordgate, Bridgwate TA7 0AP (01278 691908). A charming country cottage set in two acres of garden in an Area of Outstanding Natural Beauty and special interest, close to rivers and canal where birds and wildlife flourish. A centre for the famous Somerset Levels and all of this historic county. We offer you privacy, comfort and tranquillity, staying in en suite rooms with king-size antique four-poster beds, TV, heating and hospitality trays. Easy access, with all rooms at ground level opening directly onto the gardens. English country cooking at its best, using fresh vegetables, fruit, honey and free range eggs. Bed and Breakfast from £21pppn. Easy access Junction 24 M5. Ample secure parking. A delightful place to stay especially for that special short break. No smoking in house please. Phone or write for brochure and map. Open all year. HIGHLY RECOMMENDED. Contact: **Beverley Jenkins.**
e-mail: jenkins@thecottage.fsnet.co.uk

Leigh Farm
Pensford, Near Bristol BS39 4BA
Telephone or Fax: 01761 490281

200-year old comfy, natural stone built farmhouse. Guest lounge with open fire in cold weather; TV, video. Bedrooms with TV and beverage trays. Keys for access at all times. Double en suite, family room with cot and private bathroom. Extra bedrooms can be facilitated (subject to availability) at short notice on empty self-catering properties with private facilities. Menu available and breakfasts freshly cooked to order.

• *Working livestock farm* • *Cows with calves and growing stock* • *A few free-range pigs and chickens.*
Credit cards accepted • *Regret no pets* • *B&B from £27.00pp.*

See also Colour Advertisement

Brinsea Green Farm

Brinsea Green is a Period farmhouse surrounded by open countryside. Set in 500 acres of farmland, it has easy access from the M5, (J21), A38 and Bristol Airport. Close to the Mendip Hills, the historic towns of Bath, Bristol and Wells, plus the wonders of Cheddar Gorge and Wookey Hole. Beautifully furnished en suite/shower bedrooms offer lovely views, comfortable beds, complimentary hot drinks and biscuits, radio, alarm, toiletries, sewing kit and hair dryer for your convenience. Both guest lounge (with TV) and dining room have inglenook fireplaces providing a warm, home from home atmosphere. Choose from our wide range of books and enjoy real peace and tranquillity. Early booking recommended.

Mrs Delia Edwards,
Brinsea Green Farm
Brinsea Lane,
Congresbury, Near Bristol
BS49 5JN
Tel: (01934) 852278
Fax: (01934) 852 861

SINGLE FROM £23.00 - £28.00   DOUBLE FROM £38.00 - £45.00
e-mail: delia@brinseagreenfarm.co.uk
website: www.brinseagreenfarm.co.uk

BRISTOL
Mrs M. Hasell, The Model Farm, Norton Hawkfield, Pensford, Bristol BS39 4HA (01275 832144). Working farm. Model Farm is situated two miles off the A37 in a peaceful hamlet, nestling under the Dundry Hills. A working arable and beef farm in easy reach of Bristol, Bath, Cheddar and many other interesting places. The spacious accommodation is in two en suite rooms, one family and one double, with tea/coffee facilities. Separate dining room and lounge with colour TV for visitors. Private parking. Open all year (except Christmas and New Year). Bed and Breakfast from £20. ETC ♦♦♦

DULVERTON
Mrs Carole Nurcombe, Marsh Bridge Cottage, Dulverton TA22 9QG (01398 323197). This superb accommodation has been made possible by the refurbishment of this Victorian former ex-gamekeeper's cottage on the banks of the River Barle. The friendly welcome, lovely rooms, delicious (optional) evening meals using local produce, and clotted cream sweets are hard to resist! Open all year, and in autumn the trees that line the river either side of Marsh Bridge turn to a beautiful golden backdrop. Just off the B3223 Dulverton to Exford road, it is easy to find and, once discovered, rarely forgotten. From outside the front door footpaths lead in both directions alongside the river. Fishing available. Terms from £19 per person Bed and Breakfast or £34 per person Dinner, Bed and Breakfast.

ENGLAND / Board   Somerset **167**

EXMOOR (DULVERTON)

Mrs P. Vellacott, Springfield Farm, Ashwick Lane, Dulverton TA22 9QD (Tel & Fax: 01398 323722). At Springfield we offer you wonderful hospitality and delicious food. We farm 270 acres within the Exmoor National Park rearing sheep and cattle. Peacefully situated a one-and-a-half mile walk from the famous beauty spot of Tarr Steps, four miles from the market town of Dulverton (film location of 'The Land Girls'). Much wildlife including red deer can be seen on the farm. An ideal base for walking or touring Exmoor and North Devon coastal resorts. Riding and fishing nearby. One double room with private WC and shower, one twin/family en suite and one double en suite - all with drinks making facilities. Guests' lounge with TV, spacious dining room leading to patio and large garden. Access to rooms at all times. Ample parking (garage by request). Pets by arrangement. No smoking in farmhouse, please. Bed and Breakfast from £23.50 to £27 per person per night. Evening meals (with 24 hours notice) £15.75. Reductions for stays of three nights or more. **ETC** ♦♦♦♦
e-mail: info@springfieldfarms.co.uk   website: www.springfieldfarms.co.uk

GLASTONBURY (near)

Mrs M. White, Barrow Farm, North Wootton, near Glastonbury BA4 4HL (Tel & Fax: 01749 890245). Working farm. Barrow is a dairy farm of 146 acres. The house is 15th century and of much character, situated between Wells, Glastonbury and Shepton Mallet. It makes an excellent touring centre for visiting Somerset's beauty spots and historic places, for example, Cheddar, Bath, Wookey Hole and Longleat. Guest accommodation consists of two double rooms, one family room, one single room and one twin-bedded room, each with washbasin, TV and tea/coffee making facilities. Bathroom, two toilets; two lounges, one with colour TV; dining room with separate tables. Guests can enjoy farmhouse fare in generous variety, home baking a speciality. Bed and Breakfast, with optional four-course Dinner available. Car essential; ample parking. Children welcome; cot and babysitting available. Open all year except Christmas. Sorry, no pets. Bed and Breakfast from £18. Dinner, Bed and Breakfast from £30. **AA** ♦♦♦

MONTACUTE

Paterson and Sue Weir, Slipper Cottage, 41 Bishopston, Montacute TA15 6UX (01935 823073; mobile: 07812 145402; Fax: 01935 826868). A friendly welcome awaits you at this charming 17th century cottage, in one of Somerset's prettiest villages. Montacute House, excellent pubs and restaurants just around the corner. Tintinhull House Gardens, Barrington Court, Stourhead, Lytes Cary, Wells Cathedral, Sherborne Abbey, Glastonbury Abbey and Lyme Regis not far away. Four golf courses within ten miles. Accommodation consists of two double rooms, both with vanity basin, shaver point, colour TV, central heating and tea/coffee making facilities. Terms from £40 to £44 per room, per night including breakfast. Single occupancy £26 to £40. Sorry, no pets, no smoking. Open all year except Christmas and New Year.
FHG DIPLOMA WINNER 2001, 2002. **ETC** ♦♦♦
e-mail: pat.weir@ntlworld.co.uk   website: www.slippercottage.co.uk

NORTH PETHERTON

Mrs Sue Milverton, Lower Clavelshay Farm, North Petherton, Near Bridgwater TA6 6PJ (01278 662347). Working farm. 17th century farmhouse on a working dairy farm set in its own peaceful valley on the edge of the beautiful Quantock Hills. Off the beaten track but within easy reach of the many attractions in Somerset. Only 10 minutes from Junction 24 of the M5 and 15 minutes from Taunton. Two en suite double bedrooms and one family room with private bathroom. Experience simple pleasures - beautiful countryside, long walks, fresh air, wildlife, wild flowers, log fires, starry nights, comfy beds, peace and tranquillity, good food, good books and good humour. Bring your family and your horse! Stables available - wonderful riding on the doorstep. Horse heaven! All meals with fresh local produce - our own where possible. Doubles £22 per person per night; family room £50 per night. Evening Meals on request (£12 adult, £6 child). **AA** ♦♦♦

The Castle Hotel
Porlock, Somerset TA24 8PY
Tel & Fax: 01643 862504

The Castle Hotel is a small, fully licensed family-run hotel in the centre of the lovely Exmoor village of Porlock. It is an ideal holiday location for those who wish to enjoy the grandeur of Exmoor on foot or by car. The beautiful villages of Selworthy and Dunster with its castle are only a short distance away. There are 13 en suite bedrooms, all fully heated, with colour TV and tea/coffee making facilities. The Castle Hotel has a well-stocked bar with Real Ale. Draught Guinness and Cider. A full range of Bar Meals are available at lunchtimes and Evenings or dine in our Restaurant. Children and pets are most welcome. Family room available, cots available on request. Pool, darts and skittles.

✤ ✤ **Special Breaks available** ✤ **Extremely low rates** ✤ ✤

See also Colour Advertisement

SHERBORNE (near)
Mrs Sue Stretton, Beech Farm, Sigwells, Charlton Horethorne, Near Sherborne, Dorset DT9 4LN (Tel & Fax: 01963 220524). Comfortable, spacious farmhouse with relaxed atmosphere on our 137 acre dairy farm, also carrying beef and horses in an area with wonderful views, particularly from Corton Beacon. Located on the Somerset/Dorset border, six miles from Wincanton, four miles from Sherborne and just two miles off the A303. A centrally heated farmhouse with a double room en suite, a twin room and a family room with guest bathroom, all with TV, tea/coffee trays. Pets and horses welcome by arrangement. Bed and Breakfast £18 per person. Less 10% for two or more nights. Open all year except Christmas.

TAUNTON
The Falcon Hotel, Henlade, Taunton TA3 5DH (01823 442502; Fax: 01823 442670). You can always expect a warm welcome at this historic villa, with just the right blend of comfortable, spacious accommodation, friendly efficient staff and the personal attention of its family owners. Located one mile from the M5 motorway, it makes an ideal base for business stays, or as a touring centre for this attractive corner of the West Country. Facilities include ten en suite bedrooms with colour TV, tea/coffee making facilities, direct dial telephone, etc. Honeymoon suite, conference facilities, restaurant and ample parking. Superbly accessible to Quantock, Blackdown Hills, Exmoor, North and South Devon coasts. Our tariff is inclusive of a Full English Breakfast. **ETC ★★★, AA ★★**

THEALE
Gilly & Vern Clark, Yew Tree Farm, Theale, Near Wedmore BS28 4SN (01934 712475). This 17th century farmhouse is equidistant between Wells and Cheddar both approximately ten minutes away by car. The seaside towns of Weston, Burnham and Brean are close by and the cities of Bath and Bristol, both served with park and ride facilities, are approx. 40 minutes' drive. There is a very warm welcome awaiting you at this farm, which has been in the Clark family for over 120 years. Lovely accommodation with en suite facilities, colour TV (one room with video) and full coffee and tea making facilities. Two and three-course meals available. Children welcome; occasional pets at discretion of the owners. From £21 per person per night. Please telephone for brochure.
e-mail: enquiries@yewtreefarmbandb.co.uk

Readers are requested to mention this guidebook when seeking accommodation (and please enclose a stamped addressed envelope).

ENGLAND / Board   Somerset **169**

See also Colour Display Advertisement

WASHFORD
Mrs Sarah Richmond, Hungerford Farm, Washford, Watchet TA23 0JZ (01984 640285). Hungerford Farm is a comfortable 13th century farmhouse on a 350 acre mixed farm, three-quarters of a mile from the West Somerset Steam Railway; quarter-of-a-mile from Cleeve Abbey and Washford Mill offering local arts and crafts. Situated in beautiful countryside on the edge of the Brendon Hills and Exmoor National Park. Within easy reach of the North Devon coast, two-and-a-half miles from the Bristol Channel and Quantock Hills. Marvellous country for walking, riding, and fishing on the reservoirs. Family room and twin-bedded room, both with colour TV; own bathroom, shower. Breakfast room with TV and open fire on colder days. Children welcome at reduced rates, cot and high chair. Pets by arrangement. Bed and Breakfast from £20, reduced rates for longer stays. Evening drink included. Open February to November.
e-mail: sarah.richmond@virgin.net

WESTON-SUPER-MARE
Sunset Bay Hotel, 53 Beach Road, Weston-Super-Mare BS23 1BH (01934 623519). Sunset Bay Hotel is a non-smoking, small, family-run hotel enjoying an unrivalled position on the seafront, with superb views to Weston Bay and the Welsh coastline. A guest lounge on the first floor overlooks the bay, with games and books for the enjoyment of our guests. Breakfast is served in the dining room/bar overlooking the beach and lawns, and though we do not provide evening meals, there is a menu of hot and cold snacks. Packed lunches can be supplied on request. All rooms are en suite, or with a private bathroom, and TV, tea/coffee making facilities, hairdryers and towels are supplied in all rooms. On arrival we would like to welcome you with a complimentary tray of tea and cakes. Sunset Bay is ideal for family holidays, weekend breaks, short breaks and holidays at any time of year.
e-mail: relax@sunsetbayhotel.co.uk

WIVELISCOMBE
Jenny Cope, North Down Farm, Pyncombe Lane, Wiveliscombe, Taunton TA4 2BL (Tel & Fax: 01984 623730). In tranquil, secluded surroundings on the Somerset/Devon border. Traditional working farm set in 100 acres of natural beauty with panoramic views of over 40 miles. M5 motorway seven miles and Taunton ten miles. All rooms tastefully furnished to high standard include en suite, TV, and tea/coffee facilities. Double, twin or single rooms available. Dining room and lounge with log fires for our guests' comfort; centrally heated and double glazed. Drying facilities. Delicious home produced food a speciality. Fishing, golf, horse riding and country sports nearby. Dogs welcome. Bed and Breakfast from £25 pppn, £195 weekly. North Down Break: three nights Bed and Breakfast and Evening Meal £95 per person. ETC ♦♦♦♦ *SILVER AWARD.*
e-mail: jennycope@tiscali.co.uk

One FREE child ticket with every fare-paying adult
(Not valid for "Day our with Thomas" events) at
Avon Valley Railway
see our READERS' OFFER VOUCHERS for details

One child FREE with two full-paying adults at
The Helicopter Museum
see our READERS' OFFER VOUCHERS for details

STAFFORDSHIRE

See also Colour Display Advertisement

ECCLESHALL
M. Hiscoe-James, Offley Grove Farm, Adbaston, Eccleshall ST20 0QB (01785 280205). You'll consider this a good find! Quality accommodation and excellent breakfasts. Small traditional mixed farm surrounded by beautiful countryside. The house is tastefully furnished and provides all home comforts. Whether you are planning to book here for a break in your journey, stay for a weekend or take your holidays here, you will find something to suit all tastes among the many local attractions. Situated on the Staffordshire/Shropshire borders we are convenient for Alton Towers, Stoke-on-Trent, Ironbridge, etc. Just 15 minutes from M6 and M54; midway between Eccleshall and Newport, four miles from the A519. Reductions for children. Play area for children. Open all year. Bed and Breakfast all en suite from £24. Many guests return. Self-catering cottages available. Brochure on request.
RAC ♦♦♦ *WARM WELCOME AWARD AND SPARKLING DIAMOND AWARD.*
e-mail: accomm@offleygrovefarm.freeserve.co.uk   website: www.offleygrovefarm.co.uk

KINGSLEY
Mrs Jane S. Clowes, The Church Farm, Holt Lane, Kingsley, Stoke-on-Trent ST10 2BA (Tel & Fax: 01538 754759). The famous Alton Towers is just five and a half miles from our farm. The Churnet Valley, with steam railway, wildlife park, narrowboat trips, Nick Williams Pottery and a maze of footpaths, is a fifteen minute walk; truly a hidden paradise! The Potteries and Peak District are within eight miles. Having visited all of these, come and unwind in our spacious cottage garden or with a book by the log fire in winter. Enjoy our beautifully furnished period farmhouse built in 1700 with many thoughtful additions for your comfort. Breakfast menu using own and local produce. Totally non-smoking. Tariff: Adults £20 to £25, children 12 years and under £12. **ETC ♦♦♦,** *"WHICH? GOOD BED & BREAKFAST GUIDE."*

STOKE-ON-TRENT
Mrs Barlow, Hermitage Working Farm, Froghall, Near Cheadle ST10 2HQ (01538 266515). Farmhouse Bed and Breakfast and self-catering accommodation situated on a 75 acre mixed livestock farm. Superbly positioned and enjoying probably some of the best views in Staffordshire overlooking the picturesque Churnet Valley, affectionately known as 'Staffordshire's Little Switzerland'. The stone barn conversions are extensively equipped with some ground floor sleeping accommodation suitable for the partially disabled.
website: www.hermitagefarm.co.uk

STOKE-ON-TRENT
Mrs D. Bickle, Crowtrees Farm, Oakamoor, Stoke-on-Trent ST10 3DY (Tel & Fax: 01538 702260). 200-year-old working family farm overlooking the Churnet Valley offering very comfortably furnished accommodation in four en suite bedrooms. Family rooms available. Within easy reach of the Potteries, Peak District and Alton Towers. Non-smoking. Own entrance with access at any time. Bed and Breakfast from £22. Special short breaks available. **ETC/AA ♦♦♦♦**
e-mail: dianne@crowtreesfarm.co.uk
website: www.crowtreesfarm.co.uk

SUFFOLK

FRAMLINGHAM
Mr and Mrs Kindred, High House Farm, Cransford, Framlingham, Woodbridge IP13 9PD (01728 663461; Fax: 01728 663409). Working farm. Beautifully restored 15th Century Farmhouse on family-run arable farm, featuring exposed oak beams and inglenook fireplaces, with spacious and comfortable accommodation. One double room, en suite and one large family room with double and twin beds and private adjacent bathroom. A warm welcome awaits all, children's cots, high chairs, books, toys, and outside play equipment available. Attractive semi-moated gardens, farm and woodland walks. Explore the heart of rural Suffolk, local vineyards, Easton Farm Park, Framlingham and Orford Castles, Parham Air Museum, Saxtead Windmill, Minsmere, Snape Maltings, Woodland Trust and the Heritage Coast. Bed and Breakfast from £22.50. Reductions for children and stays of three nights or more. Self-catering available in three-bed Gamekeeper's house set in woodland. **ETC** ♦♦♦
e-mail: b&b@highhousefarm.co.uk   website: www.highhousefarm.co.uk

See also Colour Display Advertisement

FRAMLINGHAM
Mrs Jennie Mann, Fiddlers Hall, Cransford, Near Framlingham, Woodbridge IP13 9PQ (01728 663729). Working farm, join in. Signposted on B1119, Fiddlers Hall is a 14th century, moated, oak-beamed farmhouse set in a beautiful and secluded position. It is two miles from Framlingham Castle, 20 minutes' drive from Aldeburgh, Snape Maltings, Woodbridge and Southwold. A Grade II Listed building, it has lots of history and character. The bedrooms are spacious; one has en suite shower room, the other has a private bathroom. Use of lounge and colour TV. Plenty of parking space. Lots of farm animals kept. Traditional farmhouse cooking. Bed and Breakfast terms from £25 per person.

FRAMLINGHAM
Brian and Phyllis Collett, Shimmens Pightle, Dennington Road, Framlingham, Woodbridge IP13 9JT (01728 724036). Shimmens Pightle is situated in an acre of landscaped garden, surrounded by farmland, within a mile of the centre of Framlingham, with its famous castle and church. Ideally situated for the Heritage Coast, Snape Maltings, local vineyards, riding, etc. Cycles can be hired locally. Many good local eating places. Double and twin bedded rooms, with washbasins, on ground floor. Comfortable lounge with TV overlooking garden. Morning tea and evening drinks offered. Sorry, no pets or smoking indoors. Bed and traditional English Breakfast, using local cured bacon and home made marmalade. Vegetarians also happily catered for. SAE please. Open mid April to October. Bed and Breakfast from £23.50 per person. Reduced weekly rates. **ETC** ♦♦♦

WOODBRIDGE
Sue Bagnall, Abbey House, Monk Soham, Woodbridge IP13 7EN (01728 685225). Abbey House is a Victorian rectory set in ten acres of quiet Suffolk countryside in the village of Monk Soham, between Debenham and Framlingham, and within easy reach of Southwold, Lavenham and Aldeburgh. The house is surrounded by secluded gardens with ponds and woodland. The remainder of the grounds are occupied by some Jersey cows, sheep, chickens and waterfowl. Guest accommodation comprises double bedrooms, with either en suite or private bathroom and tea making facilities; exclusive use of dining room and drawing room, with log fire. Bed and Breakfast en suite £27.50 pppn (double); £30 pppn (twin); £25 pppn with private facilities. Please write or phone for further information.

SURREY

See also Colour Display Advertisement

KINGSTON-UPON-THAMES
Chase Lodge, 10 Park Road, Hampton Wick, Kingston-upon-Thames KT1 4AS (020 8943 1862; Fax: 020 8943 9363). An award-winning hotel with style and elegance, set in tranquil surroundings at affordable prices. Easy access to Kingston town centre and all major transport links; 20 minutes from Heathrow Airport; Full English breakfast and à la carte menus; licensed bar. Ideal for wedding receptions. Various golf courses within easy reach. Major credit cards accepted. From £35.50 per person Bed and Breakfast; from £50 per person Dinner, Bed and Breakfast. Full details on request. **LTB/AA/RAC ★★★, LES ROUTIERS.**
e-mail: info@chaselodgehotel.com
website: www.chaselodgehotel.com

EAST SUSSEX

BURWASH
Mrs E. Sirrell, Woodlands Farm, Burwash, Etchingham TN19 7LA (Tel & Fax: 01435 882794). Woodlands Farm stands one-third-of-a mile off the road, surrounded by fields and woods. This peaceful and beautifully modernised 16th century farmhouse offers comfortable and friendly accommodation. Sitting/dining room; two bathrooms, one en suite, double or twin-bedded rooms (one has four-poster bed) together with excellent farm fresh food. This is a farm of 108 acres with a variety of animals, and is situated within easy reach of 20 or more places of interest to visit and half-an-hour from the coast. Open all year. Central heating. Literature provided to help guests. Children welcome. Dogs allowed if sleeping in owner's car. Parking. Evening Meal optional. Bed and Breakfast from £22 (single) to £48 (double). Non-smoking. Telephone or SAE, please.

e-mail: liz_sir@lineone.net
website: www.SmoothHound.co.uk/hotels/woodlands.html

See also Colour Display Advertisement

HASTINGS
Mr and Mrs S. York, Westwood Farm, Stonestile Lane, Hastings TN35 4PG (Tel & Fax: 01424 751038). Working farm. Farm with pigs, sheep, chickens, etc. Quiet rural location off country lane half a mile from B2093 approximately two miles from seafront and town centre. Golf course nearby. Central position for visiting places of interest to suit all ages. Elevated situation with outstanding views over Brede Valley. Double, twin, family rooms with en suite and private facilities. Colour TV, tea/coffee in all rooms, two bedrooms on ground floor. Full English breakfast. Off-road parking. Bed and Breakfast from £20 to £27 per person for two persons sharing. Reduced rates for weekly booking. Also available six-berth self-catering caravan – details on request. **ETC ♦♦♦**

e-mail: york@westwood-farm.fsnet.co.uk
website: www.SmoothHound.co.uk/hotels/westwoodf.html

Admit one FREE adult or child with one adult paying full entrance price at

Paradise Park & Gardens

see our READERS' OFFER VOUCHERS for details

RYE

Jeake's House, Mermaid Street, Rye TN31 7ET (01797 222828; Fax: 01797 222623). Dating from 1689, this beautiful Listed building stands in one of England's most famous streets. Oak-beamed and panelled bedrooms overlook the marsh to the sea. Brass, mahogany or four-poster beds with linen sheets and lace; honeymoon suite. En suite facilities, TV, radio, telephone. Book-lined bar. Traditional and vegetarian breakfast served. Terms from £37 to £58 per person. Private car park. Visa and Mastercard accepted. Pets welcome. **ETC ♦♦♦♦** *SILVER AWARD*, **AA ♦♦♦♦♦** *PREMIER SELECTED*, **RAC ♦♦♦♦♦** *SPARKLING DIAMOND & WARM WELCOME AWARD, GOOD HOTEL GUIDE, CÉSAR AWARD.*

RYE

Pat and Jeff Sullivan, Cliff Farm, Iden Lock, Rye TN31 7QE (Tel & Fax: 01797 280331 – long ring please). Our farmhouse is peacefully set in a quiet elevated position with extensive views over Romney Marsh. The ancient seaport town of Rye with its narrow cobbled streets is two miles away. We are an ideal touring base although the town and immediate district have much to offer - golden beaches, quaint villages, castles, gardens etc. Comfortable guest bedrooms with washbasins and tea/coffee making facilities; two toilets; own shower; diningroom and sittingroom. Home produce. Open March to October for Bed and Breakfast from £20 per person. Reduced weekly rates. **AA ♦♦♦**
e-mail: pat@cliff-farm.co.uk
website: www.cliff-farm.co.uk

WEST SUSSEX

See also Colour Display Advertisement

BOGNOR REGIS

Aldwick Hotel, Aldwick Road, Aldwick, Bognor Regis PO21 2QU (01243 821945; Fax: 01243 821316). Bognor Regis, sunniest town in mainland Britain, provides a splendid point from which to explore the coast and countryside of West Sussex and Hampshire. The Aldwick Hotel has been caring for the needs of holidaymakers since 1947, and is well practised in providing home-from-home comforts, quality food and service. So whether visiting the seaside for sunshine; Chichester for its history, Cathedral and Festival Theatre; or Goodwood for historic car racing on circuit and hill climb, and horse racing over arguably Britain's most scenic racecourse, choosing the Aldwick Hotel will ensure your comfort for short breaks and holidays. **ETC ★★**
e-mail: info@aldwickhotel.co.uk
website: www.aldwickhotel.co.uk

Arundel Castle • *Arundel, West Sussex* • *01903 883136*
website: www.arundelcastle.org
The family home of the Dukes of Norfolk for over 850 years. Superb collection of paintings, furniture and armour; restored Victorian kitchen; grounds with chapel.

Weald & Downland Open Air Musem • *Chichester, West Sussex* • *01243 811348*
website: www.wealddown.co.uk
Over 40 historic buildings carefully re-constructed, including medieval farmstead, working flour mill, and Victorian rural school.

WARWICKSHIRE

ALCESTER
John and Margaret Canning, Glebe Farm, Exhall, Alcester B49 6EA (Tel & Fax: 01789 772202). Shakespeare named our village "Dodging Exhall" and it has somehow "dodged" the passing of time, so if you want a true taste of rural England, come and relax in our quaint old farmhouse - parts of it dating from Tudor times - with its log fires, four-poster bed and country hospitality. One double, one twin and two single rooms, all with tea/coffee trays, electric blankets. En suite rooms available. Smoking in lounge. Payphone. Laundry. Children and pets welcome. Ample parking. Bed and Breakfast from £20. Open all year except Christmas and New Year.

See also Colour Display Advertisement

STRATFORD-UPON-AVON
Mrs Julia Downie, Holly Tree Cottage, Birmingham Road, Pathlow, Stratford-upon-Avon CV37 0ES (Tel & Fax: 01789 204461). Period cottage dating from the 17th Century with antiques, paintings, collection of porcelain, fresh flowers, tasteful furnishings and friendly atmosphere. Picturesque gardens, orchard, paddock and pasture with wildlife and extensive views over open countryside. Situated 3 miles north of Stratford-upon-Avon towards Henley-in-Arden on A3400. Rooms have television, radio/alarm, hospitality trays and hairdryers. Breakfasts are a speciality. Pubs and restaurants nearby. Ideally located for Theatre, Shakespeare Country, Heart of England, Cotswolds, Warwick Castle, Blenheim Palace and National Trust Properties. Well situated for National Exhibition Centre, Birmingham, and National Agricultural Centre, Stoneleigh. Children welcome, pets by arrangement. Non-smoking. Bed & Breakfast from £27.
e-mail: john@hollytree-cottage.co.uk   website: www.hollytree-cottage.co.uk

See also Colour Display Advertisement

STRATFORD-UPON-AVON
Mrs R.M. Meadows, Monk's Barn Farm, Shipston Road, Stratford-upon-Avon CV37 8NA (01789 293714; Fax: 01789 205886). Working farm. Two miles south of Stratford-upon-Avon on the A3400 is Monk's Barn, a 75 acre mixed farm welcoming visitors all year. The farm dates back to the 16th century, although the pretty house is more recent. The double, single and twin rooms, most with en suite facilities, are provided in the main house and the cleverly converted milking parlour. The two ground floor rooms are suitable for some disabled guests. Visitors' lounge. Beautiful riverside walk to the village. Tea/coffee making facilities and colour TV in rooms. Sorry, no pets. Non-smokers preferred. Details on request. Bed and Breakfast from £18 to £20. AA ♦♦♦♦

STRATFORD-UPON-AVON
Anne and Robert Dawkes, Penryn Guest House, 126 Alcester Road, Stratford-upon-Avon CV37 9DP (01789 293718; Fax: 01789 266077). You will be warmly welcomed to Penryn which is situated within easy walking distance of Anne Hathaway's Cottage, the town centre and railway station. For guests travelling by road, a private car park is available. All rooms are en suite and furnished with your comfort in mind, including colour television, hairdryer and tea/coffee making facilities. We strive to offer the finest locally produced food from the Heart of England and guests who prefer the vegetarian option or have special dietary requirements are also well catered for. As well as double and twin rooms we have family-style accommodation sleeping up to three or four people. Fax and e-mail facilities. For further details please access our website or telephone for brochure. ETC/RAC ♦♦♦♦
e-mail: penrynhouse@btinternet.com   website: www.penrynguesthouse.co.uk

WEST MIDLANDS

WOLVERHAMPTON

Featherstone Farm Hotel, New Road, Featherstone, Wolverhampton WV10 7NW (01902 725371; Fax: 01902 731741; mobile: 07836 315258). This is a small, high-class country house hotel set in five acres of unspoiled countryside, only one mile from Junction 11 on the M6 or Junction 1 on the M54. The main house has eight en suite bedrooms with all the facilities one would expect in a hotel of distinction. Self-contained fully furnished cottages with maid service are also available. Kings Repose Indian Restaurant serving freshly prepared dishes, and licensed bar. Secure car park. Children and pets welcome.
ETC ★★★
e-mail: lewisprice@featherstonefarm.co.uk
website: www.featherstonefarm.co.uk

WILTSHIRE

BATH (near)

Mrs Dorothy Robinson, Boyds Farm, Gastard, Near Corsham SN13 9PT (Tel & Fax: 01249 713146). Welcome Host. Dorothy and Andrew Robinson warmly welcome guests to Boyds Farm which is a family-run working farm with a pedigree herd of Hereford Cattle. The farmhouse is a delightful 16th century Listed building surrounded by beautiful mature gardens. Near to Bath, Lacock, Bradford-on-Avon, Castle Combe, Stonehenge, etc. Accommodation comprises one double en suite, one family or twin with private bathroom and one double with private shower room, all well furnished with tea/coffee facilities, electric blankets, etc; guest lounge with log fire for cooler nights. Featured in the "Daily Express," "The Sunday Observer," and "Sunday Mail". Rates from £24 per person. **ETC ♦♦♦♦♦** *SILVER AWARD*.
e-mail: dorothyrobinson@boydsfarm.freeserve.co.uk

CORSHAM

Kate Waldron, Park Farm Barn, Westrop, Corsham SN13 9QF (01249 715911; mobile: 07976 827083; Fax: 01249 701107). Recently converted 18th century tithe barn with newly constructed Cotswold style bed and breakfast accommodation close by. Park Farm Barn has three en suite bedrooms which are light and spacious with apex ceilings and beams. Colour TV and tea/coffee making facilities in each room. Central heating throughout. Breakfast is served in the dining room. Park Farm Barn is an ideal base for the many interesting and historic places in and around Corsham, situated in the delightful hamlet of Westrop, one mile from Corsham and seven miles from Junction 17 on the M4. The National Trust village of Lacock is only a short drive away with a number of excellent pubs for evening meals. Castle Combe and Bradford-upon-Avon only 20 minutes, Bath ten miles. Children welcome, cot and highchair available. No smoking. Parking. Terms from £30 pppn single, £22.50 pppn double/twin. **ETC ♦♦♦**, *FARM STAY UK MEMBER*.
e-mail: thewaldrons@lineone.net
website: www.parkfarmbarn.co.uk

DEVIZES

Longwater Farm Guest House, Erlestoke, Devizes SN10 5UE (Tel & Fax: 01380 830095). Welcome to Longwater. We offer good old-fashioned hospitality but with all the comfort and facilities of a modern home. Explore the beautiful cities of Bath and Salisbury, enjoy coarse fishing in our tranquil lake, play golf on the adjacent 18-hole course, or simply relax in our gardens or conservatory overlooking our picturesque lakes and parkland. Traditional farmhouse breakfast; local inns offer excellent dinners. All rooms en suite with tea/coffee facilities, fridge,TV, radio. Twin and double rooms and family room (children over 5 years); ground floor rooms. Wheelchair-friendly – Accessibility Level 2. Pets welcome. Brochure on request. Three-day break B&B £138 for two. Available January 10th to December 20th. **ETC** ♦♦♦

MARLBOROUGH

Mrs Maggie Vigar-Smith, Wernham Farm, Clench Common, Marlborough SN8 4DR (01672 512236). This working farm is set in picturesque countryside on Wansdyke, off the A345. It is close to Marlborough, Avebury, Pewsey and the Kennet & Avon Canal. Accommodation is available in two family bedrooms, one en suite and one with private bathroom. Terms: £30 single, £44 double. **ETC** ♦♦♦ . Five caravan and camping pitches are also available.
e-mail: margglvsf@aol.com

MELKSHAM

Beechfield House Hotel and Restaurant, Beanacre, Melksham SN12 7PU (01225 703700; Fax: 01225 790118). A comfortable Victorian country house set in eight acres of beautiful gardens in a quiet country location near the National Trust village of Lacock, yet only twenty minutes away from Junction 17 of M4 motorway. The hotel has twenty-one en suite bedrooms, including four-poster and half-tester beds. Private rooms are available for conferences and meetings, private lunches and dinner parties. Banqueting for up to sixty persons. Daily lunches and dinners are available in our elegant restaurant.
e-mail: csm@beechfieldhouse.co.uk
website: www.beechfieldhouse.co.uk

SALISBURY

Mrs Suzi Lanham, Newton Farmhouse, Southampton Road, Whiteparish, Salisbury SP5 2QL (01794 884416). This historic Listed 16th century farmhouse on the borders of the New Forest was formerly part of the Trafalgar Estate and is situated eight miles south of Salisbury, convenient for Stonehenge, Romsey, Winchester, Portsmouth and Bournemouth. All rooms have pretty, en suite facilities and are delightfully decorated, six with genuine period four-poster beds. The beamed diningroom houses a collection of Nelson memorabilia and antiques and has flagstone floors and an inglenook fireplace with an original brick built bread oven. The superb English breakfast is complemented by fresh fruits, home made breads, preserves and free-range eggs. Dinner is available by arrangement, using home grown kitchen garden produce wherever possible. A swimming pool is idyllically set in the extensive, well stocked gardens and children are most welcome in this non-smoking establishment. **ETC** ♦♦♦♦♦ *SILVER AWARD*, **AA** ♦♦♦♦♦ *PREMIER SELECTED*.
e-mail: reservations@newtonfarmhouse.co.uk   **website: www.newtonfarmhouse.co.uk**

The FHG Directory of Website Addresses
on pages 345 - 373 is a useful quick reference guide for holiday accommodation with e-mail and/or website details

ENGLAND / Board   Wiltshire / Worcestershire **177**

SALISBURY

Scotland Lodge, Winterbourne Stoke, Salisbury SP3 4TF (01980 620943; Fax: 01980 621403; mobile: 07957 863183). This 16th century cottage has been transformed into a substantial house with additions in successive centuries. The front garden was turfed from the surrounding downland, which had never been ploughed, providing a profusion of wild Spring flowers including a multitude of cowslips. Within the house there is a feeling of peace and tranquillity. All rooms are en suite with bath and shower, TV and tea/coffee making facilities. Two rooms in the Victorian part are particularly large and airy, with comfortable chairs, a fridge, and one has the added benefit of a small, fully equipped kitchen which may be used for self-catering. Also available is a smaller double with en suite bath and shower. Regret no smoking in the house. Ample car parking. **ETC/AA** ♦♦♦♦

WARMINSTER

Mrs M. Hoskins, Spinney Farmhouse, Chapmanslade, Westbury BA13 4AQ (01373 832412). Off A36, three miles west of Warminster; 16 miles from historic city of Bath. Close to Longleat, Cheddar and Stourhead. Reasonable driving distance to Bristol, Stonehenge, Glastonbury and the cathedral cities of Wells and Salisbury. Pony trekking and fishing available locally. Washbasins, tea/coffee-making facilities and shaver points in all rooms. Family room available. Guests' lounge with colour TV. Central heating. Children and pets welcome. Ample parking. Open all year. Enjoy farm fresh food in a warm, friendly family atmosphere. Bed and Breakfast from £20 per night. Reduction after two nights. Evening Meal £12.

WORCESTERSHIRE

See also Colour Display Advertisement

MALVERN WELLS

Mrs J.L. Morris, Brickbarns Farm, Hanley Road, Malvern Wells WR14 4HY (016845 61775; Fax: 01886 830037). Working farm. Brickbarns, a 200-acre mixed farm, is situated two miles from Great Malvern at the foot of the Malvern Hills, 300 yards from the bus service and one-and-a half miles from the train. The house, which is 300 years old, commands excellent views of the Malvern Hills and guests are accommodated in one double, one single and one family bedrooms with washbasins; two bathrooms, shower room, two toilets; sittingroom and diningroom. Children welcome and cot and babysitting offered. Central heating. Car essential, parking. Open Easter to October for Bed and Breakfast from £16 nightly per person. Reductions for children and Senior Citizens. Birmingham 40 miles, Hereford 20, Gloucester 17, Stratford 35 and the Wye Valley is just 30 miles.

WORCESTER (near)

Sylvia and Brian Wynn, The Old Smithy, Pirton, Worcester WR8 9EJ (01905 820482). A 17th century half-timbered country house set in peaceful countryside with many interesting walks. Centrally situated, within easy reach of Stratford-upon-Avon, Cotswolds, Warwick Castle, Malvern Hills, Worcester Cathedral and Royal Worcester Porcelain. Four-and-a-half miles from Junction 7 of the M5 Motorway. Private guest facilities include lounge with inglenook log fireplace, colour TV and video, bathroom/dressing room and toilet, laundry, tea/coffee, central heating, gardens. One double bedroom and one twin bedroom. Ample parking. Bed and English Breakfast from £22; three-course Evening Meal optional extra £9.95. Fresh local produce and home cooking. Sorry, no pets or children under 12 years. Craft Workshop (Harris Tweed and knitwear). Please telephone for availability and booking. **ETC** ♦♦♦♦
e-mail: welcome@theoldsmithy.co.uk   website: www.SmoothHound.co.uk/hotels/oldsmith.html

178 Yorkshire   Board / ENGLAND

YORKSHIRE

The **FHG**
GOLF
GUIDE
**Where to Play
Where to Stay**

Available from most bookshops, **THE GOLF GUIDE** (published annually) covers details of every UK golf course – well over 2800 entries – for holiday or business golf. Hundreds of hotel entries offer convenient accommodation, accompanying details of the courses – the 'pro', par score, length etc.

In association with 'Golf Monthly' and including Holiday Golf in Ireland, France, Portugal, Spain, The USA, South Africa and Thailand

£9.99 from bookshops or from the publishers (postage charged outside UK) • FHG Publications, Abbey Mill Business Centre, Paisley PA1 ITJ

NORTH YORKSHIRE

See also Colour Display Advertisement

AMPLEFORTH
Annabel Lupton, Carr House Farm, Ampleforth, Near Helmsley YO6 4ED (01347 868526 or 07977 113197). Working farm. 'Which?' Guide; Sunday Observer recommends "Fresh air fiends' dream – good food, good walking, warm welcome". In idyllic 16th century farmhouse, sheltered in Herriot/Heartbeat countryside, half an hour to York, ideal to enjoy Moors, Dales, National Parks, coasts, famous abbeys, castles and stately homes. Romantics will love four-poster bedrooms en suite and medieval-styled bedroom in comfortable relaxing home, with large garden. Enjoy full Yorkshire Breakfasts, hearty Evening Meals – own produce used whenever possible and served in oak-panelled, beamed dining room with flagstoned floor, inglenook and original brick bread oven. Aromatherapy beauty treatments and massage available; also fitness and body-building programmes. No children under seven, no smoking and no pets. Bed and Breakfast from £22.50. Evening meal £12.50. Open all year. ETC ♦♦♦, *FARM STAY UK MEMBER.*
e-mail: enquiries@carrhousefarm.co.uk   website: www.carrhousefarm.co.uk

ASKRIGG
Mrs B. Percival, Milton House, Askrigg, Leyburn DL8 3HJ (01969 650217). Askrigg is situated in the heart of Wensleydale and is within easy reach of many interesting places – Aysgarth Falls, Hardraw Falls, Bolton Castle. Askrigg is one of the loveliest villages in the dale. This is an ideal area for touring or walking. Milton House is a lovely spacious house with all the comforts of home, beautifully furnished and decor to match. All bedrooms are en suite with colour TV and tea/coffee making facilities. Visitors' lounge, dining room. Central heating. Private parking. Milton House is open all year for Bed and Breakfast. Good pub food nearby. You are sure of a friendly welcome and a homely atmosphere. Please write or phone Mrs Beryl Percival for details and brochure. ETC ♦♦♦♦

BEDALE
Mrs D. Layfield, Little Holtby, Leeming Bar, Northallerton DL7 9LH (01609 748762). A period farmhouse with beautiful views at the gateway to the Yorkshire Dales, within easy distance of many places of great interest, just 100 yards off the A1 between Bedale and Richmond. Little Holtby has been restored and furnished to a high standard whilst still retaining its original character; polished wood floors, open fires and original beams in many of the rooms. All bedrooms have colour TV, tea/coffee making facilities and are centrally heated. One double bedroom (en suite), one four-poster room, one twin-bedded room with washbasin. Bed and Breakfast from £25 to £30pppn; Evening Meal available. ETC ♦♦♦♦ *SILVER AWARD.*
e-mail: littleholtby@yahoo.co.uk

See also Colour Display Advertisement

FILEY
Leonard & Diane Hunter, "Sea Cabin" 16 Gap Road, Hunmanby Gap, Near Filey YO14 9QP (01723 891368). Unique Bed & Breakfast accommodation. En suite for two people only. Own private lounge. Located on the clifftop with access to the golden sands of Filey Bay. Quiet location. Good Yorkshire food, 3-course English breakfast. Bookings for evening meals as required. The perfect venue for a relaxing break. Private parking. Pets welcome. By car: five minutes Filey, 10 minutes Flamborough, 15 minutes Bridlington, 20 minutes Scarborough. Please contact for brochure and terms.

FILEY

Sea Brink Hotel, 3 The Beach, Filey YO14 9LA (01723 513257; Fax: 01723 514139). Licensed seafront hotel with nine en suite rooms, many overlooking Filey Bay. Room amenities include TV, clock/radio, central heating, direct-dial telephone and tea/coffee tray. **ETC ★★**
website: www.seabrink.co.uk

GLAISDALE

Tom and Sandra Spashett, Red House Farm, Glaisdale, Near Whitby YO21 2PZ (Tel & Fax: 01947 897242). Listed Georgian farmhouse featured in "Houses of the North York Moors". Completely refurbished to the highest standards, retaining all original features. Bedrooms have bath/shower/toilet, central heating, TV and tea making facilities. Excellent walks straight from the doorstep. Friendly farm animals – a few cows, horses, geese and pretty free-roaming hens. One-and-a-half acres of gardens, sitting-out areas. Magnificent views. Interesting buildings – Listed barns now converted to two holiday cottages. Games room with snooker table. Eight miles from seaside/Whitby. Village pubs within walking distance. Stabling available for horses/dogs. Non-smoking. Please phone Tom or Sandra for more information.
e-mail: spashettredhouse@aol.com   website: www.redhousefarm.net

HARROGATE

Mrs Sue Clarke, Brimham Lodge, Brimham Rocks Road, Burnt Yates, Harrogate HG3 3HE (01423 771770; Fax: 01423 770370). Working farm, join in. The Lodge, built in 1661, was extensively refurbished in 1999 but the farmhouse retains all its original character. Our accommodation offers two twin/double rooms with private facilities. All rooms have central heating, beverage tray, hairdryer, colour TV and clock radio. There is a large sitting room with a blazing fire set in a large inglenook, with television, video and games available. A hearty farmhouse breakfast is served in the oak panelled dining room. Brimham Lodge Farm is situated in the heart of Nidderdale, with many sites of interest within a short walk or car journey. Bed and Breakfast from £20 to £25 per person. **ETC ♦♦♦♦**
e-mail: neil.clarke@virgin.net   website: www.farmhousesbedandbreakfast.com

HARROGATE

Mrs Judy Barker, Brimham Guest House, Silverdale Close, Darley, Harrogate HG3 2PQ (01423 780948). The family-run guest house is situated in the centre of Darley, a quiet village in unspoilt Nidderdale. All rooms en suite and centrally heated with tea/coffee making facilities and views across the Dales. Full English breakfast served between 7am and 9am in the dining room; a TV lounge/conservatory is available for your relaxation. Off street parking. Central for visits to Harrogate, York, Skipton and Ripon, or just enjoying drives through the Dales and Moors where you will take in dramatic hillsides, green hills, picturesque villages, castles and abbeys. Children welcome. Bed and Breakfast from £20 per person per night double, £22 per person twin or £30 single room, reductions for three nights or more. Yorkshire in Bloom Winner. **ETC ♦♦♦♦**

OTLEY

Mrs C. Beaumont, Paddock Hill, Norwood, Otley LS21 2QU (01943 465977). Converted farmhouse on B6451 south of Bland Hill. Open fires, lovely views, in the heart of the countryside. Within easy reach of Herriot, Brontë and Emmerdale country and with attractive market towns around – Skipton, Knaresborough, Otley and Ripon. Walking, bird- watching and fishing on the nearby reservoirs. Residents' lounge with TV. Comfortable bedrooms. Non-smoking accommodation available. Children welcome. Pets by arrangement. Bed and Breakfast £17, en suite £22. **ETC ♦♦♦**

PICKERING

Mrs S. Wardell, Tangalwood, Roxby Road, Thornton-le-Dale, Pickering YO18 7SX (01751 474688). Tangalwood provides a warm welcome. Very clean and comfortable accommodation and good food. Situated in a quiet part of this picturesque village, which is in a good central position for Moors, "Heartbeat" country, coast, North York Moors Railway, Flamingo Park Zoo and forest drives, mountain biking and walking. Good facilities for meals provided in the village. Accommodation in one twin and one double en suite rooms, one single; all with tea/coffee making facilities and TV; alarm clock/radio and hairdryer also provided; diningroom; central heating. Open Easter to October for Bed and Breakfast from £21 each. Private car park. Secure motorbike and cycle storage. ETC ♦♦♦♦
website: www.accommodation.uk.net/tangalwood

ROBIN HOOD'S BAY

Mrs B. Reynolds, 'South View', Sledgates, Fylingthorpe, Whitby YO22 4TZ (01947 880025). Pleasantly situated, comfortable accommodation in own garden with sea and country views. Ideal for walking and touring. Close to the moors, within easy reach of Whitby, Scarborough and many more places of interest. There are two double rooms, lounge and dining room. Bed and Breakfast from £18, including bedtime drink. Parking spaces. Phone for further details.

SCARBOROUGH

Sue and Tony Hewitt, Harmony Country Lodge, Limestone Road, Burniston, Scarborough YO13 0DG (0800 2985840). DISTINCTIVELY DIFFERENT. Peaceful and relaxing retreat, octagonal in design and set in two acres of private grounds with 360º panoramic views of the National Park and sea. Two miles from Scarborough and within easy reach of Whitby, York and the beautiful North Yorkshire countryside. Tastefully decorated, en suite, centrally heated rooms with colour TV and all with superb views. Attractive dining room, guest lounge and relaxing conservatory. Traditional English breakfast, including vegetarian. Fragrant massage available. Bed and Breakfast from £24 to £34. Non-smoking, licensed, private parking facilities. Personal service and warm, friendly Yorkshire hospitality. Spacious five-berth caravan also available for self-catering holidays. Christmas package. Please telephone or write for brochure. Children over 7 years welcome. ETC ♦♦♦♦
e-mail: tony@harmonylodge.net   website: www.harmonylodge.net

SCARBOROUGH

Simon and Val Green, Killerby Cottage Farm, Killerby Lane, Cayton, Scarborough YO11 3TP (01723 581236; Fax: 01723 585465). Simon and Val extend a warm Yorkshire welcome and invite you to share their charming farmhouse in the pleasant countryside between Scarborough and Filey. All our bedrooms are tastefully decorated and have en suite facilities, colour TV, and well-stocked beverage trays. Hearty breakfasts that will keep you going all day are served in the conservatory overlooking the lovely garden. Our 350-acre farm has diversified and we now have the Stained Glass Centre and tearoom which are open to visitors. Cayton offers easy access to Scarborough, Filey, Whitby, the North York Moors, and York. ETC ♦♦♦♦
e-mail: val@green-glass.demon.co.uk

Terms quoted in this publication may be subject to increase if rises in costs necessitate

SCARBOROUGH

Mrs V. Henson, Brinka House, 2 Station Square, Ravenscar, Scarborough YO13 0LU (01723 871470). Brinka House Bed and Breakfast is situated in Ravenscar – midway between Scarborough and Whitby. It has stunning views across to Robin Hood's Bay and is surrounded by the moors. The village boasts a variety of walks, cycle tracks, golf course, pony and llama trekking and a bus service that runs from the front door into town. A warm welcome and tasty breakfast awaits everyone, vegetarians and special diets are catered for. We have a romantic double room with a large corner bath en suite and a twin/family room en suite. All rooms have TV, drinks facilities and sea views. £19 per person per night, £25 single supplement.

SCARBOROUGH

Mrs M. Edmondson, Plane Tree Cottage Farm, Staintondale, Scarborough YO13 0EY (01723 870796). This small mixed farm is situated off the beaten track, with open views of beautiful countryside and the sea. We have sheep, hens, two ginger cats and special sheep dog "Bess". This very old beamed cottage, small but homely, has one twin with bathroom and two double en suite rooms with tea maker. Meals of very high standard served with own fresh eggs and garden produce are available. Staintondale is about half-way between Scarborough and Whitby and near the North York Moors. Pretty woodland walks nearby. Car essential. Bed and Breakfast from £23 per person per night. Also six-berth caravan available. SAE please for details, or telephone. ETC ◆◆◆

THIRSK

Joyce Ashbridge, Mount Grace Farm, Cold Kirby, Thirsk YO7 2HL (01845 597389; Fax: 01845 597872). A warm welcome awaits you on this working farm surrounded by beautiful open countryside with magnificent views. Ideal location for touring or exploring the many walks in the area. Luxury en suite bedrooms with tea/coffee facilities. Spacious guests' lounge with colour TV. Garden. Enjoy delicious, generous helpings of farmhouse fayre cooked in our Aga. Children from 12 years plus. No smoking. No pets. Bed and Breakfast from £28. Open all year except Christmas.
e-mail: joyce@mountgracefarm.com
website: www.mountgracefarm.com

THIRSK

Mrs M. Fountain, Town Pasture Farm, Boltby, Thirsk YO7 2DY (01845 537298). Working farm, join in. A warm welcome awaits on a 180 acre mixed farm in beautiful Boltby village, nestling in the valley below the Hambleton Hills, in the midst of Herriot country and on the edge of the North York Moors National Park. An 18th century stone-built farmhouse with full central heating, comfortable en suite bedrooms (one family, one twin) with original old oak beams, and tea/coffee facilities; spacious guests' lounge with colour TV. Children and pets welcome. Good home cooking, hearty English breakfast and evening meals by arrangement. Ideal walking country and central for touring the Dales, York and East Coast. Pony trekking in village. Bed and Breakfast from £20 - £25. ETC ◆◆◆

One adult travels FREE when accompanied by a fare paying adult at
Embsay & Bolton Abbey Steam Railway
see our READERS' OFFER VOUCHERS for details

WHITBY

Peter & Jane Dowson, Furnace Farm, Fryup, Lealholm, Whitby YO21 2AP (Tel & Fax: 01947 897271). A warm Yorkshire welcome to our working family farm in the peaceful Esk Valley. Close to Moors and Coast, with beautiful views. Ideal base for walking and touring. Woodland river walk on farm, day fishing available. Whitby ten miles, 'Heartbeat Country' and Steam Railway five miles, Danby Moors Centre two miles. Accommodation consists of two tastefully colour-coordinated rooms – a family room with cot available, and a double/twin. One en suite and one with private bathroom. Both rooms have hospitality trays with fresh milk, colour TV and central heating. Delicious full English Breakfast served in cosy dining room/lounge with log fires. Use of large garden. Secure cycle storage. Dogs by arrangement. Non-smoking. Open all year. B&B £22.50 to £25. ETC ♦♦♦♦, *FARM STAY UK MEMBER*.
e-mail: furnacefarm@hotmail.com

YORK

Mrs Diana Susan Tindall, Newton House, Neville Street, Haxby Road, York YO31 8NP (01904 635627). Diana and John offer all their guests a friendly and warm welcome to their Victorian End Town House, a few minutes' walk from the City Centre, York's beautiful Minster, the City Walls and museums. Situated near an attractive park with good bowling greens. York is an ideal base for touring Yorkshire Moors, Dales and coastline. Three double/twin en suite rooms, colour TV, tea/coffee tray, central heating, car park. Non-smoking. Fire certificate, Electrical Installation Certificate. Terms from £25 per person.

YORK

Mrs J.Y. Tree, Inglewood Guest House, 7 Clifton Green, York YO23 6LH (01904 653523). The Inglewood Guest House has a warm and friendly atmosphere where guests will really feel at home. The bedrooms have colour TV and some have en suite bathrooms. Open all year with central heating. Breakfast is an enjoyable experience in our pleasant diningroom with dark wooden tables and chairs. Helpful information is given on where to go and what to see. It is an ideal centre for exploring York and making day excursions to many market towns and villages around York. There are many places of historic interest also to visit. Children are welcome. Sorry, no pets. A car is not essential, but there is parking. Bed and Breakfast from £25; reductions for children. Non-smoking.
website: www.SmoothHound.co.uk/hotels/inglewood.html

YORK

Crossways Guest House, 23 Wigginton Road, York YO31 8HJ (01904 637250). Crossways Guest House is a three-storey Victorian Town House, situated ten minutes' walk from the city wall. It is an excellent base for exploring the city's famous attractions as well as touring the North York Moors and Dales. All rooms are en suite with TV and tea/coffee making. Twin room on the ground floor. Patio with a garden available for guests. City bus stop at the end of the garden. Bed and Breakfast £40 per room per night for two nights or more, £50 per room for one night, £20 -£30 per room per night single occupancy of double room. Bargain breaks out of season, prices on request. No smoking.
e-mail: info@crosswaysguesthouse.freeserve.co.uk
website: www.crosswaysguesthouse.freeserve.co.uk

When making enquiries or bookings, a stamped addressed envelope is always appreciated

YORK
June, Keith and Rob Wood, Ascot House, 80 East Parade, York YO31 7YH (01904 426826; Fax: 01904 431077). An attractive Victorian villa built in 1869 with easy access to the historic city centre by walking or by public transport. All bedrooms have central heating, colour TV and complimentary tea/coffee making facilities while the family and double rooms are en suite. Most rooms have four-poster or canopy beds. Comfortable residents' lounge with TV; attractive dining room. There is also a sauna which can be hired by the hour. York has much to offer with its ancient narrow streets, medieval churches, Roman, Viking and National Railway museums and the Minster. Private parking. Single from £26 to £56 per room per night, double £56 to £68 per room per night, including Traditional English Breakfast and VAT.
ETC/AA/RAC ♦♦♦♦, ETC *SILVER AWARD.*
e-mail: admin@ascothouseyork.com
website: www.ascothouseyork.com

YORK
Mrs Joan Liversidge, Cuckoo Nest Farm, Wilberfoss, York YO41 5NL (01759 380365). Situated seven miles east of York off the A1079 Hull road, Cuckoo Nest is a traditional red brick farmhouse on a cattle/dairy/arable farm. The house has oak-beamed rooms, a pleasant sitting room and a separate dining room. There is an en suite double room, and one double and one twin rooms, both with washbasins. Good country pubs nearby. Easy drive to coast, dales and moors. A warm welcome awaits you here. Open all year. Bed and Breakfast from £22pp.
ETC ♦♦♦

Eden Camp Modern History Museum • *Malton, North Yorkshire* • *01653 697777*
website: www.edencamp.co.uk
This award-winning museum will take you back to wartime Britain where you can experience the sights, sounds and smells of World War II.

Blacksheep Brewery Visitor Centre • *Masham, North Yorkshire* • *01765 689227*
website: www.blacksheepbrewery.com
Traditional working brewery with excellent visitor facilities including guided tours, bistro and gift shop.

PLEASE NOTE

All the information in this book is given in good faith in the belief that it is correct. However, the publishers cannot guarantee the facts given in these pages, neither are they responsible for changes in policy, ownership or terms that may take place after the date of going to press. Readers should always satisfy themselves that the facilities they require are available and that the terms, if quoted, still apply.

ENGLAND / Self-catering 185

ENGLAND
Self-catering Accommodation

See also Colour Display Advertisement

Country Holidays (0870 442 5240). BRITAIN'S FAVOURITE COTTAGE HOLIDAYS. Every kind of property for every kind of holiday. With over 3,000 quality graded cottages throughout the UK, catering from two to twenty-two, you're sure to find the right property for you. Many of our properties also accept pets so none of your family need miss out. Please telephone for your 2004 brochure.
website: www.country-holidays.co.uk

186 Cornwall Self-catering / ENGLAND

CORNWALL

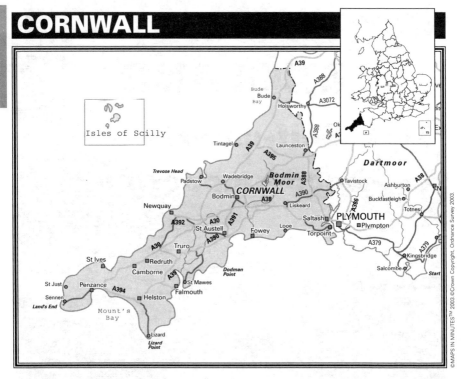

classic cottages

www.classic.co.uk

Featuring 500 hand selected coastal and country holiday homes throughout the West Country

01326 565 555

FHG PUBLICATIONS publish a large range of well-known accommodation guides. We will be happy to send you details or you can use the order form at the back of this book.

ENGLAND / Self-catering   Cornwall 187

Coombe Mill

A relaxing self-catering holiday for all the family

An idyllic Cornish hamlet of picturesque stone cottages
and quiet riverside lodges set amidst a glorious 30-acre estate.

Friendly farm animals, tractor rides, safe play area, gardens, wildlife, fishing lakes and river fishing, 4 posters, log burners, BBQs, home cooking, groceries delivered.

Indoor Pool, pony trekking and cycle hire in the village. Sandy beaches. Padstow and many varied children's activities nearby.

Open all year   Coombe Mill, St Breward, Bodmin, Cornwall PL30 4LZ

Tel: 01208 850344
mail@coombemill.com   www.coombemill.com

Penrose Burden
Holiday Cottages

St Breward, Bodmin, Cornwall PL30 4LZ
Tel: 01208 850277 & 850617 • Fax: 01208 850915
www.penroseburden.co.uk

Situated within easy reach of both coasts and Bodmin Moor on a large farm overlooking a beautiful wooded valley with own salmon and trout fishing. These stone cottages with exposed beams and quarry tiled floors have been featured on TV and are award-winners. Home-made meals can be delivered daily. All are suitable for wheelchair users and dogs are welcomed. Our cottages sleep from two to seven and are open all year. Please write or telephone for a colour brochure. Close to The Eden Project.

See also Colour Advertisement

BODMIN MOOR
Silverstream Country Holidays, Hellandbridge, Bodmin Moor PL30 4QR (01208 74408). Beautiful Bodmin Moor at Hellandbridge. Silverstream, a pet-friendly and children-welcome secluded, spacious, but not isolated selection of idyllic cottages and lodges. Situated on the Camel Trail, and near the Eden Project. Good pubs close by. Fishing, discounted golf available.
e-mail: silverstreamhols@hellandbridge.freeserve.co.uk
website: www.silverstreamcottages.co.uk

BOSCASTLE

Caroline Jackson-Gali, The Barn, Ringford Farm, St Juliot, Boscastle PL35 0BX (01840 250306; 07881 944119). A pretty two-bedroomed converted barn with slate floors, log-burning stove and antique furniture. Magnificent sea views. The barn is set in 25 acres of organic farmland with pure spring water. Coastal footpaths accessed from our own fields on the farm. Children are welcome and can help feed chickens and ducks, and groom ponies. Many wonderful beaches only a few minutes' drive away; 40 minutes' drive to the spectacular Eden Project. "An English holiday as it used to be."

BUDE

Lower Kitleigh Cottage, Week St Mary, Near Bude. Pretty Listed farmhouse in unspoilt country near magnificent coast. Newly renovated with all conveniences, yet retaining its charm, it stands in a peaceful grassy garden with picnic table and own parking. The sitting room has period furniture, inglenook fireplace, free logs and colour TV. The fully equipped kitchen has fridge/freezer, double sink, electric cooker and washer/tumble dryer. Three bedrooms with panoramic views, cots, duvets. Well-controlled dogs allowed. Riding nearby, golf, safe beaches, surfing, Cornish Moors, markets, cliff walks. All electricity inclusive, and central heating ensures a cosy stay throughout the year. Prices from £250 to £525 weekly, reductions for part week. Sleeps seven plus cot. **Mr & Mrs T. Bruce-Dick, 114 Albert Street, London NW1 7NE (0207 485 8970)**

CUSGARNE (near Truro)

Joyce and George Clench, Saffron Meadow, Cusgarne, Near Truro TR4 8RW (01872 863171). Sleeps 2. A cosy single-storey, clean, detached dwelling with own enclosed garden, within grounds of Saffron Meadow, in quiet hamlet five miles west of Truro. Secluded and surrounded by wooded pastureland. Bedroom (double bed) with twin vanity unit. Fully tiled shower/WC and LB. Comprehensively equipped kitchen/diner. Compact TV room. Storage room. Hot water galore and gas included. Metered electricity. Automatic external safety lighting. Your own ample parking space in drive. Inn, good food, a short walk. Central to Truro, Falmouth and North and South coasts. Dogs welcome. Terms from £160 to £230 per week.

FALMOUTH near

See also Colour Display Advertisement

Viscar Farm Holiday Cottages. Sleep 2-4+ cot. Set in 22 acres, the three cottages are full of character – open beamed ceilings, stone walls, inglenook fireplace, slate floors, double glazed, attractive wall lighting, pine furniture, well equipped. There is a wealth of wildlife to be seen and horses and foals on the farm. An ideal location for beaches and touring. Available all year, short winter breaks. Linen and towels provided; welcome tray. For brochure tel: **01326 340897**
e-mail: BiscarHols@amserve.net
website: www.viscarfarm-cottages.co.uk

Terms quoted in this publication may be subject to increase if rises in costs necessitate

ENGLAND / Self-catering Cornwall 189

Falmouth

Detached bungalow and gardens, shower room, bathroom and separate wc. Close to Falmouth Town Centre in residential area. Sleeps 2 to 6. Garage and parking. From £350 to £600 per week incl. Unlimited electricity and hot water.

Booking Office:
Creation Accommodation, 96 Market Street, Penryn TR10 8BH
Tel: 0800 298 6565 • Fax: 01326 375088
e-mail: hq@encompasstravel.com

HELFORD ESTUARY

Mrs S. Trewhella, Mudgeon Vean Farm, St Martin, Helston TR12 6DB (01326 231341). Leave the hustle and bustle of town life. Come and enjoy the peace and tranquillity of the Helford Estuary. Three homely cottages sleep four/six, equipped to a high standard. Open all year for cosy winter breaks. Open fires/heating. Set amidst a small 18th century organic working farm with magnificent views across an extensive valley area, surrounded by fields and woodland - a walk through the woods takes you to the Helford River. A superb location in an Area of Outstanding Natural Beauty with the rugged coastline of the Lizard Peninsula and beaches only a short drive away. Children and pets welcome. From £115 to £390 per week
e-mail: mudgeonvean@aol.com
website: www.cornwall-online.co.uk/mudgeon-vean/ctb.html

HELSTON

Jan Oates, Rosuick Farm, St Martin, Helston TR12 6DZ (01326 231302). Tucked away in our picturesque valley, in an Area of Outstanding Natural Beauty, Rosuick Farm offers a special holiday. Steeped in history, and each with its individual charm and character, the cottages offer quality and comfort. Four-poster beds, log fires, snooker table, private gardens, tennis court. Meet the animals on our fully organic farm, registered with the Soil Association. Produce is available from the farm shop. Discover the Helford River with its sailing and wonderful walks, and the many coves and beaches on The Lizard. Elmtree and Rosuick Cottage each sleep six, and Rosuick Farmhouse sleeps ten. Open all year. £90 to £850 per week.

LAUNCESTON

Cartmell Bungalow, Trelash, Warbstow, Launceston PL15 8RL. Sleeps 6. Cartmell is a dormer bungalow ideally situated for touring Devon and Cornwall - Crackington Haven five miles, Boscastle six, Tintagel and Camelford seven, Bude and Launceston 12, Plymouth 40 miles. Warbstow with bus services to Launceston and Exeter daily is just two miles away, Marshgate with shop, garage and post office three miles. Golf available at Bude and Launceston, horse riding on coastal paths just four miles away; the Tamar Otter Park, Tamar and Crowdy Lakes are nearby. Accommodation comprises two double and one twin bedroom, bathroom with bath and shower, large lounge/diner with TV and modern kitchen. Electricity included. Linen available for hire. Central heating extra. Ample parking. Sorry no pets, or children under 8. For further information please contact: **Mr & Mrs Dawe (01840 261353).**

When making enquiries or bookings, a stamped addressed envelope is always appreciated

LAUNCESTON

Mrs Heather French, Higher Scarsick, Treneglos, Launceston PL15 8UH (01566 781372) Working farm. Nestled amongst the peace and tranquillity of unspoilt Cornish countryside, this well furnished and comfortable cottage is the ideal retreat for both couples and families. Very convenient for exploring the many beaches and coves on the North Cornwall Coast yet within easy driving distance of Bodmin Moor, Dartmoor and all leisure pursuits. The accommodation has three bedrooms, two double and one twin bedded, bathroom with separate shower cubicle, a fully equipped large farmhouse kitchen, lounge with open fireplace. Tariff: £150–£450 includes bed linen, night storage heaters, electricity and a very warm welcome. Short breaks from £100. No Pets.

LAUNCESTON

See also Colour Display Advertisement

Hollyvag Farmhouse, Lewannick, Near Launceston PL15 7QH. Sleeps 5. Part of a cosy 17th century Listed farmhouse in 80 acres of fields and woods. Working farm with rare breed sheep, horses, geese, dogs and cats. Central to North and South coasts, Bodmin Moor and the fabulous Eden Project with an abundance of wildlife in the area. Golf and riding nearby. All modern conveniences including electric cooker, microwave, fridge, TV and video; laundry service FOC. Terms from £180. Also available is a luxury mobile home (sleeps four) in private idyllic location. Contact: **Mrs Anne Moore (01566 782309)**

LAUNCESTON

Mrs Kathryn Broad, Lower Dutson Farm, Launceston PL15 9SP (Tel & Fax: 01566 776456). Working farm. Sleeps 2/6. Play fetch with Fly our sheepdog or watch out for the Kingfisher as you relax or fish down by the lake or riverside. Get up late and enjoy an all day breakfast at Homeleigh Garden Centre, just 400m up the road. Enjoy the suntrap just outside the front door. Well-equipped 17th century cottage with three bedrooms, two bathrooms, Tv lounge and kitchen. Situated two miles from historic Launceston with its Norman Castle (even Tescos!) Centrally located for visiting National Trust houses and gardens, Dartmoor, Bodmin Moor and the beaches and harbours of Devon and Cornwall. Pets welcome by arrangement. Terms from £180 to £480. **ETC ★★★**

e-mail: francis.broad@btclick.com   website: www.farm-cottage.co.uk

LAUNCESTON

See also Colour Display Advertisement

Trenannick Cottages. Five delightful cottages converted from 18th century farm buildings, standing at the end of a private, tree-lined drive, in a quiet rural setting. All cottages have small private gardens, and access to barbecue area, children's playing field, and small copse. Ideal touring base for North Cornish coast, two miles from A39, with Crackington Haven, Bude, and Boscastle all nearby. Accommodation varies from two to six persons per cottage, with wheelchair access in the Roundhouse. Open throughout the year, with log fires for those colder evenings. Short Breaks available. Pets welcome in certain cottages. Rates from £130 to £475 per week. Details from **Mrs L. Harrison, Trenannick Farmhouse, Warbstow, Launceston PL15 8RP (01566 781443)**

e-mail: lorraine.trenannick@i12.com   website: www.trenannickcottages.co.uk

---

A useful index of towns and counties appears at the back of this book on pages 375 - 378. Refer also to Contents Pages 2 and 3.

ENGLAND / Self-catering   Cornwall   191

LISKEARD
Alan and Kathleen Hunstone, Rivermead Farm, Twowatersfoot, Liskeard PL14 6HT (01208 821464). Self-catering apartments and farm cottage, set in beautiful wooded Glynn Valley, amidst 30 acres of meadows and water meadows. River and lakeside walks; mile of sea trout and salmon fishing on the River Fowey by arrangement. Convenient for both coasts and moors. Pets welcome. Brochure on request.
website: www.zednet.co.uk/rivermead

LISKEARD
Boturnell Farm Cottages, St Pinnock, Liskeard PL14 4QS (01579 320880; Fax: 01579 320375). Cosy character cottages, set in the beautiful Cornish countryside. These cottages have been tastefully converted from the original farm barns and sleep up to seven people. Many original features left including stone walls and slate floors; stained glass windows. Fresh eggs from our free-range hens and ducks. Many animals including pygmy goats, horses, sheep from Pet Rescue and guinea pigs. Free access to all 25 acres of woods and fields. Children's playfield. Private spring water supply. Pets welcome, free of charge; pet crèche available. Details from **Ian & Sue Jewell.**
e-mail: sue@dogs-holiday.co.uk
website: www.dogs-holiday.co.uk

See also Colour Display Advertisement

LOOE
Mr and Mrs J. Spreckley, Tremaine Green Country Cottages, Pelynt, Near Looe PL13 2LT (01503 220333). Sleep 2-8. Tremaine Green for memorable holidays. 'A beautiful private hamlet' of 11 award-winning traditional cosy craftsmen's cottages, between Polperro and Looe. Clean, comfortable and well-equipped, with a warm and friendly atmosphere. Set in lovely grounds with country and coastal walks and The Eden Project nearby. Towels, linen, central heating and hot water included. Dishwashers in larger cottages. Power shower baths. Launderette, games room and tennis court. TV/videos. Cot and highchair available. Pubs and restaurants within easy walking distance. Terms from £112. Pets welcome. **ETC ★★★**
e-mail: stay@tremainegreen.co.uk
website: www.tremainegreen.co.uk

LOOE VALLEY
Badham Farm, St Keyne, Liskeard PL14 4RW (Tel & Fax: 01579 343572). Once part of a Duchy of Cornwall working farm, now farmhouse and farm buildings converted to a high standard to form a six cottage complex around former farmyard. Sleeping from two to ten. All cottages are well furnished and equipped and prices include electricity, bed linen and towels. Most cottages have a garden. Five acre grounds, set in delightful wooded valley, with tennis, putting, children's play area, fishing lake, animal paddock, games room with pool and table tennis. Separate bar. Laundry. Barbecue. Railcar from Liskeard to Looe stops at end of picnic area. Have a 'car free' day out. Children and well behaved dogs welcome (regret, no dogs in high season). Prices from £120 per week. **ETC ★★★**, *GREEN TOURISM AWARD*.
website: www.looedirectory.co.uk/badhamcottages.htm

**FREE or REDUCED RATE entry to Holiday Visits and Attractions –
see our READERS' OFFER VOUCHERS on pages 67 - 94**

MAWGAN PORTH

See also Colour Display Advertisement

Tredragon Lodge. Five serviced self-catering lodges between Newquay and Padstow at Mawgan Porth. 200 yards from the beach. Fully equipped, including dishwashers; daily maid service; linen provided. Mastercard and Visa accepted. For details contact **J. McLuskie (01637 881610).**
e-mail: tredragonlodge@hotmail.com
website: www.tredragonlodge.co.uk

PADSTOW

Mr Mike Benwell, Trevorrick Farm, St Issey, near Padstow PL27 7QH (01841 540574). Sleeps 2 - 5. Working farm, join in. Well-equipped stone and slate cottages on a smallholding, set in an Area of Outstanding Natural Beauty. Beautiful location overlooking Little Petherick Creek and the Camel Estuary. Ideal for walking – easy access to Padstow, Saints Way and the Camel Trail. Great for cycling (cycle hire nearby) with the signed Cornish Way and The Camel Trail. Good pub/restaurant half a mile. Heated indoor swimming pool and games room in converted barn. Ideal for children; toys/games can be provided to suit ages of children. Safe sandy/surfing beaches nearby and some excellent coastal walking. Shorts Breaks available. Open all year. All facilities on site. Pets and children welcome. Disabled and non-smoking accommodation available. Terms from £180 to £750 linen included. **ETC ★★★**
e-mail: info@trevorrick.co.uk
website: www.trevorrick.co.uk

PADSTOW

Yellow Sands Cottages, Harlyn Bay, Padstow PL28 8SE (01637 881548). Sleeps 1-6. Situated in an Area of Outstanding Natural Beauty, along the magnificent north Cornish coast, Harlyn Bay is a crescent of firm, golden sand - six other spectacular beaches are within close proximity. Surrounded by its own private grounds and gardens, we provide well-appointed cottages to sleep from one to six persons. Each property is furnished and equipped to a high standard. Appliances include cooker/hob, fridge/freezer, microwave, TV/video, CD unit and hairdryer - most have dishwasher. Cleanliness is paramount throughout. Storage heating is provided. Patio, garden and adequate parking adjacent to each property. Cot/highchair available. Linen available, electricity via £1 coin meter. Pets and children welcome. **ETC ★★★/★★★★**
e-mail: yellowsands@btinternet.com
website: www.yellowsands.co.uk

PADSTOW

Carnevas Farm Holiday Park, Carnevas Farm, St Merryn, Padstow PL28 8PN (01841 520230). Bungalow/Chalets sleep 4/6. Situated only half a mile from golden sandy beach, fishing, golf, sailing etc. Quaint harbour village of Padstow only four miles. Bungalows/chalets sleep four/six, have two bedrooms, bathroom, kitchen/diner, airing cupboard, colour TV. Caravans six-berth or eight berth, all have showers, toilets, fridge, colour TV (also separate camping and caravan facilities). Newly converted barns now available, sleep four/six persons, furnished to a high standard. Brochure on request. **ETC ★★★★**, *ROSE AWARD PARK 2003, AA THREE PENNANT SITE.*

Readers are requested to mention this guidebook when seeking accommodation (and please enclose a stamped addressed envelope).

ENGLAND / Self-catering   Cornwall   193

PENZANCE
Mrs Catherine Wall, Trenow, Relubbus Lane, St Hilary, Penzance TR20 9EA (01736 762308). Mini bungalow sleeps two within the grounds of an old country house. Lovely garden, surrounding rural area. Lounge/ diner with cooking area, fridge, cooker, colour TV etc; shower room. Linen provided. Beaches within easy reach, sporting activities, bird watching. No pets. Off-road Parking. Terms from £100 per week. Available all year. Please write or phone for further details.

PENZANCE
Mrs James Curnow, Barlowenath, St Hilary, Penzance TR20 9DQ (01736 710409). Working farm. Cottages sleep 4/5. These two cottages are on a working farm, in a little hamlet right beside St Hilary Church, with quiet surroundings and a good road approach. A good position for touring Cornish coast and most well-known places. Beaches are two miles away; Marazion two-and-a-half miles; Penzance six miles; St Ives eight; Land's End 16. Both cottages have fitted carpets, lounge/diner with TV/video; modern kitchen (fridge, electric cooker, microwave, toaster, iron); bathroom with shaver point. Electricity by £1 meter, night storage heaters extra. One cottage sleeps five in three bedrooms (one double, twin divans and one single). The second cottage sleeps four in two bedrooms (twin divans in both). Linen not supplied, but can be hired by arrangement. Cot by arrangement. Available all year. £95 to £375 weekly, VAT exempt.

PORT ISAAC
The Lodge, Treharrock, Port Isaac. Sleeps 6. Pleasant, south-facing and convenient bungalow, set in its own small, natural garden and surrounded by fields and woodland with streams. About two miles inland from Port Isaac, a sheltered, secluded spot at the end of driveway to Treharrock Manor. Rugged North Cornish cliffs with National Trust footpaths and lovely sandy coves in the vicinity. Excellent sandy surfing beach at Polzeath (five miles), also pony trekking, golf etc. in the area. South-facing sun room leads on to terrace; TV. Accommodation for six plus baby. Bathroom, toilet; sittingroom; kitchen/diner. Open all year. Linen extra. Sorry, no pets. Car essential – parking. Terms from £200 to £500 per week (heating included). SAE to **Mrs E. A. Hambly, Willow Mill, St Kew, Bodmin, Cornwall PL30 3EP (01208 841806).**

ST KEVERNE
Mrs Rosemary Peters, Trenoweth Valley Farm Cottages, St Keverne, Helston TR12 6QQ (01326 280910). Spacious, comfortable, rural cottages, fully furnished and carpeted, with well-equipped kitchen, colour TV and laundry facilities. Kitchen/diner, lounge/sitting room, shower room/toilet. Sleeping up to five persons, plus cot, each cottage has two bedrooms, with duvets and covers for each bed. Surrounded by trees and fields, there is a safe play area for young children, and a barbecue. Quiet, relaxing environment, midway between St Keverne and Porthallow. Pleasant walks; beach, village shops and inns one-and-a-half miles. Open Easter to end October. Sorry, no pets. Attractive early and late prices. Terms from £70 per week.
e-mail: rosemary@lizard-peninsula.co.uk
website: www.lizard-peninsula.co.uk

TRURO

Mrs Pamela Carbis, Trenona Farm, Ruan High Lanes, Truro TR2 5JS (01872 501339). Two renovated barns near the main farmhouse on working beef and sheep farm. Peaceful location three miles from the South Coast and close to the Eden Project and the Lost Gardens of Heligan. CHY TYAK sleeps 6-8 (plus cot) in a double master bedroom with en suite bathroom; two twin bedded rooms upstairs. Downstairs consists of an open plan kitchen/diner/lounge with high quality furnishings, pro-logic TV, video, CD player, payphone, dishwasher, fridge/freezer, washer/dryer, microwave and electric fan oven. CHY WHEL is a single cottage sleeping 6 in one double and two twin bedded rooms. Open plan kitchen/diner/lounge has all new appliances. Both properties have ample parking with room for boats, trailers and under cover storage for bicycles. Wheelchair access and pets welcome.
e-mail: info@trenonafarmholidays.co.uk   website: www.trenonafarmholidays.co.uk

TRURO

Garvinack Farm Holidays, Tregavethan, Truro TR4 9EP (01872 560385). Conveniently situated alongside the A30, between Bodmin and Redruth, and yet very secluded and peaceful, the farm is equidistant from St Agnes and Perranporth to the north, and Truro with its excellent shopping facilities, cathedral and other points of interest to the south. Four acre woodland to the rear of the house, with its three-tiered walk amongst camellias, rhododendrons and magnolias. THOMAS BUNGALOW - a compact and comfortable cottage occupying an elevated position with wonderful parkland views. Fully furnished and equipped to a high standard, accommodation comprises one double and one twin bedroom (duvets supplied), sitting room, dining room, modern kitchen with cooker, and bathroom and shower. Small secluded garden. Colour TV, laundry facilities. Conservatory. Parking. Pets by arrangement. Contact **Carol MacKenley** for further details.

WADEBRIDGE (near)

See also Colour Display Advertisement

Polgrain Holiday Cottages, Higher Polgrain, St Wenn PL30 5PR (01637 880637; Fax: 01637 881944). Beautifully converted and well-equipped barn conversions in glorious countryside location, superbly positioned to tour the spectacular north coast, this is a holiday destination which offers the best of both worlds. Polgrain is the most perfect place to relax, unwind and enjoy the peace and tranquillity of the surrounding countryside. Once a flourishing farm and mill, the main farmhouse is now our family home, while the granite barns and mill have been converted into comfortable, well-equipped holiday cottages – each with its own individual character and features. Adjoining the main farmhouse is the HEATED INDOOR POOL. Each cottage has a fully fitted kitchen including washing machine and microwave, and each living area is also equipped with colour TV, video recorder and compact disc hi-fi system. Alarm clock radios can be found in the bedrooms and all linen is provided free of charge. Central heating, power and lighting are all included within the price of the holiday. Each cottage also has its own patio, complete with furniture and brick built barbecue. Car parking. Tariffs and booking details on request. Open March – January. ETC ★★★★
e-mail: Polgrainholidaycottages@ukgateway.net   website: www.selfcateringcornwall.uk.com

---

See the *Family-Friendly Pubs & Inns*
Supplement on pages 335 - 344 for establishments
which really welcome children

ENGLAND / Self-catering Cumbria 195

CUMBRIA

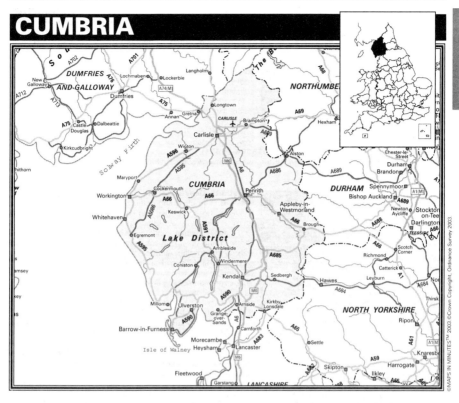

The LAKE DISTRICT and CUMBRIA

Superb, personally inspected, self catering holiday properties in beautiful rural and coastal locations from Beatrix Potter and Wordsworth country to the Borders. Cosy cottages to country houses, many welcome pets and short breaks are available.

Dales Holiday Cottages

0870 909 9500
www.dalesholcot.com

Holker Hall & Gardens • *Near Newby Bridge, Cumbria* • *015395 58328*
website: wwwholker-hall.com
A historic hall set in 25 acres of beautiful gardens, plus the Lakeland Motor Museum featuring the Campbell Bluebird Exhibition.

Cumberland Pencil Museum • *Keswick, Cumbria* • *017687 73626*
website: www.pencils.co.uk
The fascinating history of the humble pencil, from the discovery of Borrowdale graphite to present day manufacture. See the world's largest colouring pencil, Shop.

AMBLESIDE

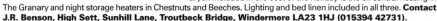

Betty Fold Apartment, Hawkshead Hill, Ambleside. Sleeps 4. This comfortable ground floor apartment has wonderful views over the valley. It has its own private entrance and is centrally heated. The accommodation comprises an open plan kitchen and living room with three piece suite, dining table and chairs, colour TV/video and well-equipped kitchen area with electric cooker, refrigerator and microwave. The double bedroom is en suite and has space for an extra small bed or cot. There is a small twin bedded room with its own bathroom, dressing room and colour TV...ideal for older children. We have plenty of maps and guide books and will happily help you plan your day. Ample private parking. Terms include heat, light, power, bed linen and towels. Contact: **Neil and Claire Salisbury, Betty Fold, Hawkshead Hill, Ambleside LA22 0PS (015394 36611).**
e-mail: csalisbury@bettyfold.fsnet.co.uk website: www.bettyfold.co.uk

AMBLESIDE

Chestnuts, Beeches & The Granary, High Wray, Ambleside. Sleep 6. Two charming cottages and one delightful bungalow converted from a former 18th century house and cornstore/tack room. Set in idyllic surroundings overlooking Lake Windermere with magnificent panoramic views of the Langdale Pikes, Coniston Old Man and the Troutbeck Fells, making this an ideal base for walking and touring. All three properties have large lounges with satellite TV and video. The Granary has a separate kitchen/diner. Chestnuts and Beeches have balconies overlooking Lake Windermere and dining areas in the large lounges. All properties have bathrooms with bath, shower, fitted kitchens with electric cooker, microwave, fridge, freezer and tumble dryer. Included in the cost of the holiday is the oil central heating in The Granary and night storage heaters in Chestnuts and Beeches. Lighting and bed linen included in all three. **Contact J.R. Benson, High Sett, Sunhill Lane, Troutbeck Bridge, Windermere LA23 1HJ (015394 42731).**

AMBLESIDE

Mr Evans, Ramsteads Coppice, Outgate, Ambleside LA22 0NH (015394 36583). Six timber lodges of varied size and design set in 15 acres of mixed woodland with wild flowers, birds and native wild animals. There are also 11 acres of rough hill pasture. Three miles south west of Ambleside, it is an ideal centre for walkers, naturalists and country lovers. No pets. Children welcome. Open March to November.

APPLEBY-IN-WESTMORLAND

David and Madeleine Adams, The Station, Milburn Road, Long Marton, Appleby CA16 6BU (0161-775 5669). WHY NOT TRY SOMETHING A LITTLE DIFFERENT? Long Marton Station, on the historic Settle - Carlisle Railway, has been painstakingly restored over the past 10 years. Situated in the unspoilt Eden Valley between the Lakes and the Pennines, the Station occupies a commanding position in half an acre of land just outside the village. There is a large lounge with original marble fireplace, dining room, kitchen, bathroom, large double bedroom with cot, and twin bedroom. Gas central heating, colour TV/video, music centre, electric cooker, microwave, fridge/freezer, washing machine, bath/shower, large lawn. Ample on-site parking. Electricity, gas, firewood, bed linen and towels (on request) included. Welcome pack on arrival. Pets by arrangement.
website: www.LongMartonStation.co.uk

A useful index of towns and counties appears at the back of this book on pages 375 - 378. Refer also to Contents Pages 2 and 3.

ENGLAND / Self-catering   Cumbria   197

APPLEBY-IN-WESTMORLAND

Mrs Edith Stockdale, Croft House, Bolton, Appleby-in-Westmorland CA16 6AW (Tel & Fax: 017683 61264). Sleep 2/5 and 10. Three cosy cottages recently converted from an old Westmorland style barn adjoining the owner's house. With an abundance of open stone work and oak beams and many original features. An excellent base for fell and country walking, horse-riding or as a touring base for the Lake District, beautiful Eden Valley, Scottish Borders, Hadrian's Wall and North Yorkshire Dales. Bed linen, towels, electricity and heating included in rent. Facilities include electric cooker, washing machine, fridge-freezer, microwave, colour TV, video, hi-fi and dishwasher. Stabling provided for anyone wishing to bring pony on holiday. Weekly terms from £160. Brochure.
website: www.crofthouse-cottages.co.uk

BOWNESS-ON-WINDERMERE

43A Quarry Rigg, Bowness-on-Windermere. Sleeps 4. Ideally situated in the centre of the village close to the Lake and all amenities, the flat is in a new development, fully self-contained, and furnished and equipped to a high standard for owner's own comfort and use. Lake views, ideal relaxation and touring centre. Accommodation is for two/four people. Bedroom with twin beds, lounge with TV and video; convertible settee; separate kitchen with electric cooker, microwave and fridge/freezer; bathroom with bath/shower and WC. Electric heating. Parking for residents. Sorry, no pets. Terms from £130 to £250. Weekends and Short Breaks also available. SAE, please, for details to **E. Jones, 45 West Oakhill Park, Liverpool, Merseyside L13 4BN (Tel & Fax: 0151-228 5799).**
e-mail: eejay@btinternet.com

See also Colour Display Advertisement

CONISTON

Coniston Country Cottages. Sleep 2-6. A range of quality cottages in superb surroundings in and around Coniston. Each cottage is well equipped and individually and tastefully furnished. Central location with easy access to the lakes and mountains. Ideal for walking, mountain-biking, climbing and sailing. Nearby in Coniston village are shops, banks, restaurants and pubs. Complimentary leisure club membership. Off-road parking. Electricity included. Private patio or garden area with each cottage. Short breaks available November to March. **Tel & Fax: 015394 41114.**
e-mail: enquiry@conistoncottages.co.uk
website: www.conistoncottages.co.uk

CONISTON

Thurston View Cottage (sleeps 4) and Thurston House (flats sleep 2/6). THURSTON VIEW COTTAGE is an old stone-miners cottage a few minutes' walk from the centre of Coniston. Fully equipped, with central heating, dishwasher, microwave, fridge/freezer etc. Garden has patio and barbecue area. No smoking or pets. Terms from £205 to £375 per week. **ETC ★★★★**. THURSTON HOUSE has been converted into spacious, comfortable apartments which are open all year (storage heaters early and late season). Children and pets welcome. Only a short walk to village centre and lake. Terms from £90 to £260 per week. **ETC ★★**. Enquiries to **Mr and Mrs Jefferson, 21 Chalegreen, Harwood, Bolton BL2 3NJ (01204 419261).**
e-mail: alan@jefferson99.freeserve.co.uk
website: www.jefferson99.freeserve.co.uk

The FHG Directory of Website Addresses
on pages 345 - 373 is a useful quick reference guide for holiday accommodation with e-mail and/or website details

See also Colour Display Advertisement

ELTERWATER
Lane Ends Cottages, Elterwater. The cottages are situated next to "Fellside" on the edge of Elterwater Common. Two cottages accommodate a maximum of four persons: double bedroom, twin bedded room; fully equipped kitchen/diningroom; bathroom. Third cottage sleeps five: as above plus single bedroom and separate diningroom. Electricity by meters. The cottages provide an ideal base for walking/touring holidays with Ambleside, Grasmere, Hawkshead and Coniston within a few miles. Parking for one car per cottage, additional parking opposite. Open all year; out of season long weekends available. Rates from £200 per week. Brochure on request (SAE please). **Mrs M. E. Rice, "Fellside", Elterwater, Ambleside LA22 9HN (015394 37678).**

KENDAL
Mrs E. Bateman, High Underbrow Farm, Burneside, Kendal LA8 9AY (01539 721927). Working farm. Sleeps 4. The cottage adjoins the 17th century farmhouse in a sunny position with wonderful views. Ideal spot for touring the Lake District and Yorkshire Dales, with many pleasant walks around. There are two bedrooms (one with double bed, the other with two singles). Children are welcome and a cot is available. Bathroom with bath, shower, toilet and washbasin. Large livingroom/kitchen with colour TV, fitted units, fridge and cooker. Electricity by £1 coin meter. Storage heaters 50p meter. Understairs store. Fitted carpets throughout. Own entrance porch. Sorry, no pets. Shops at Burneside two miles away, Kendal four miles, Windermere eight miles. Linen provided. Car essential – parking. Terms from £165 weekly. There is also a six-berth holiday caravan to let from £160 per week. Dogs allowed in caravan.

KENDAL
The Barns, Field End, Patton, Kendal. Two detached barns converted into five spacious architect-designed houses. The Barns are situated on 200 acres of farmland, four miles north of Kendal. A quiet country area with River Mint passing through farmland and lovely views of Cumbrian Hills, many interesting local walks with the Dales Way Walk passing nearby. Fishing is available on the river. The Barns consist of four houses with four double bedrooms and one house with three double bedrooms. Each house fully centrally heated for early/late holidays; lounge with open fire, diningroom; kitchen with cooker, fridge, microwave and washing machine; bathroom, downstairs shower room and toilet. Many interesting features include oak beams, pine floors and patio doors. Central to Lakes and Yorkshire Dales, National Parks. Terms from £185 to £450. Electricity at cost. Pets welcome. ETC ★★★. For brochure of The Barns apply to **Mr and Mrs E.D. Robinson, 1 Field End, Patton, Kendal LA8 9DU (01539 824220 or 07778 596863); Fax: 01539 824464.**
e-mail: robinson@fieldendholidays.co.uk   website: www.fieldendholidays.co.uk

KENDAL
Holiday Cottage, Kendal. Holiday bungalow on farm between Kendal and Windermere. Sleeps five in two bedrooms. Large lounge with TV/video. Fuel provided for multifuel stove. Cot available. Linen provided. Bathroom plus second toilet. Fully-equipped kitchen/diner with electric cooker and microwave. At the rear of the bungalow is a small private garden, and at the front, parking for two cars. Most beautiful views. Broad Oak has beef cattle and sheep, and guests are invited to meet our pet lambs when we have them. There are two shops and several places to eat locally. Sorry, no pets and no smoking. Terms from £200 to £400 per week. **Mrs D. Dobson, Broad Oak, Crosthwaite, Kendal LA8 8JL (015395 68334).**

Readers are requested to mention this guidebook when seeking accommodation (and please enclose a stamped addressed envelope).

ENGLAND / Self-catering   Cumbria 199

KESWICK
Mrs E.M. Richardson, Fold Head Farm, Watendlath, Borrowdale, Keswick CA12 5UW (017687 77255). Sleeps 6. Semi-detached farm cottage situated on banks of Watendlath tarn in this picturesque hamlet. Sleeps six in two double and one twin bedroom. All electric. Linen, towels, electricity and central heating included. Ideal centre for walking, relaxing or fly fishing for trout in the tarn, permits available. Five miles from Keswick. Car essential, parking. Open all year. Terms from £250 to £450.

KESWICK
Irton House Farm, Isel, Cockermouth, Near Keswick CA13 9ST (017687 76380). Sleeps 2/6. Farm location with superb views of lake and mountains. Family accommodation (wheelchair accessible). Children welcome. Interesting walking area and comfortable motoring. Convenient restaurant nearby, also facilities for fishing, swimming and golf. Ample parking. Please telephone for colour brochure.
e-mail: almond@farmersweekly.net
website: www.irtonhousefarm.com

See also Colour Display Advertisement

KESWICK (near)
Mrs A.M. Trafford, Brook House Cottages, Bassenthwaite Hall Farm, Bassenthwaite Village, Near Keswick CA12 4QP (Tel & Fax: 017687 76393). Working farm. Location! Location! Location! By a stream with ducks. Delightful cottages charmingly restored and cared for in this attractive hamlet near Keswick. Various cottages sleep 2-10. Ideal for reunions, or family get-togethers. Short breaks available. Excellent food at village pub. Ideally situated just two miles from Skiddaw and Bassenthwaite Lake and just six miles from Keswick and Cockermouth. Mid-week and weekend breaks from £80 to £250.Weekly £120-£750. Open all year.
e-mail: a.m.trafford@amserve.net
website: www.holidaycottageslakedistrict.co.uk

KIRKBY LONSDALE (near)
Mrs M. Dixon, Harrison Farm, Whittington, Kirkby Lonsdale, Carnforth, Lancashire LA6 2NX (015242 71415). Properties sleep 2/8. Near Hutton Roof, three miles from Kirkby Lonsdale and central for touring Lake District and Yorkshire Dales. Coast walks on Hutton Roof Crag, famous lime stone pavings. Sleeps eight people, one room with double and single bed and one room with double and cot, while third bedroom has three single beds. Bathroom. Sittingroom, diningroom and kitchen. Everything supplied but linen. Parking space. Pets permitted. Other cottages available for two to eight people. Electric cooker, fridge, kettle, iron, immersion heater and TV. Electricity and coal extra. Terms from £200 per week. SAE brings quick reply.

FHG
Visit the FHG website
www.holidayguides.com
for details of the wide choice of accommodation featured in the full range of FHG titles

HODYOAD COTTAGES

Hodyoad stands in its own private grounds, with extensive views of the surrounding fells in peaceful rural countryside. Mid-way between the beautiful Lakes of Loweswater and Ennerdale, six miles from Cockermouth and 17 from Keswick. Fell walking, boating, pony trekking and trout fishing can all be enjoyed within a three-and a half mile radius. Each cottage is fully centrally heated and has two bedrooms to sleep five plus cot. All linen provided. Lounge with colour TV. Kitchen with fitted units, cooker and fridge. Bathroom with shower, washbasin, toilet, shaver point. Laundry room with washing machine and tumble dryer. Car essential, ample parking. Sea eight miles. Open all year. From £200 to £360 per week. For further details please contact:

Mrs J. A. Cook, Hodyoad House, Lamplugh, Cumbria CA14 4TT • Tel: 01946 861338

See also Colour Advertisement

See also Colour Display Advertisement

KIRKOSWALD
Liz Webster, Howscales, Kirkoswald, Penrith CA10 1JG (01768 898666; Fax: 01768 898710). Sleeps 2/4. COTTAGES FOR NON-SMOKERS. Howscales was originally a 17th century farm. The red sandstone buildings have been converted into five self-contained cottages, retaining many original features. Set around a cobbled courtyard, the cosy, well-equipped cottages for two/four, are surrounded by gardens and open countryside. Shared laundry facilities. Well-behaved pets welcome by arrangement. Open all year, short breaks available. Colour brochure. Non-smoking. Cared for by resident owner. Ideal base from which to explore The Eden Valley, Lakes, Pennines and Hadrian's Wall. Please ring, write or see our website for details. **ETC ★★★★.** *NATIONAL ACCESSIBILITY SCHEME: CATEGORY 2.*

e-mail: liz@howscales.fsbusiness.co.uk
website: www.eden-in-cumbria.co.uk/howscales

KIRKOSWALD

Crossfield Cottages with Leisure Fishing. Tranquil quality cottages overlooking fishing lake amidst Lakeland's beautiful Eden Valley countryside. Only 30 minutes' drive from Ullswater, North Pennines, Hadrian's Wall and the Scottish Borders. You will find freshly made beds for your arrival, tranquillity and freedom to roam. Good coarse fishing for residents only; fly fishing nearby on River Eden. Cottages are clean, well-equipped and maintained. Laundry area. Pets very welcome. Exceptional wildlife and walking area. Escape and relax to your home in the country. **ETC ★★★**. SAE to **Crossfield Cottages, Kirkoswald, Penrith CA10 1EU (Tel & Fax: 01768 898711 6pm-10pm for bookings, 24hr Brochure Line).**
e-mail: info@crossfieldcottages.co.uk
website: www.crossfieldcottages.co.uk

PENRITH
Beckside Cottage, Martindale, Ullswater. Sleeps 2/4. The cottage, which is part of the 17th century farmhouse, is set close to the babbling brook in the tiny hamlet of Sandwick, on a traditional Lakeland farm. The spectacular fells surrounding and glimpse of lake Ullswater are five minutes' walk away, make it an ideal retreat or base for walking. A cosy two-bedroom cottage with oak beams and log fire awaits your arrival, with added modern touches i.e. oil central heating, fully fitted and well-equipped kitchen, shower, as well as books, videos and games to while away the evenings. A warm and friendly welcome assured. Terms from £250 to £430 depending on season, short breaks available. **ETC ★★★★.** Colour brochure available - please contact: **Andrew and Caroline Ivinson, Beckside Farm, Sandwick, Martindale, Penrith CA10 2NF (Tel & Fax: 017684 86239).**
e-mail: ivinson_becksidefarm@hotmail.com

ENGLAND / Self-catering   Cumbria **201**

STAVELEY
Margaret and William Beck, Brunt Knott Farm, Staveley, Kendal LA8 9QX (01539 821030; Fax: 01539 821221). Sleep 2/5. Four cosy cottages sympathetically converted from stone barn and stables on small secluded 17th century hill farm set above Staveley, midway between Kendal and Windermere (five miles). Retained beams/stone features. Peaceful hillside setting. Superb panoramic views over Lakeland Fells. Excellent base for walking, touring Lakes/Dales, relaxing in delightful surroundings. Walks/cycling on doorstep. Ample private parking. Laundry facilities. Resident owners. Well-equipped fitted kitchens. Duvets, bed linen provided. Oil central/electric heating. Woodburner/open fire in three cottages. Gardens with tables and benches. Children and pets welcome. Village and shops one and a half miles. Low season Short Breaks. Terms from £190 to £400 per week. Brochure. **ETC ★★★**
e-mail: margaret@bruntknott.demon.co.uk   website: www.bruntknott.demon.co.uk

See also Colour Display Advertisement

ULLSWATER
The Estate Office, Patterdale Hall Estate, Glenridding, Penrith CA11 0PJ (017684 82308; Fax: 017684 82867). Our range includes three very comfortable, large Coach Houses, two stone built Cottages with open fires, three three-bedroomed pine Lodges, six two-bedroomed cedar Chalets, a unique detached converted Dairy and two converted Bothies which make ideal, low cost accommodation for two people. All set in a private 300 acre estate between Lake Ullswater and Helvellyn and containing a working hill farm, a Victorian waterfall wood, private lake foreshore for guests to use for boating and fishing and 100 acres of designated ancient woodland for you to explore. Children welcome. Dogs by appointment in some of the accommodation. Colour TV, central heating, launderette, payphone; daytime electricity metered. Linen hire available. Weekly prices from £145.00 to £465.00. Please phone for full brochure. **ETC ★★ – ★★★**
e-mail: welcome@patterdalehallestate.com   website: www.patterdalehallestate.com

WIGTON
Mr & Mrs E. and J. Kerr, Fox Gloves, Greenrigg Farm, Westward, Wigton CA7 8AH (016973 42676). A spacious well-equipped, comfortable cottage on a working farm. Superlative setting and views, large kitchen/dining room, Aga, lounge, open fire, TV/video, three bedrooms, bathroom, separate shower room. Linen, towels, electricity, logs and coal inclusive. Children and pets very welcome. Extensive garden. Storage heaters, washing machine, dishwasher. Easy reach Lake District, Scottish Borders and Roman Wall. Sleeps two to eight people. Prices from £195–£425. Available all year. Short breaks by arrangement. *JPC PUBLICATIONS AWARD OF MERIT.*

WINDERMERE
Mrs R. Dodgson, Cragg Farm, Bowston, Burneside, Kendal LA8 9HH (01539 821249). Cragg Farm Cottage adjoins our farmhouse and is set in quiet rural surroundings, with ample parking space, giving the opportunity to walk in the countryside. Three-quarters-of-a-mile from the main Kendal to Windermere Road (A591) it is in an ideal position for visiting the Lakes and Windermere (15 minutes away) and Kendal, four miles away. The villages of Staveley and Burneside are just two miles away. The cottage is comfortable, clean and well-equipped. Lounge/diningroom with colour TV, fully equipped kitchen, one double and one twin-bedded room and bathroom. Gas fire and central heating, electricity on £1 meter. Bed linen provided. Details on request.

When making enquiries or bookings, a stamped addressed envelope is always appreciated

DERBYSHIRE

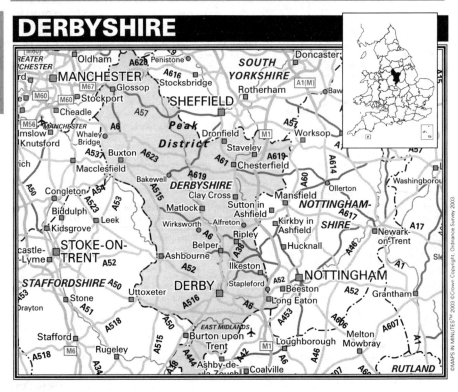

ASHBOURNE

Windlehill Farm, Sutton-on-the-Hill, Ashbourne DE6 5JH (Tel & Fax: 01283 732377). Set amidst tranquil countryside south of Ashbourne, our two beamed barns offer cosy, well-equipped accommodation on our small organic farm. THE CHOP HOUSE sleeps six people. It has three twin bedrooms, kitchen/dining room, separate living room, sheltered garden with table and seats. Prices: £180 to £420 per week. THE HAY LOFT sleeps two people. It is a first-floor apartment over the old stable and is approached by the original internal stone steps. It has a twin/double bedroom and kitchen/living room. Prices: £120 to £240 per week. Both have excellent views over the farm and countryside and are graded ETC ★★★★
e-mail: windlehill@btinternet.com   website: www.windlehill.btinternet.co.uk

ASHBOURNE near

Briar, Bluebell and Primrose Cottages. Sleep 5/6. Our Listed barn now contains three self-catering cottages. Situated in pleasant and peaceful surroundings on a working dairy farm on the outskirts of Bradley village, we offer first-class accommodation for the tourist and business person alike. Each cottage has three bedrooms, bathroom with bath and shower, and fitted kitchen, and is fully carpeted. Ample safe parking available. The market town of Ashbourne is just three miles away; Carsington Water, Dovedale, Matlock, Bakewell, Alton Towers and many stately homes are all within easy reach. This is a welcoming place to relax and explore the wonders of Derbyshire and the Peak District. Terms £150 to £400 per week depending on cottage; winter short breaks available. **ETC ★★★** and **★★★★**. B&B also available.
Details from **Mrs Janet Hinds, Yeldersley Old Hall Farm, Yeldersley Lane, Bradley, Ashbourne DE6 1PH (01335 344504).**

BAKEWELL

Burton Manor Farm Cottages, Over Haddon, Bakewell DE45 1JX (Tel & Fax: 01298 871429; mobile: 07790 966707). Sleep 2-8. Our family-run dairy/sheep farm is an ideal base for visitors, being in the heart of the Peak District. Excellent walking in all directions, with Lathkill Dale and Limestone Way nearby. The recent barn conversion consists of six cosy cottages providing quality accommodation with excellent parking. Open all year. Terms from £150 to £610 per week. ETC ★★★★. Details from **Mrs Ruth Shirt.**
e-mail: cshirt@burtonmanor.freeserve.co.uk
website: www.burtonmanor.freeserve.co.uk

See also Colour Display Advertisement

ILAM

Throwley Moor Farm and Throwley Cottage, Ilam, Near Ashbourne. Working farm, join in. Properties sleep 7/12. Our self-catering accommodation is situated on our family farm in the heart of rural England in the Peak District National Park. Within a few miles of the renowned beauty of the Manifold Valley and Dovedale. All properties are traditional farmhouses, converted into comfortable, well-equipped, spacious, holiday houses. All have cosy lounges with open fires. Kitchens are well appointed including microwaves, freezers, automatic dishwashers and washing machines and driers. Large private gardens with furniture and barbecue facilities. Despite their peaceful rural location the properties are within easy reach of Alton Towers theme park as well as Chatsworth and the historic pottery works of Stoke-on-Trent. Nearby are the charming local market towns of Ashbourne, Leek and Buxton. Tariffs include all fuel costs. Linen provided, towels, cot and high chair by arrangement. ETC ★★★/★★★★. SAE, please, for further details to **Mrs M.A. Richardson, Throwley Hall Farm, Ilam, Near Ashbourne DE6 2BB (01538 308 202/243).**
e-mail: throwleyhall@talk21.com or throwley@btinternet.com
website: www.throwleyhallfarm.co.uk

See also Colour Display Advertisement

HARTINGTON

J. Gibbs, Wolfscote Grange Farm Cottages, Hartington, Near Buxton SK17 0AX (Tel & Fax: 01298 84342). Sleep 4/6. Charming cottages nestling beside the beautiful Dove Valley in stunning scenery. Cruck Cottage is peaceful 'with no neighbours, only sheep' and a cosy 'country living' feel. Swallows Cottage offers comfort for the traveller and time to relax in beautiful surroundings. It sparkles with olde worlde features, yet has modern amenities including en suite facilities and spa bathroom. The farm trail provides walks from your doorstep to the Dales. Open all year. Weekly terms from £180 to £450 (sleep four); £180 to £550 (sleep six). ETC ★★★★
e-mail: wolfscote@btinternet.com
website: www.wolfscotegrangecottages.co.uk

Denby Pottery Visitor Centre • *Denby, Derbyshire* • *01773 740799*
website: www.denbyvisitorcentre.co.uk
Guided tours of the working factory and demonstrations of key skills.
Factory shop, Cookery Emporium, restaurant.

The FHG Directory of Website Addresses
on pages 345 - 373 is a useful quick reference guide for holiday accommodation with e-mail and/or website details

204 Derbyshire Self-catering / ENGLAND

HARTINGTON

P. Skemp, Cotterill Farm, Biggin by Hartington, Buxton SK17 0DJ (01298 84447; Fax: 01298 84664). Three stone cottages, two sleeping four, and one sleeping two. Exposed beams, two-person cottage has galleried bedroom, log burner, five-piece suite in bathroom and more. High and tasteful specification. Patio, substantial garden area, wild flower meadows and barbecue. Laundry room. Phone. Glorious location in rolling countryside. Excellent views with privacy. Half-a-mile from village and pub. Tissington Trail three-quarters of a mile, two other cycle/footpath trails within three miles, nature reserve on our land leading after one-and-a-half miles to River Dove, four miles down river is Dovedale. Footpaths/bridleways surround our farm. Highly praised, personalised information pack in each cottage giving loads of advice on attractions, walks, etc. Terms from £200 to £420 per week. **ETC ★★★★**
e-mail: enquiries@cotterillfarm.co.uk   website: www.cotterillfarm.co.uk

MATLOCK

Honeysuckle, Jasmine and Clematis Cottages, Middlehills Farm, Grange Mill, Matlock DE4 4HY (01629 650368). Relax, unwind, enjoy the peace and tranquillity in one of our warm, welcoming cottages or static caravan. JASMINE - two bedroomed, and HONEYSUCKLE - three bedroomed, are full of character – stone mullions, enclosed south-facing patios. CLEMATIS - two bedroomed, Accessible Category 2, is on one level and especially converted for less-able and wheelchair users. Large bathroom with support rails, wheel-in shower with shower seat. Also fully equipped static caravan for bargain breaks. Meet our friendly pot-bellied pig, and Bess and Ruby are ideal playmates for children of all ages.

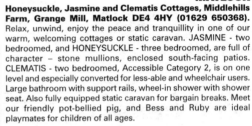

One child FREE with every paying adult at
Blue-John Cavern
see our READERS' OFFER VOUCHERS for full details

One child FREE with every full paying adult at
Crich Tramway Village
see our READERS' OFFER VOUCHERS for full details

10% discount (not valid on Special Events Days) at
Treak Cliff Cavern
see our READERS' OFFER VOUCHERS for full details

See the ***Family-Friendly Pubs & Inns***
Supplement on pages 335 - 344 for establishments which really welcome children

ENGLAND / Self-catering   Devon 205

450 Superb Cottages — The Widest Selection of Farm Cottages Throughout Devon, Cornwall & Somerset in rural and coastal locations.

Tel: 01237 479698   www.farmcott.co.uk

FHG PUBLICATIONS publish a large range of well-known accommodation guides. We will be happy to send you details or you can use the order form at the back of this book.

206 Devon Self-catering / ENGLAND

www.classic.co.uk

classic cottages

Featuring 500 hand selected coastal and country holiday homes throughout the West Country

01326 565 555

Toad Hall Cottages

200 fabulous and unusual properties situated in truly beautiful waterside, rural and village locations in Devon, Cornwall & Exmoor.

For our full colour brochure please call

08700 777345

www.toadhallcottages.com
email: thc@toadhallcottages.com

See also Colour Display Advertisement

North Devon Holiday Homes, 19 Cross Street, Barnstaple EX31 1BD (01271 376322 24-hour brochure service; Fax: 01271 346544). With our Free Colour Guide and unbiased recommendation and booking service, we can spoil you for choice in the beautiful unspoilt region around Exmoor and the wide sandy beaches and coves of Devon's beautiful National Trust Coast. Choose from 400 selected properties including thatched cottages, working farms, beachside properties with swimming pools, luxury manor houses, etc. Bargain Breaks from only £35 per person, to luxury manor house for 16 from only £995 per week. First class value assured.
e-mail: info@northdevonholidays.co.uk
website: www.northdevonholidays.co.uk

See also Colour Display Advertisement

AXMINSTER
Cider Room Cottage, Hasland Farm, Membury, Axminster. Sleeps 4. This delightfully converted thatched cider barn, with exposed beams, adjoins main farmhouse overlooking the outstanding beauty of the orchards, pools and pastureland, and is ideally situated for touring Devon, Dorset and Somerset. Bathing, golf and tennis at Lyme Regis and many places of interest locally, including Wildlife Park, donkey sanctuary and Forde Abbey. Membury Village, with its post office and stores, trout farm, church and swimming pool is one mile away. The accommodation is of the highest standard with the emphasis on comfort. Two double rooms, cot if required; shower room and toilet; sitting/diningroom with colour TV; kitchen with electric cooker, microwave, fridge, washing machine. Linen supplied if required. Pets by arrangement. Car essential. Open all year. No smoking. Terms from £135 to £270. **ETC ★★★★**.
SAE, please, to **Mrs Pat Steele, Hasland Farm, Membury, Axminster EX13 7JF (01404 881558).**

ENGLAND / Self-catering   Devon 207

See also Colour Display Advertisement

BARNSTAPLE
Lower Yelland Farm Cottages, Barnstaple. Winner of the 2002 Golden Achievement Award of Excellence for the Devon Retreat of the Year, this delightfully modernised, comfortable and quiet farm cottage is situated close to the road between Barnstaple and Bideford on the lovely Taw/Torridge estuary, immediately adjacent to the Tarka Trail. Set in its own private lawned gardens with ample courtyard parking, the cottage is ideal for family holidays and as a base for touring. It is within a mile of the sandy beach at Instow and excellent pubs and restaurants. B&B is also available and there are many leisure activities close at hand. **ETC ★★★** *SELF-CATERING*, ◆◆◆ *B&B*. Contact: **Mr Peter Day, Lower Yelland Farm, Fremington, Barnstaple EX31 3EN (01271 860101; mobile: 07803 933642).**

e-mail: peterday@loweryellandfarm.co.uk   website: www.loweryellandfarm.co.uk

See also Colour Display Advertisement

BOVEY TRACEY
John and Helen Griffiths, Lookweep Farm, Liverton, Newton Abbot TQ12 6HT (01626 833277; Fax: 01626 834412). Sleeps 5. Lookweep Farm is set within Dartmoor National Park and is perfectly placed for exploration of Dartmoor, the stunning coastline, charming villages and towns of South Devon. Shippen and Dairy cottages are two attractive, well-equipped stone cottages surrounded by open farmland and woods in this tranquil setting near Bovey Tracey and just a two mile drive from Haytor. Own gardens, ample parking, heated pool and outstanding walks right on your doorstep. Children welcome (high chairs and cots available). Pets by arrangement. Short breaks available. Mastercard and Visa accepted. Please phone or write for brochure. **ETC ★★★**

e-mail: holidays@lookweep.co.uk   website: www.lookweep.co.uk

See also Colour Display Advertisement

BRIXHAM
Devoncoast Holidays. We are a highly experienced holiday letting agency on Devon's sunny south coast. We have numerous properties on our books ranging from one-bedroom flats to large three bedroomed houses, all in sunny South Devon. We have personally inspected all of our properties and all of the accommodation is of a high standard and comes fully equipped with colour TV, microwave, full cooker and car parking. Our properties are available all year round, for mini breaks or for full week lettings. Pets and children are welcome. Many have a flat access. All of our properties are within easy reach of the coast, some have sea views. We accept all credit cards. Please telephone for a free brochure and map - 24 hour operation. **Devoncoast Holidays, P.O. Box 14. Brixham, Devon TQ5 8AB (Tel & Fax: 07050 338889).**

website: www.devoncoast.com

CHULMLEIGH
Fiona Lincoln-Gordon, Bridleway Cottages, Golland Farm, Burrinton, Umberleigh EX37 9JP (01769 520263). Sleep 2/8. Country lovers' retreat. Two cottages converted from a stone barn on small mixed, organic farm. Overlooking Taw Valley, offering exclusive fishing on coarse and trout ponds. 160 miles of Tarka Trail for cyclists and walkers 10 minutes away. The cottages have been sensitively restored to offer all home comforts. Heating and woodburners for cosy winter breaks. Many original wood features. Organic vegetables from our Veg Box Scheme. A traditional rural country base between Dartmoor and Exmoor. Country pubs. RHS Rosemoor and Trust gardens nearby; Eden Project within one-and-a-half hours. Pets welcome. Open all year. Terms from £170 to £560 per week. Short breaks welcome. **ETC ★★★**

website: www.golland.btinternet.co.uk

208 Devon   Self-catering / ENGLAND

See also Colour Display Advertisement

COLYTON
Mrs R. Gould and Mrs S. Gould, Bonehayne Farm, Colyton EX24 6SG (01404 871396 or 01404 871416). Bonehayne Farm cottage welcomes you with many olde worlde features. Spacious, fully-furnished with four-poster, microwave, laundry facilities and central heating. Family-run dairy farm on the banks of the river Coly, in a beautiful, picturesque sheltered valley. Large garden, good trout fishing, woodlands to roam and plenty of walks. Coast is only 10 minutes away.
e-mail: gould@bonehayne.co.uk
website: www.bonehayne.co.uk

COLYTON
Church Approach Cottages, Farway, Colyton EX24 6EQ. Sleep 5/6. Situated beside the village church, the cottages have been tastefully renovated to maintain the old style of the barn. With panoramic views over the Coly valley, they provide a quiet holiday and offer many interesting walks. A countryside park, riding stables and ancient monuments are all within walking distance. Honiton Golf Course, swimming pool and bowling green are four miles away. Lyme Regis, Sidmouth and Exmouth plus many other quaint scenic coastal resorts are all within half an hour's drive. Each cottage has a modern kitchen complete with washing machine and microwave as well as a conventional cooker, comfortable lounge with colour TV and video, two bedrooms and bathroom with bath and shower. Central heating.

Electricity by £1 meter. Bed linen supplied. Brochure on request. Bed and Breakfast available at our farmhouse. For further details please contact: **Sheila Lee (01404 871383/871202; Fax: 01404 871233).**
e-mail: lizlee@eclipse.co.uk

See also Colour Display Advertisement

DARTMOUTH
Watermill Cottages, Hansel, Dartmouth TQ6 0LN (01803 770219). Down a narrow lane lies a secret valley just over a mile inland from Slapton Sands. There you will find the six delightful Watermill Cottages on the banks of a small river by an old mill house. A peaceful haven with wonderful walks and freedom for children to explore. Home cooking available. Winter breaks from £95.
e-mail: graham@hanselpg.freeserve.co.uk
website: www.watermillcottages.co.uk

See also Colour Display Advertisement

HOPE COVE
Mike and Judy Tromans, Hope Barton Barns, Hope Cove, Near Salcombe TQ7 3HT (01548 561393). Sleep 2/10. Nestling in its own valley, close to the sandy cove, Hope Barton Barns is an exclusive group of 17 stone barns in two courtyards and three luxury apartments in the converted farmhouse. Heated indoor pool, sauna, gym, lounge bar, tennis court, trout lake and a children's play barn. We have 35 acres of pastures and streams with sheep, goats, pigs, chickens, ducks and rabbits. Superbly furnished and fully-equipped, each cottage is unique and they vary from a studio to four bedrooms, sleeping two to ten. Farmhouse meals from our menu. Ample parking. Golf, sailing and coastal walks nearby. Open all year. A perfect setting for family Summer holidays, a week's walking in Spring/Autumn or just a

"get away from it all" break. Free range children and well behaved dogs welcome. For a colour brochure and rental tariff, please contact Mike or Judy. Open all year. ★★★★
website: www.hopebarton.co.uk

When making enquiries or bookings, a stamped addressed envelope is always appreciated

THE SALTER FAMILY WELCOMES YOU
HALDON LODGE FARM
Kennford, Near Exeter, Devon
20 minutes from Dawlish and Teignmouth Beaches

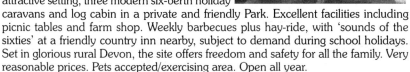

Freedom and safety for all the family

Central for South Devon coast and Exeter in an attractive setting, three modern six-berth holiday caravans and log cabin in a private and friendly Park. Excellent facilities including picnic tables and farm shop. Weekly barbecues plus hay-ride, with 'sounds of the sixties' at a friendly country inn nearby, subject to demand during school holidays. Set in glorious rural Devon, the site offers freedom and safety for all the family. Very reasonable prices. Pets accepted/exercising area. Open all year.

Relax and enjoy the scenery or stroll along the many forest lanes. Famous country inns nearby. Three coarse fishing lakes close to the Park and the attraction of ponies and horse riding at a nearby farm.

Large six-berth caravans, two bedrooms, lounge with TV, bathroom/toilet (H/C); rates from £70 to £195 High Season.

Personal attention and welcome by David & Betty Salter.
For brochure telephone 01392 832312.

See also Colour Display Advertisement

ILFRACOMBE
Jeremy and Elizabeth Sansom, Widmouth Farm, Watermouth, Nr. Ifracombe EX34 9RX (01271 863743). Widmouth Farm has 35 acres of gardens, woodland, pastures and a private beach on National Heritage Coastline. There are 10 one, two and three bedroom cottages, some early Victorian, some conversions from farm buildings. All are comfortable and well equipped. We have sheep, goats, chickens, ducks, rabbits, guinea pigs and much wildlife (seals sometimes play off our coast). The surroundings are tranquil, the views superb and access easy (on the A399 between Ilfracombe and Combe Martin). Ideal for walking (the coastal footpath runs around the property), bird watching, painting and sea fishing. Ilfracombe Golf Club in walking distance. Pets welcome. **ETC ★★★**

e-mail: holiday@widmouthfarmcottages.co.uk   website: www.widmouthfarmcottages.co.uk

---

See also Colour Display Advertisement

ILFRACOMBE (near)
Lower Campscott Farm, Lee, Near Ilfracombe EX34 8LS (01271 863479). We have a lovely farm set at the head of the Fuchsia Valley of Lee, with views across the Atlantic. Our four fully furnished cottages and two holiday homes are so popular we have erected a log cabin to accommodate all the visitors that want to keep coming to stay in this peaceful corner of Devon, surrounded by our special animals and the beautiful wildlife - Deer, Badgers, Geese and Buzzards to name a few. The beaches of Lee and Woolacombe are close by. Meals and cream teas are available, by arrangement, in our conservatory.
e-mail: holidays@lowercampscott.co.uk
website: www.lowercampscott.co.uk

Nuckwell Cottage
Churchstow, Near Kingsbridge TQ7 4NZ
Tel: 01548 550368

Picturesque stone-built cottage, sleeps 5, in peaceful and secluded setting, bordered by fields and cider orchards. Recently refurbished and retaining many of the original features, such as stone and timber floors and old beams, but with the benefit of central heating. Fully fitted kitchen with Aga (for the winter months), granite worktops, dishwasher, microwave, etc. Lounge with log burner, TV and video. Bedrooms: one double, one twin, one single. Bedding, electricity, heating and logs all inclusive. Near to beautiful sandy beaches, fantastic pubs and golf courses, etc. Exclusively for non-smokers. Sorry, no pets. Telephone for brochure and prices. *Terms from £295 to £710 per week.*

INSTOW
Tides Reach Cottage. Seafront cottage – photo shows view from garden of sandy beach and sea. Parking by the cottage. Instow is a quiet seaside village; shops, pubs and restaurants serving meals overlooking the water. Cottage has 3 bedrooms, enclosed garden, many sea views. Colour TV, washing machine, coastal walks. Dogs welcome. Other sea front cottages available.Please send SAE for colour brochure of this and other sea edge cottages to **F. T. Barnes, 140 Bay View Road, Northam, Bideford EX39 1BJ (or phone 01237 473801 for prices and dates).**

See also Colour Display Advertisement

KINGSBRIDGE (near)
Mrs J. Tucker, Mount Folly Farm, Bigbury-on-Sea, Near Kingsbridge TQ7 4AR (01548 810267). Working farm. Sleeps 2/6. A delightful family farm, situated on the coast, overlooking the sea and sandy beaches of Bigbury Bay. Farm adjoins golf course and River Avon. Lovely coastal walks. Ideal centre for South Hams and Dartmoor. The spacious wing comprises half of the farmhouse, and is completely self-contained. All rooms attractively furnished. Large, comfortable lounge with bay windows overlooking the sea; TV and video. There are three bedrooms – one family, one double and a bunk bed; two have washbasins. The kitchen/diner has a fridge/freezer, electric cooker, microwave, washing machine and dishwasher. There is a nice garden, ideal for children. Cot and babysitting available. Sorry no smoking. Reduction for two people staying in off peak weeks. Please write or telephone for a brochure.

See also Colour Display Advertisement

MORETONHAMPSTEAD
Sue Horn, Narramore Farm Cottages, Narramore Farm, Moretonhampstead TQ13 8QT (01647 440455; Fax: 01647 440031). Sleeps 2-6. Stressed out? Let Narramore work its magic on you! Six comfortable cottages situated on 107-acre horse stud/alpaca farm. A really warm pool, bubbling hot spa, games/laundry room, play area, fishing pool, boat, barbecue, small animals, plus the opportunity to badgerwatch amidst glorious countryside – all these make us special. Colour brochure. Open all year. Terms from £100 to £660. Short breaks available.
e-mail: sue@narramore.com
website: www.narramorefarm.co.uk

Readers are requested to mention this guidebook when seeking accommodation (and please enclose a stamped addressed envelope).

ENGLAND / Self-catering — Devon

COLLACOTT FARM Quality Country Cottages

Eight delightful country cottages sleeping 2-12 set around a large cobbled courtyard, amidst twenty acres of tranquil Devon countryside. All are well equipped with wood-burning stove, dishwasher, heating, bed linen, and their own individual patio and garden. A tennis court, heated swimming pool, games room, children's play area, trampoline room and BHS approved riding centre make Collacott an ideal holiday for the whole family.

**Jane & Chris Cromey-Hawke, Collacott Farm,
King's Nympton, Umberleigh, North Devon EX37 9TP
Tel: 01769 572491 • e-mail: jane@collacott.co.uk
website: www.collacott.co.uk**

See also Colour Advertisement

NORTH DEVON

Torridge House Farm Cottages, Little Torrington EX38 8PS (01805 622542). Join us on the farm – help feed the animals. If you are looking for a different, very child-friendly, highly recommended holiday you might like to consider Torridge House Farm Cottages, where young families – the under sevens are especially welcome – can join in helping feed the animals: lambs, hens, ducks, pigs, rabbits as well as chicks and ducklings. The ten cottages are welcoming, comfortable and well appointed. The small, friendly, family-run farm has panoramic views of the glorious Devon countryside. There is plenty of room to play in the gardens, a heated outdoor summer swimming pool, barbecues, pool, table tennis and tennis area. We have over 16 years experience of offering relaxed, hands-on farm holidays. To find out more phone for a brochure or visit our website. **ETC ★★★**

e-mail: holidays@torridgehouse.co.uk
website: www.torridgehouse.co.uk

OKEHAMPTON

East Hook Cottages, Okehampton. Sleep 2/6. An outstanding location in the heart of Devon, with a beautiful panoramic view of the Dartmoor National Park, on the Tarka Trail and Devon Coast to Coast Cycle Route. Three comfortably furnished country cottages with exposed beams, log fire and full of character. Quiet and peaceful, set in own large grounds with garden furniture. Ample parking. Very accessible, one mile from Okehampton, less than two miles from Dartmoor, three miles from the A30. The most central point for leisure in the West Country. Children and pets welcome. Open all year. Flexible short breaks. Terms £145 to £395 per week. Guests return yearly!
Mrs M.E. Stevens, West Hook Farm, Okehampton EX20 1RL (01837 52305).
e-mail: marystevens@westhookfarm.fsnet.co.uk

See also Colour Display Advertisement

PAIGNTON

Wulfruna Holiday Apartments, 9 Esplanade Road, Paignton TQ4 6EB (01803 212660). Situated at the end of the seafront, just across the road from the beach and green, with own private car park – just a short stroll from the main shopping centre, restaurants, entertainment, and harbour and an easy level walk from both stations. The flats are comfortably furnished and comprehensively equipped; all bed linen is supplied. Personally owned and supervised by Lynne and Ian Macrae, who take pride in providing clean, pleasant accommodation, with a warm welcome, to enable you to have a happy and enjoyable stay in Paignton. Ideally situated for trips to Dartmoor, Dartmouth and Totnes and for all the attractions of Torbay.
website: www.wulfruna.com

Admit one child FREE with each paying adult at
The Big Sheep
see our READERS' OFFER VOUCHERS for full details

212 Devon   Self-catering / ENGLAND

See also Colour Display Advertisement

PLYMOUTH
Churchwood Valley, Wembury Bay PL9 0DZ (01752 862382). Relax in one of our comfortable log cabins, set in a peaceful wooded valley near the beach. Enjoy wonderful walks in woods and along the coast. Abundance of birds and wildlife. Up to two pets per cabin. Open April to January including special Christmas and New Year Breaks. Seven times David Bellamy Gold Award Winner. **ETC ★★★★**
e-mail: **Churchwoodvalley@btinternet.com**

See also Colour Display Advertisement

SEATON
Mrs E.P. Fox, "West Ridge", Harepath Hill, Seaton EX12 2TA (Tel & Fax: 01297 22398).Sleeps 3/4. "West Ridge" bungalow stands on elevated ground above the small coastal town of Seaton. It has one-and-a-half-acres of lawns and gardens and enjoys wide panoramic views of the beautiful Axe Estuary and the sea. Close by are Axmouth, Beer and Branscombe. The Lyme Bay area is an excellent centre for touring, walking, sailing, fishing, golf, etc. This comfortably furnished accommodation is ideally suited for two to four persons. Cot can be provided. Available March to October, £195 to £425 weekly (fuel charges included). Full gas central heating. Colour TV. SAE for brochure. **ETC ★★★**
e-mail: **foxfamily@westridge.fsbusiness.co.uk**
website: **www.cottageguide.co.uk/westridge**

SIDMOUTH
Mrs B.I. Tucker, Goosemoor Farm Cottage, Newton Poppleford, Sidmouth EX10 0BL (01395 568279). Sleeps 5. Set on 25-acre mixed farm on Exeter to Lyme Regis bus route, about four miles from Sidmouth and the sea, with streams running through its meadows. Many delightful walks. Accommodation is in two bedrooms (each with washbasin), kitchen, lounge plus diner, bathroom/toilet, plus shower. Linen provided. Off-road parking. Bed and Breakfast available in adjoining farmhouse from £16.

SOUTH MOLTON
Mike and Rose Courtney, West Millbrook, Twitchen, South Molton EX36 3LP (01598 740382). Properties sleep 2/8. Adjoining Exmoor. Two fully-equipped bungalows and one farmhouse annexe in lovely surroundings bordering Exmoor National Park. Ideal for touring North Devon and West Somerset including moor and coast with beautiful walks, lovely scenery and many other attractions. North Molton village is only one mile away. All units have electric cooker, fridge/freezer, microwave and colour TV; two bungalows also have washing machines. Children's play area; cots and high chairs available free. Linen hire available. Games room. Car parking. Central heating if required. Electricity metered. Out of season short breaks. Weekly prices from £70 to £375. Colour brochure available. **ETC ★★/★★★**
e-mail: wmbselfcatering@aol.com   website: **www.westcountrynow.com**

One FREE child with full paying adult at
The Gnome Reserve & Wild Flower Garden
see our READERS' OFFER VOUCHERS for full details

ENGLAND / Self-catering   Devon   213

See also Colour Display Advertisement

SOUTH MOLTON (near)
Court Green, Bishop's Nympton, Near South Molton. Sleeps 5. A most attractive, well-equipped, south facing cottage with large garden, on edge of the village of Bishop's Nympton, three miles from South Molton. Ideal holiday centre, within easy reach of Exmoor, the coast, sporting activities and places of interest. Three bedrooms, one double, one twin-bedded with washbasin and one single. Two bathrooms with toilet. Sitting and dining rooms, large kitchen. Central heating, electric coal/wood effect fires, TV. One mile sea trout/trout fishing on river mole. Well behaved pets welcome. Terms April to October £200 to £240. **Mrs J. Greenwell, Tregeiriog, Near Llangollen, North Wales LL20 7HU (01691 600672).**

TOTNES
J. and E. Ball, Higher Well Farm and Holiday Park, Stoke Gabriel, Totnes TQ9 6RN (01803 782289). A quiet secluded farm park welcoming tents, motor caravans and touring caravans. It is less than one mile from the riverside village of Stoke Gabriel and within four miles of Torbay beaches. Central for touring South Devon. Facilities include new toilet/shower block with dishwashing and family rooms. Electric hook-ups and hard standings. Launderette, shop and payphone. Also static caravans to let from £125 per week or £18 per night. **ETC ★★★★**

See also Colour Display Advertisement

WOOLACOMBE
Chichester House Holiday Apartments, The Esplanade, Woolacombe EX34 7DJ (Tel: 01271 870761). Quiet, relaxing, fully furnished apartments situated opposite Barricane Shell Beach – central seafront position with outstanding sea and coastal views. Equipment including colour TV, fridge, cooker etc. Watch the sun go down into the sea from your own balcony. Open all year. Free parking. Pets by arrangement. Off-peak reductions. Short Break details on request. SAE to resident proprietor, **Mrs Joyce Bagnall.**

WOOLACOMBE
Cliffside Sea Front Holiday Flats. Sleep 2-6. Self-catering flats providing well-equipped comfortable accommodation. Spectacular views overlooking Baggy Point, Hartland Point and Lundy Island. Surrounded by National Trust with many coastal walks, four minutes' walk to village, two minutes' walk to beach. Pleasant garden and car parking. Reduced rates for early and late season. SAE please to **Peter and Avril Bowen, Cliffside, The Esplanade, Woolacombe EX34 7DJ (01271 870210).**
e-mail: avril.bowen@cliffside.fsworld.co.uk

WOOLACOMBE
Mr Watts, Resthaven Holiday Flats, The Esplanade, Woolacombe EX34 7DJ (01271 870248). Situated on the sea front opposite the beautiful Combesgate Beach, with uninterrupted views of the coastline. Two self-contained flats – ground floor sleeps five, first floor sleeps nine. Family, double and single bedrooms, all with washbasins. Comfortable lounges with sea views, colour TV and videos. Fully equipped electric kitchens. Bathrooms have bath with shower. Electricity by £1 meter. Payphone. Free lighting, parking, hot water and laundry facility. Terms from £160 to £800 per week. Please write, or phone, for brochure.

DORSET

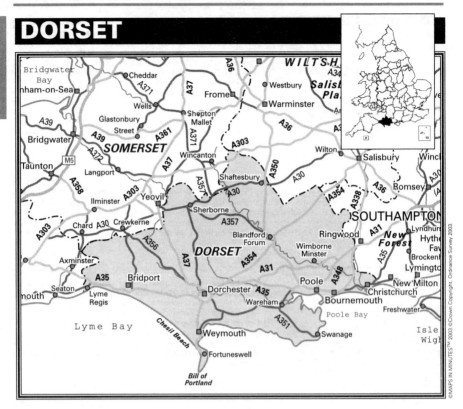

See also Colour Display Advertisement

Bournecoast (01202 428717/417757). Where the forest meets the sea, here is a peaceful place for all the family. To the north as you look, the New Forest is waiting to be explored. To the east as you look, maritime history in the making – Southampton. To the west as you look, the unspoilt beauty of the Isle of Purbeck. And to the south, there is the wide open sea – so why are you still reading this? Est. 1960, K.W. Simmons MBE.
website: ww.bournecoast.co.uk

ABBOTSBURY (near)
Character Farm Cottages, Langton Herring. Sleep 2-8. Working farm. Four character farm cottages situated in the villages of Langton Herring and Rodden, nestling on the coastline between picturesque Abbotsbury and Weymouth. This unique part of Dorset's Heritage Coast is ideal for walking, touring, bird-watching and fishing with the added attractions of Abbotsbury's world famous Swannery, The Fleet and Weymouth's safe sandy beaches. The four cottages are all comfortably furnished with features such as open fires, beams, inglenooks, walled gardens and ample parking. Pets and children welcome. Logs and linen available. Prices from £155. Enquiries: **Mrs J. Elwood, Lower Farmhouse, Langton Herring, Weymouth DT3 4JB (01305 871187; Fax: 01305 871347). ETC ★★★★**

e-mail: jane@mayo.fsbusiness.co.uk

website: www.characterfarmcottages.co.uk

ENGLAND / Self-catering Dorset 215

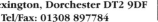

West Bexington, Dorchester DT2 9DF
Tel/Fax: 01308 897784

Mimosa

Two Wings

Tamarisk Farm

e-mail: tamarisk@eurolink.ltd.net
web: www.tamariskfarm.co.uk

On slope overlooking Chesil beach between Abbotsbury and Burton Bradstock. Three large (one for wheelchair disabled Cat. 1-M3) and two small COTTAGES, and two secluded CHALETS (not ETC graded). Terms from £105 to £650. Each one stands in own fenced garden. Glorious views along West Dorset and Devon coasts. Lovely walks by sea and inland. Mixed organic farm with arable, sheep, cattle, horses and market garden (organic vegetables, meat and wholemeal flour available). Sea fishing, riding in Portesham and Burton Bradstock, lots of tourist attractions and good markets in Bridport (6 miles), Dorchester, Weymouth and Portland, (all 13 miles). Good centre for touring Thomas Hardy's Wessex. Safe for children and excellent for dogs. Very quiet.

See also Colour Display Advertisement

BLANDFORD FORUM

Luccombe Country Holidays, Luccombe, Milton Abbas, Blandford Forum DT11 0BE (01258 880558; Fax: (01258) 881384). Superior self-catering holiday cottages, set in the heart of the beautiful and unspoilt Dorset countryside with stunning views and a peaceful, traffic free environment. Luccombe offers quality accommodation for two to eight people in a variety of converted and historic farm buildings, with original timbers and panelling. Well equipped kitchens. Large shower or bath. Cosy lounge/dining with colour TV. Bed linen, duvets, towels provided. Laundry room. Children and well behaved pets welcome. Ample parking. Disabled access. Riding, tennis, games room. Clay pigeon shooting and fishing nearby. Post office and village stores in local village. Open throughout the year. Group/family enquiries welcome. Short breaks available. Magnificent heated indoor swimming pool, sauna and gymnasium on site. **ETC ★★★★**
e-mail: info@luccombeholidays.co.uk   website: www.luccombeholidays.co.uk

BRIDPORT

Carol and Karl Mansfield, Lancombes House Holiday Cottages, West Milton, Bridport DT6 3TN (01308 485375). Lancombes House is a 200-year-old stone barn built 300 feet above sea level set in 10 acres; there are tame animals for children to play and help with including horses, ponies, goats and ducks. Farm has panoramic views to the sea only four miles away. There are four superbly converted cottages, each with its own sitting-out area, barbecue and garden furniture. They have spacious open plan living areas, most with wood burning stoves. Modern fitted kitchens, double and twin-bedded rooms. Electric central heating, shared laundry. Deep in the heart of Hardy country, this is a delightful area to explore whether on foot or horseback. There are many things to do and pets and children are very welcome. Prices start at £120 for mini-breaks; open all the year round. **ETC ★★★**
website: www.lancombeshouse.co.uk

BRIDPORT (near)

Mrs S. Norman, Frogmore Farm, Chideock, Bridport DT6 6HT (01308 456159). Working farm. Sleeps 6. Delightful farm cottage on ninety acre grazing farm set in the rolling hills of West Dorset. Superb views over Lyme Bay, ideal base for touring Dorset and Devon or rambling the many coastal and country footpaths of the area. This fully equipped self-catering cottage sleeps six. Three bedrooms. Bed linen supplied. Cosy lounge with woodburner and colour TV, French doors to a splendid columned sun verandah. Children and well behaved dogs welcome. Car essential. Open all year. Short breaks available, also Bed and Breakfast in the 17th century farmhouse. Brochure and terms free on request.

216 Dorset — Self-catering / ENGLAND

BRIDPORT/NETTLECOMBE

The Studio, The Old Station, Nettlecombe, Bridport. Sleeps 2. Enjoy a peaceful stay in beautiful countryside. Off-road parking, two-and-a-half acres of garden. The 150-year-old stone building, originally the linesmen's hut at Powerstock Station, was later enlarged, forming a fashion designer's studio. Recently double glazed, it has a bedsit, kitchen, shower room, toilet, for one to two non-smoking adult guests (no children or pets). Two single beds; duvets, bed linen and towels provided. Electricity also included (small winter surcharge). Microwave, fridge, TV, heating. Garden furniture, putting. Badger-watching at the adjacent Old Station. Terms from £140-£160 per week. Low season short stays by arrangement. SAE please: **Mrs D.P. Read, The Old Station, Powerstock, Bridport DT6 3ST (01308 485301).**

DORCHESTER (near)

Pitt Cottage, Ringstead Bay, Near Dorchester. Sleeps 6. An attractive thatched stone cottage, surrounded by farmland and situated on the edge of a small wood about a quarter mile from the sea, commanding outstanding views of Ringstead Bay on the Dorset Heritage Coast. The cottage is equipped to sleep six; three bedrooms (two beds in each), two bathrooms, sitting room with open fire and large kitchen/dining area. Cot/high chair; washing machine; TV; night storage heaters/electric radiators in all rooms. Car essential. Available from £200 per week. For details please send SAE (reference FHG) to: **Mrs S.H. Russell, 49 Limerston Street, London SW10 0BL or telephone 0207 351 9919.**

GILLINGHAM

Mrs J. Wallis, Meads Farm, Stour Provost, Gillingham SP8 5RX (01747 838265; Fax: 01258 821123). Working farm, join in. Sleeps 6. Mead Bungalow is a superior property enjoying outstanding views over Blackmore Vale. Situated one mile from A30 at the end of the lovely village of Stour Provost. Shaftesbury with its famous Gold Hill is nearby and within easy reach are Bournemouth, Weymouth and Bath. Many attractive and interesting places lie a short car ride away. Over one mile of private coarse fishing 160 yards from bungalow. Spacious accommodation sleeps six plus cot. Large lounge with colour TV, diningroom, three double bedrooms, bathroom, luxury oak kitchen with automatic washing machine etc; all electric (no meters), full central heating; linen supplied. Quarter acre lawns. Sorry no pets. **ETC ★★★★**

LYME REGIS (near)

Mrs Debby Snook, Westover Farm Cottages, Wootton Fitzpaine, Bridport DT6 6NE (01297 560451). Working farm. Sleeps 6/7. Immerse yourself in rural tranquillity. Set in an Area of Outstanding Natural Beauty, Wootton Fitzpaine nestles amidst rolling Dorset farmland. Within walking distance of the beaches and shops of Charmouth, world famous for its fossils, and three miles from the renowned Cobb at Lyme Regis. Golf, water sports and riding close by. We have two spacious, comfortable, well-furnished three-bedroomed cottages with open fires, inglenooks, heating and all amenities. Also large secluded, secure gardens with furniture, barbecues, parking. Open all year. Pets and children welcome. Logs and linen available. Guests are welcome to walk our farm. Terms from £175 to £590 per week, winter breaks available. **ETC ★★★**
e-mail: wfcottages@aol.com
website: www.lymeregis.com/westover-farm-cottages

MILTON ABBAS

See also Colour Display Advertisement

Little Hewish Barn. A 150 year-old brick and flint barn, converted to provide comfortable accommodation of a very high standard, including oil-fired central heating. There are two double bedrooms (one converts to twin), both with en suite bath/shower facilities. Spacious open-plan living/dining area features a wood-burning stove, fully-equipped kitchen, dishwasher, washer/dryer, TV/video, stereo etc. Children and well-behaved pets are very welcome. Fully-enclosed private garden and secure on-site parking. Prices are all inclusive – no hidden extras. ETC ★★★★★. **Little Hewish Barn, Milton Abbas, Blandford Forum, Dorset DT11 0DP (01258 881235; Fax: 01258 881393).**
e-mail: terry@littlehewish.co.uk

WAREHAM (near)

See also Colour Display Advertisement

"Dormer Cottage", Woodlands, Hyde, Near Wareham. Sleeps 5. This secluded cottage, cosy and modern, is a converted old barn of Woodlands House. Standing in its own grounds, it is fronted by a small wood with a walled paddock at the back. Pleasant walks in wooded forests nearby. In the midst of "Hardy Country" and ideal for a family holiday and for those who value seclusion. All linen included, beds ready made on guests' arrival and basic shopping arranged on request. Amusements at Bournemouth, Poole and Dorchester within easy reach. Five people and a baby can be accommodated in two double and one single bedrooms; cot and high chair available. Bathroom, two toilets; lounge and diningroom, colour TV. Kitchen with cooker, fridge, washing machine, small deep freeze, etc. Pets welcome. Open all year. Golf course half-mile; pony trekking, riding nearby. **SAE, please, for terms. Mrs M.J.M. Constantinides, "Woodlands", Hyde, near Wareham BH20 7NT (01929 471239).**

Sherborne Castle • *Sherborne, Dorset* • *01935 813182*
website: www.sherbornecastle.com
Built by Sir Walter Raleigh in 1594 and home to the Digby family since the early 17th century. Splendid collection of art, furniture and porcelain.

Abbotsbury Swannery
Near Bridport, Dorset • *01305 871858*
Up to 600 free-flying swans – help feed them twice daily. Baby swans hatch May/June.
AV show, coffee shop and gift shop.

PLEASE NOTE

All the information in this book is given in good faith in the belief that it is correct. However, the publishers cannot guarantee the facts given in these pages, neither are they responsible for changes in policy, ownership or terms that may take place after the date of going to press. Readers should always satisfy themselves that the facilities they require are available and that the terms, if quoted, still apply.

DURHAM

See also Colour Display Advertisement

BARNARD CASTLE
East Briscoe Farm Cottages, Baldersdale, Barnard Castle DL12 9UL (01833 650087; Fax: 01833 650027). Winner of the Northumbria Tourist Board Self-Catering of the Year 1999. In a beautiful situation central to the north of England. The six stone built cottages, sleeping two to six, offer superb accommodation on a stunning riverside estate, which offers walks and fishing. A place to relax and explore the North. Terms from £120. Open all year. Pets welcome in two of the cottages. Contact: **Emma Wilson. ETC ★★★★**, *FARM STAY UK MEMBER.*
e-mail: info@eastbriscoe.co.uk
website: www.eastbriscoe.co.uk

LANCHESTER
Mrs Ann Darlington, Hall Hill Farm, Lanchester, Durham DH7 0TA (01207 521476; Tel & Fax: 01388 730300). Two country cottages. Well-equipped and comfortable. Both cottages have one double and one twin room – sleep up to four people. Downstairs is a livingroom and large kitchen/dining room, upstairs two bedrooms and bathroom. Kitchen contains washing machine/tumble dryer, microwave and fridge/freezer. Linen and towels are provided. Both cottages are heated. The cottages are in an ideal location for Durham City and Beamish Museum. You will have a free pass for the week to visit our own open farm. Prices from £160 per week. Children welcome. Sorry no pets. Please write or telephone for brochure. **ETC ★★★**
e-mail: cottages@hallhillfarm.co.uk
website: www.hallhillfarm.co.uk

MIDDLETON-IN-TEESDALE
Mrs Scott, Westfield Cottage, Laithkirk, Middleton-in-Teesdale, Barnard Castle DL12 0PN (Tel & Fax: 01833 640942). Sleeps 6. Westfield Cottage is a Grade II Listed building very recently renovated and furnished to a high standard. Situated on a working farm in beautiful Teesdale which is excellent touring, cycling and walking country with the Pennine and Teesdale Ways close by. The Cumbrian border is about six miles away. Ample parking area; free fishing. About half a mile from the local village. Open all year. From £185-£380. **ETC ★★★★**

One child FREE with full-paying adult (not valid for Park Level Mine) at
Kilhope Lead Mining Museum
see our READERS' OFFER VOUCHERS for details

The FHG Directory of Website Addresses
on pages 345 - 373 is a useful quick reference guide for holiday accommodation with e-mail and/or website details

GLOUCESTERSHIRE

CHELTENHAM
Mr & Mrs J. Close, Coxhorne Farm, London Road, Charlton Kings, Cheltenham GL52 6UY (01242 236599). Cosy, well-equipped. Non-smoking. Self-contained apartment with open aspects, attached to the farmhouse of a 100 acre livestock farm. Situated on the eastern outskirts of Cheltenham, on the edge of the Cotswold Escarpment. Comfortably furnished, with full central heating, payphone and plenty of parking space. Electricity and bed linen included in rental. Ideal position for visiting the lovely Regency town of Cheltenham and the mellow villages of the Cotswolds. Sorry, no pets allowed. Terms £145 to £175 per week Low Season; £185 to £205 per week High Season. **ETC ★★★**

See also Colour Display Advertisement

MISERDEN
Sudgrove Cottages, Miserden GL6 7JD. One three-bedroom cottage sleeping six, and two two-bedroom cottages sleeping four on 'no through road' in the heart of the Cotswolds. Each cottage has views across fields, a garden, wood-burning stove, TV, radio/CD/tape player, electric cooker, microwave, fridge/freezer, washer/dryer. Cot/high chair available. Pub serving good food and general store/post office in Miserden (½ mile). Footpaths radiate from Sudgrove or short scenic drives lead to Cirencester, Stroud, Cheltenham or Gloucester. Explore the Cotswolds and beyond. Open all year. Weekly rates £200-£300 (two-bedroom), £225-£410 (three-bedroom). Bed linen/towels included. Electricity extra. Winter short breaks. Non-smoking available. **ETC ★★★**. Contact **Carol Ractliffe (Tel & Fax: 01285 821322).**
e-mail: enquiries@sudgrovecottages.co.uk   website: www.sudgrovecottages.co.uk

MINSTERWORTH

Mrs Carter, 'Severn Bank', Minsterworth GL2 8JH (01452 750357). **Sleeps 6.** 'Severn Bank' is a large country house set in riverside gardens, four miles west of Gloucester. Ideally situated for touring nearby Forest of Dean, Severn Vale, Cotswolds and Malverns, and is recommended viewpoint for the Severn Bore tidal wave. The area is rich in history and packed with intriguing places of interest, from caves to castles. The three bedroomed flat has kitchen/dining area, sitting room, TV and separate shower room and toilet. One of the three bedrooms is en suite. It is situated on the second floor. Sorry, but no pets or children under 12 years. No smoking. Terms per week from £250 low season to £350 high season.

MORETON-IN-MARSH

The Laurels, Moreton-in-Marsh. Modern cottage bungalow five minutes' walk from the centre of town. Many well-known picturesque villages are only a short drive away, as are the historic towns of Cheltenham, Oxford and Stratford-upon-Avon, making this Cotswold town, with its good bus and rail links, an ideal touring centre. The Laurels comprises two bedrooms, one double and one single, well-equipped kitchen with electric cooker, fridge, microwave and washing machine, bathroom and a lounge/dining room with TV and radio/CD player, that opens onto an attractive patio and garden. Ample parking. Central heating, gas, electricity, linen and towels inclusive. **ETC ★★★**. Please write or telephone for further information or to make a reservation. Contact: **Graham and Sandra Billinger, Blue Cedar House, Stow Road, Moreton-in-Marsh GL56 0DW (01608 650299).**
e-mail: gandsib@dialstart.net

STROUD

The Old Coach House, Edgecombe House, Toadsmoor Road, Brinscombe, Stroud GL5 2UE (01453 883147). Attention All Dog Lovers! Romantic 18th century cottage in the heart of the beautiful Cotswold Hills. Two double bedrooms, beams, wood-burners, outdoor heated swimming pool, patio heater and all year round, bubbling Hot Tub. Small enclosed garden plus a further 20 acres of woodland. Two dogs in the cottage, but a spacious private kennel will accommodate loads more for free! Weekends from £115 and four-night mid-week breaks from £110. Full weeks £195 – £550. Second cottage available for larger family groups or available separately from £120pw – £300. Colour brochure from **Ros Smith.**

HAMPSHIRE

LYNDHURST

Penny Farthing Hotel, Romsey Road, Lyndhurst SO43 7AA (02380 284422; Fax: 02380 284488). We have some neighbouring cottages available as hotel annexe rooms or on a self-catering basis. These have been totally refitted, much with "Laura Ashley" and offer quieter, more exclusive accommodation. The Penny Farthing is a cheerful small Hotel ideally situated in Lyndhurst village centre, the capital of the "New Forest". The hotel offers en suite single, double, twin and family rooms with direct dial telephones, tea/coffee tray, colour TV and clock radios. The hotel has a licensed bar, private car park and bicycle store. Lyndhurst has a charming variety of shops, restaurants, pubs and bistros and the "New Forest Information Centre and Museum". **ETC ★★★★**
website: www.pennyfarthinghotel.co.uk

HEREFORDSHIRE

See also Colour Display Advertisement

FELTON

The Lodge, Felton. A former Verger's cottage in a tranquil setting just eight miles north of the historic cathedral town of Hereford. Peacefully located next to the Parish Church. Guests can enjoy the pleasure of the gardens of Felton House, the stone-built former Rectory. The Lodge has been completely renovated and restored to its Victorian character but with the convenience of central heating, a modern kitchen, two shower rooms, a dining room and a sitting room with TV and video. There are three bedrooms with accommodation for five people (One double room, one twin, one single), and in addition a cot is available. Linen may be hired. Children, and pets with responsible owners, are most welcome. Private parking, patio and garden. The Lodge is a cosy, restful cottage, spotlessly clean. Short Breaks catered for and weekly terms range from £150 to £275 per week, exclusive of electricity. Brochure available. **Marjorie and Brian Roby, Felton House, Felton HR1 3PH (Tel & Fax: 01432 820366).**
e-mail: bandb@ereal.net   website: www.SmoothHound.co.uk/hotels/felton.html

See also Colour Display Advertisement

GOODRICH

Mainoaks Farm Cottages, Goodrich, Ross-on-Wye. Six units sleeping 2,4,6 & 7. Mainoaks is a 15th century Listed farm which has been converted to form six cottages of different size and individual character. It is set in 80 acres of pasture and woodland beside the River Wye in an Area of Outstanding Natural Beauty and an SSSI where there is an abundance of wildlife. All cottages have exposed beams, pine furniture, heating throughout, fully equipped kitchens with microwaves, washer/dryer etc., colour TV. Private gardens, barbecue area and ample parking. Linen and towels provided. An ideal base for touring the local area with beautiful walks, fishing, canoeing, pony trekking, golf, birdwatching or just relaxing in this beautiful tranquil spot. Open throughout the year. Short breaks available. Pets by arrangement. Brochure on request. ETC ★★★/★★★★. **Mrs P. Unwin, Hill House, Chase End, Bromsberrow, Ledbury, Herefordshire HR8 1SE (01531 650448).**
e-mail: mainoaks@lineone.net   website: www.mainoaks.co.uk

HEREFORD

Mrs S. Dixon, Swayns Diggins, Harewood End, Hereford HR2 8JU (01989 730358). This highly recommended small first floor flat is completely self-contained at one end of the main house. The bedroom, sitting room and private balcony all face south with panoramic views over farmland towards Ross and Symonds Yat. The well-equipped kitchen overlooks the garden with grand views towards Orcop Hill and the Black Mountains. Open all year, rental from £150 to £165 per week includes electricity, linen, heating, colour TV. Ideal base for exploring the beautiful Wye Valley, Herefordshire, Gloucestershire and the historic Welsh Marches. There is much to see and do in the area. Write or phone for further particulars.

KINGTON

The Harbour, Upper Hergest, Kington. Properties sleep 5/9. This bungalow is on a good second-class road facing south with beautiful views from its elevated position, across the Hergest Ridge and Offa's Dyke. The Welsh border is a mile away. Shops are two-and-a-half miles away. Kington Golf Club nearby. Accommodation for five/nine in two double rooms (one with extra single bed) downstairs and two double dormer bedrooms; two cots; bathroom, toilet; sittingroom (TV); diningroom; sun porch for relaxing; kitchen with electric cooker, microwave, fridge, food store and usual equipment. Central heating throughout. No linen. Children and pets welcome. Car essential - parking. Available all year. SAE, please, to **Mrs B.F. Welson, New House Farm, Upper Hergest, Kington, Herefordshire HR5 3EW (01544 230533).**

LEOMINSTER

Nicholson Farm Holidays. Self-catering properties on a working dairy farm. Beautiful views. Wide choice of restaurants and bar meals in the area. Supermarket 10 minutes. Excellent walking, golf, riding, carp fishing available on the farm, swimming and tennis 10 minutes. Dogs are welcome but must not remain in during the owner's absence. Non- smoking. Contact: **Mrs J. Brooke, Docklow, Leominster HR6 0SL (01568 760346).**

ROSS-ON-WYE (near)

A rendered stone cottage tucked away down a country lane in a tiny village on the edge of the Royal Forest of Dean in the Wye Valley, an Area of Outstanding Natural Beauty. Excellent acccommodation for up to 12 people. The cottage is typical of the Herefordshire countryside, but when entered, quality and high standards are very much in evidence. Five bedrooms, one with handmade oak four-poster, king-size bed; one of the bathrooms has a jacuzzi bath; two showers. Two beamed lounges with TV and video, open fires and storage heaters. Oak-fitted kitchen with dishwasher, fridge, freezer etc. Linen and towels for hire. Children and pets welcome. Ample parking. The River Wye is a haven for fishermen, with salmon, trout and coarse fishing. For the adventurous, cycling in the Royal Forest of Dean, golf, canoeing, quad biking, hovercraft, clay pigeon shooting, archery and orienteering. (Also B&B **AA/RAC** ◆◆◆◆ *SPARKLING DIAMOND AWARD*). Details from **Mrs H. Smith, The Old Kilns, Howle Hill, Ross-on-Wye HR9 5SP (Tel & Fax: 01989 562051).**

ISLE OF WIGHT

See also Colour Display Advertisement

ISLE OF WIGHT

Island Cottage Holidays. Sleep 1/14. Charming individual cottages in lovely rural surroundings and close to the sea. Over 50 cottages situated throughout the Isle of Wight. Beautiful views, attractive gardens, delightful country walks. All equipped to a high standard and graded for quality by the Tourist Board. £132 to £1195 per week. Short breaks available in low season from £89 to £395 (three nights). For a brochure please contact: **Mrs Honor Vass, The Old Vicarage, Kingston, Wareham, Dorset BH20 5LH (01929 480080; Fax: 01929 481070).** ETC ★★★/★★★★★
e-mail: enq@islandcottageholidays.com
website: www.islandcottageholidays.com

TOTLAND BAY

3 Seaview Cottages, Broadway, Totland Bay. Sleeps 5. This well-modernised cosy old coastguard cottage holds the Farm Holiday Guide Diploma for the highest standard of accommodation. It is warm and popular throughout the year. Four day winter break from £45; a week in summer £260. Located close to two beaches in beautiful walking country near mainland links. It comprises lounge/dinette/ kitchenette; two bedrooms (sleeping five); bathroom/toilet. Well furnished, fully heated, TV, selection of books and other considerations. Another cottage is also available at Cowes, Isle of Wight. Non-smokers only. **Mrs C. Pitts, 11 York Avenue, New Milton, Hampshire BH25 6BT (01425 615215).**

ENGLAND / Self-catering   Kent 223

KENT

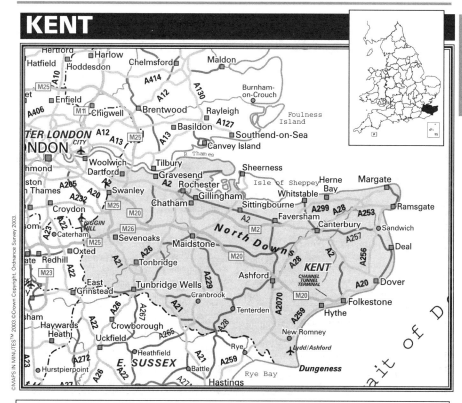

Fairhaven Holiday Cottages

Fairhaven Holiday Cottages is an independent owner-managed agency offering personally inspected holiday properties of all types in town, country and coastal areas of Kent and Sussex. For further information please visit our website
www.fairhaven-holidays.co.uk
e-mail: enquiries@fairhaven-holidays.co.uk
Telephone or fax **01634 570157**

GOUDHURST

Marion Fuller, Three Chimneys Farm Holiday Cottages, Bedgebury Road, Goudhurst TN17 2RA (Tel & Fax: 01580 212175). Set on top of a hill at the end of a one-mile track, on the edge of Bedgebury Forest, Three Chimneys is a haven of tranquillity, yet only an hour from London. The five cottages (and two Bed and Breakfast rooms) are individually and tastefully furnished. The cottages are well equipped and all bed linen is included. Central heating; telephone. There is a tennis court and the forest is perfect for visitors who like to walk or cycle. Goudhurst is centrally placed for visiting the castles and gardens of the South East. ETC ★★★★, *KENT TOURISM ALLIANCE AWARD FOR EXCELLENCE 2002/2003.*
e-mail: **marionfuller@threechimneysfarm.co.uk**
website: **www.threechimneysfarm.co.uk**

LANCASHIRE

See also Colour Display Advertisement

COLNE
Mrs Rachel Boothman, Blakey Hall Farm, Red Lane, Colne BB8 9TD (01282 863121). Two luxury apartments within easy reach of Skipton and Bronte Country. DUKE OF LANCASTER has two en suite bedrooms, well-equipped kitchen, dining and sitting area, all linen and towels provided; no smoking, no pets. DUKE OF YORK - first floor with balcony and stunning views - has two en suite bedrooms and fully fitted kitchen; large living/dining area. Bed and Breakfast also available in delightful old farmhouse alongside Leeds/Liverpool Canal. En suite bedrooms; no smoking (**ETC** ♦♦♦). Fishing and barge trips available; golf courses within easy reach.

See also Colour Display Advertisement

HIGH BENTHAM
Woodside & Parkside, High Bentham, Lancaster LA2 7BN. Sleep 6-14. Large stone barn converted into two properties with interconnecting doors so that they can be let separately for 6-8 or let together to accommodate 14. Mainly en suite bathrooms. Parkside has a ground floor bedroom and bathroom. Set in beautiful countryside yet within walking distance of the market town. Open all year. Short breaks or weekly lets. Colour brochure available. **ETC** ★★★★, *FARM STAY UK MEMBER*. Contact: **Thomas & Jane Marshall, Knowe Top, Low Bentham Road, Bentham, Lancaster LA2 7BN (Tel & Fax: 015242 62163).**
website: www.riversidecottages.co.uk

ENGLAND / Self-catering   Lancashire 225

MORECAMBE
St Ives and Rydal Mount Holiday Flats, 360-361 Marine Road, East Promenade, Morecambe LA4 5AQ (01524 411858). Situated on the sea front overlooking the bay and Lakeland hills. Ideal base for touring the Lake District and Yorkshire Dales. Large one or two bedroom flats occupying one floor, each with their own TV, electric cooker, fridge and microwave. Stair lift. Car park. SAE please for brochure to **Mrs S M Holmes**.

SOUTHPORT
Mr W.H. Core, Sandybrook Farm, 52 Wyke Cop Road, Scarisbrick, Southport PR8 5LR (Tel & Fax: 01704 880337). Welcome to our small arable farm and 18th century Barn, which has been converted into five superbly equipped holiday apartments. Many of the Barn's original features have been retained and it is furnished in traditional style but also offers all modern amenities. The Barn is situated three-and-a-half miles from the seaside town of Southport and five miles from the historic town of Ormskirk with lots of places to visit in the surrounding area. Families are welcome and cot and high chairs are available. One apartment equipped for wheelchair/disabled guests. Central heating, bed linen and towels are provided free of charge. **ETC ★★★**
e-mail: sandybrookfarm@lycos.co.uk

One FREE child per one paying adult (one voucher per child) at
Docker Park Farm
see our READERS' OFFER VOUCHERS for details

National Football Museum • Preston, Lancashire • 01772 908442
www.nationalfootballmuseum.com
The story of the world's greatest game. In two distinctive halves, it can be enjoyed by supprters of all ages. Shop and restaurant.

The FHG Directory of Website Addresses
on pages 345 -373 is a useful quick reference guide for holiday accommodation with e-mail and/or website details

---

FHG PUBLICATIONS
publish a large range of well-known accommodation guides. We will be happy to send you details or you can use the order form at the back of this book.

LINCOLNSHIRE

See also Colour Display Advertisement

ALFORD (near)
Mrs Stubbs, Woodthorpe Hall Country Cottages, Near Alford LN13 0DD (01507 450294; Fax: 01507 450885). Very well appointed luxury one and three bedroomed cottages, overlooking the golf course, all with central heating, colour TV, microwave, washer, dryer, dishwasher and fridge freezer. Woodthorpe is situated approximately six miles from the coastal resort of Mablethorpe and offers easy access to the picturesque Lincolnshire Wolds. Adjacent facilities include golf, fishing, garden centre, aquatic centre, snooker, pool and restaurant with bar and family room. ETC ★★★★
e-mail: enquiries@woodthorpehall.com
website: www.woodthorpehall.com

ALFORD (near)
Manor Farm Cottage. Comfortable cottage in rural countryside, midway between the coast and Lincolnshire Wolds. Well equipped including colour TV, video, washing machine, microwave and freezer. Rose garden including picnic table. Suitable area for pets to exercise. Pets and children welcome. Ample parking space. For further details please contact: **Mrs E.M. Farrow, Manor Farm, Strubby, Alford LN13 0LW (01507 450228).** ETC ★★

LOUTH
Shepherd's Cottage, Louth. Fall in love with the experience of staying in our charming 16th century self-catering cottage, situated in the grounds of Grimblethorpe Hall, in the heart of the Lincolnshire Wolds. Recently restored with original beams and stonework with a very spacious bedroom, lounge and kitchen/dining area. Facilities include cooker, microwave, fridge/freezer, washer/dryer, linen and bedding, towels and cloths, full central heating, television, video, garage and board games. Electricity inclusive. Fabulous walking and cycling routes nearby, including the Viking Way, and visitors may use the private trout lake. An optional evening meal can be waiting for you on your arrival and occasional picnic hampers are available. Prices from £150 per week; Short Breaks from £95. ETC ★★★★★. Contact: **Annie and Robert Codling, Grimblethorpe Hall, Grimblethorpe, Near Louth LN11 0RB (01507 313671/313440; Fax: 01507 313854).**
e-mail: enquiries@ShepherdsHolidayCottage.co.uk
website: www.ShepherdsHolidayCottage.co.uk

Free entry for one child when accompanied by full-paying adult at

Skegness Natureland Seal Sanctuary

see our READERS' OFFER VOUCHERS for details

---

*When making enquiries or bookings,
a stamped addressed envelope is always appreciated*

SKEGNESS

The Chestnuts Farm & Country Cottages, Wainfleet Road, Burgh Le Marsh PE24 5AH (Tel & Fax: 01754 810904). 'Farm, Fishing, Friendly and Fun'. Two, three and four bedroom cottages on a real farm situated on the edge of the village of Burgh le Marsh, only five miles from Skegness, yet ideal for a quiet, rural holiday. Children's play area, farm animals - horses, pigs, calves, chickens etc. Cottages have their own private fishing waters. Tennis court, plenty of space, ample parking and gardens. Full colour brochure available. Short Breaks out of season from as little as £70. Please telephone for our current price list. ETC ★★★. Contact: **Mrs J Mackinder.**
e-mail: **macka@freenetname.co.uk**
website: **www.thechestnutsfarm.co.uk**

WADDINGWORTH

Andrew and Alison Pritchard, Redhouse Farm, Waddingworth LN10 5EE (Tel & Fax: 01507 578285; mobile: 07702 678241). Working farm. Sleeps 6. This delightful, well-equipped cottage offers self-catering and Bed & Breakfast and is integral to the main farmhouse. Redhouse Farm stands within beautiful Lincolnshire countryside, overlooking St Margaret's Church, central point of Old Lincolnshire. The cottage makes the perfect base for the holidaymaker and the business person. Pets and children welcome. Weekly terms from £250 to £350, includes fuel and linen. Open all year, short breaks available. **ETC ★★★★, MEMBER FARMSTAY UK.**
e-mail: **redhousefarm@waddingworth**
website: **www.redhousecottage.co.uk**

Other specialised
FHG PUBLICATIONS

Published annually: available in all good bookshops
or direct from the publisher.

PETS WELCOME! £7.99
Recommended COUNTRY HOTELS OF BRITAIN £6.99
Recommended COUNTRY INNS & PUBS OF BRITAIN £6.99
Recommended SHORT BREAK HOLIDAYS IN BRITAIN £6.99

FHG PUBLICATIONS LTD,
Abbey Mill Business Centre,
Seedhill, Paisley, Renfrewshire PA1 1TJ
Tel: 0141-887 0428 • Fax: 0141-889 7204
e-mail: fhg@ipcmedia.com
website: www.holidayguides.com

NORFOLK

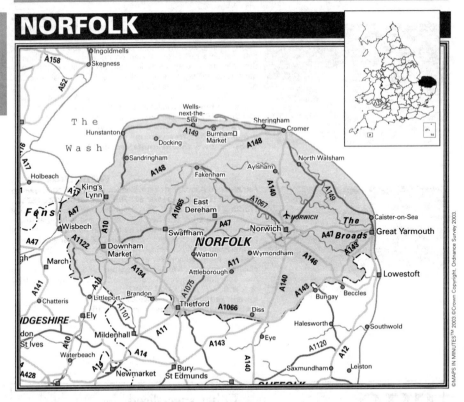

DISS

Walcot Green Farm Cottage. Ken and Nannette Catchpole welcome you to their family-run farm, set amid peaceful countryside close to the pleasant market town of Diss, an ideal base for exploring Norfolk and Suffolk. There are three bedrooms - two single and a family room with double and single bed. Linen and towels provided. Fully equipped kitchen and utility room with fridge/freezer, microwave, washing machine, tumble dryer and ironing facilities. Lounge has colour TV, video and music centre. Spacious lawned garden, patio with barbecue and garden furniture. Children welcome; cot, high chair and stair gates available. No pets and no smoking. Heated indoor swimming pool. Details from: **Mrs N. Catchpole, Walcot Green Farm, Diss IP22 3SU (Tel & Fax: 01379 652806; mobile: 07881 501862).**

e-mail: n.catchpole.wgf@virgin.net
website: www.walcotgreenfarm.co.uk

Pensthorpe Waterfowl Trust • *Fakenham, Norfolk* • *01328 851465*
Over 120 species of waterfowl from all over the world make this Europe's finest collection of endangered and exotic waterbirds, with over 200 acres of lakes, woodland and meadows to explore.

Pettitts Animal Adventure Park • *Near Great Yarmouth, Norfolk* • *01493 701403*
Three parks in one - fun for all the family. Rides, play area, adventure golf course, animals galore. Children's entertainment daily.

ENGLAND / Self-catering   Norfolk   229

MUNDESLEY-ON-SEA

47 Seaward Crest, Mundesley-on-Sea. Sleeps 4. Mundesley-on-Sea is an attractive seaside village situated centrally on the Norfolk coast, within 10 miles of the Norfolk Broads, seven miles from Cromer and 20 miles from Norwich. The clean sandy beaches stretch for miles with safe bathing and natural paddling pools. This attractive west-facing brick-built chalet is in a delightful setting with lawns, flower beds, trees and parking. Beach 500 yards away and shops 800 yards. There is an excellent golf course nearby and bowls and riding are within easy reach. Large lounge/diningroom tastefully furnished including easy chairs, settee and colour TV. Kitchenette with electric cooker, fridge, sink unit, etc. One double, one twin-bedded rooms. Fully carpeted. Bathroom and toilet. Lighting, hot water, heating and cooking by electricity (£1 slot meter). Fully equipped except for linen. Weekly terms from £120. Details, SAE, please, **Mrs J. Doar, 4 Denbury Road, Ravenshead, Nottinghamshire NG15 9FQ (01623 798032).**

SPIXWORTH

Spixworth Hall Cottages, Grange Farm, Buxton Road, Spixworth NR10 3PR (01603 898190). Delightful 18th century coachman's cottage, Lodge Cottage and award-winning stable conversions in seclusion on our own farm. Ideal for exploring Norwich, the Broads and countryside. Very well furnished and equipped, with central heating, log fires, secure gardens, games barn and children's play area, farm walks and fishing, tennis and space to unwind. We offer a warm welcome. Contact us for further details. Short Autumn to Spring weekend or midweek breaks from £150. Weekly rates from £220 to £700. National Accessibility Scheme, Level 4, CLA Farm Buildings Award, Broadlands Enhancement Award. **ETC ★★★/★★★★**

e-mail: hallcottages@btinternet.com   website: www.hallcottages.co.uk

---

50p off adult admission - 25p of child admission at
The Collectors' World of Eric St John-Foti
see our READERS' OFFER VOUCHERS for details

TWO for ONE with full-paying adult, one free visit per voucher at
Galleries of Justice
see our READERS' OFFER VOUCHERS for details

One child FREE with full-paying adult per voucher at
The Tales of Robin Hood
see our READERS' OFFER VOUCHERS for details

50p off standard admission prices for up to six people at
Dinosaur Adventure Park
see our READERS' OFFER VOUCHERS for details

NORTHUMBERLAND

Enjoy a break on the Northumberland Coast

Choose from twelve family-owned and managed cottages along the Northumberland coast.
Three-day short breaks from £70 per cottage during low season.
Beautiful rugged coastline, fishing villages little changed in 100 years, golden beaches, historic castles, wildlife, walks, cycling, fishing, golf, Alnwick Castle & Gardens, National Park, Kielder Water and Forest.

For details and bookings contact: **Heritage Coast Holidays,**
6G Greensfield Court, Alnwick, Northumberland NE66 2DE
01670 787864 24-hour enquiry line • Tel: 01665 606022 (office hours)
Fax: 01670 787336 • e-mail: paulthompson@alncom.net

Visit our website• **www.northumberland-holidays.com**

See also Colour Advertisement

One FREE adult with one paying adult at
Chester Walled Garden
see our READERS' VOUCHER OFFERS for details

ENGLAND / Self-catering   Northumberland 231

Town Foot Farm, Shilbottle, Alnwick, Northumberland NE66 2HG • Tel/Fax: 01665 575591
E-mail: crissy@villagefarmcottages.co.uk • Website: www.villagefarmcottages.co.uk

Choice of cosy cottages, airy chalets or 17th century farmhouse. Sleep between two and twelve. Perfectly situated; three miles from beaches and historic Alnwick. Fantastic facilities include an indoor forty-foot heated swimming pool, health club, sauna/steam room, sunshower, tennis court and a games room. Visit our beauty therapist. Also try fishing and riding.

Terms from £135 – £975.

VILLAGE FARM *SELF-CATERING*   Free colour brochure.   ETC ★★★ to ★★★★★

ALNWICK (near)

Briar, Rose & Clematis Cottages. Sleep 2-4+cot. Quality self-catering cottages in recent barn conversions in a courtyard setting, providing the perfect base for exploring historic Northumberland. All with log-burning stoves and modern facilities, both Rose and Briar Cottages have open plan sitting/dining room and well-equipped kitchen, with open staircase leading to double bedroom with four-poster and bathroom with over bath shower. Clematis Cottage (shown in photo; sleeps 4 + cot) includes picture windows with views to open countryside. Superb walking area, golf, horse riding, birdwatching and fishing available locally. Within easy reach of Heritage Coast and the Cheviots; Hadrian's Wall (30 miles) and Edinburgh (65 miles) within easy reach. Well-behaved pets welcome in Rose Cottage and Clematis Cottage. Contact: **Graeme and Helen Wyld, New Moor House, Edlingham, Alnwick NE66 2BT (01665 574638).**
e-mail: stay@newmoorhouse.co.uk   website: www.newmoorhouse.co.uk

BAMBURGH

Point Cottages, Bamburgh. POINT COTTAGES consist of a cluster of cottages in a superb location at the end of the Wynding, next to a beautiful golf course on the edge of Bamburgh, only a short drive away from many other attractive Links courses. Bamburgh is an unspoilt coastal village dominated by a magnificent castle and is an ideal base for visiting other parts of historic Northumbria. The cottages overlook the sea with fine views of the Farne Islands and Lindisfarne. Sandy beaches nearby. They share a large garden with lawns and a total of ten car parking spaces are provided (two per cottage). The cottages are in excellent order, have open fire or woodburning stove and are comfortably furnished. Each cottage has its own special atmosphere but all are warm, cosy and well-equipped. **ETC ★★★**. For further information, availability, prices and booking please contact: **John and Elizabeth Sanderson, 30 The Oval, Benton, Newcastle-upon-Tyne NE12 9PP (0191-266 2800 or 01665 720246 (weekends); Fax: 0191-215 1630).**
e-mail: info@bamburgh-cottages.co.uk   website: www.bamburgh-cottages.co.uk

BELFORD

Mrs K. Burn, Fenham-le-Moor Farmhouse, Belford NE70 7PN (Tel & Fax: 01668 213247). A comfortably furnished farm cottage situated in peaceful surroundings on a quiet road, half a mile from the shore and Lindisfarne Nature Reserve, an Area of Outstanding Natural Beauty. Close to Holy Island and Bamburgh, and within easy reach of the Cheviot Hills. An ideal base for golf, beaches and walking. Electricity, linen and fuel for open fire included in rent. Terms from £190 to £400 per week. **ETC ★★★★**. THE LOOKOUT– on the edge of the shore, on Lindisfarne Nature Reserve, fantastic views, studio for two. All inclusive from £160 to £320 per week
website: www.fenham-le-moor.co.uk

BERWICK-UPON-TWEED

The Boathouse, Norham, Berwick-Upon-Tweed. Sleeps 10. A delightful south-facing, 18th century house offering spacious accommodation with frontage to the River Tweed and spectacular views over the surrounding countryside. The ground floor consists of a sitting room with TV, lounge with open fire and TV, dining room, kitchen with electric cooker, fridge/freezer, microwave, automatic washing machine, tumble dryer and dishwasher; bathroom with bath, shower, basin and WC; en suite bedroom with king-size bed. First floor has three bedrooms, all with washbasins and bathroom with bath/shower, WC and washbasin. Oil central heating, duvets and linen are provided (not towels).Sports centre, golf course, beaches, places of historic interest, salmon fishing and abundant wildlife. Tariffs from £350 to £750 per week. Open all year. ETC ★★★. For further information contact **Mrs M Chantler, Great Humphries Farm, Grafty Green, Maidstone, Kent ME17 2AX (Tel & Fax: 01622 859672).**
e-mail: chantler@humphreys46.fsnet.co.uk

See also Colour Display Advertisement

BERWICK-UPON-TWEED

Mrs Carol Lang, West Ord Holiday Cottages, West Ord Farm, Berwick-upon-Tweed TD15 2XQ (01289 386631; Fax: 01289 386800). West Ord Farm sits on the banks of the River Tweed with stunning scenery and beautiful walks. Three miles from the centre of Berwick-upon-Tweed with its numerous shops, restaurants, cinema and theatre. Our seven attractive cottages, sleeping 2-6, are comfortable, warm and well-equipped, most with private gardens. Two cottages are located on the waterside, the other five are only a short walk from the riverside. Fishing for sea trout and salmon on our own beat, a hard surface tennis court and good beaches within 10 minutes' drive. Well placed for visiting Lindisfarne, the Cheviot Hills and National Park, Kelso, Jedburgh, Melrose, Hawick and many castles and stately homes that make up the rich heritage of this area. ETC ★★★★
e-mail: stay@westord.co.uk
website: www.westord.co.uk

CHATHILL

Mrs Naomi Barrett, Gardener's Cottage, Tuggal Hall, Chathill NE67 5EW (01665 589229). Gardener's Cottage is detached from the Hall and stands in a yard overlooking a paddock and fields to a view of the sea. Situated near the coast between Embleton and Beadnell it takes about five minutes by car to reach the nearest beach. Accommodation consists of one bedroom with double bed, large bathroom and lavatory on the first floor. On the ground floor there is one bedroom with twin beds, sitting room with sofa bed, open fire and colour TV. Kitchen with electric cooker, microwave and dining area, fridge and automatic washing machine. Bathroom and seperate lavatory. Bed linen can be hired by request. We regret pets cannot be taken without prior arrangement.

See also Colour Display Advertisement

HALTWHISTLE

Ald White Craig Cottages. On the edge of Northumberland National Park, a superb base for exploring Hadrian's Wall and Roman museums. Lake District, Scottish Borders and Northumberland coast all approximately one hour's drive. B&B also available. WREN'S NEST sleeps one/two persons; SMITHY COTTAGE sleeps two/three; COBBLESTONES COTTAGE sleeps four; COACH HOUSE sleeps five; SHEPHERD'S HEFT sleeps six. ETC up to ★★★★. For further information contact: **C. Zard, Ald White Craig Farm, Shield Hill, Near Hadrian's Wall, Haltwhistle NE49 9NW (01434 320565; Fax: 01434 321236).**
e-mail: whitecraigfarm@yahoo.co.uk
website: www.hadrianswallholidays.com

HALTWHISTLE

Scotchcoulthard, Haltwhistle NE49 9NH (01434 344470; Fax: 01434 344020). Situated within Northumberland National Park, Scotchcoulthard is surrounded by splendid scenery with magnificent views and not another inhabited dwelling in sight. Fully equipped, our five cottages have been professionally designed and furnished with comfort in mind. All bedrooms are en suite, and all cottages have open fires to give that warm welcome after a day out exploring. There is a large indoor heated swimming pool and a games room with full-size table tennis table, pool table, hi-fi system and a variety of toys for younger visitors. Although remote, Scotchcoulthard is not isolated - it is possible to be parked in the Metro Centre or the middle of Newcastle or Carlisle within an hour. Please send for our brochure.

Well behaved pets and horses welcome. **ETC ★★★★**
e-mail: info@scotchcoulthard.co.uk
website: www.scotchcoulthard.co.uk

MORPETH

Mr & Mrs A.P. Coatsworth, Gallowhill Farm, Whalton, Morpeth NE61 3TX (01661 881241). Working farm. Sleep 4-6. Relax in our two spacious stone-built cottages. Recently converted and modernised to give you every facility you require. Electric cooker, fridge, freezer, dishwasher, washer/dryer, microwave, colour TV. Located in the heart of Northumberland on a very tidy farm with private gardens. Bolam Lake two miles, Belsay Castle four miles, coast 20 minutes, Hadrian's Wall 30 minutes, to name only a few attractions. All linen, heating, electricity included in price. Sorry, no pets. All children welcome. Brochure on request. Terms £220 to £410.

ROTHBURY/HARBOTTLE

Mrs J.D. Blakey, Woodhall Farm Holiday Cottage, Woodhall Farm, Harbottle, Morpeth NE65 7AD (Tel & Fax: 01669 650245). Sleep 6 + Cot. Spacious, well-equipped farmhouse, set within the National Park in the Coquet Valley, an ideal location for a relaxing holiday, and a great area for cycling, walking and exploring beautiful Northumberland. Woodhall is easy to find, being situated on the main road seven miles west of Rothbury and between Sharperton and Harbottle. Pets welcome. Terms from £190 to £400 per week. Please contact for further details. **ETC ★★★**
e-mail: Blakey@woodhall65.freeserve.co.uk
website: www.woodhallcottage.co.uk

OXFORDSHIRE

PANGBOURNE (near)

"Brambly Thatch" Holiday Cottage, Coombe End Farm, Whitchurch Hill, Near Pangbourne, Reading. Brambly Thatch is an attractive, thatched, 17th century farm cottage, located on a working mixed (beef and arable) farm, at the southern end of the Chiltern Hills. The cottage is about two miles north of Pangbourne, seven miles north-west of Reading, and about 20 miles south of Oxford. London is within easy reach. With the River Thames, Chiltern beech woods and countryside nearby, there is the chance to go walking, boating, driving or picnicking. One double bedroom, one single bedroom, and bathroom/W.C. upstairs; while downstairs there are the kitchen, main living room, dining room, and third bedroom. Fully equipped kitchen, VCR, colour TV, and telephone. Small garden. No pets, except by special arrangement. Smoking discouraged. Terms from £355 to £425. Contact: **Mr J. N. Hatt, Merricroft Farming, Goring Heath, Reading, Berkshire RG8 7TA (01189 843121).**
e-mail: hatts@merricroft.demon.co.uk

234 Shropshire   Self-catering / ENGLAND

SHROPSHIRE

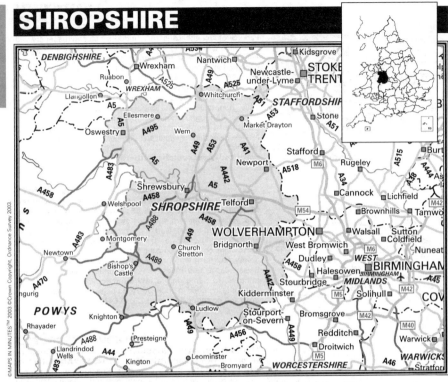

CRAVEN ARMS
Mrs B. Freeman, Upper House, Clunbury, Craven Arms SY7 0HG (01588 660629). Welcome to Horseshoe Cottage which is situated in the beautiful gardens of Upper House (17th century Listed) in Clunbury, a village of archaeological interest in a designated Area of Outstanding Natural Beauty – A. E. Housman countryside. This private self-catering cottage is completely furnished and equipped; being on one level the accommodation is suitable for elderly and disabled persons. Colour TV. Sleeps four; cot available. Children and pets welcome. Ample parking. This Welsh Border countryside is rich in medieval history, unspoilt villages and natural beauty. Enjoy walking on the Long Mynd and Offa's Dyke, or explore Ludlow and Ironbridge. £140 to £190 per week. Please write or phone for further details.

IRONBRIDGE
Virginia Evans, Church Farm, Rowton, Near Wellington, Telford TF6 6QY (Tel & Fax: 01952 770381). Sleep 2-8. Two beautifully converted barn cottages, sleeping 2-5, and a recently converted cowshed sleeping up to 8, situated 15 minutes from Shrewsbury and the World Heritage site of Ironbridge Gorge Museum. All cottages have well-equipped kitchens and are wheelchair friendly, with a bedroom and bathroom or shower room on the ground floor. Electric storage heaters. Ample parking. Pets welcome under control. Bed linen and towels available on request. **ETC ★★★**
e-mail: church.farm@bigfoot.com
website: www.virtual-shropshire.co.uk/churchfarm

LEINTWARDINE

Paul and Sallyann Swift, Oaklands Farm Cottages, Kinton, Leintwardine SY7 0LT (01547 540635). Nestled at the head of a valley with views over the River Teme and the Welsh hills, Oaklands Farm is the perfect place for those seeking a peaceful escape. Two traditional stone buildings have been sympathetically restored to provide rural charm and comfort. THE BARN (sleeps 6+2) has a large living room, a well-equipped kitchen, three bedrooms and two bathrooms. THE GRANARY (sleeps 5) has living room, kitchen/dining area, three bedrooms and bathroom. Central heating, colour TV, cot and highchair; ample parking. Bed linen provided. Pets by arrangement. Leintwardine village (half a mile) has shop, post office and pub; Ludlow 8 miles.

LUDLOW

Hazel Cottage, Duxmoor, Onibury, Craven Arms. Sleeps 4. Beautifully restored, semi-detached, yet private, period cottage, set in its own extensive cottage-style garden with its own drive and ample parking space. Amidst peaceful surroundings and panoramic views of the countryside, it is situated five miles north of historic Ludlow and one-and-a-half miles from the A49. The cottage retains all its original features and fittings with traditional decoration and is fully furnished, with antiques throughout. It comprises a comfortable living room with a Victorian range for coal and log fire; TV, wireless and telephone; dining room with bread oven; fully equipped kitchen, hall, Victorian bathroom; two bedrooms (one double and one twin-bedded) with period washbasins. Electric central heating throughout. All linen included. Tourist information. Open all year. Short Breaks available. No pets. Terms from £195 to £410 per week. ETC ★★★★. **Mrs Rachel Sanders, Duxmoor Farm, Onibury, Craven Arms SY7 9BQ (01584 856342).**

SHREWSBURY

John & Annabel Gill, Courtyard Cottages, Lower Springs Farm, Kenley, Shrewsbury SY5 6PA (Tel & Fax: 01952 510841). Situated in the Kenley Valley beneath Wenlock Edge with lovely panoramic views, two beautifully restored and converted 19th century barns in large garden overlooking stocked trout pool. Both have lounge, fitted kitchens and bathroom. The smaller conversion is ideal for two people while the larger cottage is more suitable for a party of four. All heating and hot water is included and there is private parking. Electricity is metered. Close by is the historic town of Much Wenlock with its ruined abbey, museum and interesting shops. Shrewsbury, Ironbridge, several famous gardens and local pubs and restaurants are all within easy reach. Prices range from £200 -£400 per week. ETC ★★★★

e-mail: a-gill@lineone.net
website: www.courtyardcottages.com

PLEASE NOTE

All the information in this book is given in good faith in the belief that it is correct. However, the publishers cannot guarantee the facts given in these pages, neither are they responsible for changes in policy, ownership or terms that may take place after the date of going to press. Readers should always satisfy themselves that the facilities they require are available and that the terms, if quoted, still apply.

SOMERSET

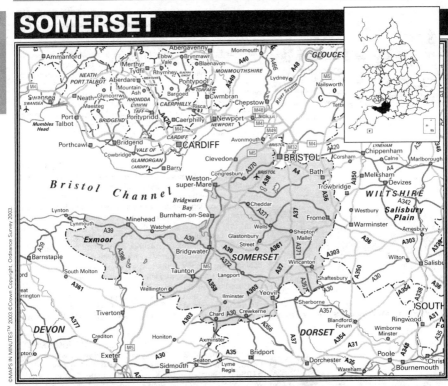

Exmoor • • The Pack Horse

Idyllic location for a self-catering holiday in the National Trust village of Allerford alongside the shallow River Aller, overlooking the famous Pack Horse Bridge. Immediate access to Exmoor and the beautiful surrounding countryside.

Variety of well-equipped apartments and family cottage arranged around a pretty courtyard. Sleeping two - six. Pets welcome. Stabling available. Ample private parking. Local amenities - Post office, stores, pub, additional restaurants/pubs etc in nearby Porlock.

Terms: £220 – £450 per week. Open all year. Short breaks available.
The Pack Horse, Allerford, Near Porlock, Somerset TA24 8HW Tel & Fax: 01643 862475
e-mail: holidays@thepackhorse.net • website: www.thepackhorse.net
See also Colour Advertisement

BATH near
Toghill House Farm, Wick, Near Bath BS30 5RT (01225 891261; Fax: 01225 892128). Situated just four miles north of Bath and within a few miles of Lacock, Castle Combe, Tetbury and the Cotswolds. The 17th century farm buildings have been converted into luxury self-catering cottages with well-equipped kitchens, TV and video. Ample car parking. Pets welcome. Separate laundry room and all bed linen, towels etc. included. B&B also available in warm and cosy 17th century farmhouse.

ENGLAND / Self-catering — Somerset

See also Colour Display Advertisement

BURNHAM-ON-SEA (Near)
Mrs W. Baker, Withy Grove Farm, East Huntspill, near Burnham-on-Sea TA9 3NP (01278 784471). Sleep 4/5. Come and enjoy a relaxing and friendly holiday "Down on the Farm" set in beautiful Somerset countryside. Peaceful rural setting adjoining River Huntspill, famed for its coarse fishing. The farm is ideally situated for visiting the many local attractions including Cheddar Gorge, Glastonbury, Weston-super-Mare and the lovely sandy beach of Burnham-on-Sea. Self-catering cottages are tastefully converted and fully equipped including colour TV. Facilities also include heated swimming pool, licensed bar and entertainment in high season, games room, skittle alley. Reasonable rates. Please write or telephone for further details.

EXMOOR
Mrs Jones, Higher Town, Dulverton TA22 9RX (01398 341272). Our property is set in 80 acres of National Park, half-a-mile from open moorland and visitors are welcome to walk over our beef and sheep farm. The bungalow is situated on its own with lovely views, lawn and parking space. It sleeps six with one bunk-bedded room, double bedroom and one bedroom with two single beds. Bedding, linen and electricity are provided. The bathroom and toilet are separate and the bath also has a shower over. The lounge has an open fire and colour TV, the kitchen has electric cooker, fridge freezer and washer dryer. Centrally heated and double glazed. SAE please for further information.

EXMOOR (near Selworthy)
Penny & Roger Webber, Hindon Organic Farm, Near Selworthy TA24 8SH (Tel & Fax: 01643 705244). Real Farm – Real Food– Relax. Escape to where the buzzards soar and red deer roam. B&B and Self-catering. Charming cottage and 18th century farmhouse on our 500-acre organic stock farm adjoining heather moors, South West coast path, and thatched village of Selworthy for 'scrummy' cream teas. All within National Trust Estate – wonderful walks and riding, bring dogs and horses. Waymarked farm trail with picnic wood. Organic lamb, Aberdeen Angus beef, free-range pork, bacon, ham, sausages, and more, all available in our farm shop. Free organic produce basket for self-catering accommodation guests; organic breakfasts also available. Minehead three miles, Dunster Castle six miles. Award winners from Exmoor National Park for conservation. ETC★★★/ ★★★★

e-mail: info@hindonfarm.co.uk
website: www.hindonfarm.co.uk

LANGPORT
Mr J. Woodborne, Muchelney Ham Farm, Muchelney Ham, Langport TA10 0DJ (Tel & Fax: 01458 250737). Sleeps 4/5. Self-catering cottages built in traditional style adjoining farmhouse. Double and family bedrooms, en suite. Large kitchen/diningroom. One further bathroom downstairs. Stable cottage has a downstairs bedroom. Electricity by coin meter. Linen included in price. Open all year. Weekly terms from £150 to £395, or from £120 to £285. ETC ★★★★ and ♣♣♣
website: www.muchelneyhamfarm.co.uk

FREE or REDUCED RATE entry to Holiday Visits and Attractions – see our READERS' OFFER VOUCHERS on pages 67 - 94

238 Somerset   Self-catering / ENGLAND

See also Colour Display Advertisement

MUCHELNEY
Mrs J. Thorne, Gothic House, Muchelney, Langport, Somerset TA10 0DW (01458 250626). Gothic House is a Victorian former farmhouse with two self-contained units available. Well-equipped kitchens with washing machine, microwave, cooker, fridge. Free central heating. Comfortably furnished sitting rooms with colour TV. Bedlinen and bathroom towels provided. It is situated on the edge of the Somerset Levels in the unspoilt village of Muchelney. Within the village are the ruins of a medieval Abbey and also the medieval priest house belonging to the National Trust. Gothic House can be found two-and-a-half miles south of Langport and is next door to well-known potter John Leach. Ideal for touring, cycling, fishing, walking and birdwatching. Terms from £160 to £295 per week. ETC ★★★
e-mail: joy-thorne@totalserve.co.uk

PORLOCK
Lucott Farm, Porlock, Minehead. Sleeps 12. Comfortable farmhouse on working Exmoor hill farm, with wood-burning fireplaces and all modern conveniences. It lies at the head of Horner Valley and guests will delight in the wonderful scenery. Excellent base for walking, pony trekking nearby. The house has three double and three twin bedrooms, bathroom with shower over bath, large sitting room, dining room, kitchen with oil-fired Aga, cloakroom and toilet, utility room with shower, and a garden. Shops and pubs three miles. Parking for five cars. All fuel and bed linen included. Terms from £400 to £900. Discount for parties of four or less. **Mrs J. Stapleford, West Lucott Farm Cottage, Ley Hill, Porlock, Minehead TA24 8LU (01643 862669).**
e-mail: fred.stapleford@talk21.com

SHEPTON MALLET
Pat and Ted Allen, Springfield Cottage Holidays, Springfield House, Maesdown Hill, Stoney Stratton, Evercreech BA4 6EG (01749 830748). Sleep 4/5 +cot. Springfield Cottages have been tastefully converted from the stables in the adjoining yard to Springfield House, a large country house set in eight acres of beautiful Somerset countryside, on the south slopes of the Mendip Hills. Ideal for bird lovers, walkers, cyclists, fishing, golfing or for visiting the many sites of historical and international interest. Historic Wells, Glastonbury and Bath are only a short drive away; many country pubs and restaurants nearby. Both cottages are well-equipped, with wheelchair access throughout the ground floor. Both have lounge/diner with bed settee; downstairs bathroom/showerroom; enclosed gardens with furniture and barbecue. Cot and high chair available. All linen provided, electricity by meter reading, payable on departure. Ample parking. Open all year. Short Breaks available. Well-behaved pets welcome. Non-smoking. Terms from £210 to £480 per week. ETC ★★★/★★★★
e-mail: Ted.Allen@btinternet.com

See also Colour Display Advertisement

SHEPTON MALLET
Knowle Farm, West Compton, Shepton Mallet BA4 4PD (01749 890482; Fax: 01749 890405). Working farm. Cottages sleep 2/5/6. Knowle Farm Cottages are converted from the old cowstall and stables, set around the old farmyard now laid out as a pleasant garden. Quiet location at the end of a private drive. Excellent views and plenty of wildlife. All cottages furnished to a high standard - bathroom (bath, shower, toilet, washbasin); fully fitted kitchen (automatic washing machine, fridge/freezer, microwave, full size cooker). Two cottages have kitchen/diner, separate lounge with colour TV, the other two have kitchen, lounge/diner, colour TV. Cot, high chair by prior arrangement. Bed linen supplied, towels by request. Surrounding area full of interesting places to visit. Five miles from Wells and Mendip Golf Clubs; the area also has a wide selection of family attractions, fishing, selection of pubs and restaurants. Around the farm plenty of walks, play area for children. Sorry no pets. Terms from £150 to £450. Car essential, ample parking. Payphone for guests. Open all year. ETC ★★★
website: www.knowle-farm-cottages.co.uk

ENGLAND / Self-catering   Somerset / Staffordshire

TAUNTON
Mrs Joan Greenway, Woodlands Farm, Bathealton, Taunton TA4 2AH (01984 623271). You can be assured of a warm and friendly welcome on our family-run dairy farm. Children are welcome and will enjoy feeding the animals. We are in the heart of beautiful unspoilt countryside within easy reach of the north and south coasts and Exmoor. The cottage sleeps five people and is furnished to a high standard to enjoy a relaxing holiday. Well equipped kitchen with use of washing machine and dryer. Bathroom with bath and shower. Electricity, central heating and bed linen included in the tariff. Terms from £135 to £350 per week. Fishing, golf and horse riding near by. Please write or phone for colour brochure.

WELLS
Mrs G. Creed, Model Farm, Model Farm Cottage, Milton, Wells BA5 3AE (01749 673363). Working farm. Sleeps 2. Set in peaceful countryside on a working farm away from traffic yet only one mile from the city centre and Wookey Hole. It is comfortably furnished with bedroom with double bed (plus single bed if required) bathroom with bath and shower, kitchen, lounge/diner and patio all on ground level. The cottage is well equipped with colour TV, washing machine, electric cooker and fridge freezer. Bed linen is provided and electricity is included in the price. Well-behaved dogs welcome. Please send for further details.

STAFFORDSHIRE

LEEK
Wren Cottage, Fairboroughs Farm, Rudyard, near Leek ST13 8PR. Built around 1550, Wren Cottage is situated on a working beef and sheep farm and was formerly a shippon (cow shed) used for young stock. It is situated in the curtilage of Fairboroughs farmhouse which has a history going back to 1230, and is Grade II Listed. Converted in 2002, the original beams and other features have been left exposed to add to the ambience of the cottage. Facilities include one double and one twin-bedded room (cot available), bathroom with bath and shower, fully-fitted kitchen with electric cooker, fridge/freezer and microwave; TV, video, radio/CD player; hairdryer, iron and ironing board; bed linen and towels. Full central heating and electric fire. Garden with furniture and barbecue. Laundry room available. Welcome tray on arrival. Close to Alton Towers and the Potteries. Sorry no smoking or pets. ETC ★★★★. Contact: **Mrs E. Lowe (01260 226341).** e-mail: **fairboroughs@talk21.com**

LEEK
Edith and Alwyn Mycock, 'Rosewood Cottage and Rosewood Flat', Lower Berkhamsytch Farm, Bottom House, Near Leek ST13 7QP (Tel & Fax: 01538 308213). Each sleeps 6. Situated in Staffordshire Moorlands, one cottage and one flat overlooking picturesque countryside. Fully equipped, comfortably furnished and carpeted throughout. Cottage, all on ground floor and with three bedrooms (one with four-poster) is suitable for the less able. An ideal base for visits to Alton Towers, the Potteries and Peak District. Patio, play area. Cot and high chair available. Laundry room with auto washer and dryer. Electricity and fresh linen inclusive. Terms from £160 to £315. **ETC ★★★**

SUFFOLK

BUNGAY

Three Ash Farm House, Bungay. Surrounded by gardens, meadows, ponds and farmland, Three Ash House is a tranquil spot to stay – no neighbours, just wide open spaces. The house sleeps six, and has two bathrooms and a farmhouse kitchen with an Aga. Come and unwind in this large, comfortable and well-equipped house. Walk, fish or birdwatch; within easy reach of the coast and many local attractions. Open all year. For details phone **Steffie 01986 896895.**

HALESWORTH

Cherry Trees at Cratfield Hall, Suffolk. Situated 25 minutes from Southwold and the Heritage Coast, deep in the Suffolk countryside, Cherry Trees offers an ideal family holiday or peaceful retreat. Accommodation comprises kitchen and dining area with dishwasher, washing machine, microwave, electric hob and oven, fridge/freezer, table seating six, high chair and vacuum cleaner. Downstairs bathroom with bath and electric shower over, basin and WC. Sitting room with open fire, three-piece suite, TV and video with children's videos. Twin bedroom with pull-out extra bed, double bedroom, washroom with wc and basin upstairs. Garage/playroom with children's games. Outside parking for two cars. Towels and linen provided. Cherry Trees stands alone set within a large garden enclosed by trees, suitable for both children and pets, and equipped with garden table and chairs, and barbecue. Open all year. Short breaks welcome.
Contact: **Chris Knox (01379 586709; Fax: 01379 588033).**
e-mail: **J.L. Knox@farming.co.uk**

ENGLAND / Self-catering Suffolk

KESSINGLAND COTTAGE Rider Haggard Lane, Kessingland

An exciting three-bedroom recently built semi-detached cottage situated on the beach, three miles south of sandy beach at Lowestoft. Fully and attractively furnished with colour TV and delightful sea and lawn views from floor-to-ceiling windows of lounge. Accommodation for up to six people. Well-equipped kitchen with electric cooker, fridge, electric immersion heater. Electricity by £1 coin meter. Luxurious bathroom with coloured suite. No linen or towels provided. Only a few yards to beach and sea fishing. One mile to wildlife country park with minitrain. Buses quarter-of-a-mile and shopping centre half-a-mile. Parking, but car not essential. Children and disabled persons welcome. Available 1st March to 7th January. Weekly terms from £50 in early March and late December to £250 in peak season.

SAE to Mr S. Mahmood, 156 Bromley Road, Beckenham, Kent BR3 6PG
Tel/Fax: 020-8650 0539
e-mail: jeeptrek@kjti.freeserve.co.uk • web: www.k-cottage.co.uk

---

See also Colour Display Advertisement

LAVENHAM
The Grove Cottages, Priory Green/Edwardstone CO10 5PP (01787 211115 or International: 0044 1787 211115). Enjoy the romantic atmosphere of your own 300-year-old farm cottage, with ancient oak beams, open log fires, period furniture, ducks, roses and a touch of luxury. Set in lovely Suffolk countryside, just 90 minutes from London or 60 minutes from Cambridge, our seven cottages are close to the beautiful medieval villages of Lavenham, Long Melford and Kersey. Bikes and canoes are available to explore 'Constable Country'. Pets are welcome. The cottages sleep from 2-6. Please visit our New Superfast Website where you will find lots of photos, information and prices, plus an Availability Calendar. Short Breaks are always welcome.
e-mail: mark@grove-cottages.co.uk
website: www.grove-cottages.co.uk

SAXMUNDHAM
Mrs Mary Kitson, White House Farm, Sibton, Saxmundham IP17 2NE (01728 660260). Working farm. Sleeps 4/6 adults; 2/4 Children. The flat is a self-contained part of late Georgian farmhouse standing in 130 acres of quiet farmland with a variety of livestock. Fishing on farm. Accommodation in three double bedrooms (two double/two single beds) plus cot; livingroom with TV; shower/toilet on first floor. Entrance hall, kitchen/diner on ground floor. Full central heating. Situated one-and-a-half miles from village shops, etc. Ten miles from coast at Dunwich, Minsmere Bird Sanctuary, Snape Maltings. Linen optional. Pets permitted. Car essential - parking. Available all year. Terms from £150 to £200 per week. SAE, please, for further details.

See also Colour Display Advertisement

SOUTHWOLD/WALBERSWICK
H.A. Adnams, Estate Agents, 98 High Street, Southwold IP18 6DP (01502 723292; Fax: 01502 724794). Furnished Holiday Cottages, Houses and Flats, available in this charming unspoilt seaside town. Convenient for sandy beaches, with safe bathing, sailing, fishing, golf and tennis. Near to 300 acres of open Common. Attractive country walks and historic churches may be found in this area, also the fine City of Norwich, the Festival Town of Aldeburgh and the Bird Sanctuary at Minsmere, all within easy driving distance. SAE, please, for brochure with full particulars.
website: www.haadnams.com

£1 per person off for up to 4 full-paying admissions at
Easton Farm Park
see our READERS' OFFER VOUCHERS for details

EAST SUSSEX

Fairhaven Holiday Cottages

Fairhaven Holiday Cottages is an independent owner-managed agency offering personally inspected holiday properties of all types in town, country and coastal areas of Kent and Sussex. For further information please visit our website

www.fairhaven-holidays.co.uk
e-mail: enquiries@fairhaven-holidays.co.uk
Telephone or fax 01634 570157

See also Colour Display Advertisement

ALFRISTON

Mr and Mrs G. Burgess, Polhills, Arlington, Polegate BN26 6SB (01323 870004). Idyllically situated on shore of reservoir and edge of Sussex Downs within easy reach of the sea. Fully furnished period cottage (approached by own drive along the water's edge) available for self-catering holidays from April to October (inclusive). Fly fishing for trout can be arranged during season. Accommodation consists of two main bedrooms; tiled bathroom. Lounge with colour TV; large well-fitted kitchen with fridge freezer, electric cooker, microwave, washing machine; dining room with put-u-up settee; sun lounge. Central heating. Linen supplied. Most rooms contain a wealth of oak beams. Children and pets welcome. Car essential. Ample parking. Shops two miles. Golf, hill climbing locally. Sea eight miles. Weekly terms from £220 to £295 (electricity included).

ARLINGTON

Mrs P. Boniface, Lakeside Farm Holiday Bungalows, Arlington, Polegate BN26 6SB (01323 870111). Situated on the edge of Arlington Reservoir, with views of the South Downs. Eastbourne, Brighton and Lewes within 15 miles; Drusillas Zoo two miles, shopping half a mile. Modern, comfortable accommodation: two double rooms, lounge, dining room, colour TV, bathroom, toilet. Well-equipped kitchen with microwave. Open April to October. Car essential, parking. Suitable for disabled guests. Children welcome; cot and high chair available. Well-controlled pets accepted. Electricity included. Weekly terms on request.
e-mail: pat@lakesidecottages.freeserve.co.uk
website: www.showpony.com/lakeside

WADHURST

Mrs Edwina Le May, The Old Stables, Ladymeads Farm, Bewlbridge Lane, Lower Cousley Wood, Wadhurst TN5 6HH (01892 783240; Fax: 01892 783562). Sleeps 2/4. Quality conversion Stables on one level, in magnificent Victorian barn, farmhouse to organic working farm on banks of Bewl Water, an Area of Outstanding Natural Beauty. Two bedrooms, two bathrooms, sitting room with sofa, kitchen area with fridge/freezer, electric cooker, microwave, washing machine, colour TV, cot, high chair. Full linen and towels included, full central heating. Non-smokers preferred. Partly walled courtyard, private drive. Bewl Water has a 13-mile-round water walk only a few minutes' walk away, nature reserve, bridlepath, sailing, cycling, fly fishing. Wealth of beautiful gardens and National Trust Properties. Convenient

one hour to the sea at Rye and Camber Sands, South Downs Way, Ashdown and Bedgebury Forests. Convenient for London (55 minutes by train), airports. Terms from £212 to £345 per week. Available all year. **ETC ★★★**
e-mail: enquiries@camrosa.co.uk

WARWICKSHIRE

STRATFORD-UPON-AVON
Crimscote Downs Farm Self-catering Accommodation. Sleeps 2 and 4. PARADISE COTTAGE is a romantic hideaway for two people in a newly converted former shepherd's retreat, with views over the downs. It is full of character, with beams and wooden floors; centrally heated throughout. The kitchen is fully equipped with microwave, dishwasher, electric cooker and washing machine. THE DAIRY is ideal for a family visit, with fully equipped kitchen, sitting room and two en suite bedrooms; centrally heated throughout. It has stunning views and is full of character with beams and wooden floors. Terms from £190 to £420. Both cottages are five and a half miles from Stratford-upon-Avon. No smoking. Ample parking. Pets by prior arrangement. ETC ★★★. Contact: **Mrs J James, The Old Coach House, Whitchurch Farm, Wimpston, Stratford-upon-Avon CV37 8NS (01789 450275).** website: www.stratford-upon-avon.co.uk/crimscote.htm

WILTSHIRE

LACOCK (near Bath)
The Cheese House & The Cyder House. Situated on a working farm, both these beautiful self-catering properties were converted in 1994, with great care taken to preserve their natural charm. THE CYDER HOUSE sleeps up to four persons and has the original cyder press on the ground floor, separating the kitchen from the sitting room. There are two single bedrooms and one double, and shower room with wash basin and W.C. Wooden floors throughout, all rooms have either night storage heaters or panel heaters. THE CHEESE HOUSE sleeps up to five persons and consists of an open living/dining room with arch to fitted kitchen. One double and one single bedroom on first floor with shower room with wash basin and W.C, and a further twin-bedded room on the second floor with galleried sitting area with books, TV and games. Both properties have been traditionally furnished with co-ordinating fabrics and attention to detail. Each has parking area and separate garden with seating and barbecue. Sorry no pets. Non-smoking. Short Breaks available. **Sue and Philip King, Wick Farm, Lacock, Chippenham SN15 2LU (01249 730244; Fax: 01249 730072).** ETC ★★★★. *WELCOME HOST, FARM STAY UK MEMBER.*
e-mail: kingsilverlands2@btopenworld.com   website: www.cheeseandcyderhouses.co.uk

TROWBRIDGE
John and Elizabeth Moody, Gaston Farm, Holt, Trowbridge BA14 6QA (01225 782203). The self-contained accommodation is part of a farmhouse, which dates from the 16th century, on the edge of the village of Holt with views across open farmland. Within 10 miles of Bath, Bradford-on-Avon two miles, Lacock eight miles. Private fishing on River Avon available. The apartment consists of a large lounge/dining room with open fire and sofa which converts into a double bed; two generously proportioned bedrooms upstairs, one twin-bedded, one with a double bed, both with washbasins; a separate toilet (downstairs); a large kitchen in the single storey wing, fitted with light oak finish units, electric cooker, microwave, refrigerator and automatic washing machine; shower room which opens off the kitchen. Off road parking. Choice of pubs in village. Terms £170 to £195. Brochure and further details available.

YORKSHIRE

YORKSHIRE'S DALES, MOORS & COAST

Superb, personally inspected, self catering holiday properties in beautiful rural and coastal locations including the Calendar Girls and Brontë, Heartbeat and Herriot areas. Cosy cottages to country houses, many welcome pets and short breaks are available.

Dales Holiday Cottages

0870 909 9500

www.dalesholcot.com

EAST YORKSHIRE

See also Colour Display Advertisement

KILHAM
Mrs P.M. Savile, Raven Hill Farm, Kilham, Driffield YO25 4EG (01377 267217). Working farm. Sleeps 8+2 plus cots. With delightful views overlooking the Yorkshire Wolds, ideally situated for touring the East Coast, Bridlington, Scarborough, Moors and York, this secluded and private four-bedroomed farmhouse is set in its own acre of woodland lawns and orchard, with garden furniture, summerhouse and children's play area. Games room in converted Granary in the main farm area 200 yards away. Clean and comfortable and very well equipped including dishwasher, microwave, automatic washing machine and dryer; two bathrooms, payphone, TV and video. Fully centrally heated. Beds are made up for your arrival; cots and high chair available. Three miles to the nearest village of Kilham with Post Office, general stores, garage and public houses. Available all year. Terms from £230 - £380 per week (low season) to £380 - £540 per week (high season). Brochure on request. ETC ★★★★

NORTH YORKSHIRE

See also Colour Display Advertisement

ASKRIGG
Fern Croft, 2 Mill Lane, Askrigg. Sleeps 4. A modern cottage enjoying quiet location on edge of village with open fields rising immediately behind. Attractive and compact, this Wensleydale village is an ideal centre for the Dales, with facilities for everyday needs, including two shops, Post Office, restaurant and a couple of pubs. Furnished to a high standard for four, ground floor accommodation comprises large comfortable lounge/diner with colour TV and well-equipped kitchen. Upstairs there are two double bedrooms with a double and twin beds respectively, and modern bathroom. Storage heating included, other electricity by meter. Regret no pets. Terms from £140 to £270 weekly. Brochure: **Mr and Mrs K. Dobson (01689 838450).**

ASKRIGG (Wensleydale)
Mrs E. Scarr, Coleby Hall, Askrigg, Leyburn DL8 3DX (01969 650216). Working farm. Sleeps 5 plus cot. Situated in Wensleydale, half-a-mile from Bainbridge and one mile from Askrigg, Coleby Hall is a 17th century gabled farmhouse with stone mullioned windows, the west end being to let. A stone spiral staircase leads to two bedrooms; linen provided. The kitchen is equipped with electric cooker, fridge, crockery, etc., and coal fire. The lounge has an inglenook coal fire and TV. Oil-fired central heating throughout. Coleby has lovely views and is an ideal situation for walking, fishing and driving round the Yorkshire Dales. Children and pets welcome. Terms from £180 per week.
website: www.colebyhall.co.uk

One FREE child for each two paying adults at

The Deep

see our READERS' OFFER VOUCHERS for details

246 North Yorkshire — Self-catering / ENGLAND

See also Colour Display Advertisement

COVERDALE

Westclose House (Allaker), West Scrafton, Coverdale, Leyburn DL8 4RM. Stone farmhouse with panoramic views, high in the Yorkshire Dales National Park (Herriot family's house in 'All Creatures Great and Small' on TV). Three bedrooms (sleeps 6-8), sitting and dining rooms with wood-burning stoves, kitchen, bathroom, WC. House has electric storage heating, cooker, microwave, fridge, washing machine, colour TV, telephone. Garden, large barn, stables. Access from lane, private parking, no through traffic. Excellent walking from front door, near Wensleydale. Pets welcome. Self-catering from £400 per week. For bookings telephone: **020 8567 4862**
e-mail: ac@adriancave.com
website: www.adriancave.com/yorks

GRASSINGTON (near)

Mrs Judith M. Joy, Jerry and Ben's, Hebden, Skipton BD23 5DL (01756 752369; Fax: 01756 753370). Properties sleep 3/6/8/9. Jerry and Ben's stands in two acres of grounds in one of the most attractive parts of the Yorkshire Dales National Park. Seven properties; Ghyll Cottage (sleeps eight); Mamie's Cottage (sleeps eight); Paradise End (sleeps six); Robin Middle (sleeps six); High Close (sleeps nine); Cruck Rise (sleeps six); Raikes Side (sleeps two/three). All have parking, electric cooker, microwave, toaster, fridge, colour TV, electric heating and immersion heater; lounge, dining area, bathroom with shower; cots if required. Fully equipped, including linen if requested. Washing machine and telephone available. Ghyll and Mamie's Cottages now have dishwashers. Well behaved pets accepted. Open all year. Fishing and bathing close by. Terms from £98 to £425. SAE, please for detailed brochure. Suitable for some disabled guests.
e-mail: dawjoy@aol.com   website: www.yorkshirenet.co.uk/stayat/jerryandbens

See also Colour Display Advertisement

HARDRAW

Cissy's Cottage, Hardraw, Hawes. Sleeps 4. A delightful 18th century cottage of outstanding character. Situated in the village of Hardraw with its spectacular waterfall and Pennine Way. Market town of Hawes one mile. This traditional stone built cottage retains many original features including beamed ceilings and an open fire. Sleeping four in comfort, it has been furnished and equipped to a high standard using antique pine and Laura Ashley prints. Equipped with dishwasher, microwave and tumble dryer. Outside, a south-facing garden, sun patio with garden furniture, and a large enclosed paddock make it ideal for children. Cot and high chair if required. Open all year. Terms £120-£295 includes coal, electricity, linen and trout fishing. For brochure, contact **Mrs Belinda Metcalfe, Southolme Farm, Little Smeaton, Northallerton DL6 2HJ (01609 881302/881052).**

HARROGATE

Mrs Janet Hollings, Dougill Hall, Summerbridge, Harrogate HG3 4JR (01423 780277). Working farm. Sleeps 4. Dougill Hall is of Georgian design, built in 1722 by the Dougill family who lived on this farm from 1496 to 1803. It is in Nidderdale, half-a-mile from the village of Summerbridge, just by the River Nidd, where there is fishing available for visitors. There are good facilities for horse riding, tennis, swimming, squash, etc. Well situated for the walking enthusiast and within easy reach of the Dales, the beautiful and ancient city of York, Fountains Abbey, How Stean Gorge and many other places of interest. The Old Cooling House flat sleeps up to four people. Well equipped, with electric cooker and fridge, iron, vacuum cleaner. Linen by arrangement. Car essential, parking. Terms from £135 to £220. SAE please for details.

FREE or REDUCED RATE entry to Holiday Visits and Attractions – see our READERS' OFFER VOUCHERS on pages 67 - 94

Helme Pasture Cottages and Lodges
Old Spring Wood

Hartwith Bank • Summerbridge • Harrogate • North Yorkshire HG3 4DR
Tel: (01423) 780279 • Fax: (01423) 780994
e-mail: info@helmepasture.co.uk
web: www.helmepasture.co.uk

★ Four Star accommodation in the heart of the Yorkshire Dales.
★ Exclusive Scandinavian Lodges in natural English woodland.
★ Converted Dales Farmhouse – mind your head on beams!
★ Excellently equipped. Central heating. Colour TV. Payphone. Laundry.
★ Extensive private grounds, magnificent views. Adjacent parking.
★ Splendid walking and touring country. ★ 29 acres of conservation woodland.
★ Ideal centre – Harrogate, York, Dales, Herriot/Brontë country, Nat.Parks/Trust.
★ Warm personal welcome ★ Welcome Host Award.
★ Pets welcome ★ Barbecue Area ★ David Bellamy Environmental Award.

Mobility Level 1

See also our advert on Inside Back Cover

248 North Yorkshire — Self-catering / ENGLAND

HARROGATE

Mrs Hardcastle, Southfield Farm, Darley, Harrogate HG3 2PR (01423 780258). Two well-equipped holiday cottages on a farm in an attractive area between Harrogate and Pateley Bridge. An ideal place to explore the whole of the dale with York and Herriot country within easy driving distance. Riverside walks, village shop and post office within quarter-of-a-mile, and local pub one mile away. Each cottage has two bedrooms, one double and one with bunk beds. Games room. Large lawn for ball games, with garden chairs and barbecue. Pets welcome. Ample car parking. Prices from £170 to £200 low season, £200 to £270 high season.

HELMSLEY (near)

Mrs Rickatson, Summerfield Farm, Harome, York Y62 5JJ (01439 748238). Working farm. Sleeps 6. Enjoy walking or touring in North York Moors National Park. Lovely area 20 miles north of York. Comfortable and well-equipped farmhouse wing with electric cooker, fridge, microwave and automatic washing machine. Sit beside a log fire in the evenings. Linen supplied. Trout stream on farm. Children and dogs welcome. Weekly terms £95 to £230. Mid-week and weekend bookings are possible. For further information phone or write for leaflet.

LEYBURN

Park Grange Farm Cottage. A working farm situated just a mile from the picturesque market town of Leyburn, Wensleydale. Comfortable self-catering cottage. Superb views of beautiful countryside. Ideal for walking, cycling, fishing, horse-riding, playing golf and touring the Dales. The cottage comprises two double rooms, one bunk-bed room and a double bed-settee if required. The kitchen is equipped with cooker, fridge, dishwasher and washer. Children, dogs and horses welcome. Grazing/stabling for your equine friends, and kennels available if you wish to bring working dogs on holiday. We cater for special occasions, and include a Yorkshire welcome pack with each booking. Short breaks available. For brochure and rates, contact: **Pam Sheppard, Low Gill Farm, Agglethorpe, Leyburn DL8 4TN (01969 640258).**
e-mail: pamsheppardlgf@aol.com

LOW BENTHAM

Mrs L.J. Story, Holmes Farm, Low Bentham, Lancaster LA2 7DE (015242 61198). Sleeps 4. Attractively converted and well equipped stone cottage adjoining 17th century farm house. In a secluded position surrounded by 127 acres of beautiful pastureland. Central heating, fridge, TV, washing machine, games room. Ideal base for visiting Dales, Lake District and coast. **ETC ★★★★**

One adult travels FREE when accompanied by a fare paying adult at
Embsay & Bolton Abbey Steam Railway
see our READERS' OFFER VOUCHERS for details

ENGLAND / Self-catering North Yorkshire **249**

MARTON/KIRKBYMOORSIDE

Mr & Mrs A.W. Turnbull, Oak Lodge, White Thorn Farm, Rook Barugh, Kirkbymoorside YO62 6PF (01751 431298). Charming, detached former stable with open beams and log burners, tastefully furnished and well equipped throughout. On a family-run farm (beef, cows, sheep) surrounded by open countryside with easy access to bridleways and footpaths. Centrally situated for the North York Moors with its famous steam railway (four miles); York 27 miles, coast 22 miles, Castle Howard just 20 minutes. Available all year. Terms from £200 to £375 per week. ETC ★★★
e-mail: turnbull@whitethornfarm.fsnet.co.uk
website: www.cottageguide.co.uk/oak-lodge

RICHMOND

Dyson House Farm, Newsham, Richmond DL11 7QP (01833 627365). Sleeps 6. A personal welcome from the owners living in the adjoining farmhouse awaits visitors to the converted barn. Midway between Richmond and Barnard Castle it is the ideal base for touring Swaledale, Teesdale, Cumbria, Durham, York and the surrounding areas where there are numerous museums, castles, antique shops and markets. One double and one twin bedroom and bathroom are on the first floor. The ground floor has a twin bedroom (two steps up), shower room, large lounge, large kitchen/diner and utility. The enclosed patio makes it ideal for children. Two pub/restaurants ten minutes' walk. Dogs welcome, £10 each. Colour brochure available. Terms from £210 – £425 per week. ETC ★★★★
e-mail: dysonbarn@tinyworld.co.uk
website: www.cottageguide.co.uk/dysonhousebarn

ROBIN HOOD'S BAY (near)

Ken and Nealia Pattinson, South House Farm, Fylingthorpe, Whitby YO22 4UQ (01947 880243). Glorious countryside in North York Moors National Park. Five minutes' walk to beach at Boggle Hole. Super large farmhouse sleeps 10. Four spacious cottages sleeping two to six. All inclusive and fully equipped. Gardens. Parking. Terms from £180 to £1500.
e-mail: kmp@bogglehole.fsnet.co.uk
website: www.southhousefarm.co.uk

SCARBOROUGH

Mr and Mrs T.M. Bull, Gowland Farm, Gowland Lane, Cloughton, Scarborough YO13 0DU (01723 870924). Sleep 2/7. Four charming converted stone barns situated within the beautiful North York Moors National Park, enjoying wonderful views of Harwood Dale and only two miles from the coast. The cottages have been sympathetically converted from traditional farm buildings, furnished and fitted to a very high standard, retaining the old features as well as having modern comforts. They are fully carpeted, warm and cosy with central heating and double glazing. Electric fire and colour TV in all lounges. Well-equipped kitchens. All linen and bedding provided (duvets). Large garden with plenty of car parking space. Garden furniture and laundry facilities. Sorry, no pets. Open all year. From £135 to £525 per week. White Rose Award Self-Catering Holiday of the Year runner up 1993.
e-mail: GowlandFarm@aol.com
website: www.gowlandfarm.co.uk

The FHG Directory of Website Addresses
on pages 345 - 373 is a useful quick reference guide for holiday accommodation with e-mail and/or website details

SKIPTON

Mrs Brenda Jones, New Close Farm, Kirkby Malham, Skipton BD23 4DP (01729 830240; Fax:01729 830179). Sleeps 5. A supa dupa cottage on New Close Farm in the heart of Craven Dales with panoramic views over the Aire Valley. Excellent area for walking, cycling, fishing, golf and touring. Two double and one single bedrooms; bathroom. Colour TV and video. Full central heating and double glazing. Bed linen, towels and all amenities included in the price. Low Season £250, High Season £300; deposit required. Sorry, no young children, no pets. Non-smokers preferred. The weather can't be guaranteed but your comfort can. *FHG DIPLOMA AWARD WINNER.*
e-mail: brendajones@newclosefarmyorkshire.co.uk
website: www.newclosefarmyorkshire.co.uk

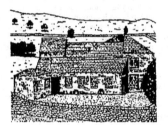

SKIPTON

The Pearson Family, Cawder Hall Cottages, Cawder Hall, Cawder Lane, Skipton BD23 2QQ (01756 791579; Fax: 01756 797036). Sleeps 2/6. Enjoy the peace and quiet of our warm, welcoming cottages just one mile from Skipton, with its thriving street market, medieval castle and church. Surrounded by fields and animals, each cottage is well equipped (colour TV, video, microwave) and is suitable for disabled guests. There is a lawned garden, barbecue, phone, laundry room and children's play area. Linen, gas and electricity are included in the price, as are cots and high chairs. Open all year. Prices from £120 to £340 per week.
website: www.cawderhallcottages.co.uk

STAITHES

Garth End Cottage, Staithes. Sleeps 5/6. Georgian cottage situated on sea wall in this old fishing village in the North Yorkshire Moors National Park. Excellent walking centre. Small sandy beach with numerous rock pools. Cottage has feature fireplace, beamed ceilings, pine panelled room, well-equipped kitchen including microwave. Warm, comfortable, well-equipped with central heating, electricity and bed linen included in rent. Two lounges, front one with picture window giving uninterrupted panoramic views of sea, harbour and cliffs. Dining kitchen; bathroom with toilet; three bedrooms - one double, one twin, one single (two with sea views). Colour TV and video. Front terrace overlooking the sea. Sorry, no pets. Terms from £220. **Apply Mrs Hobbs (01132 665501).**

WHITBY

Mrs O. Hepworth, Land of Nod Farm, Near Whitby YO21 2BL (01947 840325). Sleeps 6 plus cot. This 250-year-old sandstone cottage is an annexe to the main farmhouse, situated on a 50-acre working farm in the North Yorkshire Moors National Park. Whitby is around nine miles away. Goathland & "Heartbeat" Country about the same, villages on the coast, like Staithes and Runswick Bay are closer, around three miles. The cottage looks over farmland, with splendid views to the south and east across the widening valley. Parking for two cars, a private garden and patio area. The cottage consists of a kitchen/diner, lounge with colour TV and electric fire, shower room, and a bathroom. Three bedrooms, two double and one with twin beds. Bed linen and night storage heaters are included in the hire, electricity is on a £1.00 slot meter, (with a £5.00 credit on entry). We prefer to keep the cottage non-smoking, however smoking is permitted in the entrance porch. Prices for 2004 start from £106 to £210 per week, pets £14 a week extra. For availability and prices, please ring or e-mail.
colin@thecottage-ugthorpe.freeserve.co.uk   **www.thecottage-ugthorpe.freeserve.co.uk**

Eden Camp Modern History Museum • *Malton, North Yorkshire* • *01653 697777*
website: www.edencamp.co.uk
This award-winning museum will take you back to wartime Britain where you can experience the sights, sounds and smells of World War II.

ENGLAND / Self-catering   North Yorkshire **251**

Valley View Farm
Old Byland, Helmsley, York, North Yorkshire YO6 5LG
Telephone: 01439 798221

Four holiday cottages sleeping two, four and six persons respectively. Each with colour TV, video, washer, dishwasher, microwave. Peaceful rural surroundings on a working farm with pigs, sheep and cattle. Winter and Spring Breaks available. Short Breaks from £90 and High Season weeks up to £495. Bed and Breakfast also available (ETC ◆◆◆◆). Please telephone for brochure and further details to: Mrs Sally Robinson.
e-mail: sally@valleyviewfarm.com   website: www.valleyviewfarm.com

WHITBY
Nick Eddleston, Greenhouses Farm Cottages, Greenhouses Farm, Lealholm, Near Whitby YO21 2AD (01947 897486). The three cottages have been converted from the traditional farm buildings. The old world character has been retained with the thick stone walls, exposed beams and red pantile roofs typical of North Yorkshire. Set in the tiny hamlet of Greenhouses and enjoying splendid views over open countryside, the cottages offer a very quiet and peaceful setting for a holiday. All the cottages are equipped with colour TV, electric cooker, fridge/freezer, microwave and automatic washing machine. Linen, fuel and lighting are all included in the price. There are ample safe areas for children to play. Sorry, no pets. Prices from £188 to £509 per week. Winter Breaks from £142.

YORK
Orillia Cottages, Stockton-on-the-Forest, York. Four converted farmworkers' cottages in a courtyard setting at the rear of the 300-year-old farmhouse in Stockton-on-the-Forest; three miles from York. Golf course nearby, pub 200 yards away serves food. Post Office, newsagents and general stores within easy reach. Convenient half-hourly bus service to York and the coast. Fully furnished and equipped for two to eight, the cottages comprise lounge with colour TV, etc; kitchen area with microwave oven, grill and hob. Bedrooms have double bed or twin beds. Gas central heating. Non-smokers preferred. Children and pets welcome. Available all year. Short Breaks may be available. Terms from £195 to £495 weekly includes heating, linen, etc. Contact: **Mr & Mrs G.Hudson, Orillia House, 89 The Village, Stockton-on-the-Forest, York YO3 9UP (01904 400600).** (B&B also available ETC ◆◆◆◆)
website: www.orilliacottages.co.uk

YORKSHIRE DALES NATIONAL PARK
Hawes, Bainbridge and West Burton in Wensleydale. Sleep 4 to 7. Four lovely old Dales stone cottages of character with beamed ceilings, open fires, Laura Ashley prints and many personal touches. Beautifully maintained, the cottages have oil fired central heating and well-equipped farmhouse kitchens with Rayburn/Aga. Warm and cosy with every comfort. Peacefully situated in the Yorkshire Dales National Park with spectacular views over Wensleydale, come in delightful village settings. Lovely old-fashioned walled gardens with barbecue areas. Private parking. Free trout fishing on farm. Open all year. Children and pets welcome. SAE for terms and prompt reply. Contact: **Mrs A. Fawcett, Mile House Farm, Hawes, Wensleydale DL8 3PT (01969 667481); Fax: 01969 667425).**
e-mail: milehousefarm@hotmail.com
website: www.wensleydale.uk.com

A useful index of towns and counties appears at the back of this book on pages 375 - 378. Refer also to Contents Pages 2 and 3.

WEST YORKSHIRE

See also Colour Display Advertisement

HOLMFIRTH
Summerwine Cottages, Shepley, Near Holmfirth, Huddersfield. Sleep 2/4. Part of a beautifully converted 17th century farmhouse, set in six acres of Pennine farmland, deep in the heart of 'Summer Wine' country. Sympathetically restored in the mid 1980s, the cottages have continued to be very popular with ramblers, walkers and country loving people who just want to 'get away from it all'. Fully self-contained, each has access via patio doors to a lovely enclosed rose garden. Furnishings and decor are to a high standard and all cottages have TV, video, cooker, washer/dryer, microwave, iron, lounge suite and dining table, etc. Each has central heating, double glazing and off-road parking. Cot, high chair available. Short breaks available. Price range £150 to £325 per week. ETC ★★★. For more information please contact: **Mrs Susan Meakin, West Royd Farm, Marsh Lane, Shepley, Huddersfield HD8 8AY** (01484 602147; Fax: 01484 609427).
e-mail: summerwinecottages@lineone.net   website: www.summerwinecottages.co.uk

HUDDERSFIELD
Ashes Farm Cottages. Sleep 4-8. Surrounded by open country yet near town, these two 17th century Listed barns, converted and furnished to a high standard make highly individual cottages. Both have gas central heating, fully-equipped kitchens with cooker, microwave, fridge/freezer, washing machine and tumble dryer. Cruck Cottage has one double and two single bedrooms, the Barn House will sleep six to eight in one double, two twin bedrooms (two en suite) and double sofa bed. Another bedroom/bathroom wing is available on request. All linen inclusive, ample parking. Please contact us for a brochure or more details, or visit our website. ETC ★★★-★★★★. Contact: **Mrs Barbara Lockwood, Ashes Common Farm, Ashes Lane, Almondbury, Huddersfield HD4 6TE (Tel & Fax: 01484 426507).**
e-mail: enquiries@ashescommonfarm.co.uk   website: www.ashescommonfarm.co.uk

---

TWO for ONE at
The Colour Museum
see our READERS' OFFER VOUCHERS for details

"ONE for ONE" free admission at
Museum of Rail Travel
see our READERS' OFFER VOUCHERS for details

See the *Family-Friendly Pubs & Inns*
Supplement on pages 335 - 344 for establishments
which really welcome children

CORNWALL

St Ives Bay Holiday Park

CALL OUR 24hr BROCHURE LINE **0800 317713**

The park on the beach

CHALETS • CARAVANS • CAMPING

St Ives Bay Holiday Park is set in sand dunes which run down to its own sandy beach. Many units have superb sea views. There is a large indoor pool and 2 clubs with FREE entertainment on the Park

www.stivesbay.co.uk

BUDE

Willow Valley Holiday Park, Bush, Bude EX23 9LB (01288 353104). Our camp site, which is only two miles from Bude and the sandy surfing beaches, is set in a beautiful valley. There is a small river meandering through the site which adds to its beauty. We are only a small site, with two pitches on four acres of land and, as these are not arranged in rows but around the edges of the site, there are always plenty of open spaces. We have toilets, showers, dishwashing area and a laundry. We also have a children's adventure playground which is in full view of most pitches, but not set amongst them. Dogs on leads are very welcome and we have seven acres of land in which they can run free. We also have a wide variety of pets on site including chickens, ducks, rabbits and peacocks. Open 31st March to 31st October, but enquiries are welcome anytime. For further details please write or telephone for a brochure and price list.

ST AUSTELL

See also Colour Display Advertisement

Trencreek Farm Holiday Park, Hewaswater, St Austell PL26 7JG (01726 882540). A peaceful, family-run holiday park with self-catering and camping facilities, all with country views and within easy reach of the sea. We can provide two and three bedroom units to sleep up to eight, and fully equipped self-catering tents to sleep six. We have a heated swimming pool, tennis court, and fishing lakes, etc, with kids entertainment in the main season. Children will love our free roaming and friendly animals. One of Cornwall's favourite family holiday parks.
e-mail: trencreekfarm@aol.com
website: www.trencreek.co.uk

The Eden Project • *Near St Austell, Cornwall* • *01726 811911*
website: www.edenproject.com
A gateway into the fascinating interaction of plants and people. Two gigantic geodesic conservatories - the Humid Tropics Biome and the Warm Temperate Biome - set amidst landscaped outdoor terraces.

National Maritime Museum • *Falmouth, Cornwall* • *01326 313388*
website: www.nmmc.co.uk
A gateway to the maritime world with interactive displays of boats and their place in the nation's life.

CUMBRIA

See also Colour Display Advertisement

AMBLESIDE

Greenhowe Caravan Park, Great Langdale, Ambleside LA22 9JU (015394 37231; Freephone: 0800 071 7231; Fax: 015394 37464). Greenhowe is a permanent Caravan Park with self-contained holiday accommodation. Subject to availability, holiday homes may be rented for short or long periods from 1st March until mid-November. The park is situated in the Lake District half-a-mile from Dungeon Ghyll at the foot of the Langdale Pikes. It is an ideal centre for climbing, fell walking, riding, swimming and water skiing. Please ask about our short breaks. Please telephone for a free colour brochure. ETC ★★★★, *DAVID BELLAMY SILVER CONSERVATION AWARD, WELCOME HOST.*

BRAMPTON

Mrs O.R. Campbell, Irthing Vale Caravan Park, Old Church Lane, Brampton, Near Carlisle CA8 2AA (016977 3600). Popular with tourists whose prime concern is cleanliness, peace and quietness with the personal attention of the owner, this four-and-a-half acre park has pitches for 20 touring caravans, motorised caravans plus space for camping. There is a small site shop, laundry room, mains water and drainage and electric hook-ups. In fact all the amenities one would expect on a quiet, modern caravan park. We are very close to Hadrian's (Roman) Wall and convenient for having days out discovering romantic Scottish Border country. The ideal site for walking, sailing, fishing and golf. Open 1st March until 31st October. Terms from £9 per car/caravan plus two persons. Special reductions for hikers and cyclists. **AA ★★★**, *AA THREE PENNANTS, CARAVAN AND CAMPING CLUB LISTED SITE.*
e-mail: glennwndrby@aol.com
website: www.ukparks.co.uk/irthingvale

CONISTON

Scarr Head Caravans and Campsite. Small working farm at the foot of the Coniston mountains, just two miles south of Coniston village where there is a good range of shops, hotels and restaurants. Hawkshead, Ambleside, Bowness and Windermere are easily accessible by car. Three permanent caravans, two four-berth with two bedrooms, and one two-berth with one bedroom. All have shower, toilet and washbasin, galley style kitchen with gas cooker, fridge, small freezer and electric kettle, comfortable lounge with gas fire, colour TV and dining area. Mains electricity - fuel costs and hot water included in hire charge. Small laundry room on site. Linen not provided. Small campsite for up to five touring caravans or camper vans, facilities include standpipe water tap, dishwasher drain, elsan disposal point, flush toilets, hot water, shower and shaver and hairdryer points. Please telephone for further details. Contact: **S.J. and Mrs J.F. Halton, Scarr Head Bungalow, Torver, Near Coniston LA21 8BP (015394 41576 or 41328).**
e-mail: scarr.head@virgin.net

CONISTON

Mrs E. Johnson, Spoon Hall, Coniston LA21 8AW (015394 41391). Caravans sleep 6. Three 6-berth caravans situated on a 50 acre working hill farm one mile from Coniston, overlooking Coniston Lake. All have flush-toilet, shower, gas cookers, fires and water heaters, electric lighting and fridge plus colour TV. Children are welcome. Pets are allowed free. Available March to October. Pony trekking arranged from farm. Weekly terms on request.

One child FREE with two paying adults at
Cars of the Stars Motor Museum
see our READERS' OFFER VOUCHERS for full details

256 Cumbria / Derbyshire   Caravan & Camping / ENGLAND

PENRITH
R & A Taylforth, Side Farm, Patterdale, Penrith CA11 0NP (017684 82337). Camping on the shores of Lake Ullswater for tents and motor caravans (sorry, no towing caravans), surrounded by the beautiful scenery of the Lake District. Activities on the lake include swimming, sailing, boating, canoeing and fishing; steamer cruises. Modern toilet block, showers, washing facilities, shaving, hair drying points, washing machines and dryers. Dogs allowed provided they are kept on a lead. Convenient for touring the Lake District National Park. Fresh milk and eggs are available at the farm, with shops and post office in nearby Patterdale; regular bus services. Terms - Adults £4.50 per night; reductions for children; vehicles £1, boats/trailers/motorbikes 50p. Open Easter to November.

SILLOTH-ON-SOLWAY
M.C. Bowman, Tanglewood Caravan Park, Causeway Head, Silloth-on-Solway CA5 4PE (016973 31253). Tanglewood is a family-run park on the fringes of the Lake District National Park. It is tree-sheltered and situated one mile inland from the small port of Silloth on the Solway Firth, with a beautiful view of the Galloway Hills. Large modern holiday homes are available from March to October, with car parking beside each home. Fully equipped except for bed linen, with end bedroom, central heating in bedrooms, electric lighting, hot and cold water, toilet, shower, gas fire, fridge and colour TV, all of which are included in the tariff. Touring pitches also available with electric hook-ups and water/drainage facilities, etc. Play area. Licensed lounge with adjoining children's play room. Pets welcome free but must be kept under control at all times. Full colour brochure available. **ETC ★★★, AA** *THREE PENNANTS* website: www.tanglewoodcaravanpark.co.uk

DERBYSHIRE

BUXTON near
Mr and Mrs J. Melland, The Pomeroy Caravan Park, Street House Farm, Flagg, Near Buxton SK17 9QG (01298 83259). Working farm. This site for 30 caravans is situated five miles from Buxton, in the heart of the Peak District National Park. Ideal base for touring by car or walking. Site adjoins northern end of now famous Tissington and High Peak Trail. Only nine miles from Haddon Hall and ten from Chatsworth House. Landscaped to the latest model standards for caravan sites; tourers and campers will find high standards here. Toilet block with showers, washing facilities and laundry; mains electric hook-up points. Back-packers welcome. Large rally field available. Children welcome; dogs on lead. Touring rates £6.50 to £7.00 for two people per night. Open Easter to end of October. SAE for brochure please. **ETC ★★**

One child FREE with every paying adult at

Blue-John Cavern

see our READERS' OFFER VOUCHERS for full details

DEVON

HALDON LODGE FARM,
Kennford, Near Exeter EX6 7YG
Tel: (01392) 832312

In an attractive setting, three six-berth holiday caravans and log cabin in a private and friendly park. Fully equipped kitchen, lounge with TV, bathroom, toilet, H/C. Rates from £70 to £195 per week high season; tourers and campers welcome.

Excellent facilities. Open all year. Pets welcome.

Exeter and South Devon beaches 15 minutes, horse riding from a nearby farm. Three well-stocked coarse fishing lakes close by, also the attraction of barbecues and hayrides to a friendly country inn during school holidays.

Personal welcome given by David & Betty Salter.

ASHBURTON

Parkers Farm Holiday Park, Ashburton TQ13 7LJ (01364 652598; Fax: 01364 654004). A friendly, family-run farm site, set in 400 acres and surrounded by beautiful countryside. 12 miles to the sea and close to Dartmoor National Park. Ideal for touring Devon/Cornwall. Perfect for children and pets with all farm animals, play area and plenty of space to roam, also large area for dogs. Holiday cottages and caravans fully equipped except for linen. Level touring site with some hard standings. Electric hook-up. Free showers in fully tiled block, laundry room and games room. Small family bar, restaurant, shop and phone. Prices start from £90 Low Season to £480 High Season. Good discounts for couples. To find us: From Exeter take A38 to Plymouth till you see "26 miles Plymouth" sign; take second left at Alston Cross signposted to Woodland and Denbury. **ETC ★★★**, *AA FOUR PENNANTS, BRITISH FARM TOURIST AWARD. 2003 GOLD AWARD FOR QUALITY AND SERVICE. SILVER DAVID BELLAMY CONSERVATION AWARD. PRACTICAL CARAVAN TOP 100 PARKS 2003.*
e-mail: parkersfarm@btconnect.com   website: www.parkersfarm.co.uk

See also Colour Display Advertisement

COLYTON

Bonehayne Farm, Colyton EX24 6SG. Working farm. Enjoy a relaxing holiday deep in the tranquil Devon countryside. Bonehayne is a 250-acre family farm. Our six-berth luxury caravan is situated in the farmhouse garden. It is south-facing and overlooks the banks of the River Coly. It is quiet and tranquil and the caravan enjoys lovely surrounding views. Two miles from quaint little town of Colyton; four miles to coast. Children welcome – we have spacious lawns and animals to see. Good trout fishing, woodlands and walks. Laundry rooms, picnic tables, barbecue, deck chairs. Bed and Breakfast also available. Details from **Mrs S. Gould (01404 871416) and Mrs R. Gould (01404 871396).**
e-mail: gould@bonehayne.co.uk
website: www.bonehayne.co.uk

See also Colour Display Advertisement

WOOLACOMBE

Mrs Gilbert, North Morte Farm Caravan and Camping, Dept. FHG, Mortehoe, Woolacombe EX34 7EG (01271 870381). The nearest camping and caravan park to the sea, in perfectly secluded beautiful coastal country. Our family-run park, adjoining National Trust land, is only 500 yards from Rockham Beach, yet only five minutes' walk from the village of Mortehoe with a Post Office, petrol station/garage, shops, cafes and pubs – one of which has a children's room. Four to six berth holiday caravans for hire and pitches for tents, dormobiles and touring caravans, electric hook-ups available. We have hot showers and flush toilets, laundry room, shop and off-licence; Calor gas and Camping Gaz available; children's play area. Dogs accepted but must be kept on lead. Open Easter to end September. Brochure available. **ETC ★★★★**

DORSET

REDLANDS FARM CARAVAN PARK

...for Personal Service and Easiest Access to Weymouth Beach...

Very conveniently situated in a semi-rural location backing onto open fields, yet not too far from the town centre and 1½ miles from the seafront. Buses stop just outside the park entrance and serve not only the town centre but much of Dorset. Ideal for day trips exploring the lovely countryside.

- Thirty 4 - 8 berth modern luxury caravans for hire with all services plus colour TV and fridge
- Friendly family-run park • Launderette facilities • Supermarkets close by • Personal supervision
- Caravan sales • Children and Pets welcome • Plenty of official footpaths and country walks to explore • Car parking alongside caravans • Open March to November
- Terms per week £130 - £420

SAE for enquiries.

REDLANDS FARM CARAVAN PARK
DORCHESTER ROAD, WEYMOUTH,
DORSET DT3 5AP

Tel: 01305 812291 • Fax: 01305 814251

Redlands Sports Club is opposite the park where club, bar and sports facilities are available.
Membership open to all visitors.

See also Colour Advertisement.

See also Colour Display Advertisement

WIMBORNE
Woolsbridge Manor Farm Caravan Park, Three Legged Cross, Wimborne BH21 6RA (01202 826369). Situated approximately three-and-a-half-miles from the New Forest market town of Ringwood – easy access to the south coast. Seven acres level, semi-sheltered, well-drained spacious pitches. Quiet country location on a working farm, ideal and safe for families. Showers, mother/baby area, laundry room, washing up area, chemical disposal, payphone, electric hook-ups, battery charging. Children's play area on site. Site shop. Dogs welcome on leads. Fishing adjacent. Moors Valley Country Park golf course one mile. Pub and restaurant 10 minutes' walk. **AA** *THREE PENNANTS*, **ETC ★★★**

Sherborne Castle • *Sherborne, Dorset* • *01935 813182*
website: www.sherbornecastle.com
Built by Sir Walter Raleigh in 1594 and home to the Digby family since the early 17th century. Splendid collection of art, furniture and porcelain.

Abbotsbury Swannery
Near Bridport, Dorset • *01305 871858*
Up to 600 free-flying swans – help feed them twice daily. Baby swans hatch May/June.
AV show, coffee shop and gift shop.

KENT

Residential Park Homes, Leisure Homes and Tourist Park. Beautiful setting for a peaceful and relaxing holiday, set in the heart of the Kent countryside. An ideal base for visiting the many attractions nearby, from historic castles to quaint villages. Electric hook-ups available. A friendly welcome awaits you. Open March to October. Terms available on request.
Tel: 01580 291216 • e-mail: info@campingsite.co.uk
web: www.campingsite.co.uk

Woodlands Park
Tenterden Road, Biddenden
Kent TN27 8BT

Other specialised
FHG PUBLICATIONS

Published annually: available in all good bookshops or direct from the publisher.

PETS WELCOME! £7.99
Recommended **COUNTRY HOTELS** OF BRITAIN £6.99
Recommended **COUNTRY INNS & PUBS** OF BRITAIN £6.99
Recommended **SHORT BREAK HOLIDAYS** IN BRITAIN £6.99

**FHG PUBLICATIONS LTD,
Abbey Mill Business Centre,
Seedhill, Paisley, Renfrewshire PA1 1TJ
Tel: 0141-887 0428 • Fax: 0141-889 7204**
e-mail: fhg@ipcmedia.com
website: www.holidayguides.com

Visit the **FHG** website
www.holidayguides.com
for details of the wide choice of accommodation featured in the full range of FHG titles

NORTHUMBERLAND

Budle Bay Campsite

**WAREN MILL
BAMBURGH
NORTHUMBERLAND NE70 7EE**
Tel: 01668 214 598 (High Season)
or 01668 213 362
• 250 Pitches for Tourers & Tents
• Seasonal Touring Pitches • Electric Hook-up & Hard Stand.
• Winter Storage & Towage Services

On-site facilities include toilets and showers (free of charge), chemical disposal, launderette, snack bar, payphone, playpark, and during peak season (weather permitting) we have a bouncy castle and other rides for the children, as well as a number of small animals in Pets Corner. Sun bed hire is also available.

Situated in the north of Northumberland within easy reach of England's finest stretches of coastline, close to the Scottish border, there is something for everyone here. You can explore the North's tumultuous past, enjoy a round of golf, or go climbing, canoeing, wind-surfing or horse riding. Angling, hillwalking and watching the abundant wildlife are just some of the more peaceful pastimes on offer. There are plenty of good local pubs to visit, in Belford and Bamburgh. Early booking is strongly advised. Season runs from the beginning of March to the end of October. Storage available for the winter months. Please ask for details.

**Mrs Phyl Carruthers, Bluebell Farm, Belford, Northumberland NE70 7QE
Tel: 01668 213362 • E-mail: phyl.carruthers@virgin.net**

HEXHAM
**Mrs Archer, St Oswalds Farm, Wall, Hexham NE46 4HB
(01434 683231/681307).** Two six-berth caravans situated on small working farm on Hadrian's Wall on the B6318, five miles north of the market town of Hexham. Panoramic views over beautiful countryside. Both caravans have shower, flush toilets, TV, fridge; electricity and gas inclusive. Price from £120 to £185 per week. Please ring for details.

Grace Darling Museum • *Bamburgh, Northumberland* • *01668 214465*
Commemorates the rescue by Grace and her father of the nine survivors of the wreck of the Forfarshire. Many original relics, including the cable used in the rescue, plus books, paintings etc.

The FHG Directory of Website Addresses
on pages 345 - 373 is a useful quick reference guide for holiday accommodation with e-mail and/or website details

SOMERSET

CHEDDAR

Broadway House Holiday Touring Caravan and Camping Park, Cheddar BS27 3DB (01934 742610; Fax: 01934 744950). SELF-CATERING. Cheddar Gorge - "England's Grand Canyon." A totally unique four star caravan and camping family experience. One of the most interesting inland parks in the West Country. A family business specialising in family holidays. Visit our llama and parrot. Prices include the use of the heated outdoor swimming pool and entrance to the Bar/Family room. Activities from the park include fishing archery, shooting; bike hire; table tennis, crazy golf, boules, croquet, skate-board park, BMX track. **ETC ★★★★, AA** 5 PENNANTS, **RAC** APPOINTED, DAVID BELLAMY GOLD AWARD.
e-mail: enquiries@broadwayhouse.uk.com   website: www.broadwayhouse.uk.com

DULVERTON

Mrs M.M. Jones, Higher Town, Dulverton TA22 9RX (01398 341272). Working farm. Caravans sleep 8. Our farm is situated half-a-mile from open moorland, one mile from the Devon/Somerset border and four miles from Dulverton. 80 acres of the farm is in the Exmoor National Park. We let two caravans which are quarter-of-a-mile apart and do not overlook each other, and have lovely views, situated in lawns with parking space. Both are eight berth, with a double end bedroom, bunk bedroom, shower, flush toilet, hot/cold water and colour TV. The caravans are modern and fully equipped except linen. Cot and high chair available. One caravan new for season 1999 with three bedrooms. Visitors are welcome to watch the milking or walk over our beef and sheep farm. Riding and fishing nearby. Open May to October. Price from £115, includes gas and electricity.

SUFFOLK

SUDBURY
Mrs A. Wilson, Willowmere Camping Park, Bures Road, Sudbury CO10 0NN (01787 375559). This neat little site could be suitable for a weekend or as a touring base for inland Suffolk. It has just 40 pitches, 24 with electric points. Site has single toilet block of good quality and well maintained, with free hot water in the washbasins and showers. No other on-site amenities apart from milk, cold drinks, etc. Village shops half-a-mile away. Open Easter to October. AA, HPA. Terms per unit with two persons from £10.

EAST SUSSEX

See also Colour Display Advertisement

RYE (near)
Camber Sands, Camber, Near Rye TN31 7RT (0870 442 9284; Fax: 01797 225 756). Camber Sands faces seven miles of award-winning Blue Flag golden beach in East Sussex. This beautiful region is steeped in history, with unspoilt Sussex towns like Rye. The park itself has wonderful leisure facilities including four indoor pools, sauna, spa bath and solarium and presents a first-rate entertainment programme. Four fun pools with amazing whirlpool. Amusements centre. Dylan the Dinosaur children's club and outdoor play area. Family Fun Bar. Indoor games, competitions, pool and satellite TV. Bouncy Castle. Well-stocked convenience store. Fast-food cafe. Fishing, golf driving range nearby. ETC ★★★
e-mail: holidays@gbholidayparks.co.uk
website: www.gbholidayparks.co.uk

TYNE & WEAR

See also Colour Display Advertisement

WHITLEY BAY
The Links, Whitley Bay, Tyne and Wear NE26 4RR (0870 442 9282; Fax: 0191 297 1033). Whitley Bay is an immensely popular park that sits on the edge of a well-known seaside resort with a whole array of restaurants, cafes and bars. The walk from the park through to the resort is along a pleasant promenade with lovely views out towards St Mary's Lighthouse and a long stretch of beach. Facilities include a lovely indoor pool and inviting bars offering entertainment, Dylan the Dinosaur children's club and outdoor play area. Local sea fishing opportunities. Multi-sports court. Well-stocked convenience store. Cafe and popular takeaway. ETC ★★★★
e-mail: holidays@gbholidayparks.co.uk
website: www.gbholidayparks.co.u

TWO Gold All Day Passes for the price of ONE at
The New Metroland
see our READERS' OFFER VOUCHERS for details

NORTH YORKSHIRE

just 5 miles ...*from the centre of York!*

NEW 2003

This all-new park, which is open all year, has superb facilities including a full length Golf Driving Range and a 9 hole Putting Course.

welcome to our leisure park

Tel: **01904 499275**
www.yorkcaravansite.co.uk

Come and see us soon... ...*Perfect relaxation*

See also Colour Advertisement

One adult travels FREE when accompanied by a fare paying adult at
Embsay & Bolton Abbey Steam Railway
see our READERS' OFFER VOUCHERS for details

Eden Camp Modern History Museum • *Malton, North Yorkshire* • *01653 697777*
website: www.edencamp.co.uk
This award-winning museum will take you back to wartime Britain where you can experience the sights, sounds and smells of World War II.

Blacksheep Brewery Visitor Centre • *Masham, North Yorkshire* • *01765 689227*
website: www.blacksheepbrewery.com
Traditional working brewery with excellent visitor facilities including guided tours, bistro and gift shop.

The **FHG**
GOLF
GUIDE
Where to Play
Where to Stay

Available from most bookshops, **THE GOLF GUIDE** (published annually) covers details of every UK golf course – well over 2800 entries – for holiday or business golf. Hundreds of hotel entries offer convenient accommodation, accompanying details of the courses – the 'pro', par score, length etc.

In association with 'Golf Monthly' and including Holiday Golf in Ireland, France, Portugal, Spain, The USA, South Africa and Thailand

£9.99 from bookshops or from the publishers (postage charged outside UK) • FHG Publications, Abbey Mill Business Centre, Paisley PAI ITJ

ENGLAND

Activity Holidays

DEVON

HALDON LODGE FARM,
Kennford, Near Exeter EX6 7YG
Tel: (01392) 832312

In an attractive setting, three six-berth holiday caravans and log cabin in a private and friendly park. Fully equipped kitchen, lounge with TV, bathroom, toilet, H/C. Rates from £70 to £195 per week high season; tourers and campers welcome.

Excellent facilities. Open all year. Pets welcome.

Exeter and South Devon beaches 15 minutes, horse riding from a nearby farm. Three well-stocked coarse fishing lakes close by, also the attraction of barbecues and hayrides to a friendly country inn during school holidays.

Personal welcome given by David & Betty Salter.

ASHBURTON
Parkers Farm Holiday Park, Ashburton TQ13 7LJ (01364) 652598; Fax: 01364 654004). A friendly, family-run farm site, set in 400 acres and surrounded by beautiful countryside. 12 miles to the sea and close to Dartmoor National Park. Ideal for touring Devon/Cornwall. Perfect for children and pets with all farm animals, play area and plenty of space to roam, also large area for dogs. Holiday cottages and caravans fully equipped except for linen. Level touring site with some hard standings. Electric hook-up. Free showers in fully tiled block, laundry room and games room. Small family bar, restaurant, shop and phone. Prices start from £90 Low Season to £480 High Season. Good discounts for couples. To find us: From Exeter take A38 to Plymouth till you see "26 miles Plymouth" sign; take second left at Alston Cross signposted to Woodland and Denbury. **ETC ★★★, AA** *FOUR PENNANTS. BRITISH FARM TOURIST AWARD. 2002 GOLD AWARD FOR QUALITY AND SERVICE. SILVER DAVID BELLAMY CONSERVATION AWARD. PRACTICAL CARAVAN TOP 100 PARKS 2002*
e-mail: parkersfarm@btconnect.com   website: www.parkersfarm.co.uk

---

Admit one child FREE with each paying adult at
The Big Sheep
see our READERS' OFFER VOUCHERS for full details

SCOTLAND
Board Accommodation

Ratings You Can Trust

ENGLAND

The **English Tourism Council** (formerly the English Tourist Board) has joined with the **AA** and **RAC** to create a new, easily understood quality rating for serviced accommodation, giving a clear guide of what to expect.

HOTELS are given a rating from One to Five **Stars** – the more Stars, the higher the quality and the greater the range of facilities and level of services provided.

GUEST ACCOMMODATION, which includes guest houses, bed and breakfasts, inns and farmhouses, is rated from One to Five **Diamonds**. Progressively higher levels of quality and customer care must be provided for each one of the One to Five Diamond ratings.

HOLIDAY PARKS, TOURING PARKS and CAMPING PARKS are now also assessed using **Stars**. Standards of quality range from a One Star (acceptable) to a Five Star (exceptional) park.

Look out also for the new **SELF-CATERING** Star ratings. The more **Stars** (from One to Five) awarded to an establishment, the higher the levels of quality you can expect. Establishments at higher rating levels also have to meet some additional requirements for facilities.

SCOTLAND

Star Quality Grades will reflect the most important aspects of a visit, such as the warmth of welcome, efficiency and friendliness of service, the quality of the food and the cleanliness and condition of the furnishings, fittings and decor.

**THE MORE STARS,
THE HIGHER THE STANDARDS.**

The description, such as Hotel, Guest House, Bed and Breakfast, Lodge, Holiday Park, Self-catering etc tells you the type of property and style of operation.

WALES

Places which score highly will have an especially welcoming atmosphere and pleasing ambience, high levels of comfort and guest care, and attractive surroundings enhanced by thoughtful design and attention to detail

STAR QUALITY GUIDE FOR

HOTELS, GUEST HOUSES AND FARMHOUSES
SELF-CATERING ACCOMMODATION
(Cottages, Apartments, Houses)
CARAVAN HOLIDAY HOME PARKS
(Holiday Parks, Touring Parks, Camping Parks)

★★★★★ Exceptional quality
★★★★ Excellent quality
★★★ Very good quality
★★ Good quality
★ Fair to good quality

In England, Scotland and Wales, all graded properties are inspected annually by Tourist Authority trained Assessors.

ABERDEEN, BANFF & MORAY

KEITH

Mrs Jean Jackson, The Haughs Farm, Keith AB55 6QN (Tel & Fax: 01542 882238). The Haughs is a traditional mixed farm engaged in rotational cropping and cattle and sheep production. The spacious old farmhouse has a light cheerful dining room with excellent views. Ground floor bedrooms, three en suite, all with tea/coffee facilities and colour TV. The farm is situated just half-a-mile outside Keith and off the A96 Inverness road on the Whisky Trail; Falconry Centre eight miles. Open April to October. Bed and Breakfast from £19 to £21; Evening Meal £13. **STB ★★★** *GUEST HOUSE*, **AA ◆◆◆◆**

PORTSOY

Mrs Helen Christie, The Boyne Hotel, 2 North High Street, Portsoy AB45 2PA (01261 842242). This cosy, privately owned, coastal village hotel has recently been refurbished to a high standard. The hotel boasts twelve en suite bedrooms, two dining rooms, a TV and video lounge, public bar and a cocktail lounge bar complete with a small dance floor. Meals are served daily using the finest local produce. Portsoy has lovely sandy beaches and a natural outdoor pool. Situated on the Moray Firth Coast, it is an ideal centre for touring North East Scotland. Activities include golf, pony trekking, bird watching, sea angling, curling and bowls. Follow the Whisky, Castle and Coastal trails. Visit the Agricultural Heritage Centre, Baxters Visitor Centre and Portsoy Boat Festival. **STB ★★** *HOTEL*.
e-mail: enquiries@boynehotel.co.uk
website: www.boynehotel.co.uk

ARGYLL & BUTE

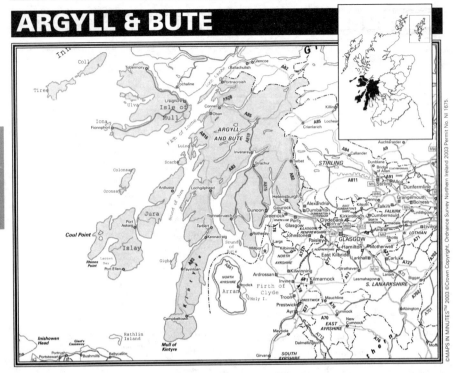

CARRADALE
Mrs D. MacCormick, Mains Farm, Carradale, Campbeltown PA28 6QG (01583 431216). Working farm. From April to October farmhouse accommodation is offered at Mains Farm, five minutes' walk from safe beach, forestry walks with views of Carradale Bay and Arran. Near main bus route and 15 miles from airport. Golf, sea/river fishing, pony trekking, canoeing locally. Comfortable accommodation in one double, one single, one family bedrooms; guests' sitting/dining room with coal/log fire; bathroom, toilet. Heating in rooms according to season. Children welcome at reduced rates, cot and high chair available. Pets by prior arrangement. The house is not suitable for disabled visitors. Good home cooking and special diets catered for. Bed and Breakfast from £17.50. Tea making facilities in rooms. **STB ★★** *B&B*.

CARRADALE
Mr A. Milstead, Dunvalanree, Port Righ, Carradale, Kintyre PA28 6SE (01583 431226; Fax: 01583 431339). Dunvalanree was built in 1939 and has been welcoming guests ever since. The owners' advertising grab line is "at the waters edge", and it would be difficult to imagine a place closer to the sea with great views to the golf course and Arran hills across Kilbrannan Sound. Alyson has been awarded both 'Taste of Scotland' and two RAC Dining Awards and has been accredited by the Vegetarian Society. In 2001 Dunvalanree was voted by guests to be the best hotel in the local tourist area. The area abounds with wildlife (there are often seals in the bay), and history (this is where Robert the Bruce landed in 1306), or just come and chill out. From £55 per person for Dinner, Bed and Breakfast. Room for disabled guests. Also self-catering cottage for two available. **STB ★★★★** *SMALL HOTEL*, **RAC ♦♦♦♦♦**
e-mail: fhg@dunvalanree.com website: www.dunvalanree.com

SCOTLAND / Board — Argyll & Bute

See also Colour Display Advertisement

DALMALLY

Rockhill Waterside Country House, Ardbrecknish, By Dalmally PA33 1BH (01866 833218). 17th century guest house in spectacular waterside setting on Loch Awe with breathtaking views to Ben Cruachan, where comfort, peace and tranquillity reign supreme. Small private Highland estate breeding Hanoverian competition horses. 1200 metres free trout fishing. Five delightful rooms with all modern facilities. First-class highly acclaimed home cooking with much home-grown produce. Wonderful area for touring the Western Highlands, Glencoe, the Trossachs and Kintyre. Ideal for climbing, walking, bird and animal watching. Boat trips locally and from Oban (30 miles) to Mull, Iona, Fingal's Cave and other islands. Dogs' Paradise! Also self-catering cottages.
www.rockhillhanoverianstud.co.uk

HELENSBURGH

Mrs Elizabeth Howie, Drumfork Farm, Helensburgh G84 7JY (01436 672329). Traditional sandstone farmhouse, extensively refurbished; all rooms en suite, some with sea views. Organic food served and we offer packed lunches, afternoon teas and high teas. The Victorian seaside town of Helensburgh, with its wide streets and stylish architecture, is port of call for the paddle steamer, 'Waverley', and the site of the Hill House by Charles Rennie Mackintosh. Open all year. Babysitting available. Bed and Breakfast from £18 pppn. Non-smoking. STB ★★★ B&B.
e-mail: drumfork@supanet.com

LOCHGOILHEAD

Mrs Rosemary Dolan, The Shorehouse Inn, Lochgoilhead PA24 8AJ (01301 703340). Friendly informal Inn, fully licensed, has five letting rooms, central heating and double glazing. There are two family, two double, and one single bedrooms; a bar of unusual character and a licensed restaurant. Home cooking, bar meals. Formerly the old manse on a historic site with lochside and panoramic views looking southward down Loch Goil, situated in the village on the shore. Local amenities include water sports, fishing, pony trekking, tennis, bowls, golf, swimming pool, curling in winter and a good area for hill walking. Some rooms with private facilities. Fully licensed. One hour travel time from Glasgow. Open all year round. Ideal for winter or summer breaks. Rates from £18 per person Bed and Breakfast, en suite £23 per person; £6 supplement for single occupancy of double room.

See also Colour Display Advertisement

OBAN

Mrs J. Currie, Hawthorn, 5 Keil Crofts, Benderloch, Oban PA37 1QS (01631 720452). A warm welcome awaits you in this delightful bungalow set in 20 acres of farmland where we breed our own Highland cattle which graze at the front. It is a peaceful location as we are set back from the road, and an ideal spot for touring, with the main ferry terminal at Oban just 10 minutes away. Our luxurious rooms have their own special sitting room attached where you can enjoy your coffee or a glass of wine in peace.
e-mail: junecurrie@hotmail.com
website: www.hawthorncottages.co.uk

20% DISCOUNT on all admissions at
Oban Rare Breeds Farm Park
see our READERS' OFFER VOUCHERS for details

AYRSHIRE & ARRAN

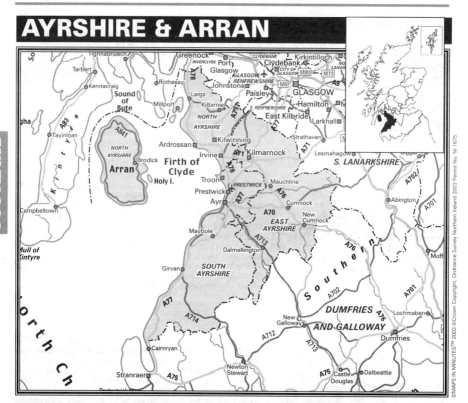

See also Colour Display Advertisement

AYR

Mrs Agnes Gemmell, Dunduff Farm, Dunure, Ayr KA7 4LH (01292 500225; Fax: 01292 500222). Welcome to Dunduff Farm where a warm, friendly atmosphere awaits you. Situated just south of Ayr at the coastal village of Dunure, this family-run beef and sheep unit of 600 acres is only 15 minutes from the shore providing good walks and sea fishing and enjoying close proximity to Dunure Castle and Park. Accommodation is of a high standard yet homely and comfortable. Bedrooms have washbasins, radio alarm, tea/coffee making facilities, central heating, TV, hair dryer and en suite facilities (the twin room has private bathroom). There is also a small farm cottage available sleeping two/four people. Bed and Breakfast from £25 per person; weekly rate £170. Cottage from £250 per week. Colour brochure available. **STB ★★★★ B&B, AA/RAC ◆◆◆◆◆**
e-mail: gemmelldunduff@aol.com
website: www.gemmelldunduff.co.uk

KILMARNOCK

Mrs Nancy Cuthbertson, West Tannacrieff, Fenwick, Kilmarnock KA3 6AZ (01560 600258; mobile: 07773 226332; Fax: 01560 600914). A warm welcome awaits all guests at our dairy farm, situated in the peaceful Ayrshire countryside. Relax in spacious well-furnished en suite rooms with all modern amenities, colour TV and tea/coffee making facilities. Large parking area and garden. Situated off the A77 on the B751 road to Kilmaurs, so easily accessible from Glasgow, Prestwick Airport and the south. An ideal base for exploring Ayrshire's many tourist attractions. Enjoy a hearty breakfast with home-made breads and preserves and home-baking for supper. Children welcome. Terms from £20 per person. Brochure available. **STB ★★★★ B&B.**
e-mail: westtannacrieff@btopenworld.com
website: www.SmoothHound.co.uk/hotels/westtannacrieff.htm

BORDERS

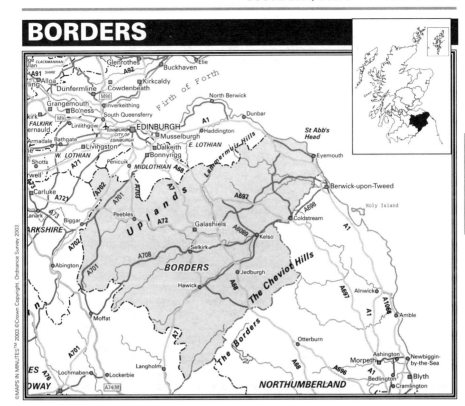

KELSO

Mrs Debbie Playfair, Morebattle Tofts Farm, Kelso TD5 8AD (01573 440364; Fax: 01573 440634). Working farm. Elegant 18th century farmhouse set amongst the Cheviot foothills where a warm welcome awaits you. Three acres of gardens and a woodland with tennis court. Ideally situated for touring the Borders. Accommodation includes two elegantly furnished double rooms en suite and twin room with private bathroom. Beautiful drawing room for guests' own use with TV. The working farm is noted for its pedigree cattle and sheep. Situated seven miles south of Kelso. Fishing, golf and wonderful walking. Bed and Breakfast from £25 per person. Reductions for children. Write or telephone for booking details and directions.
e-mail: debbytofts@aol.com
website: www.scotland2000.com/morebattle

TRAQUAIR

Mrs J. Caird, The Old School House, Traquair, Innerleithen EH44 6PL (Tel & Fax: 01896 830425). The Old School House has been recently modernised. Stands above picturesque Traquair village, with spectacular views of the River Tweed valley. The Southern Upland Way passes close by; perfect walking and riding country. Nearby is Innerleithen Golf Course, historic Traquair House and Kailzie Garden with fishing lake. Salmon and trout fishing on Tweed; horses can be hired or bring your own. Peebles is an attractive Border town with splendid woollen shops and a swimming pool. Edinburgh 35 minutes by car. Children and dogs welcome; stabling available; resident cats, dogs, ponies, hens and sometimes puppies. Log fire; home-cooked evening meals on request.

e-mail: caird@old-schoolhouse.NDO.co.uk
website: www.old-schoolhouse.NDO.co.uk

DUMFRIES & GALLOWAY

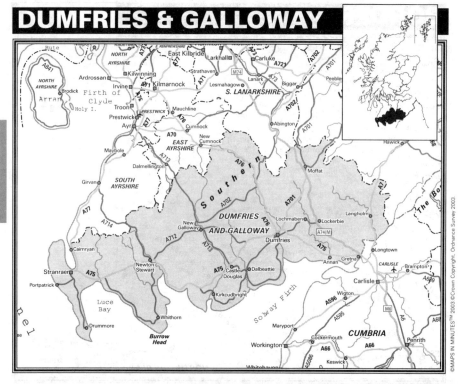

CANONBIE
Miss G. Matthews, Four Oaks, Canonbie DG14 0TF (013873 71329). Bed and Breakfast accommodation in comfortable, peaceful family home, with open views of lovely rolling countryside and farmland. Near the village of Canonbie, off the A7 just north of Carlisle, providing an excellent base for touring the Borderlands. Near River Esk. Accommodation provided in one twin room en suite, one double room with en suite bathroom with bath and shower. Cot available. Visitors' lounge with TV, tea/coffee making facilities. Garden and good parking. Terms £20 to £22. **STB ★★★ B&B**

CROSSMICHAEL (Galloway)
Mr James C. Grayson, Culgruff House Hotel, Crossmichael DG7 3BB (01556 670230). Culgruff is a former Baronial Mansion standing in its own grounds of over 35 acres, overlooking the beautiful Ken Valley and the loch beyond. The hotel is comfortable, ideal for those seeking a quiet, restful holiday. An excellent position for touring Galloway and Burns country. The hotel is half-a-mile from A713 Castle Douglas to Ayr road, four miles from Castle Douglas and A75 to Stranraer. Many places of interest in the region - picturesque Solway coast villages, gardens, castles (including Culzean), the Ayrshire coast. For holiday activities - tennis, riding, pony trekking, bowls, golf, fishing (salmon, fly, coarse and sea), boating, water ski-ing, windsurfing, swimming etc. Lovely walks. All rooms have washbasins (some

en suite), electric blankets, tea/coffee facilities; ample bathroom/toilet facilities. All bedrooms have TVs. Large family rooms available. One of the lounges has colour TV; dining room. Central heating. Cot. Non-smoking accommodation if required. Car advisable, parking. Bed and Breakfast from £15 per person in large family rooms, doubles from £23.50 per person. Open from Easter to October. Restricted October to Easter. Home of author James Crawford.

GRETNA
Mr Gary Beattie, Guards Mill Farm, Gretna DG16 5JA (01461 338358). Modern farmhouse accommodation in separate units on this family-run mixed farm. One double and one family room, both with shower en suite, TV, radio, tea/coffee making facilities and central heating. Convenient for M74/M6. Parking available. Non-smoking. Children welcome. Open March to November. B&B £18 per person per night. Short breaks available. STB ★★ B&B.

STRANRAER
Mrs. J. Waugh, East Challoch Farmhouse, Dunragit, Stranraer DG9 8PY (01581 400391). East Challoch farmhouse is situated seven miles from Stranraer and has beautiful views overlooking Luce Bay. We offer home from home comfortable spacious accommodation. All bedrooms have colour TV, tea/coffee making facilities, central heating and all have en suite bathrooms. A cosy lounge with a real log fire is there to relax in and dinner is available by request. An ideal area for exploring gardens, walking, cycling, fishing, birdwatching and golf. Pony trekking is within one mile. A self catering cottage is also available on the farm. Send for colour brochures. Bed and Breakfast from £20 per person. STB ★★★ B&B.

DUNDEE & ANGUS

BRECHIN
Rosemary Beatty, Brathinch Farm, By Brechin DD9 7QX (01356 648292; Fax: 01356 648003). Working farm. Brathinch is an 18th century farmhouse on a family-run working arable farm, with a large garden, situated off the B966 between Brechin and Edzell. Rooms have private or en suite bathroom, TV and tea/coffee making facilities. Shooting, fishing, golf, castles, stately homes, wildlife, swimming and other attractions are all located nearby. Easy access to Angus Glens and other country walks. Double £20, twin £21, single £22 - £25. Open all year. We look forward to welcoming you.
STB ★★★ B&B.
e-mail: adam.brathinch@btinternet.com

Sensation Science Centre • Dundee • 01382 228800
website: www.sensation.org.uk
A unique 4-star visitor attraction devoted to the five senses, with over 60 hands-on exhibits, live science shows and workshops.

FREE or REDUCED RATE entry to Holiday Visits and Attractions — see our READERS' OFFER VOUCHERS on pages 67 - 94

EDINBURGH & LOTHIANS

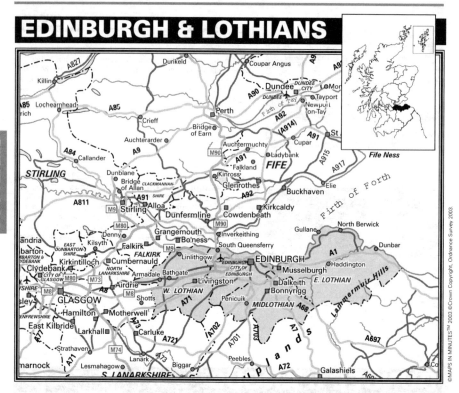

MUSSELBURGH

Inveresk House, Inveresk Village, Musselburgh EH21 7UA (0131-665 5855; Fax: 0131-665 0578). Historic Mansion house and award-winning Bed & Breakfast. Family-run "home from home". Situated in three acres of garden and woodland. Built on the site of a Roman settlement from 150 AD, the remains of a bathhouse can be found hidden in the garden. Three comfortable en suite rooms. Original art and antiques adorn the house. Edinburgh's Princes Street seven miles from Inveresk House. Good bus routes. Families welcome. Off-street parking. Telephone first. Price from £40 per person. Family room £100 to £120.
e-mail: chute.inveresk@btinternet.com
website: http://travel.to/edinburgh

See also Colour Display Advertisement

PATHHEAD

FAIRSHIELS

Mrs Anne Gordon, "Fairshiels", Blackshiels, Pathhead EH37 5SX (01875 833665). We are situated on the A68, three miles south of Pathhead at the picturesque village of Fala. The house is an 18th century coaching inn (Listed building). All bedrooms have washbasins and tea/coffee making facilities; one is en suite. All the rooms are comfortably furnished. We are within easy reach of Edinburgh and the Scottish Borders. A warm welcome is extended to all our guests – our aim is to make your stay a pleasant one. Cost is from £18.50 per person; children two years to 12 years £11.50, under two years FREE.

SCOTLAND / Board Fife **275**

FIFE

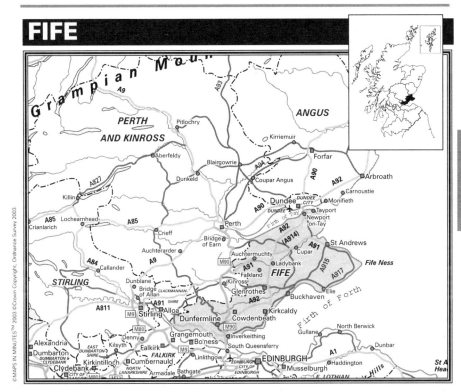

ST ANDREWS

Mrs Anne Duncan, Spinkstown Farmhouse, St Andrews KY6 8PN (Tel & Fax: 01334 473475). Working farm. Only two miles from St Andrews on the picturesque A917 road to Crail, Spinkstown is a uniquely designed farmhouse with views of the sea and surrounding countryside. Bright and spacious, it is furnished to a high standard. Accommodation consists of double and twin rooms, all en suite, with tea/coffee making facilities and colour TV; diningroom and lounge. Substantial farmhouse breakfast to set you up for the day. The famous Old Course, historic St Andrews and several National Trust properties are all within easy reach, as well as swimming, tennis, putting, bowls, horse riding, country parks, nature reserves, beaches and coastal walks. Plenty of parking available. Bed and Breakfast from £24.
STB ★★★★ *B&B, AA* ◆◆◆◆

e-mail: anne@spinkstown.com   website: www.spinkstown.com

Scotland's Secret Bunker • *Near St Andrews, Fife* • *01333 310301*
website: www.secretbunker.co.uk
An amazing labyrinth built 100ft below ground, from where the country would have been run in the event of nuclear war. The command centre with its original equipment can be seen, AV theatre and two cinemas.

---

*When making enquiries or bookings,
a stamped addressed envelope is always appreciated*

HIGHLANDS

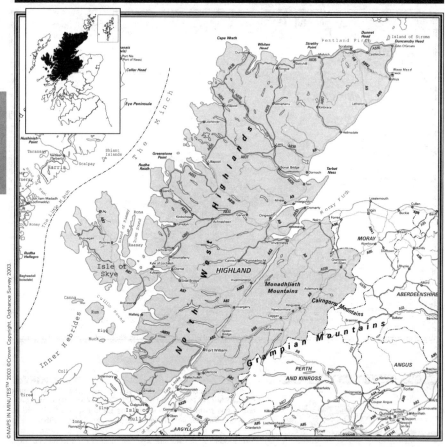

HIGHLANDS (NORTH)

ARDGAY
Mrs Moffat, Sgodachail, Braelangwell, Ardgay IV24 3BP (01863 755322). Warm Highland welcome in a peaceful location with views over the river to the beautiful hills. Ideal for nature lovers. The house is situated in a typical Highland glen where the hills and sky dominate the land, scenery unique to this part of Scotland. Accommodation comprises three bedrooms, one with private bathroom, two twin bedrooms share a bathroom. Situated six miles from Ardgay village, two miles from Croick Church, the centre of the Highland clearances. Railway station is six miles away. No bus service. Activities include golf, horse riding and fishing with permits. Bed & Breakfast is £16; £18 including private facilities. No evening meals.

HIGHLANDS (SOUTH)

Dunain Park Hotel

A small, luxury, family-owned and run country house hotel, secluded in beautiful gardens. Two miles from Inverness, five miles from Loch Ness. High standards of comfort and service; cuisine is Scottish/French. Open fires, over 200 malt whiskies. Indoor heated swimming pool, sauna. Accommodation includes 6 suites, four-poster bedroom, two cottages.

DUNAIN PARK HOTEL, INVERNESS IV3 8JN
www.dunainparkhotel.co.uk
e-mail: dunainparkhotel@btinternet.com

Tel: 01463 230512
Fax: 01463 224532

See also Colour Advertisement

INVERNESS
Mrs E. MacKenzie, The Whins, 114 Kenneth Street, Inverness IV3 5QG (01463 236215). Comfortable, homely accommodation awaits you here 10 minutes' walking distance from town centre, bus and railway stations, Inverness being an excellent touring base for North, West and East bus and railway journeys. Bedrooms have TV and tea making facilities, washbasin and heating off-season. Bathroom has a shared shower and toilet. Two double/twin rooms from £17 per person per night. Write or phone for full details. Non-smoking.

INVERNESS
Glen Mhor Hotel, 8-13 Ness Bank, Inverness IV2 4SG (01463 234 308; Fax: 01463 713170). Established in 1957, the Glen Mhor Hotel is situated in a beautiful, tranquil location on the River Ness in the heart of Inverness. Our business and leisure visitors have enjoyed friendly, attentive service from Management and Staff, many with many years' service well into double figures. We are just a few minutes' walk away from the city centre, railway station, Eden Court Theatre and other attractions. The bedrooms are spread over four adjacent properties, all of the same high standard and individually decorated. Our restaurants, Nico's and The Riverview, are by far the longest established Seafood Restaurants in Inverness and are renowned for the excellence of the Made In Scotland cuisine. Innovative, international and traditional themes on poultry, beef, lamb, vegetarian and game in season.

e-mail: glenmhorhotel@btconnect.com   website: www.glen-mhor.com

INVERNESS
The Waterside Hotel, 19 Ness Bank, Inverness IV2 4SF (01463 233065; Fax: 01463 241075). Beautifully located on the river bank and within five minutes' walk of the city centre, The Waterside is a family-owned and professionally run hotel where Management and Staff will ensure all your needs are catered for. The new owners, Mr and Mrs Manson, have recently refurbished the Function Suite as well as refitting the reception and function area and it is intended that by March 2004 all the bedrooms will have undergone significant upgrading to maintain the hotel's position at the upper end of the three star hotel market. The Waterside Brasserie, with its fabulous river views, and the Cocktail Bar offer freshly prepared and imaginatively presented food with an impressive range of wines, beers, malts and spirits. A sound base to tour the Highlands, offering a warm welcome and Highland hospitality.
e-mail: info@thewatersideinverness.com   website: www.thewatersideinverness.com

---

A useful index of towns and counties appears at the back of this book on pages 375 - 378. Refer also to Contents Pages 2 and 3.

PERTH & KINROSS

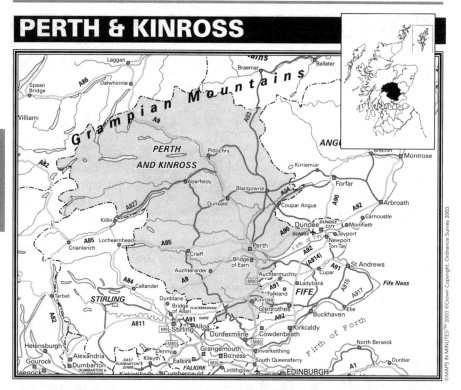

BRIDGE OF CALLY
Mrs Josephine MacLaren, Blackcraig Castle, Bridge of Cally PH10 7PX (01250 886251 or 0131-551 1863). A beautiful castle of architectural interest situated in spacious grounds. Free trout fishing on own stretch of River Ardle. Excellent centre for hill walking, golf and touring – Braemar, Pitlochry (Festival Theatre), Crieff, Dunkeld, etc. Glamis Castle within easy reach by car. Three double, two twin, two family and one single bedroom, all with washbasin; two bathrooms, three toilets and one shower. Cot, high chair. Dogs welcome free of charge. Car essential – free parking. Open for guests from 1st July to 7th September. £27 per person per night includes full Breakfast plus night tea/coffee and home baking at 10pm in the beautiful drawing room which has a log fire. Reduced rates for children under 14 years. Enquiries November to end June to **1 Inverleith Place, Edinburgh EH3 5QE.**

FHG PUBLICATIONS publish a large range of well-known accommodation guides. We will be happy to send you details or you can use the order form at the back of this book.

STIRLING & THE TROSSACHS

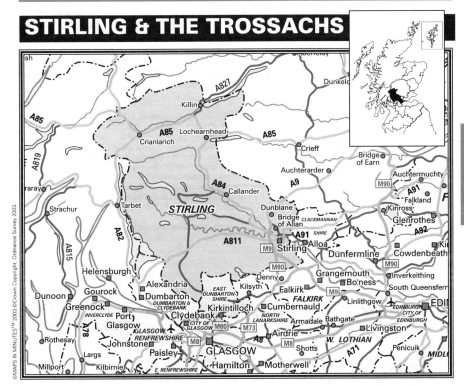

BLAIRLOGIE

Mrs Margaret Logan, Blairmains Farm, Manor Loan, Blairlogie, Stirling FK9 5QA (01259 761338). Working farm. Charming, traditional stone farmhouse set in attractive gardens on a working dairy farm with a herd of pedigree Holstein cattle. Adjacent to a picturesque conservation village and close to the Wallace Monument and Stirling University. Three-and-a-half miles from Stirling. Edinburgh airport is 30 minutes' drive and Glasgow airport 45 minutes. Ideal base for touring and walking. Accommodation is in one double and two twin rooms with shared bathroom. Very comfortable TV lounge. Ample private parking at this non-smoking establishment. Children welcome. Sorry no pets. Bed and Breakfast terms – double or twin £20; single £22 to £25. Room only £18. A warm Scottish welcome awaits you.

The Falkirk Wheel • *Falkirk, Stirlingshire* • *08700 500208*
website: *www.thefalkirkwheel.co.uk*
Measuring 115ft. the world's only rotating boatlift links the Forth & Clyde and Union Canals using state-of-the-art engineering. Visitor centre and boat trips.

FREE or REDUCED RATE entry to Holiday Visits and Attractions – see our READERS' OFFER VOUCHERS on pages 67 - 94

SCOTTISH ISLANDS

Isle of Coll

ARINAGOUR
Ruth Sturgeon, Tigh-na-Mara FHG, Arinagour, Isle of Coll PA78 6SY (01879 230354). This licensed guest house offers spectacular views to Mull and the Treshnish Isles. Explore magnificent sandy beaches, visit the RSPB Reserve - perhaps spot an elusive corncrake? Roam amidst a profusion of wild flowers or relax in the lounge whilst keeping a watchful eye for otters and admire the ever changing moods of the sea. All rooms have washbasin, electric blankets, tea/coffee making facilities and mini bar. Interesting 9 hole golf course and fishing nearby; cycle hire available. Bed and Breakfast from £23, Evening Meal £15. A self-catering cottage is also available.
e-mail: ruth@tighnamara.info

Isle of Skye

PORTREE
The Royal Hotel, Portree, Isle Of Skye IV51 9BU (01478 612525; Fax: 01478 613198). Set overlooking the picturesque harbour of Portree, The Royal Hotel offers you a quiet, relaxing retreat during your stay on Skye. Recently refurbished, offering new standards in comfort and style. Accommodation consists of 21 well appointed rooms, some equipped to accommodate families, most overlooking the harbour and featuring private bathroom facilities and colour TV. Room service is available as well as a fitness centre and sauna for guests to use. The Royal Hotel offers a wide and varied menu serving sea food, lamb, venison and tender Highland beef. Vegetarians are also catered for. There is something for everyone; from walking, climbing and watersports. **STB ★★★ HOTEL. RAC ★★**
e-mail: info@royal-hotel-skye.com
website: www.royal-hotel-skye.com

Talisker Distillery • *Isle of Skye* • 01478 640314
The only distillery on the island, set in an area of great natural beauty. Talisker is one of the six 'classic malts'– friendly guides reveal some of the mysteries of its production, with a sample to taste before you leave.

The FHG Directory of Website Addresses
on pages 345 - 373 is a useful quick reference guide for holiday accommodation with e-mail and/or website details

SCOTLAND
Self-catering Accommodation

SCOTLAND from BORDERS to HIGHLANDS

Superb, personally inspected, self catering holiday properties in beautiful rural and coastal locations including Burns country, Cowal, the West Coast & Isles and Speyside. Cosy cottages to country houses, many welcome pets and short breaks are available.

Dales Holiday Cottages

0870 909 9500
www.dalesholcot.com

ABERDEEN, BANFF & MORAY

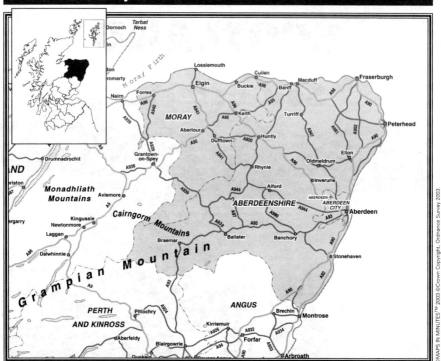

ABERDEEN

See also Colour Display Advertisement
The Robert Gordon University, Business & Vacation Accommodation, Schoolhill, Aberdeen AB10 1FR (01224 262134; Fax: 01224 262144). The Robert Gordon University in the heart of Aberdeen offers a variety of accommodation in the city centre to visitors from June through to August. Aberdeen is ideal for visiting Royal Deeside, castles and historic buildings, playing golf or touring the Malt Whisky Trail. The city itself is a place to discover and Aberdonians are friendly and welcoming people. We offer 2-Star self-catering accommodation for individuals or groups at superb rates in either en suite or shared facility flats. Each party has exclusive use of their own flat during their stay. The flats are self-contained, centrally heated, fully furnished and suitable for children and disabled guests. All flats have colour TV, microwave, bedlinen, towels, all cooking utensils and a complimentary "welcome pack" of basic groceries. There are laundry and telephone facilities on site as well as ample car parking spaces. *ASSC MEMBER.*
e-mail: p.macinnes@rgu.ac.uk   website: www.scotland2000.com/rgu

FORRES

See also Colour Display Advertisement
Tulloch Lodges. Peace, Relaxation and Comfort in beautiful Natural Surroundings. One of the loveliest self-catering sites in Scotland. Modern, spacious, attractive and beautifully equipped Scandinavian lodges for up to six in glorious woodland/water setting. Perfect for the Highlands and Historic Grampian, especially the Golden Moray Coast and the Golf, Castle and Malt Whisky Trails. **STB ★★★/★★★★** £240 to £675 per week. *SELF-CATERING.* For a brochure contact: **Tulloch Lodges, Rafford, Forres, Moray IV36 2RU (01309 673311; Fax: 01309 671515).** *ASSC MEMBER.*
e-mail: enquiries@tullochlodges.com
website: www.tullochlodges.com

SCOTLAND / Self-catering — Aberdeenshire, Banff & Moray

INVERURIE

> See also Colour Display Advertisement

Mr and Mrs P. A. Lumsden, Kingsfield House, Kingsfield Road, Kintore, Inverurie AB51 0UD (01467 632366; Fax: 01467 632399). 'The Greenknowe' is a comfortable detached and renovated cottage in a quiet location at the southern edge of the village of Kintore. It is in an ideal situation for touring castles, historic sites and distilleries, or for walking, fishing and even golf. The cottage is all on one level with a large south-facing sittingroom overlooking the garden. It sleeps four people in one double and one twin room. A cot is available. Parking adjacent. Open from March to November. Prices from £275 to £475 per week, inclusive of electricity (the cottage is all-electric) and linen. Walkers Welcome Scheme. STB ★★★ SELF-CATERING. ASSC MEMBER.
e-mail: kfield@clara.net

TURRIFF

> See also Colour Display Advertisement

Forglen Country Cottages. 10 cottages, sleep 6-9. The Estate lies along the beautiful Deveron River and our traditional stone cottages nestle in individual seclusion. Visitors can explore one of the ancient baronies of Scotland. The sea is only nine miles away, and the market town of Turriff only two miles, with its golf course, swimming pool, etc. Places of interest including the Cairngorms, Aviemore, picturesque fishing villages and castles, all within easy reach on uncrowded roads. See our Highland cattle. Six miles of own walks. Terms from £159 weekly. Special winter lets. Children and reasonable dogs welcome. **STB** inspected. Wildlife haven. **Mrs P. Bates, Holiday Cottages, Forglen Estate, Turriff, Aberdeenshire AB53 4JP (01888 562918/562518; Fax: 01888 562252).**
website: www.forglen.co.uk

TWO for the price of ONE entry to exhibition (based on full adult rate only) at
The Grassic Gibbon Centre
see our READERS' OFFER VOUCHERS for details

Ballindalloch Castle • *Ballindalloch, Moray* • *01807 500206*
website: www.ballindallochcastle.co.uk
16th century castle, home of the Macpherson-Grant family since 1546 with many interesting artefacts. Famous Aberdeen-Angus herd, gardens, tearoom and shop.

The **FHG**
GOLF GUIDE
Where to Play
Where to Stay

Available from most bookshops, **THE GOLF GUIDE** (published annually) covers details of every UK golf course – well over 2800 entries – for holiday or business golf. Hundreds of hotel entries offer convenient accommodation, accompanying details of the courses – the 'pro', par score, length etc.

In association with 'Golf Monthly' and including Holiday Golf in Ireland, France, Portugal, Spain, The USA, South Africa and Thailand

£9.99 from bookshops or from the publishers (postage charged outside UK) • **FHG Publications, Abbey Mill Business Centre, Paisley PAI ITJ**

ARGYLL & BUTE

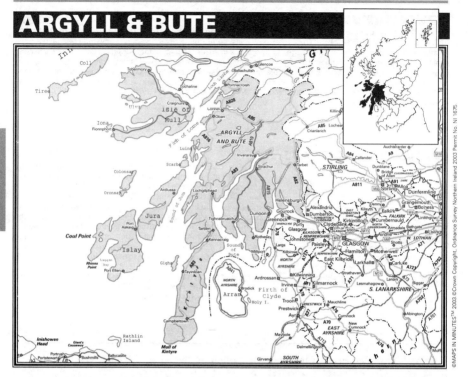

See also Colour Display Advertisement

APPIN

Ardtur Cottages, Appin. Two adjacent cottages in secluded surroundings on promontory between Port Appin and Castle Stalker, opposite north end of Isle of Lismore. Ideal centre for hill walking, climbing etc.(Glencoe and Ben Nevis half hour drive). Direct access across the field to sea (Loch Linnhe). Tennis court available by arrangement. Boat hire, pony trekking, fly fishing all available locally. Accommodation in first cottage is suitable for eight people in one double and three twin-bedded rooms, large dining/sittingroom/kitchenette and two bathrooms. Second cottage accommodates six people in one double and two twin-bedded rooms, dining/sittingroom/kitchenette and bathroom. Everything is provided except linen. Shops one mile; sea 200 yards. Pets allowed. Car essential, parking. Open March/October.
Terms from £165 to £375 weekly. SAE, please for full details to **Mrs J. Pery, Ardtur, Appin PA38 4DD (01631 730223 or 01626 834172)**
e-mail: pery@eurobell.co.uk

20% DISCOUNT on all admissions at

Oban Rare Breeds Farm Park

see our READERS' OFFER VOUCHERS for details

Situated on beautiful Seil Island with wonderful views of surrounding countryside. These lovingly restored cottages (one detached and one attached to the main croft house) retain their traditional character while incorporating all modern facilities. The cottages are near to each other and ideal for two families on holiday together. Seil is one of the most peaceful and tranquil spots in the West Highlands, with easy access to neighbouring Isles of Luing and Easdale. Oban, the hub for trips to Mull and Iona, is half an hour's drive away over the famous 18th century "Bridge Over The Atlantic". Wonderful area for hillwalking, cycling, fishing and bird watching.
Short breaks from £35.00 per day.

KILBRIDE CROFT
BALVICAR, ISLE OF SEIL, ARGYLL PA34 4RD
CONTACT: MARY & BRIAN PHILLIPS
TEL: 01852 300475
e-mail: kilbridecroft@aol.com
website: www.kilbridecroft.fsnet.co.uk

See also Colour Advertisement

Self-catering Holidays in Unspoilt Argyll at
THE HIGHLAND ESTATE OF ELLARY AND CASTLE SWEEN

One of the most beautiful areas of Scotland with a wealth of historical associations such as St Columba's Cave, one of the first places of Christian worship in Britain, also Castle Sween, the oldest ruined castle in Scotland, and Kilmory Chapel where there is a fascinating collection of Celtic slabs.

PEACE, SECLUSION, OUTSTANDING SCENERY AND COMPLETE FREEDOM TO PURSUE INDIVIDUAL HOLIDAY PASTIMES.

Loch, sea and burn fishing, swimming, sailing and observing a wide variety of wildlife can all be enjoyed on the estate and there are many attractive paths and tracks for the walker. Various small groups of cottages, traditional stone-built as well as modern, are strategically scattered throughout the estate. All have wonderful views and are near to attractive stretches of shore; in many cases there is safe anchorage for boats close by. Most of the cottages accommodate 6, but one will take 8. All units are fully equipped except linen. TV reception is included.
For further details, brochure and booking forms please apply to: **ELLARY ESTATE OFFICE**
By Lochgilphead, Argyll PA31 8PA
01880 770209/770232
or 01546 850223
info@ellary.com   www.ellary.com

FHG PUBLICATIONS
publish a large range of well-known accommodation guides. We will be happy to send you details or you can use the order form at the back of this book.

286 Argyll & Bute — Self-catering / SCOTLAND

See also Colour Display Advertisement

DALMALLY
Mr & Mrs E. Crawford, Blarghour Farm, Lochaweside, By Dalmally PA33 1BW (01866 833246; Fax: 01866 833338). At Blarghour, a working hill farm on the shores of lovely Loch Awe, the holiday guest has a choice of high quality, well appointed, centrally heated, double glazed accommodation of individual character, each enjoying its own splendid view over loch and mountain in this highly scenic area. Barn House sleeps two, Stable House accommodates four, Barr-beithe Lower sleeps five and Barr-beithe Upper sleeps six. All have fitted kitchens with fridge/freezer, washing machine, microwave and electric cooker; telephone and TV. The cottages at Barr-beithe also include a dishwasher, and a cot and highchair are also available. Linen and towels are supplied. Parking beside each house. Barn and Stable Houses are unsuitable for children under five years. No pets allowed. Open all year. The area, centrally situated for touring, offers opportunities for walking, bird-watching, boating and fishing. Golf is available at Dalmally and Inveraray. Colour brochure sent on request.
e-mail: blarghour@btconnect.com   website: www.self-catering-argyll.co.uk

See also Colour Display Advertisement

DALMALLY
Mrs E. Fellowes, Inistrynich, Dalmally PA33 1BQ (01838 200256; Fax: 01838 200253). Two cottages overlooking Loch Awe, surrounded by beautiful scenery, making the perfect retreat for a peaceful holiday. Garden Cottage (sleeps 8), Millside Cottage (sleeps 4). Dalmally five miles, Inveraray 11 miles, Oban 28 miles. Both have garden area, convector heaters in all rooms, open fire in living rooms, electric cooker, fridge, immersion heater, electric kettle, iron, vacuum cleaner, washing machine, colour TV. Cot and high chair by request. Dogs allowed by arrangement. Car essential, ample parking. Ideal for touring mainland and Inner Hebrides. Good restaurants, hill walking, forest walks, fishing, boat hire, pony trekking. NT gardens and golf within easy reach. Open Easter to November. Colour brochure available. STB★★★ *SELF CATERING*.
e-mail: dlfellowes@supanet.com   website: www.loch-awe.com/inistrynich

See also Colour Display Advertisement

OBAN
Cologin Country Chalets. Set in a tranquil glen less than three miles from Oban, our cosy chalets and atmospheric country pub/restaurant are a winning combination. Enjoy the waymarked forest trails in the hills above our farm, or relax in front of the fire and sample home-cooked local produce in the pub. The attractions of Oban – "Gateway to the Islands" – are minutes away. Pets and children are welcome – we have a playpark, games byre, and 17,000 acres to walk the dog. Disabled access chalets are available. Free fishing on our hill loch; boats and rods provided. Short breaks from £30, weekly lets from £180 to £510. STB ★★★ to ★★★★ *SELF CATERING*. **Mrs Linda Battison, Cologin House, Lerags Glen, By Oban PA34 4SE (01631 564501; Fax: 01631 566925).** *ASSC MEMBER*.
e-mail: cologin@west-highland-holidays.co.uk   website: www.west-highland-holidays.co.uk

OBAN (By)

Eleraig Highland Lodges, Kilninver, By Oban PA34 4UX (Tel & Fax: 01852 200225). Sleep 4/7. These seven well-equipped, widely spaced chalets are set in breathtaking scenery in a private glen 12 miles south of Oban, close to Loch Tralaig, with free brown trout fishing and boating - or bring your own boat. Peace and tranquillity are features of the site, located within an 1800 acre working sheep farm. Walkers' and bird-watchers' paradise. Children and pets are especially welcome. Cots and high chairs available. Gliding, water skiing and other sports, pastimes and evening entertainment are available locally. Car parking by each chalet. Open March to November. From £205 per week per chalet including electricity and bed linen. Colour brochure from resident owners **Anne and Robin Grey**. STB ★★★ and ★★ *SELF-CATERING*.
website: www.scotland2000.com/eleraig

SCOTLAND / Self-catering — Argyll & Bute

See also Colour Display Advertisement

TARBERT

Amanda Minshall, Dunmore Court, Kilberry Road, Near Tarbert, Argyll PA29 6XZ (01880 820654). Five cottages in architect design conversion of home farm on the estate of Dunmore House. Spacious accommodation for 2-8 persons. All have stone fireplaces for log fires. Bird-watching, fishing and walking. Easy access to island ferries. Pets welcome. Open all year. Colour brochure. From £175-£490. **STB** ★★ *SELF CATERING*. *ASSC MEMBER*
e-mail: dunmorecourtsc@aol.com
website: www.dunmorecourt.com

TAYNUILT

Inverawe House, Taynuilt PA35 1HU (01866 822446; Fax: 01866 822274). **Cottages sleep 2/6.** Three delightful cottages, accommodating 2-6 people. The cottages are fully equipped with laundry facilities, freezers, open fires and gardens to enjoy. Set amidst the most breathtaking of scenery, overlooking the River Awe, Inverawe is ideally situated for holidays. With walking, fishing, golf and tennis on the door step, it is a paradise for all country lovers. It is brilliant for touring Argyll, with Glencoe in the north or Crinan Canal and the standing stones in Kilmartin in the south. Oban, our local coastal town, is 17 miles. It is the gateway to the islands and offers many day excursions - a visit to Mull and Duart Castle is a must. Ideal for the family and pets are very welcome. Inverawe lets you completely relax and get away from it all.
e-mail: holidays@inverawe.co.uk
website: www.inverawe-fisheries.co.uk

TAYNUILT

Jenifer Moffat, Airdeny Chalets, Glen Lonan, Taynuilt PA35 1HY (01866 822648). Airdeny Chalets – secluded, peaceful, ideal for touring Highlands and Islands, walking, cycling and golf. Three holiday chalets situated on private land. Taynuilt one mile, Oban 12 miles; wonderful views of Ben Cruachan and Glen Etive. The chalets sleep four/six and are equipped to a very high standard. Parking at each chalet. Ideal safe family setting. Dogs welcome by prior arrangement. Owner resident. Prices from £195 to £395.
e-mail: jenifer.moffat@airdenychalets.co.uk
website: www.airdenychalets.co.uk

FHG

Other specialised **FHG PUBLICATIONS** published annually: available in all good bookshops or direct from the publisher.

PETS WELCOME! £7.99
Recommended **COUNTRY HOTELS** OF BRITAIN £6.99
Recommended **COUNTRY INNS & PUBS** OF BRITAIN £6.99
Recommended **SHORT BREAK HOLIDAYS** IN BRITAIN £6.99

FHG Publications Ltd, Abbey Mill Business Centre,
Seedhill, Paisley, Renfrewshire PA1 1TJ
Tel: 0141-887 0428 • Fax: 0141-889 7204
e-mail: fhg@ipcmedia.com • website: www.holidayguides.com

AYRSHIRE & ARRAN

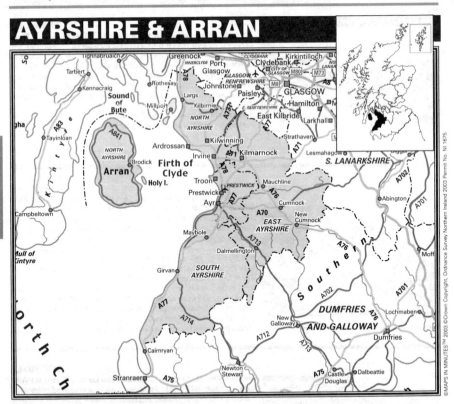

BALLANTRAE

Mrs M. Drummond, Balnowlart Farm, Ballantrae KA26 0LA (01465 831343). Working farm. Sleeps 6. Luxury country lodge situated in lovely Stinchar Valley near old fishing village of Ballantrae, with shopping facilities, sea fishing, tennis court, putting green, bowling, golf courses within easy reach. Beautiful scenery, places of historic interest, many unspoilt beaches, with rock formations said to be among the oldest in the world. Ideal spot for touring Burns Country and Alloway, with panoramic views at Glen Trool in Bonnie Galloway. Daily sailings from Stranraer and Cairnryan to Northern Ireland. Accommodation for six comprises sitting/dining room with open fires (fuel included), three bedrooms (two double, one twin), bathroom with electric shower, fully equipped kitchen, immerser. Heating, metered electricity, telephone. Tastefully furnished throughout. Linen included. Ample parking – car essential. Pets by arrangement. Available all year. Terms from £130 per week. **STB ★★★ SELF-CATERING.**

KILMARNOCK

Mrs M. Howie, Hillhouse Farm, Grassyards Road, Kilmarnock KA3 6HG (Tel & Fax: 01563 523370). Bungalow situated in open countryside on a working farm two miles east of Kilmarnock. Easy access to Ayrshire coast, numerous golf courses, Glasgow and Loch Lomond. The bungalow is fully equipped for six people and comprises three bedrooms, cot if required, lounge with colour TV and fire; kitchen with electric cooker, fridge/freezer, washer/dryer, etc.; bathroom with shower. Garden. Storage heaters. Linen and towels supplied. Weekly rates £200 to £320. **STB ★★★ SELF-CATERING.** Bed and Breakfast available in farmhouse from £20. **STB ★★★★ B&B.**

The Island of Arran

See also Colour Display Advertisement

ARRAN
Arran HideAways, Invercloy House, Brodick, Isle of Arran KA27 8AJ. Choice of properties on the island, available throughout the year. All villages, all dates. Self-catering and bunk house accommodation available. STB Quality Assured. Short breaks available. Major credit cards accepted. Please ask for our brochure. On-line booking and availability. Our staff are here to help you seven days a week. **Call 01770 302303/302310.** *ASSC MEMBER.*
e-mail: holidays@arran-hideaways.co.uk
website: www.arran-hideaways.co.uk

KILMORY
Kilbride Farmhouse. Sleeps 5-7 adults, 2 children. Adjacent to a working farm. Located towards the south end of the Isle of Arran, with extensive gardens towards the front and a secluded and enclosed yard to the rear, ideal for family holidays. Kilbride enjoys sea views towards Ireland and Ailsa Craig to the South and towards Campbeltown and those romantic sunsets over Kintyre to the West. The long, sandy beach of Torrylinn is nearby, whilst the hills, golf courses and other attractions are only a short drive away. Accommodation comprises on first floor: two twin rooms, one single, bunk room with bunk-bed, bathroom with shower and bath,W.C. and wash hand basin. Ground floor: sitting room with open fire, sofa and TV/video, kitchen with oil-fired stove, electric hob and oven, microwave, and farmhouse dining table. Shower room/cloakroom. Spacious garage with games table(s). Prices from £510 per week. Enquiries: **Arran Estate Office, Douglas Park, Brodick, Isle of Arran KA27 8EJ (01770 302203, Fax: 01770 302813).**
e-mail: hazelwood.arran@virgin.net   website: www.arranland.net/farmhouse.html

PIRNMILL
Mrs Dale, The Wee Rig, Pirnmill, By Brodick, Isle of Arran KA27 8HP (01770 850228). Situated on a slightly elevated site, within a spacious garden to the side of the main house, in a unique secluded position flanked by sheltering woodlands but with fine open outlook to panoramic views and sunsets over the Kilbrannan Sound to Kintyre. Across the road the low tide reveals a clean sandy expanse which is habitat to various seabirds. Wider exploration of our unspoiled picturesque island, termed "Scotland in miniature" offers much variety with rugged mountains, rolling farmlands, interesting bird/wildlife, castles, distillery, golf (seven courses), walking, cycling, ponies plus various visitor centres, swimming facilities, etc. An overall sense of peace and relaxation which we warmly welcome you to share with us. Terms from £240 per week. **STB ★★★** *SELF-CATERING.*

TWO for the price of ONE at
Dunaskin Heritage Centre
see our READERS' OFFER VOUCHERS for details

TWO for the price of ONE at
Scottish Maritime Museum
see our READERS' OFFER VOUCHERS for details

BORDERS

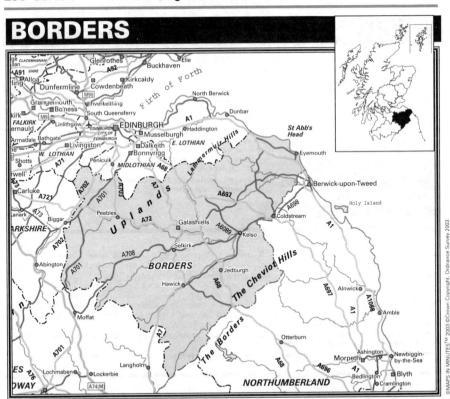

ASHKIRK

Wendy and Chris Davies, Synton Mains Holiday Cottages, Synton Mains Farm, Ashkirk, Selkirk TD7 4PA (Tel & Fax: 01750 32388). Sleep 6+6. Two beautifully renovated, semi-detached farm cottages positioned to one side of a farm steading, located in the heart of the Scottish Borders, an ideal base for touring and sightseeing. Both cottages are well furnished and extremely well-equipped, with double glazing, oil central heating and woodburning stoves. Lawned to front and sides; terrace with patio furniture. One cottage is suitable for disabled, having double bedroom downstairs with en suite bathroom, shower available for wheelchair users. We have our own golf driving range, small private loch for fishing; horse riding and golf available locally. Pets welcome by arrangement. Terms from £170 to £360 per week.

e-mail: Syntonmains@Tinyworld.co.uk
website: www.Syntonmains-holidaycottages.co.uk

See also Colour Display Advertisement

JEDBURGH

Mill House, Letterbox and Stockman's Cottages. Three recently renovated, quality Cottages, each sleeping four, on a working farm three miles from Jedburgh. Ideal centres for exploring, sporting holidays or getting away from it all. Each cottage has two public rooms (ground floor available). Minimum let two days. Terms £190–£330. Open all year. Bus three miles, airport 54 miles. **STB ★★★★ SELF-CATERING. Mrs A. Fraser, Overwells, Jedburgh TD8 6LT (01835 863020; Fax: 01835 864334). ASSC MEMBER.**
e-mail: abfraser@btinternet.com
website: www.overwells.co.uk

PEEBLES

Mrs R. Smith, Chapelhill Farm, Peebles EH45 8PQ (01721 720188; Fax: 01721 729734). Three delightful cottages on working farm situated in quiet, peaceful location with superb country views. The popular town of Peebles with its many shops, hotels, pubs and restaurants is less than a mile away. Edinburgh just 30 minutes by car. All cottages have central heating throughout, electric cooker, microwave and washing machine. Heating and bed linen included in price. Garden and garden furniture. Ample parking. Children most welcome. Dogs by arrangement. Many golf courses, beautiful walks, fishing, horse riding, cycling etc. All nearby. Brochures available. Prices from £150-£320 per week. Farmhouse B&B also available. STB ★★★ SELF CATERING.

DUMFRIES & GALLOWAY

PORTPATRICK

Mr A.D. Bryce, "Alinn", Portpatrick DG9 8JW (01776 810277). Seafront situation with unrestricted views of harbour and boats, overlooking small sandy beach with safe bathing. Golf, bowling, tennis and sea angling, scenic cliff walks and ideal country roads for touring. Shops and restaurants nearby. Area is of great historical and archaeological interest and enjoys a mild climate. Cottage with two bedrooms. Electric heating, cooking etc. Prepayment coin meter. Terms from £150 to £215 per week. Parking at door. Please write or telephone for further details.

DUNDEE & ANGUS

BROUGHTY FERRY

Kingennie Fishings and Holiday Lodges, Kingennie, Broughty Ferry DD5 3RD (01382 350777; Fax: 01382 350400). The four modern Lodges provide luxury self-catering holiday accommodation; all have colour TV and are well insulated and centrally heated. Set in secluded woodland, they enjoy views over the fishing ponds below, where experts and beginners alike can try their skills. GLENCLOVA, sleeping up to seven has been specially designed for disabled visitors, GLENISLA and GLENESK, sleeping four to six, both enjoy lovely views. THE BARD'S NEUK is situated in a quiet secluded corner site. The nearby towns, villages, beaches and countryside around the area provide many fascinating and enjoyable trips all of which can be covered within a day. Pets welcome. Weekly terms from £230 to £465 for Esk, Clova and Isla Lodges; from £363 to £765 for The Bard's Neuk. STB ★★★★ SELF-CATERING.
e-mail: kingennie@easynet.co.uk   website: www.kingennie-fishings.com

KIRRIEMUIR (by)

D. Smith, Scobshaugh Farm, Cortachy, By Kirriemuir DD8 4QH (01575 540214; Fax: 01575 540355). Sleep 5, 6. Modern farmhouse and farm cottage on working farm five miles from Kirriemuir on B955 road to Glen Clova. Both houses approximately one mile from main road. Bed linen and towels are provided and terms are from £180 to £250 per week, electricity and heating extra. Children very welcome, sorry no dogs. Please phone or fax for more details.

Sensation Science Centre • *Dundee* • *01382 228800*
website: www.sensation.org.uk
A unique 4-star visitor attraction devoted to the five senses, with over 60 hands-on exhibits, live science shows and workshops.

HIGHLANDS

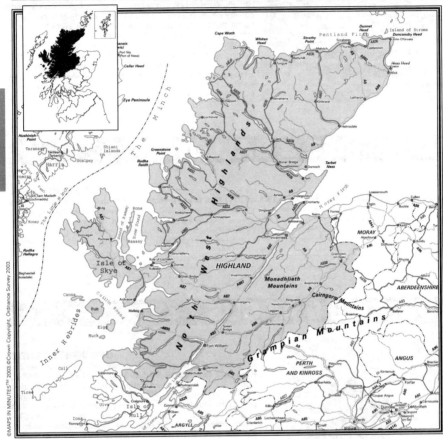

The FHG GOLF GUIDE
Where to Play Where to Stay

Available from most bookshops, THE GOLF GUIDE (published annually) covers details of every UK golf course – well over 2800 entries – for holiday or business golf. Hundreds of hotel entries offer convenient accommodation, accompanying details of the courses – the 'pro', par score, length etc.

In association with 'Golf Monthly' and including Holiday Golf in Ireland, France, Portugal, Spain, The USA, South Africa and Thailand

£9.99 from bookshops or from the publishers (postage charged outside UK) • FHG Publications, Abbey Mill Business Centre, Paisley PA1 1TJ

HIGHLANDS (NORTH)

ARDGAY

Mrs M.C. MacLaren, The Poplars, Ardgay, Sutherland IV24 3BG (01863 766302). Sleeps 6. Detached cottage standing in its own grounds with private parking. Fully furnished except for linen, accommodation comprises one double, one king and one bedroom with bunk beds (all with duvets and covers); sitting room with open fire, electric fire and TV; bathroom with shower; kitchen/dining room with electric cooker, washing machine, refrigerator, microwave, kettle, toaster and iron, together with cutlery, pans, crockery and radio. The cottage is clean and comfortable. Immersion heater for hot water; electric fires in all rooms. Dornoch Cathedral (where Madonna and Guy Ritchie were married), Royal Dornoch Golf Course and beautiful safe sandy beaches only 14 miles away. Skibo Castle, Tain, Brora and Golspie golf courses all within easy reach. Angling, mountain biking, hill walking, wildlife and forest walks all available locally. Tariff £150 to £220 per week.

JOHN O' GROATS

Stable Cottage. Sleeps 6. Standing adjacent to a Listed former mill, which boasts the oldest Highland military bridge (1651), Stable Cottage enjoys panoramic views across the Pentland Firth, with wonderful sunsets, a photographer's paradise. Located in a rural hamlet and within walking distance of the local shop, restaurants and passenger ferry service to Orkney. Nearby the towering cliffs and seastacks of Dunnet and Duncansby Head provide an ideal location for walking and bird-watching. Quaint harbours and an abundance of clean, safe, golden beaches to explore. Accommodation comprises three double bedrooms (one en suite), bathroom with toilet and washbasin, open-plan kitchen/dining/ seating area - fully furnished and well equipped. Electric heating, colour TV, washing machine, microwave, fridge and electric cooker. Ample parking space is available. STB ★★★ SELF CATERING. Contact Mrs Sina Houston, Mill House, John O' Groats, By Wick, Caithness KW1 4YR (01955 611239).

STRATHNAVER

Mrs C.M. MacLeod, Achnabourin, Strathnaver, Near Bettyhill KW11 6UA (01641 561210). Comfy country cottage situated beside the River Naver in the lovely Strathnaver Valley, six miles from coast and village of Bettyhill, 14 miles from Tongue, both with lovely sandy beaches. An ideal base for touring the rugged north coast of Scotland or for just enjoying the local walks and scenery. Trout fishing available. Two double and one twin-bedded rooms, sitting room with open or electric fire, kitchen with electric cooker, fridge, deep freeze, microwave, automatic washing machine, toaster, etc; bathroom. Fully equipped except linen. Open March to October. Rates from £150 to £180 per week. Electricity extra. For full details send SAE.

One FREE adult or child with adult paying full entrance price at
Highlands and Rare Breeds Farm
see our READERS' OFFER VOUCHERS for details

HIGHLANDS (MID)

Achnahaird Farm Cottages are situated right beside a large, sandy beach and sand dunes, with stunning panoramic views of the bay and the mountains beyond.
CUL MOR, CUL BEAG and SUILVEN COTTAGES, a recent conversion of a 200 years' old traditional Highland Lodge, offer quality STB 4-star accommodation, sleeping 2-4 guests. All have full oil-fired central heating and open fire, making these cottages a comfortable retreat at any time of the year
THE FARM COTTAGE, sleeping 5, is a spacious well-equipped STB 3-star family cottage with cosy multi-fuel stove in the lounge. All bed linen and towels are supplied in all cottages.
Children and well-behaved pets are welcome.
Price range £250 -£420 per week.

For further details contact: Mrs Marilyn Mackenzie, Achnahaird, Achiltibuie, Ross-shire IV26 2YT
Tel/Fax: 01854 622245 • e-mail: Mackenzie@achnahaird.freeserve.co.uk • web: www.achnahairdfarm.com
See also Colour Advertisement

Conchra Farm Cottages
Open all year
STB ★★ Self-catering

See also Colour Advertisement

Comfortable, fully modernised traditional farm cottages adjacent to working farm. Tranquil lochside setting, convenient for exploring Skye and the Highlands. Fully equipped; central heating, electricity and bed linen incl. Excellent value for money and ideal for families, walking and activity holidays.

Gardener's Cottage • 2 single, one double, one twin   **£175-£415 per week**
Shepherd's Cottage • one family, one twin
Farmer's Cottage • one double, one single, one family. For details contact:

Conchra Farm Cottages, Tigh-na-Coille, Argyll IV40 8DZ
Tel & Fax: 01599 555474 • www.conchracottages.co.uk
e-mail: enquiries@conchracottages.co.uk

See also Colour Display Advertisement   **POOLEWE**
Innes Maree Bungalows, Poolewe IV22 2JU (Tel & Fax 01445 781454). Only a few minutes' walk from the world-famous Inverewe Gardens in magnificent Wester Ross. A purpose-built complex of six superb modern bungalows, all equipped to the highest standards of luxury and comfort. Each bungalow sleeps six with main bedroom en suite. Children and pets welcome. Terms from £190 to £425 inclusive of bed linen and electricity. Brochure available. **STB ★★★★** *SELF-CATERING*. ASSC MEMBER.
e-mail: fhg@poolewebungalows.com   website: www.poolewebungalows.com

---

See also Colour Display Advertisement   **ULLAPOOL (near)**
Broomview & Sunset. Enjoy peace and tranquillity in the North West Highlands in the comfort of our accommodation. These properties overlook picturesque Loch Broom where panoramic views and spectacular sunsets can be seen. Broomview is on the ground floor. One double en suite bedroom, one double and one single bedroom both with wash hand basins. Bathroom, utility, spacious, well-equipped kitchen/dining room, lounge with colour TV and video. Sunset is on the upper floor with a double and single bedroom, shower room, utility, kitchen and lounge with colour TV and video. Ideal base for touring. Children welcome. Sorry, no pets. Colour brochure available. Broomview from £250 to £365, Sunset £195 to £290. **STB ★★★★** *SELF-CATERING*.
For further information contact: **Mrs Linda Renwick, Spindrift, Keppoch Farm, Dundonnell, By-Garve, Ross-shire IV23 2QR** (Tel & Fax: 01854 633267).

HIGHLANDS (SOUTH)

See also Colour Display Advertisement

ARISAIG

Arisaig House Cottages. Luxurious, secluded accommodation in mature woodland. Set in an area of breathtaking coastal and hill scenery, and wonderful sandy beaches. Mountain bike hire and fishing on Loch Morar can be arranged. Golf seven miles, swimming pool 13 miles. Hard tennis court. Day trips to the Small Isles and to Skye. Various properties, sleeping from two to eight persons. On-line booking. Details from: **Andrew Smither, Arisaig House, Beasdale, Arisaig, Inverness-shire PH39 4NR (Tel & Fax: 01687 462 686).** *ASSC MEMBER.*
e-mail: enquiries@arisaighouse-cottages.co.uk
website: www.arisaighouse-cottages.co.uk

See also Colour Display Advertisement

CULLODEN (By Inverness)

Blackpark Farm, Westhill, Inverness IV2 5BP (01463 790620; Fax: 01463 794262). This newly-built holiday home is located one mile from Culloden Battlefield with panoramic views over Inverness and beyond. Fully equipped with many extras to make your holiday special, including oil-fired central heating to ensure warmth on the coldest of winter days. Ideally based for touring the Highlands including Loch Ness, Skye etc. Extensive information is available on our website. A Highland welcome awaits you. *ASSC MEMBER.*
e-mail: i.alexander@blackpark.co.uk   website: www.blackpark.co.uk

FORT WILLIAM

Ben View Self Catering. Sleeps 6. A fully-equipped detached house with garage and small garden. It is ideally situated on the A82 Glasgow - Inverness road, only three minutes' walk from Fort William town centre, bus and rail stations and the Leisure Centre. The accommodation comprises one double room with en suite facilities, two twin-bedded rooms and a shower room with WC. The house has a well equipped fitted kitchen and a spacious, luxurious dining/lounge area with log fire. Bedding is provided and a travel cot is available on request. Starter pack is also available if desired. **Mrs Smith, Ben View Guest House, Belford Road, Fort William PH33 6ER (01397 772017).**
e-mail: BenView@gowanbrae.co.uk
website: www.benviewguesthouse.co.uk

FORT WILLIAM

Great Glen Holidays, Torlundy, Fort William PH33 6SW (01397 703015: Fax 01397 703304). Sleeps 4/6. Eight timber chalets situated in woodland with spectacular mountain scenery. These spacious two bedroom lodges are attractively furnished with linen provided. On working Highland farm. Riding, fishing and walking on farm. Ideal for family holidays and an excellent base for touring; four miles from town. Prices from £250 to £480 per week. **STB ★★** *SELF-CATERING.*
e-mail: chris@greatglenchalets.demon.co.uk
website: www.greatglenchalets.demon.co.uk

FREE entry to 'Heather Story" exhibition at
Speyside Heather Garden & Visitor Centre
see our READERS' OFFER VOUCHERS for details

296 Highlands (South) / Lanarkshire   Self-catering / SCOTLAND

See also Colour Display Advertisement

KINCRAIG
Loch Insh Log Chalets, Kincraig PH21 1NU (01540 651272). Just six miles south of Aviemore these superb log chalets are set in 14 acres of woodland in the magnificent Spey Valley, surrounded on three sides by forest and rolling fields with the fourth side being half a mile of beach frontage. Free watersports hire for guests, 8.30-10am/4-5.30pm daily. Sailing, windsurfing, canoeing, salmon fishing, archery, dry ski slope skiing. Hire/instruction available by the hour, day or week mid-April to end of October. Boathouse restaurant on the shore of Loch Insh offering coffee, home-made soup, fresh salads, bar meals, children's menu and evening à la carte. Large gift shop and bar. Three children's adventure areas, three kilometres lochside/woodland walk/interpretation trail, ski slope, mountain bike hire and stocked trout lochan are open all year round. Ski, snowboard hire and instruction available December to April. *ASSC MEMBER.*
e-mail: office@lochinsh.com
website: www.lochinsh.com

See also Colour Display Advertisement

NEWTONMORE
Crubenbeg Holiday Cottages, Newtonmore PH20 1BE (01540 673566; Fax: 01540 673509). Rural self-catering cottages in the central Highlands where one can relax and stroll from the doorstep or take part in the choice of many sporting activities in the area. We have a children's play area, a games room, pond stocked with trout for fishing and a barbecue. Pets welcome. STB ★★★★ *SELF CATERING.*
e-mail: enquiry@crubenbeg.com
website: www.crubenbeg.com

See also Colour Display Advertisement

ONICH
Cuilcheanna Cottages and Caravans, Onich, Fort William PH33 6SD. Three cottages and eight caravans (6 x 2003 models) situated on a small peaceful site. The cottages are built to the highest standards with electric heating, double glazing and full insulation. Tastefully furnished and fully equipped, each cottage has a large picture window in the main living area which look out over Loch Leven and Glencoe. Adjacent car parking. Laundry room and phone box on site. Only a short walk from the centre of Onich and an ideal base from which to explore the West Highlands. Paradise for hillwalkers. The caravans also have full facilities. Whether your stay with us is a long one, or just a few days, we shall do our best to ensure that it is enjoyable. Weekend Breaks available, winter rates, off season discounts. *ASSC MEMBER.*
For further details please telephone **01855 821526** or **01855 821310.**

LANARKSHIRE

See also Colour Display Advertisement

BIGGAR (Clyde Valley)
Carmichael Country Cottages, Carmichael Estate Office, Westmains, Carmichael, Biggar ML12 6PG (01899 308336; Fax: 01899 308481). Working farm, join in. Sleep 2/7. These 200-year-old stone cottages nestle among the woods and fields of our 700-year-old family estate. Still managed by the descendants of the original Chief of Carmichael. We guarantee comfort, warmth and a friendly welcome in an accessible, unique, rural and historic time capsule. We farm deer, cattle and sheep and sell meats and tartan – Carmichael of course! Children and pets welcome. Open all year. Terms from £190 to £535. 15 cottages with a total of 32 bedrooms. We have the ideal cottage for you. Private tennis court and fishing loch; cafe, farm shop and visitor centre. STB ★★/★★★★
SELF-CATERING. ASSC MEMBER. FARM STAY UK MEMBER.
e-mail: chiefcarm@aol.com   website: www.carmichael.co.uk/cottages

PERTH & KINROSS

See also Colour Display Advertisement

DUNKELD (By)
Laighwood Holidays, Butterstone, By Dunkeld PH8 0HB (01350 724241; Fax: 01350 724212). Properties sleep 2/8. A de luxe detached house, comfortably accommodating eight, created from the West Wing of a 19th century shooting lodge with panoramic views. Two popular cottages sleeping four to six, situated on our hill farm, with beautiful views. Two well-equipped apartments adjoining Butterglen House near Butterstone Loch. Butterstone lies in magnificent countryside (especially Spring/Autumn), adjacent to Nature Reserve (ospreys). Central for walking, touring, historic houses, golf and fishing. Private squash court and hill loch (wild brown trout) on the farm. Sorry no pets. Terms: House £424 to £660; Cottages and Apartments £165 to £375 per week. **STB** ★★★ to ★★★★ *SELF-CATERING. ASSC MEMBER.*
e-mail: holidays@laighwood.co.uk
website: www.laighwood.co.uk

KENMORE
Mr Robin Menzies, Mains of Taymouth Cottages, Kenmore, Aberfeldy PH15 2HN (01887 830226; Fax: 01887 829059). Mains of Taymouth Cottages are set in magnificent Highland Perthshire by the village of Kenmore amidst the finest scenery Scotland has to offer. We are surrounded by lovely walks, good fishing, Kenmore Golf Course is on our doorstep and activities abound from water sports and mountain biking to Highland Adventure safaris. Our five cottages are based around an 18th century courtyard and vary from a cosy two-bedroomed cottage to an extensive luxury four-bedroom with en suite facilities, large garden, sauna and hot tub. All cottages are traditional stone built and tastefully modernised with full central heating, open fires, dishwashers and all other mod cons you would possibly need. The cottages are in a quiet private setting with easy access to the golf course and restaurant and everything the area has to offer.
e-mail: info@taymouth.co.uk
website: www.taymouth.co.uk

SCOTTISH ISLANDS

Orkney

DEERNESS
Mrs M. Eunson, Staye, Deerness KW17 2QH (01856 741240). Sleeps 8. Farmhouse, situated in a quiet, rural area, with sandy beaches nearby and only ten miles from Kirkwall. Five minutes' walk to shop and post office, with ferry 25 miles away, and airport seven. Four bedrooms; one king-size, one double and two twin, with cot also supplied. Fully equipped kitchen/diningroom. Oil central heating, electricity charged at 7p per unit. All bed linen supplied. Ample parking. Sorry, no pets. Terms from £220 to £320 per week. **STB** ★★★ *SELF-CATERING.*

SCOTLAND
Caravans & Camping

ARGYLL & BUTE

KINLOCHLEVEN

Mrs Patsy Cameron, Caolasnacon Caravan & Camping Park, Kinlochleven PA40 4RS (01855 831279). There are 20 static six-berth caravans for holiday hire on this lovely site with breathtaking mountain scenery on the edge of Loch Leven - an ideal touring centre. Caravans have electric lighting, Calor gas cookers and heaters, toilet, shower, fridge and colour TV. There are two toilet blocks with hot water and showers and laundry facilities. Children are welcome and pets allowed. Open from April to October. Milk, gas, soft drinks available on site; shops three miles. Sea loch fishing, hill walking and boating; boats and rods for hire, fishing tackle for sale. Weekly rates from £200 for vans; 10% reductions on two week bookings. Tourers from £9.35 nightly. Seven and a half acres for campers - rates from £6.25 nightly.

DUMFRIES & GALLOWAY

NEWTON STEWART

Whitecairn Farm Caravan Park, Glenluce, Newton Stewart DG8 0NZ (01581 300267). Peacefully set by a quiet country road, one-and-a-half-miles from the village of Glenluce with panoramic views over the rolling Galloway countryside to Luce Bay. This family-run park offers a choice of two different caravan types sleeping up to six, all of a high standard and fully equipped except for linen. Amenities include shop, children's play area, launderette, telephone, toilet blocks and shower rooms. Electric hook-ups on touring pitches. The six acre site offers freedom for children of all ages and dogs are welcome under strict control. Colour brochure available. Open all year. STB ★★★★ HOLIDAY PARK.

PORTPATRICK

Adam and Liz Mackie, Galloway Point Holiday Park, Portpatrick, Stranraer DG9 9AA (01776 810561). This David Bellamy Silver Award park, family owned and managed, offers panoramic views over the Irish Sea and has a plethora of historic sites and gardens in the area for you to visit. Galloway Point makes an ideal base for touring the area, walking, golf and fishing holidays. We also have new luxurious caravan holiday homes for hire and a small selection for sale. This family-owned park is an excellent choice for short breaks as well as main holidays in Bonnie Galloway. A warm family welcome awaits you. **RAC, AA** 3 PENNANTS, DAVID BELLAMY SILVER AWARD, BRITISH HOLIDAY & HOME PARKS ASSOCIATION.

HIGHLANDS (SOUTH)

ARISAIG
A. Simpson, Camusdarach, Arisaig, Inverness-shire PH39 4NT (01687 450221). 'Camusdarach' is the ideal base to explore the beautiful scenery of the 'Road to the Isles' and the West Highlands. The grassy site, surrounded by mature trees, has 42 pitches for tents or vans including 11 electric hook-ups. A unique shower/toilet block has sheltered washing-up sinks, a laundry and a separate room with disabled and baby changing facilities. A foot path leads you on the short walk to the fabulous beaches featured in 'Local Hero'. Local shops, restaurants and ferries are within easy reach at Arisaig (four miles) and Mallaig (six miles). Traigh Golf Course is only one mile away. Pitch fees, based on two people with car: tents from £8 per night, caravans from £10 per night, serviced pitches available. *ASSC MEMBER*
e-mail: camdarach@aol.com
website: www.camusdarach.com

PERTH & KINROSS

COMRIE
West Lodge Caravan Park, Comrie PH6 2LS (01764 670354). Two to six berth caravans for hire fully equipped with gas cooker, running water, toilet, electric fridge, lighting, colour TV and gas fire. Crockery, cutlery, cooking utensils, blankets and pillows are provided. Sheets and towels can be hired. All caravans have showers. Pitches available for tents, tourers and motor homes. One modern shower block on site, complete with washing machine, tumble dryer, showers and hot and cold running water; shop. Fishing, golf, tennis, bowling, hill-walking and canoeing all within easy reach. Watersports available on nearby Loch Earn. Ideal for touring, 23 miles north of Stirling and 23 miles west of Perth. Terms from £25 to £39 nightly, £150 to £245 weekly; VAT, electricity and gas included. Open 1st April to 31st October. **STB** ★★★★ *SELF-CATERING*.

KILLIN
Cruachan Farm Caravan and Camping Park, Cruachan, Killin FK21 8TY (01567 820302). Family-run site of 10 acres adjacent to farm, set amidst beautiful Highland scenery. Ideal central situation for touring; walking, fishing and golf nearby. Licensed restaurant and coffee shop on site. Children and pets welcome. Open mid-March to October. Terms: (per night) touring caravans £7.50, motor caravans £7, car and tent £7. Holiday caravans for hire, also Lodge House for self catering lets. Reduced rates off season. Brochure available. New amenities for 2003 – loos, showers, indoor wash-up, laundry machines.
e-mail: info@cruachanfarm.co.uk
website: www.cruachanfarm.co.uk

**FREE or REDUCED RATE entry to Holiday Visits and Attractions –
see our READERS' OFFER VOUCHERS on pages 67 - 94**

FHG Diploma Winners 2003

Each year we award a small number of diplomas to holiday proprietors whose services have been specially commended by our readers. The following were our FHG Diploma Winners for 2003.

England

DERBYSHIRE
Mr Tatlow
Ashfield Farm, Calwich
Near Ashbourne
Derbyshire DE6 2EB

DEVON
Mrs Tucker
Lower Luxton Farm, Upottery
Near Honiton
Devon EX14 9PB

♦

Royal Oak
Dunsford Near Exeter
Devon EX6 7DA

GLOUCESTERSHIRE
Mrs Keyte
The Limes, Evesham Road
Stow-on-the-Wold
Gloucestershire GL54 1EN

HAMPSHIRE
Mrs Ellis, Efford Cottage,
Everton, Lymington,
Hampshire SO41 0JD

♦

R. Law
Whitley Ridge Hotel
Beauly Road, Brockenhurst
Hampshire SO42 7QL

HEREFORDSHIRE
Mrs Brown
Ye Hostelrie, Goodrich
Near Ross on Wye
Herefordshire HR9 6HX

NORTH YORKSHIRE
Charles & Gill Richardson
The Coppice, 9 Studley Road
Harrogate
North Yorkshire HG1 5JU

♦

Mr & Mrs Hewitt
Harmony Country Lodge
Limestone Road, Burniston,
Scarborough
North Yorkshire YO13 0DG

Wales

POWYS
Linda Williams
The Old Vicarage
Erwood, Builth Wells
Powys LD2 3SZ

Scotland

ABERDEEN, BANFF & MORAY
Mr Ian Ednie
Spey Bay Hotel
Spey Bay
Fochabers
Moray IV32 7PJ

PERTH & KINROSS
Dunalastair Hotel
Kinloch Rannoch
By Pitlochry
Perthshire PH16 5PW

HELP IMPROVE BRITISH TOURISM STANDARDS

As recommendations are submitted from readers of the FULL RANGE of FHG titles the winners shown above may not necessarily appear in this guide.

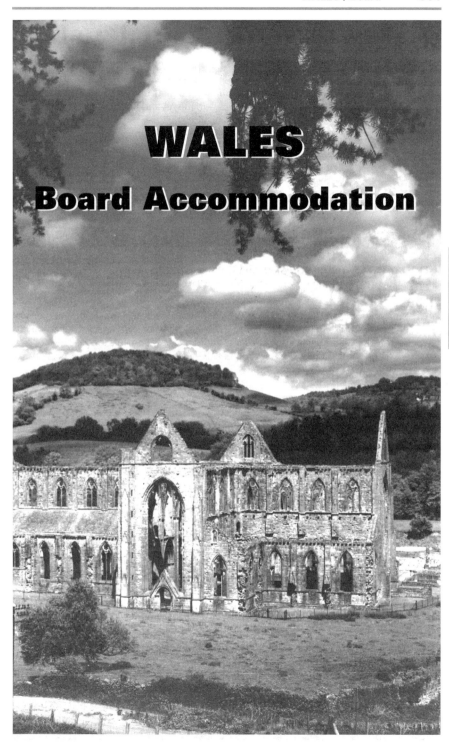

Ratings You Can Trust

ENGLAND

The **English Tourism Council** (formerly the English Tourist Board) has joined with the **AA** and **RAC** to create a new, easily understood quality rating for serviced accommodation, giving a clear guide of what to expect.

HOTELS are given a rating from One to Five **Stars** – the more Stars, the higher the quality and the greater the range of facilities and level of services provided.

GUEST ACCOMMODATION, which includes guest houses, bed and breakfasts, inns and farmhouses, is rated from One to Five **Diamonds**. Progressively higher levels of quality and customer care must be provided for each one of the One to Five Diamond ratings.

HOLIDAY PARKS, TOURING PARKS and CAMPING PARKS are now also assessed using **Stars**. Standards of quality range from a One Star (acceptable) to a Five Star (exceptional) park.

Look out also for the new **SELF-CATERING** Star ratings. The more **Stars** (from One to Five) awarded to an establishment, the higher the levels of quality you can expect. Establishments at higher rating levels also have to meet some additional requirements for facilities.

SCOTLAND

Star Quality Grades will reflect the most important aspects of a visit, such as the warmth of welcome, efficiency and friendliness of service, the quality of the food and the cleanliness and condition of the furnishings, fittings and decor.

THE MORE STARS, THE HIGHER THE STANDARDS.

The description, such as Hotel, Guest House, Bed and Breakfast, Lodge, Holiday Park, Self-catering etc tells you the type of property and style of operation.

WALES

Places which score highly will have an especially welcoming atmosphere and pleasing ambience, high levels of comfort and guest care, and attractive surroundings enhanced by thoughtful design and attention to detail

STAR QUALITY GUIDE FOR

HOTELS, GUEST HOUSES AND FARMHOUSES
SELF-CATERING ACCOMMODATION
(Cottages, Apartments, Houses)
CARAVAN HOLIDAY HOME PARKS
(Holiday Parks, Touring Parks, Camping Parks)

★★★★★ Exceptional quality
★★★★ Excellent quality
★★★ Very good quality
★★ Good quality
★ Fair to good quality

In England, Scotland and Wales, all graded properties are inspected annually by Tourist Authority trained Assessors.

ANGLESEY & GWYNEDD

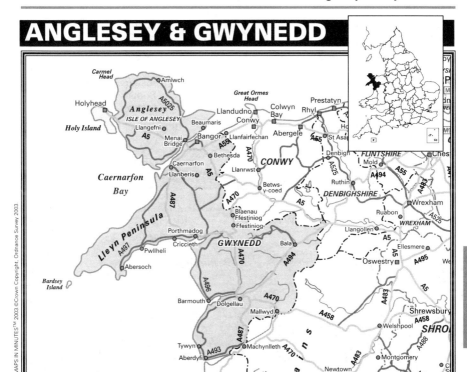

HARLECH

Mrs G.M. Evans, Glanygors, Llandanwg, Harlech LL46 2SD (01341 241410). This detached house with two acres of land is situated 400 yards from a sandy beach, and has beautiful views of the mountains. It is one-and-a-half miles from Harlech Castle, golf club and swimming pool, and within a quarter-mile of train station. Ideal place for bird-watching. Private access to beach. Presenting good home-cooking in a homely and relaxed atmosphere and run by a Welsh-speaking family. Open all year. Central heating and electric blankets for winter months. Accommodation comprises one double, one twin and one family bedrooms, all with washbasin, TV and tea-making facilities; bathroom, toilet; TV lounge and diningroom. Reduced rates for children. Bed and Breakfast from £18 to £20 per night.

LLANERCHYMEDD

Margaret and Richard Hughes, Llwydiarth Fawr, Llanerchymedd, Isle of Anglesey LL71 8DF (01248 470321/470540). Llwydiarth Fawr is a stylish, secluded and special place to stay. Guests invariably appreciate its air of spaciousness, its quiet luxury, its superior standards, its antiques, its warmth of welcome, its delicious breakfast and its unbeatable value for money. The bedrooms are furnished to the highest standards, all en suite with colour TV, tea/coffee making facilities and central heating. Llwydiarth Fawr's central location makes it the perfect base from which to explore all of Anglesey, or just enjoy the relaxing setting. Nature walks, a lake for private fishing and bird watching are all available within the grounds, while children can play in complete security in the farmland surroundings. Open all year except Christmas. Non-smoking. Bed & Breakfast from £25 to £30 per night.

NORTH WALES

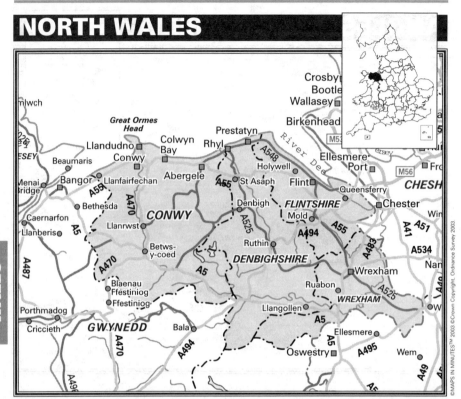

BETWS-Y-COED

Jim and Lilian Boughton, Bron Celyn Guest House, Lon Muriau, Llanrwst Road, Betws-y-Coed LL24 0HD (01690 710333; Fax: 01690 710111). A warm welcome awaits you at this delightful guest house overlooking the Gwydyr Forest and Llugwy/Conwy Valleys and village of Betws-y-Coed in Snowdonia National Park. Ideal centre for touring, walking, climbing, fishing and golf. Also excellent overnight stop en route for Holyhead ferries. Easy walk into village and close to Conwy/Swallow Falls and Fairy Glen. Most rooms en suite, all with colour TV and beverage makers. Lounge. Full central heating. Garden. Car park. Open all year. Full hearty breakfast, packed meals, snacks, evening meals - special diets catered for. Bed and Breakfast from £22 to £30, reduced rates for children under 12 years. Special out of season breaks. **WTB ★★★ GUEST HOUSE.**

e-mail: welcome@broncelyn.co.uk

website: http://www.broncelyn.co.uk

COLWYN BAY

Lyndale Hotel and Restaurant, Abergele Road, Colwyn Bay LL29 9AB (01492 515429). Centrally situated near Old Colwyn Village, the Lyndale, with sea views, is in an ideal location. All North Wales attractions, including Snowdonia National Park Anglesey, Caernarfon, Conway, LLandudno and Colwyn Bay, are within easy reach. All bedrooms with full en suite facilities, colour TV, in-house video, radio, telephones, tea/coffee making facilities and central heating, offering a high standard of comfort. The restaurant has an excellent reputation for high quality cuisine. Fully licensed and open all year. Private car park. Bed and Breakfast from £29 per person. **AA ★★, RAC ★★**

CARMARTHENSHIRE

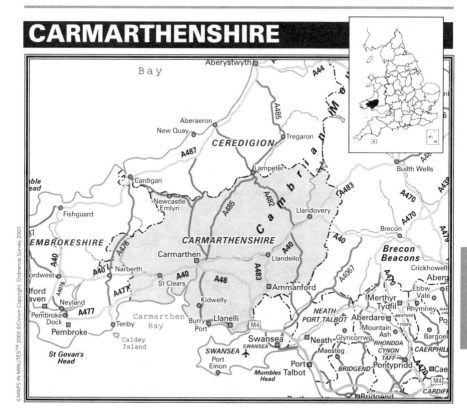

WHITLAND
Mrs O. Ebsworth, Brunant Country House, Whitland SA34 0LX (Tel & Fax: 01994 240421). 'Never enough time to enjoy this to the full, never enough words to say how splendid it was.' – John Carter (Wish You Were Here). Welcome to our 200-year-old farmhouse, centrally situated for touring, beaches, walking or just relaxing. Comfortable spacious bedrooms, all en suite, tea/coffee facilities, TV, hairdryers. Good home cooking, comfortable lounge, separate tables in dining room. No smoking. Open all year except Christmas and New Year. Bed & Breakfast £25 to £27. Evening meal £15.

WHITLAND
Mrs A. Windsor, Forest Farm, Whitland SA34 0LS (01994 240066). Forest Farm is a mixed livestock farm, situated on the A40 (en route to Fishguard for Ireland) in the rolling hillside of the Taf Valley, with beautiful walks around the farm and woodlands and fishing on the River Taf, which runs through the farm (salmon and trout). Within easy reach of the coastal areas (Tenby and Saundersfoot) and shopping areas of Carmarthen and Swansea. Close to several National Trust properties and within easy reach of Oakwood and other pleasure parks. A homely atmosphere, fully centrally heated. TV lounge for guests, diningroom with separate tables – good home-cooked breakfast. Plenty of good restaurants and pubs nearby. En suite bedrooms. Ample parking space. B&B from £20.

CEREDIGION

ABERYSTWYTH

Marine Hotel, The Promenade, Marine Terrace, Aberystwyth SY23 2BX (Freephone: 0800 0190020; Tel: 01970 612444; Fax: 01970 617535). Large seafront hotel with a lift to all floors. Bars, restaurant, bistro and lounges all on ground level. This family-run hotel is highly recommended for its warm, friendly atmosphere, good home cooking, and attention to guests' comfort. The 42 en suite refurbished bedrooms have TV and tea/coffee making facilities, and most have magnificent views of Cardigan Bay. Complimentary use of leisure suite with sauna, steam room, jacuzzi and gym. The hotel has facilities for disabled guests. Bargain breaks and mini-holidays offer excellent value. Golf parties welcome. **WTB ★★ HOTEL.**
e-mail: marinehotel1@btconnect.com
website: www.marinehotelaberystwyth.co.uk

LAMPETER

Ann and Huw Jenkins, Pantycelyn, Llanwnnen, Lampeter SA48 7LW (01570 434455). We invite you to enjoy this peaceful unspoiled branch of the Teify Valley, five miles west of Lampeter. Pantycelyn, in 11 acres of meadows, is within easy reach of Cardigan Bay's Heritage Coast and the tranquillity of the Cambrian Mountains; an ideal base for all of Ceredigion's abundant attractions. We promise a warm welcome, comfortable beds (with en suite facilities in all rooms), and memorable breakfasts. We are entirely non-smoking and have ample local information; and friendly Welsh Cobs. Access is easy, with private parking. Bed and Breakfast £22 to £24. Well behaved dogs welcome. More details available on website. **WTB ★★★ GUEST HOUSE.**
e-mail: HuwAnnJ@aol.com
website: www.pantycelyn-wales.com

PEMBROKESHIRE

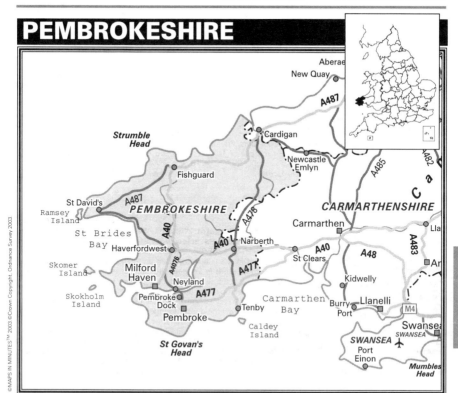

BROADHAVEN

Mrs F. Morgan, Albany Guest House, 27 Millmoor Way, Broadhaven, Haverfordwest SA62 3JJ (01437 781051; Fax: 01437 781050. Albany is a friendly, family-run Bed & Breakfast. Three en suite rooms, double, single or twin, all with tea/coffee making facilities, TV, central heating, and access at all times (some rooms have sea views). Parking. Two minutes from sandy beach of Broadhaven and leading to Little Haven. Within walking distance are shop/Post Office, cafe, pub/restaurant and Coastal Path. Windsurfing, swimming, diving and boat trips to Skomer and Grassholm bird islands (puffins, razorbills etc); seal pups in bays September/October. Coastal bus May to September. Nearby are St David's, Tenby, Oakwood etc and sandy beaches.
WTB ★★★ GUEST HOUSE.
e-mail: info@albanyguesthouse.fsnet.co.uk
website: www.albanyguesthouse.co.uk

Marine Life Centre • *St David's, Pembrokeshire* •*01437 721665*
All-weather attraction giving a unique insight into the undersea world. Simulation of underwater caves, shipwreck tank and touch tanks; gift shop, refreshments, play areas.

Pembroke Castle • *Pembroke, Pembrokeshire* • *01646 681510*
The birthplace of Henry VII, this is the oldest castle in West Wales, dating back to the 13th century, with a fine five-storey circular keep. Exhibitions, displays, videos and tableaux give a fascinating insight into history and heritage.

308 Pembrokeshire   Board / WALES

BROADHAVEN (near)
Sandra Davies, Barley Villa, Walwyns Castle, Near Broadhaven, Haverfordwest SA62 3EB (01437 781254). Our 20 acre smallholding with friendly horses offers peace, tranquillity and walks and overlooks Rosemoor Nature Reserve in Pembrokeshire's National Park. Our spacious house, furnished for the comfort of our guests, has three bedrooms, two of which are en suite, complete with hospitality trays; lounge/dining room with colour TV, coal fire and board games for restful evenings. We are centrally situated for visiting Pembokeshire's many sandy bays, famous bird islands, coastal paths and historic places. Many sport and leisure activities within easy travelling distance. We offer hearty breakfasts, packed lunches, special diets. Private car and boat parking. Non-smoking establishment catering for adults and young persons over the age of 14 years. Bed and Breakfast from £23 to £27 en suite. Comfortable two-bedroomed caravan also available for hire. **WTB ★★★** *FARM.*
e-mail: sandra.barleyvilla@btinternet.com   website: www.barleyvilla.co.uk

HAVERFORDWEST
Mrs Margaret Williams, Skerryback, Sandy Haven, St Ishmaels, Haverfordwest SA62 3DN (01646 636598; Fax: 01646 636595). Our 18th century farmhouse is a working farm set in a sheltered garden adjoining the Pembrokeshire coast footpath. It is an ideal situation for walkers and bird lovers to explore the secluded coves and sandy beaches of the area, or take a boat trip to see the puffins on Skomer Island. The two attractive double rooms, both en suite, look out across horses grazing in the meadow; the guests' lounge has a colour TV and central heating backed up by log fires on chilly evenings. A welcoming cup of tea/coffee on arrival plus hospitality trays in the bedrooms. Skerryback breakfasts are a real treat, the perfect way to start a day of strenuous walking or just relaxing on the nearest beach. Bed and Breakfast £22.50 to £30. **WTB ★★★** *FARMHOUSE* .
e-mail: skerryback@pfh.co.uk   website: www.pfh.co.uk/skerryback

See also Colour Display Advertisement

HAVERFORDWEST
Mrs M. E. Davies, Cuckoo Mill Farm, Pelcomb Bridge, St David's Road, Haverfordwest SA62 6EA (01437 762139). Working farm. There is a genuine welcome to our mixed working family farm. Quietly set in beautiful countryside surrounded by animals and wild life. Comfortable, well-appointed accommodation. Bedrooms with tea/coffee tray, radio, TV and en suite. Excellent quality food using home and local produce. Families welcome. Deductions for children and Senior Citizens. Open January to December. Pretty flowers, lawns in relaxed surroundings. Personal attention. Unrestricted access. Ideally situated in central Pembrokeshire for coastline walks. Sandy beaches. Bird islands, castles, city of St David's, Tenby. Bed and Breakfast; Bed, Breakfast and Evening Dinner. Terms on application. **WTB ★★★** *FARM, GOLD WELCOME HOST AWARD, TASTE OF WALES.*

MARTINS HAVEN/MARLOES
Mrs Christina Chetwynd, East Hook Farm, Marloes, Haverfordwest SA62 3BJ (01646 636291). Farm on Pembrokeshire Coast Path offering Bed and Breakfast, camping, caravans, cycle hire, sea fishing, bird-watching and walking. Convenient for boat trips to Skomer and Skokholm Islands and next to Marloes Mere Nature Reserve. 110 acres of natural unspoilt beauty. Bedrooms with washbasin, TV and tea/coffee making facilities available. Reception room on site. Transport to Martins Haven for boat trips, diving and Marine Nature Reserve. Bed and Breakfast £20 per person per night. Children welcome.

POWYS

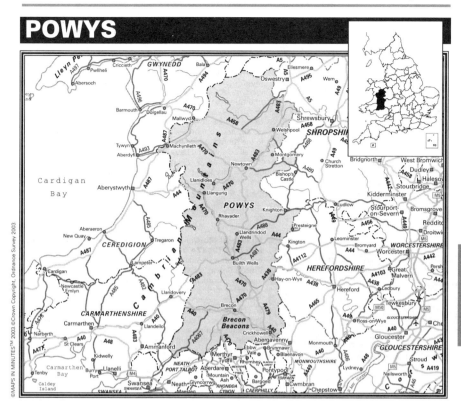

BRECON

Mrs M. J. Mayo, Maeswalter, Heol Senni, Near Brecon LD3 8SU (01874 636629). Maeswalter is a 300-year-old farmhouse in the mountainous Brecon Beacons National Park. There are four tastefully decorated bedrooms: two double en suite, one standard double and a family room sleeping three. The comfortable lounge/diningroom features exposed timbers. Visitors can roam freely through the grounds where there are seats to sit and admire the scenery and wildlife. Also private apartment (en suite double bedroom and private sittingroom). The bedrooms have colour TV and beverage tray with tea/coffee making facilities, chocolate and biscuits. Rates per room: en suite double £50 per night, standard double £36, family room sleeping three £60 per night; private en suite on the ground floor £60 per night. Reductions for longer stays.

BRECON

Mrs A. Harpur, Llanbrynean Farm, Llanfrynach, Brecon LD3 7BQ (01874 665222). Llanbrynean is a fine, traditional, Victorian farmhouse peacefully situated on the edge of the picturesque village of Llanfrynach, three miles south-east of Brecon. We are in an ideal spot for exploring the area - the Brecon Beacons rise behind the farm and the Brecon/Monmouth canal flows through the fields below. We are a working family sheep farm with wonderful pastoral views and a large garden. The house is spacious and comfortable with a friendly, relaxed atmosphere. We have two double en suite bedrooms and one twin with private bathroom. All have tea/coffee facilities. There is a sitting room with log fire. Bed and Breakfast from £20 per person. Excellent pub food within easy walking distance.

BRECON

Gwyn and Hazel Davies, Caebetran Farm, Felinfach, Brecon LD3 0UL (Tel & Fax: 01874 754460). Working farm, join in.
A warm welcome, a cup of tea and home-made cakes await you when you arrive at Caebetran. Well off the beaten track, where there are breathtaking views of the Brecon Beacons and the Black Mountains and just across a field is a 400 acre common, ideal for walking, bird-watching or just relaxing. Ponies and sheep graze undisturbed, while buzzards soar above you. Visitors are welcome to see the cattle and sheep on the farm. The farmhouse dates back to the 17th century and has been recently modernised to give the quality and comfort visitors expect today. There are many extras in the rooms to give that special feel to your holiday. The rooms are all en suite and have colour TV and tea making facilities. The dining room has separate tables, there is also a comfortable lounge with colour TV and video. Caebetran is an ideal base for exploring this beautiful, unspoilt part of the country with pony trekking, walking, birdwatching, wildlife, hang-gliding and so much more. For a brochure and terms please write, telephone or fax. "Arrive as visitors and leave as our friends". Winners of the 'FHG Diploma' for Wales 1998 and 1999. *WELCOME HOST*.
e-mail: hazelcaebetran@aol.com

BRECON

Mrs Carol Morgan, Blaencar Farm, Sennybridge, Brecon LD3 8HA (01874 636610). Enjoy the warmth and quality of a true Welsh welcome on a working family farm in the heart of the Brecon Beacons National Park. Eight miles west of Brecon, this lovingly refurbished farmhouse with a wealth of charm and character offers superior accommodation and comfort for discerning guests looking for something special. Three luxurious en suite bedrooms have all facilities. The peace and tranquillity of this quiet, accessible location provides an ideal base for relaxation, touring and exploring in unspoilt countryside. Friendly country pub a pleasant 15 minute walk. **WTB ★★★★★ FARM, TASTE OF WALES MEMBER, WELCOME HOST GOLD.**
e-mail: carol@blaencar.co.uk
website: www.blaencar.co.uk

BRECON

Mrs Eileen Williams, Upper Farm, Llechfaen, Brecon LD3 7SP (01874 665269). Working farm. A modernised farmhouse offering Bed and Breakfast only, situated just off the A40 Brecon to Abergavenny road, two miles from Brecon town. A 64-acre dairy farm in the heart of the National Park directly facing Brecon Beacons. Ideal for touring, with golf, trekking and fishing nearby and many Welsh craft shops to visit. Two double and one family bedrooms with washbasin and tea/coffee making facilities; bathroom, toilet; sittingroom; diningroom. Cot, babysitting, reduced rates for children. Open all year. Car essential - parking. No pets. Rates from £15 to £18.

BUILTH WELLS

C. Davies, Gwern-y-Mynach, Llanafan Fawr, Builth Wells LD2 3PN (01597 860256). Working farm. Gwern-y-Mynach Farm is a working sheep farm near Builth Wells in mid-Powys where golf, rugby, bowls, cricket and a new sports hall are all available. Our house is centrally heated throughout. Guest accommodation comprises one single room and one double room with bathroom en suite. Situated in a lovely area, ideal for walking, enjoying the open mountains and watching the Red Kites in flight. Also nearby the oldest pub in Powys – The Red Lion, voted best pub in Powys for food. Please write or telephone for further information. Bed & Breakfast single from £16; double en suite from £18 per person. Closed over Christmas.

Child FREE when accompanied by full-paying adult at
Celtica
see our READERS' OFFER VOUCHERS for details

GLADESTRY

Mrs M.E. Hughes, Stonehouse Farm, Gladestry, Kington, Herefordshire HR5 3NU (01544 370651). Working farm. Large Georgian farmhouse, modernised whilst retaining its character, situated on Welsh border with Offa's Dyke Footpath going through its 380 acres of mixed farming. Beautiful unspoiled area for walking. Many places of interest within driving distance such as Elan Valley Dams, Devil's Bridge, Llangorse Lake, Kington golf course. Guests are accommodated in one double and one twin-bedded rooms, with washbasins; bathroom, two toilets; sitting and diningroom. Homely informal atmosphere with home produced food and home cooking. Vegetarian meals on request. Good food available nearby at village inn. Children welcome. Babysitting available. Bed and Breakfast from £16.50; Evening Meals by arrangement.

See also Colour Display Advertisement

LLANDRINDOD WELLS

Mrs Ruth Jones, Holly Farm, Howey, Llandrindod Wells LD1 5PP (Tel & Fax: 01597 822402). Tastefully restored Tudor farmhouse on working farm in peaceful location. En suite bedrooms with breathtaking views over fields and woods, colour TV, beverage trays. Two lounges with log fires. Renowned for excellent food. Wonderful area for wildlife, walking, cycling, near Red Kite feeding station. Safe parking. Bed, Breakfast and Evening meal weekly from £215 to £240. Bed and Breakfast from £22 to £26 per day. Brochure on request. **WTB ★★★** *FARM*, **AA ♦♦♦♦**, *TASTE OF WALES TOURISM AWARD, FARM STAY UK MEMBER.*

LLANIDLOES

Mrs L. Rees, Esgairmaen, Y Fan, Llanidloes SY18 6NT (01686 430272). "Croeso Cynnes" a warm welcome awaits you at Esgairmaen, a working farm one mile from Clywedog reservoir where fishing and sailing can be enjoyed, an ideal base for walking, bird watching and exploring nearby forests. The house commands magnificent views of unspoilt countryside, only 29 miles from the coast. One double and one family room, both en suite with tea/coffee making facilities. Central heating. Open April to October. Children and pets welcome. Camping also available. We offer peace and tranquillity.

LLANWRTHWL

Gaynor Tyler, Dyffryn Farm, Llanwrthwl, Llandrindod Wells LD1 6NU (01597 811017; Fax: 01597 810609). Idyllically situated amidst the magnificent scenery of the Upper Wye Valley, Dyffryn, dating from the 17th century, is an ideal base from which to explore this unspoilt area of 'Wild Wales' with its wonderful walking, cycling, pony-trekking, bird-watching and fishing. The beautiful Elan Valley is close by; Rhayader four miles. Slate floors, beams, stone walls and woodburning stoves all add their charm to this serene old house. We have two double and one single bedroom, en suite facilities and a lovely relaxing hayloft lounge. A cosy self-catering cottage is also available. Enjoy our wholesome food and a warm welcome. No smoking. Bed and Breakfast from £22 to £26. Self-catering from £155 to £300. Brochure available. **WTB ★★★** *FARM*.

e-mail: stay@dyffrynfarm.co.uk
website: www.dyffrynfarm.co.uk

Terms quoted in this publication may be subject to increase if rises in costs necessitate

MACHYNLLETH
Gwernstablau, Llanwrin, Machynlleth SY20 8QH (01650 511688). Gwernstablau is a tranquil 17th century farmhouse set in its own five acre grounds. It tastefully combines the old world charm of a wealth of beamed ceilings and open log fires with the convenience of modern central heating and en suite accommodation. Visitors can enjoy a leisurely wander around the gardens, feed the ducks or just sit and relax by the stream. Dinner can be enjoyed in the distinctive dining room with its galleried landing, crystal chandelier and antique furniture.
website: www.gwern-stablau.com

MONTGOMERY
Ceinwen Richards, The Drewin Farm, Churchstoke, Montgomery SY15 6TW (Tel & Fax: 01588 620325). A family-run mixed farm set on hillside overlooking panoramic views of the most beautiful countryside. The Drewin is a charming 17th century farmhouse retaining much of its original character with oak beams and large inglenook fireplace, separate lounge; twin and family rooms, both en suite and all modern amenities with colour TV. Full central heating. Offa's Dyke footpath runs through the farm - a wonderful area for wildlife. Ideal base for touring the many beauty spots around. Good home cooking and a very warm welcome await our visitors. Bed and Breakfast from £22 to £25; Bed, Breakfast and Evening Meal from £34. Featured in The Travel Show. Holder of Essential Food Hygiene Certificate and Farmhouse Award from Wales Tourist Board, 1999/2000 winner of AA Best Breakfast in Wales Award. Open April to October. **WTB ★★★★ FARM, AA ♦♦♦♦**
e-mail: ceinwen@drewin.freeserve.co.uk

NEWTOWN
Mrs Joy Evans, Upper Ffrydd Farm, Caersws, Newtown SY17 5QS (01686 688963). A warm welcome awaits you at our traditional family farmhouse with its beautiful oak beams, inglenook fire places and charming en suite bedrooms with colour TV. Set in unspoilt countryside we are an ideal base for exploring mid-Wales where there is plenty to see and do, including historic market towns to explore, reservoirs with breathtaking views of valleys and mountains, railways, castles, walks, pony treks, golf courses and if you still have time we are only 50 minutes to the quiet coastline of west Wales. At the end of the day our working farm offers a relaxed atmosphere, hospitality at its best and of course - delicious home-cooking. Bed & Breakfast from £24.
WTB ★★★★ FARM.

PENYBONT-FAWR
Mrs Anne Evans, Glanhafon, Penybont-Fawr SY10 0EW (01691 860377). Working farm. Secluded farmhouse in the Upper Tanat Valley, ideal for a peaceful break. Glanhafon is a working sheep farm with hill walks on the farm. Bordering the Berwyn Mountains, it is a wonderful area for walking, bird-watching, or touring, with Lake Vyrnwy, RSPB Centre, and Pistyll Falls - one of the seven wonders of Wales- just seven miles away. Many other places of interest within easy reach, including Powys and Chirk Castle, Snowdonia, Erddig and the market towns of Shrewsbury and Oswestry. There are three attractive bedrooms, all en suite, with tea making facilities. Guests' own sittingroom. Ample parking. Children and pets welcome. Open Easter till October. Bed and Breakfast from £18. **WTB ★★★ FARM.**

**When making enquiries or bookings,
a stamped addressed envelope is always appreciated**

SOUTH WALES

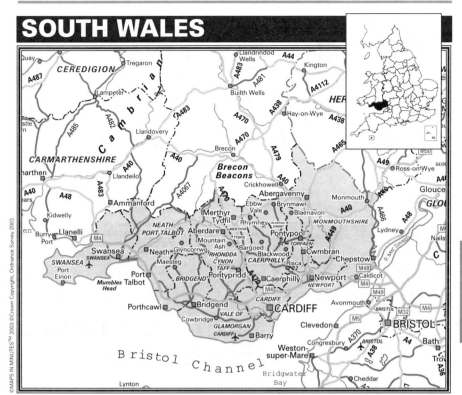

COWBRIDGE (near)

Mrs Sue Beer, Plas Llanmihangel, Llanmihangel, Near Cowbridge CF71 7LQ (01446 774610). Plas Llanmihangel is the finest medieval Grade I Listed manor house in the beautiful Vale of Glamorgan. We offer a genuine warmth of welcome, delightful accommodation, first class food and service in our wonderful home. The baronial hall, great log fires, the ancient tower and acres of beautiful historic gardens intrigue all who stay in this fascinating house. Its long history and continuous occupation have created a spectacular building in romantic surroundings unchanged since the sixteenth century. A great opportunity to experience the ambience and charm of a past age. Guests are accommodated in three double rooms. Bed and Breakfast from £28. High quality home-cooked Evening Meal available on request. **WTB ★★★** *GUEST HOUSE, CONSUMER ASSOCIATION'S 'WHICH?' GOOD BED & BREAKFAST GUIDE.*
e-mail: plasllanmihangel@ukonline.co.uk

MONMOUTH

Rosemary and Derek Ringer, Church Farm Guest House, Mitchel Troy, Monmouth NP25 4HZ (01600 712176). A spacious and homely 16th century former farmhouse (Grade II Listed) with oak beams and inglenook fireplaces, set in large attractive garden with stream. An excellent base for visiting the Wye Valley, Forest of Dean and Black Mountains. All bedrooms have washbasins, tea/coffee making facilities and central heating; most are en suite. Own car park. Colour TV. Non-smoking. Terrace and barbecue area. Bed and Breakfast from £22 to £26 per person. Evening Meal by arrangement. **WTB ★★** *GUEST HOUSE,* **AA ♦♦♦**

MONMOUTH

Mrs Rosemary Townsend, Lugano, Llandogo, Monmouth NP25 4TL (01594 530496; Fax: 01594 530956). Lugano is a modern bungalow standing in its own beautiful gardens just off the A466 between Monmouth and Chepstow. Accommodation comprises one family/twin room and two double rooms (one en suite), all the non-smoking bedrooms tastefully furnished and decorated, with washbasins, TV and tea/coffee making facilities. There is a large collection of books and tourist literature which guests are welcome to borrow. The conservation village of Lugano is in the heart of the Wye Valley, an Area of Outstanding Natural Beauty, within easy reach of the Forest of Dean, Tintern Abbey and the Brecon Beacons. B&B from £21 per person per night. Brochure available. **WTB ★★★** *B&B*.
e-mail: TOWNSEND@lugano.freeserve.co.uk

NEATH

Mrs S. Brown, Green Lantern Guest House, Hawdref Ganol Farm, Cimla, Neath SA12 9SL (01639 631884). Family-run 18th century luxury centrally heated farmhouse, set in its own 45 acres with beautiful scenic views over open countryside. Close to Afan Argoed and Margam Parks; 10 minutes from M4; one mile from birthplace of Richard Burton. Ideal for walking, cycling, horse riding from farm. Colour TV. Tea/coffee making facilities in all rooms, en suite availability. Pets welcome by arrangement. We offer luxury accommodation at an affordable price. Safe off-road parking. Central for Swansea, Neath and Port Talbot. New à la carte and grill restaurant. Want to be impressed, try us. Terms from £23, reductions for children. **WTB ★★★★** *B&B*, **AA** ♦♦♦♦♦
e-mail: caren@cimla.fsbusiness.co.uk
website: www.thegreenlanterns.co.uk

PONTYPOOL

Mr and Mrs Jayne, Mill Farm, Cwmafon, Near Pontypool NP4 8XJ (Tel & Fax: 01495 774588). Caroline and Clive Jayne welcome you to experience complete tranquillity in their 15th century farmhouse situated in 30 acres of gardens, grounds and woodlands. Enjoy the comfort of rooms furnished with antiques, with breakfast until noon. Relax in the indoor heated pool situated in the large comfortable lounge. Ideal centre for walking, touring, visiting historic sites. Bed and hearty Welsh Breakfast £25 per person. Adults only. **AA** ♦♦♦

SWANSEA

Carlton Hotel, 654-656 Mumbles Road, Mumbles, Gower, Swansea SA3 4EA (Tel & Fax: 01792 360450). A warm and friendly welcome awaits you at the Carlton Hotel, in the village of Mumbles on the Gower Peninsula. The hotel is located on the sea front, offering panoramic views across Swansea Bay, and is a short walk from the attractions of Mumbles and the picturesque village of Oystermouth. The Carlton has 20 en suite bedrooms all with TV, tea/coffee making facilities, radio clock alarms and central heating. Fredrick's Restaurant provides a varied menu, snacks and a comprehensive wine list; well stocked bar. Excellent facilities for water skiing, sailing and power boating opposite the hotel. Swansea's modern city centre, with shops, cinemas, night clubs etc. is a short trip from the hotel. Well behaved pets welcome.
e-mail: mail@carltonmumbles.co.uk
website: www.carltonmumbles.co.uk

WALES
Self-catering Accommodation

ANGLESEY & GWYNEDD

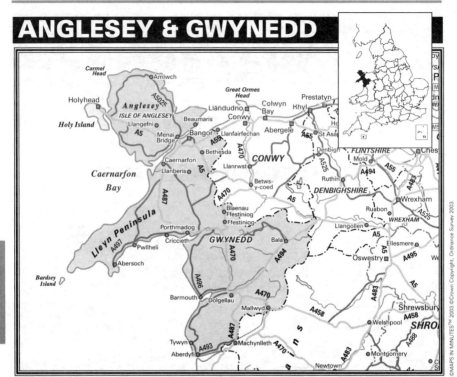

AROUND THE MAGNIFICENT WELSH COAST
Away from the Madding Crowd • Near safe sandy beaches

A small specialist agency with over 41 years experience of providing quality self-catering, offers privacy, peace and unashamed luxury.
The first Wales Tourist Board Self-Catering Award Winner. Highest residential standards.
Dishwashers, Microwaves, Washing Machines, Central Heating. No Slot meters.
LOG FIRES • LINEN PROVIDED • PETS WELCOME FREE!

All in coastal areas famed for scenery, walks, wild-flowers, birds, badgers and foxes.
Free colour brochure from F.G. Rees "Quality Cottages", Cerbid, Solva, Haverfordwest, Pembrokeshire SA62 6YE
Telephone: (01348) 837871 • Website: www.qualitycottages.co.uk

---

One child FREE with two adults at
Museum of Childhood Memories
see our READERS' OFFER VOUCHERS for details

BRYN BRAS CASTLE

Welcome to beautiful Bryn Bras Castle – enchanting castle Apartments, elegant Tower-House within unique romantic turreted Regency Castle (Listed Building) in the gentle foothills of Snowdonia. Centrally situated amidst breathtaking scenery, ideal for exploring North Wales' magnificent mountains, beaches, resorts, heritage and history. Near local country inns/restaurants, shops. Each spacious apartment is fully self-contained, gracious, peaceful, clean, with distinctive individual character, comfortable furnishings, generously and conveniently appointed from dishwasher to fresh flowers, etc. Inclusive of VAT. Central heating, hot water, linen. 32 acres of tranquil landscaped gardens, sweeping lawns, woodland walks of natural beauty, panoramic hill walks overlooking the sea, Anglesey and Mount Snowdon. Mild climate. Enjoy the comfort, warmth, privacy and relaxation of this castle of timeless charm in truly serene surroundings. Open all year, including for Short Breaks. Sleep 2-4 persons. **Regret no young children. Brochure sent with pleasure**

Llanrug, Near Caernarfon, North Wales LL55 4RE • Tel & Fax: Llanberis (01286) 870210
e-mail: holidays@brynbrascastle.co.uk • website: www.brynbrascastle.co.uk

Listed Building Grade II★

See also Colour Advertisement

ABERSOCH

Quality Cottages. Around the magnificent Welsh coast. Away from the madding crowd. Near safe sandy beaches. A small specialist agency offering privacy, peace and unashamed luxury. Wales Tourist Board 1989 Award Winner. Residential standards - dishwashers, microwaves, washing machines, central heating, log fires, no slot meters. Linen provided. Pets welcome free. All in coastal areas famed for scenery, walks, wild flowers, birds, badgers and foxes. Free colour brochure. **S.C. Rees, Quality Cottages, Cerbid, Solva, Haverfordwest, Pembrokeshire SA62 6YE (01348 837871).**
website: www.qualitycottages.co.uk

BALA (near)

Rhyd Fudr, Llanuwchllyn, Near Bala. Sleeps 6-8. Stone farm cottage set in an isolated position with views of five mountain peaks and Bala Lake. Accommodation comprises three bedrooms, plus cot; two sittingrooms; sun room; kitchen; bathroom. Garage. Multi-fuel burning stove and most modern conveniences but no TV. Fully-equipped including washing machine and telephone. Linen not supplied. Mountain stream and lovely walks on the doorstep. Sea, 45 minutes by car; Snowdon, one hour. Children welcome. Terms from £200. Apply: **Mrs J. H. Gervis, Nazeing Bury, Nazeing Road, Nazeing, Essex EN9 2JN (01992 892331) or Mrs G. E. Evans, Pant-y-Ceubren, Llanuwchllyn, Bala (01678 540252).**
e-mail: j.h.gervis@aol.com

CRICCIETH

Quality Cottages. Around the magnificent Welsh coast. Away from the madding crowd. Near safe sandy beaches. A small specialist agency offering privacy, peace and unashamed luxury. Wales Tourist Board 1989 Award Winner. Residential standards - dishwashers, microwaves, washing machines, central heating, log fires, no slot meters. Linen provided. Pets welcome free. All in coastal areas famed for scenery, walks, wild flowers, birds, badgers and foxes. Free colour brochure. **S.C. Rees, Quality Cottages, Cerbid, Solva, Haverfordwest, Pembrokeshire SA62 6YE (01348 837871).**
website: www.qualitycottages.co.uk

DOLGELLAU

Mrs Doris Jones, Abergwynant Farm and Trekking Centre, Penmaenpool, Dolgellau LL40 1YF (01341 422377). In the world today with all the stress and pressures of modern living there are few holidays more relaxing or refreshing than a get-away-from-it-all rural retreat in Wales. Nestling in a suntrap, amidst the meadows and mountains of Snowdonia National Park, Abergwynant Farm has been lovingly converted into a holiday centre, providing many activities such as fishing, horse riding, birdwatching and walking. There are six self-catering premises available, all with bathroom, shower and toilet, electric cooker, fridge, microwave and colour TV. Electricity meter. Please bring your own linen and towels. Please telephone for further details or brochure. **WTB ★★★** *SELF-CATERING.*

318 Anglesey & Gwynedd — Self-catering / WALES

This 17th century farmhouse is situated on a working farm in Dinas on the Lleyn Peninsula, 10 minutes' drive to Pwllheli for shopping; pub, restaurant and supermarket in Nefyn (3 miles). Accommodation consists of large, old beamed lounge with coal fire, TV/video, electric fire, oil-fired central heating (all fuel included in rental). Kitchen/diner has electric cooker, microwave, fridge/freezer, automatic washing machine. Two double, two twin bedrooms, sleeping 8 (duvets/bed linen included). Cot & highchair available. Bathroom with bath/overhead shower, wash basin & toilet. Large enclosed garden with garden furniture & BBQ. Owners live in a discreet rear annexe. Caravan also available. Private parking for four cars. Well behaved pets welcome. Ideal location for coastal walks. Only 10 minutes drive to 27 hole golf course at Morfa Nefyn.

nyffryn Bella
dinas, pwllheli, Gwynedd LL53 8ua

Mr & Mrs Williams
01758 770275

PORTHMADOG
Mrs M. J. Thomas, Pensyflog Farm, Porthmadog LL49 9PW (01766 513055). Spacious country farmhouse on the outskirts of the popular holiday town of Porthmadog and within easy access of a number of good beaches and hill walks. Comfortable accommodation, traditionally furnished, with lots of character and exposed beamed ceilings. Bathroom with overhead shower, separate toilet. Colour TV. Cafes, shops and pubs approximately half-a-mile. Ample parking on tarmac yard. Children welcome.

PWLLHELI
Deuglawdd, Aberdaron, Pwllheli LL53 8BN. The cottage is situated on a working farm, within easy walking distance of the charming village of Aberdaron in an Area of Outstanding Natural Beauty, with lots of coastal walks, rocky coves and sandy beaches. Fishing, surfing and the Island of Bardsey are just some of the many attractions. The cottage sleeps eight in one double and three single rooms on the first floor, with one double bedroom, living/dining area, kitchen and bathroom on the ground floor. Colour TV, video, microwave, washing machine, oil fired central heating, electricity by £1 meter. Bedding and towels provided. Available all year. Contact: **Graham on 01257 480396.**

PWLLHELI
Marine View, The Promenade, South Beach, Pwllheli LL53 5AL (01758 612758). Situated in a quiet, sunny position on the sea front commanding an excellent view of Cardigan Bay and the Cambrian mountain range, centrally situated for touring with Snowdonia National Park nearby. Accommodation comprises lounge; kitchen; two doubles on the first floor; toilet and bathroom. One mile of sandy beach, ideal for bathing and wind surfing. Golf, tennis, fishing and marina for boating not far from house. Ideal for a quiet relaxing holiday. Free parking. Terms from £150 per week.

WALES / Self-catering　　North Wales 319

NORTH WALES

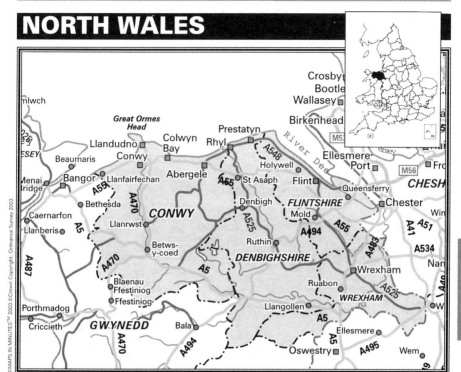

See also Colour Display Advertisement

North Wales Holiday Cottages & Farmhouses (08707 559888). Spring Breaks, Summer Holidays, Autumn Leaves or Winter Weekends ... whatever time of year you choose, our wide selection of self-catering properties throughout North Wales is sure to include just the right place for you.
website: www.northwalesholidaycottages.co.uk

BETWS-Y-COED
Jim and Lilian Boughton, Bron Celyn, Lôn Muriau, Llanrwst Road, Betws-y-Coed LL24 0HD (01690 710333; Fax: 01690 710111). Our cosy 200-year-old converted coach house has been tastefully refurbished and offers accommodation for up to four persons. Upstairs: one double room with space for a cot, and one bunk-bedded room with full length/width bunk beds. All bed linen is provided but not towels. Downstairs: lounge with colour TV and video, and wood-burning stove (ample supply of chopped timber available). Kitchen with fridge, electric cooker, microwave, toaster and water heater. Shower room and toilet. Electric storage heaters fitted throughout. Open all year. Ideal centre for walking, climbing, fishing or simply just relaxing! Terms £150 to £325 per week. Short Breaks available.
e-mail: welcome@broncelyn.co.uk　　website: http://www.broncelyn.co.uk

BETWS-Y-COED
Mrs E. Thomas, Bryn Farm, Nebo, Llanrwst LL26 0TE (01690 710315). Sleeps 2. Self-contained fully equipped farmhouse flat sleeping two on a beef and sheep farm. Situated in the Snowdonia National Park and approximately five miles from Betws-y-Coed with beautiful rural views. The accommodation comprises small double bedroom and large bathroom upstairs. Ground floor has a kitchen/diner/lounge including microwave, fridge/freezer, TV and video. Central heating in winter. Small patio with garden furniture at front of property. Ideally situated for peace and quiet. Excellent base for country walks. Sorry no pets. Short Breaks available out of season. Open all year except Christmas and New Year.

CARMARTHENSHIRE

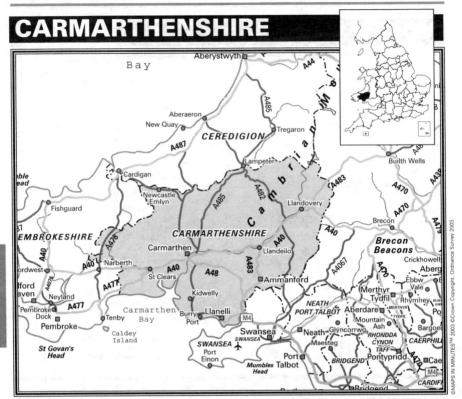

PENDINE

Mrs Sara Ellis, Sunnybank Cottage, Pendine SA33 4PS (01994 453431). Sleeps up to 5. A semi-detached cottage in a tranquil setting, really tucked away from it all. The owner has an organic garden and a wildlife area with ponds. Pendine Sands is just a ten minute drive away and Marros Beach a mile and a half walk. The cottage is fully equipped and consists of a kitchen, living/dining area, two bedrooms (one double, one bunkbeds) and bathroom. Night storage heaters and log burning stove for those cold winter nights. Room for parking. Pets allowed. Pub two miles. Shops ten-minute drive. Rates from £200 to £400 including fuel, power and linen. Open all year. Short breaks available. **WTB ★★★** *SELF-CATERING.*

Visit the FHG website
www.holidayguides.com
for details of the wide choice of accommodation featured in the full range of FHG titles

CEREDIGION

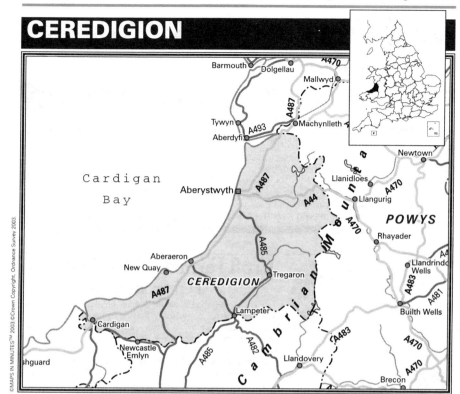

ABERPORTH
Quality Cottages. Around the magnificent Welsh coast. Away from the madding crowd. Near safe, sandy beaches. A small specialist agency offering privacy, peace and unashamed luxury. Wales Tourist Board 1989 Award Winner. Residential standards - dishwashers, microwaves, washing machines, central heating, log fires, no slot meters. Linen provided. Pets welcome free. All in coastal areas famed for scenery, walks, wild flowers, birds, badgers and foxes. Free colour brochure. **S.C. Rees, Quality Cottages, Cerbid, Solva, Haverfordwest, Pembrokeshire SA62 6YE (01348 837871).**
website: www.qualitycottages.co.uk

CARDIGAN (near)
Quality Cottages. Around the magnificent Welsh coast. Away from the madding crowd. Near safe sandy beaches. A small specialist agency offering privacy, peace and unashamed luxury. Wales Tourist Board 1989 Award Winner. Residential standards - dishwashers, microwaves, washing machines, central heating, log fires, no slot meters. Linen provided. Pets welcome free. All in coastal areas famed for scenery, walks, wild flowers, birds, badgers and foxes. Free colour brochure. **S.C. Rees, Quality Cottages, Cerbid, Solva, Haverfordwest, Pembrokeshire SA62 6YE (01348 837871).**
website: www.qualitycottages.co.uk

LLANGRANNOG
Quality Cottages. Around the magnificent Welsh coast. Away from the madding crowd. Near safe sandy beaches. A small specialist agency offering privacy, peace and unashamed luxury. Wales Tourist Board 1989 Award Winner. Residential standards - dishwashers, microwaves, washing machines, central heating, log fires, no slot meters. Linen provided. Pets welcome free. All in coastal areas famed for scenery, walks, wild flowers, birds, badgers and foxes. Free colour brochure. **S.C. Rees, Quality Cottages, Cerbid, Solva, Haverfordwest, Pembrokeshire SA62 6YE (01348 837871).**
website: www.qualitycottages.co.uk

PEMBROKESHIRE

Quality Cottages

AROUND THE MAGNIFICENT WELSH COAST

Away from the Madding Crowd • Near safe sandy beaches

A small specialist agency with over 41 years experience of providing quality self-catering, offers privacy, peace and unashamed luxury. The first Wales Tourist Board Self-Catering Award Winner. Highest residential standards.

Dishwashers, Microwaves, Washing Machines, Central Heating. No Slot meters.

LOG FIRES • LINEN PROVIDED • PETS WELCOME FREE!

All in coastal areas famed for scenery, walks, wild-flowers, birds, badgers and foxes.

Free colour brochure from F.G. Rees "Quality Cottages", Cerbid, Solva, Haverfordwest, Pembrokeshire SA62 6YE

Telephone: (01348) 837871 • Website: www.qualitycottages.co.uk

---

Croft Farm & Celtic Cottages
• Pembrokeshire •

Croft makes the ideal place for a main holiday or short break. Delightful barn conversions provide superbly comfortable accommodation. Enjoy the luxury indoor heated pool, sauna, spa pool and gym facilities. Close to sandy beaches, bays and coastal National Park. Good walking country. Indoor and outdoor play areas. Colourful gardens. Friendly farm animals. Pets welcome.

**For a brochure please contact Andrew and Sylvie Gow,
Croft Farm & Celtic Cottages, Croft, Near Cardigan, Pembrokeshire SA43 3NT
Tel/Fax: 01239 615179 • www.croft-holiday-cottages.co.uk
• e-mail: croftfarm@compuserve.com**

See also Colour Advertisement

Marine Life Centre • *St David's, Pembrokeshire* •*01437 721665*
All-weather attraction giving a unique insight into the undersea world. Simulation of underwater caves, shipwreck tank and touch tanks; gift shop, refreshments, play areas.

Pembroke Castle • *Pembroke, Pembrokeshire* • *01646 681510*
The birthplace of Henry VII, this is the oldest castle in West Wales, dating back to the 13th century, with a fine five-storey circular keep. Exhibitions, displays, videos and tableaux give a fascinating insight into history and heritage.

Manor House Wild Animal Park • *Near Tenby, Pembrokeshire* • *01646 651201*
www.manorhousewildanimalpark.co.uk
Set in landscaped grounds round an 18th century manor. Lots of animals, including a 'close encounters' unit, plus daily falconry displays.

A useful index of towns and counties appears at the back of this book on pages 375 - 378. Refer also to Contents Pages 2 and 3.

WALES / Self-catering — Pembrokeshire

AMROTH
Furzewood, Granary & Stables Cottage, Amroth. In a spectacular setting of nine acres overlooking the bay with views to Caldey Island and the Gower, all our cottages offer 5 star comfort all year round. Just minutes from the safe sandy beach, Amroth village and the Pembrokeshire Coast Path and adjacent to Colby Estate, with its lovely sheltered wooded walks. We welcome children, pets and their owners! We have a large safe garden play area and fields to walk the dogs. Short Breaks available out of season. For brochure contact **Mrs Green, Furzewood Farm, Amroth, Pembrokeshire SA67 8NQ. (01834 814674)** WTB ★★★★★ *SELF CATERING*
e-mail: info@amrothcottages.co.uk
website: www.amrothcottages.co.uk

AMROTH (near)
Carol Lloyd, East Llanteg Farm, Llanteg, Amroth SA67 8QA (01834 831336). Two charming cottages privately situated and ideally located for exploring Pembrokeshire. The resorts of Saundersfoot and Tenby are close at hand with the seaside resort of Amroth and the coastal path just minutes away. Each cottage sleeps four to five adults; cots and high chairs are also provided. All facilities including fully fitted kitchen, central heating and colour television are included. There is ample private parking plus a lawned garden area and patio with garden furniture provided. Farmhouse B&B also available. WTB ★★★★★ *SELF-CATERING*.
e-mail: john@pembrokeshireholiday.co.uk
website: www.pembrokeshireholiday.co.uk

BOSHERTON
Quality Cottages. Around the magnificent Welsh coast. Away from the madding crowd. Near safe sandy beaches. A small specialist agency offering privacy, peace and unashamed luxury. Wales Tourist Board 1989 Award Winner. Residential standards - dishwashers, microwaves, washing machines, central heating, log fires, no slot meters. Linen provided. Pets welcome free. All in coastal areas famed for scenery, walks, wild flowers, birds, badgers and foxes. Free colour brochure. **S.C. Rees, Quality Cottages, Cerbid, Solva, Haverfordwest, Pembrokeshire SA62 6YE (01348 837871).**
website: www.qualitycottages.co.uk

FISHGUARD
Jane Stiles, Killoskehane, Letterston, Haverfordwest SA62 5TN (01348 840879). Sleep 2-12. Pembrokeshire Coast – Newport to St David's. Charming, individual cottages situated near sandy beaches, rocky bays and spectacular cliff walks. Traditional stone-built cottages or modern properties, many with central heating and wood-burning stoves. All furnished to high residential standards, fully equipped and personally supervised. Watersports, golf, birdwatching and wild flowers. Boat trips to the islands. Explore the Preseli Mountains, castles, cromlechs and Iron Age forts. Visit art galleries and craft workshops, relax in country pubs and quality restaurants. Pets and children welcome.
e-mail: janestiles@virgin.net
website: www.pembrokeshireholidays.co.uk

GOODWICK
Mrs Rosemary Johns, Carne Farm, Goodwick SA64 0LB (01348 891665). Working farm, join in. Sleeps 6. Stone cottage adjoining farmhouse, sleeps six in three bedrooms, also a spacious residential caravan for six with two bedrooms, each with its own garden where children can play safely. In peaceful countryside on 350 acre dairy and sheep farm between Fishguard and Strumble Head, three miles from the sea. Within easy reach of many beaches by car, ideal for walking and bird-watching. No linen supplied. Children welcome. Washing machine in cottage. TV, microwave, cots, high chairs. Baby sitting available. You can be sure of a warm welcome and visitors can feed calves and watch the milking.

NEWGALE

Quality Cottages. Around the magnificent Welsh coast. Away from the madding crowd. Near safe sandy beaches. A small specialist agency offering privacy, peace and unashamed luxury. Wales Tourist Board 1989 Award Winner. Residential standards - dishwashers, microwaves, washing machines, central heating, log fires, no slot meters. Linen provided. Pets welcome free. All in coastal areas famed for scenery, walks, wild flowers, birds, badgers and foxes. Free colour brochure. **S.C. Rees, Quality Cottages, Cerbid, Solva, Haverfordwest, Pembrokeshire SA62 6YE (01348 837871).**
website: www.qualitycottages.co.uk

ST DAVID'S

Quality Cottages. Around the magnificent Welsh coast. Away from the madding crowd. Near safe sandy beaches. A small specialist agency offering privacy, peace and unashamed luxury. Wales Tourist Board 1989 Award Winner. Residential standards - dishwashers, microwaves, washing machines, central heating, log fires, no slot meters. Linen provided. Pets welcome free. All in coastal areas famed for scenery, walks, wild flowers, birds, badgers and foxes. Free colour brochure. **S.C. Rees, Quality Cottages, Cerbid, Solva, Haverfordwest, Pembrokeshire SA62 6YE (01348 837871).**
website: www.qualitycottages.co.uk

SOLVA

Quality Cottages. Around the magnificent Welsh coast. Away from the madding crowd. Near safe sandy beaches. A small specialist agency offering privacy, peace and unashamed luxury. Wales Tourist Board 1989 Award Winner. Residential standards - dishwashers, microwaves, washing machines, central heating, log fires, no slot meters. Linen provided. Pets welcome free. All in coastal areas famed for scenery, walks, wild flowers, birds, badgers and foxes. Free colour brochure. **S.C. Rees, Quality Cottages, Cerbid, Solva, Haverfordwest, Pembrokeshire SA62 6YE (01348 837871).**
website: www.qualitycottages.co.uk

TENBY

Quality Cottages. Around the magnificent Welsh coast. Away from the madding crowd. Near safe sandy beaches. A small specialist agency offering privacy, peace and unashamed luxury. Wales Tourist Board 1989 Award Winner. Residential standards - dishwashers, microwaves, washing machines, central heating, log fires, no slot meters. Linen provided. Pets welcome free. All in coastal areas famed for scenery, walks, wild flowers, birds, badgers and foxes. Free colour brochure. **S.C. Rees, Quality Cottages, Cerbid, Solva, Haverfordwest, Pembrokeshire SA62 6YE (01348 837871).**
website: www.qualitycottages.co.uk

See also Colour Display Advertisement

WHITLAND

Mrs Angela Colledge, Gwarmacwydd, Llanfallteg, Whitland SA34 0XH (01437 563260; Fax: 01437 563839). Gwarmacwydd is a country estate of over 450 acres, including two miles of riverbank. Come and see a real farm in action, the hustle and bustle of harvest, newborn calves and lambs. Children are welcomed. On the estate are six character stone cottages. Each cottage has been lovingly converted from traditional farm buildings, parts of which are over 200 years old. Each cottage is fully furnished and equipped with all modern conveniences. All electricity and linen included. All cottages are heated for year-round use. Colour brochure available. Five cottages **WTB** ★★★★ *SELF-CATERING.*
e-mail: info@a-farm-holiday.org
website: www.a-farm-holiday.org

FHG PUBLICATIONS publish a large range of well-known accommodation guides. We will be happy to send you details or you can use the order form at the back of this book.

POWYS

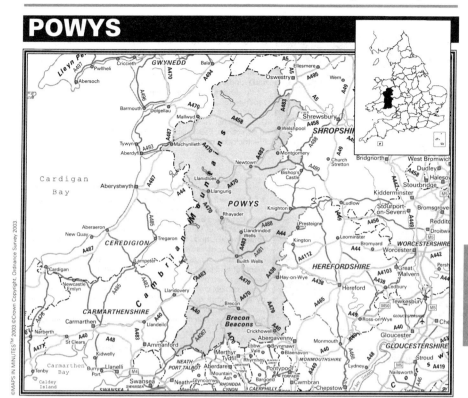

LLANDRINDOD WELLS

e-mail: unwind@gaercottage.co.uk

Phillip and Patricia Harley, Gaer Cottage, Hundred House, Llandrindod Wells LD1 5RU (Tel & Fax: 01982 570208). Gaer Cottage is a comfortable, well equipped, recently restored Welsh cottage. It has oil-fired central heating throughout. There are large south- facing windows and a conservatory. The kitchen and utility are well stocked with pots and pans for up to eight people. There is a fan oven, microwave, fridge/freezer, dishwasher and automatic washing machine. The lounge is very spacious providing a dining table with seating for eight, comfortable chairs and a bed-settee. There is a TV and video. Upstairs there are two en suite bedrooms; one has a double bed and the other has three single beds, two of which can join together to form a double. Non-smoking. Bed and Breakfast available in farmhouse.
WELCOME HOST, CYCLISTS WELCOME.
website: www.gaercottage.co.uk

LLANDRINDOD WELLS

Mrs Ruth Jones, Holly Farm, Howey, Llandrindod Wells LD1 5PP (Tel & Fax: 01597 822402). Tastefully restored Tudor farmhouse on working farm in peaceful location. En suite bedrooms with breathtaking views over fields and woods, colour TV, beverage trays. Two lounges with log fires. Renowned for excellent food. Wonderful area for wildlife, walking, cycling, near Red Kite feeding station. Safe parking. Bed, Breakfast and Evening meal weekly from £220 to £245. Bed and Breakfast from £22 to £26 per day. Brochure on request. **WTB ★★★ *FARM*, AA ♦♦♦♦, *TASTE OF WALES TOURISM AWARD, FARM STAY UK MEMBER.***

OSWESTRY (near)
Mr and Mrs Breeze, Lloran Isaf, Llansilin, Near Oswestry SY10 7QX (01691 791376/780318). Working farm.
Beautiful bungalow set on a working farm in its own valley which has wonderful scenery and walks. Kitchen with microwave, washer/dryer, fridge, cooker; lounge/dining area with colour TV and wood-burning stove (small charge for logs). Three bedrooms – two double and one single (duvets supplied but no linen); separate toilet and bathroom. Fitted carpets and electric heating in bedrooms and lounge; garden furniture in enclosed garden. One and a half miles from village, wonderful touring area with lots of attractions. Pets welcome. Sorry, no children. Terms from £100. Electricity by meter reading. **WTB ★★★** *SELF-CATERING.*

TALYBONT-ON-USK
1 Caerfanell Place, Talybont-on-Usk, Brecon. Talybont-on-Usk is a small village nestling below the Beacons in the National Park. Cottage is built of traditional Welsh slate and stone, situated in the centre of village with garden leading to River Caerfanell. Totally refurbished - three bedrooms sleep seven; bathroom and toilet upstairs and shower room and toilet downstairs; comfortable lounge with colour, free to view channel TV, video recorder and cosy wood/coal stove for winter or chilly nights. A washing machine, dryer, dishwasher, fridge, freezer, large dual fuel Range cooker, coffee machine and microwave are complemented by a full range of smaller kitchen essentials. Chalet in garden with gas BBQ for outdoor use. Roadside parking. Excellent village pubs serve a wide selection of beers. Short Breaks available out of season. Canal trips available nearby as are many other sporting activities. Terms from £215 to £450 per week. Winter fuel supplement of £20 October to April, payable with rent. Linen and duvets provided. No pets. Apply: **Mrs F.I. Smith, Holt's Farm House, Coopers Lane, Fordcombe, Near Tunbridge Wells, Kent TN3 0RN (01892 740338).**

Powis Castle and Garden • *Near Welshpool, Powys* • *01938 554336*
Perched on a rock above gardens of great historical and horticultural importance, the medieval castle contains a superb collection of paintings and furniture and a collection of treasures from India.

King Arthur's Labyrinth • *Machynlleth, Powys* • *01654 761584*
website: www.kingarthurslabyrinth.com
A boat ride along a beautiful subterranean river takes you to the Labyrinth, carved from rock, where the tales of King Arthur are re-told. New 'Bard's Quest' challenges you to go in search of the lost legends hidden in the Maze of Time.

Two for the price of one at
National Cycle Collection
see our READERS' OFFER VOUCHERS for details

WALES
Caravan & Camping

ANGLESEY & GWYNEDD

BENLLECH
Golden Sunset Holidays, Benllech Bay, Anglesey LL74 8SW (01248 852345). Beautiful caravan and camping park overlooking the sea with miles of glorious sands. Modern caravans for hire each having flush toilet and shower. Farmhouse for rent. Touring caravans welcome, electric hook-ups available. Organised camps for schools, Scouts, Guides etc., are catered for, having their own separate well sheltered fields. Special quotations on request. The village of Benllech has a good range of shops, pubs and post office. Dogs on lead only. Donkey and pony rides for children. Open April to end of September. Send for free brochure.

NORTH WALES

ABERGELE
Mr and Mrs T.P. Williams, Pen Isaf Caravan Park, Llangernyw, Abergele LL22 8RN (01745 860276). This small caravan site in beautiful unspoilt countryside is ideal for touring North Wales and is situated 10 miles from the coast and 12 miles from Betws-y-Coed. The eight-berth caravans are fully equipped except for linen and towels and have shower, flush toilet, hot and cold water, Calor gas cooker, electric light and fridge. Fresh eggs and milk can be obtained from the farm on which this 20 caravan site is situated. Children especially will enjoy a holiday here, there being ample space and facilities for fishing and pony riding. Pets are allowed but must be kept under control. Open March to October. Terms on application with SAE, please.

CEREDIGION

ABERPORTH
Mrs S. Jones, Manorafon Caravan Park, Sarnau, Llandyssul SA44 6QH (01239 810564). Sleeps 6. Quiet, peaceful site of five caravans and two log chalets, fully equipped including linen (except towels); all caravans six-berth with end bedrooms. All essential facilities provided. Bathroom facilities with hot water on tap in each van; Calor gas cooker, electric lighting and heating. Toilets and washbasins, showers, shaving points. Calor and Camping Gaz sold. Available March to January. Children welcome. Only half-a-mile from the pleasant Penbryn beach and nine miles from the market towns of Cardigan and Newcastle Emlyn. Half-acre for campers and tourers.
e-mail: info@manorafonholidaypark.co.uk website: www.manorafonholidaypark.co.uk

---

One child FREE with two paying adults. Guide dogs welcome at
Alice in Wonderland Centre
see our READERS' OFFER VOUCHERS for details

IRELAND

Co. GALWAY • Board

ORANMORE
Mrs Cannon, Cartroon Farm, Galway Coast Road, Oranmore (00 353 91 794345). Spacious farmhouse in scenic surroundings overlooking Galway Bay. Situated one mile west of Oranmore and four-and-a-half miles east of Galway City just off N18 and N6 roads. Ideal base for touring Connemara, Burren, Cliffs of Moher and indeed the whole of the West of Ireland. Galway City and Airport eight minutes' drive. Galway Bay Golf and Country Club five minutes, also horse riding, fishing and sailing locally. Dairy farm, other farm animals and domestic poultry also kept. Good food and accommodation in four bedrooms, all en suite. Prices 30 euros per person sharing; single 35 euros.
e-mail: cartroonfarmhouse@eircom.net
website: http://homepage.eircom.net/~cartroonfarmhouse/

Co. KERRY • Self-catering

LAURAGH
Creveen Lodge Caravan and Camping Park, Healy Pass Road, Lauragh (00 353 64 83131; from Ireland 064 83131). Attractive two-storey dormer-style farmhouse attached to proprietors' residence, 200 yards from roadside, with magnificent views of sea and countryside. The 80-acre mixed farm is conveniently situated for fishing, mountain climbing, Derreen Gardens, shops and old Irish pub: 16 miles south of Kenmare. Accommodation for six/eight persons in three double and one single room, all with washbasin; cot. Sittingroom with large stone fireplace, TV; separate diningroom. Kitchen has gas cooker; full oil-fired central heating and storage heating; washing machine and dryer. Everything supplied including linen. Children and pets welcome; high chair, and babysitting arranged. Car essential - parking. Available all year. April, May and October 200 euros; June and September 260 euros; July and August 400 euros per week; rest of the year by 160 euros. Gas and electricity extra.
e-mail: info@creveenlodge.com
website: www.creveenlodge.com

Co. KERRY • Caravan & Camping

See also Colour Display Advertisement

KILLORGLIN
West's Caravan Park, Killarney Road, Killorglin, Co. Kerry (00 353 66 9761240). Mobile homes for hire on family-run park situated on banks of River Laune overlooking Ireland's highest mountain. Pool table, table-tennis, tennis, laundry. Town one mile. Ideal touring centre for Ring of Kerry, Dingle Peninsula, Cork, Blarney Stone, Killarney National Park and Tralee. From £150 to £350 (sterling p.w.). Ferry and mobile home prices available.

COUNTRY INNS

FHG Other specialised **FHG PUBLICATIONS**
Published annually: available in all good bookshops or direct from the publisher.

PETS WELCOME! £7.99
Recommended **COUNTRY HOTELS** OF BRITAIN £6.99
Recommended **COUNTRY INNS & PUBS** OF BRITAIN £6.99
Recommended **SHORT BREAK HOLIDAYS** IN BRITAIN £6.99

FHG Publications Ltd, Abbey Mill Business Centre,
Seedhill, Paisley, Renfrewshire PA1 1TJ
Tel: 0141-887 0428 • Fax: 0141-889 7204
e-mail: fhg@ipcmedia.com • website: www.holidayguides.com

BEDFORDSHIRE

See also Colour Display Advertisement

LEIGHTON BUZZARD

The Globe Inn, Globe Lane, Stoke Road, Old Linslade, Leighton Buzzard LU7 7TA (01525 373338; Fax: 01525 860551). Situated on the edge of the Grand Union Canal, The Globe Inn is an idyllic pub/restaurant for all age groups to enjoy, for a special occasion or just a casual meeting. Entertain the little ones on our outside play area, and feed them with their own special menu. Our traditional and friendly atmosphere warms everyone's hearts, as does our exceptional quality food. Our restaurant is open seven days a week, and booking is highly recommended. Seafood dishes are our speciality, and our chef ensures the home-cooked aspect is kept with his pies and puddings. Our evenings are enhanced by candlelight, and during the winter months open fires add to the warm welcome. Enjoy our range of well-kept cask-conditioned ales with a meal in the bar, or some fine wine in our traditional restaurant.

FHG

Other specialised
FHG PUBLICATIONS

Published annually: available in all good bookshops or direct from the publisher.

PETS WELCOME! £7.99
Recommended **COUNTRY HOTELS** OF BRITAIN £6.99
Recommended **COUNTRY INNS & PUBS** OF BRITAIN £6.99
Recommended **SHORT BREAK HOLIDAYS** IN BRITAIN £6.99

**FHG PUBLICATIONS LTD,
Abbey Mill Business Centre,
Seedhill, Paisley, Renfrewshire PA1 ITJ
Tel: 0141-887 0428 • Fax: 0141-889 7204
e-mail: fhg@ipcmedia.com
website: www.holidayguides.com**

See the *Family-Friendly Pubs & Inns*
Supplement on pages 335 - 344 for establishments which really welcome children

CUMBRIA

Talkin Village, Brampton, Cumbria CA8 1LE
Tel: 016977 3452 • Fax: 016977 3396
e-mail: info@blacksmithstalkin.co.uk
website: www.blacksmithstalkin.co.uk

The Blacksmith's Arms offers all the hospitality and comforts of a traditional country inn. Enjoy tasty meals served in the bar lounges, or linger over dinner in the well-appointed restaurant. The inn is personally managed by the proprietors, Anne and Donald Jackson, who guarantee the hospitality one would expect from a family concern. Guests are assured of a pleasant and comfortable stay. There are eight lovely, en suite bedrooms. Peacefully situated in the beautiful village of Talkin, the inn is convenient for the Borders, Hadrian's Wall and the Lake District. There is a good golf course, walking and other country pursuits nearby..

See also Colour Advertisement

See also Colour Display Advertisement

POOLEY BRIDGE
The Sun Inn, Pooley Bridge, Penrith CA10 2NN (017684 86205; Fax: 017684 86913). Dating from the mid 1700s, the inn has nine bedrooms, all en suite, comprising five doubles, one twin, two singles and a family room. There is a no smoking policy in the bedrooms and also in the 30-seater dining room, the lobby and the lounge bar. The Public bars attract the colourful local people, walkers, fishermen and sportsmen who enjoy rugby and football on our big screen. The inn enjoys a certain atmosphere, especially in busy times during the season. Visitors are encouraged to enjoy the inn and the area in winter when we offer special rates. Children and dogs are most welcome.
e-mail: michaeljane66@btopenworld.com

DEVON

See also Colour Display Advertisement

LYDFORD
The Castle Inn Hotel and Restaurant, Lydford, Okehampton EX20 4BH (01822 820241; Fax: 01822 820454). One of the finest traditional wayside inns in the West Country, this romantic Elizabethan hostelry is featured in Conan Doyle's 'The Hound of the Baskervilles'. First-class food in a bar and restaurant with slate floors, bowed ceilings, low, lamp-lit beams and fascinating antiques; dining by candlelight from imaginative table d'hôte and à la carte menus. Guest rooms, decorated in individual style, are beautifully furnished and equipped. A wonderful place to shake off the cobwebs of urban existence and appreciate the really worthwhile things of life.
e-mail: castleinnlyd@aol.com

See also Colour Display Advertisement

TOTNES
Sea Trout Inn, Staverton, Near Totnes, Devon TQ9 6PA (01803 762274; Fax: 01803 762506). The Inn has two well-appointed bars with oak beams and real log fires, both pleasant places to relax and unwind after a day's walking or touring. 10 bedrooms, delightfully decorated in a comfortable cottage style, have private bathrooms, central heating, direct-dial telephone, tea/coffee making facilities and colour TV. Guests dining in the Hotel may choose from the award winning restaurant or the relaxing and leisurely atmosphere of the bars or, on warmer summer days, the attractive patio garden. An extensive menu ranges from light snacks to full meals, with vegetarian dishes always available. **ETC ★★, AA TWO ROSETTES.**
website: www.seatroutinn.com

GLOUCESTERSHIRE

See also Colour Display Advertisement

BOURTON-ON-THE-WATER
The Old New Inn, Bourton-on-the-Water GL54 2AF (01451 820467; Fax: 01451 810236). The Old New Inn is a traditional country inn. It has log fires and three bars where guests can enjoy a drink and a chat. In the heart of the Cotswolds, close to the River Windrush, Bourton-on-the-Water is an ideal centre for a country holiday. All rooms are en suite and all have TV and tea/coffee making facilities. The Hotel has a spacious lounge for residents. There is a car park and a large attractive beer garden. A comprehensive table d' hôte dinner menu is available in the evening – bar meals are served at lunch times and evening. RAC ★★
e-mail: reception@theoldnewinn.co.uk
website: www.theoldnewinn.co.uk

See also Colour Display Advertisement

BRISTOL
The Bowl Inn & Lilies Restaurant, 16 Church Road, Lower Almondsbury, Bristol BS32 4DT (01454 612757; Fax: 01454 619910). Whether travelling on business or just taking a break, you will find all the comforts of modern life housed in this historic 12th century village inn. 13 bedrooms, one four-poster, all en suite with TV, central heating, tea and coffee making facilities and hairdryers. Real ales, fine wines, extensive bar menu and à la carte restaurant. Located just five minutes from Junction 16 off the M5. ETC ★★
e-mail: reception@thebowlinn.co.uk
website: www.thebowlinn.co.uk

HERTFORDSHIRE

See also Colour Display Advertisement

HERTFORD
Salisbury Arms Hotel, Fore Street, Hertford, Hertfordshire SG14 1BZ (01992 583091; Fax: 01992 552510). Hertford's oldest hostelry offers guests excellent food, traditional local ales and an extensive list of wines available by the glass and bottle in surroundings that have character and charm complemented by great service. The wood panelled, air-conditioned restaurant has excellent value table d'hôte and à la carte menus that offer a combination of traditional and contemporary dishes. The rooms are all en suite with satellite TV, two specially designed for those who require disabled facilities. Green fee discounts are available to guests at many of the surrounding golf clubs. Central London is 35 minutes away by train. ETC/AA ★★★
e-mail: reception@salisbury-arms-hotel.co.uk
www.salisbury-arms-hotel.co.uk

Visit the **FHG** website
www.holidayguides.com
for details of the wide choice of accommodation featured in the full range of FHG titles

WEST SUSSEX

Horse & Groom
17th Century Inn with Restaurant & Accommodation

Located in the quiet West Sussex village of East Ashling, the Horse & Groom is a traditional 17th Century inn with separate en suite accommodation in a converted barn and new wing.

Only a few miles from the historic city of Chichester, it makes the perfect place to stay for an unforgettable break, to simply relax and unwind.

The bar has all the charm of a traditional English country pub, with original flagstones and a baker's oven set into the wall. It offers an excellent selection of real ales, chilled lagers, fine wines and spirits for your enjoyment.

The light and airy restaurant makes a wonderful place to enjoy lunch or have dinner, and for lighter meals, bar snacks are also available.

For a memorable break or short overnight stay we offer 11 en suite twin/double rooms, each with colour television and tea/coffee making facilities. Five rooms have been converted from the adjoining old flint barn.

Open January – December, Bed & Breakfast from £40 per room (single), £60 (double)

Horse & Groom, East Ashling, near Chichester, West Sussex PO18 9AX
Tel: 01243 575339 • Fax: 01243 575560 • E-mail: horseandgroomea@aol.com
www.horseandgroom.sageweb.co.uk • www.thehorseandgroomchichester.com

---

Other specialised **FHG PUBLICATIONS**
Published annually: available in all good bookshops or direct from the publisher.

PETS WELCOME! £7.99
Recommended **COUNTRY HOTELS** OF BRITAIN £6.99
Recommended **COUNTRY INNS & PUBS** OF BRITAIN £6.99
Recommended **SHORT BREAK HOLIDAYS** IN BRITAIN £6.99

FHG Publications Ltd, Abbey Mill Business Centre, Seedhill, Paisley, Renfrewshire PA1 1TJ
Tel: 0141-887 0428 • Fax: 0141-889 7204
e-mail: fhg@ipcmedia.com • website: www.holidayguides.com

WILTSHIRE

AA ★★
Courtesy & Care Award
RAC ★★

YOUNG'S

THE LAMB AT HINDON
Hindon, Near Salisbury, Wiltshire SP3 6DP
Tel: 01747 820573 • Fax: 01747 820605 • e-mail: lambinnhotel@youngs.co.uk

The fascinating history of this ancient inn is related in its brochure, which reveals among other intriguing facts that it was once the headquarters of a notorious smuggler. No such unlawful goings-on today – just good old-fashioned hospitality in the finest traditions of English inn-keeping. Charmingly furnished single, double and four-poster bedrooms provide overnight guests with cosy country-style accommodation, and the needs of the inner man (or woman!) will be amply satisfied by the varied, good quality meals served in the bar and restaurant. Real ales can be enjoyed in the friendly bar, where crackling log fires bestow charm and atmosphere as well as warmth.

WALES

POWYS

LLANWRTYD WELLS

The Neuadd Arms Hotel, Llanwrtyd Wells LD5 4RB (01591 610236; Fax: 01591 610610). Llanwrtyd Wells has fabulous facilities for walking and mountain biking (way-marked trails), pony trekking and riding, fishing, birdwatching, or sightseeing. A warm welcome is guaranteed at this 19th century hotel. Relax in the comfortable lounge bar, the traditional farmers' Bell Bar, the residents' TV lounge, or in the games room. Upstairs, comfortable, well-appointed bedrooms ensure sound repose after the day's activities; most have en suite facilities, colour TV and radio. Excellent reputation for good home-cooked food, served in the attractive restaurant overlooking the town square and surrounding hills. Interesting events are organised in the town throughout the year, including the 'Man versus Horse' Marathon and the World Bog Snorkelling Championships. *GOOD BEER GUIDE.* **RAC ★**
e-mail: Lindsay@neuaddarms.fsnet.co.uk   website: www.neuaddarmshotel.co.uk

Family-Friendly Pubs & Inns

"Family-Friendly"
Pubs, Inns & Hotels

This is a selection of establishments which make an extra effort to cater for parents and children. The majority provide a separate children's menu or they may be willing to serve small portions of main course dishes on request; there are often separate outdoor or indoor play areas where the junior members of the family can let off steam while Mum and Dad unwind over a drink.

For full details of facilities offered, please contact the individual establishments.

Family-Friendly Pubs & Inns

half portions
children's menu
garden or play area
baby-changing facilities
high chairs
family room

COMPTON SWAN HOTEL
Compton, Near Newbury
Berkshire RG20 6NJ
Tel: 01635 578269
www.comptonswan.co.uk

THE CROOKED INN
Stoketon Cross, Trematon
Cornwall PL12 4RZ
Tel: 01752 848177

WHITE MARE COUNTRY HOUSE HOTEL & PUB
Beckermet
Cumbria CA21 2XS
Tel: 01946 841246
www.whitemare.co.uk

KING GEORGE IV INN
Eskdale, Holmrook
Cumbria CA19 1TS
Tel: 01946 723262
www.kinggeorge-iv.co.uk

RUSLAND POOL HOTEL
Haverthwaite, Ulverston
Cumbria LA12 8AA
Tel: 01229 861384
www.ruslandpool.co.uk

QUEENS ARMS INN
Warwick-on-Eden, Carlisle
Cumbria CA4 8PA
Tel: 01228 560699
www.queensarms.uk.com

KNOCKERDOWN INN
Near Carsington Water,
Ashbourne, Derbyshire DE6 1NQ
Tel: 01629 540209
www.theknockerdown.co.uk

Family-Friendly Pubs & Inns

BERESFORD ARMS HOTEL
Station Road, Ashbourne
Derbyshire DE6 1AA
Tel: 01335 300035
www.beresford-arms.demon.co.uk

DOLPHIN INN
Kingston, Near Bigbury,
Devon TQ7 4QE
Tel: 01548 810314

KINGS ARMS INN
Stockland, Near Honiton
Devon EX14 9BS
Tel: 01404 881361
www.kingsarms.net

GEORGE HOTEL
Broad Street, South Molton
Devon EX36 3AB
Tel: 01769 572514
www.s-molton.freeserve.co.uk

OLD WELL INN
The Bank, Barnard Castle
Co Durham DL12 8PH
Tel: 01833 690130
www.oldwellinn.co.uk

THE CRICKETERS
Clavering, Saffron Walden
Essex CB11 4QT
Tel: 01799 550442
www.thecricketers.co.uk

KING'S HEAD INN
Birdwood, Near Huntley
Gloucestershire GL19 3EF
Tel: 01452 750348

THE FIVE ALLS INN
Filkins, Near Lechlade
Gloucestershire GL7 3JQ
Tel: 01367 860306
www.dursley-cotswolds-uk.com

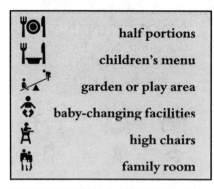

half portions
children's menu
garden or play area
baby-changing facilities
high chairs
family room

BASKERVILLE ARMS
Clyro, Near Hay-on-Wye
Herefordshire HR3 5RZ
Tel: 01497 820670
www.baskervillearms.co.uk

HOPTON ARMS
Ashperton, Near Ledbury
Herefordshire HR8 2SE
Tel: 01531 670520
www.hoptonarms.co.uk

WINDMILL INN HOTEL
Steyne Road, Bembridge
Isle of Wight PO35 5UH
Tel: 01983 872875
www.windmill-inn.com

LIGHTHOUSE INN
Capel-le-Ferne, Folkestone
Kent CT18 7HT
Tel: 01303 223300
www.lighthouse-inn.co.uk

SWAN & ROYAL HOTEL
Castle Street, Clitheroe
Lancashire BB7 2BX
Tel: 01200 423130
www.swanandroyal.co.uk

SHIREBURN ARMS
Hurst Green, Clitheroe
Lancashire BB7 9QY
Tel: 01254 826518
www.shireburnarmshotel.com

FARMHOUSE TAVERN
Morecambe Road, Lancaster
Lancashire LA1 5JB
Tel: 01524 69255

Family-Friendly Pubs & Inns

MOORCOCK INN
Waddington, Near Clitheroe
Lancashire BB7 3AA
Tel: 01200 422333
www.moorcockinn.co.uk

MONCKTON ARMS
Glaston, Uppingham
Rutland LE15 9BP
Tel: 01572 822326
www.rutnet.co.uk

KING'S ARMS INN
Top Street, Wing
Rutland LE15 8SE
Tel: 01572 737634
www.thekingsarms-wing.co.uk

WHITE HART INN
Lydgate, Oldham
Greater Manchester OL4 4JJ
Tel: 01457 872566

YE OLDE RED LION
Brook Street, Cromer
Norfolk NR27 9HD
Tel: 01263 514964
www.yeolderedlionhotel.co.uk

BLUE BOAR INN
Sprowston, Norwich
Norfolk NR7 8RL
Tel: 01603 426802
www.blueboarnorwich.co.uk

CAT INN
Cheswick, Berwick-upon-Tweed
Northumberland TD15 2RL
Tel: 01289 387251

COOK & BARKER INN
Newton-on-the-Moor, Felton
Northumberland NE65 9JY
Tel: 01665 575234
www.cookandbarkerinn.co.uk

Family-Friendly Pubs & Inns

half portions
children's menu
garden or play area
baby-changing facilities
high chairs
family room

MASONS ARMS
Stamford, Rennington
Northumberland NE66 3RX
Tel: 01665 577275
www.masonsarms.net

INN FOR ALL SEASONS
The Barringtons, Burford
Oxfordshire OX18 4TN
Tel: 01451 844324
www.innforallseasons.com

BLOWING STONE INN
Kingston Lisle, Wantage
Oxfordshire OX12 9QL
Tel: 01367 820288
www.theblowingstoneinn.com

FALCON HOTEL
St John Street, Bridgnorth
Shropshire WV15 6AG
Tel: 01746 763134
www.thefalconhotel.co.uk

THE BEAR HOTEL
Hodnet, Near Market Drayton
Shropshire TF9 3NH
Tel: 01630 685214
www.bearhotel.org.uk

LONGVILLE ARMS
Longville-in-the-Dale
Shropshire TF13 6TD
Tel: 01694 771206

THE WHEATSHEAF
Combe Hay, Bath
Somerset BA2 7EG
Tel: 01225 833504

Family-Friendly Pubs & Inns

KING'S ARMS INN
Bishopton, Montacute
Somerset TA15 6UU
Tel: 01935 822513
www.greeneking-inns.co.uk

PENSCOT INN
Shipham, Near Cheddar
Somerset BS25 1TW
Tel: 01934 842659

HALFWAY HOUSE INN
Chilthorne Domer, Yeovil
Somerset BA22 8RE
Tel: 01935 840350
www.halfwayhouseinn.com

THE CROWN
High Street, Southwold
Suffolk IP18 6DP
Tel: 01502 722275
www.adnams.co.uk

DOLPHIN INN
Thorpeness, Aldeburgh
Suffolk IP16 4NA
Tel: 01728 454994
www.thorpeness.co.uk

THE BELL INN
Ferry Road, Walberswick
Suffolk IP18 6TN
Tel: 01502 723109
www.blythweb.co.uk/bellinn

THE PLOUGH INN
Coldharbour, Near Dorking
Surrey RH5 6HD
Tel: 01306 711793
www.ploughinn.com

INGLENOOK HOTEL
Pagham, Bognor Regis
West Sussex PO21 3QB
Tel: 01243 262495
www.the-inglenook.com

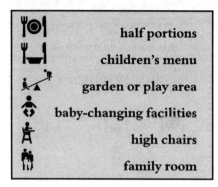

OLDE COACH HOUSE
Ashby St Ledgers, Near Rugby
Warwickshire CV23 8UN
Tel: 01788 890349

BATH ARMS - LONGLEAT
Horningsham, Warminster
Wiltshire BA12 7LY
Tel: 01985 844308
www.batharms-longleat.co.uk

SOMERSET ARMS
Church Street, Maiden Bradley
Wiltshire BA12 7HW
Tel: 01985 844207
www.somersetarms.co.uk

MANOR ARMS
Abberley Village
Worcestershire WR6 6BN
Tel: 01299 896507
www.themanorarms.co.uk

THE WHEATSHEAF
Carperby, Leyburn
North Yorkshire DL8 4DF
Tel: 01969 663216
www.wheatsheafinwensleydale.co.uk

THE YORKSHIRE LASS
Harrogate Road, Knaresborough
North Yorkshire HG5 8DA
Tel: 01423 862962
www.knaresborough.co.uk

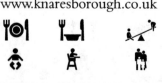

THREE SISTERS HOTEL
Brow Top Road, Haworth
West Yorkshire BD22 9PH
Tel: 01535 643458

Family-Friendly Pubs & Inns

BURNETT ARMS HOTEL
High Street, Banchory
Aberdeenshire AB31 5TD
Tel: 01330 824944
www.burnettarms.co.uk

GRANT ARMS HOTEL
Monymusk, Inverurie
Aberdeenshire AB51 7HJ
Tel: 01467 651226

THE WHEATSHEAF
Swinton, Duns
Berwickshire TD11 3JJ
Tel: 01890 860257
www.wheatsheaf-swinton.co.uk

ANNANDALE ARMS
High Street, Moffat
Dumfriesshire DG10 9HF
Tel: 01683 220013
www.AnnandaleArmsHotel.co.uk

THE INN AT LATHONES
By Largoward, St Andrews
Fife KY9 1JE
Tel: 01334 840494

THE PRIORY HOTEL
The Square, Beauly
Inverness-shire IV4 7BX
Tel: 01463 782309
www.priory-hotel.com

LOCH TUMMEL INN
Strathtummel, By Pitlochry
Perthshire PI I16 5RP
Tel: 01882 634272

KENMORE HOTEL
The Square, Kenmore
Perthshire PH15 2NU
Tel: 01887 830205
www.kenmorehotel.com

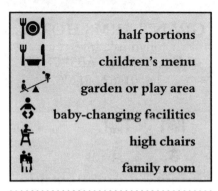

THE DOVEY INN
Aberdovey
Gwynedd LL35 0EF
Tel: 01654 767332
www.doveyinn.com

FAIRY GLEN HOTEL
Beaver Bridge, Betws-y-Coed
Gwynedd LL24 0SH
Tel: 01690 710269
www.fairyglenhotel.co.uk

ELEN'S CASTLE HOTEL
Dolwyddelan
Gwynedd LL25 0EJ
Tel: 01690 750207

WHEATSHEAF INN
Betws-yn-Rhos, Abergele
Conwy LL22 8AW
Tel: 01492 680218

THE WOLFE INN
Wolfscastle, Haverfordwest
Pembrokeshire SA62 5LS
Tel: 01437 741662
www.thewolfe.info

CASTLE VIEW HOTEL
Bridge Street, Chepstow
Monmouthshire NP16 5EZ
Tel: 01291 620349
www.hotelchepstow.co.uk

THE BELL AT SKENFRITH
Skenfrith
Monmouthshire NP7 8UH
Tel: 01600 750235
www.skenfrith.co.uk

… WEBSITE DIRECTORY 345

DIRECTORY OF WEBSITE AND E-MAIL ADDRESSES

A quick-reference guide to holiday accommodation with an e-mail address and/or website, conveniently arranged by country and county, with full contact details.

•LONDON

Guesthouse
MacDonald Hotel, 45-46 Argyle Square,
LONDON WC1H 8AL
020 7837 3552
• e-mail: fhg@macdonaldhotel.com
• website: www.macdonaldhotel.com

Hotel
The Elysee Hotel, 20-26 Craven Terrace,
LONDON W2 8EL
020 7402 7633
• e-mail: information@elyseehotel-london.co.uk
• website: www.elyseehotel-london.co.uk

Hotel / B & B
Lincoln House Hotel, 33 Gloucester Place,
LONDON W1V 8HY
020 7486 7630
• e-mail: reservations@lincoln-house-hotel.co.uk
• website: www.lincoln-house-hotel.co.uk

Guesthouse / Hotel
Barry House Hotel, 12 Sussex Place,
Hyde Park, LONDON W2 2TP
020 7723 7340
• e-mail: RSB@barryhouse.co.uk
• website: www.barryhouse.co.uk

Hotel / B & B
Elizabeth Hotel, 37 Eccleston Square,
LONDON SW1V 1PB
020 7828 6812
• e-mail: info@elizabethhotel.com
• website: www.elizabethhotel.com

Hotel
Queens Hotel, 33 Anson Road,
Tufnell Park, LONDON N7
020 7607 4725
• e-mail: queens@stavrouhotels.co.uk
• website: www.stavrouhotels.co.uk

Hotel
Athena Hotel, 110-114 Sussex Gardens,
Hyde Park, LONDON W2 1UA
020 7706 3866
• e-mail: athena@stavrouhotels.co.uk
• website: www.stavrouhotels.co.uk

Hotel
Gower Hotel, 129 Sussex Gardens,
Hyde Park, LONDON W2 2RX
020 7262 2262
• e-mail: gower@stavrouhotels.co.uk
• website: www.stavrouhotels.co.uk

B & B
Sohel & Anne Armanios, 67 Rannoch Road,
Hammersmith, LONDON W6 9SS
020 7385 4904
• website: www.thewaytostay.co.uk

B & B / Hotel / Self-Catering
Windsor House Hotel, 12 Penywern Road,
LONDON SW5 9ST
020 7373 9087
• e-mail: bookings@windsor-house-hotel.com
• website: www.windsor-house-hotel.com

•BERKSHIRE

Hotel
Clarence Hotel, 9 Clarence Road,
WINDSOR, Berkshire SL4 5AE
01753 864436
• website: www.clarence-hotel.co.uk

•CAMBRIDGESHIRE

Guest House
Dykelands Guest House, 157 Mowbray Road, CAMBRIDGE,
Cambridgeshire CB1 7SP
01223 244300
• e-mail: dykelands@fsbdial.co.uk
• website: www.dykelands.com

Guest House
Victoria Guest House,
57 Arbury Road, CAMBRIDGE,
Cambridgeshire CB4 2JB
01223 350086
• e-mail: victoriahouse@ntlworld.com
• website: www.SmoothHound.co.uk/hotels/victori3.html

346 WEBSITE DIRECTORY

• CHESHIRE

Guest House / Self-Catering
Mrs Joanne Hollins, Balterley Green Farm,
Farm Deans Lane, BALTERLEY, Crewe
Cheshire CW2 5QJ
01270 820 214
• e-mail: greenfarm@balterley.fsnet.co.uk
• website: www.greenfarm.freeserve.co.uk

Guest House / Self-Catering
Mrs Angela Smith, Mill House and Granary,
Higher Wych, MALPAS,
Cheshire SY14 7JR
01948 780362
• e-mail: angela@videoactive.co.uk
• website: www.millhouseandgranary.co.uk

• CORNWALL

Self-Catering
Fiona & Martin Nicolle,
Classy Cottages, Cornwall
07000 423000
• website: www.classycottages.co.uk

Self-Catering
Cornish Traditional Cottages, Blisland,
BODMIN, Cornwall PL30 4HS
01208 821666
• e-mail: info@corncott.com
• website: www.corncott.com

Self-Catering
Tregatherall Farm,
BOSCASTLE, Cornwall PL35 0EQ
01840 250177
• e-mail: tregatherall@ipl.co.uk
• website: www.ipl.co.uk/tregatherall/

Self-Catering
Mr Charles Tippet,
Mineshop Holiday Cottages, Crackington
Haven, BUDE, Cornwall EX23 0NR
01840 230178
• e-mail: tippett@mineshop.freeserve.co.uk
• website: www.crackingtoncottages.co.uk

Self-Catering / Caravan & Camping
Willow Valley Holiday Park,
Bush, BUDE, Cornwall EX23 9LB
01288 353104
• e-mail: willowvalley@talk21.com
• website: www.caravansitecornwall.co.uk

Caravan & Camping
Cornish Coasts Caravan & Camping Park,
Middle Penlean, Poundstock,
Widemouth Bay, BUDE, Cornwall EX23 0EE
01288 361380
• e-mail: info@cornishcoasts.co.uk
• website: www.cornishcoasts.co.uk

Self-Catering
Mr Ian Goodman,
Hilton Farm Holiday Cottages,
Marhamchurch, BUDE, Cornwall EX23 0HE
01288 361521
• e-mail: ian@hiltonfarmhouse.freeserve.co.uk
• website: www.hiltonfarmhouse.co.uk

Caravan & Camping
Widemouth Bay Caravan Park,
Near BUDE, Cornwall
01271 866666
• website:
www.johnfowlerholidays.com/widemouth_bay.asp

Hotel / Self-Catering
Wringford Down Hotel, CAWSAND,
Torpoint, Cornwall PL10 1LE
01752 822287
• e-mail: a.molloy@virgin.net
• website: www.cornwallholidays.co.uk

Hotel
Rosemullion Hotel, Gyllyngvase Hill,
FALMOUTH,
Cornwall TR11 4DF
01326 314690
• e-mail: gail@rosemullionhotel.demon.co.uk
• website:
www.s-h-systems.co.uk/hotels/rosemullion.html

Caravan & Camping
Boscrege Caravan & Camping Park,
Ashton, HELSTON, Cornwall TR13 9TG
01736 762231
• e-mail: enquiries@caravanparkcornwall.com
• website: www.caravanparkcornwall.com

Guest House
Greystones Guest House, 40 West End,
Porthleven, HELSTON TR13 9JL
01326 565583
• e-mail: neilvwoodward@hotmail.com

Self-Catering
Kathryn Broad, Lower Dutson Farm,
LAUNCESTON, Cornwall PL15 9SP
01566 776456
• e-mail: francis.broad@btclick.com
• website:
www.chycor.co.uk/cornish-farmholidays

WEBSITE DIRECTORY 347

Self-Catering
Celia Hutchinson,
Caradon Country Cottages, East Taphouse,
LISKEARD, Cornwall PL14 4NH
01579 320355
* e-mail: celia@caradoncottages.freeserve.co.uk
* website: www.caradoncottages.co.uk

Self-Catering
Kaye & Bill Chapman, Well Meadow
Cottage, Coldrinnick Farm, Duloe,
LISKEARD, Cornwall
01503 220251
* e-mail: kaye@coldrinnick.fsnet.co.uk
* website: www.cornishcottage.net

Self-Catering
Sue Jewell, Boturnell Farm Cottages,
St Pinnock, LISKEARD, Cornwall PL14 4QS
01579 320880
* e-mail: boturnell-barns@breathemail.net
* website: www.dogs-holiday.co.uk

Self-Catering
Mrs S. Clemens, Lametton Barton,
St Keyne, LISKEARD, Cornwall PL14 4SQ
01579 343434
* website:
  www.stayincornwall.co.uk/lametton.htm

B & B / Self-Catering
Paul Brumpton, Talehay Holiday Cottages,
Pelynt, near LOOE, Cornwall PL13 2LT
01503 220252
* e-mail: paul@talehay.co.uk
* website: www.talehay.co.uk

B & B
Mrs Dawn Rundle, Lancallan Farm,
MEVAGISSEY, St Austell,
Cornwall PL26 6EW
01726 842284
* e-mail: dawn@lancallan.fsnet.co.uk

Hotel
Golden Bay Hotel, Pentire Avenue,
Pentire, NEWQUAY,
Cornwall TR7 1PD
01637 873318
* e-mail: enquiries@goldenbayhotel.co.uk
* website: www.goldenbayhotel.co.uk

Guest House / Self-Catering
Trewerry Mill Guest House, Trewerry Mill,
Trerice, St Newlyn East, NEWQUAY,
Cornwall TR8 5GS
01872 510345
* e-mail: trewerry.mill@which.net
* website: www.trewerrymill.co.uk

Holiday Park
Treloy Tourist Park, NEWQUAY,
Cornwall TR8 4JN
01637 872063/876279
* e-mail: holidays@treloy.co.uk
* website: www.treloy.co.uk

Hotel
White Lodge Hotel, Mawgan Porth Bay,
Near NEWQUAY, Cornwall TR8 4BN
01637 860512
* e-mail: adogfriendly@aol.com
* website: www.dogfriendlyhotel.co.uk

Guest House
Dewolf Guest House, 100 Henver Road,
NEWQUAY, Cornwall TR7 3BL
01637 874746
* e-mail: holidays@dewolfguesthouse.com
* website: www.dewolfguesthouse.com

B & B / Hotel
Mr Simon Chapman, Camilla House Hotel,
12 Regent Terrace, PENZANCE,
Cornwall TR18 4DW
01736 363771
* e-mail: visitus@camillahouse-hotel.co.uk
* website: www.penzance.co.uk/camilla/

Farmhouse B & B
Rose Farm, Chyannal, Buryas Bridge,
PENZANCE, Cornwall
01736 731808
* e-mail: lally@rosefarmcornwall.co.uk
* website: www.rosefarmcornwall.co.uk

Inn
Crumplehorn Inn, POLPERRO,
Cornwall PL13 2RJ
01503 272348
* e-mail: host@crumplehorn-inn.co.uk
* website: www.crumplehorn-inn.co.uk

Visit the FHG website
www.holidayguides.com
for details of the wide choice of accommodation
featured in the full range of FHG titles

Caravan & Camping / Holiday Park
Globe Vale Holiday Park, Radnor,
REDRUTH, Cornwall
01209 891183
- e-mail: globe@ukgo.com
- website: www.globe.ukgo.com

Caravan & Camping / Holiday Park
Chiverton Park, Blackwater, ST AGNES,
Cornwall TR4 8HS
01872 560667
- e-mail: info@chivertonpark.co.uk
- website: www.chivertonpark.co.uk

Hotel / Inn
Mrs J. Treleaven, Driftwood Spars Hotel,
Trevaunance Cove, ST AGNES,
Cornwall TR5 0RT
01872 552428 / 553323
- e-mail: driftwoodspars@hotmail.com
- website: www.driftwoodspars.com

B & B
Mrs Liz Berryman, Polgreen Farm,
London Apprentice, ST AUSTELL,
Cornwall PL26 7AP
01726 75151
- e-mail: polgreen.farm@btclick.com
- website: www.polgreenfarm.co.uk

Holiday Park
St Ives Bay Holiday Park, ST IVES BAY,
Cornwall TR27 5BH
0800 317713 (24hr brochure line)
- e-mail: enquiries@stivesbay.co.uk
- website: www.stivesbay.co.uk

Hotel
Rosevine Hotel, Porthcurnick Beach,
ST MAWES, Cornwall
01872 580206
- e-mail: info@rosevine.co.uk
- website: www.rosevine.co.uk

Hotel
Dalswinton House, ST MAWGAN,
Near Newquay, Cornwall TR8 4EZ
01637 860385
- e-mail: dalswinton@bigwig.net
- website: www.dalswinton.com

Self-Catering
Mr & Mrs C.W. Pestell, Hockadays,
Tregenna, near Blisland, ST TUDY,
Cornwall PL30 4QJ
01208 850146
- e-mail:
holidays@hockadaysholidaycottages.co.uk
- website: www.hockadaysholidaycottages.co.uk

Hotel & Self-Catering Lodges
St Mellion Hotel, Golf & Country Club,
St Mellion, Near SALTASH, Cornwall
01579 351351
- e-mail: stmellion@americangolf.uk.com
- website: www.st-mellion.co.uk

Caravan & Camping
Wheal Rose Caravan & Camping Park,
Wheal Rose, SCORRIER,
Near Redruth, Cornwall
01209 891496
- e-mail: les@whealrosecaravanpark.co.uk
- website: www.whealrosecaravanpark.co.uk

Hotel
Willapark Manor Hotel, Bossiney,
TINTAGEL, Cornwall PL34 0BA
01840 770782
- e-mail: nick@willapark.co.uk
- website: www.willapark.co.uk

Guest House
Sara Hawkins, Bosayne Guest House,
Atlantic Road, TINTAGEL,
Cornwall PL34 0DE
01840 770514
- e-mail: clark@clarky100.freeserve.co.uk
- website: www.bosayne.co.uk

Self-Catering
Mrs Sandy Wilson, Salutations,
Atlantic Road, TINTAGEL,
Cornwall PL34 0DE
01840 770287
- website: www.salutationstintagel.co.uk

Caravan Park
C.R. Simpkins, Summer Valley Touring Park,
Shortlanesend, TRURO, Cornwall TR4 9DW
01872 277878
- e-mail: res@summervalley.co.uk
- website: www.summervalley.co.uk

Self-Catering
Mrs Sue Zamaria, Colesent Cottages,
St Tudy, WADEBRIDGE, Cornwall PL30 4QX
01208 850112
- e-mail: welcome@colesent.co.uk
- website: www.colesent.co.uk

Please mention this guide when enquiring about accommodation

• CUMBRIA

Hotel
Rothay Manor, Rothay Bridge,
AMBLESIDE, Cumbria LA22 0EH
015394 33605
• e-mail: hotel@rothaymanor.co.uk
• website: www.rothaymanor.co.uk

Caravan Park
Greenhowe Caravan Park, Great Langdale,
AMBLESIDE, Cumbria LA22 9JU
015394 37231
• e-mail: enquiries@greenhowe.com

B & B
Mr Jack Halliday, The Anchorage,
Rydal Road, AMBLESIDE,
Cumbria LA22 9AY
015394 32046
• e-mail: info@anchorageonline.force9.co.uk
• website: www.anchorageonline.force9.co.uk/

Hotel
Appleby Manor Country House Hotel,
Roman Road, APPLEBY-IN-WESTMORLAND,
Cumbria CA16 6JB
017683 51571
• e-mail: reception@applebymanor.co.uk
• website: www.applebymanor.co.uk

Self-Catering / Holiday Homes
Lakelovers, Belmont House, Lake Road,
BOWNESS-ON-WINDERMERE,
Cumbria LA23 3BJ
015394 88855
• e-mail: bookings@lakelovers.co.uk
• website: www.lakelovers.co.uk

B & B
Elaine Packer, The Hill, Gilsland,
BRAMPTON, Cumbria CA8 7SA
016977 47214
• e-mail: info@hadrians-wallbedandbreakfast.com
• website:
www.hadrians-wallbedandbreakfast.com

Hotel
Bridge Hotel, BUTTERMERE,
Cumbria CA13 9UZ
017687 70252
• e-mail: enquiries@bridge-hotel.com
• website: www.bridge-hotel.com

Guest House
Dalegarth Guest House, Hassness Estate,
BUTTERMERE, Cumbria CA13 9XA
017687 70233
• e-mail: dalegarth.buttermere@rdplus.net
• website: www.dalegarthguesthouse.co.uk

Self-Catering
Loweswater Holiday Cottages, Scale Hill,
Loweswater, COCKERMOUTH,
Cumbria CA13 9UX
01900 85232
• website:
www.loweswaterholidaycottages.co.uk

Hotel
Rob Treeby, Ivy House Hotel, Ivy House,
Main Street, HAWKSHEAD, Cumbria
015394 36204
• e-mail: rob@ivyhousehotel.com
• website: www.ivyhousehotel.com

Farm & Self-Catering
Mrs S. Beaty, Garnett House Farm,
Burneside, KENDAL, Cumbria
01539 724542
• e-mail: info@garnetthousefarm.co.uk
• website: www.garnetthousefarm.co.uk

Farmhouse B & B
Mrs Swindlehurst, Tranthwaite Hall,
Underbarrow, near KENDAL,
Cumbria LA8 8HG
015395 68285
• e-mail: tranthwaitehall@aol.com
• website: www.tranthwaitehall.co.uk

Self-Catering
Mrs Val Sunter, "Dora's Cottage",
c/o Higher House Farm, Oxenholme Lane,
Natland, KENDAL, Cumbria LA9 7QH
015395 61177
• website: www.shortbreaks-uk.co.uk/514

Hotel
Derwentwater Hotel, Portinscale, KESWICK,
Cumbria CA12 5RE
017687 72538
• e-mail: info@derwentwater-hotel.co.uk
• website:
www.derwentwater.hotel.dial.pipex.com

B&B
Highside Farm, Bassenthwaite, KESWICK
Cumbria CA12 4QG
017687 76952/76328
• e-mail: deborah@highside.co.uk
• website: www.highside.co.uk

Self-Catering
Brook House Cottage Holidays,
Bassenthwaite Village,
Near KESWICK, Cumbria
017687 76393
• e-mail: a.m.trafford@amserve.net
• website:
www.holiday.cottageslakedistrict.co.uk

350 WEBSITE DIRECTORY

Self-Catering
Keswick Cottages, Kentmere, How Lane,
KESWICK, Cumbria CA12 5RS
017687 73895
• e-mail: info@keswickcottages.co.uk
• website: www.keswickcottages.co.uk

B & B
Mrs S. Park, Langdale, 14 Leonard Street,
KESWICK, Cumbria CA12 4EL
017687 73977
• website: www.langdaleguesthouse.com

Self-Catering
16 Hewetson Court, Main Street,
KESWICK, Cumbria
01786 814955
• e-mail: martyn_d2@hotmail.com

Caravan & Camping
Mrs L. Lamb, Burns Caravan & Camping
Site, St Johns in the Vale, KESWICK,
Cumbria CA12 4RR
01768 779225
• e-mail: llamb@callnetuk.com

B & B
Val Bradley, Rickerby Grange, Portinscale,
KESWICK, Cumbria CA12 5RH
017687 72344
• e-mail: val@ricor.co.uk
• website: www.ricor.co.uk

Self-Catering
Watendlath Guest House and Barrowside &
Swinside Cottages,
c/o Mrs Walker, 15 Acorn Street, KESWICK,
Cumbria CA12 4EA
01768 774165
• e-mail: info@watendlathguesthouse.co.uk
• website: www.watendlathguesthouse.co.uk

Guest House
Ian Townsend and Annie Scally, Latrigg
House, St Herbert Street,
KESWICK, Cumbria CA12 4DF
017687 73068
• e-mail: info@latrigghouse.com
• website: www.latrigghouse.com

Self-Catering
Mrs S.J. Bottom, Crossfield Cottages,
KIRKOSWALD, Penrith, Cumbria CA10 1EU
01768 898711
• e-mail: info@crossfieldcottages.co.uk
• website: www.crossfieldcottages.co.uk

Hotel & Inn
The Shepherd's Arms Hotel,
Ennerdale Bridge,
LAKE DISTRICT NATIONAL PARK,
Cumbria CA23 3AR
01946 861249
• e-mail: enquiries@shepherdsarmshotel.co.uk
• website: www.sheperdsarmshotel.co.uk

B & B
Jenny Wickens, Garth Row,
LOWICK GREEN, Ulverston,
Cumbria LA12 8EB
01229 885633
• e-mail: b&b@garthrow.freeserve.co.uk
• website: www.garthrow.co.uk

Guest House / B & B
Mr & Mrs C. Smith, Mosedale House,
MOSEDALE, Mungrisdale,
Cumbria CA11 0XQ
01768 779371
• e-mail: mosedale@northlakes.co.uk
• website: www.mosedalehouse.co.uk

Guest House / Self-Catering
Near Howe Country House Hotel,
MUNGRISDALE, Penrith,
Cumbria CA11 0SH
017687 79678
• e-mail: nearhowe@btopenworld.co.uk
• website: www.nearhowe.co.uk

Caravan & Camping / Self-Catering
Park Foot Caravan & Camping Park,
Howtown Road, Pooley Bridge, PENRITH,
Cumbria CA10 2NA
017684 86309
• e-mail: park.foot@talk21.com
• website: www.parkfootullswater.co.uk

Guest House
Mrs M. Whittam, Netherdene Guest House,
Troutbeck, Near PENRITH,
Cumbria CA11 0SJ
017684 83475
• e-mail: netherdene@aol.com
• website: www.netherdene.co.uk

Guest House
Elle Jackson, Albany House,
5 Portland Place, PENRITH,
Cumbria CA11 7NQ
01768 863072
• e-mail: info@albany-house.org.uk
• website: www.albany-house.org.uk

WEBSITE DIRECTORY 351

Self-Catering / Caravan & Camping
Mr & Mrs Burnett, Fell View, Glenridding,
PENRITH, Cumbria CA11 0PJ
01768 482342; Evening: 01768 867420
• e-mail: enquiries@fellviewholidays.com
• website: www.fellviewholidays.com

Self-Catering / Caravan & Camping
Tanglewood Caravan Park, Causewayhead,
SILLOTH, Cumbria CA7 4PE
016973 31253
• e-mail: tanglewoodcaravanpark@hotmail.com
• website: www.tanglewoodcaravanpark.co.uk

Guest House / Self Catering
Mrs Jones, Primrose Cottage, Orton Road,
TEBAY, Cumbria CA10 3TL
01539 624791
• e-mail: info@primrosecottagecumbria.co.uk
• website: www.primrosecottagecumbria.co.uk

Self-Catering
High Dale Park House, Satterthwaite,
ULVERSTON, Cumbria CA12 8LJ
01229 860226
• e-mail: peter@lakesweddingmusic.com
• website: www.lakesweddingmusic.com

Guest House
Mr & Mrs Tyson, Hollywood Guest House,
Holly Road, WINDERMERE,
Cumbria LA23 2AF
015394 42219
• website: www.hollywoodguesthouse.co.uk

Self-Catering
Mr & Mrs Dodsworth, Birthwaite Edge,
Birthwaite Road, WINDERMERE,
Cumbria LA23 1BS
015394 42861
• e-mail: fhg@lakedge.com
• website: www.lakedge.com

Self-Catering
J.R. Benson, High Sett, Sun Hill Lane,
Troutbeck Bridge, WINDERMERE,
Cumbria LA23 1HJ
015394 42731
• e-mail: info@accommodationlakedistrict.com
• website: www.accommodationlakedistrict.com

•DERBYSHIRE

Farmhouse B & B / Self-Catering
Mrs M.A. Richardson, Throwley Hall Farm,
Ilam, ASHBOURNE, Derbyshire DE6 2BB
01538 308202
• e-mail: throwleyhall@talk21.com
• website: www.throwleyhallfarm.co.uk

Guest House
Mr & Mrs Hyde, Braemar Guest House,
10 Compton Road, BUXTON,
Derbyshire SK17 9DN
01298 78050
• e-mail: buxtonbraemar@supanet.com
• website: www.cressbrook.co.uk/buxton/braemar

Self-Catering
R.D. Hollands, Wheeldon Trees Farm,
Earl Sterndale, BUXTON,
Derbyshire SK17 0AA
01298 83219
• e-mail: hollands@earlsterndale.fsnet.co.uk
• website: www.wheeldontreesfarm.co.uk

Hotel
Biggin Hall Hotel, Biggin-by-Hartington,
BUXTON, Derbyshire SK17 0DH
01298 84451
• e-mail: enquiries@bigginhall.co.uk
• website: www.bigginhall.co.uk

Inn
Nick & Fiona Clough, The Devonshire Arms,
Peak Forest, near BUXTON,
Derbyshire SK17 8EJ
01298 23875
• e-mail: fiona.clough@virgin.net
• website: www.devarms.com

Farm / Self-Catering
J. Gibbs, Wolfscote Grange, HARTINGTON,
near Buxton, Derbyshire SK17 0AX
01298 84342
• e-mail: wolfscote@btinternet.com
• website: www.wolfscotegrangecottages.co.uk

FHG PUBLICATIONS
publish a large range of well-known accommodation guides. We will be happy to send you details or you can use the order form at the back of this book.

• DEVON

Self-Catering
Toad Hall Cottages,
DEVON
08700 777345
• website: www.toadhallcottages.com

Self-Catering
Waters Reach, West Quay, APPLEDORE, Devon. C/o Viv and Peter Foley
01707 657644
• e-mail: viv@vfoley.freeserve.co.uk

Holiday Park
Parkers Farm Holiday Park,
Higher Mead Farm, ASHBURTON, Devon
01364 652598
• e-mail: parkersfarm@btconnect.com
• website: www.parkersfarm.co.uk

Self-Catering
North Devon Holiday Homes,
19 Cross Street, BARNSTAPLE,
Devon EX31 1BD
01271 376322
• e-mail: info@northdevonholidays.co.uk
• website: www.northdevonholidays.co.uk

Farm B & B / Self-Catering
Peter Day, Lower Yelland Farm, Fremington,
BARNSTAPLE, Devon EX31 3EN
01271 860101
• e-mail: peterday@loweryellandfarm.co.uk
• website: www.loweryellandfarm.co.uk

Self-Catering
Mr Ridge, Braddon Cottages, Ashwater,
BEAWORTHY, Devon EX21 5EP
01409 211350
• e-mail: holidays@braddoncottages.co.uk
• website: www.braddoncottages.co.uk

Hotel
Sandy Cove Hotel, Combe Martin Bay,
BERRYNARBOR, Devon EX34 9SR
01271 882243 / 882888
• e-mail: rg/4003483@aol.com
• website: www.exmoor-hospitality-inns.co.uk

Self-Catering / Organic Farm
Little Comfort Farm Cottages,
Little Comfort Farm, BRAUNTON,
North Devon EX33 2NJ
01271 812414
• e-mail: jackie.milsom@btclick.com
• website: www.littlecomfortfarm.co.uk

B & B
Mrs Roselyn Bradford, St Merryn,
Higher Park Road, BRAUNTON,
Devon EX33 2LG
01271 813805
• e-mail: ros@st-merryn.co.uk
• website: www.st-merryn.co.uk

Self-Catering
Devoncourt Holiday Flats, Berryhead Road,
BRIXHAM, Devon TQ5 9AB
01803 853748
• e-mail: devoncourt@devoncoast.com

Guest House
Mr John Parry, Woodlands Guest House,
Parkham Road, BRIXHAM,
South Devon TQ5 9BU
01803 852040
• e-mail: Dogfriendly2@aol.com
• website: www.dogfriendlyguesthouse.co.uk

Self-Catering
Wheel Farm Country Cottages, Berry Down,
COMBE MARTIN, Devon EX34 0NG
01271 882106
• e-mail: holidays@wheelfarmcottages.co.uk
• website: www.wheelfarmcottages.co.uk

Self-Catering
Mrs S.R. Ridalls, The Old Bakehouse,
7 Broadstone, DARTMOUTH,
Devon TQ6 9NR
01803 834585
• e-mail: pioneerparker@aol.com
• website: www.oldbakehousedartmouth.co.uk

Farm / B & B
Mrs Karen Williams, Stile Farm, Starcross,
EXETER, Devon EX6 8PD
01626 890268
• e-mail: info@stile-farm.co.uk
• website: www.stile-farm.co.uk

Farmhouse B & B
Mrs J. Bragg, Marianne Pool Farm,
Clyst St George, EXETER, Devon EX3 0NZ
01392 874939
• website:
www.s-h-systems.co.uk/hotels/mariannepool.html

B & B
Mrs Sally Glanville, Rydon Farm, Woodbury,
EXETER, Devon EX5 1LB
01395 232341
• website:
www.hotelon.com/uk/s-w/b&b/rydon-farm.htm

WEBSITE DIRECTORY 353

Self-Catering
Christine Duncan, Raleigh Holiday Homes,
24 Raleigh Road, EXMOUTH,
Devon EX8 2SB
01395 266967
• e-mail: c.e.duncan@amserve.net

Farmhouse B&B
Mrs Alison Homa, Mullacott Farm,
Mullacott Cross, ILFRACOMBE,
Devon EX34 8NA
01271 866877
• e-mail: relax@mullacottfarm.co.uk
• website: www.mullacottfarm.co.uk

Farm / Self-Catering
Mrs E. Sansom, Widmouth Farm,
Watermouth, Near ILFRACOMBE,
Devon EX34 9RX
01271 863743
• e-mail: holiday@widmouthfarmcottages.co.uk
• website: www.widmouthfarmcottages.co.uk

Self-Catering
Karen Jackson, Torcross Apartment Hotel,
Torcross, KINGSBRIDGE, Devon
01548 580206
• e-mail: enquiries@torcross.com
• website: www.torcross.com

Hotel
Buckland-Tout-Saints Hotel & Restaurant,
Goveton, KINGSBRIDGE, Devon TQ7 2DS
01548 853055
• e-mail: buckland@tout-saints.co.uk
• website: www.tout-saints.co.uk

Guest House
Tricia & Alan Francis, Glenville House,
2 Tors Road, LYNMOUTH,
North Devon EX35 6ET
01598 752202
• e-mail: tricia@glenvillelynmouth.co.uk
• website: www.glenvillelynmouth.co.uk

Guest House
Mrs J. Parker, Tregonwell, The Olde Sea
Captain's House, 1 Tors Road, LYNMOUTH,
Exmoor National Park, Devon EX35 6ET
01598 753369
• website:
www.SmoothHound.co.uk/hotels/tregonwl.html

Inn
The Exmoor Sandpiper Inn, Countisbury,
LYNMOUTH, Devon EX35 6NE
01598 741263
• e-mail: info@exmoor-sandpiper.co.uk

Farm / B & B
Great Sloncombe Farm,
MORETONHAMPSTEAD,
Newton Abbot, Devon TQ13 8QF
01647 440595
• e-mail: hmerchant@sloncombe.freeserve.co.uk
• website: www.greatsloncombefarm.co.uk

Self-Catering
Mrs Whale, Roselands, Totnes Road,
Ipplepen, NEWTON ABBOT, Devon
01803 812701
• e-mail: enquiries@roselands.net
• website: www.roselands.net

B & B
Mrs Rosemary Ward, Parsonage Farm,
Iddesleigh, OKEHAMPTON,
Devon EX19 8SN
• website:
www.devon-holiday.com/parsonage-farm/

Farm Guest House
Mrs Ann Forth, Fluxton Farm,
OTTERY ST MARY, Devon EX11 1RJ
01404 812818
• website:
www.s-h-systems.co.uk/hotels/fluxtonfarm.html

Guest House
The Lamplighter Hotel, 103 Citadel Road,
The Hoe, PLYMOUTH, Devon PL1 2RN
01752 663855
• e-mail: lamplighterhotel@ukonline.co.uk

Self-Catering / Caravan & Camping
Harford Bridge Holiday Park, Peter Tavy,
TAVISTOCK, Devon PL19 9LS
01822 810349
• e-mail: enquiry@harfordbridge.co.uk
• website: www.harfordbridge.co.uk

Guest House
Mrs Arnold, The Mill, Washfield,
TIVERTON, Devon EX16 9PD
01884 255207
• e-mail: arnold5@washfield.freeserve.co.uk
• website: www.washfield.freeserve.co.uk

Guest House
Aveland Hotel, Aveland Road,
Babbacombe, TORQUAY, Devon TQ1 3PT
01803 326622
• e-mail: avelandhotel@aol.com
• website: www.avelandhotel.co.uk

354 WEBSITE DIRECTORY

Self-Catering
Mrs H. Carr, Sunningdale Apartments,
11 Babbacombe Downs Road, TORQUAY,
Devon TQ1 3LF
• website: www.sunningdaleapartments.co.uk

Self-Catering
Mrs J. Ford, Flear Farm Cottages,
East Allington, TOTNES, Devon TQ9 7RF
01548 521227
• e-mail: flearfarm@btinternet.com
• website: www.flearfarm.co.uk

Self-Catering
J. Lincoln-Gordon, Golland Farm,
Burrington, UMBERLEIGH, Devon EX37 9JP
01769 520263
• e-mail: golland@btinternet.com
• website: www.golland.btinternet.co.uk

Self-Catering
Jane Cromey-Hawke, Collacott Farm,
Kings Nympton, UMBERLEIGH,
Devon EX37 9TP
01769 572491
• e-mail: jane@collacott.co.uk
• website: www.collacott.co.uk

Guest House
Sunnymeade Country Hotel, Dean Cross,
West Down, WOOLACOMBE,
Devon EX34 8NT
01271 863668
• e-mail: info@sunnymeade.co.uk
• website: www.sunnymeade.co.uk

Self-Catering/ Camping
Dartmoor Country Holidays,
Magpie Leisure Park, Bedford Bridge,
Horrabridge, YELVERTON, Devon PL20 7RY
01822 852651
• website: www.dartmoorcountryholidays.co.uk

•DORSET

Guest House
Caroline Pielesz, The Walnuts,
2 Prout Bridge, BEAMINSTER, Dorset
01308 862211
• e-mail: caroline@thewalnuts.co.uk

Guest House
S. Barling, Mayfield Guest House,
46 Frances Road, BOURNEMOUTH, Dorset
BH1 3SA
01202 551839
• e-mail: accom@mayfieldguesthouse.com
• website: www.mayfieldguesthouse.com

Hotel / Guest House
Southernhay Hotel, 42 Alum Chine Road,
Westbourne, BOURNEMOUTH,
Dorset BH4 8DX
01202 761251
• e-mail: enquiries@southernhayhotel.co.uk
• website: www.southernhayhotel.co.uk

Hotel
Fircroft Hotel, Owls Road, BOURNEMOUTH,
Dorset BH5 1AE
01202 309771
• e-mail: info@fircrofthotel.co.uk
• website: www.fircrofthotel.co.uk

Hotel / Guest House
Westcotes House Hotel,
9 Southbourne Overcliff Drive,
BOURNEMOUTH, Dorset BH6 3TE
01202 428512
• website: www.westcoteshousehotel.co.uk

Caravan & Camping
Martin Cox, Highlands End Holiday Park,
BRIDPORT, Eype, Dorset DT6 6AR
01308 422139
• e-mail: holidays@wdlh.co.uk
• website: www.wdlh.co.uk

Self-Catering
Westover Farm Cottages,
Wootton Fitzpaine, Near LYME REGIS,
Dorset DT6 6NE
01297 560451
• e-mail: wfcottages@aol.com
• website: www.lymeregis.com/westover-farm-cottages/

Guest House / Self-Catering
White Horse Farm, Middlemarsh,
SHERBORNE, Dorset DT9 5QN
01963 210222
• e-mail: enquiries@whitehorsefarm.co.uk
• website: www.whitehorsefarm.co.uk

Hotel
The Knoll House, STUDLAND BAY,
Dorset BH19 3AW
01929 450450
• e-mail: enquiries@knollhouse.co.uk
• website: www.knollhouse.co.uk

Please mention this guide when enquiring about accommodation

WEBSITE DIRECTORY 355

B&B
Mrs Jill Miller, Lower Fifehead Farm,
Fifehead, St Quinton, STURMINSTER
NEWTON, Dorset DT10 2AP
01258 817335
• website: www.ruraldorset.co.uk

Touring Park
Wareham Forest Touring Park, North Trigon,
WAREHAM, Dorset BH20 7NZ
01929 551393
e-mail: holiday@wareham-forest.co.uk
website:
http://freespace.virgin.net/wareham.forest

Self-Catering on Working Farm
Josephine Pearse, Tamarisk Farm Cottages,
WEST BEXINGTON, Dorchester,
Dorset DT2 9DF
01308 897784
• e-mail: tamarisk@eurolink.ltd.net
• website: www.tamariskfarm.co.uk

Self-Catering
Mrs J. Elwood, Lower Farmhouse,
Langton Herring, WEYMOUTH,
Dorset DT3 4JB
01305 871187
• e-mail: jane@mayo.fsbusiness.co.uk
• website: www.characterfarmcottages.co.uk

•DURHAM

Self-Catering
Peter Wilson, East Briscoe Farm,
Baldersdale, BARNARD CASTLE,
Co Durham DL12 9UL
01833 650087
• e-mail: fhg@eastbriscoe.co.uk
• website: www.eastbriscoe.co.uk

Hotel / Golf
Ramside Hall Hotel, Carrville, DURHAM,
Co Durham DH1 1TD
0191 3865282
• e-mail: info@ramsidehallhotel.co.uk
• website: www.ramsidehallhotel.co.uk

Self-Catering
Raby Estates Holiday Cottages,
Upper Teesdale Estate Office,
MIDDLETON-IN-TEESDALE, Barnard Castle,
Co Durham DL12 0QH
01833 640209
• e-mail: teesdaleestate@rabycastle.com
• website: www.rabycastle.com

•GLOUCESTERSHIRE

Lodge
Ian Gibson, Thornbury Golf Lodge, Bristol
Road, Thornbury, BRISTOL, Gloucestershire
01454 281144
• e-mail: info@thornburygc.co.uk
• website: www.thornburygc.co.uk

B & B
Mrs G. Jeffrey, Brymbo, Honeybourne Lane,
Mickleton, CHIPPING CAMPDEN,
Gloucestershire GL55 6PU
01386 438890
• e-mail: enquiries@brymbo.com
• website: www.brymbo.com

Farmhouse B & B
Mrs D. Gwilliam, Dryslade Farm,
English Bicknor, COLEFORD,
Gloucestershire, GL16 7PA
01594 860259
• e-mail: dryslade@agriplus.net
• website: www.drysladefarm.co.uk

Inn
The Wild Duck, EWEN, Gloucestershire
01285 770310
• e-mail: wduckinn@aol.com
• website: www.thewildduck.co.uk

Farmhouse B & B
Suzie Paton, Milton Farm, FAIRFORD,
Gloucestershire GL7 4HZ
01285 712205
• e-mail: milton@farmersweekly.net
• website: www.milton-farm.co.uk

Guest House / Farm
Gunn Mill Guest House, Lower Spout Lane,
MITCHELDEAN, Gloucestershire GL17 0EA
01594 827577
• e-mail: info@gunnmillhouse.co.uk
• website: www.gunnmillhouse.co.uk

B & B
Mrs F.J. Adams, Aston House,
Broadwell, MORETON-IN-MARSH,
Gloucestershire GL56 0TJ
01451 830475
• e-mail: fja@netcomuk.co.uk
• website:
www.netcomuk.co.uk/~nmfa/aston_house.html

Farmhouse B & B
Robert Smith, Corsham Field Farmhouse,
Bledington Road, STOW-ON-THE-WOLD,
Gloucestershire GL54 1JH
• e-mail: farmhouse@corshamfield.co.uk
• website: www.corshamfield.co.uk

B & B
Mrs Williams, Abbots Court, Church End,
Twyning, TEWKESBURY, Gloucestershire
GL20 6DA
01684 292515
• e-mail: bernie@abbotscourt.fsbusiness.co.uk
• website:
  www.glosfarmhols.co.uk/abbots-court/

B & B
Mrs Wendy Swait, Inschdene,
Atcombe Road, SOUTH WOODCHESTER,
Stroud, Gloucestershire GL5 5EW
01453 873254
• e-mail: malcolm.swait@repp.co.uk
• website: www.inschdene.co.uk

•HAMPSHIRE

B & B
Mrs Arnold-Brown, Hilden B&B,
Southampton Road, Boldre,
BROCKENHURST, Hampshire SO41 8PT
01590 623682
• website: www.newforestbandb-hilden.co.uk

Caravan & Camping
Kingfisher Caravan Park, Browndown Road,
Stokes Bay, GOSPORT,
Hampshire PO13 9BG
023 9250 2611
• e-mail: info@kingfisher-caravan-park.co.uk
• website: www.kingfisher-caravan-park.co.uk

Caravan & Campsite
Hayling Island Family Campsites,
Copse Lane, HAYLING ISLAND, Hampshire
023 9246 2479, 023 9246 4695, 023 9246 3684
• e-mail: lowertye@euphony.net
• website: www.haylingcampsites.co.uk

B & B
Mr & Mrs Farrell, Honeysuckle House,
24 Clinton Road, LYMINGTON,
Hampshire SO41 9EA
01590 676635
• e-mail: derekfarrell1@btopenworld.com
• website:
  www.newforest.demon.co.uk/honeysuckle.htm

Hotel
Woodlands Lodge Hotel, Bartley Road,
Woodlands, NEW FOREST,
Hampshire SO40 7GN
023 8029 2157
• e-mail: reception@woodlands-lodge.co.uk
• website: www.woodlands-lodge.co.uk

B & B
Mr & Mrs T. Jelley, Appledore Cottage,
Holmsley Road, Wootton, NEW MILTON,
Hampshire, BH25 5TR
01425 629506
• e-mail: info@appledorecottage.co.uk
• website:
  www.newforest-online.co.uk/appledore

•HEREFORDSHIRE

Hotel
The Steppes, Ullingswick,
Near HEREFORD, HR1 3JG
01432 820424
• e-mail: info@steppeshotel.co.uk
• website: www.steppeshotel.co.uk

B & B / Farm
Mrs D Sinclair, Holly House Farm,
Allensmore, HEREFORD,
Herefordshire HR2 9BH
01432 277294
• e-mail: hollyhousefarm@aol.com
• website: www.hollyhousefarm.org.uk

B & B
Mrs Gill Andrews, Webton Court
Farmhouse, KINGSTONE,
Herefordshire HR2 9NF
01981 250220
• e-mail: gill@webton.fsnet.co.uk

B & B
Mrs S.W. Born, The Coach House, Putley,
LEDBURY, Herefordshire HR8 2QP
01531 670684
• e-mail: wendyborn@putley-coachhouse.co.uk
• website: www.putley-coachhouse.co.uk

Self-Catering
Mrs Jane Viner, Docklow Manor, Docklow,
LEOMINSTER, Herefordshire HR6 0RX
01568 760668
• e-mail: jane@docklowmanor.freeserve.co.uk
• website: www.docklow-manor.co.uk

B & B
Mrs I. Pritchard, Olchon Cottage Farm,
LONGTOWN, Herefordshire HR2 0NS
01873 860233
• website: www.golden-valley.co.uk/olchon/

Guest House / Farm
Mrs Drzymalski, Thatch Close, Llangrove,
ROSS-ON-WYE, Herefordshire HR9 6EL
01989 770300
• e-mail: thatch.close@virgin.net
• website: www.thatchclose.com

WEBSITE DIRECTORY 357

•ISLE OF WIGHT

Caravan & Camping
Castlehaven Caravan Site, Niton, Near Ventnor, Isle of Wight, PO38 2ND
01983 855556
• e-mail: caravans@castlehaven.co.uk
• website: www.castlehaven.co.uk

•KENT

Caravan & Camping
Woodlands Park, Tenterden Road, BIDDENDEN, Kent
01580 291216
• e-mail: woodlandsp@aol.com
• website: www.campingsite.co.uk

Self-Catering
Marion Fuller, Three Chimneys Farm, Bedgebury Road, GOUDHURST, Kent TN17 2RA
• e-mail: marionfuller@threechimneysfarm.co.uk
• website: www.threechimneysfarm.co.uk

Farm B & B / Camping
Julia Soyke, Manor Court Farm, Ashurst, TUNBRIDGE WELLS, Kent TN3 9TB
01892 740279
• e-mail: jsoyke@jsoyke.freeserve.co.uk
• website: www.manorcourtfarm.co.uk

•LEICESTERSHIRE

Guest House
The Highbury Guest House, 146 Leicester Road, LOUGHBOROUGH, Leicestershire LE11 2AQ
01509 230545
• e-mail: emkhighbury@supanet.com
• website: www.thehighburyguesthouse.co.uk

•LINCOLNSHIRE

B & B
Jenny Dixon, 19 West Street, Kings Cliffe, PETERBOROUGH, Lincolnshire PE8 6XB
01780 470365
• e-mail: kjhl-dixon@hotmail.com
• website: kingjohnhuntinglodge.com

Hotel
Petwood Hotel, Stixwood Road, WOODHALL SPA, Lincolnshire
01526 352411
• e-mail: reception@petwood.co.uk
• website: www.petwood.co.uk

•NORFOLK

Self-Catering
Sand Dune Cottages, Tan Lane, CAISTER-ON-SEA, Great Yarmouth, Norfolk
01493 720352
• e-mail: sand.dune.cottages@amserve.net
• website: www.eastcoastlive.co.uk/sites/sandunecottages.php

Farmhouse B & B
Mrs Jenny Bell, Peacock House, Peacock Lane, Old Beetley, DEREHAM, Norfolk NR20 4DG
• e-mail: PeackH@aol.com
• website: www.SmoothHound.co.uk/hotels/peacockh.htm

Self-Catering
Nannette Catchpole, Walcot Green Farm, DISS, Norfolk IP22 5SU
01379 652806
• e-mail: n.catchpole.wgf@virgin.net
• website: www.walcotgreenfarm.co.uk

FHG PUBLICATIONS LTD
publish a large range of well-known accommodation guides.
We will be happy to send you details or you can use the order form at the back of this book.

WEBSITE DIRECTORY

Self-Catering
Idyllic Cottages at Vere Lodge,
South Raynham, FAKENHAM,
Norfolk NR21 7HE
01328 838261
• e-mail: major@verelodge.co.uk
• website: www.idylliccottages.co.uk

Self-Catering
Blue Riband Holidays, HEMSBY,
Great Yarmouth, Norfolk NR29 4HA
01493 730445
• website: www.BlueRibandHolidays.co.uk

Farmhouse B & B
Mrs Lynda Mack, Hempstead Hall, HOLT,
Norfolk NR25 6TN
01263 712224
• website: www.broadland.com/hempsteadhall

Guest House B & B
Mrs Christine Lilah Thrower, Whincliff,
Cromer Road, MUNDESLEY-ON-SEA,
Norfolk NR11 8DU
01263 721554
• e-mail: whincliff@freeuk.com
• website: http://whincliff.freeuk.com

Self-Catering
Mr & Mrs Moore, Mangreen Farm Holiday
Cottages, STANFIELD, Dereham,
Norfolk NR20 4HZ
01328 700272
• e-mail: bettymick@compuserve.com
• website: www.mangreen.co.uk

Inn
The Lifeboat Inn and Old Coach House,
Ship Lane, THORNHAM, Norfolk PE36 6LT
01485 512236
• website: www.llifeboatinn.co.uk

• NORTHUMBERLAND

Self-Catering
Village Farm Self-Catering, Town Foot Farm,
Shilbottle, ALNWICK,
Northumberland NE66 2HG
01665 575591
• e-mail: crissy@villagefarmcottages.co.uk
• website: www.villagefarmcottages.co.uk

Self-Catering
Mrs Helen Wyld, New Moor House,
Edlingham, ALNWICK,
Northumberland NE66 2BT
01665 574638
• e-mail: stay@newmoorhouse.co.uk
• website: www.newmoorhouse.co.uk

Hotel
The Cobbled Yard Hotel Ltd, 40 Walkergate,
BERWICK-UPON-TWEED,
Northumberland TD15 1DJ
01289 308407
• e-mail: cobbledyardhotel@berwick35.fsnet.co.uk
• website: www.cobbledyardhotel.com

Caravans
D.J. Caravan Holidays (Haggerston Castle),
c/o Mr J. Lane, 11 Wallis Street, Penshaw,
Houghton-le-Spring DH4 7HB
• e-mail: joseph_lane1@hotmail.com
• website: www.djcaravanholidays.com

• OXFORDSHIRE

B & B
Carol Ellis, Wynford House, 79 Main Road,
Long Hanborough, BLADON,
Oxfordshire OX29 8JX
01993 881402
• website: www.accommodation.net/wynford.htm

Inn
The Kings Head Inn, The Green,
BLEDINGTON, Oxfordshire
01608 658365
• e-mail: kingshead@orr-ewing.com
• website: www.kingsheadinn.net

Guest House / B & B
Gorselands Hall, Boddington Lane,
North Leigh, WITNEY,
Oxfordshire OX29 6PU
01993 882292
• e-mail: hamilton@gorselandshall.com
• website: www.gorselandshall.com

Guest House
Mrs Elizabeth Simpson, Field View, Wood
Green, WITNEY, Oxfordshire OX28 1DE
01993 705485
• e-mail: bandb@fieldview-witney.co.uk
• website: www.fieldview-witney.co.uk

WEBSITE DIRECTORY 359

•SHROPSHIRE

Farm B & B
Mrs M. Jones, Acton Scott Farm,
Acton Scott, CHURCH STRETTON,
Shropshire SY6 6QN
01694 781260
• e-mail: bandb@actonscottfarm.co.uk
• website: www.actonscottfarm.co.uk

Guest House
Ron & Jenny Repath, Meadowlands,
Lodge Lane, Frodesley, DORRINGTON,
Shropshire SY5 7HD
01694 731350
• e-mail: meadowlands@talk21.com
• website: www.meadowlands.co.uk

B & B
Ravenscourt Manor, Woofferton,
LUDLOW, Shropshire SY8 4AL
01584 711905
• e-mail: ravenscourtmanor@amserve.com
• website:
www.s-h-systems.co.uk/hotels/ravenscourt.html

Self-Catering
Clive & Cynthia Prior, Mocktree Barns
Holiday Cottages, Leintwardine, LUDLOW,
Shropshire SY7 0LY
01547 540441
• e-mail: mocktreebarns@care4free.net
• website: www.mocktreeholidays.co.uk

Guest House & Self-Catering
Mrs E. Purnell, Ravenscourt Manor,
Woofferton, LUDLOW, Shropshire SY8 6AL
01584 711905
• e-mail: ravenscourtmanor@amserve.com
• website:
www.smoothhound.co.uk/ravenscourt

Inn
M.A. Tennant, The Talbot Inn, High Street,
MUCH WENLOCK, Shropshire TF13 6AA
01952 727077
• e-mail: maggie@talbotinn.idps.co.uk
• website: www.the-talbot-inn.co.uk

B & B
Mrs P. Morrissey, Top Farm House, Knockin,
Near OSWESTRY, Shropshire SY10 2HN
01691 682582
• e-mail: p.a.m@knockin.freeserve.co.uk
• website: www.topfarmknockin.co.uk

Hotel
Pen-y-Dyffryn Country Hotel, OSWESTRY,
Shropshire SY10 7JD
01691 653700
• e-mail: stay@peny.co.uk
• website: www.peny.co.uk

B & B
Lythwood Hall Bed & Breakfast,
2 Lythwood Hall, Lythwood, Bayston Hill,
SHREWSBURY, Shropshire SY3 0AD
07074 874747
• e-mail: lythwoodhall@amserve.net

Self-Catering
Mrs V. Evans, Church Farm, Rowton,
Near Wellington, TELFORD,
Shropshire TF6 6QY
01952 770381
• e-mail: church.farm@bigfoot.com
• website:
www.virtual-shropshire.co.uk/churchfarm

•SOMERSET

Guest House / Farm/ Self-Catering
Jackie & David Bishop, Toghill House Farm,
Wick, BATH, Somerset BS30 5RT
01225 891261
• website: www.toghillhousefarm.co.uk

B & B
Mrs C. Bryson, Walton Villa,
3 Newbridge Hill, BATH, Somerset BA1 3PW
01225 482792
• e-mail: walton.villa@virgin.net
• website: www.walton.izest.com

Self-Catering / Caravan & Camping
T.M. Hicks, Diamond Farm, Weston Road,
BREAN, Near Burnham-on-Sea,
Somerset TA8 2RL
01278 751263
• e-mail: trevor@diamondfarm42.freeserve.co.uk
• website: www.diamondfarm.co.uk

Caravan & Camping
Beachside Holiday Park, Coast Road,
BREAN SANDS, Burnham-on-Sea,
Somerset TA8 2QZ
01278 751346
• e-mail: beachside@breansands.fsnet.co.uk
• website: www.beachsideholidaypark.co.uk

Farm B&B / Self-catering
Delia Edwards, Brinsea Green Farm, Brinsea
Lane, Congresbury, Near BRISTOL,
North Somerset BS49 5JN
01934 852278
• e-mail: delia@brinseagreenfarm.co.uk
• website: www.brinseagreenfarm.co.uk

WEBSITE DIRECTORY

B & B
Mrs Alexander, Priors Mead,
23 Rectory Road, BURNHAM-ON-SEA,
Somerset TA8 2BZ
01278 782116
- e-mail: priorsmead@aol.com
- website: www.priorsmead.co.uk

B & B / Self-Catering
Butcombe Farm, Aldwick Vale, BUTCOMBE,
Near Blagdon, Somerset BS40 7UW
01761 462380
- e-mail: info@butcombe-farm.demon.co.uk
- website: www.butcombe-farm.demon.co.uk

Caravan & Camping Park
Broadway House Holiday Touring Caravan &
Camping Park, CHEDDAR,
Somerset BS27 3DB
01934 742610
- e-mail: enquiries@broadwayhouse.uk.com
- website: www.broadwayhouse.uk.com

B & B
Mrs C. Bacon, Honeydown Farm,
Seaborough Hill, CREWKERNE,
Somerset TA18 8PL
01460 72665
- e-mail: cb@honeydown.freeserve.co.uk
- website: www.honeydown.freeserve.co.uk

Hotel
Yarn Market Hotel, 25-33 High Street,
DUNSTER, Somerset TA24 6SF
01643 821425
- e-mail: yarnmarket.hotel@virgin.net
- website: www.yarnmarkethotel.co.uk

Inn
Exmoor White Horse Inn, EXFORD,
Somerset TA24 7PY
01643 831229
- website: www.exmoor-hospitality-inns.co.uk

Self-Catering
Mr Hughes, West Withy Farm Holiday
Cottages, Upton, Near Wiveliscombe,
EXMOOR, Somerset TA4 2JH
01398 371258
- e-mail: westwithyfarm@exmoor-cottages.com
- website: www.exmoor-cottages.com

Self-Catering / B & B
Mrs Joan Atkins, 2 Edgcott Cottage,
Exford, EXMOOR, Somerset TA24 7QG
01643 831564
- e-mail: info@stilemoorexmoor.co.uk
- website: www.stilemoorexmoor.co.uk

Farm / Self-Catering
Mrs Styles, Wintershead Farm, Simonsbath,
EXMOOR, Somerset TA24 7LF
01643 831222
- e-mail: info@wintershead.co.uk
- website: www.wintershead.co.uk

Farm Self-Catering & Camping
Westermill Farm, Exford, EXMOOR,
Somerset TA24 7NJ
01643 831238
- e-mail: holidays@westermill-exmoor.co.uk
- website: www.exmoorfarmholidays.co.uk

Self-Catering
Mrs N. Hanson, Woodcombe Lodges,
Bratton, MINEHEAD,
Somerset TA24 8SQ
01643 702789
- e-mail: nicola@woodcombelodge.co.uk
- website: www.woodcombelodge.co.uk

B & B
Mr P.R. Weir, Slipper Cottage,
41 Bishopston, MONTACUTE,
Somerset TA15 6UX
01935 823073
- e-mail: sue.weir@totalise.co.uk
- website: www.slippercottage.co.uk

B & B
Mr & Mrs Painter, Blorenge House,
57 Staplegrove Road, TAUNTON, Somerset
TA1 1DG
01823 283005
- e-mail: enquiries@blorengehouse.co.uk
- website: www.blorengehouse.co.uk

Farm / B & B
Yew Tree Farm, THEALE, Near Wedmore,
Somerset BS28 4SN
01934 712475
- e-mail: enquiries@yewtreefarmbandb.co.uk
- website: www.yewtreefarmbandb.co.uk

**FREE or REDUCED RATE
entry to Holiday Visits and Attractions
see our READERS' OFFER VOUCHERS**

Self-Catering
Croft Holiday Cottages, 2 The Croft, Anchor Street, WATCHET, Somerset TA23 0BY
01984 631121
• e-mail: croftcottages@talk21.com
• website: www.cottagessomerset.com

Farm / B & B
Mrs Sheila Stott, 'Lana', Hollow Farm, Westbury-sub-Mendip, WELLS, Somerset
01749 870635
• e-mail: sheila@stott.2366

Hotel
Braeside Hotel, 2 Victoria Park, WESTON-SUPER-MARE, Somerset BS23 2HZ
01934 626642
• e-mail: braeside@tesco.net
• website: www.braesidehotel.co.uk

• STAFFORDSHIRE

Farm B & B / Self-Catering
Mrs M. Hiscoe-James, Offley Grove Farm, Adbaston, ECCLESHALL, Staffordshire ST20 0QB
01785 280205
• e-mail: accom@offleygrovefarm.freeserve.co.uk
• website: www.offleygrovefarm.co.uk

Guest House
Ruth Franks, The Beehive, Churnet View Road, OAKAMOOR, Staffordshire ST10 3AE
01538 702420
• e-mail: thebeehiveoakamoor@btinternet.com
• website: www.thebeehiveguesthouse.co.uk

• SUFFOLK

Guest House
Kay Dewsbury, Manorhouse, The Green, Beyton, BURY ST EDMUNDS, Suffolk IP30 9AF
01359 270960
• e-mail: manorhouse@beyton.com
• website: www.beyton.com

B & B / Self-Catering
Tim & Sarah Kindred, High House Farm, Cransford, FRAMLINGHAM, Woodbridge, Suffolk IP13 9PD
01728 663461
• e-mail: info@highhousefarm.co.uk
• website: www.highhousefarm.co.uk

Farmhouse / Caravan Site
Fiddlers Hall, Cransford, FRAMLINGHAM, Woodbridge, Suffolk IP13 9PQ
• e-mail: johnmann@suffolkonline.com
• website: www.fiddlershall.com

Self-Catering
Kessingland Cottages, Rider Haggard Lane, KESSINGLAND. Contact: S. Mahmood, 156 Bramley Road, Beckenham, Kent BR3 6PG
020 8650 0539
• e-mail: jeeptrek@kjti.freeserve.co.uk
• website: www.k-cottage.co.uk

Self-Catering
Southwold Self-Catering Properties. H.A. Adnams, 98 High Street, SOUTHWOLD, Suffolk IP18 6DP
01502 723292
• e-mail: haadnams_lets@ic24.net
• website: www.haadnams.com

Self-Catering
Mr M. Scott, The Grove, Priory Green, Edwardstone, Lavenham, SUDBURY, Suffolk CO10 5PP
01787 211115
• e-mail: mark@grove-cottages.co.uk
• website: www.grove-cottages.co.uk

Hotel
The Crown & Castle, Orford, WOODBRIDGE, Suffolk IP12 2LJ
01394 450205
• e-mail: info@crownandcastle.co.uk
• website: www.crownandcastle.co.uk

• SURREY

Hotel
Chase Lodge Hotel, 10 Park Road, Hampton Wick, KINGSTON-UPON-THAMES, Surrey KT1 4AS
020 8943 1862
• e-mail: info@chaselodgehotel.com
• website: www.chaselodgehotel.com

Self-Catering
Mrs J.A. Vause, Woodend, High Cotts Lane, WEST CLANDON, Surrey GU4 7XA
01483 222644
• e-mail: deevause@amserve.net
• website: www.hillcrest-mortehue.co.uk

visit the FHG website
www.holidayguides.com

•EAST SUSSEX

Self-Catering
Eva Morris, Pekes, CHIDDINGLY,
East Sussex
020 7352 8088
• e-mail: pekes.afa@virgin.net
• website: www.pekesmanor.com

Hotel
Beauport Park Hotel, Battle Road,
HASTINGS, East Sussex TN38 8EA
01424 851222
• e-mail: reservations@beauportprkhotel.demon.co.uk
• website: www.beauportparkhotel.co.uk

Self-Catering
Beach Cottages, Claremont Road,
SEAFORD BN25 2QQ.
Contact: Julia Lewis, 47 Wandle Bank,
London, SW19 1DW
020 8542 5073
• website: www.beachcottages.info

•WEST SUSSEX

Caravan & Camping
Wicks Farm Holiday Park, Redlands Lane,
West Wittering, CHICHESTER,
West Sussex PO20 8QD
01243 513116
• e-mail: wicks.farm@virgin.net
• website: www.wicksfarm.co.uk

B & B
Mrs M.R. Milton, Beacon Lodge B&B,
London Road, WATERSFIELD,
West Sussex RH20 1NH
01798 831026
• e-mail: beaconlodge@hotmail.com
• website: www.beaconlodge.co.uk

•WARWICKSHIRE

Guest House
Linhill Guest House, 35 Evesham Place,
STRATFORD-UPON-AVON,
Warwickshire CV37 6HT
01789 292879
• e-mail: linhill@bigwig.net
• website: www.linhillguesthouse.co.uk

Guest House / B & B
Julia Downie, Holly Tree Cottage,
Pathlow, STRATFORD-UPON-AVON,
Warwickshire CV37 0ES
01789 204461
• e-mail: john@hollytree-cottage.co.uk
• website: www.hollytree-cottage.co.uk

Guest House
Mr & Mrs Learmount,
Green Haven Guest House,
217 Evesham Road,
STRATFORD-UPON-AVON,
Warwickshire CV37 9AS
01789 297874
• e-mail: information@green-haven.co.uk
• website: www.green-haven.co.uk

Self-Catering
Rayford Caravan Park, Riverside,
Tiddington Road,
STRATFORD-UPON-AVON,
Warwickshire CV37 7BE
01789 293964
• e-mail: info@stratfordcaravans.co.uk
• website: www.stratfordcaravans.co.uk

Guest House
Mr & Mrs D. Clapp, The Croft,
Haseley Knob, WARWICK,
Warwickshire CV35 7NL
01926 484447
• e-mail: david@croftguesthouse.co.uk
• website: www.croftguesthouse.co.uk

B & B / Self-Catering
Mrs Elizabeth Draisey, Forth House,
44 High Street, WARWICK,
Warwickshire CV34 4AX
01926 401612
• e-mail: info@forthhouseuk.co.uk
• website: www.forthhouseuk.co.uk

FHG PUBLICATIONS LTD
publish a large range of well-known accommodation guides.
We will be happy to send you details or you can use the
order form at the back of this book.

WEBSITE DIRECTORY 363

•WEST MIDLANDS

Hotel
Mr Price, Featherstone Farm Hotel,
New Road, Featherstone, WOLVERHAMPTON,
West Midlands WV10 7NW
01902 725371
• website:
www.featherstonefarm.co.uk/index.html

•WILTSHIRE

Farmhouse / Board
Mrs D. Robinson, Boyds Farm, Gastard,
Near Corsham, BATH, Wiltshire SN13 9PT
01249 713146
• e-mail:
dorothyrobinson@boyds.farm.freeserve.co.uk

Self-Catering
Mrs S. King, Wick Farm, LACOCK,
Chippenham, Wiltshire SN15 2LU
01249 730244
• e-mail: kingsilverlands2@btinternet.com
• website: www.cheeseandcyderhouses.co.uk

Guest House
Alan & Dawn Curnow, Hayburn Wyke Guest
House, 72 Castle Road, SALISBURY,
Wiltshire SP1 3RL
01722 412617
• e-mail: hayburn.wyke@tinyonline.co.uk
• website: www.hayburnwykeguesthouse.co.uk

•WORCESTERSHIRE

Guesthouse / Farm
Mrs S Harrison, Middleton Grange,
Salwarpe, DROITWICH SPA,
Worcestershire WR9 0AH
01905 451678
• e-mail: salli@middletongrange.com
• website: www.middletongrange.com

•EAST YORKSHIRE

B & B
Paws-a-While, KILNWICK PERCY,
East Yorkshire YO42 1UF
01759 301168
• e-mail: paws.a.while@lineone.net
• website: www.pawsawhile.net

•NORTH YORKSHIRE

Self-Catering
Recommended Cottages, North Yorkshire
08700 718 718
• website: www.recommended-cottages.co.uk

B & B / Self-Catering
Mrs E.J. Moorhouse,
The Courtyard at Duke's Place,
Bishop Thornton, HARROGATE,
North Yorkshire HG3 3JY
01765 620229
• e-mail: jakimoorhouse@onetel.net.uk

Caravan & Camping
Bainbridge Ings, Caravan & Camping Site,
HAWES, North Yorkshire DL8 3NU
01969 667354
• e-mail: janet@bainbridge-ings.co.uk
• website: www.bainbridge-ings.co.uk

Farm B & B / Self-Catering
John & Felicity Wiles,
Sinnington Common Farm,
KIRKBYMOORSIDE, York,
North Yorkshire YO62 6NX
01751 431719
• e-mail: felicity@scfarm.demon.co.uk
• website: www.scfarm.demon.co.uk

Farm Self-Catering
A.W. & A. Turnbull, Whitethorn Farm,
Rook Barulth, KIRKBYMOORSIDE,
York, North Yorkshire
01751 431298
• e-mail: turnbull@whitethornfarm.fsnet.co.uk
• website: www.cottageguide.co.uk/oak-lodge

Farmhouse B & B
Mrs Julie Clarke, Middle Farm,
Woodale, Coverdale, LEYBURN,
North Yorkshire DL8 4TY
01969 640271
• e-mail: julie-clarke@amserve.com
• website:
www.yorkshirenet.co.uk/stayat/middlefarm

Self-Catering
Coronation and Forge Valley Cottages,
c/o Mr David Beeley, Barn House, Westgate,
OLD MALTON, North Yorkshire YO17 7HE
01653 698251
• e-mail:
enquiries@coronationfarmcottage.co.uk
• website: www.coronationfarmcottage.co.uk

364 WEBSITE DIRECTORY

B & B / Self-Catering
Mrs Sandra Pickering, "Nabgate",
Wilton Road, Thornton-le-Dale, PICKERING,
North Yorkshire YO18 7QP
01751 474279
• website: www.nabgateguesthouse.co.uk

Guest House
Mrs Ella Bowes, Banavie, Roxby Road,
Thornton-Le-Dale, PICKERING, North
Yorkshire YO18 7SX
01751 474616
• e-mail: ella@banavie.fsbusiness.co.uk
• website: www.banavie.uk.com

Hotel
Ganton Greyhound, Main Street, Ganton,
Near SCARBOROUGH,
North Yorkshire YO12 4NX
01944 710116
• e-mail: gantongreyhound@supanet.com
• website: www.gantongreyhound.com

Guest House
Sue & Tony Hewitt,
Harmony Country Lodge,
80 Limestone Road, Burniston,
SCARBOROUGH, North Yorkshire YO13 0DG
0800 2985840
• e-mail: tony@harmonylodge.net
• website: www.harmonylodge.net

Touring Caravan Park
Cayton Village Caravan Park, Mill Lane,
Cayton, SCARBOROUGH,
North Yorkshire YO11 3NN
• e-mail: info@caytontouring.co.uk
• website: www.caytontouring.co.uk

Hotel
Mrs M.M Abbott, Howdale Hotel,
121 Queen's Parade, SCARBOROUGH,
North Yorkshire YO12 7HU
01723 372696
• e-mail: mail@howdalehotel.co.uk
• website: www.howdalehotel.co.uk

Farmhouse B & B / Self-Catering
Mrs Heather Simpson, Low Skibeden
Farmhouse & Cottage, SKIPTON,
North Yorkshire
01756 793849
• website:
www.yorkshirenetco.uk/accgde/lowskibeden

Self-Catering
Mrs Jones, New Close Farm,
Kirkby Malham, SKIPTON,
North Yorkshire BD23 4DP
01729 830240
• e-mail:
brendajones@newclosefarmyorkshire.co.uk
• website: www.newclosefarmyorkshire.co.uk

Self-Catering
Mrs Knowlson, Thrush House,
SUTTON-ON-FOREST, York,
North Yorkshire YO61 1ED
• e-mail: kmkholcottyksuk@aol.com
• website:
www.holidayskmkholcotts-yks.uk.com

Hotel
The Golden Fleece Hotel, Market Place,
THIRSK North Yorkshire
01845 523108
• e-mail: goldenfleece@bestwestern.co.uk
• website: www.goldenfleecehotel.com

Self-Catering
Anne Fawcett,
Mile House Farm Country Cottages,
Mile House Farm, Hawes, WENSLEYDALE,
North Yorkshire DL8 3PT
01969 667481
• e-mail: milehousefarm@hotmail.com
• website: www.wensleydale.uk.com

Self-Catering
Mrs Sue Cooper, St Edmunds, The Green,
Crakehall, Bedale, WENSLEYDALE,
North Yorkshire DL8 1HP
01677 423584
• e-mail:
stedmundscountrycottages@hotmail.com
• website: www.crakehall.org.uk

Self-Catering
Westclose House (Allaker),
WEST SCRAFTON, North Yorkshire
c/o Mr A Cave,
020 8567 4862
• e-mail: ac@adriancave.com
• website: www.adriancave.com/yorks

FHG PUBLICATIONS LTD publish a large range of well-known accommodation guides. We will be happy to send you details or you can use the order form at the back of this book.

Self-Catering
White Rose Holiday Cottages,
c/o Mrs Roberts, 5 Brook Park, Sleights,
Near WHITBY, North Yorkshire YO21 1RT
01947 810763
• e-mail: enquiries@whiterosecottages.co.uk
• website: www.whiterosecottages.co.uk

Self-Catering
Mrs N. Pattinson, South House Farm,
Fylingthorpe, WHITBY,
North Yorkshire YO22 4UQ
01947 880243
• e-mail: kmp@bogglehole.fsnet.co.uk
• website: www.southhousefarm.co.uk

B & B / Self-Catering / Holiday Caravans
Mr & Mrs Tyerman, Partridge Nest Farm,
Eskdaleside, Sleights, WHITBY,
North Yorkshire YO22 5ES
01947 810450
• e-mail: barbara@partridgenestfarm.com
• website: www.partridgenestfarm.com

B & B
Mrs Sally Robinson, Valley View Farm,
Old Byland, Helmsley, YORK,
North Yorkshire YO6 5LG
01439 798221
• e-mail: sally@valleyviewfarm.com
• website: www.valleyviewfarm.com

Guest House / Self-Catering
Mr Gary Hudson, Orillia House,
89 The Village, Stockton on Forest,
YORK, North Yorkshire YO3 9UP
01904 400600
• e-mail: orillia@globalnet.co.uk
• website: www.orilliahouse.co.uk

Self-Catering
Mr N. Manasir, York Lakeside Lodges, Moor
Lane, YORK, North Yorkshire YO24 2QU
01904 702346
• e-mail: neil@yorklakesidelodges.co.uk
• website: www.yorklakesidelodges.co.uk

•WEST YORKSHIRE

Self-Catering
Summerwine Cottages, West Royd Farm,
Marsh Lane, Shepley, near HOLMFIRTH,
Huddersfield, West Yorkshire
01484 602147
• e-mail: summerwinecottages@lineone.net
• website: www.summerwinecottages.co.uk

•SCOTLAND

•ABERDEEN, BANFF & MORAY

Guest House
E. Robertson,
Aberdeen Springbank Guesthouse,
6 Springbank Terrace, ABERDEEN,
Aberdeenshire AB11 6LS
01224 592048
• e-mail: betty@springbank6.fsnet.co.uk
• website:
www.aberdeenspringbankguesthouse.co.uk
or www.aberdeen-guesthouse.co.uk

B & B
Mrs E. Malim, Invercairn House, BRODIE,
by Forres, Moray IV36 2TD
01309 641261
• e-mail: invercairnhouse@supanet.com
• website: www.invercairnhouse.co.uk

B & B
Mrs H. Massie, Milton of Grange Farm,
FORRES, Morayshire IV36 0TR
01309 676360
• e-mail: hildamassie@aol.com
• website: www.forres-accommodation.co.uk

•ARGYLL & BUTE

Inn
Mr D. Fraser, Cairndow Stagecoach Inn,
CAIRNDOW, Argyll PA26 8BN
01499 600286
• e-mail: cairndowinn@aol.com

B & B
Mrs D. MacCormick, Mains Farm,
CARRADALE, Campbeltown,
Argyll PA28 6QG
01583 431216
• e-mail:
maccormick@mainsfarm.freeserve.co.uk

Guest House
A.J. Burke, Orchy Bank, DALMALLY,
Argyll PA33 1AS
01838 200370
• e-mail: aj.burke@talk21.com
• website:
www.loch-awe.com/orchybank/

Self-Catering
Mrs Isabella Crawford, Blarghour Farm Cottages, Loch Awe-side, By DALMALLY, Argyll PA33 1BW
01866 833246
- e-mail: blarghour@btconnect.com
- website: www.self-catering-argyll.co.uk

B & B / Self-Catering
R. Gayre, Minard Castle B&B/Self-Catering, Minard, INVERARAY, Argyll PA32 8YB
01546 886272
- e-mail: reinoldgayre@minardcastle.com
- website: www.minardcastle.com

Self-Catering
B & M Phillips, Kilbride Croft, Balvicar, ISLE OF SEIL, Argyll PA34 4RD
01852 300475
- e-mail: kilbridecroft@aol.com
- website: www.kilbridecroft.fsnet.co.uk

Self-Catering
Castle Sween Bay (Holidays) Ltd, Ellery, LOCHGILPHEAD, Argyll PA31 8PA
01880 770202
- e-mail: info@ellary.com
- website: www.ellary.com

Self-Catering
Linda Battison, Cologin House, Lerags Glen, OBAN, Argyll PA3 4SE
01631 564501
- e-mail: cologin@west-highland-holidays.co.uk
- website: www.west-highland-holidays.co.uk

B & B
Mrs C. MacDonald, Bracker, Polvinister Road, OBAN, Argyll
01631 564302
- e-mail: cmacdonald@connectfree.co.uk
- website: www.bracker.co.uk

Hotel
Willowburn Hotel, Clachan Seil, by OBAN, Argyll PA34 4TJ
01852 300276
- e-mail: willowburn.hotel@virgin.net
- website: www.willowburn.co.uk

Self-Catering
Isolated Seashore Cottage, c/o John Rankin, 12 Hamilton Place, Perth, Tayside
01738 632580
- e-mail: john@claddie.co.uk
- website: www.claddie.co.uk

• AYRSHIRE & ARRAN

B & B
Mrs Wilcox, Fisherton Farm, Dunure, AYR, Ayrshire KA7 4LF
01292 500223
- e-mail: lesleywilcox@hotmail.com
- website: www.fishertonfarm.homestead.com

Self-Catering
Arran Hideaways, Invercloy House, Brodick, ISLE OF ARRAN
01770 302303
- e-mail: info@arran-hideaways.co.uk
- website: www.arran-hideaways.co.uk

B & B
Mrs Watson, South Whittlieburn Farm, Brisbane Glen, LARGS, Ayrshire KA30 8SN
01475 675881
- e-mail: largsbandb@southwhittlieburnfarm.freeserve.co.uk
- website: www.SmoothHound.co.uk/hotels/whittlie.html

• BORDERS

Self-Catering
Mrs J. Gray, Saughs Farm Cottages, Saughs Farm, BAILEY, Newcastleton, Borders TD9 0TT
016977 48346
- e-mail: skylark@onholiday.co.uk
- website: www.skylarkcottages.co.uk

Self-Catering
Mrs A. Fraser, Overwells, Jedburgh, ROXBURGH, Roxburghshire
01835 863020
- e-mail: abfraser@btinternet.com
- website: www.overwells.co.uk

• DUMFRIES & GALLOWAY

Hotel
The Urr Valley Hotel, Ernspie Road, CASTLE DOUGLAS, Dumfries & Galloway DG7 3JG
01556 502 188
- e-mail: info@urrvalleyhotel.co.uk
- website: www.urrvalley.demon.co.uk

WEBSITE DIRECTORY 367

Farm
Celia Pickup, Craigadam,
CASTLE DOUGLAS,
Dumfries & Galloway DG7 3HU
01556 650233
• e-mail: enquiry@craigadam.com
• website: www.craigadam.com

Self-Catering
Mr Ball, Barncrosh Leisure Co Ltd,
Barncrosh, CASTLE DOUGLAS,
Dumfries & Galloway DG7 1TX
01556 680216
• e-mail: enq@barncrosh.co.uk
• website: www.barncrosh.co.uk

Self-Catering
Catherine McDowall, Shawhill Farmhouse,
DUNDRENNAN,
Dumfries & Galloway DG6 4QT
• e-mail: mail@shawhill-cottages.co.uk
• website: www.shawhill-cottages.co.uk

Self-Catering
Rusko Holidays,
GATEHOUSE OF FLEET, Castle Douglas,
Dumfries & Galloway DG7 2BS
01557 814215
• e-mail: gilbey@rusko.demon.co.uk
• website: www.ruskoholidays.co.uk

B & B
June Deakins, Annandale House, MOFFAT,
Dumfriesshire DG10 9SA
01683 221460
• e-mail: june@annandalehouse.com
• website: www.annandalehouse.com

•DUNDEE & ANGUS

Farmhouse B & B
Rosemary Beatty, Brathinch Farm,
by BRECHIN, Angus DD9 7QX
01356 648292
• e-mail: adam.brathinch@btinternet.com

Self-Catering
Jenny Scott, Welton Farm,
The Welton of Kingoldrum, KIRRIEMUIR,
Angus DD8 5HY
01575 574743
• website: www.cottageguide.co.uk/thewelton

•EDINBURGH & LOTHIANS

Guest House
Kenneth Harkins, 78 East Main Street,
BLACKBURN, By Bathgate,
West Lothian EH47 7QS
01506 655221
• e-mail: cruachan.bb@virgin.net
• website: www.cruachan.co.uk

Guest House
Mr & Mrs McWilliams,
Ben Craig Guest House, 3 Craigmillar Park,
EDINBURGH, Lothians EH16 5PG
0131 667 2593
• e-mail: bencraighouse@dial.pipex.com
• website: www.bencraighouse.co.uk

B & B
McCrae's B&B, 44 East Claremont Street,
EDINBURGH, Lothians EH7 4JR
0131 556 2610
• e-mail: mccraes.bandb@lineone.net
• website: http://website.lineone.net/~mccraes.bandb

Guest House
Mrs Kay, Blossom House, 8 Minto Street,
EDINBURGH EH9 1RG
0131 667 5353
• e-mail: blossom_house@hotmail.com
• website: www.blossomguesthouse.co.uk

Guest House
D. Green, Ivy Guest House,
7 Mayfield Gardens, Newington,
EDINBURGH, Lothians EH9 2AX
0131 667 3411
• e-mail: don@ivyguesthouse.com
• website: www.ivyguesthouse.com

Guest House
International Guest House,
37 Mayfield Gardens, EDINBURGH,
Lothians EH9 2BX
0131 667 2511
• e-mail: intergh@easynet.co.uk
• website: www.accommodation-edinburgh.com

Please mention this guide when enquiring about accommodation

Hotel
Shirley Mowat, Dunstane House Hotel,
4 West Cootes, Haymarket, EDINBURGH
0131 337 6169
- e-mail: reservations@dunstanehousehotel.co.uk
- website: www.dunstanehousehotel.co.uk

B & B
Mr & Mrs R. Inglis, Thornton,
Edinburgh Road, LINLITHGOW,
Lothians EH49 6AA
01506 844693
- e-mail: inglisthornton@hotmail.com
- website: www.thornton-scotland.co.uk

•HIGHLANDS

Self-Catering
A. Simpson, Camusdarach Enterprises,
Camusdarach, ARISAIG,
Inverness-shire PH39 4NT
01687 450221
- e-mail: camdarach@aol.com
- website: www.camusdarach.com

Hotel
The Boat Hotel, BOAT OF GARTEN,
Inverness-shire PH24 3BH
01479 831258
- e-mail: info@boathotel.co.uk
- website: www.boathotel.co.uk

Guest House
Mrs Lynn Benge,
The Pines Country Guest House, Duthil,
CARRBRIDGE, Inverness-shire PH23 3ND
01479 841220
- e-mail: lynn@thepines-duthil.fsnet.co.uk
- website: www.thepines-duthil.fsnet.co.uk

B & B
Mrs Brenda Graham, "Caledonian Cottage",
Station Road, FORT AUGUSTUS,
Inverness-shire PH32 4AY
01320 366401
- e-mail: brenda@ipw.com
- website: www.ipw.com/calcot

Hotel
Allt-Nan-Ros Hotel, Onich, FORT WILLIAM,
Inverness-shire PH33 6RY
01855 821210
- e-mail: fhg@allt-nan-ros.co.uk
- website: www.allt-nan-ros.co.uk

Hotel
Clan Macduff Hotel, Achintore Road,
FORT WILLIAM, Inverness-shire PH33 6RW
01397 702341
- e-mail: reception@clanmacduff.co.uk
- website: www.clanmacduff.co.uk

Self-Catering
Linnhe Lochside Holidays, Corpach,
FORT WILLIAM PH33 7NL
01397 772376
- e-mail: holidays@linnhe.demon.co.uk
- website: www.linnhe-lochside-holidays.co.uk

Guest House
Norma E. McCallum, The Neuk, Corpach,
FORT WILLIAM, Inverness-shire PH33 7LR
01397 772244
- e-mail: theneuk@fortwilliamguesthouse.com
- website: www.theneuk.fsbusiness.co.uk

Self-Catering
Great Glen Holidays, Torlundy, FORT
WILLIAM, Inverness-shire
01397 703015
- e-mail: chris@greatglenchalets.demon.co.uk
- website: www.greatglenchalets.demon.co.uk

Self-Catering
Mr William Murray,
Springwell Holiday Homes, Onich,
FORT WILLIAM, Inverness-shire PH33 6RY
01855 821257
- e-mail: info@springwellholidayhomes.co.uk
- website: www.springwellholidayhomes.co.uk

B & B
Mrs M. MacLean, Innishfree, Lochyside,
FORT WILLIAM, Inverness-shire PH33 7NX
01397 705471
- e-mail: mburnsmaclean@aol.com
- website: www. innishfree.co.uk

Hotels
The Freedom of the Glen Family of Hotels,
Onich, near FORT WILLIAM,
Inverness-shire PH33 6RY
0871 222 3415
- e-mail: reservations@freedomglen.com
- website: www.freedomglen.co.uk

Self-Catering
Miss Jean Ellice, Taigh-an-Lianach,
Aberchalder Farm, INVERGARRY,
Inverness-shire PH35 4HN
01809 501287
- website: www.ipw.com/aberchalder

Guest House / Self-Catering
Nick & Patsy Thompson, Insh House,
KINCRAIG, Kingussie
01540 651377
• e-mail: inshhouse@btinternet.com
• website: www.kincraig.com/inshhouse

Guest House
Gary Clulow, Sunset Guest House, MORAR,
by Mallaig, Inverness-shire PH40 4PA
01687 462259
• e-mail: sunsetgh@aol.com
• website: www.sunsetguesthouse.co.uk

Self-Catering Chalets / B & B
D.J. Mordaunt, Mondhuie, NETHY BRIDGE,
Inverness-shire PH25 3DF
01479 821062
• e-mail: david@mondhuie.com
• website: www.mondhuie.com

Guest House
Mrs J. MacLean, Foresters Bungalow,
Inchree, ONICH, Fort William,
Inverness-shire PH33 6SE
• website: www.s-h-systems.co.uk/
hotels/forestersbungalow.html

Self-Catering
Mr A. Urquhart, Crofters Cottages,
15 Croft, POOLEWE, Ross-shire IV22 2JY
01445 781268
• e-mail: croftcottages@btopenworld.com
• website: www.croftcottages.btinternet.co.uk

Hotel
Mrs Campbell, Rhiconich Hotel,
RHICONICH, by Lairg, Sutherland IV27 4RN
01971 521224
• e-mail: rhiconichhotel@aol.com
• website: www.rhiconichhotel.co.uk

Self-Catering
Wildside Highland Lodges, By Loch Ness,
WHITEBRIDGE, Inverness-shire IV2 6UN
01456 486373
• e-mail: info@wildsidelodges.com
• website: www.wildsidelodges.com

•LANARKSHIRE

Self-Catering
Carmichael Country Cottages,
Carmichael Estate Office, Westmains,
Carmichael, BIGGAR, Lanarkshire ML12 6PG
01899 308336
• e-mail: chiefcarm@aol.com
• website: www.carmichael.co.uk/cottages

•PERTH & KINROSS

Self-Catering
Loch Tay Lodges, Remony,
ABERFELDY, Perthshire
01887 830209
• e-mail: remony@btinternet.com
• website: www.lochtaylodges.co.uk

Guest House
Janet Greenfield, "Annfield Guest House",
North Church Street, CALLANDER,
Perthshire
01877 330204
• e-mail: janet-greenfield@amserve.com

Guest House
J. Clifford, Merlindale, Perth Road,
CRIEFF, Perthshire
01764 655205
• e-mail: merlin.dale@virgin.net
• website: www.merlindale.co.uk

Self-Catering
Laighwood Holidays, Laighwood,
Butterstone, By DUNKELD,
Perthshire PH8 0HB
01350 724241
• e-mail: holidays@laighwood.co.uk
• website: www.laighwood.co.uk

Self Catering
Mrs Hunt, Wester Lix Holiday Cottages,
Wester Lix, KILLIN, Perthshire FK21 8RD
01567 820990
• e-mail: gill@westerlix.co.uk
• website: www.westerlix.co.uk

B & B
Mrs P. Honeyman, Auld Manse Guest House,
Pitcullen Crescent, PERTH, Perthshire PH2 7HT
01738 629187
• e-mail: trishaatauldmanse@hotmail.com
• website: www.guesthouseperth.com

Guest House
Jacky Catterall, Tulloch, Enochdhu,
by PITLOCHRY, Perthshire PH10 7PW
01250 881404
• e-mail: maljac@tulloch83.freeserve.co.uk
• website: www.maljac.com

**Visit the FHG website
www.holidayguides.com**

•STIRLING & TROSSACHS

Caravan & Camping
Riverside Caravan Park, Dollarfield,
DOLLAR, Clackmannanshire FK14 7LX
01259 742896
- e-mail: info@riverside-caravanpark.co.uk
- website: www.riverside-caravanpark.co.uk

B & B
Mrs Strain, Hawthorndean, Wallacestone
Brae, Reddingmuirhead, FALKIRK,
Stirlingshire FK2 0DQ
- e-mail: eileenstrain@yahoo.co.uk

Guest House
Mrs Betty Ward, Ashbank Guest House,
105 Main Street, Redding, FALKIRK,
Stirlingshire FK2 9UQ
01324 716649
- e-mail: ashbank@guest-house.freeserve.co.uk
- website: www.bandbfalkirk.com

•ISLE OF SKYE

Guest House / B & B
Fiona Scott, Blairdhu House, Old Kyle Farm
Road, KYLEAKIN, Isle of Skye IV41 8PR
01599 534760
- e-mail: info@blairdhuhouse.co.uk
- website: www.blairdhuhouse.co.uk

•WALES

Self-Catering
Quality Cottages, Cerbid, Solva,
HAVERFORDWEST,
Pembrokeshire SA62 6YE
01348 837871
- website: www.qualitycottages.co.uk

•ANGLESEY & GWYNEDD

Country House
Jim and Marion Billingham, Preswylfa,
ABERDOVEY, Gwynedd LL35 0LE
01654 767239
- e-mail: info@preswylfa.co.uk
- website: www.preswylfa.co.uk

B & B
Mrs Murphy, Ingledene, Ravenspoint Road,
Trearddur Bay, ANGLESEY LL65 2YU
01407 861026
- e-mail: info@ingledene.co.uk
- website: www.ingledene.co.uk

B & B
Mrs J. Bown, Drws-y-Coed,
Llannerch-y-medd, ANGLESEY LL71 8AD
01248 470473
- e-mail: drws.ycoed@virgin.net
- website:
www.SmoothHound.co.uk/hotels/drwsycoed.html

Self-Catering within a Castle
Bryn Bras Castle, Llanrug,
near CAERNARFON Gwynedd LL55 4RE
01286 870210
- e-mail: holidays@brynbrascastle.co.uk
- website: www.brynbrascastle.co.uk

Self-Catering / Caravan
Plas-y-Bryn Chalet Park, Bontnewydd,
CAERNARFON, Gwynedd LL54 7YE
01286 672811
- e-mail: philplasybryn@aol.com
- website:
www.plasybrynholidayscaernarfon.co.uk

Hotel
Prince of Wales Hotel, Bangor Street,
CAERNARFON, Gwynedd
01286 673367
- e-mail: info@prince-of-wales-hotel.co.uk
- website: www.prince-of-wales-hotel.co.uk

Guest House
Mrs M.A. Parker, Seaspray Guest House,
4 Marine Terrace, CRICCIETH,
Gwynedd LL52 0EF
- e-mail: manya.parker@btopenworld.com
- website: www.seasprayguesthouse.co.uk

Self-Catering
Anwen Jones, Rhos Country Cottages,
Betws Bach, Ynys, CRICCIETH,
Gwynedd LL52 0PB
01758 720047
- e-mail: cottages@rhos.freeserve.co.uk
- website: www.rhos-cottages.co.uk

Guest House
Mrs M. Bamford, Ivy House,
Finsbury Square, DOLGELLAU,
Gwynedd LL40 1RF
01341 422535
- e-mail: marg.bamford@btconnect.com
- website: www.ukworld.net/ivyhouse

Self-Catering / Caravans
Minffordd Luxury Cottages & Caravans,
Minfford, DULAS, Isle of Anglesey LL70 9HJ
01248 410678
• e-mail: enq@minffordd-holidays.com
• website: www.minffordd-holidays.com

B & B
Mrs G. McCreadie, Deri Isaf,
DULAS BAY, Anglesey LL70 9DX
01248 410536
• e-mail: mccreadie@deriisaf.freeserve.co.uk
• website: www.deriisaf.freeserve.co.uk

Farm B & B
Judy Hutchings, Tal y Foel, DWYRAN,
Anglesey, Gwynedd LL61 6LQ
01248 430377
• e-mail: riding@talyfoel.u-net.com
• website: www.tal-y-foel.co.uk

Self-Catering
Mrs S. Edwards, Dwyfach Cottages,
Pen-y-Bryn, Chwilog, PWLLHELI,
Gwynedd LL53 6SX
01766 810208
• e-mail: llyredwards@ukonline.co.uk
• website: www.dwyfach.co.uk

•NORTH WALES

Hotel
Fairy Glen Hotel, Beaver Bridge,
BETWS-Y-COED, Conwy,
North Wales LL24 0SH
01690 710269
• e-mail: fairyglenhotel@amserve.net
• website: www.fairyglenhotel.co.uk

Guest House
Mr M. Wilkie, Bryn Bella Guest House,
Lôn Muriau, Llanrwst Road,
BETWS-Y-COED, Gwynedd LL24 0HD
01690 710627
• e-mail: welcome@bryn-bella.co.uk
• website: www.bryn-bella.co.uk

Guest House / Self-Catering
Jim & Lilian Boughton,
Bron Celyn Guest House, Lôn Muriau,
Llanrwst Road, BETWS-Y-COED,
North Wales LL24 0HD
01690 710333
• e-mail: welcome@broncelyn.co.uk
• website: www.broncelyn.co.uk

B & B
Christine Whale, Brookside House,
Brookside Lane, Northop Hall,
near CHESTER CH7 4HN
01244 821146
• e-mail: christine@brooksidehouse.fsnet.co.uk
• website: www.brooksidehouse.fsnet.co.uk

Guest House
Sychnant Pass House, Sychnant Pass Road,
CONWY, North Wales LL32 8BJ
01492 596868
• e-mail: bresykes@sychnant-pass-house.co.uk
• website: www.sychnant-pass-house.co.uk

Hotel
Caerlyr Hall Hotel, Conwy Old Road,
Dwygyfylchi, CONWY,
North Wales LL34 6SW
01492 623518
• website: www.caerlyrhallhotel.co.uk

Guest House
Mr & Mrs Watson Jones, Glan Heulog Guest
House, Woodlands, Llanrwst Road, CONWY
01492 593845
• e-mail: glanheulog@no1guesthouse.freeserve.co.uk
• website: www.walesbandb.com

Self-Catering
Cottage, CONWAY c/o Mrs G.M. Simpole,
105 Haygreen Road, Terrington-St-Clement,
Kings Lynn, Norfolk PE34 4PU
01553 828897
• e-mail: gsimpole@care4free.net
• website: www.comestaywithus.com/
wales-hotels/sc-full/brongain.html

Hotel
Moreton Park Lodge, Gledrid, Chirk,
WREXHAM, LL14 5DG
01691 776666
• e-mail: reservations@moretonpark.com
• website: www.moretonpark.com

Please mention this guide when enquiring about accommodation

372 WEBSITE DIRECTORY

•CARMARTHENSHIRE

B & B
Miss S Czerniewicz, Pant y Bas, Pentrefelin, LLANDEILO, Carmarthenshire, SA19 6SD
01558 822809
- e-mail: anna@pantybas.fsnet.co.uk
- website: www.southwestwalesbandb.co.uk

•CEREDIGION

Self-Catering
Gilfach Holiday Village, Llwyncelyn, Near ABERAERON, Ceredigion SA46 0HN
01545 580288
- e-mail: info@stratfordcaravans.co.uk
- website: www.stratfordcaravans.co.uk

Self-Catering
Mrs Tucker, Penffynnon, ABERPORTH, Ceredigion SA43 2DA
01239 810387
- e-mail: jann@aberporth.com
- website: www.aberporth.com

• PEMBROKESHIRE

Self-Catering
John Lloyd, East Llanteg Farm Holiday Cottages, Llanteg, near AMROTH, Pembrokeshire SA67 8QA
01834 831336
- e-mail: john@pembrokeshireholiday.co.uk
- website: www.pembrokeshireholiday.co.uk

Farm B & B
Mrs Margaret Williams, Skerryback, Sandy Haven, St Ishmaels, HAVERFORDWEST, Pembrokeshire SA62 3DN
01646 636598
- e-mail: skerryback@pfh.co.uk
- website: www.pfh.co.uk/skerryback

Caravan Park
Scamford Caravan Park, Keeston, HAVERFORDWEST, Pembrokeshire SA62 6HN
01437 710204
- e-mail: holidays@scamford.com
- website: www.scamford.com

Caravan & Camping
Brandy Brook Caravan & Camping Site, Rhyndaston, Hayscastle, HAVERFORDWEST, Pembrokeshire
01348 840272
- e-mail: f.m.rowe@btopenworld.com

Self-Catering
T.M. Hardman, High View, Catherine Street, ST DAVIDS, Pembrokeshire SA62 6RT
01437 720616
- e-mail: enquiries@lowermoorcottages.co.uk
- website: www.lowermoorcottages.co.uk

Farm Guest House
Mrs Morfydd Jones, Lochmeyler Farm Guest House, Llandeloy, Pen-y-Cwm, near SOLVA, St David's, Pembrokeshire SA62 6LL
01348 837724
- e-mail: stay@lochmeyler.co.uk
- website: www.lochmeyler.co.uk

•POWYS

Self-Catering
Mrs Ann Phillips, Tylebrythos Farm, Cantref, BRECON, Powys LD3 8LR
01874 665329
- e-mail: ann@wernymarchog.co.uk
- website: www.wernymarchog.co.uk

Farm
Gilfach Farm, Sennybridge, BRECON, Powys LD3 8TY
01874 636818
- e-mail: sm@mip.co.uk
- website: www.breconbeaconsriding.co.uk

Farm Self-Catering
Mrs E. Bally, Lane Farm, Painscastle, BUILTH WELLS, Powys LD2 3JS
01497 851605
- e-mail: jbally@btclick.com
- website: www.lane-farm.co.uk

Self-Catering
Mrs Jones, Penllwyn Lodges, GARTHMYL, Powys SY15 6SB
01686 640269
- e-mail: penllwynlodges@supanet.com
- website: www.penllwynlodges.co.uk

WEBSITE DIRECTORY

Self-Catering
Peter & Jackie Longley, Neuadd Farm,
Penybont, LLANDRINDOD WELLS,
Powys LD1 5SW
01597 851032
* e-mail: jackie@neuaddfarm.fsnet.co.uk
* website: www.neuaddfarm.co.uk

Motel / Caravans
The Park Motel, Crossgates,
LLANDRINDOD WELLS, Powys LD1 6RF
01597 851201
* e-mail: lisa@theparkmotel.freeserve.co.uk
* website: www.theparkmotel.freeserve.co.uk

B & B
Mrs V.J. Madeley, Greenfields, Kerry,
NEWTOWN, Powys SY16 4LH
01686 670596
* e-mail: info@greenfields-bb.co.uk
* website: www.greenfield-bb.co.uk

B & B
Laura Kostoris, Erw yr Danty,
TALYBONT-ON-USK, Brecon,
Powys LD3 7YN
01874 676498
* e-mail: kosto@ukonline.co.uk
* website: wiz.to/lifestyle/

•SOUTH WALES

Guest House / Self-Catering
Mrs Norma James, Wyrloed Lodge,
Manmoel, BLACKWOOD, Caerphilly, Gwent
01495 371198
* e-mail: norma.james@btinternet.com
* website: www.btinternet.com/~norma.james/

Sports Centre / Hotel
Welsh Institute of Sport, Sophia Gardens,
CARDIFF
029 20 300500
* e-mail: wis@scw.co.uk
* website: www.sports-council-wales.co.uk

Hotel
Mr & Mrs J. Llewellyn, Cwrt-y-Gaer,
Wolvesnewton, CHEPSTOW NP16 6PR
01291 650700
* e-mail: john.ll@talk21.com
* website: www.cwrt-y-gaer.co.uk

B & B
Sue Beer, Plas Llanmihangel,
Llanmihangel, near COWBRIDGE,
Vale of Glamorgan CF71 7LQ
01446 774610
* e-mail: plasllanmihangel@ukonline.co.uk

Narrowboat
Castle Narrowboats, Church Road Wharf,
GILWERN, Monmouthshire NP7 0EP
01873 830001
* e-mail: castle.narrowboats@btinternet.com
* website: www.castlenarrowboats.co.uk

Hotel
Culver House Hotel, Port Eynon,
GOWER, Swansea, South Wales SA3 1NN
01792 390755
* e-mail: info@culverhousehotel.co.uk
* website: www.culverhousehotel.co.uk

Guest House
Chapel Guest House, Church Road,
ST BRIDES, Wentloog, near Newport,
Gwent NP10 8SN
01633 681018
* e-mail: chapelguesthouse@hotmail.com
* website: www.SmoothHound.co.uk/

•IRELAND

Co. Clare

Self-catering
Ballyvaughan Village & Country Holiday
Homes, Main Street, BALLYVAUGHAN,
Co. Clare
00 353 65 9051977
* e-mail: vchh@iol.ie
* website: www.ballyvaughan-cottages.com

Co. Dublin

Golf Club
The Royal Dublin Golf Club,
North Bull Island Nature Reserve,
DOLLYMOUNT, Dublin 3
00 353 1 833 6346
* e-mail: info@theroyaldublingolfclub.com
* website: www.theroyaldublingolfclub.com

Visit the FHG website
www.holidayguides.com

THE FHG DIPLOMA

HELP IMPROVE BRITISH TOURIST STANDARDS

You are choosing holiday accommodation from our very popular FHG Publications.
Whether it be a hotel, guest house, farmhouse or self-catering accommodation, we think you will find it hospitable, comfortable and clean, and your host and hostess friendly and helpful.

Why not write and tell us about it?

As a recognition of the generally well-run and excellent holiday accommodation reviewed in our publications, we at FHG Publications Ltd. present a diploma to proprietors who receive the highest recommendation from their guests who are also readers of our Guides. If you care to write to us praising the holiday you have booked through FHG Publications Ltd. – whether this be board, self-catering accommodation, a sporting or a caravan holiday, what you say will be evaluated and the proprietors who reach our final list will be contacted.

The winning proprietor will receive an attractive framed diploma to display on his premises as recognition of a high standard of comfort, amenity and hospitality. FHG Publications Ltd. offer this diploma as a contribution towards the improvement of standards in tourist accommodation in Britain. Help your excellent host or hostess to win it!

FHG DIPLOMA

We nominate

Because

Name ....

Address...

....

Telephone No...

Index of towns and counties
Please also refer to Contents pages 2 and 3.

Abbotsbury	DORSET	Bodmin	CORNWALL
Aberdeen	ABERDEEN, BANFF & MORAY	Bodmin Moor	CORNWALL
Abergele	NORTH WALES	Bognor Regis	WEST SUSSEX
Aberporth	CEREDIGION	Boscastle	CORNWALL
Abersoch	ANGLESEY & GWYNEDD	Bosherton	PEMBROKESHIRE
Aberystwyth	CEREDIGION	Bourton-on-the-Water	GLOUCESTERSHIRE
Achiltibuie	HIGHLANDS	Bovey Tracey	DEVON
Alcester	WARWICKSHIRE	Bowness-on-Windermere	CUMBRIA
Alford	LINCOLNSHIRE	Brampton	CUMBRIA
Alfriston	EAST SUSSEX	Braunton	DEVON
Allerford	SOMERSET	Brechin	DUNDEE & ANGUS
Alnwick	NORTHUMBERLAND	Brecon	POWYS
Ambleside	CUMBRIA	Bridge of Cally	PERTH & KINROSS
Ampleforth	NORTH YORKSHIRE	Bridgwater	SOMERSET
Amroth	PEMBROKESHIRE	Bridport	DORSET
Appin	ARGYLL & BUTE	Bridport/Nettlecombe	DORSET
Appleby-in-Westmorland	CUMBRIA	Bristol	SOMERSET
Ardgay	HIGHLANDS (NORTH)	Bristol	GLOUCESTERSHIRE
Arinagour	ISLE OF COLL	Brixham	DEVON
Arisaig	HIGHLANDS (SOUTH)	Broadhaven	PEMBROKESHIRE
Arlington	EAST SUSSEX	Broadstairs	KENT
Arran	AYRSHIRE & ARRAN	Brockenhurst	HAMPSHIRE
Ashbourne	DERBYSHIRE	Bromyard	HEREFORDSHIRE
Ashbrittle	SOMERSET	Broughty Ferry	DUNDEE & ANGUS
Ashburton	DEVON	Bude	CORNWALL
Ashkirk	BORDERS	Builth Wells	POWYS
Askrigg	NORTH YORKSHIRE	Bungay	SUFFOLK
Axminster	DEVON	Burnham-on-Sea	SOMERSET
Ayr	AYRSHIRE & ARRAN	Burwash	EAST SUSSEX
Bakewell	DERBYSHIRE	Buttermere	CUMBRIA
Bala	ANGLESEY & GWYNEDD	Buxton	DERBYSHIRE
Ballantrae	AYRSHIRE & ARRAN	Caernarvon	ANGLESEY & GWYNEDD
Bamburgh	NORTHUMBERLAND	Caldbeck	CUMBRIA
Bampton	DEVON	Cambridge	CAMBRIDGESHIRE
Banbury	OXFORDSHIRE	Canonbie	DUMFRIES & GALLOWAY
Barnard Castle	DURHAM	Canterbury	KENT
Barnstaple	DEVON	Cardigan	CEREDIGION
Baslow	DERBYSHIRE	Carlisle	CUMBRIA
Bath	SOMERSET	Carradale	ARGYLL & BUTE
Bath	WILTSHIRE	Cartmel Fell	CUMBRIA
Bedale	NORTH YORKSHIRE	Cerne Abbas	DORSET
Belford	NORTHUMBERLAND	Charmouth	DORSET
Belton-in-Rutland	LEICESTERSHIRE	Chathill	NORTHUMBERLAND
Benllech	ANGLESEY & GWYNEDD	Cheddar	SOMERSET
Berwick-upon-Tweed	NORTHUMBERLAND	Cheltenham	GLOUCESTERSHIRE
Betws-y-Coed	NORTH WALES	Chester	CHESHIRE
Bexington	DORSET	Chichester	WEST SUSSEX
Biddenden	KENT	Chinley	DERBYSHIRE
Bideford	DEVON	Chipping Campden	GLOUCESTERSHIRE
Biggar (Clyde Valley)	LANARKSHIRE	Chorley	LANCASHIRE
Bishop's Castle	SHROPSHIRE	Chulmleigh	DEVON
Blairlogie	STIRLING & THE TROSSACHS	Church Stretton	SHROPSHIRE
Blandford Forum	DORSET	Clacton-on-Sea	ESSEX

Index of Towns/Counties

Town	County
Clun	SHROPSHIRE
Cockermouth	CUMBRIA
Colchester	ESSEX
Colne	LANCASHIRE
Colwyn Bay	NORTH WALES
Colyton	DEVON
Comrie	PERTH & KINROSS
Congleton	CHESHIRE
Congresbury	SOMERSET
Coningsby	LINCOLNSHIRE
Coniston	CUMBRIA
Consett	DURHAM
Corsham	WILTSHIRE
Coverdale	NORTH YORKSHIRE
Cowbridge	SOUTH WALES
Craven Arms	SHROPSHIRE
Crediton	DEVON
Criccieth	ANGLESEY & GWYNEDD
Croft	PEMBROKESHIRE
Crossmichael	DUMFRIES & GALLOWAY
Culloden	HIGHLANDS (SOUTH)
Cusgarne	CORNWALL
Dalmally	ARGYLL & BUTE
Dartmouth	DEVON
Deerness	ORKNEY
Devizes	WILTSHIRE
Diss	NORFOLK
Dolgellau	ANGLESEY & GWYNEDD
Dorchester	DORSET
Dovedale	DERBYSHIRE
Dover	KENT
Dulverton	SOMERSET
Dunkeld	PERTH & KINROSS
Eccleshall	STAFFORDSHIRE
Elterwater	CUMBRIA
Ely	CAMBRIDGESHIRE
Exeter	DEVON
Exmoor	SOMERSET
Exmouth	DEVON
Fairford	GLOUCESTERSHIRE
Fakenham	NORFOLK
Falmouth	CORNWALL
Felton	HEREFORDSHIRE
Filey	NORTH YORKSHIRE
Fishguard	PEMBROKESHIRE
Forres	ABERDEEN, BANFF & MORAY
Fort William	HIGHLANDS (SOUTH)
Fowey	CORNWALL
Framlingham	SUFFOLK
Furzehill	DORSET
Gainsborough	LINCOLNSHIRE
Gillingham	DORSET
Gladestry	POWYS
Glaisdale	NORTH YORKSHIRE
Glastonbury	SOMERSET
Glossop	DERBYSHIRE
Goodrich	HEREFORDSHIRE
Goodwick	PEMBROKESHIRE
Goudhurst	KENT
Grassington	NORTH YORKSHIRE
Great Torrington	DEVON
Gretna	DUMFRIES & GALLOWAY
Halesworth	SUFFOLK
Haltwhistle	NORTHUMBERLAND
Hardraw	NORTH YORKSHIRE
Harlech	ANGLESEY & GWYNEDD
Harrogate	NORTH YORKSHIRE
Hartington	DERBYSHIRE
Hartland	DEVON
Hastings	EAST SUSSEX
Haverfordwest	PEMBROKESHIRE
Helensburgh	ARGYLL & BUTE
Helford Estuary	CORNWALL
Helmsley	NORTH YORKSHIRE
Helston	CORNWALL
Henley-on-Thames	OXFORDSHIRE
Hereford	HEREFORDSHIRE
Hertford	HERTFORDSHIRE
Heswall	CHESHIRE
Hexham	NORTHUMBERLAND
High Bentham	LANCASHIRE
Highclere	BERKSHIRE
Hindon	WILTSHIRE
Holmfirth	WEST YORKSHIRE
Holt	NORFOLK
Honiton	DEVON
Hope Cove	DEVON
Horncastle	LINCOLNSHIRE
Huddersfield	WEST YORKSHIRE
Hyde	CHESHIRE
Ilam	DERBYSHIRE
Ilfracombe	DEVON
Instow	DEVON
Inverness	HIGHLANDS (SOUTH)
Inverurie	ABERDEEN, BANFF & MORAY
Ironbridge	SHROPSHIRE
Isle of Seil	ARGYLL & BUTE
Ivybridge	DEVON
Jedburgh	BORDERS
John O' Groats	HIGHLANDS (NORTH)
Keith	ABERDEEN, BANFF & MORAY
Kelso	BORDERS
Kendal	CUMBRIA
Kenmore	PERTH & KINROSS
Kessingland	SUFFOLK
Keswick	CUMBRIA
Kettering	NORTHAMPTONSHIRE
Kilham	EAST YORKSHIRE
Killin	PERTH & KINROSS
Killorglin	CO. KERRY
Kilmarnock	AYRSHIRE & ARRAN
Kilmory	AYRSHIRE & ARRAN
Kincraig	HIGHLANDS (SOUTH)

Index of Towns/Counties 377

King's Lynn	NORFOLK	Melton Mowbray	LEICESTERSHIRE
King's Nympton	DEVON	Mevagissey	CORNWALL
Kingsbridge	DEVON	Middleton-in-Teesdale	DURHAM
Kingsley	STAFFORDSHIRE	Milton Abbas	DORSET
Kingston-upon-Thames	SUFFOLK	Minsterworth	GLOUCESTERSHIRE
Kington	HEREFORDSHIRE	Miserden	GLOUCESTERSHIRE
Kinlochleven	ARGYLL & BUTE	Monmouth	SOUTH WALES
Kirk Langley	DERBYSHIRE	Montacute	SOMERSET
Kirkby Lonsdale	CUMBRIA	Montgomery	POWYS
Kirkoswald	CUMBRIA	Montrose	DUNDEE & ANGUS
Kirriemuir	DUNDEE & ANGUS	Morecambe	LANCASHIRE
Knutsford	CHESHIRE	Moretonhampstead	DEVON
Lacock	WILTSHIRE	Moreton-in-Marsh	GLOUCESTERSHIRE
Lampeter	CEREDIGION	Morpeth	NORTHUMBERLAND
Lamplugh	CUMBRIA	Muchelney	SOMERSET
Lanchester	DURHAM	Mullion	CORNWALL
Langport	SOMERSET	Mundesley-on-Sea	NORFOLK
Launceston	CORNWALL	Musselburgh	EDINBURGH &
Lauragh	CO. KERRY		LOTHIANS
Lavenham	SUFFOLK	Nantwich	CHESHIRE
Leek	STAFFORDSHIRE	Neath	SOUTH WALES
Leighton Buzzard	BEDFORDSHIRE	New Forest	HAMPSHIRE
Leintwardine	SHROPSHIRE	Newbiggin on Lune	CUMBRIA
Leominster	HEREFORDSHIRE	Newbury	BERKSHIRE
Leyburn	NORTH YORKSHIRE	Newgale	PEMBROKESHIRE
Lifton	DEVON	Newport	ISLE OF WIGHT
Liskeard	CORNWALL	Newport	SHROPSHIRE
Llandrindod Wells	POWYS	Newquay	CORNWALL
Llanerchymedd	ANGLESEY &	Newton Stewart	DUMFRIES & GALLOWAY
	GWYNEDD	Newtonmore	HIGHLANDS (SOUTH)
Llangranog	CEREDIGION	Newtown	POWYS
Llanidloes	POWYS	Norfolk Broads	NORFOLK
Llanwrthwl	POWYS	North Petherton	SOMERSET
Llanwrtyd Wells	POWYS	Northwich	CHESHIRE
Lochgilphead	ARGYLL & BUTE	Norwich	NORFOLK
Long Hanborough	OXFORDSHIRE	Oban	ARGYLL & BUTE
Longtown	HEREFORDSHIRE	Okehampton	DEVON
Looe	CORNWALL	Onich	HIGHLANDS (SOUTH)
Looe Valley	CORNWALL	Oranmore	CO. GALWAY
Louth	LINCOLNSHIRE	Oswestry	SHROPSHIRE
Low Bentham	NORTH YORKSHIRE	Otley	NORTH YORKSHIRE
Ludlow	SHROPSHIRE	Otterton	DEVON
Lydford	DEVON	Oxford	OXFORDSHIRE
Lyme Regis	DORSET		
Lymington	HAMPSHIRE	Padstow	CORNWALL
Lyndhurst	HAMPSHIRE	Paignton	DEVON
Lynmouth	DEVON	Pangbourne	OXFORDSHIRE
Lynton	DEVON	Pathhead	EDINBURGH & LOTHIANS
Machynlleth	POWYS	Peebles	BORDERS
Malvern Wells	WORCESTERSHIRE	Pendine	CARMARTHENSHIRE
Marlborough	WILTSHIRE	Penrith	CUMBRIA
Martins Haven/Marloes	PEMBROKESHIRE	Penybont-Fawr	POWYS
Marton/Kirkbymoorside		Penzance	CORNWALL
	NORTH YORKSHIRE	Pickering	NORTH YORKSHIRE
Matlock	DERBYSHIRE	Pirnmill	AYRSHIRE & ARRAN
Mawgan Porth	CORNWALL	Plymouth	DEVON
Melbourne	DERBYSHIRE	Pontypool	SOUTH WALES
Melksham	WILTSHIRE	Poole	DORSET

Index of Towns/Counties

Poolewe	HIGHLANDS (MID)	Tarbert	ARGYLL & BUTE
Pooley Bridge	CUMBRIA	Taunton	SOMERSET
Porlock	SOMERSET	Tavistock	DEVON
Port Isaac	CORNWALL	Taynuilt	ARGYLL & BUTE
Porthmadog	ANGLESEY & GWYNEDD	Telford	SHROPSHIRE
Portland	DORSET	Tenby	PEMBROKESHIRE
Portpatrick	DUMFRIES & GALLOWAY	Tewkesbury	GLOUCESTERSHIRE
Portree	ISLE OF SKYE	Theale	SOMERSET
Portsoy	ABERDEEN, BANFF & MORAY	Thirsk	NORTH YORKSHIRE
Pwllheli	ANGLESEY & GWYNEDD	Thorpe Fendykes	LINCOLNSHIRE
		Tigh-na-Coille	HIGHLANDS
Ravenglass	CUMBRIA	Tintagel	CORNWALL
Richmond	NORTH YORKSHIRE	Tiverton	DEVON
Robin Hood's Bay	NORTH YORKSHIRE	Todmorden	LANCASHIRE
Roseland Peninsula	CORNWALL	Torquay	DEVON
Ross-on-Wye	HEREFORDSHIRE	Totland Bay	ISLE OF WIGHT
Rothbury/Harbottle	NORTHUMBERLAND	Totnes	DEVON
Rye	EAST SUSSEX	Traquair	BORDERS
		Troutbeck	CUMBRIA
St Agnes	CORNWALL	Trowbridge	WILTSHIRE
St Andrews	FIFE	Truro	CORNWALL
St Austell	CORNWALL	Tunbridge Wells	KENT
St David's	PEMBROKESHIRE	Turriff	ABERDEEN, BANFF & MORAY
St Ives	CORNWALL	Ullapool	HIGHLANDS (MID)
St Keverne	CORNWALL	Ullswater	CUMBRIA
St Mawes	CORNWALL		
Salcombe	DEVON	Waddingworth	LINCOLNSHIRE
Salisbury	WILTSHIRE	Wadebridge	CORNWALL
Sandy	BEDFORDSHIRE	Wadhurst	EAST SUSSEX
Saxmundham	SUFFOLK	Wareham	DORSET
Scarborough	NORTH YORKSHIRE	Warminster	WILTSHIRE
Seaton	DEVON	Washford	SOMERSET
Shepton Mallet	SOMERSET	Watford	HERTFORDSHIRE
Sherborne	DORSET	Weardale	DURHAM
Shillingstone	DORSET	Wells	SOMERSET
Shrewsbury	SHROPSHIRE	Westcliff-on-Sea	ESSEX
Sidmouth	DEVON	Weston-super-Mare	SOMERSET
Silloth-on-Solway	CUMBRIA	Weymouth	DORSET
Skipton	NORTH YORKSHIRE	Whitby	NORTH YORKSHIRE
South Molton	DEVON	Whitland	CARMARTHENSHIRE
Southampton	HAMPSHIRE	Whitland	PEMBROKESHIRE
Southport	LANCASHIRE	Whitsand Bay/Downderry	CORNWALL
Southport	MERSEYSIDE	Whitley Bay	TYNE & WEAR
Southwold	SUFFOLK	Wicken	CAMBRIDGESHIRE
Spixworth	NORFOLK	Wigton	CUMBRIA
Staithes	NORTH YORKSHIRE	Wimborne	DORSET
Stanley	DURHAM	Winchester	HAMPSHIRE
Stanton-on-the-Wolds	NOTTINGHAMSHIRE	Windermere	CUMBRIA
Staveley	CUMBRIA	Wisbech	CAMBRIDGESHIRE
Stoke-on-Trent	STAFFORDSHIRE	Whitsand Bay	CORNWALL
Stow-on-the-Wold	GLOUCESTERSHIRE	Wiveliscombe	SOMERSET
Stranraer	DUMFRIES & GALLOWAY	Wolverhampton	WEST MIDLANDS
Stratford-upon-Avon	WARWICKSHIRE	Woodbridge	SUFFOLK
Strathnaver	HIGHLANDS (NORTH)	Woodstock	OXFORDSHIRE
Stroud	GLOUCESTERSHIRE	Woolacombe	DEVON
Studland	DORSET	Worcester	WORCESTERSHIRE
Sudbury	SUFFOLK	Wymondham	NORFOLK
Swanage	DORSET	York	NORTH YORKSHIRE
Swansea	SOUTH WALES	Yorkshire Dales National Park	NORTH YORKSHIRE

OTHER FHG TITLES FOR 2004

FHG Publications have a large range of attractive holiday accommodation guides for all kinds of holiday opportunities throughout Britain. They also make useful gifts at any time of year. Our guides are available in most bookshops and larger newsagents but we will be happy to post you a copy direct if you have any difficulty. POST FREE for addresses in the UK. We will also post abroad but have to charge separately for post or freight.

SELF-CATERING HOLIDAYS ☐
in Britain
Over 1000 addresses throughout for self-catering and caravans in Britain.

BED AND BREAKFAST STOPS ☐
Over 1000 friendly and comfortable overnight stops. Non-smoking, Disabled and Special Diets Supplements.

BRITAIN'S BEST HOLIDAYS ☐
A quick-reference general guide for all kinds of holidays.

Recommended
WAYSIDE AND COUNTRY INNS of Britain ☐
Pubs, Inns and small hotels.

Recommended
COUNTRY HOTELS ☐
of Britain
Including Country Houses, for the discriminating.

Recommended
SHORT BREAK HOLIDAYS in Britain ☐
"Approved" Accommodation for quality bargain breaks.

CHILDREN WELCOME! ☐
Family Holidays and Days Out guide.
Family holidays with details of amenities for children and babies.

The FHG Guide to
CARAVAN & CAMPING HOLIDAYS, ☐
Caravans for hire, sites and holiday parks and centres.

PETS WELCOME! ☐
The original and unique guide for holidays for pet owners and their pets.

The **GOLF GUIDE** –
Where to play Where to stay
In association with GOLF MONTHLY. Over 2800 golf courses in Britain with convenient accommodation. Holiday Golf in France, Portugal, Spain, USA, South Africa and Thailand.

£9.99 ☐

Tick your choice and send your order and payment to
FHG PUBLICATIONS, ABBEY MILL BUSINESS CENTRE,
SEEDHILL, PAISLEY PA1 1TJ
TEL: 0141- 887 0428; FAX: 0141- 889 7204
e-mail: fhg@ipcmedia.com
Deduct 10% for 2/3 titles or copies; 20% for 4 or more.

Send to: NAME ....

ADDRESS ....

....

....

POST CODE ....

I enclose Cheque/Postal Order for £ ....

SIGNATURE...DATE ....

Please complete the following to help us improve the service we provide. How did you find out about our guides?:

☐ Press   ☐ Magazines   ☐ TV/Radio   ☐ Family/Friend   ☐ Other